# Multisystem Skills and Interventions in School Social Work Practice

Edited by

**Edith M. Freeman**
**Cynthia G. Franklin**
**Rowena Fong**
**Gary L. Shaffer**
**Elizabeth M. Timberlake**

Foreword by

**Paula Allen-Meares**

NASW PRESS
National Association of Social Workers
Washington, DC

Josephine A. V. Allen, PhD, ACSW, *President*
Josephine Nieves, MSW, PhD, *Executive Director*

©1998 by the NASW Press, Inc.

**Library of Congress Cataloging-in-Publication Data**

Multisystem skills and interventions in school social work practice /
   edited by Edith M. Freeman . . . [et al.].
      p.  cm.
    Includes bibliographical references and index.
    ISBN 0-87101-295-2 (pbk. : alk. paper)
    1. School social work--United States.  I. Freeman, Edith M.
  II. National Association of Social Workers.
  LB3013.4.M85  1998
  371.4'6--dc21
                             98-25903
                                CIP

Printed in the United States of America

# Contents

# Foreword

This compilation of articles—authored by leading writers, practitioners, academicians, and advocates—is an excellent addition to the rich literature on the interface of social work and education. Over the course of this 20th century, we have seen social work practice in schools expand in directions that have reflected new knowledge. The entire field of child and adolescent development has emerged. Multiple theories have arisen about how schools should respond to both internal forces, such as changing demographics, and external forces, such as taxpayer demands for greater fiscal accountability in education and legislative mandates for inclusion of vulnerable groups of pupils and families in regular education services. There have been shifting views on how communities evolve over time, given their financial and human capital resources and their migratory patterns. Clearly, during the next century we will continue to witness even more profound transformations in the school and in society, spurred on by advances in information technology and by changing employment opportunities in the labor market, including the displacement of workers who are employed in today's traditional occupations.

In keeping with the ecological perspective that serves as the grounding framework of this book, no level of practice or size of systems is ignored; large, intermediate, and small systems are presented as targets of change and as repositories of resources. To promote positive developmental and learning outcomes and to create functional health support systems for children and their families, 21st-century school social work practitioners will need knowledge about a spectrum of multilevel interventions. These social workers will be expanding approaches to classrooms and small groups, empowering groups, finding ways to improve and sustain community development, strategizing about multicultural organizing, writing grant applications and proposals, advocating in political and legislative arenas, and creating processes to link support systems and integrate social work services on behalf of children and families.

The chapters presented in this book cover the breadth of social work practice with school-age children and their families as well as the multiple and complex systems in which these clients interact functionally and dysfunctionally. The authors do not shy away from the needs of vulnerable groups of children: those who are truant, homeless, or have disabilities; students of color; victims of sexual and physical abuse; those who are HIV-positive or are battling full-blown AIDS; and those who feel great emotional despair and contemplate suicide.

*Multisystem Skills and Interventions in School Social Work Practice* is grounded in a strengths-based perspective that replaces our pathology preoccupation with a focus on the normative. It offers proactive techniques for practitioners to draw on for individual and systemic change.

—*Paula Allen-Meares, PhD*
*Dean and Professor*
*School of Social Work*
*University of Michigan, Ann Arbor*

# Introduction

The school social work field is in a major transition as a result of momentous changes in many important areas. Public education has undergone numerous shifts in its curricula, programs, and policies. The reauthorization of IDEA (Individuals with Disabilities Education Act) by the 105th Congress concerning inclusion (P.L. 101-476) and the requirements to serve children with disabilities from birth to age five (P. L. 99-457) are but two recent examples of significant policy changes in education. A number of social welfare policy reforms have developed that are affecting the quantity and quality of health, mental health, child welfare, and economic resources available to meet the needs of children and families. Such changes will influence the role of schools—and that of school social workers—in addressing those needs when they affect family functioning and students' school performance.

Technological advances, including management information systems and social and medical life supports for children with disabilities, now allow schools to better educate and monitor the special needs of students and the effectiveness of specialized services in meeting those needs. Within the profession of social work itself, there has been a renewed emphasis on implementing a strengths perspective and empowerment ideals for helping clients resolve environmental and social justice issues. Indeed, there is a movement within the profession to modify its language so that it is more consistent with these values. Some social workers are now using the term "consumer" instead of "client" and have replaced problem-oriented terms, such as "treatment" and "diagnosis," with concepts of solution-focused practice, such as "miracle questions" and "exceptions to the problem."

These changes are substantive. Along with the related transition in school social work, they represent opportunities and risks, both to the field and to the children and families it serves. Opportunities include using this transition to study the shifting needs of children, families, schools, and communities and to implement the skills necessary for effective practice in this new era. The risks, often associated with periods of great change, involve ignoring and denying the emerging needs and adopting a "status quo" philosophy by continuing to use strategies that are ineffective in addressing those needs.

*Multisystem Skills and Interventions in School Social Work Practice* offers school social workers the opportunity to increase their understanding of the emerging needs of students, families, schools, and communities and of the skills and competencies necessary for working effectively with these consumers collectively. To facilitate this process, the book is organized into five sections that contain chapters primarily focused on practice at various systems levels, including practice with individuals, families, groups and classrooms, communities, and large systems and also policy. Thus, it emphasizes skills and competencies in school–community practice from a systems perspective, a resource that school social workers around the country have requested repeatedly.

The book's other features include

- a view of children–families–schools–communities as consumers and equal partners and stakeholders in defining and resolving issues of concern
- a strengths-based, solution-focused approach to assessment and intervention
- a problem-relevant but non–pathology-oriented focus on the normative and non-normative issues that children and families encounter
- an ecological perspective that requires a combination of simultaneous multisystems interventions for effectiveness
- creativity in addressing social justice issues in a variety of situations that delimit the opportunities and hopes of children and families related to their disabling conditions, ethnicity, gender, sexual orientation, age, religion, socioeconomic status, or geographic location
- an emphasis on comprehensive early intervention and prevention services that are accessible in the school, in the community, or in both areas.

These features and the range of diverse chapters in this book should make it useful to school social workers and community practitioners with varying years of practice experience. Beginning practitioners can use it as a guide for developing an effective foundation for practice, and more experienced practitioners can use it as a tool for helping hone their existing practice skills. The book can be used by graduate and undergraduate schools of social work as a text for courses in school social work, child and family specializations, community practice, direct practice, and—particularly related to its systems perspective—for human behavior in the social environment courses. It can be a resource to helping professionals in other fields as well, such as school counselors, school psychologists, clinical and community psychologists, psychiatric nurses, mental health professionals, and preventionists.

As school social workers and other professionals use this reader to transition into the 21st century, *Multisystem Skills and Interventions in School Social Work Practice* may become a benchmark for noting a historical shift in children's and families' needs and related services. Benchmarks often reflect an uncommon awareness of some of the current forces that signal change while characteristically offering a vision of future possibilities and dreams. We believe this reader more than fulfills these criteria of change.

—Edith M. Freeman,
MSW, PhD
professor
School of Social Welfare
University of Kansas
Lawrence

—Cynthia G. Franklin,
PhD, LMSW-ACP
associate professor
University of Texas
at Austin

—Rowena Fong,
MSW, EdD
associate professor
University of Hawaii
Honolulu

—Gary L. Shaffer, PhD
associate professor and
director of field education
University of North
Carolina at Chapel Hill

—Elizabeth M.
Timberlake, DSW, BCD
ordinary professor
of social work
Catholic University
of America
Washington, DC

# Part I

# SKILLS AND INTERVENTIONS FOR PRACTICE WITH INDIVIDUALS

# Part I: Skills and Interventions for Practice with Individuals

School social workers are often challenged in their work with individual students to maintain a strengths perspective in spite of the presence of severe problems and concerns. These practitioners may be even more challenged in their efforts to understand the context of students' concerns and problems, because important aspects of the context are often not observable during individual counseling sessions. Yet, students and family members may need individual services because of the nature and intensity of a problem or their inability to use the services in a different modality, at least initially. A child severely traumatized by sexual abuse or one with extremely violent behavior in the presence of peers are examples of typical situations encountered by school social workers that may require individual services.

Chapters in this section address these dilemmas in practice with individuals. Some chapters delineate clearly the skills needed to implement a strengths perspective for intervening with acting-out high school students, for assessing special education students using a portfolio approach, and for providing culturally specific developmental services to students of color. These chapters also indicate how some of the services and skills used with individual students can lead to systems change within schools by changing the labeling and negative perceptions of students by school staff.

Other chapters in this section are designed to help school social workers improve their practice skills with individuals related to the context of children's and adolescents' concerns. The focus is on identifying and changing students' coping and problem-solving abilities as well as environmental or contextual factors, for example, in the school, in the foster care system, in the housing system, and in the general community. Helping school social workers identify and change both individual and contextual factors is important. This approach to individual practice helps decrease the victim blaming and labeling that often is reinforced by more traditional approaches to individual practice. Simultaneously, it provides practitioners with examples of how to skillfully work with children and youths individually who are engaged in violence, who are experiencing out-of-home placements or homelessness, who are truant, and who are struggling with disabilities.

# 1    How to Interview for Client Strengths

Peter De Jong and Scott D. Miller

rticles calling for a "strengths perspective" in social work practice have begun to appear in the professional literature. Although the roots of the strengths perspective reach deep into the history of social work, it was not until 1989 that Weick, Rapp, Sullivan, and Kisthardt first incorporated the words "strengths perspective" into the title of an article. In their article, these authors addressed social work's past emphasis on problems and pathologies and the difficulties this emphasis created for practice, and they offered the ingredients of an alternative strengths perspective. In 1992 Saleebey published a collection of articles in which several authors explained, in considerable detail, the assumptions and principles of strengths-based practice with at-risk populations.

The strengths perspective rests on the following assumptions (Saleebey, 1992): First and foremost, despite life's problems, all people and environments possess strengths that can be marshaled to improve the quality of clients' lives. Practitioners should respect these strengths and the directions in which clients wish to apply them. Second, client motivation is fostered by a consistent emphasis on strengths as the client defines these. Third, discovering strengths requires a process of cooperative exploration between clients and workers; "expert" practitioners do not have the last word on what clients need. Fourth, focusing on strengths turns the practitioner's attention away from the temptation to "blame the victim" and toward discovering how clients have managed to survive even in the most inhospitable of circumstances. And, fifth, all environments—even the most bleak—contain resources.

These assumptions are grounded in the poststructural notion that social workers must increasingly respect and engage clients' ways of viewing themselves and their worlds in the helping process. Or, to put it differently, the strengths perspective asserts that the client's "meaning" must count for more in the helping process, and scientific labels and theories must count for less. This shift toward a deeper respect for the frame of reference of a particular client is especially important in this era of practice with increasingly diverse groups.

The literature about applying the strengths perspective to practice settings contains philosophy, practice principles, and general areas to explore for possible strengths. Notably lacking, however, are specific interview questions the worker can use to elicit client strengths. Authors who do address how to determine client strengths recommend using an inventory of potential areas of strength (Cowger, 1992; Rapp, 1992) based on a set of categories that the worker brings to the client. These categories may or may not reflect the categories the client uses to organize his or her experiences.

This article presents a set of interviewing questions that we believe are appropriate to the philosophy and practice principles of the strengths perspective, including the commitment to work within the client's frame of reference. These questions, collectively known as the solution-focused approach to interviewing, have evolved over 20 years of work by de Shazer and his colleagues at the Brief Family Therapy Center in Milwaukee (Berg & Miller, 1992; de Shazer, 1988; de Shazer et al., 1986). Although originally developed for use in individual, couples, and family therapy, the questions have evolved to the point at which they are useful in a variety of practice settings and client concerns. Indeed, we are persuaded that they are useful alternatives in any practice setting previously calling for problem solving with clients. This article presents the two key concepts behind solution-focused interviewing: the questions themselves and a discussion of how these questions fit with the key concepts of the strengths perspective.

## SOLUTION–FOCUSED INTERVIEWING

Solution-focused interviewing turns on two practice activities. The first is the development of well-formed goals with the client within the client's frame of reference; the second is the development with the client of solutions based on "exceptions."

### Well-Formed Goals

Berg and Miller (1992), drawing on their practice experience, identified seven characteristics of well-formed goals:

1. Goals are important to the client. Goals are well formed when they belong to the client and are expressed in the client's language; they are not well formed when, first of all, they are thought appropriate by the worker and are expressed in the worker's categories. This characteristic constitutes a practice principle that rests on the belief that clients whose goals are respected are more motivated than those whose goals are overlooked. The principle is not compromised except in cases in which the worker, after exploring for client strengths and coping capacities, is convinced that the client is overwhelmed or a danger to self or others.

2. The goals are small. Small goals are easier to achieve than large ones. For example, it is easier to "fill out one job application" than to "get a job."

3. The goals are concrete, specific, and behavioral. Goals so characterized help both client and worker know when progress is occurring. Accordingly, "going out to lunch with a friend twice a week" is preferable to "getting more involved with others."

4. The goals seek presence rather than absence. Clients, when asked about their goals, often tell workers what they want eliminated from their lives, for example, "feeling discouraged." Practice outcomes are improved when clients are helped to express their goals as the presence of something—for example, "taking walks"—rather than the absence of something.

5. The goals have beginnings rather than endings. Clients also tend initially to conceptualize their goals as end points, for example, "having a happy

marriage." Workers, aware that achieving goals is a process, can help by encouraging clients to conceptualize the first steps to their desired ends, such as "asking my husband to pick a place for next summer's vacation."

6. The goals are realistic within the context of the client's life. This characteristic speaks for itself and is usually achieved automatically in the course of developing goals with the preceding characteristics. However, when uncertain, the worker can explore with the client what it is in the client's life that tells the client that this particular goal makes sense for him or her.

7. The goals are perceived by the client as involving "hard work." Encouraging clients to think about their goals in this way is both realistic and useful for protecting the client's dignity. It is realistic, because goals call for changes in the client, and change is difficult. It protects the client's dignity because, first, if the client achieves the goal, the achievement is noteworthy and, second, if the client does not, it means only that there is still more hard work to be done.

This conceptualization of well-formed goals implies that they are negotiated between worker and client. It suggests that clients rarely enter the helping relationship with well-formed goals and that workers do not have the right or the power to determine which goals are appropriate for clients. Instead, practitioner and client must labor together to define achievable goals within the client's frame of reference.

## Exceptions

Exploring for exceptions represents the second main interviewing activity in the solution-focused approach. Exceptions are those occasions in the client's life when the client's problem could have occurred but did not. For example, if a couple complains of a troubled relationship because of "constant fighting," the solution-focused worker asks the couple to describe those times when they were together during which they did not fight or, at least, fought less destructively.

Solution-focused questioning by workers is quite persistent, but it avoids in-depth exploration of client problems. Workers focus on the who, what, when, and where of exception times instead of the who, what, when, and where of problems. The consequence is a growing awareness in both workers and clients of the clients' strengths relative to their goals, rather than the clients' deficiencies relative to their problems. Once these strengths are brought to awareness and thereby made available, clients can mobilize them to create solutions tailor-made for their lives.

## INTERVIEWING QUESTIONS

In a solution-focused approach, interviewing for well-formed goals and interviewing for client strengths go hand-in-hand to increase the chances of uncovering those strengths most appropriate to the client's goals.

### Interviewing for Well-Formed Goals

The relationship between client and social worker usually focuses first on the client's concerns or problems. Clients insist on telling their workers "what's wrong" with their lives. It is important for workers to listen to these concerns and then, once they have established that there is not an emergency, to turn the conversation toward developing well-formed goals. The "miracle" question is a good way to begin the negotiation (de Shazer, 1988). The worker might ask the following:

> Suppose while you are sleeping tonight a miracle happens. The miracle is that the problem that has you here talking to me is somehow solved. Only you don't know that because you are asleep. What will you notice different tomorrow morning that will tell you that a miracle has happened?

This question is the starting point for a whole series of satellite questions designed to take the client's attention away from difficulties and to focus it on imagining a future when the problem is solved. The following satellite questions might be used:

- What is the very first thing you will notice after the miracle happens?
- What might your husband or wife (child, friend) notice about you that would give him or her the idea that things are better for you?
- When he or she notices that, what might he or she do differently?
- When he or she does that, what would you do?
- And when you do that, what will be different around your house?

The intent of these questions is to help the client formulate, in detail, what will be "different" in his or her life when the miracle happens. As the client struggles to describe these differences, the client also often develops both an expectation of change and a growing sense of the goals toward which to direct effort.

The satellite questions mirror the characteristics of well-formed goals. Thus, when a client responds to the miracle question, "I'd have a sense of peace," the worker might ask, "What might your husband notice different about you that would tell him that you are beginning to 'have a sense of peace'?" With this question, the worker is attempting to help the client develop more concrete goals that are more the beginning of something rather than the end and that respect the client's language. Or, to give another example, when a client responds to the miracle question with, "I'd cry less," the worker would ask, "What would be there instead of the crying?" recognizing that well-formed goals are the presence of something rather than the absence.

### Interviewing for Client Strengths

*Exception-Finding Questions.* Exception-finding questions are used by the worker to discover a client's present and past successes in relation to the client's goals. Eventually these successes are used to build solutions. Examples of exception-finding questions are as follows:

> You said that when the "miracle" happens, you and your husband would notice yourselves "communicating more about your days and hugging each other more." Are there times now or in the past when the two of you were able to do that?
>
> *       *       *
>
> Okay, if I remember correctly, you said you would know that you did not need to see me anymore when you were "drinking less and spending more time

> with your wife, kids, and nondrinking buddies." So, when was the last time you were "drinking less and . . ."?

Sometimes clients are not yet able to describe how their life will be different when the problem is solved; they can talk only about their problems. In these situations a worker can still explore for exceptions but must do so by working from the problem instead of from an answer to the miracle question:

> I'm wondering, are there days when you feel "less scared about the future" [client's definition of the problem]? When was the last time you had a better day? What was different about that day that made it better? Where did that happen? Who was there with you? What might [those people] have noticed you doing differently that would tell them that you were doing better?

Once exceptions are brought to light—in easily the majority of the cases—the worker then explores how they happened. In particular, the worker attempts to clarify, as concretely as possible, what the client may have contributed to making the exceptions happen. Whatever contributions the worker and client together can bring into the client's awareness represent client strengths. Here is an example of a conversation wherein a worker and a client uncover a client's contribution to making exceptions happen:

> *Worker:* I am curious about those days when you are "less scared about your future." What do you think you do differently on those days?
> *Client:* I'm not sure [pause], maybe wash the car and rake leaves.
> *Worker:* What else?
> *Client:* Well, yesterday I did check the want ads for another job.

When a worker and client together uncover an exception along with the client's strengths that contributed to the exception, the worker affirms and amplifies those strengths in a way that is consistent with the worker's individual style and sense of proportion:

> *Worker:* So on better days you do things like "washing the car, raking the yard, and checking the want ads for a better job." And those things help. They seem like a good idea. Where did you get the idea to do all that? [or: Was doing these things something new for you? Was it hard for you to do those things?]

***Scaling Questions.*** Scaling questions are a clever way to make complex features of a client's life more concrete and accessible for both client and worker. They usually take the form of asking the client to give a number from 0 through 10 that best represents where the client is at some specified point. The worker usually designates 10 as the positive end of the scale, equating higher numbers with more positive outcomes and experiences. Here is an example:

> *Worker:* At this point, I want to ask you to rank something between 0 and 10. Let's say that 0 was where you were at with this problem when you first made the call to come in and see me and 10 means your problem is solved. Give me a number that says where you are right now.
> *Client:* Hmm. I guess about a 2 or 3.

Almost any aspect of a client's life can be scaled, including progress toward finding a solution, confidence about finding a solution, motivation to work on a solution, severity of a problem, the likelihood of hurting self or another person, self-esteem, and so on. Once the client answers with numbers greater than 0, the worker can follow up with questions that uncover, affirm, and amplify the client's strengths, as the continuation of the scaling question demonstrates:

> *Worker:* So you are at a 2 or 3 right now. What's different that tells you that you're doing better now than when you first called?
> *Client:* Well, I decided to come here, and I started thinking about how I might tell my boss that I need some time off.
> *Worker* [perceiving the client's sense of satisfaction]: That's great. Was it hard for you to "decide to come here"? [also:] Where did you get the idea to "decide to come here"? Is that the way you start to find a solution—"to start thinking about" what you need to do differently?

*Coping Questions.* In the authors' practice experience, more than 80 percent of clients are able to work productively at developing goals and identifying exceptions. However, like all workers, we encounter clients who are feeling hopeless and seem able to talk only about how horrible their present is and how bleak their future looks. Sometimes these clients are experiencing an acute crisis that gives rise to their hopelessness, and at other times the hopelessness represents a persistent pattern of self-expression and relating to others. In both cases, coping questions can be helpful in uncovering client strengths.

These questions accept the client's perceptions and then move on to ask how the client is able to cope with such overwhelming circumstances and feelings. For example,

> *Worker* [empathizing and responding to a client who is describing a long-standing depression and one discouraging event after another in her life]: I can see that you have many reasons to feel depressed; there have been so many things that haven't worked out the way you wished. I'm wondering how you have managed to keep going? How have you been able to get up each morning and face another day?
> *Client:* I really don't know.
> *Worker:* I'm amazed. With all . . . [worker refers to the discouragements in client's terms], I don't know how you make it. How do you do it?
> *Client:* I surprise myself sometimes, too; sometimes I'd just like to end it all. But I can't. Who would take care of my kids?
> *Worker:* Is that how you do it—think about how much your kids need you? You must care a lot about them. Tell me more about what you do to take care of them [worker explores for parenting strengths and motivation].

As the worker helps the client to uncover coping strengths, the client's mood and confidence usually rise. Sometimes new ideas for coping emerge that the client has never thought of before. However, it is also common for the client to return to problem descriptions and associated feelings of discouragement. As this occurs, the worker respectfully listens, empathizes, and then gently returns the client to a focus on strengths exploration and affirmation.

*"What's Better?" Questions.* "What's better?" questions are not so much a distinct set of questions as an approach to beginning later sessions by continuing the work of building solutions and uncovering client strengths. Instead of beginning later sessions with a review of homework tasks assigned or even the client's estimate of progress, a solution-focused worker simply asks, "What's

happening in your life that's better?" This is done for two reasons: First, it optimizes the chances of bringing to light exceptions that have occurred since the last visit with the worker. Second, it recognizes that the lives of clients, including their goals, are in process, not necessarily being the same today as yesterday. Consequently, the "what's better?" approach increases the chances of uncovering exceptions and associated strengths that are the most meaningful and useful to the client at the present moment.

Exploring for "what's better" is the same as exploring for exceptions. And, as with exceptions, clients may or may not have difficulty answering the questions. Therefore, workers will have to be more or less persistent, accordingly. The following is an example of an interaction involving a client seeking help with anxiety symptoms:

> *Worker* [first question of the second session]: So, tell me, what's happening that's better?
> *Client:* Well, I'm not sure; I mean, I still get the shakes. But maybe they're not quite as bad.
> *Worker:* Oh, "not quite as bad." Some relief must feel good.
> *Client:* Yeah, it does, but they still come back, and when they do, I'm miserable.
> *Worker:* I'm sure you are—you've described to me how tough it can be for you to get through. [pause] Now, I'm wondering about when was the last time the "shakes" were "not quite as bad"? [also:] What was different about that time? How did it happen? What might [your friend] have noticed that you do differently that helped you [through that morning]? On a scale of 0 to 10 with 10 equal to "every chance," what are the chances of your having another morning like that in the next couple of days? What gives you that level of confidence? What's the most important thing for you to remember to increase the chances of having more mornings when the "shakes are not quite as bad"?

In solution-focused interviewing, it is customary for the worker to take a brief break before the end of an interview and prepare feedback for the client. The feedback consists mainly of affirming the client's well-formed goals (insofar as they exist) and highlighting thoughts, actions, and feelings of the client (gleaned from the exploration of exceptions) that already are contributing to either reaching the goals or coping with life's hardships or traumas. These thoughts, actions, and feelings constitute the client's strengths on the road to client-devised solutions expressed in the client's categories.

## FIT BETWEEN SOLUTION-FOCUSED INTERVIEWING AND THE STRENGTHS PERSPECTIVE

There are six key concepts behind the strengths perspective (Saleebey, 1992) to be operationalized in the worker–client relationship: empowerment, membership, regeneration and healing from within, synergy, dialogue and collaboration, and suspension of disbelief. Solution-focused clinicians must convey these concepts to their clients in practice.

### Empowerment

Drawing on Rappaport (1990), Saleebey (1992) explained that empowering clients means creating a context in which clients can "discover the considerable power within themselves" (p. 2) to handle their own problems, rather than—even with the best of intentions—telling clients what they need or ought to do to overcome their difficulties. The matter of whose "definitions of reality" take precedence in this process is critical. Those who practice social work from the strengths perspective try to empower their clients by encouraging them to define their own worlds, problems, aspirations, and strengths to create more satisfying lives.

Solution-focused interviewing honors a worker's commitment to use client meanings. For example, when a client states that her problem "might be depression," the solution-focused worker responds with, "What is happening in your life that tells you that you 'might be depressed'?" Similarly, the same worker would encourage the client to work at defining her own goals, exceptions, levels of confidence and motivation to solve her depression, and eventual degrees of progress—all in her own language. The client is empowered by the worker's creating a context that requires her to draw on two of her most important and unique human capacities: conceptualizing her own world and making decisions about how to live in it.

## Membership

Frequently the clients of social workers are cut off from their cultural and geographic roots, feel vulnerable, experience discrimination, or are otherwise alienated; therefore, they lack a sense of belonging (Saleebey, 1992). In part because alienated people lack the sense of belonging, they are also out of touch with their strengths and possibilities. Consequently, in a beginning effort to foster a sense of membership in alienated clients, Saleebey wrote, "Certain things are required of us [workers] at the outset"(p. 9): (1) working collaboratively with clients, (2) affirming client perceptions and stories, (3) recognizing the survival efforts and successes of clients, and (4) fostering client links to contexts in which client strengths can flourish.

The solution-focused interviewing questions discussed earlier demonstrate how practitioners can meet Saleebey's first three requirements. Regarding the fourth, we have found that in our work with clients, the miracle, exception-finding, "what's better?" and coping questions all uncover useful possibilities for linking clients to affirming contexts.

## Regeneration and Healing from Within

Regeneration and healing bring to mind wellness and how to achieve it rather than disease and how to overcome it. Although there is an undeniable reality to physical disease, many of the human difficulties social workers encounter in practice, including some physical diseases, are most effectively addressed by helping clients discover and apply "their own (inner and outer) resources for healing" (Saleebey, 1992, p. 10). Solution-focused interviewers concentrate on regeneration and healing from within. Because they ask clients to define their own goals and the exceptions to their difficulties, they help clients uncover their own resources for better lives and promote in them expectations of positive change. The latter, by itself, is a strong agent for change.

## Synergy

A synergic relationship is one in which the participants, by virtue of their inter-action, are able to create a larger, more beneficial result than either could have created alone using individual resources. Such a relationship potentially can exist at or between any of the several levels at which people interact—from the level of individuals to that of large collectivities.

The strengths perspective asserts that both inner and outer human resources are expandable through synergic relationship. We believe that solution-focused interviewing increases the possibility of synergic relationship in two respects.

*Between Client and Worker.* First, in solution-focused work each party con-tributes differently to the interaction. The client provides content—a personal story, values, beliefs, perceptions, wishes, definitions of reality—expressed in his or her own way. The worker brings an understanding of the structure of the change process—the necessity of developing well-formed goals and building solutions from exceptions—along with the interviewing questions that reflect his or her understanding. The practitioner assists the client's participation by affirming the client's frame of reference and the strengths that emerge in the interaction. In the end, more often than not, the mix produces a synergic expan-sion of the client's inner resources.

*Between Client and the Client's Context.* Second, the strengths perspective is as committed to enhancing the relationships between clients and their contexts as it is to expanding the inner resources of clients (although the two often occur together). When solution-focused workers ask their questions, they always do so in relation to the social context of their clients. Satellite questioning opens up possibilities for different, more synergy-enhancing interactions between clients and their social contexts and thus contributes to creating "new and often unex-pected patterns and resources" (Saleebey, 1992, p. 11).

## Dialogue and Collaboration

To truly hold a dialogue with a client is to explore and affirm the "otherness" of the client. Solution-focused interviewing does just this. In drawing out the client's perceptions and strengths, the worker is continually respecting and affirming the client's otherness.

To collaborate with a client is to negotiate and consult with the client, not to provide expert answers. When clients insist on returning to problem talk or ask-ing for answers from the worker, the worker listens, empathizes, and gently returns them to defining their goals for a more desirable future and examining the significance of exceptions in their lives.

## Suspension of Disbelief

Although suspension of disbelief may seem to have drawbacks in the short run, it offers great hope of a synergic, empowering relationship between client and worker over the long haul. This concept of the strengths perspective challenges workers to avoid the long-standing tendency in the profession to distrust the perceptions and statements of clients about themselves and their circumstances.

Solution-focused interviewing, too, is premised on a belief that respecting the client's perceptions and statements is the best antidote to what the profession calls "client resistance" (de Shazer, 1984). Once the client experiences acceptance and affirmation from the worker, the likelihood of productive work increases.

## CONCLUSION

It is hard to imagine a tighter fit between philosophy and practice than that between the strengths perspective and solution-focused interviewing questions. This article makes a case for that fit at the micro level of work with individuals, couples, and families, the level at which the interviewing questions were first developed and applied. Recently, applications have been made in work with groups (Selekman, 1991) and organizations (Sparks, 1989).

Saleebey (1992) boiled the philosophy of the strengths perspective down to the following challenge:

> At the very least, the strengths perspective obligates workers to understand that, however downtrodden or sick, individuals have survived (and in some cases even thrived). They have taken steps, summoned up resources, and coped. We need to know what they have done, how they have done it, what they have learned from doing it, what resources (inner and outer) were available in their struggle to surmount their troubles. People are always working on their situations, even if just deciding to be resigned to them; as helpers we must tap into that work, elucidate it, find and build on its possibilities. (pp. 171–172)

The miracle question, exception-finding questions, scaling questions, coping questions, and "what's better?" questions are invaluable resources for meeting Saleebey's challenge in day-to-day social work practice.

## REFERENCES

Berg, I. K., & Miller, S. D. (1992). *Working with the problem drinker: A solution-focused approach.* New York: W. W. Norton.

Cowger, C. D. (1992). Assessment of client strengths. In D. Saleebey (Ed.), *The strengths perspective in social work practice* (pp. 139–147). New York: Longman.

de Shazer, S. (1984). The death of resistance. *Family Process, 23,* 79–93.

de Shazer, S. (1988). *Clues: Investigating solutions in brief therapy.* New York: W. W. Norton.

de Shazer, S., Berg, I. K., Lipchik, E., Nunally, E., Molnar, A., Gingerich, W. C., & Weiner-Davis, M. (1986). Brief therapy: Focused solution development. *Family Process, 25,* 202–221.

Rapp, C. A. (1992). The strengths perspective of case management with persons suffering from severe mental illness. In D. Saleebey (Ed.), *The strengths perspective in social work practice* (pp. 45–58). New York: Longman.

Rappaport, J. (1990). Research methods and the empowerment social agenda. In P. Tolan, C. Keys, F. Chertak, & L. Jason (Eds.), *Researching community psychology* (pp. 51–53). Washington, DC: American Psychological Association.

Saleebey, D. (Ed.). (1992). *The strengths perspective in social work practice.* New York: Longman.

Selekman, M. (1991). The solution-oriented parenting group: A treatment alternative that works. *Journal of Strategic and Systemic Therapies, 10,* 36–49.

Sparks, P. M. (1989). Organizational tasking: A case report. *Organizational Development Journal, 7,* 51–57.

Weick, A., Rapp, C., Sullivan, W. P., & Kisthardt, W. (1989). A strengths perspective for social work practice. *Social Work, 34,* 350–354.

*An earlier version of this chapter was presented at the 39th Annual Program Meeting of the Council on Social Work Education, February 1993, New York.*

*This chapter was originally published in the November 1995 issue of* Social Work, *Vol. 40, pp. 729–736.*

# 2 The Getting Better Phenomenon: Videotape Applications of Previously At-Risk High School Student Narratives

Glenn Carley

The intervention project used in this article began with the simple observation that some students go through lengthy periods of behavioral conflict in high school, and then, quietly, they improve. The improved student no longer is sent to the office, no longer is suspended, and no longer is referred to special services personnel for counseling. This "getting better phenomenon" is sometimes observed, rarely acknowledged, and usually chalked up to maturity. The improvement may be seen as post-at-risk behavior—that is, as part of a behavioral sequence that includes conflict, resolution, and stability.

This article describes an intervention project that sought to identify the students who had improved, to videotape and collect their narratives, and to edit the narratives and show the videos to various populations within the school system. The goal was to sensitize the viewing audience to the person behind the at-risk behavior at a time when he or she was no longer at risk.

## USE OF VIDEOTAPE IN THERAPY

In narrative language, we could say that "getting better" is the phase when the student is practicing a new story. The story includes healthier behaviors of getting along or of surviving in school. This places de Shazer's (1985) notion of the "crystal ball" technique into an immediate context. In the crystal ball technique, the client visualizes a future without complaint and thereby does something different so that this vision of the future can become a reality. "Getting better" is the point in which the vision is being practiced.

The idea of videotaping the new story makes sense, because at this point in their narratives, the students are permitted to speak from the solution and to further visualize how that solution will unfold into future, healthy possibilities. Characteristically, the students then may take on the roles of consultant and teacher of ways to successfully navigate high school.

This approach shifts White and Epston's (1990) "problem-saturated" description of self and others to a solution-saturated description of expected future outcomes. Videotaping serves the twofold purpose of reinforcing the student's new narrative and, with permission, of punctuating that story of health and replaying it for other populations in a language that is the student's own. This is the true "joint discovery" (Gallant, 1993) between older and younger students and between adults that is part of a constructivist approach to "understanding the way people are making sense of themselves and their interactions with others" (p. 120).

Laybourne (1975) aptly described the impact of video feedback on his class: "One can sense its raw power, its latent capability to address areas of behavior that are seldom explicitly explored" (p. 54). Noble, Egan, and McDowell (1977) hypothesized that children were "better able to describe themselves both verbally and nonverbally . . . after video feedback of themselves in action" (p. 62). Ehrgood (1979) described video feedback in terms of skill acquisition. Booth and Fairbank (1983) studied the effectiveness of videotape feedback as a procedure for increasing on-task behavior. They also found that the ability to replay a sequence of behavior as many times as possible was extremely helpful in staff and parent training. Michel and Blitstein (1979) found that the "conscious use" of videotape in a group work setting facilitated the correction of distorted body images, low self-esteem, lack of capacity for self-observation, and poor peer relationships in their sample.

## STUDENTS TEACHING STUDENTS PROJECT

In the Students Teaching Students project, videotape was used to capture the life experience of a young person in the emotional context of his or her story. The story was then made portable and available to a wider audience within the school system. Both the participants and "audience" are members of the same story in its broader sense. This is a pragmatic application of Kral's (1988b) discussion of the ripple effect on a school system that shows the interconnectedness between small positive changes in a larger system.

The project took place in a high school of 2,100 young people. The school is one of 18 high schools and 88 elementary schools in the Dufferin–Peel Roman Catholic Separate School Board, a relatively large school system in the province of Ontario with an enrollment of 73,000 students. This system was seen as the unit of study (and as a story to study), with each high school serving as an untapped resource of young people with specific insights to offer the entire system. The author, a school social worker, was assigned to the high school three days a week. The project consisted of five phases: awareness, referral, interviews, videotaping, and application.

### Awareness

During the awareness phase the author identified and discussed the phenomenon of "getting better" with staff and students at school. This dialogue is supported by Fullan's (1991) views on how to successfully approach educational change. Effective implementation involves an exchange of reality through interaction with others.

### Referral

In the referral phase staff were asked to generate a list of students who, in their perception, had improved over the past several semesters. The breakdown of the referral sources and the number of students they referred is as follows: vice principals (11), teachers (3), guidance counselors (2), school social workers (6), school psychologists (2), youth workers (3), and attendance secretary (1). Of the 28 students referred to the project, 25 were selected for interviews.

## Interviews

During the interviewing phase, the author met with each student and explained the project. The students were told who referred them and why. They were invited to videotape their story with the understanding that it would be screened as a teaching tool. They would be given a copy of their interview, and their consent to participate could be revoked at any time. In the interview, the author asked each student for his or her opinion as to why he or she had improved. Their responses included the following:

- "I don't know, I just did it."
- "I got my driver's license, and I needed to use my dad's car."
- "My girlfriend helped."
- "My cheerleading coach kept telling me I could do it."
- "I looked around and saw my friends all graduating, and I didn't want to be here forever."
- "I wanted to get my education on my time, not theirs [the teachers']."

These themes reflect the coming of age or maturity functions of increased responsibility, new relationships, a willingness to listen to and accept teacher feedback, and a new type of peer pressure that laments the "lost time" of previous misbehavior. This type of student-generated wisdom about "getting better" in high school is the type of "story" the project sought to discover and recycle for a younger audience. The author thanked each student for attending and congratulated them on their improvement.

## Videotaping

Five of the 25 young people interviewed volunteered to be taped. The taping involved one to two meetings with each student in the author's office at the high school. A semistructured interview was designed to elicit a narrative from each student that described the passage from at-risk behavior to where they saw themselves at that point and to where they predicted themselves going.

The interview style used in taping was based on the solution-focused and narrative literature that describes theoretical frameworks as a basis for asking "questions which enhance a self-perception of competence" (Durrant, 1992, p. 4). Kral's (1988a) description of "rating" desired behavior was reflected in the question, "On a scale of 1 to 10—10 is high (things are going well at school), 1 is low (lots of hassles)—what number would you give yourself now?" This question was helpful in providing a benchmark at various points in the student's story. The author tried to avoid becoming mired in detailed descriptions of the problems in the student's school narrative; White's (1988–89) notion of externalizing the problem—that is, making the problem a separate entity outside of the person—was helpful.

Videotaping in the present and playing back the result allows the person a repeated (and therefore reinforced) ability to talk back in time to the problems of the old story and thereby further distance his or her relationship from what used to be. This is the historicism that White (1988) discovered in his unique outcome questions. Nonetheless, the true focus of this new story was on lessons learned, knowledge gained, advice for other students who are thinking about "heading into trouble," and suggestions to adults about what helped or what would have helped.

Tomm's (1987) perspective that specific questions can enable self-healing was particularly useful to this project. It was impossible to ignore the terrible grief and anger students expressed in their narratives when they described their recognition that they were "not getting better" at high school.

The end result of the videotaping phase was a series of five interviews, which the author edited down into four 15-minute "stories" dubbed together to form an hour-long presentation. Copies were given to each student to screen with their friends, with their parents, or on their own. Students were given the option to reconsent to use the videotape as a teaching tool or to revoke consent and keep the tape. One of the five chose to revoke consent and keep the tape.

## Application

Once the narratives were on videotape, the tapes were used in a variety of direct service and organizational or systems ways within the school system.

*Direct Service.* The videotapes were shown to individual students, groups of teachers, or classrooms of students as an intervention. For example, in the role of attendance counselor, the author screened the school narratives individually with four young people who were chronically absent from school. The tape provided a vehicle for discussion of school problems and created more openings for change during an interview. Another school social worker screened the material with five grade 8 classes in two schools as a vehicle for discussing the transition to high school. She reported that consistently the students asked many questions about rules, lockers, skipping, suspensions, class timetables, and homework. The students applauded the presentation when it was over, and the worker felt that this helped her gain more role credibility as a part of the support staff in the school.

Another social worker screened segments of the tapes at a staff meeting with 90 teachers present. During a rather emotional debriefing, one vice principal reported that the video stories had changed her view on how she was going to deal with "bad kids."

*Systems.* Several systems applications involved screening the narratives with school superintendents and trustees. The author was able to demonstrate how young people can reclaim their health at school with staff who would not necessarily be able to hear their story. The myth of the "bad student" was easily challenged in this forum.

## IMPLICATIONS FOR SCHOOL SOCIAL WORK PRACTICE

The Students Teaching Students project listened to and recorded student voices, enabling viewers to observe education at its fundamental point: the student–teacher relationship. One of the outcomes of videotaping school narratives was to "discover," preserve, and replay for the system the fact that small acts of recognition by a teacher can have a profound impact on a student. This message was a common feature in each of the taped narratives, and it had enormous value as a feedback tool. For example, students were given the opportunity to write thank you notes to the teachers who had made a difference. The teachers, in turn, were moved by this simple act of being recognized. In most cases they did not realize that they had made an impression. For the students, the ability to thank teachers who mattered (as opposed to hate teachers who did not) helped emphasize the healthier aspects of the narrative and the sense that they had "conquered" high school. Teachers were reminded of how powerful their use of self can be in the classroom in both negative and positive ways.

The author observed that there was a great deal of residual grief in some of the videotaped narratives. Perhaps expressing anger allowed students' feelings of sadness to be more available. The negative emotional effects on students of doing poorly at school are seldom discussed. For these students, the presentation of the completed tape emerged as a ritual or graduation of sorts. White and Epston (1990) might classify the tape as an "alternative" document that "signals the person's arrival at a new status in the community, one that brings with it new responsibilities and privileges . . . which have the potential of incorporating a wider readership and of recruiting an audience to the performance of new stories" (p. 191).

## CONCLUSION

The enlisting of students (and parents) as partners in the educational process is receiving more attention. For example, Ontario's Royal Commission on Learning report (Begin et al., 1994) agreed that "students, particularly from grade 7 on, have insights into their schools, principals, teachers, and courses that no one else possibly can, and everyone can learn from those insights. Instead of remaining passive participants in their own lives [young people are] formally entitled to have their views heard" (p. 46).

Rather than leaving students alone when they have improved, it is important that school personnel take the time to listen to and, if possible, to videotape narratives of young people who are getting better at high school. In this way, we can affirm their growth and recycle or replay their stories as a teaching tool for specific populations within a school system. This process is one small way of augmenting the relevance of education in both teachers' and students' lives.

## REFERENCES

Begin, M., Caplan, G., Bharti, M., Glaze, A., Murphy, D., & DiCecco, R. (1994). *For the love of learning: Report of the Royal Commission on Learning* (short version). Toronto: Ministry of Education and Training, The Queen's Printer for Ontario.

Booth, S. K., & Fairbank, D. W. (1983). Video feedback as a behavioral management technique. *Behavioral Disorders, 9*(1), 55–58.

de Shazer, S. (1985). *Keys to solution in brief therapy.* New York: W. W. Norton.

Durrant, M. (1992). *Brief therapy approach with adolescents and their families.* Epping, Australia: Eastwood Family Therapy Centre.

Ehrgood, A. H. (1979, November–December). The camera and the self. *Journal of Physical Education and Recreation,* p. 70.

Fullan, M. (1991). *The new meaning of educational change*. New York: Teachers College Press.

Gallant, J. P. (1993). New ideas for the school social worker in the counseling of children and families [Trends & Issues]. *Social Work in Education, 15,* 119–125.

Kral, R. (1988a). A little quick step: The "5 'D' Process" for solution-focused brief therapy. *Family Therapy Case Studies, 3*(1), 14.

Kral, R. (1988b). *Strategies that work: Techniques for solution in the schools*. Milwaukee: Wisconsin Institute of Family Issues, Brief Family Therapy Center.

Laybourne, K. (1975, September). The mirror image of classroom video. *Media and Methods,* pp. 54–63.

Michel, J., & Blitstein, S. (1979). Use of videotape feedback with severely disturbed adolescents. *Child Welfare, 58,* 245–252.

Noble, G., Egan, P., & McDowell, S. (1977). Changing the self concepts of seven-year-old deprived urban children by creative drama or video feedback. *Social Behavior and Personality, 5*(1), 55–64.

Tomm, K. (1987). Interventive interviewing: Part II. Reflexive questioning as a means to enable self-healing. *Family Process, 26,* 167–182.

White, M. (1988, Winter). The process of questioning: A therapy of literary merit? *Dulwich Centre Newsletter,* pp. 37–46.

White, M. (1988–89, Summer). The externalizing of the problem and the re-authoring of lives and relationships. *Dulwich Centre Newsletter,* pp. 3–21.

White, M., & Epston, D. (1990). *Narrative means to therapeutic ends*. New York: W. W. Norton.

*This chapter is dedicated to A. M. Carley.*

*This chapter was originally published in the April 1997 issue of* Social Work in Education, *Vol. 19, pp. 115–120.*

# 3 Female Gang Members: A Profile of Aggression and Victimization

Christian E. Molidor

> It was my job to go out and find some girl and make sure she came back to the house with me after school, and it didn't matter how the fuck I got her back there. [I'd] tell her there was a party, tell her there were drugs, tell her there was some boy there that liked her. . . . Then, when she got there, the guys would have sex with her whether she wanted to or not. Mostly I'd just watch and laugh; sometimes I'd join in or have sex with myself.
>
> —*16-year-old female gang member*

Serious criminal behavior committed by female gang members has steadily increased over the past two decades and is becoming more common (Campbell, 1987; Spergel, 1992; Taylor, 1993). The number of serious crimes by teenage girls increased by more than 50 percent between 1968 and 1974; serious crimes by teenage boys increased less than 10 percent (Campbell, 1984). Between 1960 and 1978, arrests of girls younger than 18 increased by 265 percent for all offenses and 393 percent for violent crimes; arrests of boys for violent crimes increased by 82 percent (Giordano, 1978). As female gang members became more liberated and independent during the 1980s, they took on roles more comparable to male gang members. According to Taylor (1993), "Female gang members now are hard-core and deadly" (p. 45). Fishman (1992), who has studied female gang membership since the 1960s, reported that "female gang members today have become more entrenched, more violent, and more and more oriented to male crime" (p. 28).

Although statistics indicate that teenage girls are becoming more involved in serious criminal activity, female gang members have largely been ignored (Chesney-Lind, 1989; Covey, Menard, & Franzese, 1992). The majority of material written about female gang membership is incomplete and outdated, most having been written in the 1970s or earlier. Thrasher's (1927) initial study of more than 1,000 Chicago gangs included only one page of discussion about female gang participation. The extensive theories explaining male gang participation include poor economic conditions (Perkins, 1987; Zatz, 1987), drug use and marketing (Spergel & Curry, 1990), family dysfunction (Teilmann & Landry, 1981), peer pressure (Campbell, 1984; Hagedorn, 1989), and poor self-esteem (Chesney-Lind, 1989; Huff, 1990). Theories about female gang participation focus on girls' social ineptness, physical unattractiveness, or psychological impairments (Bowker & Klein, 1983; Rosenbaum, 1991; Spergel, 1992). "The bulk of the literature, then, has perpetuated the notion that personal maladjustments characterize the female delinquent" (Giordano, 1978, p. 126).

Perhaps one reason why so few theories explain female gang participation is that the female role is often described by male gang members to male researchers and interpreted by male academics, rather than being described by the girls themselves (Horowitz, 1986). Thus, in addition to problems with the paucity of theories explaining female gang membership, one must also be concerned about the reliability of the information (Campbell, 1987). Only recently have authors begun to question the girls themselves about their motives for gang participation (Campbell, 1987; Spergel, 1992; Taylor, 1993).

Because the literature presents female gang members as secondary participants, no research has been conducted on the ecological factors surrounding their lives. This descriptive study explores the ecology of female gang participation to uncover themes from which to develop a comprehensive model. This article discusses the contextual factors that motivate girls to join a gang; the extent of the girls' criminal behavior; and the physical, sexual, and psychological abuses the girls experience from other gang members. Implications for social work and future research are discussed.

## METHOD

### Study Design

Data were obtained from a convenience sample of 15 female gang members. The young women, who were in a secure residential treatment facility in Texas, consented to participate in in-depth structured interviews about their experiences in the gang. The interviews were done in the social work "cabin." Each participant had complete privacy and was able to speak freely. Interviewers explained the purpose of the interview to each participant, assured her anonymity, and obtained her consent to conduct and audiotape the interview. The structure of the interview was developed from Quicker's (1983) social structural view of female juvenile delinquency, which proposes the examination of macrolevel and exolevel issues as well as microlevel issues.

### Participants

Of the 36 young women then living at the facility, 15 identified themselves as active members (had been initiated) of several diverse gangs across Texas and New Mexico. All 15 consented to being interviewed. Each had been out of contact with their gangs while in the facility but still considered themselves gang members. All had a record of one to six arrests for various criminal behaviors and had been sent to the facility either by their parents or by the state (when custody had been taken away from their parents).

Six participants were white, five were Hispanic, three were African American, and one was American Indian. Their ages ranged from 13 to 17, consistent with the literature, which suggests that the majority of gang members are between ages 14 and 18 (Covey et al., 1992; Huff, 1990; Monti, 1993), although there is evidence that gang members are recruiting members as young as eight to 10 (Johnstone, 1983; McKinney, 1988). One 14-year-old confirmed the young age at which gang membership begins:

> Basically, I was born into the gang. My mother and stepfather were leaders in the gang, and I was always there. For my first birthday I got a tattoo on my arm that says "Crips." I'll be one of them till I die. Most girls aren't born into the gang, usually they start hangin' with us at around nine or 10.

## RESULTS

### Education

One theme that emerged from the interviews is the lack of formal education. Because they were in the treatment facility, all of the young women participated in school. However, before coming to the facility, the young women were at least two academic years behind their peers. Only three had completed ninth grade. The young women showed a consistent pattern of falling through the cracks in the school system; most had a history of suspensions for fighting or drug or weapon possession on the school grounds. After their suspensions were completed, they never returned to school or were truant so often that they failed. Several had attended alternative schools or attempted home schooling, but the results were the same. Each had quit attending school and began to hang out with her gang on a daily basis with no follow-up by her parents or the school system.

The young women's experiences while in school sounded more like descriptions of a combat zone than a learning environment. Their recollections included knife fights in the halls, intimidation of classmates and teachers, drug use, truancy, and vandalism:

> There was this place in the back of the school, under the stairway. None of the teachers ever went there. That's where we would meet anyone who was looking [for a fight]. We went there every day. . . . Casper [gang member's name] would be talkin' shit with someone. I'd walk up behind him and grab his hair and pull down hard—I'm talkin' hard and fast—and knee him in the back. (17-year-old)

*     *     *

> Hey, school's a dangerous place. You gotta do what ya gotta do—fist, blade, or pop [gun]. (15-year-old)

The majority of the young women carried a knife to school on a daily basis. Although few reported owning a gun, the majority reported that they had easy access to one. In addition, the young women often carried the gun of one of their "boyfriends," because the women were less likely to be searched.

### Family and Neighborhood Life

Another theme was severely dysfunctional family life. Covey et al. (1992) described the environment in which the majority of gang members grow up: "In particular, the poorer and less-educated [gang member] is concentrated in central city slum areas, where they are isolated from legitimate economic opportunity, education, and mainstream society generally" (p. 17).

Responses to questions about their parents' marital situation referred to domestic violence, divorce, and remarriage. Often the young women's birth parents were never married. The young women related stories of extensive alcohol and drug use by parents, stepparents, or boyfriends living in the home. They also indicated that severe physical or sexual abuse by relatives began at an early age:

> I remember this one Thanksgiving dinner. As usual, everybody got real drunk and . . . started fighting. My uncle was yelling at my stepdad and cousin about some shit, and he pulls out a gun and shoots it right there in the house. I was so scared. I thought, "Shit, he's gonna kill somebody right here," and I was hoping it was gonna be my stepdad. If my uncle had known what that son-of-a-bitch had done to me [sexual abuse], he would have blown his head off right there. (17-year-old)

In addition, the majority of the young women's neighborhoods were rife with poverty, alcohol and drug use and distribution, and gang violence. Although three reported coming from middle-class and upper-middle-class communities, the majority described their neighborhoods as slums, projects, ghettos, or pits. These low-socioeconomic neighborhoods provided few alternatives and little opportunity for the young women to better their situations.

## Gang Initiation

Gang initiation rites have been documented by other researchers (Covey et al., 1992; Cummings & Monti, 1993; Moore, 1993). Usually the initiation is extremely painful and humiliating, which the gang justifies as deterring spying by rival gang members and ensuring that whoever is trying to get in is doing it for the good of the gang rather than solely for sex or protection. The gang leader determines the type of initiation.

The female gang member may have several initiation rites to endure. The most common are to "walk the line," "pull a train," get tattoos, participate in a robbery, or participate in a drive-by shooting. To walk the line is a form of beating. The young woman walks through a double line of gang members who severely punch and kick her until she comes to the end of the line. The rite can also be done in a circle in which the young woman fights five to 12 gang members for a set period of time. Winning the fight is not expected; rather, the goal is to show her strength and toughness.

> When I walked the line, there were about 14 or 16 of my homies [gang members] there. Some just used their fists or were kicking me, but I remember that one homeboy had on brass knuckles that broke my nose, and this one girl hit me with a stick. (13-year-old)

To pull a train means to have sex with multiple male gang members. One young woman reported that she had sex with 11 male members in one night. At times, the sexual initiation may be voluntary, but often it resembles rape:

> We were in this abandoned building drinking and getting high. There was me and four other guys. Slick [gang name] tells me he thinks it's time I got V'd [initiated] into the family. I knew what he meant, and I told him I didn't think so. So he pulls out this knife and tells me he does think so. So I said OK, and we

> went into this back room and he did me. Then, the other three did me after him. The last guy was this big fat pig. I got sick and started throwing up all over the place. God, that really pissed him off, and he ended up beating the shit outta me. (16-year-old)

Part of any initiation involves somehow permanently identifying oneself as part of the gang, most commonly with a tattoo. The young women had tattoos declaring "Crips till I die," "Blood or Bloodbath," or "Widows not Wanderers" or depicting an image such as a spider (identifying the Black Widows):

> My tattoo is like my colors. It shows where I belong and who my family is, except it never rubs off. (15-year-old)

## Reasons for Joining

Two themes emerged as reasons for joining a gang: belonging to a family and the feeling of power. Although their statements were varied, the young women spoke of "belonging to a family that cared":

> My gang is my family; I'm accepted, and I know I can always count on them. (13-year-old)

> \*      \*      \*

> My family [gang] makes me feel like I'm a somebody. When we're hanging, people respect me. (16-year-old)

Conflict with and ambivalence toward the family of origin are aspects of normal adolescent development (Erikson, 1980; Molidor, 1995): "The teenager feels tense and anxious in the presence of the parents and feels safe only when apart from them. Instead of admitting any dependence and love, they take an attitude that is exactly the opposite" (Freud, 1936, p. 236). The healthy teenager struggles with the issues surrounding individuation and separation and slowly develops a more individual sense of self apart from the family. However, although it appeared that physically the young women were ready to begin separating from their parents, they were not yet ready or able to become psychologically or emotionally independent. They consequently turned to the gang members.

In addition, many female gang members experience a sense of internal powerlessness (Campbell, 1987). The external power of the gang provides them with, in their terms, protection and respect:

> They're [students in school] afraid of our gang [the Black Widows], and because I'm in the gang, people show me respect and won't mess with me. I like that feeling of power. (16-year-old)

One young woman said she had been selling drugs and felt it was too dangerous to do alone:

> I needed back-up bad, and the Crips [her gang] gave it to me. When I was hangin' with the Crips, nobody messed with me then. They respected me. (15-year-old)

The power and protection from the gang helped the young women feel respected by others. However, after further questioning, they agreed that this respect was fear. People fear what the gang will do to them if they fail to obey or show respect.

## Fear and Paranoia

In discussing the most negative aspect of being in a gang, the theme was universal: fear and paranoia. Ironically, making others feel afraid (power) was seen as one of the best parts about being in a gang, and the constant fear associated with being in a gang was seen as the worst part:

> The worst part of being in the gang has to be the paranoia. It's there all the time. I mean all the time, even at your own house. You don't never know when you're gonna get hit. You're always watching your back to see if there's any asshole behind you to knock you up, or if one of your homies is playing [betraying] you. It don't go away. I been here [residential facility] for a year and two months, and I still keep a watch out. (17-year-old)

During the interviews, the young women often referred to the experience of paranoia about the never-ending threat of being "hit" (shot, stabbed, beaten) at any moment:

> I was just walking to the store with my little bro'. He's only nine. . . . Then out from the alley comes a car filled with about five or six gangsters. I'd never seen any of them. I didn't know even one. But two of them took a shot at me as they drove by. Neither of us was hit, but my bro' got scratched up pretty bad 'cause I pushed him down so hard to get out of the way. (14-year-old)

The young women related that it is not unusual to have a family member or friend shot at or stabbed by a rival gang in retaliation for some real or perceived affront.

## Physical and Sexual Abuse

In addition to physical violence perpetrated by rival gangs, the young women feared violence from their own gang. Results from a modified version of Straus's (1979) Conflict Tactics Scale indicated that they endured physical abuse such as being slapped, punched, kicked, and choked; threatened with a weapon; and severely beaten.

A common theme in the gang and female delinquency literature is that male members view female members as sex objects (Campbell, 1984; Covey et al., 1992; Huff, 1990; Monti, 1993). An example of the type and frequency of sexual abuse experienced from within the gang came from one 16-year-old:

Q: OK, let me see if I've gotten all of this. You've said that you have experienced different types of sexual abuse including being made to dance on tables in just your bra and underwear, making Playboy-type home videos, [performing] oral sex in front of other gang members, and [having] intercourse at any given time, is that right?

A: Yeah, that about sums it up.

Q: And you say that any one of the guys can just snap his finger at any time and tell you to have sex with him and you'd have to do it?

A: Yep.

Q: That must be very humiliating.

A: It is, but it comes with the show.

Q: What if you turned it around, and you snapped your finger and told one of the males that you wanted him to perform some kind of sexual act in front of the others? Would he have to do it?

A *(Laughing):* You gotta be kidding. I wouldn't dare do that. If I did, depending on who it was, I'd probably pay in spades [be beaten severely].

*Q:* OK, say in any given month, how often would you say something sexually humiliating happens to you?

*A:* A month? Let's say in a day. In a 24-hour period of time, I might have to have sex or do something two or three times.

## Criminal Behavior

Early literature on delinquency indicated that teenage girls were more frequently the offenders of status criminal behavior (for example, truancy, shoplifting, violating curfew, and writing graffiti) and that teenage boys more often committed more serious crimes (Bowker & Klein, 1983; Monti, 1993; Moore, 1993). More recent findings suggest a dramatic increase in more serious criminal activities by teenage girls, including drive-by shootings, armed robberies, muggings, automobile thefts, and drug sales and distribution (Bowker & Klein, 1983; Campbell, 1984; Covey et al., 1992; Molidor, 1995; Teilmann & Landry, 1981).

When questioned about why this change is occurring, one 17-year-old replied, "It's simple. I got a gun." In the past, gang fighting was done with fists and knives, and female members could be at a disadvantage. No matter how big and muscular the opponent, using a gun evens out the odds:

> Oh, he thought he was some bad shit. Yeah, he thought he was on me. I'll tell you, he thought different when I pulled out my piece. (17-year-old)

## DISCUSSION

To view these young women as victims is justifiable. Most have been victims of violence and sexual abuse from parents and relatives since early childhood. They have been victims of poor economic conditions and the cycle of poverty and of overburdened and understaffed school systems that have failed to recognize them as at risk. In addition, the young women have become victims of the physical and sexual violence within their own gangs.

However, to view these young women only as victims is not accurate. Although the literature portrays female gang members as little more than sex objects, the role of teenage girls in gangs is evolving. They now are the perpetrators of serious crimes.

The stories of these young women are illuminating but represent the experiences of only 15 gang members incarcerated for asocial behavior. The themes of female gang membership in this article must be studied more extensively on a larger scale. Even so, the information collected from these young women gives context to female gang participation, challenges some commonly held assumptions about female gang behaviors, and may confirm the experiences of some social work practitioners working with teenage girls.

## IMPLICATIONS FOR SOCIAL WORK

The themes that emerged in this article have implications for social workers. First, social workers can develop school-based programs that encourage affiliation and membership that would substitute for gang membership. Such programs can include sports teams, art and educational groups, and peer-interest groups. By belonging to these alternative groups, teenage girls can establish their identity, gratify social needs, and increase their sense of acceptance and recognition by their peers.

Also, school systems have an obligation to create a safe environment in which students can learn. Programs can be designed to monitor more closely the school buildings and grounds for violence. Health, physical education, or specially designed classes can address and identify victims of physical, psychological, and sexual abuse. Social workers working with teachers can identify and treat the students while they are at school and report perpetrators to law enforcement agencies. This creates an environment of trust among a variety of systems.

Second, social workers need to focus prevention and intervention efforts on younger children. By focusing on only the high school population, social workers will have missed the girls who have already become gang members. If the majority of hard-core gang members begin associating with gangs at age 11 and drop out of school by the 10th grade, then programs must target elementary school and middle-school students.

Third, social workers need to direct interventions toward the family. This task can be extremely difficult because families of gang members or juvenile delinquents are difficult to engage in treatment (Spergel, 1995). The families of the young women in this article were former or current gang members or single parents who were overwhelmed, addicted to drugs, or themselves abused. Often these families had no idea of the trouble their children were in or how to handle the situation if they found out.

Social workers can develop community-based parent-training classes and outreach programs. Helping parents acquire new skills can increase positive communication between them and their children and eliminate the need for the children to seek an alternative family. Also, in cases in which children cannot continue to live with their families, foster families trained in the special needs of at-risk teenagers must be available.

Finally, all citizens have the right to live in their communities without the fear of being shot or stabbed. Community awareness of the ease with which weapons are available needs to increase. Legislators, working with law enforcement and other agencies, need to enact stricter laws that target those who distribute weapons, especially to minors.

## POSTSCRIPT

Six weeks after the completion of the interviews, three of the girls in the facility grabbed a female staff member, stabbed her nine times, and escaped from the residential facility. They were apprehended the next day. Two of the girls are currently serving 10 years for aggravated assault, and one has been released back into the program.

## REFERENCES

Bowker, L. H., & Klein, M. K. (1983). The etiology of female juvenile delinquency and gang membership: A test of psychological and social structural explanations. *Adolescence, 18,* 739–751.

Campbell, A. (1984). *The girls in the gang.* New York: Basil Blackwell.

Campbell, A. (1987). Self-definition by rejection: The case of gang girls. *Social Problems, 34,* 451–466.

Chesney-Lind, M. (1989). Girls' crime and a woman's place: Toward a feminist model of female delinquency. *Crime and Delinquency, 35,* 5–29.

Covey, H. C., Menard, S., & Franzese, R. J. (1992). *Juvenile gangs.* Springfield, IL: Charles C Thomas.

Cummings, S., & Monti, D. J. (1993). Preface. In S. Cummings & D. Monti (Eds.), *Gangs: The origins and impact of contemporary youth gangs in the United States* (pp. vii–x). Albany: State University of New York Press.

Erikson, E. H. (1980). *Identity and the life cycle.* New York: W. W. Norton.

Fishman, L. T. (1992, March). *The Vice Queens: An ethnographic study of black female gang behavior.* Paper presented at the annual meeting of the American Society of Criminology, Chicago.

Freud, A. (1936). *The ego and the mechanisms of defense.* New York: International Universities Press.

Giordano, P. C. (1978). Girls, guys, and gangs: The changing, social context of female delinquency. *Journal of Criminal Law and Criminology, 69,* 126–132.

Hagedorn, J. M. (1989). *People and folks.* Chicago: Lake View Press.

Horowitz, R. (1986). Remaining an outsider: Membership as a threat to research rapport. *Urban Life, 1,* 409–430.

Huff, R. (1990). Youth gangs and public policy. *Crime and Delinquency, 35,* 238–251.

Johnstone, J. W. (1983). Recruitment to a youth gang. *Youth and Society, 14,* 281–300.

McKinney, K. C. (1988). *Juvenile gangs: Crime and drug trafficking.* Washington, DC: Office of Juvenile Justice and Delinquency Prevention.

Molidor, C. E. (1995). Gender differences of psychological abuse in high school dating relationships. *Child and Adolescent Social Work Journal, 12,* 238–251.

Monti, D. J. (1993). Origins and problems of gang research in the United States. In S. Cummings & D. Monti (Eds.), *Gangs: The origins and impact of contemporary youth gangs in the United States* (pp. 3–26). Albany: State University of New York Press.

Moore, J. (1993). Gangs, drugs and violence. In S. Cummings & D. Monti (Eds.), *Gangs: The origins and impact of contemporary youth gangs in the United States* (pp. 27–48). Albany: State University of New York Press.

Perkins, U. E. (1987). *Explosion of Chicago's black street gangs: 1900–present.* Chicago: Third World Press.

Quicker, J. C. (1983). *Homegirls.* San Pedro, CA: International Universities Press.

Rosenbaum, J. L. (1991). Female crime and delinquency. In S. E. Brown, F. Esbensen, & G. Geis (Eds.), *Criminology: Explaining crime and its context* (pp. 521–524). Cincinnati: Anderson.

Spergel, I. A. (1992). Youth gangs: An essay review. *Social Service Review, 6,* 121–140.

Spergel, I. A. (1995). *The youth gang problem: A community approach.* New York: Oxford University Press.

Spergel, I. A., & Curry, G. D. (1990). Strategies and perceived effectiveness in dealing with the youth gang problem. In C. R. Huff (Ed.), *Gangs in America* (pp. 127–144). Newbury Park, CA: Sage Publications.

Straus, M. A. (1979). Measuring intrafamily conflict and violence: The Conflict Tactics Scale (CTS). *Journal of Marriage and the Family, 45,* 75–88.

Taylor, C. S. (1993). Female gangs: A historical perspective. In C. S. Taylor (Ed.), *Girls, gangs, women, and drugs* (pp. 13–47). East Lansing: Michigan State University Press.

Teilmann, K. S., & Landry, P. H. (1981). Gender bias in juvenile justice. *Journal of Research in Crime and Delinquency, 18,* 47–80.

Thrasher, F. (1927). *The gang.* Chicago: University of Chicago Press.

Zatz, M. S. (1987). Chicano youth gangs and crime: The creation of a moral panic. *Contemporary Crises, 11,* 129–158.

*An earlier version of this chapter was presented at the annual meeting of the NASW Texas Chapter, November 1994, Corpus Christi. The author thanks Richard Dangel and Marjie Barrett for their invaluable assistance with this project.*

*This chapter was originally published in the May 1996 issue of* Social Work, *Vol. 41, pp. 251–257.*

# 4 A Critical Review of Strategies to Reduce School Violence

Rudolph Alexander, Jr., and Carla M. Curtis

The topic of crime and violence permeates U.S. society and has been part of the public debate for years. To provide better reporting of the incidences of crime and violence, the federal government now surveys households to compile its crime index (Bynum & Thompson, 1992). The government also now surveys and reports the amount of crime and violence occurring in schools (Bastian & Taylor, 1991; Pearson & Toby, 1991). As more attention focuses on school violence (Sharp, 1993), policymakers have become more concerned and have instituted strategies to reduce its incidence.

Because information and knowledge tend to be scattered throughout the literature, we compiled and critically reviewed macro and micro intervention strategies used by school personnel to reduce school violence from the psychology, education, sociology, human relations, and social work literature, and we make recommendations for school social workers. In differentiating between micro and macro interventions, we drew on a discussion by Meenaghan (1987), who stated that in macro practice social workers do not work directly with individuals and groups; macro intervention involves planning, administration, evaluation, and community organizing. From Meenaghan's perspective, we define *macro interventions* in a school context as interventions in which practitioners attempt to create an environment conducive to ameliorating school violence, such as smaller schools or classrooms or preventive strategies. *Micro interventions*, on the other hand, are interventions in which practitioners work directly with parents, students, or school personnel to reduce school violence.

## WHAT IS SCHOOL VIOLENCE?

Kelly and Pink (1982) defined *school violence* as disrespect to teachers and administrators, theft, and physical assaults. Other studies have used more broadly defined indicators of youth aggression, including such factors as extreme competitiveness, quarrels with peers, and verbal and physical assaults (Bandura, 1973; Moyer, 1987; Ross, 1981; Steward & Kelso, 1987). However, some researchers have stressed that studies involving the extent of school violence as a dependent measure should narrowly define this concept and focus on the most serious behavior (Alexander & Langford, 1992; Dentler, 1977). This view is consistent with the federal government's definition, which includes rape, robbery, and simple and aggravated assaults (Bastian & Taylor, 1991). Contrary to the violent incidents depicted in the media, simple assaults committed without weapons that result in minor injuries represent the largest percentage of violent crimes in schools (Bastian & Taylor, 1991).

## STRATEGIC INTERVENTIONS

### Macro Interventions

*Smaller Schools.* Several researchers have used an ecological perspective to study school violence and have recommended macro interventions as a result of their findings. For example, Gottfredson and Gottfredson (1985) compared the amount of criminal victimization in large and small schools and recommended forming smaller schools as an intervention strategy in reducing violence. Similarly, Blyth, Thiel, Bush, and Simmons (1980) reported that students had a higher rate of victimization when they attended a large school than when they attended a smaller school. These researchers urged either building smaller schools or reducing the number of students attending large schools. Although subsequent research has shown the beneficial effects of small classes on student behavior (Russell, 1990), little evidence exists to show that school policymakers have heeded these researchers' recommendations.

*Increased Security.* School policymakers have endeavored to reduce school violence by increasing security. Some school security consultants stressed violence prevention and an effective response once a violent act had occurred (Vertermark & Blauvelt, 1978). Borrowing from other security-conscious environments, consultants recommended that school administrators should adopt target hardening procedures (for example, using security devices and personnel efficiently to prevent criminal activity) as the key to prevention. Six school periods were marked as common times when violence occurs—before school opening, during the school day, during after-school activities, during evening activities, during weekend activities, and during periods when the school is closed. Consultants recommended using teachers, parent volunteers, students, and security staff to monitor these periods. If a crime occurs on school property, an administrator's response should be geared toward identifying the perpetrator to law enforcement officials (Vertermark & Blauvelt, 1978).

Similarly, Quarles (1989), a criminal justice professor, reviewed the literature and also recommended target hardening procedures for school officials. He wrote that teachers who were observant tended to be victimized less often than nonobservant teachers. Observant teachers made eye contact, suggesting to potential offenders that these teachers were aware of them. Moreover, Quarles recommended that teachers walk down the middle of the hall instead of the edges to increase the distance an offender must come to initiate an attack. Also, teachers were urged to respond assertively to remarks that carried sexual overtones. "If you create an environment that increases the amount of time necessary to steal from you, or rob, rape, assault, or abuse you, the criminal will look for a softer, easier victim" (p. 12).

*Other Preventive Strategies.* One suggestion for curbing classroom violence urged teachers to send a student for help, get the names of participants and witnesses in case criminal charges are later made, disperse crowds because students like excitement and the dynamics exacerbate problems, keep calm, and follow the school policy regarding the reporting of incidents (Chernow & Chernow, 1989). Furthermore, a panel of school experts has recommended that schools conduct safety assessments, reviewing how school policies are enforced with respect to violent students, how staff are trained, and how the school can promote a positive climate (U.S. Department of Education, 1992).

Emphasizing preventive measures to curb gangs, Rich (1992) stated that educators can divert students from joining gangs by establishing "an organized atmosphere of learning and living in school" (p. 38). Moreover, administrators should create a climate in which norms and values are positively viewed and improve ways of instilling positive socialization during school hours. Alternative schools could be established for delinquent and violent students. Rich noted that alternative schools, more than traditional schools, have comprehensive goals, are smaller and less bureaucratic, and have more adjustable curricula. Radin (1989) stated that the Education of the Handicapped Act Amendments of 1986 (P.L. 99-457) requires preventive strategies for at-risk students.

*Suspensions and Expulsions.* School officials have used traditional suspensions and expulsions as a means of deterring students from committing crimes on school property. However, former Senator Birch Bayh held hearings on school violence in the 1970s and found that some school administrators had been suspending and expelling students for minor offenses, making these measures counterproductive (Bayh, 1978). Besag (1989) stressed that harsh and punitive disciplinary measures aggravate the potential for violence rather than control it. More recently, Alexander (1993) examined the policy of permanent school expulsion as a way to control school violence and concluded that this policy is counterproductive.

## Micro Interventions

Although some preventive macro strategies have been used, they have not been enthusiastically embraced as the answer for school violence; instead, schools and professionals have tended to use micro intervention strategies.

*Commission on Youth Violence.* The American Psychological Association (APA) (1993) created the Commission on Youth Violence (CYV) to review its literature on youth violence and to summarize strategies to reduce it. CYV noted that a plethora of intervention programs had been launched; however, many programs were created essentially for service delivery without theoretical justification or intention to study program effectiveness. The programs were aimed at perpetrators, victims, and witnesses of violence. Some programs were preventive in nature. Other programs were designed to alleviate the psychological trauma and were "targeted toward changing individuals, [whereas] others seek to change the systems and settings that influence behavior, such as the family, peers, schools, and community" (APA, 1993, p. 53). Although these interventions into various systems were discussed from a psychological perspective, these discussions have applicability for social work practice because social work has had a long history of intervening in these systems.

CYV stated that the most scientifically conducted research of effectiveness had shown that the most efficacious interventions were those that reduced risk factors of "detrimental life circumstances" and those that strengthened children and families. Specifically, prevention programs during the early life of children reduced factors that increased the risk for violence and clinical dysfunctions during childhood and adolescence. CYV recommended home visitor programs for at-risk families that included prenatal and postnatal counseling with parents. Additionally, CYV supported preschool programs that met children's intellectual, emotional, and social needs, including developing children's cognitive and decision-making processes.

With respect to school-based programs, CYV noted that the most effective programs were those for children in whom the violence was not yet deeply ingrained. For this group, primary prevention programs can improve prosocial behaviors by fostering nonviolent norms, decreasing the opportunity for violent acts, and inhibiting the aggressive acts that manifest themselves during childhood and adolescence. These programs can help instill in students better coping skills so that when normal crises develop, students will respond more appropriately:

> Primary prevention programs of the type that promote social and cognitive skills seem to have the greatest impact on attitudes about violent behavior among children and youth. Skills that aid children in learning alternatives to violent behaviors include social perspective-taking, alternative solution generation, self-esteem enhancement, peer negotiation skills, problem-solving skills training, and anger management. (APA, 1993, p. 56)

The recommendations from the CYV were derived from the psychology literature, and the CYV did not identify particular studies. Although the CYV stated that some of the studies from the psychology literature were not based on sound research methodology, it did not differentiate specific studies or cite any specific authors.

*Cognitive–Behavioral Approach.* Wells and Miller (1993) discussed assaults on students and teachers and recommended a cognitive-behavioral approach for intervention. This affective aggression model considers the linkages between stimuli, unconditioned responses, conditioned responses, and contingencies. The behavior exhibited by an adolescent indicates to the school professional where to intervene, conforming to the social work principle of starting where the client is. For example, the school professional, depending on where the student was in the cycle, should intervene by teaching avoidance techniques; helping a student recognize arousal; teaching cognitive, self-management, or coping strategies; and offering positive reinforcement.

Similarly, Horne, Glaser, Sayger, and Wright (1992) described a model for the prevention of serious conduct disorders in children and recommended many intervention strategies, including social competence, peer counseling, academic remediation, behavioral self-control strategies, training educators, parent training in child management skills, social learning, family therapy, parent individual therapy, couple or single-parent counseling, and parent education. Also, Nystrom (1989), a school social worker, posited an empowerment model for school social workers consisting of five components: (1) empowerment of individuals, (2) reduction of learned helplessness, (3) enhancement of internal locus of control,

(4) reframing, and (5) consultation. Nystrom did not indicate that his model was appropriate for addressing school violence, but the model does indicate that it was appropriate for parent training, which could be used to help address school violence.

Mace and Shea (1989) stated that some student problems can be addressed early before more-intrusive and more-restrictive interventions are used. They recommended a behavioral self-management intervention strategy consisting of self-management, self-evaluation, self-reinforcement, and self-instruction. This model is appropriate for schools because it is time efficient and allows more students to be served; uses least-restrictive positive techniques; and allows input from students, teachers, and special services providers in the design, administration, and evaluation. However, this model, like Horne et al.'s (1992) and Nystrom's (1989), did not involve empirical research studies. Some researchers have examined the effects of intervention with control studies or studies involving the use of multivariate analysis in which statistical control groups were used. As an example, Loeber and Dishion (1984) studied boys who fought at home and school and found that boys who fought in both environments were more antisocial, had poorer parenting, had more marital discord at home, had families with poorer problem-solving skills, and were more likely to experience parental rejection than three comparison groups of boys who were nonfighters, who fought at home only, and who fought at school only. Loeber and Dishion stressed preventive intervention in early childhood because behavioral patterns tend to be more ingrained the longer they exist. Although they noted that some studies have reported successful interventions involving parents and teachers, this intervention was costly in time and resources.

Alexander and Langford (1992) studied fighting among students but did not differentiate between environments. Using social learning as a theoretical groundwork, Alexander and Langford found that the peer group and the family were important reinforcers for fighting. The researchers recommended intervention with parents and fighters through group treatment. Alexander and Langford's model stressed conflict resolution skills, which is consistent with other researchers who have advocated mediation (Rubenstein & Feldman, 1993; Tolson, McDonald, & Moriarty, 1992).

Other researchers have used empirical studies to test the effectiveness of intervention in decreasing the amount of school violence. One study by Doescher and Sugawara (1992), grounded in social learning theory, found that prosocial home-based and school-based interventions were effective in reducing the level of disruptive behavior. However, the effects were short-lived, and neither the home-based nor the school-based intervention produced long-term results. In another study Hammond (1990) tested the Positive Adolescent Choices Training (PACT), a school-based intervention for aggressive African American students grounded in cognitive–behavioral theory. Compared with a matched untreated group, PACT students had less aggressive behaviors and fewer suspensions and expulsions related to aggressive behaviors.

Although not presenting a model of intervention or empirical results, other professionals have discussed in policy papers methods directed at reducing student violence. Bryant and Zayas (1986) advocated for an ecological, multimodal model of intervention with children who had dysfunctional behavior by intervening with the students, family, and community. Fine and Gardner (1991) advocated a family empowerment perspective in counseling and home-based services.

A school system in Norway, spurred by the suicides of two students who were victims of bullying, developed an intervention strategy consisting of a videotape for class viewing and discussion and a booklet for teachers and parents. Additionally, other interventions consisted of drama and role playing, involvement of students in problem solving and cooperation, and assertiveness training for student victims. A three-year follow-up study of the effectiveness of the program found that the intervention resulted in a significant decrease in the amount of bullying (Cowie, Boulton, & Smith, 1992).

Another program consisted of a class assignment in which students were asked to monitor the amount of violence that they saw on television (Karlin & Berger, 1992). Students analyzed and discussed with their classmates what they had witnessed. Although no empirical studies were conducted on the project, the authors, two experienced teachers, maintained that the assignments had a major impact on sensitizing students to the amount of violence in American society. As a result, the students promised to work toward combating violence.

*Corporal Punishment.* Besides making students more aware of the amount of violence in society, some school systems have endorsed, paradoxically, corporal punishment to correct disruptive student behavior. However, a growing group of professionals have condemned corporal punishment (Hyman & Lally, 1982; Payne, 1989; Radin, 1988; Richett & Hudson, 1979; Schrage, 1986; Straus, 1991). Straus's condemnation was based on cultural spillover theory—that "violence in one sphere of life tends to engender violence in other spheres, and that this carry-over process transcends the bounds between legitimate and criminal use of force" (p. 137). Straus studied data from the National Family Violence Survey, which consisted of 3,300 children and 6,000 couples, and found that physical punishment may have a short-term effect in lessening offending behavior but that it had some long-term negative consequences, such as an increased probability of delinquency in adolescents and abusive behaviors in adults inside and outside of the home.

*Teacher Conduct.* Some professionals have examined teacher conduct that may trigger student violence. Researchers observed that some teachers had more disruption in their classes than other teachers, and the lack of crisis intervention skills by the teachers was a critical factor (Bell & Semmel, 1978). A teacher's lack of sensitivity to differences in students' tolerance levels contributed to some classroom violence (Wells, 1978). Teachers need classroom management skills and must know how to resolve disagreements peacefully, how to break up a fight, how to deal with a student with a weapon, and how to deal with habitual offenders or gang members and must be familiar with the legal rights and duties of students and teachers (U.S. Department of Education, 1992). DeCecco and Roberts (1978) proposed a negotiating model for teachers and students to reduce the incidence of violence: Both parties should be given an opportunity for direct verbal expression of anger over specific issues; to analyze the conflict in terms of the issues as stated by each party and the possible violation of each party's civil rights; to agree with common statements of the issues; to agree to gains and concessions for each side; to agree to the allocation of responsibilities for implementing agreements; and to agree to the conditions for evaluating implementation of agreements.

Teachers also can contribute to some violence in their classes by not being cognizant of the origin of their disciplining methods. For instance, Kaplan (1992) administered a punishment history inventory to teachers and was able to discern two groups of teachers: teachers who used punitive measures in class and those who did not. Using discriminant analysis, Kaplan found that teachers who used punitive measures in class were significantly more likely than teachers who did not to have been punished as children without being asked the circumstances. Further, punishing teachers were more likely to have been prohibited from questioning parental authority. Punishing teachers were less likely to report that their parents explained the reasons for various rules and the effects of noncompliance with rules on others and were less likely to be praised for prosocial behaviors and to be heard by their parents. Punishing teachers were more likely to have been screamed at by their parents, spanked with belts, bruised by spankings, and physically punished after age 12. These findings have implications for teacher training, and teachers should focus on the origins of their views regarding disciplining in the classroom.

In another study, Robinson (1992) argued that teachers' beliefs about appropriate gender behavior determined their classroom methods and responses regarding boys and girls. The author examined only the effect on girls and found that teachers' attitudes had a major impact on girls' motivation, self-esteem, reputations, and career aspirations. Moreover, stereotyped beliefs about men and women determined the disciplinary measures taken by teachers, especially male teachers.

### Combinations of Interventions

Seeming to recognize the advantages of combining macro and micro intervention strategies, some professionals have called for "whole-school policies" that encompass the involvement of all central characters (Tattum & Tattum, 1992). As an example, one article advocated the random selection of parents to serve on school boards so that the community could take ownership of school problems (Pink & Kapel, 1978). Bayh (1978) wrote that the best solution to school violence was active participation by the entire education community.

## STRATEGIES FOR SCHOOL SOCIAL WORKERS

The literature provides direction for school social workers in carrying out their roles, describes promising intervention techniques for addressing violent or inappropriately aggressive students, and provides guidance for further research. Within the context of the four school social work roles cited by Ginsburg (1990) of child therapist, consultant to school personnel, family practitioner, and broker for community resources, this critical review suggests strategies to reduce school violence that can be used by school social workers.

Of particular interest are studies by Loeber and Dishion (1984), Tolson et al. (1992), Hammond (1990), and Doescher and Sugawara (1992) because each used comparison groups. Alexander and Langford (1992) used a multivariate design that provided statistical controls. These five empirically based studies provide trustworthy knowledge for school social workers.

The literature also provides conceptual models about school violence that are ripe for rigorous research studies. The models by Wells and Miller (1993), Horne et al. (1992), and Mace and Shea (1989) look promising, but the authors did not report any empirical support for their models. Nystrom (1989) reported a case study to support his empowerment model, but it lacked grounding in sound research methodology. The Commission on Youth Violence (APA, 1993) acknowledged that some of the psychology literature lacked scientific rigor, and social work professionals have made similar comments about social work practice models (Fraser, 1993; Hopps, 1989). This void in the literature provides an opportunity for school social workers to conduct studies that will upgrade the knowledge base for the profession and increase the status of social work research.

School social workers are in an ideal environment to develop and test innovative interventions. Unlike other treatment settings that generally forbid random assignment to experimental and control groups, schools that want effective interventions for aggressive students should be more willing to permit true experiments. Researchers know that some treatment may work for some individuals but not others; thus, an experimental design that tests intensities of treatment or compares two or more treatments for different students would provide a powerful research design for determining what works for whom. Additionally, because community involvement has been cited as a critical component of stopping school violence, it also may be included in the research design. If school social workers do not have the expertise to conduct this type of research, they can solicit the help and collaboration of social work researchers who are employed in research institutions.

## REFERENCES

Alexander, R., Jr. (1993). *Permanent expulsion of students for drug and violent offenses.* Manuscript submitted for publication.

Alexander, R., Jr., & Langford, L. (1992). Throwing down: A social learning test of student fighting. *Social Work in Education, 14,* 114–124.

American Psychological Association. (1993). *Violence & youth: Psychology's response.* Washington, DC: Author.

Bandura, A. (1973). *Aggression: A social learning analysis.* Englewood Cliffs, NJ: Prentice Hall.

Bastian, L. D., & Taylor, B. M. (1991). *School crime: A national crime victimization survey report.* Washington, DC: U.S. Government Printing Office.

Bayh, B. (1978). School violence and vandalism: Problems and solutions. *Journal of Research and Development in Education, 11*(2), 2–7.

Bell, R., & Semmel, E. (1978). Training specialists to work with disruptive students: Rationale and models. In National Institute of Education (Ed.), *School crime and disruption: Prevention models* (pp. 143–151). Washington, DC: U.S. Government Printing Office.

Besag, V. E. (1989). *Bullies and victims in schools: A guide to understanding and management.* Philadelphia: Open University Press.

Blyth, D. A., Thiel, K. S., Bush, D. M., & Simmons, R. G. (1980). Student as victim. *Youth & Society, 11,* 369–388.

Bryant, C., & Zayas, L. H. (1986). Initial moves with school–family conflict: Entering, engaging, and contracting. *Child and Adolescent Social Work, 3*, 87–100.

Bynum, J. E., & Thompson, W. E. (1992). *Juvenile delinquency: A sociological perspective* (2nd ed.). Boston: Allyn & Bacon.

Chernow, C., & Chernow, F. B. (1989). *Classroom discipline survival guide for middle/junior high teachers.* West Nyack, NY: Center for Applied Research in Education.

Cowie, H., Boulton, M. J., & Smith, P. K. (1992). Bullying: Pupil relationships. In N. Jones & E. B. Jones (Eds.), *Learning to behave* (pp. 85–101). London: Kogan.

DeCecco, J., & Roberts, J. (1978). Negotiating school conflict to prevent student delinquency. In National Institute of Education (Ed.), *School crime and disruption: Prevention models* (pp. 135–141). Washington, DC: U.S. Government Printing Office.

Dentler, R. A. (1977). School violence: Building an R & D agenda. In J. M. McPortland & E. L. McDill (Eds.), *Violence in schools: Perspectives, programs, and positions* (pp. 137–142). Lexington, MA: D.C. Heath.

Doescher, S. M., & Sugawara, A. I. (1992). Impact of prosocial home- and school-based interventions on preschool children's cooperative behavior. *Family Relations, 41*, 200–204.

Education of the Handicapped Act Amendments of 1986, P.L. 99-457, 100 Stat. 1145.

Fine, M. J., & Gardner, P. A. (1991). Counseling and education services for families: An empowerment perspective. *Elementary School Guidance and Counseling, 26*, 33–44.

Fraser, M. W. (1993). Scholarship in social work: Imperfect methods, approximate truths, and emerging challenges. In *Toward relevant and useful scholarship in a fragmented world: Proceedings of the Sixth National Symposium on Doctoral Research and Social Work Practice* (pp. 1–35). Columbus: Ohio State University, College of Social Work.

Ginsburg, E. H. (1990). *Effective interventions: Applying learning theory to school social work.* New York: Greenwood Press.

Gottfredson, G. D., & Gottfredson, D. C. (1985). *Victimization in schools.* New York: Plenum Press.

Hammond, R. W. (1990, August). *Positive Adolescent Choices Training (PACT): Preliminary findings of the effects of a school-based violence prevention program for African-American adolescents.* Paper presented at the Annual Meeting of the American Psychological Association, Boston.

Hopps, J. (1989). Research and practice: Searching for a partnership. In *Fifth National Symposium of Doctoral Research and Social Work Practice* (pp. 1–14). Columbus: Ohio State University, College of Social Work.

Horne, A. M., Glaser, B. A., Sayger, T. V., & Wright, L. B. (1992). Behavior-disordered children: Home and school interventions. *Contemporary Education, 64*, 10–15.

Hyman, I. A., & Lally, D. (1982). Discipline in the 1980s: Some alternatives to corporal punishment. *Children Today, 11*, 10–13.

Kaplan, C. (1992). Teachers' punishment histories and their selection of disciplining strategies. *Contemporary Educational Psychology, 17*, 258–265.

Karlin, M. S., & Berger, R. (1992). *Discipline and the disruptive child: A new, expanded practical guide for elementary teachers.* West Nyack, NY: Parker.

Kelly, D. H., & Pink, W. T. (1982). School crime and individual responsibility: The perpetuation of a myth. *Urban Review, 14*, 47–63.

Loeber, R., & Dishion, T. J. (1984). Boys who fight at home and school: Family conditions influencing cross-setting consistency. *Journal of Consulting and Clinical Psychology, 52*, 759–768.

Mace, F. C., & Shea, M. C. (1989). Behavioral self-management with at-risk children. *Special Services in the Schools, 3–4*, 43–64.

Meenaghan, T. M. (1987). Macro practice: Current trends and issues. In A. Minahan (Ed.-in-Chief), *Encyclopedia of social work* (18th ed., Vol. 2, pp. 82–89). Silver Spring, MD: National Association of Social Workers.

Moyer, K. E. (1987). *Violence and aggression: A physiological perspective.* New York: Paragon House.

Nystrom, J. (1989). Empowerment model for delivery of social work services in public schools. *Social Work in Education, 11*, 160–170.

Payne, M. A. (1989). Use and abuse of corporal punishment: A Caribbean view. *Child Abuse & Neglect, 13,* 389–401.

Pearson, F. S., & Toby, J. (1991). Fear of school-related predatory crime. *Sociology and Social Research, 75,* 117–125.

Pink, W. T., & Kapel, D. E. (1978). Decentralizing reconsidered: School crime prevention through community involvement. In National Institute of Education (Ed.), *School crime and disruption: Prevention models* (pp. 115–122). Washington, DC: U.S. Government Printing Office.

Quarles, C. L. (1989). *School violence: A survival guide for school staff.* Washington, DC: National Education Association.

Radin, N. (1988). Alternatives to suspension and corporal punishment. *Urban Education, 22,* 476–495.

Radin, N. (1989). School social work practice: Past, present, and future trends. *Social Work in Education, 11,* 213–225.

Rich, J. M. (1992). Predicting and controlling school violence. *Contemporary Education, 64,* 35–39.

Richett, D. M., & Hudson, J. R. (1979). The socio-legal history of child abuse and neglect: An analysis of the policy of children's rights. *Journal of Sociology and Social Welfare, 6,* 849–875.

Robinson, K. H. (1992). Classroom discipline: Power, resistance and gender—A look at teacher perspectives. *Gender and Education, 4,* 273–287. (From *Sociology of Education Abstracts, 1993, 29,* Abstract No. 93S/068)

Ross, A. O. (1981). *Child behavior therapy: Principles, procedures, and empirical basis.* New York: John Wiley & Sons.

Rubenstein, J. L., & Feldman, S. S. (1993). Conflict-resolution behavior in adolescent boys: Antecedents and adaptational correlates. *Journal of Research on Adolescence, 3,* 41–66.

Russell, A. (1990). The effects of child-staff ratio on staff and child behavior in preschools: An experimental study. *Journal of Research in Childhood Education, 4,* 77–90.

Schrage, G. (1986). The law governing control and discipline of behavior-disordered students. *School Social Work Journal, 10,* 64–75.

Sharp, D. (1993, October 25). Teachers taking a beating: Physical assaults are grim reality. *USA Today,* p. 3A.

Steward, R. B., & Kelso, J. (1987). A two-year follow-up of boys with aggressive conduct disorder. *Psychopathology, 20,* 296–304.

Straus, M. A. (1991). Discipline and deviance: Physical punishment of children and violence and other crime in adulthood. *Social Problems, 38,* 133–152.

Tattum, D., & Tattum, E. (1992). Bullying: A whole-school response. In N. Jones & E. B. Jones (Eds.), *Learning to behave* (pp. 67–84). London: Kogan.

Tolson, E. R., McDonald, S., & Moriarty, A. R. (1992). Peer mediation among high school students: A test of effectiveness. *Social Work in Education, 14,* 86–93.

U.S. Department of Education. (1992). *Schools free of drugs and violence: Questions and answers on reaching national education goal 6* [Microfiche 354427]. Washington, DC: Author.

Vertermark, S. D., & Blauvelt, P. D. (1978). *Controlling crime in school: A complete security handbook for administrators.* West Nyack, NY: Parker.

Wells, D., & Miller, M. J. (1993). Adolescent affective aggression: An intervention model. *Adolescence, 28,* 781–791.

Wells, R. (1978). Teacher survival in the classroom. *Journal of Research and Development in Education, 11*(2), 64–73.

*This chapter was originally published in the April 1995 issue of* Social Work in Education, *Vol. 17, pp. 73–82.*

# A Comprehensive Afrocentric Rites of Passage Program for Black Male Adolescents

Aminifu R. Harvey and Julia B. Rauch

**M**any adolescents engage in risky behaviors that may have harmful, even fatal, consequences for themselves and others (Carnegie Corporation of New York, 1995; Irwin & Ingra, 1994). The leading causes of adolescent injury and death—motor vehicle crashes, homicide, and suicide—are behavior related (*Healthy People 2000,* 1991, 1995). The problem of risk behaviors is particularly acute among African American male adolescents who live in high-risk environments.

Empirical research suggests that risks tend to cluster in the same individual and reinforce one another and that risk behaviors often have common antecedents in childhood experience and educational failure (Irwin & Ingra, 1994; Jessor, 1992). These observations suggest that generic interventions that address more than one behavior or predisposing factor are preferable to approaches that target only one risk factor or that use only one method of intervention.

This article describes a multifaceted Afrocentric rites of passage model of intervention with African American male youths living in high-risk environments. Before describing the model, the article reviews the health status of African American male adolescents; two frameworks that are useful in social work practice with African Americans, cultural competence and empowerment; and Afrocentric theory and Afrocentric social work practice. The article concludes by identifying steps that health-based and other social workers can take to introduce Afrocentric elements into their practices and organizational settings.

## HEALTH OF AFRICAN AMERICAN MALE ADOLESCENTS

The homicide rate for black youths ages 15 to 24 jumped from 96.2 per 100,000 in 1984 to 114.8 in 1989; the rate for white youths the same ages rose from 11.2 per 100,000 in 1984 to 12.8 in 1989 (National Center for Health Statistics, 1994). The number of black men age 13 and older who died from AIDS transmitted through intravenous drug use jumped from 674 in 1985 to 2,050 in 1993, greater than the increase of 223 to 787 for their white counterparts (*Black Americans,* 1995). Between 1980 and 1992, the suicide rate among young black males increased 300 percent, more than twice the increase (120 percent) among all teenagers (Carnegie Corporation of New York, 1995).

Even though African American youths in general use alcohol and drugs less than white youths, substance abuse is epidemic in poor black neighborhoods

(*Black Americans*, 1995). Black youths are more likely than white youths to use cocaine and to use emergency rooms for drug-related reasons (Children's Defense Fund, 1995). Gonorrhea and syphilis are more prevalent among black teenagers than among white or Hispanic teenagers (Irwin, Brindis, Brodt, Bennett, & Rodrigues, 1991).

Black male teenagers are also at risk for mental health problems. In 1989 the Institute of Medicine estimated that the rate of mental disorders was 12 percent for all children under age 18 but in excess of 20 percent for those living in urban ghettos. A study of children living in violent communities suggested that children are psychologically harmed by an erosion of their sense of personal safety and security, generalized emotional distress, depersonalization, and a diminished future orientation (Isaacs, 1992). Unfortunately, current data regarding the prevalence of depression and other mental health problems among African American youths are unavailable (*Healthy People 2000*, 1995).

Access to and use of health services is problematic for black male adolescents (American Academy of Pediatrics, 1994; Irwin et al., 1991). The barriers to health care are many (American Academy of Pediatrics, 1994; Carnegie Corporation of New York, 1995). Removal of some, such as lack of health insurance, is contingent on changes in the political arena.

Other barriers to health care are rooted in the behaviors of health practitioners and organizations (Cross, Bazron, Dennis, & Isaacs, 1989). They include conduct that manifests—or is perceived as manifesting—racism, classism, and cultural insensitivity. These barriers are amenable to change through interventions targeted at the organizational and individual levels. Because of their generalist skills and sensitivity to issues of diversity, social workers are equipped to initiate and lead efforts to reduce racist, classist, and ethnocentric barriers to health care.

## CULTURAL COMPETENCE

A culturally competent system of care "acknowledges and incorporates—at all levels—the importance of culture, the assessment of cross-cultural relations, vigilance toward the dynamics that result from cultural differences, the expansion of cultural knowledge, and the adaptation of services to meet culturally-unique needs" (Cross et al., 1989, p. 17). Cultural competence can be envisioned as a continuum with negative and positive poles (Figure 5-1) (Cross et al., 1989).

The negative pole is cultural destructiveness, or attitudes, policies, and practices that harm culture and, consequently, individuals within the culture. At the

*Figure 5-1*

**Cultural Competence Continuum**

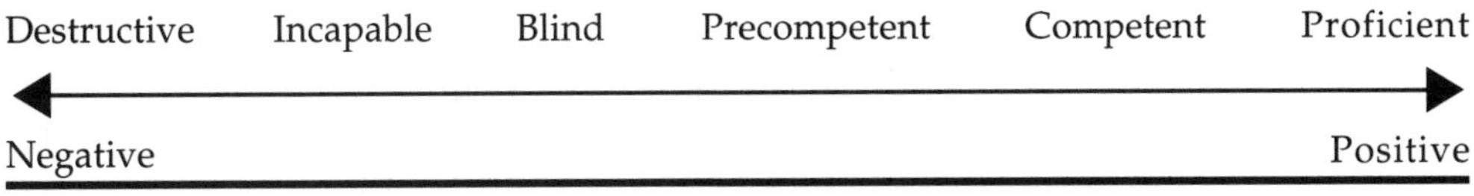

| Destructive | Incapable | Blind | Precompetent | Competent | Proficient |
|---|---|---|---|---|---|

Negative ————————————————————————————————→ Positive

point of cultural incapability, the system is biased, believes that the dominant group is superior, and is paternalistic toward populations perceived as inferior. Culturally blind practitioners and agencies believe that all people are the same and that dominant helping approaches are universally applicable. Culturally precompetent agencies and practitioners recognize weaknesses in serving diverse populations, desire to improve, and act to do so (for example, by hiring community residents).

Basic cultural competence occurs when organizations and practitioners respect difference; engage in ongoing cultural self-assessment; expand their cultural knowledge and skills; and adapt services to fit the community's culture, situation, and perceived needs. With cultural proficiency, the group's culture is esteemed and new approaches are developed on the basis of deep cultural knowledge. All health organizations and practitioners are at points along this continuum. Social work change agents need to assess their own and their organization's location on the continuum.

## EMPOWERMENT

Solomon (1976) affirmed empowerment as a process and goal for oppressed people. She defined *empowerment* as "a process whereby the social worker engages in a set of activities with the client or client system that aim to reduce the powerlessness that has been created by negative valuations based on membership in a stigmatized group" (p. 19). She defined *powerlessness* as "the inability to manage emotions, skills, knowledge, and/or material resources in a way that effective performance of valued social roles will lead to personal gratification" (p. 16).

Solomon (1976) hypothesized that powerlessness is derived from direct and indirect power blocks. Institutional agents apply direct power blocks. For example, the health care or other service system may fail to provide adequate community-based health services. Consequently, individuals' health and functioning are diminished. Indirect power blocks are incorporated into individuals' developmental experiences. For example, a parent may foster low self-esteem by denigrating a dark-skinned child's color (Harvey, 1995b). Lacking self-confidence, the child may give up when school work is difficult and may not develop basic reading, writing, and arithmetic skills.

The concept of indirect power blocks is akin to internalized racism, but broader. As in internalized racism, indirect power blocks connote rejection of self and others like oneself because of race. Indirect power blocks, in addition, connote inability to function in important roles because of psychological, interpersonal, skill, knowledge, and resource management deficits.

Solomon (1976) posited that direct and indirect power blocks interact to generate powerlessness. In the aforementioned scenario, for example, the child might continue to fail because the school does not provide adequate instruction (direct power block). Behavioral and emotional problems may emerge (indirect power blocks), further impeding learning. Solomon's model implies that intervention needs to address psychological factors, interpersonal skills, knowledge deficits, technical skills, and resource management. The goal is to enable oppressed people to transcend direct power blocks to create satisfying lives and become part of an empowered community. The approach is congruent with research findings that multiple adolescent risk behaviors tend to cluster in the same individuals and require multifaceted, rather than categorical, interventions (Carnegie Corporation of New York, 1995; Irwin & Ingra, 1994; Jessor, 1992).

## AFROCENTRIC SOCIAL WORK

Afrocentric social work is one way of implementing Solomon's (1976) model. Afrocentric social work provides multifaceted interventions, recognizing that any single intervention is by itself inadequate to mitigate direct and indirect power blocks. Afrocentrism provides a culturally specific paradigm for serving African Americans. Although currently used primarily by black social workers, Afrocentric theory and practice are tools that all social workers can use.

Afrocentric social workers contend that aspects of European American–based practice are inappropriate for black people. In their view, the African ethos, as transmuted into African American culture, has been and is central to African Americans' ability to survive racist oppression. Systematic efforts to destroy and denigrate African culture have harmed African Americans. Members of this group have been forcefully separated from their roots by slavery, and racism has imposed an alien culture on them. For example, European American culture has socialized African Americans to believe that light skin and straight hair are beautiful and that dark skin and kinky hair are ugly (Harvey, 1995b).

African Americans experience the "paradox of blackness." They are penalized when their behaviors are congruent with African and African American culture. When their behaviors are congruent with European American culture, they are rewarded. For example, a child who speaks "black English" in school may be labeled as slow or ignorant, whereas the teacher considers the child who speaks standard English as innately more intelligent. Similarly, it is insulting to call a person of African descent "a black, kinky-haired African"; that is, to describe a person by his or her natural characteristics is offensive. The paradox of blackness fosters self-hatred and self-destructiveness. Consequently, consciousness raising regarding racism and its effects is an important component of Afrocentric social work. In Afrocentric practice, treatment—conceived of as healing—takes place within and through positive, rewarding connections with African and African American culture and with other people of African descent.

### African Worldview

Afrocentrism is predicated on traditional African philosophy that predates European and Arab influences (Schiele, 1994). Two core elements are spirituality (Pinkett, 1993) and interconnectedness (Myers, 1988). "Spirituality" refers to the universal creative force that is manifested in all natural phenomena. Unlike European American thought, traditional African thought did not distinguish between the spiritual and material. It viewed all elements of the universe as linked by the nonmaterial, invisible substance of spirituality.

Spirituality supports belief in interconnectedness—that is, interdependence—within the wholeness of the universe. Because all natural phenomena contain an aspect of the universal creative force, all natural things are joined and sacred. Guided by this belief, an African worldview defines the human life task as striving to be "God-like," that is, living a life grounded in virtue and morality. Constructive, harmonious human interchange is cherished. Human dysfunction arises when humans are alienated from mutually supportive relationships. It follows that dysfunction is remediated by connecting people to each other.

Spiritually rooted, Afrocentric social work helps individuals connect with and manifest the universal creative force within them. Individuals are encouraged to prize the African and African American values of equality, cooperation, reconciliation, respect, and sharing. Connectedness is nurtured through groups. Recognizing that the effects of indirect power blocks are not easily vanquished, Afrocentric practitioners intervene over a sufficient duration to permit internalization of a positive sense of self, of other African Americans, and of African and African American heritage. The aim is respect of self, family, and community.

## Adolescent Rites of Passage

Another African concept is that life is transitional. People who have died—ancestors—continue to live as spiritual energies that exist to assist living people. Traditional African societies structured the transition from childhood to adulthood through rites of passage at puberty. During these rites, the ancestors were invoked to guide the child through this life process with the assistance of the elders in the community.

The community sequestered youths, under the guidance of elders, for months or even years to provide them with the knowledge, consciousness, and skills needed for adulthood (Erny, 1968). When the elders evaluated the youths as having mastered the necessary learning, the community commemorated their entry into adulthood by a ceremony during which the initiates pledged to carry on communal life and the community agreed to assist the initiates in their new roles. Some features of rites of passage programs for youths include being sequestered, participating in experiences to develop a sense of "we-ness," paying deference to elders, participating in ceremonies to mark milestones in the transformational process, and accomplishing life skills tasks (Harvey, 1995a; Hill, 1992).

## MAAT CENTER PROGRAM

*Ma'at*, an ancient Egyptian word, means an ethical way of life (Karenga, 1990). The goal of the MAAT Program is empowerment of black male adolescents through a nine-month rites of passage program. The MAAT Center, located in Washington, DC, serves boys ages 11 to 19 years referred by the courts and emotionally and behaviorally disturbed youths ages 11 to 19 years referred by the mental health and school systems. The MAAT Program provides a multifaceted, therapeutic program to 15-member youth groups.

To secure a cohort that can jointly proceed through the program, intake is open for limited periods. The referring person tells the youth and his family of the referral. Staff then contact the family to arrange the first interview, which optimally includes the youth, his family, and the referring person. The location is flexible based on the family's preference. It may be the home, the office of the referral person, or the MAAT Center. Participation is voluntary for youths and families, even in the case of court-referred youths.

The first eight weeks are an orientation for the youths and include an orientation session for parents or guardians and referring agency personnel. The invitation to adults communicates that the youths' transformation is a communal effort and signifies to the youths that they are affiliated with caring elders. A major component of the MAAT Center is the after-school program, held for two hours, three days per week. It offers modules on knowledge and behaviors for living; module topics include manhood development, sexuality, and drugs. Modules on creative arts, math, and science are also offered. After each module is completed, the youths develop topic-related projects, such as the production of culturally oriented T-shirts, anti-substance abuse buttons, videotapes, and concerts. Thus, the youths have a tangible product that signifies their learning experience as a group.

The MAAT Program stresses parent and caretaker involvement. Family enhancement and empowerment buffet dinners are held monthly. The objectives of the dinners are to empower adults to advocate on behalf of their families and to work toward community improvement. The dinners convey to parents that they are valued and that the program is hospitable and nurturing. This message is necessary because initially most parents distrust the MAAT Program because of previous negative experiences with human services organizations. Staff demonstrate their caring to parents through ongoing outreach. For example, they telephone parents when a youth does something well.

Another MAAT Program component is casework and counseling. Depending on need, children and family members are linked to a variety of health, educational, legal, and social services. The staff, which includes a clinical social worker as well as nonprofessionals, also provides formal, informal, and crisis counseling. Thus, the MAAT Program serves not only the youths, but also their parents and siblings.

Outreach is vital. If a youth does not attend a scheduled activity, staff seek him out at home or on the street. The MAAT Program owns a van and can transport youths to and from activities. This facilitates attendance and ensures safety when youths are traversing rival neighborhoods. Transportation time fosters informal dialogue among the youths and with staff, giving staff an opportunity to provide guidance in a more natural environment.

### Rites of Passage Model: *Nguzo Saba*

The Afrocentric ethos is crystallized in the *Nguzo Saba* (Karenga, 1965), or the Seven Principles. The principles and their definitions are given in Table 5-1. The *Nguzo Saba* provide youths with behavioral guidelines.

The MAAT Program implements the *Nguzo Saba* through various interventions and techniques. *Umoja*, which means unity or interconnectedness, is expressed through group activities. Each meeting begins with youths and staff forming a unity circle. They hold hands, say a nondenominational prayer, and pour a libation in respect to the ancestors, requesting their presence at the sacred

*Table 5-1*

**Rites of Passage Model: *Nguzo Saba* ("Seven Principles")**

| Principle | Translation | Definition |
|---|---|---|
| *Umoja* | Unity or interconnectedness | To strive and maintain unity in the family, community, nation, and race |
| *Kujichagulia* | Self-determination | To define ourselves, name ourselves, and speak for ourselves instead of being defined and spoken for by others |
| *Ujima* | Collective work and responsibility | To build and maintain our community together and to make our brothers' and sisters' problems our problems and to solve them together |
| *Ujama* | Cooperative economics | To build and own stores, shops, and other businesses and to profit from them |
| *Nia* | Purpose | To take as our collective vocation the building and developing of our community to restore our people to their traditional greatness |
| *Kuumba* | Creativity | To always do as much as we can, in the way we can, to restore our people to their traditional greatness |
| *Imani* | Faith | To believe in our parents, our teachers, our leaders, our people, and ourselves and in the righteousness and victory of our struggle |

event. This ritual conveys to the youths that they and their meeting matter. *Umoja* is also implemented after the orientation by a weekend transformational retreat. The full nine-month program ends with a closing retreat for the youths or the youths and their families and a community celebration at which the youths demonstrate the things they have learned and the skills they have developed while in the program.

*Kujichagulia*, or self-determination, means to define one's self within African and African American culture. At the first retreat, in accord with African custom, youths choose an African name based on their birthdays. This act is intended to begin the process of rejecting internalized racism and affirming African roots. Adopting an African name also symbolizes the possibility of change and of becoming responsible for one's self, family, and community. The youths mark their passage to manhood by giving themselves another African name, based on their personality, at the closing retreat. Parents and guardians may also attend this retreat and adopt African names.

*Ujima*, or collective work and responsibility, is experienced through cooperative activities and household maintenance skills instruction at the *Ujima ya Fundisha* House, where the youths learn plumbing, painting, and electrical repair. The youths as a group may also perform community service activities, such as serving lunch to homeless people.

*Ujama*, cooperative economics, occurs through entrepreneurship. For example, a group of older youths negotiated a contract to design and produce sweatshirts for a local African American bank. The youths learned business skills, enabling them to handle aspects of the contracting, bookkeeping, and production.

*Nia*, or purpose, provides reasons to live constructively. The MAAT Program teaches youths that they are "gifts of God," placed here at this place and at this time with talents that they are obliged to cultivate.

*Kuumba*, or creativity, is defined as the ability to problem solve through finding alternative solutions. One *kuumba* teaching strategy is the ancestral transformation exercise, in which a group facilitator

- asks each participant to choose a historical figure
- provides a written biographical sketch of the person
- directs participants to think, behave, and feel like the person
- sets the scene for a values clarification role play, such as being approached by a drug dealer to buy drugs or be a lookout
- directs the participant to behave in the role play as would the historical figure
- facilitates group discussion of the role play and its implications for participants' lives.

*Imani*, or faith, refers to trust in oneself, family, friends, and community. *Imani* is also the belief that tomorrow can be better, no matter how bleak things are today. *Imani* is reinforced through learning the historical struggles of African Americans and "Negro spirituals," which teach about the African American tradition of faith.

### Program Evaluation

The MAAT Program model has incorporated two evaluation methods. The first is a process evaluation, in which an evaluator attends each program component on a regular basis to ensure that the program is being implemented as proposed. The second method of evaluation is a pre- and posttest administered to all participants, including youths and parents or guardians. The evaluation instruments are designed to test the effectiveness of the program components as previously described.

## AFROCENTRISM AND SOCIAL WORK PRACTICE IN HEALTH AND OTHER SETTINGS

Afrocentric theory and practice offer tools that health care workers and organizations can use to engage African American male adolescents in preventive and primary health care. Agency-level strategies consist of the following:

- recognizing that failure to engage African American youths may manifest practitioner and organizational racism, classism, and cultural ignorance

- changing ways of thinking and speaking about African American youths, from individual modes that label the person (as in DSM-IV [American Psychiatric Association, 1994] diagnoses) to ecological modes that comprehend youths as coping with high-risk, oppressive situations
- using an ecological perspective to recognize and build on strengths in context (for example, seeing that a youth who is selling drugs may be working hard to support his mother and siblings)
- hiring staff who live in the community and, if that is not possible, hiring staff who esteem African and African American culture and desire to learn about the community
- training staff in Afrocentric principles, programs, and techniques
- locating Afrocentric programs offered by African American churches, agencies, fraternities and sororities, and so forth and making referrals to them, including their staff in activities, and using their staff as program consultants
- using specific Afrocentric techniques, such as the ancestral transformation exercise
- using pictures, fabrics, accessories, music, food, and so forth to create a culturally welcoming environment
- providing caring outreach.

The escalating death rates of African Americans has been labeled *"maafa"* (Richards, 1989), a term that refers to genocide. It is similar in meaning to the Jewish Holocaust. Admittedly, addressing this public health crisis will require national commitment; comprehensive interventions targeted at individuals, families, communities, and institutions; and cooperation among all levels of government and private organizations (Carnegie Corporation of New York, 1995; *Healthy People 2000,* 1991, 1995). When the nation will have the will to expend the resources needed to stop *maafa* is uncertain. In the meantime, at least some youths may have the opportunity to survive through reconnection to their heritage and nourishment of their personal resources.

## REFERENCES

American Academy of Pediatrics. (1994). *Report highlights: Report of the AAP Task Force on Minority Children's Access to Pediatric Care.* Elk Grove Village, IL: Author.

American Psychiatric Association. (1994). *Diagnostic and statistical manual of mental disorders* (4th ed.). Washington, DC: Author.

*Black Americans: A statistical source book.* (1995). Palo Alto, CA: Information Publications.

Carnegie Corporation of New York. (1995). *Great transitions: Preparing adolescents for a new century* (Concluding Report of the Carnegie Council on Adolescent Development). New York: Author.

Children's Defense Fund. (1995). *The state of America's children, 1995.* Washington, DC: Author.

Cross, T. L., Bazron, B. J., Dennis, K. W., & Isaacs, M. R. (1989). *Towards a culturally competent system of care: A monograph on effective services for minority children who are severely emotionally disturbed.* Washington, DC: Georgetown University Child Development Center, Child and Adolescent Service System Program Technical Assistance Center.

Erny, P. (1968). *Childhood and cosmos: The social psychology of the black African child.* New York: New Perspectives.

Harvey, A. R. (1995a). Afro-centric model of prevention with African American adolescent males: The MAAT Rites of Passage Program. In J. Rauch (Ed.), *Community-based, family-centered services in a changing health care environment: Selected papers from a conference held June 6 & 7, 1994, Baltimore, Maryland* (pp. 115–130). Baltimore: University of Maryland at Baltimore, School of Social Work.

Harvey, A. R. (1995b). The issue of skin color in psychotherapy with African Americans. *Families in Society, 76*(1), 3–10.

*Healthy people 2000: Midcourse review and 1995 revisions.* (1995). Washington, DC: U.S. Department of Health and Human Resources, U.S. Public Health Service.

*Healthy people 2000: National health promotion and disease prevention objectives: Full report with commentary* (U.S. Department of Health and Human Services Publication No. PHS 91-50212). (1991). Washington, DC: U.S. Government Printing Office.

Hill, P. (1992). *Coming of age: African American male rites of passage.* Chicago: African American Images.

Institute of Medicine. (1989). *Research on children and adolescents with mental, behavioral and developmental disorders* (National Academy of Sciences Report of a Study of the Committee of the Division of Mental Health and Behavioral Medicine). Washington, DC: National Academy Press.

Irwin, C. E., Brindis, C. D., Brodt, S. E., Bennett, T. A., & Rodrigues, R. Q. (1991). *The health of America's youth: Current trends in health status and utilization of health services.* San Francisco: University of California at San Francisco.

Irwin, C. E., Jr., & Ingra, V. (1994). Adolescent risk-taking behavior. In H. M. Wallace, R. P. Nelson, & P. J. Sweeney (Eds.), *Maternal and child health practice* (4th ed., pp. 585–601). Oakland, CA: Third Party.

Isaacs, M. R. (1992). *Violence: The impact of community violence on African American children and families.* Arlington, VA: National Center for Education in Maternal and Child Health.

Jessor, R. (1992). Risk behavior in adolescence: A psychosocial framework for understanding and action. In D. E. Rogers & E. Ginsberg (Eds.), *Adolescents at risk* (pp. 19–33). Boulder, CO: Westview Press.

Karenga, M. (1965). *Kwanzaa: Origin, concepts and practice.* Los Angeles: Kawaida Publications.

Karenga, M. (1990). Towards a sociology of Maatian ethics: Literature and context. In M. Karenga (Ed.), *Reconstructing kemetic culture: Papers, perspectives, projects* (pp. 66–96). Los Angeles: University of Sankore Press.

Myers, L. J. (1988). *Understanding an Afro-centric world view: Introduction to an optimal psychology.* Dubuque, IA: Kendall/Hunt.

National Center for Health Statistics. (1994). *Health United States, 1994.* Hyattsville, MD: U.S. Public Health Service.

Pinkett, J. (1993). Spirituality in the African-American community. In L. L. Goddard (Ed.), *An African-centered model of prevention for African-American youth at high risk* (Child and Adolescent Service System Program Tech. Rep. No. 6, pp. 79–86). Rockville, MD: U.S. Department of Health and Human Services.

Richards, D. M. (1989). *Let the circle be unbroken: The implications of African spirituality in the diaspora.* Trenton, NJ: Red Sea Press.

Schiele, J. H. (1994). Afrocentricity as an alternate world view for equality. *Journal of Progressive Human Services, 5*(1), 5–25.

Solomon, D. (1976). *Black empowerment: Social work in oppressed communities.* New York: Columbia University Press.

*The work on which this chapter is based was partially funded by grant H86-SPO 4729 from the Center for Substance Abuse Prevention.*

*This chapter was originally published in the February 1997 issue of* Health & Social Work, *Vol. 22, pp. 30–37.*

# 6 Addressing the Needs of Foster Children: The Foster Youth Services Program

Robert H. Ayasse

T he past decade has seen a variety of social ills escalate, including drug abuse, family violence, and homelessness. As a result, the number of children placed in foster care due to abuse, neglect, and prenatal drug exposure has increased rapidly (National Center on Child Abuse and Neglect, 1988). In California the number of children placed in out-of-home care increased 83 percent from 1985 to 1990 (Child Welfare Research Center, 1991), and the total number of children placed through the public child welfare agencies in the state rose from 33,285 children in 1984 to more than 84,000 children in 1994 (Barth, Courtney, Needell, & Jonson-Reid, 1994).

This rapid increase has overburdened the foster care and child welfare systems and created a shortage of appropriate foster homes for children in need (Schneider, 1989). Even when the foster care system is not overburdened, the dictates of the legal system can result in a child being placed in emergency foster homes or temporary shelters or being sent to different counties, states, or relatives as the jurisdictional and custodial matters relating to foster care placement are settled. In addition, foster children have special needs that stem from being neglected and abused that can result in burnout in foster care providers and in multiple placements.

Along with the emotional trauma of repeated separations from caretakers, this instability has a powerful effect on the school adjustment of foster children. Frequent foster home changes can mean frequent changes in schools and adjustments to new friends, teachers, and group norms both in and outside of the classroom. Foster children also often need to adjust to new educational expectations and curricula that vary from school to school and changes in the pace at which material is taught. These changes can be bewildering and discouraging to a child. Teachers and foster parents may not be able to recognize learning disabilities or other problems that were not fully assessed at the last school or that may have been assessed and not communicated to the new school or foster parent. This article discusses the efforts of California's Foster Youth Service (FYS) programs to alleviate the educational and emotional problems of foster children; it also discusses the unique social work services of the Mt. Diablo Unified School District FYS program.

## EDUCATIONAL PROBLEMS OF FOSTER CHILDREN

The social and emotional problems that stem from being abused and neglected, combined with a transient home life in the foster care system, have a powerful effect on many foster children's ability to learn. These problems become very apparent in school settings when they are not addressed in a comprehensive manner by either the social services or school systems. In 1990 a survey by the Children's Services Division of the State of Oregon assessed the educational performances of children in long-term foster care (White, Carrington, & Freeman, 1990). This study found that children who had multiple foster placements during the school year were less likely to be above grade level or to be involved in extracurricular activities than children who had a sustained period of time in one school. The children who had experienced multiple placements and who were identified as needing special education were also less likely to be receiving those services than children with more stable placements.

The Oregon study also found that only 60 percent of the foster children in the survey were performing at or above grade level, compared with 80 percent of all schoolchildren, and although 39 percent of foster children had Individual Education Plans (IEPs), only 16 percent received special education services (White et al., 1990). In Oregon, 9 percent of all schoolchildren received special education services (White et al., 1990), and nationally the percentage of children in need of special education ranged from 11 percent to 12 percent (Murphy, 1986).

The discrepancy between the number of foster children identified as needing special education and the number actually receiving services can be partly explained by the fact that information about foster children's educational needs is not tracked by their caseworkers in any consistent fashion. Thus, when a child changes foster homes and schools, the knowledge of his or her educational needs often stays with the prior home or school. This problem was illustrated in a recent demographic study that indicated that the number of foster children who needed special education was grossly underdocumented by child welfare caseworkers (Goerge, Van Voorhis, Grant, Casey, & Robinson, 1992). The study found that school records in Illinois indicated that about 30 percent of foster children received special education, whereas the caseworkers' records indicated that only about 5 percent did. The study also found that foster children with a handicapping condition suffered disproportionately from emotional disturbance as their primary handicapping condition (Goerge et al., 1992).

## BEHAVIOR PROBLEMS OF FOSTER CHILDREN

Although placement in multiple foster homes can be emotionally damaging to a child and can lead to a greater number of behavior problems (Marcus, 1991), foster children may also exhibit behavioral and emotional problems that stem primarily from their histories of neglect and abuse. Although some foster children who have learned important survival skills display minimal behavior and adjustment problems, many other children display aggressive behavior, language delays (Kinard, 1980; Martin, 1972), low self-esteem (Martin & Beezley, 1977), and disruptive behavior (Smith, Berkman, & Fraser, 1980). These problems in turn often seriously affect foster home stability (Proch & Taber, 1985) and school performance (Wodarski, Kurtz, Gaudin, & Howing, 1990).

Wodarski et al. (1990) assessed maltreated school-age children through multimodal and multisource measures to evaluate their academic, emotional, and adaptive functioning. Their findings indicated that the abused children in the study displayed severe problems at home and in the community, including "academic deficits, problem behaviors, lowered self-esteem, delinquency, elevated feelings of aggression, and pervasive adjustment difficulties in a variety of contexts" (p. 510). The neglected children, although not significantly more emotionally impaired than a comparison group, also displayed severe academic delays. Neglected children had more pervasive deficits in school than abused children, including depressed test scores (specifically in language skills), low teacher assessments of academic performance, and high rates of absenteeism. Both the "abused and neglected children had experienced grade repeats at more than twice the rate of the nonmaltreated children" (p. 510). Wodarski et al. stated further: "The problems of older abused or neglected children are particularly apparent in the school environment. Because of their unique position in communities, schools offer an appropriate setting for broad-based interventions aimed at ameliorating the academic and emotional deficits of the older maltreated child." (p. 511)

The importance of providing support at school for older foster children was further bolstered by a national evaluation of foster care independent living programs conducted by Westat (1991) for the U.S. Department of Health and Human Services in 1990 and 1991. This study found that of former foster children who had been discharged from foster care $2\,^1/_2$ to four years previously, only 54 percent completed high school, only 49 percent were employed at the time of the interview, and only 17 percent were completely self-supporting. In addition, 40 percent were a cost to the community (that is, they received some form of government income assistance) at the time of the interview, and 60 percent of the young women had given birth to a child. This same study also found that youths who had completed high school were more likely to secure stable employment and have a higher level of self-sufficiency after discharge from foster care than youths who had not completed high school, regardless of whether they had received any type of skills training (Westat, 1991).

## FOSTER YOUTH SERVICES

Foster Youth Services is a program designed specifically to help foster children with their educational needs. Four of the FYS programs in California have been in operation since 1972. They are the survivors of a multidistrict demonstration project for foster child services. The programs had maintained a precarious year-to-year existence until they received official recognition of their effectiveness in legislation enacted in California in 1981. At that time Senate Bill 831 placed into statute the findings of the legislature as follows:

> 1. It is essential to recognize, identify and plan for the critical and unique needs of children residing in licensed community care facilities.

2. A high percentage of these foster children are working substantially below grade level, are being retained at least one year in the same grade level, and become school dropouts.

3. Without a program specifically designed to meet their individual needs, foster children are frequently dysfunctional human beings at great penal and welfare costs.

4. The legislature . . . finds and declares that the instruction, counseling and related services for foster children which provide program effectiveness and potential cost savings shall be a state priority. (State of California, 1981, p. 2823)

Since 1981 the FYS programs have helped give more than 18,000 foster children the opportunity to experience success in school. In 1992 two new FYS programs were added in California, bringing the statewide total to six.

In a report to the U.S. Department of Health and Human Services, the Children's Services Foundation described the program as follows:

Each FYS program provides four core service components: school placement/ student advocacy, tutoring, counseling, and employment readiness. . . . FYS recognizes that foster students are often adrift in the educational system. Records are often lost or misplaced when a child's placement is changed. The child must move to a new school without planning and preparation, and proper assessments or testing may not get done because the child didn't attend a particular school long enough to participate in the process. Test results from prior schools may not be transferred in a timely fashion, resulting in a child being placed in an inappropriate school program, which may in turn exacerbate emotional and behavioral problems. Credits for courses fully or partially completed are often omitted from transcripts, jeopardizing chances for accumulating sufficient credits to graduate.

It is unlikely that the school staff, substitute caregiver or placement worker will have the time, the expertise, or the inclination to make sure that the educational needs and rights of each foster child are properly addressed.

FYS staff, however, have the ability and the authority to see that records are obtained and perfected, that educational testing assessment is provided as required, that placement in the right school program occurs expeditiously, and that every child receives the support and assistance they need to compete on an equal footing with their classmates.

FYS programs are also notable from an interagency perspective, establishing the school as the natural focus for identifying and integrating foster children's academic and behavioral problems and needs. FYS actively seeks out persons and organizations that influence foster children's lives—foster family, group home staff, social workers, probation officers, etc.—into the children's day-to-day routine during and after school. (Fitzharris, 1989, pp. 6–7)

## DIRECT SERVICE METHODS

### Tracking Records and Tutoring

The most essential service provided by the FYS programs is the tracking of school transcripts, immunization records, IEP documents, and past credits for each child entering the district. Each child with an IEP must have an available biological parent or legal guardian or be assigned an educational representative to advocate for their special educational needs. Once the child's records are tracked and an appropriate school placement is located, the primary method by which FYS provides direct services to foster children is through one-to-one tutoring on a weekly or twice-weekly basis. Tutoring is tailored to the needs of each child on the basis of both academic performance and tests such as the Peabody Individual Achievement Test (Markwardt, 1989) and needs expressed by the child, teacher, or caretaker. When it is clear that tutoring alone will not be enough to help a child succeed in school, the FYS tutor helps facilitate a special education assessment.

It is not unusual for foster children to bring a variety of social and behavioral problems into the tutoring sessions; the tutor or the FYS social worker must also address these problems. Although each FYS staff member uses different methods to deal with particular emotional or behavioral problems, he or she generally takes a supportive role and provides as much encouragement and empathy to the child as possible.

For younger children who have not developed adequate self-control in the tutoring sessions or who have difficulty operating according to the social and behavioral expectations of their classroom, the FYS tutors sometimes develop behavior modification plans. As students in high school and middle school become older and more independent, intervention plans are geared toward encouraging more independent behavior and accepting more adult responsibilities. Helping students adapt to the challenges of high school and employment counseling takes precedence over the more remedial approach for elementary school students.

The FYS program staff place a high premium on helping students graduate from high school or attain an equivalent diploma. However, they also recognize that preparing foster youths for independence must be an ongoing process starting when the child enters the school and social services system for the first time. Early remedial intervention, counseling, and support can prevent the child from needing more intensive help later in life, when they may be too far behind or too alienated from the system to graduate from high school and subsequently achieve self-sufficiency.

## Mt. Diablo FYS Social Work Services

Although records tracking, tutorial assistance, and some counseling are provided in all of the FYS programs, the Mt. Diablo Unified School District (MDUSD) is the only district that employs a social worker. In 1989 the MDUSD established a position titled "social services liaison" in cooperation with the Contra Costa County Social Services Department to facilitate communication between the school and social services systems. The creation of this position was a unique effort in interagency cooperation and bridging of services gaps.

The social services liaison in the MDUSD is employed on a half-time basis and supervises between one and three part-time master's-level social work interns (depending on availability). Together they constitute a small social work staff for the 250 or more foster children in the district. The social work interns' services are most often focused at those schools with the highest concentration of foster children, and the liaison provides some direct services and addresses services gaps throughout the district at large.

The social work staff provides individual counseling to foster children to support them through the various difficulties they may encounter in the foster care system. They also work with tutors, teachers, school administrators, and foster parents to help modify the behavior of students with social and emotional problems. This work sometimes involves counseling the students; consulting with social workers, FYS tutors, and foster parents; arranging family meetings; and arranging school–teacher–parent meetings. The FYS social workers often gather information from all the people involved with the foster child, including the child, to gain a greater understanding of the etiology of the child's problems. From this information, the FYS social worker may help develop a behavioral modification plan or advocate for a change in the child's school program to suit his or her needs.

To support the role of the tutors, the FYS social workers consult with the tutors confronting problems during tutoring sessions. Children often reveal problems they are having in the foster home or on home visits to a FYS tutor whom they have grown to trust and with whom they have developed a special rapport. In many instances it is more appropriate for the tutor to provide counseling than for a stranger to deal with those needs. In those instances, the FYS social worker can consult with the tutor to respond appropriately to the child's needs. In crisis situations the social worker provides a crucial role by consulting with and coordinating all the varying adult professionals who work with the child.

In some cases when it appears that a child with school difficulties may soon be reunified with his or her biological family, the social worker can facilitate parent-teacher meetings and family counseling sessions focused on the child's school needs. This improves communication between the school and parent, provides for consistent expectations and rules for the child through the transition back to the biological family, and helps bring the parents up to speed on their child's day-to-day academic and social functioning.

In addition to individual counseling, the FYS social workers also run support groups for students in primary, middle, and high schools. These groups have been successful in providing support and helping students find new ways of solving problems. In addition, the groups have been helpful in lessening the isolation that many foster children feel when they are ashamed of their family status or of being in foster care. Many older foster children do not want anyone to know that they are in foster care, and it is helpful for them to know that there are others in their school in similar situations.

The MDUSD social services liaison has also been employed half-time by the Contra Costa County Social Services Department. One benefit of bridging the two systems with one person is that it allows the person to gain an insider's knowledge of the foster care and juvenile justice systems. This knowledge is useful for helping school staff understand the possible problems the child is facing in the juvenile court process and foster care, such as emotionally disruptive home visits, questionable foster care practices, and sudden placement changes. Conversely, knowledge of the school system is also very useful when helping caseworkers advocate for the educational needs of the children on their caseloads. The FYS social worker is often a mediator between the caseworker and the school staff when conflicts arise over the needs of their respective programs. Being a member of both camps helps the social worker develop the best possible program to meet the child's needs.

## CASE EXAMPLES

### Tommy

The level of social worker intervention and number of other professionals needed to help a foster child in school can vary from situation to situation. For example, Tommy, a third-grade boy in long-term foster care, was having difficulty with being organized in class and returning completed homework on time. The FYS staff consulted with the teacher and foster parent to identify where and how these problems were occurring. It was discovered that Tommy was doing his homework but would leave it at home, on the bus, or somewhere between home and school. It was also discovered that Tommy's forgetfulness and classroom difficulties were linked to his birth mother making sudden unplanned appearances or canceling visits at the last moment.

Intervention involved consulting with Tommy's caseworker to see if visits with his mother could be structured or controlled better. The FYS tutor also made up a contract between the student and the teacher that they both signed setting a time goal for when the homework would be turned in, setting up a certain place in his backpack where Tommy could carry his homework, and arranging positive reinforcement for bringing the homework to school. In Tommy's case, reinforcement was given by earning points to get a toy kite from the tutor. The contract also stipulated that Tommy had to do his homework at recess time when it was not completed and turned in on time. The teacher and foster parent regularly sent notes to the tutor indicating whether the homework was turned in or giving a legitimate reason for the homework not being done. These interventions helped Tommy become more successful in class and in general allowed him to be more focused on school tasks.

### Jane

A teenage student, Jane, was having attendance problems and had learning disabilities that prevented her from functioning well in a regular classroom. Also, because Jane had previously been truant from school so often, she had lost so many credits that it would be very difficult for her to graduate from a comprehensive high school without an eight-period-a-day schedule. With her rate of failure in the past, Jane's social worker, foster parents, school counselors, and teachers were skeptical about her ability to function at a comprehensive high school. However, after the social worker talked with Jane, it was very clear that she had many friends in the comprehensive high school that she was attending, felt that she did not want to be stigmatized by going to an alternative education program, and insisted that she wanted to graduate with a high school diploma from a comprehensive high school.

In a counseling session with the FYS social worker, Jane revealed that the reason she had skipped classes so often in the past was because she had been put into a full-time special education program and found the work unchallenging, was embarrassed to be there, and therefore made little effort. The FYS staff advocated on Jane's behalf to have her placed in a regular school program with two special education resource classes that would be a little more educationally challenging.

A contract was arranged with Jane, the essence of which stated that as long as she attended school regularly and received passing grades she would be able to attend this comprehensive high school. However, if she were to fail any classes she would need to go to an alternative high school to have enough credits to graduate before her 19th birthday. Tutoring was arranged to help her with nonresource classes, and counseling was arranged to help with stress, study habits, and occasional crises. In addition, services were coordinated with Jane's caseworker and the county-run Independent Living Skills Program that she was involved in to ensure consistency in helping Jane prepare for life after foster care. As a result, Jane was able to pass all of her subjects and maintain a part-time job for which she also received credit. Shortly after graduation she obtained a full-time job and moved into a shared rental apartment.

## PROGRAM EFFECTIVENESS

The effectiveness of FYS has been studied by a variety of different measures from 1985 to 1989. In a study by Seashore in 1985, foster parents, teachers, and social services and probation caseworkers were surveyed on their assessment of the program's effectiveness. Using a scale ranging from much better to much worse, the majority of caseworkers who had experience with both districts with a FYS program and districts without a program judged FYS districts to be much better than districts lacking FYS in the following dimensions: placing a child in school promptly, placing a child in the appropriate school programs or classes, providing for specific education needs, identifying student problems early, and facilitating academic progress. In their overall evaluation the majority of respondents indicated that the program had been highly effective (Seashore, 1985).

In 1986, the California Health and Welfare Agency reported to the legislature and the governor that there was significant academic growth among students receiving tutorial assistance and that 70 percent of the seniors receiving FYS completed high school (compared with 50 percent in the general foster youth population). In 1988, the California Department of Education discovered that 92 percent of FYS students gained at least one month of academic growth for every month of tutoring, with an average rate of growth of 3.2 months per month tutored. Of the total 1,722 students enrolled in the four FYS programs, only 0.1 percent were expelled. Gains were maintained in program effectiveness in 1990 despite a 25 percent increase in the number of students served.

In 1989, two studies were conducted simultaneously by the Children's Services Foundation (Fitzharris, 1989), one a comparative analysis of credits earned and the other an analysis of the rate of academic achievement. The first study found that foster youth students in high school who received FYS interventions earned 10.1 credits more per semester than other foster students in a school district with no FYS program. The second study revealed that FYS tutoring resulted in an increase in the level of academic functioning of approximately 2½ months for each month of tutoring provided, with certain categories of foster care students achieving at a rate of more than five months for each month of tutoring provided.

These studies clearly demonstrate the effectiveness of FYS in helping improve academic performance, decrease maladaptive behavior, lower dropout rates, and thus aid more successful transitions to employment or higher education. Long-term follow-up studies have not been done but would be greatly helpful in examining whether these short-term gains have lasting effects for those involved in FYS programs.

## CONCLUSION

When a child is placed in foster care, his or her care is entrusted to a new family and, often, a new school whose knowledge of that child's development may be sketchy or nonexistent. Social workers most often assume that the task of attending to the child's educational needs will be handled by the school or the foster parent. But the school system often assumes that each student is accompanied by a parent or responsible adult who is knowledgeable about the student and who can take an active part in assisting the child with school requirements and advocating for special needs. Combining these false assumptions with the trauma foster children experience before, during, and sometimes after they are placed in a new home and a new school is a recipe for disaster. It is no surprise that foster children have higher rates of school failure, behavioral problems, and dropping out.

FYS programs are designed to fill the gaps in services that many foster children experience. In addition to attending to the individual needs of foster children in their districts, the FYS programs provide an important link for coordinating services and facilitating communication between schools and social services. Given that foster children spend three to five hours a day in school compared with only a few hours a month with their social services caseworker, the schools provide the most natural arena for attending to the needs of children. This school-based model of interagency cooperation enriches the efficiency and effectiveness of both the social services' and the schools' efforts to care for the growth and development of foster children.

The FYS program is very inexpensive—the cost ranges from $300 to $1,100 per year per student. When considering the costs of chronic unemployment, welfare dependency, homelessness, or incarceration, it is clear that FYS can be extremely cost effective by helping students graduate from high school and go on to successfully emancipate from foster care. Moreover, the benefits of increased self-esteem, feelings of accomplishment, and hope for the future cannot possibly be measured.

## REFERENCES

Barth, R. P., Courtney, M., Needell, B., & Jonson-Reid, M. (1994). *Performance indicators for child welfare services in California.* Berkeley: University of California at Berkeley, Child Welfare Research Center.

California Department of Education. (1988). *Biennial report to the legislature on the foster youth services program.* Sacramento: Author.

California Health and Welfare Agency. (1986). *Foster youth services: A report to the legislature and the governor superintendent of public instruction and department of youth authority.* Sacramento: Author.

Child Welfare Research Center. (1991). *Child welfare symposium on multi-state foster care study: California data.* Berkeley: University of California at Berkeley, School of Social Welfare, Family Welfare Research Group.

Fitzharris, T. L. (1989). *Evaluation of the foster youth services program: Report to the Stuart Foundations.* Sacramento, CA: Children's Services Foundation.

Goerge, R. M., Van Voorhis, J., Grant, S., Casey, K., & Robinson, M. (1992). Special education experiences of foster children: An empirical study. *Child Welfare, 71,* 419–437.

Kinard, E. M. (1980). Emotional development in physically abused children. *American Journal of Orthopsychiatry, 50,* 686–696.

Marcus, R. F. (1991). The attachments of children in foster care. *Genetic, Social, and General Psychology Monographs, 117,* 365–394.

Markwardt, F. C. (1989). *Peabody Individual Achievement Test* (rev.). Circle Pines, MN: American Guidance Service.

Martin, H. P. (1972). The child and his development. In C. H. Kempe & R. E. Helfer (Eds.), *Helping the battered child and his family* (pp. 93–114). Philadelphia: J. B. Lippincott.

Martin, H. P., & Beezley, P. (1977). Behavioral observation in abused children. *Developmental Medicine and Child Neurology, 19,* 373–378.

Murphy, D. (1986). The prevalence of handicapping conditions among juvenile delinquents. *Remedial and Special Education, 7*(3), 7–17.

National Center on Child Abuse and Neglect. (1988). *Study findings: Study of national incidence and prevalence of child abuse and neglect.* Washington, DC: U.S. Government Printing Office.

Proch, K., & Taber, M. A. (1985). Placement disruption: A review of research. *Children and Youth Services Review, 7,* 309–320.

Schneider, J. T. (1989). Foster care: Fraught with data gaps and inadequate services. In California Assembly, Office of Research (Ed.), *California children, California families* (pp. 3–5). Sacramento, CA: Joint Publications Office.

Seashore, M. (1985). *The effectiveness of foster youth services in four California school districts.* San Francisco: San Francisco State University, School of Behavioral Sciences, Public Research Institute.

Smith, C. P., Berkman, D. J., & Fraser, W. M. (1980). *A preliminary national assessment of child abuse and neglect and the juvenile justice system: The shadows of distress.* Washington, DC: U.S. Department of Justice, Office of Juvenile Justice and Delinquency Prevention.

State of California. (1981). *Statutes of California and digests of measures* (Legislative Session 1981–1982, Vol. 2). Sacramento, CA: State Printing Office.

Westat. (1991). *A national evaluation of Title IV-E—Foster care independent living programs for youth, phase 2, final report* (Vol. 1, Report to Department of Health and Human Services, Administration for Children, Youth, and Families). Washington, DC: U.S. Department of Health and Human Services.

White, J., Carrington, J., & Freeman, P. (1990). *A study of the educational status of foster children in Oregon: Research and statistics.* Portland: Oregon Department of Human Resources, Children's Services Division.

Wodarski, J. S., Kurtz, P. D., Gaudin, J. M., & Howing, P. T. (1990). Maltreatment and the school-age child: Major academic, socioemotional, and adaptive outcomes. *Social Work, 35,* 506–513.

*This chapter was originally published in the October 1995 issue of* Social Work in Education, *Vol. 17, pp. 207–216.*

# 7 Decelerating Self-Stimulating and Self-Injurious Behaviors of a Student with Autism: Behavioral Intervention in the Classroom

Barbara Peo Early

All special education students are entitled under the Education for All Handicapped Children Act of 1975 (P.L. 94-142) to an individualized plan of educational and supportive services to promote the fulfillment of their educational potential. Students with severe disabilities such as autism challenge school social workers to develop innovative ways to provide those services. The social work literature indicates that social workers have not written about behavioral techniques in the treatment of self-injurious behavior (Underwood & Thyer, 1990). Social workers often lack training in such techniques (Thyer & Maddox, 1988), whereas special education teachers are familiar with behavioral approaches.

The case study discussed in this article traces a social worker's efforts to develop an effective intervention for a student with autism in a special education setting. It illustrates the monitoring and measurement of the process through the use of a single-subject research design. The study may serve as a pilot for a more rigorous single-subject design in the future.

The study sought to answer the question, Will a behavioral social work intervention in the classroom setting combining differential reinforcement of incompatible behavior with response-cost reduce the maladaptive self-stimulating and self-injurious behaviors of a student with autism? The second question of interest was, Will the intervention increase this student's tolerance for correction or criticism in the classroom?

## LITERATURE REVIEW

Early infantile autism was described as a distinct syndrome in the 1940s by Kanner (1943). As distinct symptoms of people with autism, he identified the inability to relate to others, delayed and noncommunicative speech, stereotypical behaviors, intense insistence on environmental consistency, and absence of the capacity to use symbol or metaphor. Kanner assumed that the etiology of autistic disturbance was within the early child–parent interaction.

Bettelheim (1967) advanced this theory by suggesting that autistic behavior was defensive against parental rejection. Later, the psychogenic model gave way to the contemporary assumption of a neurobiological basis for autism (Rimland, 1964). Thus, traditional counseling techniques have yielded to more structured educational approaches to teaching new and adaptive behaviors to people with autism; extinguishing maladaptive ones; and enhancing self-control, independence, and social acceptance (Groden & Baron, 1988).

## MALADAPTIVE BEHAVIORS IN AUTISM

Of particular concern in this case study are two types of maladaptive behaviors typical in people with autism: self-stimulating behavior and self-injurious behavior (Schreibman, 1988). Self-stimulating (or stereotypical) behavior is persistent and repetitive and appears to serve no obvious function. Self-stimulating behaviors include rocking, hand flapping, grimacing, tapping, or repeating vocal or word patterns.

Self-injurious behavior is sometimes an exaggeration of self-stimulating behavior and includes slapping of the leg or face, hand biting, and head banging. Rojahn (1986) found that approximately two-thirds of people engaged in self-injurious behavior also displayed some stereotypical behavior. The study further noted an apparent association between rocking and self-hitting, suggesting that the self-injurious behavior may arise from the less dangerous rocking behavior.

Self-injurious behavior has been found to be maintained by four types of variables: social attention, opportunity to gain tangible consequences, escape from unpleasant situations, and internal sensory stimulation (Durand & Crimmins, 1988). Thus, behaviors that seem senseless may indeed be functional for the person and provide him or her with some form of reinforcement (Romanczyk, 1986).

## EXTINCTION OF MALADAPTIVE BEHAVIORS

If maladaptive behaviors are maintained by internal and environmental reinforcers, it can be assumed that some extinction procedure, involving the withdrawal of reinforcement, should be effective in decreasing them. Rincover and Devany (1982) removed the sensory stimulation for three child clients with self-injurious behavior. They blocked the sensation produced by head banging by having one child wear a helmet and by placing gloves on the hands of another child who scratched herself, blocking the sensory experience of scratching. These procedures resulted in immediate and dramatic decreases in self-injurious behavior.

Favell, McGimsey, and Schell (1982) found that much self-injurious behavior took place when the client was alone, thus ruling out social attention or escape from demands as maintaining conditions. They surmised that sensory stimuli reinforced the behavior, and so they introduced self-stimulating play to provide alternative sensory input.

Self-injurious behavior has been successfully treated in people with mental retardation with a more formalized form of alternative behavior—differential reinforcement of incompatible behavior (DRI) (Azrin, Besalel, Jamner, & Caputo, 1988). DRI involves prompting and reinforcing adaptive behaviors that compete with self-injurious ones. For example, hands are kept occupied with something that makes it impossible to use them to hurt. It is assumed that the incompatible responses lower the motivation of the client to engage in these responses (Romanczyk, 1986).

DRI requires that the substitute behavior be appropriately potent to suppress the maladaptive behavior. Thus, incompatible behaviors may have to be initially taught and continually prompted (Jones & Baker, 1988).

The effectiveness of DRI is enhanced by combining it with other operant techniques, particularly with interruption (Azrin et al., 1988; Underwood, Figueroa, Thyer, & Nzeocha, 1989). In interruption, a trainer sits close enough to the client to restrain an arm or head in the process of self-injury. After a short interval, the arm or head is released and DRI continues.

Although interruption has been found to be effective in institutional settings, it could be distracting or inappropriate during a classroom lesson. The present study reflects an attempt to augment DRI with other behavioral techniques that are both effective and yet compatible with a special education classroom setting. The classroom is conceptualized as a primary niche in the life space of the student–client with autism. It is a microcosm of the work environment for which many students with disabilities are preparing.

## THE CLIENT

This case study focuses on Matthew, a 20-year-old physically mature white male who met the criteria for autism in the DSM-IV (American Psychiatric Association, 1994). He attended a special education day school for seriously emotionally disturbed students. As he approached the end of his special education career, he continued to be inhibited in his social and vocational progress by persistent self-stimulating and occasional self-injurious behavior. Matthew was liked by students and school personnel. He was socially engaged and sought praise and attention. Matthew lived at home with supportive family members who hoped that when he finished school, he would move to a supervised group living situation and hold a job.

Matthew's most recent psychological evaluation placed him within the borderline range of intelligence with severe deficits in receptive and expressive language. He was able to communicate about the present situation, but could only describe or evaluate what happened earlier or anticipate what might happen later, stereotypically and by rote. Academically, Matthew worked on functional English and math skills. A review of Matthew's daily class notes indicated that he had received As in all activities and seldom lost any privileges. In addition to academic classes, the school provided Matthew with a vocational training program.

Of greatest concern to both school personnel and parents were Matthew's various maladaptive behaviors that occurred to some degree daily, increasing in low interest or nonstructured situations and decreasing when he was actively engaged in high interest or routine activities. Self-stimulating behaviors included hand flicking, "self-talk" (repetitive, nonfunctional word patterns), and stereotyped noises. Self-injurious behaviors ranged from mild chest thumping and skin picking to repeated violent head hitting, eye squeezing, and hand biting.

On rare occasions, Matthew had tantrums, turning over a desk or chair. He was always remorseful afterward. Some of Matthew's behaviors resulted in noticeable injury, and others interfered with his ability to focus on school work.

As a result of Matthew's behaviors, others distanced themselves from him, threatening his capacity to work in the community.

Curiously, Matthew's classroom behavioral program did not address these maladaptive behaviors directly, in part because Matthew became upset and initiated maladaptive behaviors when his daily academic and behavioral grades were less than perfect As. Thus, a second area of concern was Matthew's low tolerance for correction.

## PROCEDURE AND MEASURES

### Traditional Counseling Period Outside the Classroom

Matthew's individualized education plan (IEP) mandated counseling services to augment his special education. The goals of counseling included the minimizing of maladaptive or inappropriate behaviors and the building of adaptive, socially appropriate ones.

The social worker began weekly sessions of traditional one-to-one counseling with Matthew in a small counseling room, where the content of the hour was left to him. Appropriate behaviors were socially reinforced with praise, and maladaptive or inappropriate ones were ignored. Although not specifically measured, neither positive social reinforcement nor extinction through withdrawal of attention contributed to increase of adaptive or decrease of maladaptive behaviors.

It became clear that when Matthew left the highly structured setting of the classroom and entered one in which he was responsible for providing the content activity, he engaged in an uninhibited stream of self-talk accompanied by persistent stereotypical gestures. For example, Matthew created elaborate reenactments of TV game shows. In fact, to get a word in edgewise, the social worker had to persuade him to allow her to enter his world via "commercial breaks." Even then, most of Matthew's responses were incongruous.

### Modifying the Approach

Social work intervention attempts to focus on the transactions between clients and their social and physical environments (Germain, 1979). Most clients are able to include the laboratory of a counseling situation in their environmental niche. There they can recall and discuss earlier interactions in their life space and anticipate future ones. They generalize from insight and skills gained in the counseling lab to their larger life space.

For Matthew, traditional counseling was too removed from his life space. Positive reinforcement plus extinction procedures in a traditional counseling situation had been unsuccessful in modifying Matthew's behavior. His communication and time difficulties prevented him from including the counseling venue in his niche, and he could not generalize from it to his life space. Rather than dismiss Matthew as an inappropriate candidate for individual counseling, an alternative way to help him focus his attention on classroom behavior was to provide counseling in his classroom niche (Brower, 1988), with its familiar external structure, routine, and content.

The social worker suggested a behavioral, in vivo intervention using a combination of positive reinforcement techniques with mildly punitive ones in the life space of the classroom. This new approach combined the content of an academic lesson provided by the teacher with an operant conditioning process administered by the social worker. Teams of professionals from various disciplines interact cooperatively in schools in part because each respects the domain of the other. To accept the suggestion that the social worker enter his classroom on a regular basis necessitated a good deal of trust and self-confidence on the part of the special education teacher. He agreed to the social worker's entering his domain to try a different approach in helping his student.

The research design that emerged was A-B-C-D. However, the interventive method was not determined in advance. Rather, it developed through a process of trial and error. Progress was monitored by repeated measures in a single-system design. The intervention addressed the following hypothesis: A weekly behavioral program, provided in classroom during an academic lesson, will contribute to reduction of maladaptive behavior and to an increase in tolerance of correction.

### Measures

The measurement instrument was a chart of maladaptive target behaviors Matthew had assisted in assembling. The chart also listed several similar but adaptive behaviors suggested by the social worker that were incompatible with the maladaptive ones. The rows consisted of the target behaviors, and the columns were composed of six five-minute intervals representing the 30-minute lesson period (Figure 7-1). During each interval, the social worker made hash marks on the chart within Matthew's view to record the frequency of behaviors. Progress was recorded by multiple measures over 29 weeks.

## TREATMENT PERIOD A: DIFFERENTIAL REINFORCEMENT OF OTHER BEHAVIOR PLUS NEGATIVE FEEDBACK

During treatment period A, the social worker sat next to Matthew's desk during a regular 30-minute academic lesson and recorded Matthew's maladaptive and adaptive behaviors on the chart. Matthew was told that when he raised his hand to hit his head, he could use the upraised hand to stroke his hair instead of hitting.

When Matthew was sitting quietly, he often jiggled his leg. Leg jiggling was considered incompatible with maladaptive behaviors and could substitute for more socially distracting self-stimulating behaviors like self-talk or noises. When the social worker observed that Matthew was beginning to engage in self-stimulating or self-injurious behavior, she prompted him with, "What can you do with your hand instead?"

It was assumed that the measurement process itself, along with mild verbal disapproval, would act as a form of negative feedback or mild social punishment and would weaken the maladaptive behavior. Seeing the hash marks for the adaptive behaviors, along with receiving verbal approval, were intended to constitute differential reinforcement of incompatible behaviors and to strengthen those behaviors. No additional reinforcement was offered.

*Figure 7-1*

**Target Behavior Chart**

| Behavior | 5-Minute Intervals | | | | | |
|---|---|---|---|---|---|---|
| | 1 | 2 | 3 | 4 | 5 | 6 |
| **Negative**<br><br>Biting self<br>Burping<br>Hitting self<br>Flicking<br>Noises<br>Spitting<br>Self-talk<br>Picking lips<br>Squeezing eyes | | | | | | |
| **Positive**<br><br>Hand at cheek<br>Jiggles leg<br>Rubs hair<br>Rubs hand<br>Rubs eyelashes<br>Deep breathing | | | | | | |

## TREATMENT PERIOD B: RESPONSE–COST PLUS PRIMARY REINFORCEMENT

Later, the in-class approach was modified to involve a more directly decelerating procedure—response-cost—in which Matthew would lose something of value for each maladaptive behavior. Fearing self-injurious behavior tantrums, the teachers had been reluctant to take anything away from Matthew. Matthew's lack of tolerance for correction resulted in his almost always earning and keeping all his daily points. Furthermore, attention from the social worker and teachers was maintaining some of the maladaptive behaviors Matthew displayed.

As is typical for people with his disability, Matthew insisted on perfection and continuity, so a new IEP counseling goal was for him to begin to tolerate an evaluation of "less than perfect," a necessary skill for successful independent living. Responding in part to Matthew's intolerance of correction, a response-cost system was paired with DRI, building tolerance for a partial loss by providing some tangible reinforcer for partial success.

Based on the typical range of maladaptive behaviors Matthew previously displayed during five-minute intervals, the social worker gave him 25 popsicle sticks at the beginning of each interval. She removed a stick whenever he displayed a maladaptive behavior. At the end of each five-minute interval, the 25 sticks were replaced and the process began again. At the end of the class period, he could exchange the remaining sticks per five-minute interval for peanuts. That is, when he kept all 25 sticks during an interval, he earned five peanuts; as he lost sticks, he lost an equivalent number of peanuts. The hash marks and disapproval continued for the maladaptive behaviors, as did the differential reinforcement of incompatible adaptive behaviors in the form of hash marks and praise.

## TREATMENT PERIOD C: RESPONSE–COST—PRIMARY REINFORCEMENT

In treatment period C the fading of reinforcement procedures began. The number of sticks was reduced from 25 to five and the number of peanuts from five to three per five-minute interval. Gradually, the number of peanuts was reduced to only one per interval, so Matthew could earn no more than six peanuts for the entire lesson period. Also, the social worker continued to reinforce the adaptive behaviors with praise.

## TREATMENT PERIOD D: FURTHER FADING OF PRIMARY REINFORCEMENT

After Matthew's classroom behavior had stabilized for four months with one peanut as reward for each five-minute interval, the primary reinforcement was faded entirely. Fading was accomplished by introducing one of six intervals in which no peanut was offered and then gradually increasing the number of intervals in which Matthew could earn no peanuts. During treatment period D, verbal praise continued.

## ANALYSIS

### Treatment Period A

During the four sessions of treatment period A, the total number of maladaptive behaviors that Matthew displayed per 30-minute session ranged from 55 to 202. During this period, the mean number of maladaptive behaviors per five-minute interval varied widely from 9.2 to 33.5 (Figure 7-2).

It was apparent that the first approach, combining feedback for maladaptive and adaptive behaviors with disapproval for maladaptive and praise for adaptive, was not effective in decelerating the negative behaviors. Inspection of the graphed data indicates that the mean number of maladaptive behaviors per interval varied radically. Matthew's behavior appeared to respond to the structure of the classroom activity rather than to the intervention. In fact, the intended negative feedback may have positively reinforced the maladaptive behaviors, because whenever the social worker neglected to record a behavior, Matthew reminded her to record it.

Because the graph of treatment period A (Figure 7-2) indicates that the initial treatment was not effective in inhibiting the maladaptive target behaviors, this period may be viewed as a baseline against which the next period of treatment could be measured.

### Treatment Period B

The first day the new response-cost plus primary reinforcement system was implemented (week 5), Matthew displayed immediate improvement. He committed only two maladaptive behaviors during the first interval of the session;

*Figure 7-2*

**Treatment Periods A and B: Maladaptive Behaviors Displayed per Five-Minute Interval**

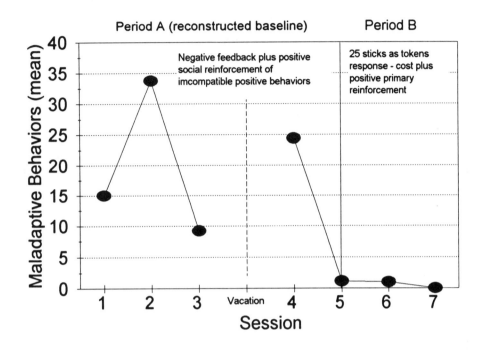

four during the second interval; one during the third; and zero during the fourth, fifth, and sixth. Thus, the mean number of maladaptive behaviors per interval was 1.16. Of a possible 30 peanuts, Matthew received 23. In spite of the removal of tokens and loss of peanuts, he did not initiate any self-injurious behavior or tantrums.

Visual analysis of the graphed data (Figure 7-2) indicates that Matthew's behavior changed dramatically from treatment period A (in which negative and positive feedback were coupled with differential reinforcement of incompatible adaptive behaviors) to treatment period B (where the response-cost system was introduced). The change was so rapid (a total of only one maladaptive behavior during session 6 and none during session 7) that it was clear Matthew could easily earn all the peanuts, have nothing to work toward, and become physically satiated. So, within two weeks, the approach was modified again.

**Treatment Period C**

During period C, despite Matthew's being able to earn no more than six peanuts for the entire lesson, even that small number was adequately reinforcing to maintain his practically flawless performance. He displayed no more than three negative behaviors during the entire 30-minute class for the next 14 sessions. The numbers dropped so precipitously that from this point on, the numbers of maladaptive behaviors are reported as totals per 30-minute session, rather than the mean number per five-minute interval (Figure 7-3).

Although Matthew objected mildly to the reduction in tokens and reinforcers, he accepted the change with no incident. He reassured himself with comments like, "I didn't get all the peanuts, but that's OK," indicating a growing tolerance for "less than perfect" evaluation. In addition, the adaptive behaviors continued to be reinforced with praise. Matthew sometimes performed those behaviors in an exaggerated, stereotyped manner and usually did so while mentioning the behavior: "Rubbing my hair, OK?"

Matthew's ability to inhibit maladaptive behavior was further demonstrated when he added a new self-injurious behavior—lip picking. The new behavior was immediately added to the list, and as sticks were lost, Matthew quickly eliminated the behavior.

### Treatment Period D

As primary reinforcement began to be eliminated in the first session of treatment period D, Matthew displayed no maladaptive behaviors (see Figures 7-4 and 7-5). The following week, Matthew could earn no peanuts during two of the six intervals, yet he continued to inhibit all maladaptive behaviors. During

*Figure 7-3*

**Treatment Period C: Maladaptive Behaviors Displayed per 30-Minute Period**

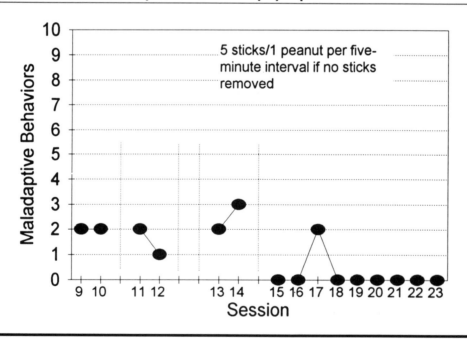

Figure 7-4

**Treatment Period D: Maladaptive Behaviors Displayed per 30-Minute Period**

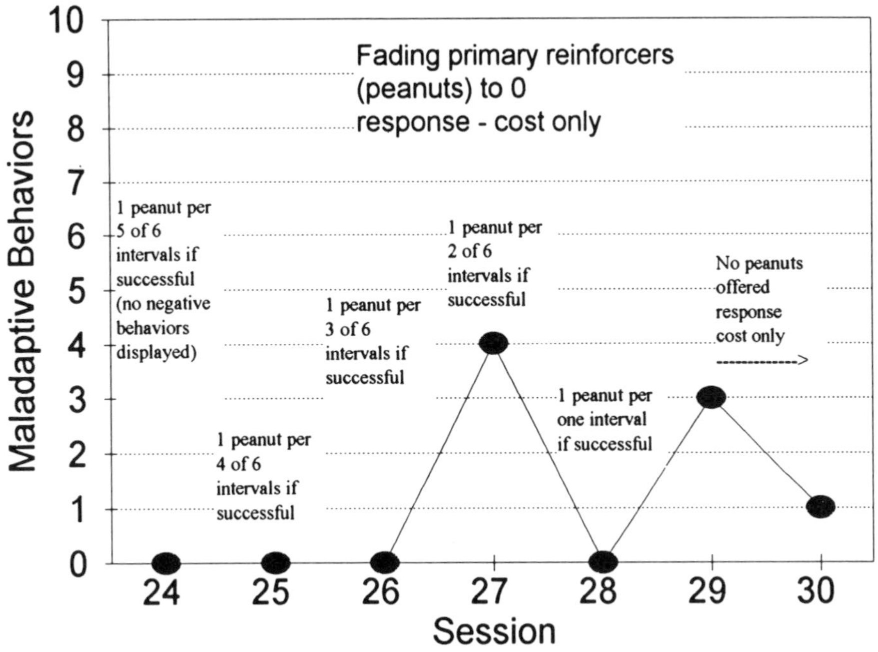

week 26, no peanuts were offered in three of the six intervals, and Matthew's behavior remained entirely appropriate. Only in week 27, when Matthew could earn peanuts during only two of the six intervals, did maladaptive behaviors re-emerge—a total of four during the entire 30-minute period. By week 29, no peanuts were offered, praise continued, and Matthew was able to maintain control with only minimal maladaptive behaviors displayed before the school year and intervention ended.

Despite Matthew's virtual elimination of maladaptive behaviors while the social worker was engaged in the program with him, he reverted to a quiet flow of inappropriate behaviors, largely of the self-stimulatory type, when the worker prepared to leave the room. If he was neither involved in the response-cost intervention nor engaged in high-interest activities (such as using the computer), the constant flow of self-talk and stereotypical hand and facial gestures returned to dominate his behavior. This observation indicates that the learned skill of inhibiting maladaptive behaviors had not generalized beyond the structured counseling period.

## DISCUSSION AND IMPLICATIONS

This study represents an experimental process over a period of 29 weeks in which variations of operant conditioning methods were tried, their results measured,

*Figure 7-5*

**Treatment Period D: Maladaptive Behaviors Displayed per Five-Minute Interval**

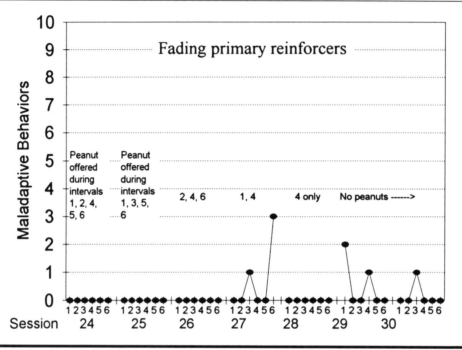

and the methods then adapted to improve results. The study revealed that Matthew was able to inhibit his maladaptive behaviors during interaction with the social worker once response-cost was paired with DRI. The addition of response-cost also contributed to Matthew's increased tolerance of correction, despite his usual insistence on sameness and perfection and his teachers' past reluctance to remove tokens or privileges. In replicating this design with similar clients, school social workers would not have to spend as much time or go through all the steps. They could move more quickly in working with a student to develop a response-cost and DRI system that uses the minimum of prompts and reinforcers that are effective.

Some might argue that the use of negative feedback, mild verbal disapproval, and response-cost are punitive methods and should be avoided unless all positive methods have proved ineffective. Yet school personnel had lavishly reinforced Matthew's adaptive behavior, both informally through praise and formally in the form of As. Positive reinforcement alone did not build adequate adaptive behaviors to inhibit the maladaptive ones. Moreover, the level of "punishment" used by the social worker was clearly consistent with the culture of the classroom, where tolerance of correction is required of all students and privileges are lost routinely. Finally, the negative techniques were always coupled with positive ones.

Despite the demonstrable effectiveness of the intervention in reducing negative behaviors and increasing tolerance for correction during the time the social worker was with Matthew, his failure to generalize the new adaptive behaviors beyond the stimulus control of the social worker may reflect the fact that among the variables found to maintain self-injurious behavior, internal sensory stimulation is extraordinarily potent (Durand & Crimmins, 1988). Thus, when Matthew was neither engaged in high-interest activities nor actively being engaged by the social worker or others, he stimulated himself with the very behaviors that interfered with more adaptive functioning.

This observation suggests that for school personnel working with students with severe developmental disabilities, effectiveness need not be restricted to mastery through generalization of all new adaptive behaviors; effectiveness may also be achieved through maintenance of some adaptive social behaviors during low-interest activities through controlling the social environment. To maximize effectiveness, however, environmental control requires teachers, job coaches, and parents to use similar tactics in all aspects of the student's environment to assist him or her in maintaining adaptive behaviors. The school social worker should, following development with the student of a successful classroom intervention, seek to generalize the method through consultation with the team of family members and professionals involved with the student.

## CONCLUSION

This case study provides an example of how social workers practicing in school settings can apply the concepts of the ecological perspective of person-in-environment to understand the functioning of severely disabled student–clients and to provide effective treatment within the host system and other aspects of the student's environment. The classroom setting may be seen as an important part of the life space of the student–client that the social worker may enter to intervene rather than withdrawing the client from the classroom niche in which he or she is comfortable and in which there is opportunity for direct involvement with the client's social functioning.

School social workers enhance their capacity to be effective even with severely disabled students within the host setting of the school by integrating techniques of operant conditioning from the behavioral practice theory of special education with the social work ecological perspective. Behavioral practice theory supports change through control of environmental stimuli and consequences, and ecological practice supports both helping clients by changing the environment to be more supportive of client needs and helping clients adapt to their environments. With this integration of theory, the school social worker may help structure environmental niches that support and maintain the adaptive behavior of each client so that all clients may learn and grow to the best of their ability.

## REFERENCES

American Psychiatric Association. (1994). *Diagnostic and statistical manual of mental disorders* (4th ed.). Washington, DC: Author.

Azrin, N. H., Besalel, V. A., Jamner, J. P., & Caputo, J. N. (1988). Comparative study of behavioral methods of treating self-injury. *Behavioral Residential Treatment, 3*, 119–152.

Bettelheim, B. (1967). *The empty fortress.* New York: Free Press.

Brower, A. (1988). Can the ecological model guide social work practice? *Social Service Review, 62,* 411–429.

Durand, Y. M., & Crimmins, D. B. (1988). Identifying the variables maintaining self-injurious behavior. *Journal of Autism and Developmental Disorders, 18*(1), 99–117.

Education for All Handicapped Children Act of 1975, P.L. 94-142, 89 Stat. 773.

Favell, J. E., McGimsey, J. F., & Schell, R. M. (1982). Treatment of self-injury by providing alternative sensory activities. *Analysis and Intervention in Developmental Disabilities, 2,* 83–104.

Germain, C. (1979). *Social work practice: People and environments.* New York: Columbia University Press.

Groden, G., & Baron, M. G. (Eds.). (1988). *Autism: Strategies for change.* New York: Gardner Press.

Jones, R.S.P., & Baker, L.J.V. (1988). The differential reinforcement of incompatible responses in the reduction of self-injurious behaviour: A pilot study. *Behavioural Psychotherapy, 16,* 323–328.

Kanner, L. (1943). Autistic disturbances of affective contact. *Nervous Child, 2,* 217–250.

Rimland, B. (1964). *Infantile autism.* New York: Appleton-Century-Crofts.

Rincover, A., & Devany, J. (1982). The application of sensory extinction procedures to self-injury. *Analysis and Intervention in Developmental Disabilities, 2,* 67–81.

Rojahn, J. (1986). Self-injurious and stereotypic behavior of noninstitutionalized mentally retarded people: Prevalence and classification. *American Journal of Mental Deficiency, 91,* 268–276.

Romanczyk, R. G. (1986). Self-injurious behavior: Conceptualization, assessment, and treatment. *Advances in Learning and Behavioral Disabilities, 2,* 29–56.

Schreibman, L. (1988). *Autism.* Newbury Park, CA: Sage Publications.

Thyer, B. A., & Maddox, K. (1988). Behavioral social work: Results of a national survey on graduate curricula. *Psychological Reports, 63,* 239–242.

Underwood, L. A., Figueroa, R. G., Thyer, B. A., & Nzeocha, A. (1989). Interruption and DRI in the treatment of self-injurious behavior among mentally retarded and autistic self-restrainers. *Behavior Modification, 13,* 471–481.

Underwood, L., & Thyer, B. (1990). Social work practice with the mentally retarded: Reducing self-injurious behaviors using non-aversive methods. *Arete, 15*(1), 14–23.

*This chapter was originally published in the October 1995 issue of* Social Work in Education, *Vol. 17, pp. 244–255.*

# 8 Using Portfolios to Assess Students' Academic Strengths: A Case Study

Jean C. Karoly and Cynthia G. Franklin

For the past several years, performance-based assessment, sometimes called "portfolio assessment," has been discussed in educational evaluation as an alternative or supplement to traditional assessment tools such as standardized tests. This trend is largely the result of a general dissatisfaction with relying solely on standardized tests to assess students' progress and skill levels (Nweke, 1991). Portfolio assessment has been reported to offset the negative aspects of standardized testing by personalizing evaluation and producing structures for individualized learning (Arter & Spandel, 1992; Grady, 1992; Jongsma, 1989; McClure, 1992; Moss, 1994; Wiggins, 1991; Wolf, 1991). Standardized tests are not objective or fair for all children; results tend to differ for students from various cultural backgrounds (Defabio, 1993). However, test scores are often given the greatest weight in labeling, tracking, and retention decisions that will affect a child's entire academic career. Children who are designated "unready" or "slow learners" on the basis of standardized tests often suffer a narrowing of their educational opportunities (Perrone, 1991).

Because portfolio assessments can increase the educational opportunities of children, this method for evaluating the educational progress of students should be of special interest to school social workers. Portfolio assessments can easily be incorporated into the psychosocial evaluations of school social workers and can be used by social workers as well as school diagnosticians and psychologists to improve academic assessments of children. This article illustrates how portfolio assessment can improve the strengths-based assessment of a child's academic competencies using a case study conducted by an associate psychologist who received consultation on the use of this approach from a social worker.

## LITERATURE REVIEW

Wolf (1991) defined *portfolio assessment* as a "depository of artifacts" that at some point requires "a written reflection by the developer on the significance or contributions of those artifacts to the attributes of interest" (p. 36). The compilation of artifacts, or portfolio, is an assortment of various documents; some may be paper-and-pencil tests or classroom observations, and others may be projects, constructions, videotapes, audiotapes, poems, artwork, or stories produced by the student (Nweke, 1991).

Portfolios reflect a shift in educational assessment from a behaviorist framework of learning involving the acquisition of a sequence of component skills through drills and practice to a constructivist lens that regards learning as complex, contextual, and collaborative (McClure, 1992). Portfolio assessment is supported by newer learning theories that recognize a wide diversity in the pace and style of cognitive and learning development among children from various cultures (Grady, 1992; Resnick & Resnick, 1992).

Investigators of the portfolio technique have raised the issue of metacognition as part of the student learning process (Grady, 1992; McClure, 1992; Paulson & Paulson, 1990; Wolf, 1991). McClure observed that in metacognitive functions, students "evaluate in a systematic way their learning on a particular project or across a set of tasks" (p. 37). Although McClure indicated that these reflections are most often written, others (DeWitt, 1991; Grady, 1992; Rosenblatt, 1991) have insisted that they can be oral presentations, remarks, or ruminations supplemented by teacher annotations.

Two assumptions underlie the use of the portfolio: (1) Judgments based on portfolios are more reliable and valid because of the comprehensive and inclusive nature of the samples (Messick, 1994; Paulson & Paulson, 1990), and (2) portfolios, when used as a supplement to other methods of measuring learning, will improve the reliability and validity of the evidence (Moss, 1992). No definitive studies conclusively support the claims of either assumption, but a study conducted by Nweke (1991) indicated that achievement measured by a portfolio is related to achievement determined by other measures such as the American College Testing exam, college grade-point averages, and essays. Nweke cautioned, however, that the nature of that relationship indicates when they exclude paper-and-pencil tests, portfolios should be used as supplements to rather than substitutes for standardized tests.

Standards for evaluating performance-based assessments are usually developed after portfolio work has been systematically collected (McClure, 1992; Paulson & Paulson, 1990). This is in sharp contrast to standardized testing, which sets specific criteria or develops normative samples for comparisons before students are evaluated. The rationale for portfolio assessment is that standards should be locally and realistically established only after student work has been gathered (Paulson & Paulson, 1990). Defabio (1993) stated that in portfolio assessment, the objective is not to assign grades to individual products but to appraise the portfolio holistically as an index of the student's progress as a thinker and learner. This type of assessment is more akin to qualitative or naturalistic evaluation (Guba, 1985; Jordan & Franklin, 1995; Mishler, 1990). Walters and Gardner (1991) insisted that portfolios cannot be reduced to numerical grades but must be approached qualitatively through a multidimensional evaluation.

Defabio (1993) recommended that portfolio work be assessed along certain domains or dimensions of standards. She advocated the use of teacher and student narratives, with evaluative comments regarding these domains as evidenced in the products of the portfolio. The final grade is negotiated between the student and the teacher. Among the dimensions proposed as benchmarks for evaluation are range (applying learned concepts to a wide range of data), flexibility (evidence of performance in varied and changing conditions), and variety (demonstration of a spectrum of skills). Moss (1994) stated that portfolio assessments can be evaluated better against a hermeneutical framework grounded in a holistic interpretation by evaluators (such as teachers) who are familiar with the context in which the tasks were performed and whose interpretations evolve from a dialogue and debate among all of the evaluators.

## CASE STUDY

### Background

An associate psychologist working in the Judson School District near San Antonio, Texas, conducted a routine re-evaluation of a 10-year-old African American male special education student following the guidelines mandated by the Texas Education Agency, which requires that school districts assess special education students in specified domains primarily with psychometric instruments. The student was being served in a self-contained behavior adjustment class for students with severe behavior problems. The standard psychometric procedures in the evaluation included the Wechsler (1991) Intelligence Scale for Children—Third Edition, the Woodcock–Johnson (1990) Psychoeducational Battery—Revised, the Holtzman (1961) Inkblot Technique, the Self-Report of Personality (Reynolds & Kamphaus, 1992), and the Personality Inventory for Children—Revised (Lachar, 1992). In addition, the associate psychologist conducted a clinical interview and consulted teacher and parent information checklists developed by the school district.

The student was initially diagnosed by another school district as having dysthymia and overanxious disorder. Since the first grade the student had been in self-contained classrooms to manage his severe temper tantrums and aggressive behavior; he was never assigned to a less-restrictive mainstream setting with students who were not developmentally disabled. The student enrolled in the Judson School District in the middle of the 1992–93 school year, at which time he was placed in a behavior adjustment class on his home elementary campus. He had an intact family that included his birth parents, who were blue-collar workers, and two younger sisters.

The results of the psychological assessment indicated that the student had average intellectual functioning and academic skills ranging from marginally average to below average and deficits in his math and writing skills. Projective data suggested that the student perceived his environment as threatening, had difficulty with interpersonal relationships, and fantasized excessively. Some of his inkblot responses were morbid, including "evil people plotting to destroy the world," "evil fighting evil," and "people and animals who are dead or messed up." Parent and teacher checklists provided corollary information about the student, indicating frequent daydreaming, peer conflicts, periods of mood lability and explosive outbursts, and feelings of helplessness. The diagnoses of dysthymia and overanxious disorder were continued.

When the associate psychologist met with the teachers to conduct a planning meeting for the student's individual education plan, she anticipated that they would spend an extensive amount of time developing a discipline plan and that it was unlikely that the student would be mainstreamed. Contrary to her expectations, however, the student had been mainstreamed extensively in the regular classroom and was doing very well. His teachers anticipated a full-time placement in the regular classroom within a month, relating that the student was earning Bs in all subjects and that his behavior was appropriate in the regular classroom, although he was still aggressive and disruptive in the special education classroom. His special education teacher and two regular education teachers had been coordinating a plan to assist the student in the transition from the self-contained to the regular classroom. Because of the discrepancy between the findings from the standardized assessment data and the teachers' reports, a portfolio assessment was undertaken with the help of the teachers and a social worker.

When the associate psychologist first approached the teachers about conducting the portfolio assessment on the student, she anticipated that the teachers would not welcome the intrusiveness of the observations, the time lost during conference periods for interviews, or the lengthy sessions analyzing the portfolio. To her astonishment, the teachers were pleased that an assessment staff member was willing to consider their professional judgments about a student that were not consonant with the results of a formal assessment.

Three 90-minute observations were scheduled for the student, two in the regular classroom and one in the special education classroom. Notes were taken during the observations. Three 60-minute interviews were conducted with each teacher. These interviews were open-ended, loosely structured, and guided only by the topic of the student. The interviews were conversational and free flowing, encouraging the teachers to identify what they perceived as important issues about the student and his performance. The flexibility of the interviews facilitated the emergence of new and unanticipated information.

## Portfolio Contents

The portfolio consisted of three notebooks of documents and several items that the student had designed and constructed. One aspect of his development in which there was a progression of skills was his written composition. Documents included early and final drafts of essays, themes, stories, and research projects. When the evaluators examined the range of the student's writing samples, it was obvious that his writing skills had evolved from constructing simple, ungrammatical sentences to composing more elaborate and descriptive sentences with correct usage and then to organizing ideas with the same topic into paragraphs. The student's compositions included both compound and complex sentences with appropriate verb and pronoun agreement. This development was in marked contrast to his writing samples on the Woodcock–Johnson Psychoeducational Battery, some of which included sentence fragments.

The portfolio included several constructed items—a pyramid, an Indian village, a wooden stool, a weathervane, a small battery-operated race car, and a terrarium. Each item demonstrated a multiplicity of skills and was accompanied by a written narrative by the student describing the item and how it was constructed. To construct the wooden stool and the pyramid, the student was required to make many math computations, which he illustrated on diagrams. All of the computations were done by hand (one teacher did not permit calculators) and were beside an illustration drawn to scale. The student also described the use of a protractor for the pyramid and a level for the stool. The written description of the car included a discussion of electromagnetic principles. One teacher reported that this project had not been assigned but that the student had asked to work on a project in his free time when they were studying a unit on electromagnetic energy. The teacher said that she and the class became interested in his project, noting that the student had taught the children about the concept of electromagnetism more effectively than her class presentations.

Several documents included both written and illustrated book reports. In some the student had drawn detailed pictures depicting scenes from the books. For example, a watercolor portrait of a scene from a children's book about King Henry VIII included a drawing of the Tower of London and beside it a guillotine dripping in blood. For other book reports the student had drawn a series of comic strips in crayon to show consecutive sequences of events in the stories. One comic strip included in the final frame a drawing of the student himself saying, "I'm a Caldecott winner!" (The illustrator of the book the student was describing was awarded the Caldecott medal for his work.)

Other entries included several photograph displays. One showed the different stages of construction of props used in a class play about the Alamo. The student had been the project manager in designing an Alamo backdrop, which he organized very well. An Alamo profile, a barracks scene, and a small chapel were all developed by the student's team. His photographic history of the props was of great interest to the other children. The student took all of the photographs included in the portfolio.

There was also an assortment of quizzes and major exams. The student's performance on these items was variable, ranging from As and Bs on social studies, science, reading, English, and math word-problem tests to Cs and Ds on math calculation and English usage tests. On the samples in which the student earned good grades, the content was complex and required the application of many skills. The samples with low grades were tests of isolated skills that were not linked to a larger project or product.

## Portfolio Assessment

The portfolio was evaluated jointly by the associate psychologist and the three teachers. The products were judged using a hermeneutical framework grounded in a holistic interpretation by the teachers, who were familiar with the context in which the tasks were performed and whose interpretations evolved from a dialogue and debate among everyone. Therefore, unlike the psychometric evaluation, the student was truly being evaluated within the classroom milieu. Similar to the findings of Moss (1994), the evaluators debated the merits of certain products. Final decisions were the result of a consensus, although in contested cases the opinions of the teachers usually prevailed because they were more familiar with the context in which the work was performed.

## FINDINGS

Several interesting findings emerged from the portfolio assessment. The student's frequent fantasizing, which was regarded as pathological in the traditional assessment, was an asset for him in the classroom. Both regular teachers reported that the student usually daydreamed aloud before his writing assignments. This behavior seemed to reflect his unique style of organizing a task and outlining his composition. The special education teacher regarded the student's rich fantasy life as a coping style for dealing with demands at school. The student kept a journal in the special education class that included interesting anecdotes and revealed his internal reflections about important issues (for example, Why do some children hurt other children's feelings?). The special education and one regular teacher reported that when the student was "timed out" for misbehavior, he often talked out his problems aloud to characters in books, plays, and posters.

Another of the student's strengths was a combination of high intelligence and creativity. Despite the marginally average and below-average scores the student earned on his Woodcock–Johnson Psychoeducational Battery, he was regarded by his teachers as above grade level and capable of producing unusual and high-quality work. One teacher reported that the student earned a top rating on his Texas Assessment of Academic Skills writing sample and described his compositions as full of elaboration and insight. For library week, he wrote a coherent and entertaining short story, and he made numerous interesting and thorough oral presentations in class about topics in social studies and science.

During the interviews both regular education teachers indicated that the student responded well to their correction in the classroom because he wanted to "fit in" and "not stand out." All three teachers observed that the student was also a "follower" who was greatly influenced by the peer models around him and was highly susceptible to peer provocation. If others were working quietly and cooperatively, he did also. This influence was further supported by the student himself during a regular classroom observation when the teacher was giving a 15-minute timed test in math. Aware that the student had difficulty sitting still and concentrating for 15 minutes, the teacher quietly called the student to her desk and asked him whether he needed more time to complete his test. He replied that he preferred to take the test in the allotted period "just like everybody else." The two regular education teachers noted also that other students extinguished some inappropriate behaviors simply by telling him to stop. This fact was evident during one observation in a regular classroom when the student, while working in a group, got off of the task and began drawing and coloring. A male classmate, who was a leader and an athlete, nudged him gently and said quietly, "Put that away and pay attention, man!"

Finally, the portfolio assessment uncovered that all three teachers had built in opportunities for the student for movement during their class periods and some choices about planning his work. They believed that both the movement and the power to make some decisions made him more invested in his school work.

For behaviors that were difficult for the student to demonstrate on a sustained basis, they asked for successive approximations of these behaviors such as paying attention for 10 minutes and remaining quiet until the teacher stops talking. At the end of the day, both regular teachers discussed with the student the extent to which he had complied with their expectations.

## IMPLICATIONS FOR SCHOOL SOCIAL WORK PRACTICE

Portfolio assessment can illuminate the academic and personal strengths of students that are missed in a traditional psychometric assessment. The discrepancy between the student's performance on the psychometric tests and his accomplishments in the classroom were largely the result of the social embeddedness of the tasks. Findings indicate that the student needed to see the task as reflecting his membership in a regular classroom and as part of a larger integrated whole rather than just an isolated drill. This was shown by his desire to fit in with his peers. The portfolio illustrated that the student did well on work that he saw as either directed toward a purpose or producing a product. For assignments including drills of facts or computations in which he was unable to see an immediate goal or outcome, he was poorly motivated to do well.

As shown in the portfolio documents, the student's general academic functioning was characterized by higher-level thinking skills, clear and coherent written expression, and an ability to read well and reflect on his readings. These results could not be identified by a psychometric assessment, which is limited to sampling only isolated skills in a single evaluation and does not address contextual issues. Of course, the immense value of a contextual assessment and analysis is not new to school social workers. This case example simply highlights the importance of individualizing assessments and including as a part of each student's assessment an evaluation of adaptive skills in the context of person-in-environment interactions. Information on a student's strengths in relevant social contexts is normally included in a school social worker's psychosocial evaluations.

Findings from the case study led the associate psychologist to conclude that all students should have their assessment augmented by some type of portfolio or performance-based evaluation. Time and money constraints, however, may not permit such an action. It is advisable to commit the additional time and money to a performance-based assessment for a student whose traditional evaluations do not match the realities of that student as constructed by his or her teachers.

Performance-based, contextual assessments can highlight the academic and personal strengths of students—strengths that may be overlooked or even judged pathological when viewed exclusively through the lens of traditional psychometric measures. School social workers may wish to consider how they can use portfolios in their own assessments and to encourage other assessment specialists to do so. It should also be noted that Moss (1994) cautioned practitioners that neither a psychometric nor a hermeneutic approach to assessments alone will ensure truth or fairness. Rather, a review of the underlying assumptions of both paradigms permits "a better informed choice" (p. 10).

## REFERENCES

Arter, J., & Spandel, V. (1992). Using portfolios of student work in instruction and assessment. *Educational Measurement, 11,* 36–44.

Defabio, R. (1993). *Characteristics of student performance as factors in portfolio assessment.* Albany, NY: National Research Center on Literature Teaching and Learning. (ERIC Document Reproduction Service No. ED 355 566)

DeWitt, K. (1991, April 24). Vermont gauges learning by what's in the portfolio. *New York Times,* p. B7.

Grady, E. (1992). *The portfolio approach to assessment.* Bloomington, IN: Phi Delta Kappa. (ERIC Document Reproduction Service No. ED 356 273)

Guba, E. (1985). *Naturalistic inquiry.* Newbury Park, CA: Sage Publications.

Holtzman, W. (1961). *Holtzman Inkblot Technique.* New York: Psychological Corporation.

Jongsma, K. (1989). Portfolio assessment (questions and answers). *Reading Teacher, 43,* 264–265.

Jordan, C., & Franklin, C. (1995). *Clinical assessment for social workers: Quantitative and qualitative methods.* Chicago: Lyceum/Nelson-Hall.

Lachar, D. (1992). *Personality Inventory for Children—Revised.* Los Angeles: Western Psychological Services.

McClure, R. (1992, April). *Alternate forms of student assessment.* Paper presented at the Annual Meeting of the American Educational Research Association, San Francisco. (ERIC Document Reproduction Service No. ED 347 209)

Messick, S. M. (1994). The interplay of evidence and consequences in the validation of performance assessments. *Educational Researcher, 23,* 13–23.

Mishler, E. (1990). Validation in inquiry-guided research. *Harvard Educational Review, 60,* 415–442.

Moss, P. (1992). Shifting conceptions of validity in educational measurement: Implications for performance assessment. *Review of Educational Research, 62,* 229–258.

Moss, P. (1994). Can there be validity without reliability? *Educational Researcher, 23,* 5–12.

Nweke, W. (1991, November). *What type of evidence is provided through the portfolio assessment method?* Paper presented at the Annual Meeting of the Mid-South Educational Research Association, Lexington, KY. (ERIC Document Reproduction Service No. ED 340 719)

Paulson, L., & Paulson, P. (1990, August). *How do portfolios measure up?* Paper presented at the Annual Meeting of the Northwest Evaluation Association, Union, WA. (ERIC Document Reproduction Service No. ED 324 329)

Perrone, V. (1991). *Expanding student assessment.* Washington, DC: National Education Association.

Resnick, L., & Resnick, D. (1992). Assessing the thinking curriculum: New tools for educational reform. In B. Gifford & M. C. O'Connor (Eds.), *Cognitive approaches to assessment* (pp. 31–56). Boston: Kluwer-Nijhoff.

Reynolds, C., & Kamphaus, R. (1992). *Self-Report of Personality.* Circle Pines, MN: American Guidance Services.

Rosenblatt, L. (1991). Literature—S.O.S.! *Language Arts, 68,* 444–448.

Walters, J., & Gardner, H. (1991). *Portfolios of student projects* (Report to the Lilly Endowment). Cambridge, MA: Harvard University, Project Zero.

Wechsler, D. (1991). *Wechsler Intelligence Scale for Children—Third Edition.* San Antonio, TX: Psychological Corporation.

Wiggins, G. (1991). Standards, not standardization. *Educational Leadership, 46,* 35–39.

Wolf, K. (1991). *The schoolteacher's portfolio.* Stanford, CA: Stanford University Press.

Woodcock, R., & Johnson, B. (1990). *Woodcock–Johnson Psychoeducational Battery—Revised.* Allen, TX: DLM Teaching Resources.

*This chapter was originally published in the July 1996 issue of* Social Work in Education, *Vol. 18, pp. 179–186.*

# 9 Aggressive Behavior in Childhood and Early Adolescence: An Ecological–Developmental Perspective on Youth Violence

Mark W. Fraser

**V**iolence is a major social and health problem that affects large numbers of children and families. Teenagers account for only 10 percent of the population, but they are victims in nearly 25 percent of all violent crimes (Allen-Hagen & Sickmund, 1993; Moone, 1994). Although only about one in five violent crimes is committed by a youth, youths have become markedly more involved in violent acts over the past decade (Snyder & Sickmund, 1995). Between 1984 and 1993, the number of juveniles arrested for murder rose 168 percent, and weapons violations rose 126 percent (Children's Defense Fund, 1995).

On the basis of self-report and victimization data, it is not clear whether youths are fighting more than in the past. But it is clear that their fights are resulting more often in injury and death because of the use of firearms (Rosenberg, 1995). The convergence of youthful impulsivity, the growing availability of handguns, the declining socioeconomic conditions of many families, and the emergence of street subcultures based on crack and other illicit drugs has made adolescence far deadlier. The problem is widespread, and although data suggest that there are important differences by race and ethnicity, sex, and region (including urban versus rural), violence touches many families and communities (for reviews, see Fraser, 1995; Prothrow-Stith, 1995).

The problem may get worse. In the early 1980s birth rates declined and the size of the teenage birth cohort grew smaller, so there were fewer children at risk-prone ages for delinquency and violence. This is about to change, because birth rates are on the rise. Over the next 10 years, the number of teenagers in the population will increase by approximately 22 percent (Krauss, 1994; Reno, 1995). Thus, even if the rate at which it occurs does not change, the seeds have been sown for increases in youth violence.

Use of physical force in such a way that it produces injury or death—perhaps the simplest definition of violence—encompasses a wide range of acts, including child abuse, gang fighting, hate crimes, sexual assault, spouse battering, suicide, terrorism, and war (Fraser, 1995). To be sure, institutions also engage in acts that injure or kill (for example, the dumping of toxic wastes). The focus of this article, however, is on street crime, a type of violence that includes fighting;

use of handguns or other weapons to resolve disputes; murder; and predatory acts such as aggravated assault, rape, and robbery.

Violent behavior of this nature rarely develops spontaneously. It often has roots in early childhood. Not surprisingly, violent behavior appears to be relatively stable for children who become aggressive at an early age. Moreover, early aggressive behavior has a strong and significant relationship with long-term life outcomes, including the development of criminal careers where physical force is used routinely (Elliott, 1994; Farrington, Loeber, et al., 1993; Nagin & Farrington, 1992).

Recent research suggests that a small percentage of families account for a disproportionately large volume of violence. Early offenders are likely to come from families in which assaultive and predatory behavior runs across generations (Farrington, Loeber, et al., 1993). In juvenile justice, a small number of youths account for a disproportionately large volume of offenses against people and property (Elliott, 1994). These children and their families use a large percentage of resources in the child welfare, mental health, and juvenile justice fields (Henggeler & Borduin, 1990). And although some children stop serious aggressive behavior as they mature and others are helped by treatment, many who avoid deep involvement in the court system go on to lead lives characterized by heavy drinking, polydrug use, sexual promiscuity, reckless driving, marital violence, and occupational marginality (Elliott, 1994; Farrington, Loeber, et al., 1993).

It is a bleak picture, and the long-term price of violence is incalculably high. Costs to victims of medical treatment, rehabilitation, and lost productivity plus direct costs to the justice system are estimated to exceed $60 billion annually (Roth & Moore, 1995). Moreover, even with treatment, the prognosis for many violent children and their families is poor (Prothrow-Stith, 1995). Across both community-based and residential services, failure rates are high when children enter treatment because of aggressive behavior (Henggeler, 1989; Kazdin, 1987, 1995). The development of new service strategies to treat aggressive behavior in childhood and early adolescence is a major national challenge. New strategies are needed both to improve the effectiveness of existing programs and to address the growing youth violence problem. Although there are many perspectives on youth violence (for example, social control, labeling, strain, psychoanalytic, and Marxist theories), this article discusses the etiology of aggressive behavior and violence from an ecological–developmental perspective and describes the implications of recent research for strengthening early intervention services for children and their families.

## SOCIAL DEVELOPMENT AND EARLY AGGRESSION

A child's social development is deeply rooted in opportunities, skills, and recognition that accrue through early interactions with family members, peers, teachers, neighbors, ministers, coaches, and many others (for example, Catalano & Hawkins, 1996; Hawkins, Catalano, & Associates, 1992). Throughout the life course, successful family, school, and work experiences have bases in early childhood opportunities for social participation and the development of a broad range of social and cognitive skills that promote building attachments to other children and adults. If, because of social or economic conditions, children lack opportunities for and role models of successful social participation, they may be seriously disadvantaged in developing skills that will promote success in school, work, and other life settings.

An ecological–developmental perspective focuses on opportunities for positive social participation and skills to promote building successful relationships with peers and adults who are committed to conventional lines of action (Tolan, Guerra, & Kendall, 1995). As Maas (1986) argued, an ecodevelopmental view emphasizes

> the processes through which people become increasingly able to interact competently and responsibly—that is, with recognition of others' needs—in an increasing array of social contexts. The greater the number of contexts with which people can cope, the fewer the situations in which they are overwhelmed by feelings of helplessness and stress. The more often they engage in socially responsive interaction, the more likely they are to help to generate or sustain a caring and sharing society. (p. 3)

From this perspective, youth violence is seen as the result of an impoverished opportunity structure, inadequate training in critical social and cognitive skills, the perception that there is social and concrete utility in aggressive behavior, and the lack of indigenous rewards for prosocial activities in the social environment.

Longitudinal studies in Colorado, Hawaii, New York, Oregon, Pennsylvania, Washington, and other states and countries afford increasingly vivid glimpses of the ecological conditions that disrupt social development and increase risk for ungovernability, delinquency, substance abuse, and violence (Brook, Whiteman, & Finch, 1992; Dishion, Patterson, Stoolmiller, & Skinner, 1991; Elliott, 1994; Hawkins, Catalano, Morrison, et al., 1992; Loeber et al., 1993; Thornberry, Lizotte, Krohn, Farnworth, & Jang, 1994; Werner, 1992). Many of these studies are distinguished by oversampling of children from low-income areas or from a variety of ethnic backgrounds. Many of the studies also include large numbers of female subjects, ensuring that tests for gender differences can be made and, if warranted, separate developmental models constructed for girls and boys (for example, Tremblay et al., 1992). Unlike clinical studies of conduct disorder, where biological involvement may be comparatively greater, or studies of schoolchildren in suburban communities, where the incidence of serious aggressive behavior may be low, these longitudinal studies help elucidate the developmental processes and environmental conditions that lead to aggressive behavior in children from a variety of backgrounds. Further, they provide important clues about how services might be refined for work with children whose behavior is hostile and aggressive.

### Family Environment

Perhaps more than any other setting in the social ecology of childhood, conditions, processes, and experiences in the family shape the behavior of children. From a family perspective, emerging research suggests that children in some homes are trained, literally but unintentionally, to respond to authority with hostility (Patterson, DeBaryshe, & Ramsey, 1989; Reid & Patterson, 1989).

Central to the sequence of events that reinforces aggression in some families is inconsistent parental supervision of children, use of harsh punishment, failure to set limits, neglect in rewarding prosocial behavior, and a coercive style of parent–child interaction (Patterson, Capaldi, & Bank, 1991). When an oppositional child engages in an aggressive behavior, most parents will intervene. However, developmental research shows that some parents do not intervene consistently. Moreover, when they do intervene, it is often with excessive force and negative affect. They yell, threaten, grab, push, yank, and hit to coerce children into compliance.

Although families that use this style of coercive child management often have many strengths, children in these homes learn poor problem-solving skills from their parents (Patterson, 1982; Weiss, Dodge, Bates, & Pettit, 1992). When faced with an undesired request (for example, "Please turn off the TV"), children respond mimetically with yelling, threatening, grabbing, crying, stomping of feet, hitting, and otherwise escalated behavior to achieve a desired goal (for example, keeping the TV turned on). More skillful parents at such a point will take decisive and preemptive action (for example, time-out or loss of a privilege). But parents who employ a coercive style of discipline—and who may be overcome by environmental stresses such as poverty, simply worn out from trying to make ends meet by working multiple jobs, or incapacitated by the abuse of psychoactive substances—are more likely to withdraw, give a neutral response, or passively grant consent.

This appears to be a common parenting pattern in homes where children are aggressive and defiant: When they do not respond with disproportional force, parents acquiesce (Patterson, 1992). Because coercion is modeled and acquiescence frequently follows a child's protestations (for example, "I won't turn off the TV! You can't make me!"), children learn that aggression pays off, that it has social and sometimes concrete utility. Parental acquiescence rewards a child's aggressive reaction and increases the chances that he or she will use similar strategies in subsequent interactions. By reacting to a parental request with an aggressive response that is modeled on parental problem solving, the child escapes punishment (hence the name "escape conditioning"), controls the social exchange, and continues desired behaviors (Patterson, 1995). In short, aggressive behavior becomes rewarding for children in families in which parents use a coercion–acquiescence style of child management (Dishion, Andrews, & Crosby, 1995; Dodge, Bates, & Pettit, 1990). For children who have high biological risk (through, for example, exposure to lead) or who are unusually provocative as a result of attention deficit or other disorders, this pattern of parent–child interaction may exacerbate conduct problems.

Without intervention, this pattern is thought to generalize from minor, developmentally expected opposition to increasingly serious noncompliance and aggressive behavior (Patterson, 1992; Patterson, Reid, & Dishion, 1992). Moreover, it may generalize from home to school, where it becomes part of a child's social repertoire with peers and teachers. From this perspective, parents unintentionally train their children to use aggression to achieve social goals. Although they may not realize that they are doing it, and although they are deeply troubled by their child's increasing defiance, they prepare the child to respond to authority with aggression. This gives many young children an early start toward an aggressive, confrontational, and potentially violent interpersonal style (Patterson, 1995; Patterson, Crosby, & Vuchinich, 1992).

## Social Consequences of Early Aggression

From toddlerhood through adolescence, confrontation with authority and aggressive behavior have serious consequences (Farrington, 1991; Farrington, Loeber, & Van Kammen, 1990; Loeber, 1996; Loeber, Stouthamer-Loeber, Van Kammen, & Farrington, 1991). Although more life course research is needed, early physical aggression and conflict with authority are often associated with the initiation of delinquency and, for some children, with behavior that escalates from minor to serious offenses. At the same time, reductions in aggression and oppositional behavior are associated with reductions over time in delinquent behavior (Loeber et al., 1991).

Many children who are ungovernable and delinquent have histories of coercive, intimidating social relations that begin in early years and that limit social opportunities with other children and adults (Kupersmidt & Coie, 1990). Early play and friend making often demonstrate this pattern. In the eyes of elementary school children, some aggressive acts warrant social censure, whereas others do not. From a series of multicultural studies, researchers have described two basic types of aggression, each eliciting a different response from children (Dodge, 1991). "Reactive" aggression involves the defensive use of force. When children are perceived as defending themselves, they are usually viewed positively by their peers. In contrast, "proactive" aggression is defined as the nondefensive use of force. When children initiate proactive aggressive contact, it is viewed negatively by peers. Children who are proactively aggressive regard physically coercive acts as socially effective. They consider it normal to use force to obtain the use of a toy, swing seat, wagon, or teeter-totter. They use aggression and coercion to meet instrumental goals (Dodge & Coie, 1987).

Compounding matters, some aggressive children are simply bullies. Beyond the strategic use of aggression to get the things that they want, they use aggression to establish social dominance (Olweus, 1993a). Whether boy or girl, bullies use force both to obtain social position and to secure desired objects (Sharp & Smith, 1994). Proactive aggression of both the instrumental and bullying types leads to increasing peer rejection (Newcomb, Bukowski, & Pattee, 1993; Parker & Asher, 1987) and isolates children from prosocial peers.

Rejection, however, appears to vary by age. After a series of studies involving samples that included many children from low-income and diverse ethnic backgrounds, Coie, Dodge, Terry, and Wright (1991) concluded, "[From] the beginning years of school, children actively dislike instrumental aggression in peers and will reject those children who use instrumental aggression at the outset of establishing new relationships" (p. 821). For first graders, reactive aggression and bullying may be part and parcel of establishing a social order (Bierman, Smoot, & Aumiller, 1993; Boulton & Underwood, 1992; Olweus, 1993a). Although instrumental aggression results in peer rejection, reactive and bullying aggression are more common in the early years of school, and somewhat surprisingly, they do not encounter the same level of social censure (see also Coie, Dodge, & Kupersmidt, 1990; Feldman & Dodge, 1987).

By the second and third grades, children appear to demand more social competence of their friends (Dodge, Coie, Pettit, & Price, 1990; Feldman & Dodge, 1987; Kupersmidt & Patterson, 1991; Underwood, Coie, & Herbsman, 1992). Among socially accepted children, problem solving with less resort to physical coercion is expected. Among children who are rejected by their peers, aggression is more likely to be used to achieve social goals (Bierman et al., 1993). In addition, rejected children are more likely to escalate aggression when they are the target of aggressive acts such as teasing or taunting. They are quick to fight and slow to employ negotiation, bargaining, and other forms of problem solving. For girls as well as boys, the result is increasing rejection by other children. Thus, aggressive behavior has the consequence of isolating children from learning opportunities in socially skilled peer groups and, because children are then beyond the influence of prosocial peer groups, of increasing the risk of subsequent problems in the school and community (Coie, Lochman, Terry, & Hyman, 1992; Kupersmidt, Coie, & Dodge, 1990).

### Other Factors in Early Aggression

Although family factors and peer rejection are involved in much aggressive behavior, extrafamilial and unique personal conditions also predispose children toward coercive and potentially violent means of achieving social goals (Brown, Esbensen, & Geis, 1991; Reiss & Roth, 1993; Rutter, 1979). In one of every five American families, normal child development is undermined by poverty. Poverty decreases the essential resources necessary for social development—shelter, food, clothing, and health care—and increases stressors that impede effective parenting and problem solving.

At the individual level, a host of constitutional or biological conditions can affect a child's capacity to learn and respond to others in the social environment. Such conditions include brain damage and other neuropathology; imbalances of neurochemicals such as the neurotransmitter serotonin; imbalances of trace minerals; imbalances of hormones such as testosterone; low IQ; and unremediated hyperactivity, impulsivity, and attention deficit disorders (for reviews, see Booth & Osgood, 1993; Farrington, Loeber, et al., 1993; Johnson, 1996). Because of learning impairments, children may be tracked from early childhood into circumstances that increase the risk of poor school adjustment and achievement, association with aggressive or socially rejected children, and early experimentation with sex and drugs (Loeber et al., 1993; Reiss & Roth, 1993). Although it is clear that there is much individual variation in the pathways that lead from early childhood aggressive behavior to violence, this combination of a weak or inadequate home life, poor school adjustment, and rejection by peers is sometimes called the "Early Starter" model (Loeber et al., 1993; Patterson, 1992, 1995; Patterson & Yoerger, 1993).

## AGGRESSIVE BEHAVIOR IN EARLY ADOLESCENCE

In contrast to aggressive behavior that emerges early in childhood, aggressive behavior that begins in early or middle adolescence appears to have somewhat more diverse roots. Sometimes called the "Late Starter" model, it is often marked more directly by the influence of contextual and systemic factors outside the family (Patterson, 1992; Patterson & Yoerger, 1993; Simons, Wu, Conger, & Lorenz, 1994), including school, neighborhood, and peer conditions such as hostile relations with teachers, peer pressure for early sexual activity, and involvement with a gang (Bjerregaard & Smith, 1993; Cernkovich & Giordano, 1992).

Separate from the family, school-related factors such as a teacher's grading practices, classroom management skills, and teaching strategies exert important environmental influences on a child's bonding with school and his or her risk of developing aggressive behavior in early adolescence (O'Donnell, Hawkins, & Abbott, 1995). In the school, teaching practices delimit children's opportunities for success in conforming activities. Teachers establish rules that guide the social interactions of children with other children and that determine how rewards are given for academic achievement, including rewards for successful social participation in study, task, and project groups. Classroom practices that promote social development create many opportunities for success and provide recognition for students of varying abilities and backgrounds (Office of Juvenile Justice and Delinquency Prevention, 1995). Classroom practices that limit opportunities and constrain recognition to a small number of students do little to promote commitment to conventional activities of those who are not rewarded and may be as potentially damaging to social development as coercive parenting. Research increasingly shows that the school climate and teaching practices are strongly related to children's educational expectations, commitment to school, and academic achievement and, in a larger sense, to their behaviors in the community (Hawkins et al., 1992; Hawkins, Catalano, Morrison, et al., 1992; O'Donnell et al., 1995).

Further, at the peer and neighborhood levels, ecological factors such as the local social and economic infrastructure often delimit the learning opportunities afforded children. In a study of 479 white and African American seventh-grade boys in Pittsburgh, Peeples and Loeber (1994) found that the delinquent behavior of boys from low-income neighborhoods did not differ by race or ethnicity once hyperactivity, parental supervision, and neighborhood characteristics were controlled. In this and other studies (for example, Farrington, Sampson, & Wikstrom, 1993; Kupersmidt, Griesler, DeRosier, Patterson, & Davis, 1995), neighborhood conditions appeared to exert an effect on behavior that was independent of individual and family influences. For children who grow up in neighborhoods where schools are weak (for example, underfinanced with poorly trained staffs and little community involvement), where opportunities for success in conventional activities are blocked, where adults are committed to illicit activities, and where gangs offer alternative social roles and financial rewards, violence may be a product of a social context in which force and coercion are used routinely to resolve disputes and protect property. Gang-related violence, in particular, appears to be more strongly associated with local economic, school, and peer factors than with biological and family factors (Klein, 1995; Spergel, 1992, 1995).

Thus, aggressive behavior that begins in adolescence is often characterized less by family characteristics and more by failure at school, the presence of an illegitimate opportunity structure, association with delinquent peers, and in some communities the prestige and illicit money that reward gang membership (Simons et al., 1994). Compared with the development of aggressive behavior that starts in early childhood, the social development of aggressive behavior that starts in early adolescence presents challenges that more directly involve many different systems—the school, the peer group, and the neighborhood.

## PREVENTING YOUTH VIOLENCE: AN ECOLOGICAL–DEVELOPMENTAL PERSPECTIVE

To improve rates of success in prevention and early intervention, strategies must be developed to better address the full complexity of influences that lead to aggressive behavior in the social ecology of childhood and early adolescence. Because youth violence is highly correlated with early childhood defiance and aggression, intervention that stalls the development of early childhood oppositional and coercive behavior may have preventive effects (Earle, 1995; Zigler, Taussig, & Black, 1992). Although early childhood aggressive behavior appears to have roots in fewer systems than aggressive behavior that emerges in adolescence, neither early nor late aggression has a single cause. And once in a child's social repertoire, aggressive behavior affects relationships at school and in the peer group.

To be sure, no set of local strategies is likely to change the broad societal conditions—poverty, racial discrimination, and media violence—that affect large numbers of children and weaken social developmental processes (for reviews, see Danish & Donohue, 1996; Hampton & Yung, 1996). However, in the absence of major social and structural reforms (for example, Gil, 1996), recent research provides important clues for how to configure community-based youth violence prevention programs.

### Communities

A multiple impact strategy that systematically assesses and targets a range of community factors that place children at risk should guide prevention and early intervention efforts. Many different kinds of efforts are required to prevent youth violence, and no single "off-the-shelf" strategy or program can be relied on across all communities. (For brief descriptions of more than 100 off-the-shelf violence prevention programs, see the U.S. Department of Justice, Partnership Against Violence Web site at http://www.usdoj.gov/pavnet.html.) Within the unique character and conditions of individual communities, both the physical and social environmental factors that affect children should be addressed.

In some communities, children must be disarmed. Laws making it illegal for children to carry handguns may need to be more vigorously enforced. In other communities, problem-oriented policing that focuses on "hot spots" of violence or gang conflict may be needed. In the longer term, the social processes that place children at risk must be addressed. Intervention for children who demonstrate early aggressive behavior should strengthen families and help children develop skills that promote successful relationships in preschool and elementary school (Schweinhart, Barnes, & Weikart, 1993; Yoshikawa, 1994). Early intervention for late-start aggressive behavior should also involve families but should take place in the context of broader efforts to support children across all developmental settings and to engage children in prosocial peer groups.

Although scholars and researchers speak in terms of early and late pathways to violent behavior, there appears to be a heterogeneity of developmental risk factors. Recent research focuses less on time-invariant attributes or traits and more on dynamic processes in the environment. Building on an ecological–developmental perspective, findings can be used to design and mark the success of interventions. This approach is beginning to reap rewards in family treatment (Borduin et al., 1995; Dishion & Andrews, 1995), school reforms (Hawkins et al., 1992; Hawkins, Catalano, Morrison, et al., 1992; Tremblay, Pagani-Kurtz, Masse, Vitaro, & Pihl, 1995), and peer-related skills training (Lochman, 1992).

But mounting ecologically and developmentally based interventions is a complex undertaking because risk factors vary across and within communities. In a study of 866 elementary-school boys and girls from low-income neighborhoods in a large midwestern city, for example, Guerra, Huesmann, Tolan, Van Acker, and Eron (1995) found that poverty—a risk factor for many social problems—affects different children differently. Across the entire sample, a significant zero-order relationship between poverty and aggression washed out when controls for stress from life events (for example, serious illness), stress from neighborhood violence (for example, witnessing a shooting), and beliefs approving the use of aggression (for example, "In general, it's OK to use violence.") were entered into regression equations. These findings suggest that poverty affects behavior through both stressful life experiences and accrued beliefs that support the use of physical force. However, the pattern was not the same for boys and girls. Moreover, it was significantly different for boys and girls from different racial and ethnic backgrounds. Neighborhood violence was a significant predictor across white ($n = 168$), Hispanic ($n = 383$), and African American ($n = 315$) subgroups, but poverty exerted a direct effect on violence only for the white children. Aggressive normative beliefs was a significant predictor only for Hispanic children, whereas for African American children, a complex interaction between individual and school-level poverty emerged.

Such findings suggest that the specific risks and strengths (sometimes called "protective factors") in communities must be assessed as a part of the interventive process. As Hawkins (1995) argued, using a social development perspective "calls for first identifying the factors that put young people at risk for violence in order to reduce or eliminate these factors and strengthen the protective factors that buffer the effects of exposure to risk" (p. 11). Building on the emerging core of longitudinal research and on community risk assessments, interventions should be tailored to local differences in the individual, family, school, and neighborhood conditions that place children at risk of violence. In the spirit of community practice in social work, violence prevention initiatives must begin with broad participatory problem solving. Based on information about local risk and protective factors, community residents develop a set of tactics—such as increasing the number of community policing officers or establishing programs for gang "wannabes"—that mobilize resources, reduce fear of victimization, and alter social developmental processes for children.

## Families

Services should address family-related risk factors. Across many communities, changes in social and economic conditions have dramatically affected parenting and support systems related to effective parenting. For many families, parental problem solving and child management skills are the linchpins in helping children develop prosocial relationships with peers and in preparing children with the skills to be successful in school (Henggeler & Borduin, 1990, 1995; Kazdin, 1995). In the context of family traditions and culture, family-centered activities should focus on lowering expressive and incendiary parent–child interchanges, setting graduated sanctions for defiant behavior, providing effective alternatives to harsh discipline, and increasing consistency in rewarding desirable behavior and ensuring consequences for aggressive behavior (Patterson, Dishion, & Chamberlain, 1993). In circumstances in which parents are unable to constrain their own abusive or illegal behavior, protective action to place children in foster or group care may be required, but substitute care too should be characterized by a family-centered approach, and long-term, stable, and safe living arrangements.

## Schools

Services should address school-related risk factors. For communities where school-related risk factors are high, school-based prevention and early intervention strategies should be developed to promote children's attachments to prosocial peers, involvement in school activities, and academic achievement. School strategies should strengthen a child's skills for school involvement and academic achievement, promote involvement in school activities, and decrease truancy and school-related misconduct (Hawkins, Doueck, & Lishner, 1988; Maguin & Loeber, 1996; O'Donnell, Hawkins, Catalano, Abbott, & Day, 1994). To help turn the school into a successful life setting for children, services should be designed to promote home–school collaboration, assist parents in rewarding children's desirable school behaviors and (mildly) providing consequences for disruptive behaviors, ensure that a child who may be eligible for special assistance is properly assessed and assigned, locate children who are truant (and assist in returning them to school or home), help students with homework, create opportunities for children to participate in school clubs or sports (arrange transportation and supervision), and monitor children at after-school activities (Kelley & McCain, 1995; Kurtz & Barth, 1989; McMahon & Peters, 1990; Posner & Vandell, 1994).

For some older children whose behavior is influenced by years of negative school experiences, these activities may not be enough. Changing the school into a successful experience for middle or high school youths may require addressing students' views of the value of academic achievement and sense of self-efficacy and encouraging their beliefs in their capacity to be effective in the school setting. If children have long-term conventional goals (for example, to own a business or to become a clerk, doctor, social worker, or teacher), the discrepancy between these goals and current behavior can be used as a motivational tool to leverage a plan for change (Miller & Rollnick, 1991). Recognition of discrepancies between goals and behavior plus the development of a family-supported plan help break the self-defeating, negative belief systems that often build as a result of social rejection, academic marginality, and the seductive messages of gang recruiters. Within the family, parents should be encouraged to actively support a child's hope that positive change can occur in his or her life. Once engendered, the belief that change can occur is thought to act as a secondary reinforcer for developing skills to promote success in the school environment (Grolnick & Slowiaczek, 1994).

## Peers

Services should address peer-related risk factors. Street violence is often correlated with peer-related factors such as gang involvement or, in the absence of organized gangs, association with peers who hold favorable attitudes toward problem behavior. Peer-related strategies should be linked to family and school interventions. Underpinning efforts to help both early- and late-start aggressive children, services should strengthen bonds of attachment to prosocial peers; weaken negative beliefs and values, including the belief that violence is an effective means for achieving personal goals; and weaken bonds of attachment with peers who employ aggression or violence in problem solving. For elementary and middle-school children, service plans should include developmentally appropriate skills training in processing social information (Lochman & Dodge, 1994). In the context of family and neighborhood history, lore, culture, and tradition, this should include training in processing social cues, drawing appropriate inferences about the intent of others' actions, identifying situation-specific goals, generating alternative social responses, evaluating the likely outcomes of responses, and enacting selected strategies (Crick & Dodge, 1994; Fraser, 1996).

As has been done in some family-based service programs, parents should be encouraged to set peer-related treatment goals, make explicit their own (prosocial) beliefs and values, and define peer-focused interventions (Henggeler & Borduin, 1990; Henggeler, Melton, & Smith, 1992). Together, the family might select settings and activities in which children are likely to avoid trouble. Parents should play a major role in identifying appropriate and inappropriate peer behaviors and in approving a child's peers. If joining a new peer group becomes a treatment goal, a child's strengths might be listed, a group that fits those strengths selected, and a strategy for approaching and joining the group discussed (Henggeler, 1994). In family-centered intervention, a peer-related focus may be as important in producing positive outcomes as activities that focus explicitly on parents' child management skills (personal communication with S. W. Henggeler, professor and director, Family Services Research Center, Medical University of South Carolina, November 17, 1995).

One of the enduring enigmas in focusing on the peer correlates of aggressive behavior is the problem of serving high-risk children in groups. Research strongly suggests that the strategy of placing aggressive children in groups with one another promotes aggressive behavior (Dishion & Andrews, 1995; Feldman, Caplinger, & Wodarski, 1983). Moderately aggressive children appear to learn from more aggressive, dominant children. Nevertheless, placing aggressive children together in groups is a common practice in schools, mental health centers, youth training programs, and other settings. Efforts are needed to engineer new group work approaches that avoid placing aggressive children together in small groups. These new approaches should be premised on the principle that children will learn from their peers, and thus services should help aggressive children develop bonds of attachment with prosocial children.

### Neighborhoods

Services should address neighborhood-related risk factors. Ecological–developmental research shows clearly that context counts. When neighborhoods are characterized by easy access to drugs and firearms, by attitudes and media favorable to violence, by high poverty, and by low levels of community attachment, the risks are high for children (Hawkins, 1995). In such communities, goals should focus on providing opportunities for children to build attachments with prosocial peers and adults. To the extent possible, services should reinforce traditional elders in businesses, churches, and community agencies.

For middle and high school youths, neighborhood-based services should include after-school mentoring, tutoring, or apprenticeship programs that build bonds of attachment with adults who are committed to conventional lines of action, that strengthen youths' vocational interests and skills, and that reinforce commitment to nonviolent, prosocial goals (Hamilton, 1990). Teenagers should be given opportunities to work or volunteer at the neighborhood level. Community programs that build children's attachments to prosocial adults and peers by creating opportunities to help more needy (and often younger) youths have reported positive effects on children's self-esteem, success in school, and comportment (Calhoun, 1994). Coupled with community mobilization and law enforcement reforms such as community policing, service strategies that involve the neighborhood should build hope, a sense of control over one's environment, expectations for success in school and work, and a stake in conformity (Chavis & Wandersman, 1990; Office of Juvenile Justice and Delinquency Prevention, 1995; Weingart, Hartmann, & Osborne, 1994).

## CONCLUSION

Across the country, thousands of programs focus on children who are aggressive, ungovernable, and assaultive. The activities provided by these programs range from child psychotherapy and counseling to midnight basketball and wilderness-challenge camping trips. Most programs represent the thoughtful efforts of professionals, advocates, and policymakers to address the angry aggression they see in young people. Most also are provided in the absence of any evidence of effectiveness (Kazdin, 1995).

There is, however, growing promise in recent research on the effectiveness of some kinds of services for children (Lipsey & Wilson, 1993; Mulvey, Arthur, & Reppucci, 1993; Prothrow-Stith, 1995; Weisz, Weiss, Han, Granger, & Morton, 1995). In primary prevention with young children (Earle, 1995; Yoshikawa, 1994; Zigler et al., 1992), early intervention with children who have demonstrated aggressive, defiant behavior (Lochman, 1992; Olweus, 1993a, 1993b), and the treatment of serious juvenile offenders (Borduin et al., 1995; Gordon, Graves, & Arbuthnot, 1995; Kazdin, Siegel, & Bass, 1992), studies suggest that many of the social conditions and developmental processes that produce violence can be changed. Combinations of strategies delivered across a variety of home, school, and other settings and coupled, where necessary, with substance abuse treatment have increased children's prosocial behaviors and reduced problem behavior, including both self-reports and official reports of illegal behaviors (see also Conduct Problems Prevention Research Group, 1992; Henggeler et al., 1992, 1995; Henggeler, Melton, Smith, Schoenwald, & Hanley, 1993; Kazdin, Esveldt-Dawson, French, & Unis, 1987a, 1987b).

In more fully addressing the factors that promote aggressive behavior and violence, these programs share many features:

- Service is provided in the context of consistent and graduated sanctions (both positive and negative) for behavior. Aggressive or violent behavior is swiftly confronted and given consequences.
- Services occur in the life settings where children or parents work, play, and learn. Or, as in the case of residential treatment, services involve the family throughout the treatment and reunification process.
- Services are based on local information about risk and protective factors. They are sensitive and relevant to cultural and racial differences within and across communities.
- In helping family members assume responsible roles, services are skills focused—strengthening problem-solving, information processing, and parenting skills.
- Services for children promote school involvement and academic success.
- Services often help families secure the absolute environmental essentials for human development—safe housing, adequate food, appropriate clothing, and basic health care.

Recent longitudinal studies of the social development of children and this small body of research on the effectiveness of programs with risk-focused strategies suggest that intervention to control and reduce aggressive behavior in childhood and early adolescence may have preventive effects on youth violence. Focused on many different systems, these programs attempt to converge combinations of strategies on the risk factors that potentiate aggressive behavior and violence (for example, Hawkins, 1995; Hawkins, Catalano, & Associates, 1992; Henggeler & Borduin, 1995; Prothrow-Stith & Weissman, 1991). Although the strategies they use cannot fully offset the effects of poverty, guns, and racism (for example, Bernard, 1990; Van Soest & Bryant, 1995; Wilson, 1987), they attack the problem of violence by attempting to alter early social processes that guide many children toward school failure and peer rejection. And in so doing, they offer new promise for many young children who have learned to survive in their families, in their schools, and on the streets by confronting authority with aggression.

## REFERENCES

Allen-Hagen, B., & Sickmund, M. (1993, July). *Juveniles and violence: Juvenile offending and victimization* (Fact Sheet No. 3). Washington, DC: U.S. Department of Justice, Office of Juvenile Justice and Delinquency Prevention.

Bernard, T. J. (1990). Angry aggression among the "truly disadvantaged." *Criminology, 28,* 73–96.

Bierman, K. L., Smoot, D. L., & Aumiller, K. (1993). Characteristics of aggressive-rejected, aggressive-nonrejected, and rejected-nonaggressive boys. *Child Development, 64,* 139–151.

Bjerregaard, B., & Smith, C. (1993). Gender differences in gang participation, delinquency, and substance use. *Journal of Quantitative Criminology, 9,* 329–355.

Booth, A., & Osgood, D. W. (1993). The influence of testosterone on deviance in adulthood: Assessing and explaining the relationship. *Criminology, 31,* 93–117.

Borduin, C. M., Mann, B. J., Cone, L. T., Henggeler, S. W., Fucci, B. R., Blaske, D. M., & Williams, R. A. (1995). Multisystemic treatment of serious juvenile offenders: Long-term prevention of criminality and violence. *Journal of Consulting and Clinical Psychology, 63,* 569–578.

Boulton, M. J., & Underwood, K. (1992). Bully/victim problems among middle school children. *British Journal of Educational Psychology, 62*(1), 73–87.

Brook, J. S., Whiteman, M. M., & Finch, S. (1992). Childhood aggression, adolescent delinquency, and drug use: A longitudinal study. *Journal of Genetic Psychology, 153,* 369–383.

Brown, S., Esbensen, F., & Geis, G. (1991). *Criminology: Explaining crime and its context.* Cincinnati: Anderson.

Calhoun, J. (1994, April). *Violence in the lives of children: Strategies for intervention.* Paper presented at the 71st Annual Meeting of the American Orthopsychiatric Association, Alexandria, VA.

Catalano, R. F., & Hawkins, J. D. (1996). The social development model: A theory of antisocial behavior. In J. D. Hawkins (Ed.), *Delinquency and crime: Current theories* (pp. 149–197). New York: Cambridge University Press.

Cernkovich, S. A., & Giordano, P. C. (1992). School bonding, race, and delinquency. *Criminology, 30,* 261–291.

Chavis, D. M., & Wandersman, A. (1990). Sense of community in the urban environment: A catalyst for participation and community development. *American Journal of Community Psychology, 18*(1), 55–81.

Children's Defense Fund. (1995). *The state of America's children yearbook: 1995.* Washington, DC: Author.

Coie, J. D., Dodge, K. A., & Kupersmidt, J. (1990). Peer group behavior and social status. In S. R. Asher & J. D. Coie (Eds.), *Peer rejection in childhood* (pp. 17–59). New York: Cambridge University Press.

Coie, J. D., Dodge, K. A., Terry, R., & Wright, V. (1991). The role of aggression in peer relations: An analysis of aggression episodes in boys' play groups. *Child Development, 62,* 812–826.

Coie, J. D., Lochman, J. E., Terry, R., & Hyman, C. (1992). Predicting early adolescent disorder from childhood aggression and peer rejection. *Journal of Consulting and Clinical Psychology, 60,* 783–792.

Conduct Problems Prevention Research Group. (1992). A developmental and clinical model for the prevention of conduct disorder: The FAST Track Program. *Development and Psychopathology, 4,* 509–528.

Crick, N. R., & Dodge, K. A. (1994). A review and reformulation of social information-processing mechanisms in children's social adjustment. *Psychological Bulletin, 115,* 74–101.

Danish, S. J., & Donohue, T. R. (1996). Understanding the media's influence on the development of antisocial and prosocial behavior. In R. L. Hampton, P. Jenkins, & T. P. Gullotta (Eds.), *Preventing violence in America* (pp. 133–155). Thousand Oaks, CA: Sage Publications.

Dishion, T. J., & Andrews, D. W. (1995). Preventing escalation in problem behaviors with high-risk young adolescents: Immediate and 1-year outcomes. *Journal of Consulting and Clinical Psychology, 63,* 538–548.

Dishion, T. J., Andrews, D. W., & Crosby, L. (1995). Adolescent boys and their friends in early adolescence: I. Relationship characteristics, quality and interactional process. *Child Development, 66,* 139–151.

Dishion, T., Patterson, G., Stoolmiller, M., & Skinner, M. (1991). Family, school, and behavioral antecedents to early adolescent involvement with antisocial peers. *Developmental Psychology, 27,* 172–180.

Dodge, K. A. (1991). The structure and function of reactive and proactive aggression. In D. J. Pepler & K. H. Rubin (Eds.), *The development and treatment of childhood aggression* (pp. 210–218). Hillsdale, NJ: Lawrence Erlbaum.

Dodge, K. A., Bates, J. E., & Pettit, G. S. (1990). Mechanisms in the cycle of violence. *Science, 250,* 1678–1683.

Dodge, K. A., & Coie, J. D. (1987). Social information processing factors in reactive and proactive aggression in children's peer groups. *Journal of Personality and Social Psychology, 53,* 1146–1158.

Dodge, K. A., Coie, J. D., Pettit, G. S., & Price, J. M. (1990). Peer status and aggression in boys' groups: Developmental and contextual analyses. *Child Development, 61,* 1289–1309.

Earle, R. B. (1995, October). Helping to prevent child abuse and future criminal consequences: Hawai'i Healthy Start. In *Program focus* (Publication No. NCJ 156216, pp. 11–12). Washington, DC: U.S. Department of Justice, National Institute of Justice.

Elliott, D. E. (1994). Serious violent offenders: Onset, developmental course, and termination. *Criminology, 32,* 1–21.

Farrington, D. P. (1991). Childhood aggression and adult violence: Early precursors and later-life outcomes. In D. J. Pepler & K. H. Rubin (Eds.), *The development and treatment of childhood aggression* (pp. 5–29). Hillsdale, NJ: Lawrence Erlbaum.

Farrington, D. P., Loeber, R., Elliott, D. S., Hawkins, J. D., Kandel, D. B., Klein, M. W., McCord, J., Rowe, D. C., & Tremblay, R. E. (1993). Advancing knowledge about the onset of delinquency and crime. In B. B. Lahey & A. E. Kazdin (Eds.), *Advances in clinical child psychology* (Vol. 13, pp. 283–342). New York: Plenum Press.

Farrington, D. P., Loeber, R., & Van Kammen, W. B. (1990). Long-term criminal outcomes of hyperactivity–impulsivity–attention deficit and conduct problems in childhood. In L. N. Robins & M. Rutter (Eds.), *Straight and devious pathways from childhood to adulthood* (pp. 62–81). New York: Cambridge University Press.

Farrington, D. P., Sampson, R. J., & Wikstrom, P. O. (Eds.). (1993). *Integrating individual and ecological aspects of crime.* Stockholm, Sweden: Liber Forlag.

Feldman, E., & Dodge, K. A. (1987). Social information processing and sociometric status: Sex, age, and situation effects. *Journal of Abnormal Child Psychology, 15,* 211–227.

Feldman, R. A., Caplinger, T. E., & Wodarski, J. S. (1983). *The St. Louis conundrum: The effective treatment of antisocial youths.* Englewood Cliffs, NJ: Prentice Hall.

Fraser, M. W. (1995). Violence. In R. L. Edwards (Ed.-in-Chief), *Encyclopedia of social work* (19th ed., Vol. 2, pp. 2453–2460). Washington, DC: NASW Press.

Fraser, M. W. (1996). Cognitive problem-solving and aggressive behavior among children. *Families in Society, 77*(1), 19–31.

Gil, D. G. (1996). Preventing violence in a structurally violent society: Mission impossible. *American Journal of Orthopsychiatry, 66,* 77–84.

Gordon, D. A., Graves, K., & Arbuthnot, J. (1995). The effect of functional family therapy for delinquents on adult criminal behavior. *Criminal Justice and Behavior, 22*(1), 60–73.

Grolnick, W. S., & Slowiaczek, M. L. (1994). Parents' involvement in children's schooling: A multidimensional conceptualization and motivational model. *Child Development, 65,* 237–252.

Guerra, N. G., Huesmann, L. R., Tolan, P. H., Van Acker, R., & Eron, L. D. (1995). Stressful events and individual beliefs as correlates of economic disadvantage and aggression among urban children. *Journal of Consulting and Clinical Psychology, 63,* 518–528.

Hamilton, S. F. (1990). *Apprenticeship for adulthood*. New York: Free Press.

Hampton, R. L., & Yung, B. R. (1996). Violence in communities of color: Where we were, where we are, and where we need to be. In R. L. Hampton, P. Jenkins, & T. P. Gullotta (Eds.), *Preventing violence in America* (pp. 53–86). Thousand Oaks, CA: Sage Publications.

Hawkins, J. D. (1995). Controlling crime before it happens: Risk-focused prevention. *National Institute of Justice Journal, 229,* 10–18.

Hawkins, J. D., Catalano, R. F., Jr., & Associates. (1992). *Communities that care*. San Francisco: Jossey-Bass.

Hawkins, J. D., Catalano, R. F., Morrison, D. M., O'Donnell, J., Abbott, R. D., & Day, L. E. (1992). The Seattle Social Development Project: Effects of the first four years on protective factors and problem behaviors. In J. McCord & R. E. Tremblay (Eds.), *Preventing antisocial behavior: Interventions from birth through adolescence* (pp. 139–161). New York: Guilford Press.

Hawkins, J. D., Doueck, H. J., & Lishner, D. M. (1988). Changing teaching practices in mainstream classrooms to improve bonding and behavior of low achievers. *American Educational Research Journal, 25,* 31–50.

Henggeler, S. W. (1989). *Delinquency in adolescence*. Newbury Park, CA: Sage Publications.

Henggeler, S. W. (1994). *Treatment manual for family preservation using multisystemic therapy*. Charleston: Medical University of South Carolina, Family Services Research Center.

Henggeler, S. W., & Borduin, C. M. (1990). *Family therapy and beyond: A multisystemic approach to treating the behavior problems of children and adolescents*. Pacific Grove, CA: Brooks/Cole.

Henggeler, S. W., & Borduin, C. M. (1995). Multisystemic treatment of serious juvenile offenders and their families. In I. M. Schwartz & P. AuClaire (Eds.), *Home-based services for troubled children* (pp. 113–130). Lincoln: University of Nebraska Press.

Henggeler, S. W., Melton, G. B., & Smith, L. A. (1992). Family preservation using multisystemic therapy: An effective alternative to incarcerating serious juvenile offenders. *Journal of Consulting and Clinical Psychology, 60,* 953–961.

Henggeler, S. W., Melton, G. B., Smith, L. A., Schoenwald, S. K., & Hanley, J. H. (1993). Family preservation using multisystemic treatment: Long-term follow-up to a clinical trial with serious juvenile offenders. *Journal of Child and Family Studies, 2,* 283–293.

Henggeler, S. W., Schoenwald, S. K., Brondino, M. J., Cunningham, P. B., Das, S., Donkervoet, J., Lashus, B. A., Penman, J., Pickrel, S. G., Price, M. P., Rowland, M. D., Sanders, F., Swenson, M. E., & West, L. (1995, October). *Multisystemic therapy using home-based services: A clinically effective and cost-effective strategy for treating serious clinical problems in youth*. Charleston: Medical University of South Carolina, Department of Psychiatry and Behavioral Sciences, Family Services Research Center.

Johnson, H. C. (1996). Violence and biology: A review of the literature. *Families in Society, 77*(1), 3–18.

Kazdin, A. E. (1987). Treatment of antisocial behavior in children: Current status and future directions. *Psychological Bulletin, 102,* 187–203.

Kazdin, A. E. (1995). *Conduct disorders in childhood and adolescence* (2nd ed.). Thousand Oaks, CA: Sage Publications.

Kazdin, A. E., Esveldt-Dawson, K., French, N. H., & Unis, A. S. (1987a). Effects of parent management training and problem-solving skills training combined in the treatment of antisocial child behavior. *Journal of the American Academy of Child and Adolescent Psychiatry, 26,* 416–424.

Kazdin, A. E., Esveldt-Dawson, K., French, N. H., & Unis, A. S. (1987b). Problem-solving skills training and relationship therapy in the treatment of antisocial child behavior. *Journal of Consulting and Clinical Psychology, 55,* 76–85.

Kazdin, A. E., Siegel, T. C., & Bass, D. (1992). Cognitive problem-solving skills training and parent management training in the treatment of antisocial behavior in children. *Journal of Consulting and Clinical Psychology, 60,* 733–747.

Kelley, M. L., & McCain, A. P. (1995). Promoting academic performance in inattentive children: The relative efficacy of school–home notes with and without response cost. *Behavior Modification, 19,* 357–375.

Klein, M. W. (1995). *The American street gang: Its nature, prevalence, and control*. New York: Oxford University Press.

Krauss, C. (1994, November 13). The nation: No crystal ball needed on crime. *New York Times* (Late Edition—Final, Section 4), p. 4.

Kupersmidt, J. B., & Coie, J. D. (1990). Preadolescent peer status, aggression, and school adjustment as predictors of externalizing problems in adolescence. *Child Development, 61,* 1350–1362.

Kupersmidt, J. B., Coie, J. D., & Dodge, K. A. (1990). The role of poor peer relationships in the development of disorder. In S. R. Asher & J. D. Coie (Eds.), *Peer rejection in childhood* (pp. 274–305). New York: Cambridge University Press.

Kupersmidt, J. B., Griesler, P. C., DeRosier, M. E., Patterson, C. J., & Davis, P. W. (1995). Childhood aggression and peer relations in the context of family and neighborhood factors. *Child Development, 66,* 360–375.

Kupersmidt, J. B., & Patterson, C. J. (1991). Childhood peer rejection, aggression, withdrawal, and perceived competence as predictors of self-reported behavior problems in preadolescence. *Journal of Abnormal Child Psychology, 19,* 427–449.

Kurtz, D. P., & Barth, R. P. (1989). Parent involvement: Cornerstone of school social work practice. *Social Work, 34,* 407–413.

Lipsey, M. W., & Wilson, D. B. (1993). The efficacy of psychological, educational, and behavioral treatment: Confirmation from meta-analysis. *American Psychologist, 48,* 1181–1209.

Lochman, J. E. (1992). Cognitive–behavioral intervention with aggressive boys: Three-year follow-up and preventive effects. *Journal of Consulting and Clinical Psychology, 60,* 426–432.

Lochman, J. E., & Dodge, K. A. (1994). Social–cognitive processes of severely violent, moderately aggressive, and nonaggressive boys. *Journal of Consulting and Clinical Psychology, 62,* 366–374.

Loeber, R. (1996). Developmental continuity, change, and pathways in male juvenile problem behaviors and delinquency. In J. D. Hawkins (Ed.), *Delinquency and crime: Current theories* (pp. 1–27). New York: Cambridge University Press.

Loeber, R., Stouthamer-Loeber, M., Van Kammen, W. B., & Farrington, D. P. (1991). Initiation, escalation, and desistance in juvenile offending and their correlates. *Journal of Criminal Law and Criminology, 82*(1), 36–82.

Loeber, R., Wung, P., Keenan, K., Giroux, B., Stouthamer-Loeber, M., Van Kammen, W. B., & Maughan, B. (1993). Developmental pathways in disruptive child behavior. *Development and Psychopathology, 5,* 103–133.

Maas, H. S. (1986). *From crib to crypt: Social development and responsive environments as professional focus*. New Brunswick, NJ: Rutgers University Press.

Maguin, E., & Loeber, R. (1996). Academic performance and delinquency. In M. Tonry (Ed.), *Crime and justice: A review of research* (pp. 145–264). Chicago: University of Chicago Press.

McMahon, R. J., & Peters, R. D. (Eds.). (1990). *Behavior disorders of adolescence: Research, intervention, and policy in clinical and school settings*. New York: Plenum Press.

Miller, W. R., & Rollnick, S. (1991). *Motivational interviewing: Preparing people to change addictive behavior*. New York: Guilford Press.

Moone, J. (1994, June). *Juvenile victimization: 1987–1992* (Fact Sheet No. 17). Washington, DC: U.S. Department of Justice, Office of Juvenile Justice and Delinquency Prevention.

Mulvey, E. P., Arthur, M. W., & Reppucci, N. D. (1993). The prevention and treatment of juvenile delinquency: A review of the research. *Clinical Psychology Review, 13*(2), 133–167.

Nagin, D. S., & Farrington, D. P. (1992). The stability of criminal potential from childhood to adulthood. *Criminology, 30,* 235–260.

Newcomb, A. F., Bukowski, W. M., & Pattee, L. (1993). Children's peer relations: A meta-analysis review of popular, rejected, neglected, controversial, and average sociometric status. *Psychological Bulletin, 113,* 99–128.

O'Donnell, J., Hawkins, J. D., & Abbott, R. D. (1995). Predicting serious delinquency and substance use among aggressive boys. *Journal of Consulting and Clinical Psychology, 63,* 529–537.

O'Donnell, J., Hawkins, J. D., Catalano, R. F., Abbott, R. D., & Day, L. E. (1994). *Preventing school failure, drug use, and delinquency among low-income children: Effects of a long-term prevention project in elementary schools*. Seattle: University of Washington, School of Social Work, Social Development Research Group.

Office of Juvenile Justice and Delinquency Prevention. (1995, June). *Juvenile Justice Bulletin: Guide for implementing the comprehensive strategy for serious, violent, and chronic juvenile offenders* (Publication No. NCJ 153571). Washington, DC: Office of Justice Programs.

Olweus, D. (1993a). *Bullying at school: What we know and what we can do*. Oxford, England: Blackwell Publishers.

Olweus, D. (1993b). Bully/victim problems among school children: Long-term consequences and an effective intervention program. In S. Hodgins (Ed.), *Mental disorder and crime* (pp. 317–349). Newbury Park, CA: Sage Publications.

Parker, J. G., & Asher, S. R. (1987). Peer relations and later personal adjustment: Are low-accepted children at risk? *Psychological Bulletin, 102*, 357–389.

Patterson, G. R. (1982). *Coercive family processes*. Eugene, OR: Castalia Publishing.

Patterson, G. R. (1992). Developmental changes in antisocial behavior. In R. D. Peters, R. J. McMahon, & V. L. Quinsey (Eds.), *Aggression and violence throughout the life span* (pp. 52–82). Newbury Park, CA: Sage Publications.

Patterson, G. R. (1995). Coercion as a basis for early age of onset for arrest. In J. McCord (Ed.), *Coercion and punishment in long-term perspectives* (pp. 81–105). New York: Cambridge University Press.

Patterson, G. R., Capaldi, D., & Bank, L. (1991). An early starter model for predicting delinquency. In D. J. Pepler & K. H. Rubin (Eds.), *The development and treatment of childhood aggression* (pp. 139–168). Hillsdale, NJ: Lawrence Erlbaum.

Patterson, G. R., Crosby, L., & Vuchinich, S. (1992). Predicting risk for early police arrest. *Journal of Quantitative Criminology, 8*, 335–355.

Patterson, G. R., DeBaryshe, B. D., & Ramsey, E. (1989). A developmental perspective on antisocial behavior. *American Psychologist, 44*, 329–335.

Patterson, G. R., Dishion, T. J., & Chamberlain, P. (1993). Outcomes and methodological issues relating to treatment of antisocial children. In T. R. Giles (Ed.), *Handbook of effective psychotherapy* (pp. 43–87). New York: Plenum Press.

Patterson, G. R., Reid, J. B., & Dishion, T. J. (1992). *Antisocial boys*. Eugene, OR: Castalia Publishing.

Patterson, G. R., & Yoerger, K. (1993). Developmental models for delinquent behavior. In S. Hodgins (Ed.), *Mental disorder and crime* (pp. 140–172). Newbury Park, CA: Sage Publications.

Peeples, F., & Loeber, R. (1994). Do individual factors and neighborhood context explain ethnic differences in juvenile delinquency? *Journal of Quantitative Criminology, 10*, 141–157.

Posner, J. K., & Vandell, D. L. (1994). Low-income children's after-school care: Are there beneficial effects of after-school programs? *Child Development, 65*, 440–456.

Prothrow-Stith, D. B. (1995). The epidemic of youth violence in America: Using public health prevention strategies to prevent violence. *Journal of Health Care for the Poor and Underserved, 6*(2), 95–101.

Prothrow-Stith, D. B., & Weissman, M. (1991). *Deadly consequences: How violence is destroying our teenage population and a plan to begin solving the problem*. New York: HarperCollins.

Reid, J. B., & Patterson, G. R. (1989). The development of antisocial behaviour patterns in childhood and adolescence. *European Journal of Personality, 3*, 107–119.

Reiss, A. J., Jr., & Roth, J. A. (Eds.). (1993). *Understanding and preventing violence*. Washington, DC: National Academy Press.

Reno, J. (1995). *Juvenile offenders and victims: A national report*. Washington, DC: U.S. Department of Justice.

Rosenberg, M. L. (1995). Violence in America: An integrated approach to understanding and prevention. *Journal of Health Care for the Poor and Underserved, 6*(2), 102–112.

Roth, J. A., & Moore, M. H. (1995, October). Reducing violent crimes and intentional injuries. In *Research in action* (Publication No. NCJ 156089). Washington, DC: U.S. Department of Justice, National Institute of Justice.

Rutter, M. (1979). Protective factors in children's responses to stress and disadvantage. In M. W. Kent & J. E. Rolf (Eds.), *Primary prevention of psychopathology: Vol. 3. Social competence in children* (pp. 49–74). Hanover, NH: University Press of New England.

Schweinhart, L. L., Barnes, H. V., & Weikart, D. P. (1993). *Significant benefits: The High/Scope Perry School Study through age 27.* Ypsilanti, MI: High/Scope Press.

Sharp, S., & Smith, P. K. (Eds.). (1994). *Tackling bullying in your school.* New York: Routledge.

Simons, R. L., Wu, C., Conger, R. D., & Lorenz, F. O. (1994). Two routes to delinquency: Differences between early and late starters in the impact of parenting and deviant peers. *Criminology, 32,* 247–276.

Snyder, H. N., & Sickmund, M. (1995, May). *Juvenile offenders and victims: A focus on violence* (Publication No. NCJ 153570). Washington, DC: Office of Justice Programs, Office of Juvenile Justice and Delinquency Prevention, National Center for Juvenile Justice.

Spergel, I. A. (1992). Youth gangs: An essay review. *Social Service Review, 66,* 121–140.

Spergel, I. A. (1995). *The youth gang problem: A community approach.* New York: Oxford Press.

Thornberry, T. P., Lizotte, A. J., Krohn, M. D., Farnworth, M., & Jang, S. J. (1994). Delinquent peers, beliefs, and delinquent behavior: A longitudinal test of interactional theory. *Criminology, 32,* 47–83.

Tolan, P. H., Guerra, N. G., & Kendall, P. C. (1995). A developmental–ecological perspective on antisocial behavior in children and adolescents: Toward a unified risk and intervention framework. *Journal of Consulting and Clinical Psychology, 63,* 579–584.

Tremblay, R. E., Masse, B., Perron, D., Leblanc, M., Schwartzman, A. E., & Ledingham, J. E. (1992). Early disruptive behavior, poor school achievement, delinquent behavior, and delinquent personality: Longitudinal analyses. *Journal of Consulting and Clinical Psychology, 60,* 64–72.

Tremblay, R. E., Pagani-Kurtz, L., Masse, L. C., Vitaro, F., & Pihl, R. O. (1995). A bimodal preventive intervention for disruptive kindergarten boys: Its impact through mid-adolescence. *Journal of Consulting and Clinical Psychology, 63,* 560–568.

Underwood, M. K., Coie, J. D., & Herbsman, C. R. (1992). Display rules for anger and aggression in school-age children. *Child Development, 63,* 366–380.

Van Soest, D., & Bryant, S. (1995). Violence reconceptualized for social work: The urban dilemma. *Social Work, 40,* 549–557.

Weingart, S. N., Hartmann, F. X., & Osborne, D. (1994, October). Case studies of community anti-drug efforts. In *Research in brief* (Publication No. NCJ 149316, pp. 1–2, 14–15). Washington, DC: National Institute of Justice.

Weiss, B., Dodge, K. A., Bates, J. E., & Pettit, G. S. (1992). Some consequences of early harsh discipline: Child aggression and a maladaptive social information processing style. *Child Development, 63,* 1321–1335.

Weisz, J. R., Weiss, B., Han, S. S., Granger, D. A., & Morton, T. (1995). Effects of psychotherapy with children and adolescents revisited: A meta-analysis of treatment outcome studies. *Psychological Bulletin, 117,* 450–468.

Werner, E. E. (1992). The children of Kauai: Resiliency and recovery in adolescence and adulthood. *Journal of Adolescent Health, 13,* 262–268.

Wilson, W. J. (1987). *The truly disadvantaged.* Chicago: University of Chicago Press.

Yoshikawa, H. (1994). Prevention as cumulative protection: Effects of early family support and education on chronic delinquency and its risks. *Psychological Bulletin, 115,* 28–54.

Zigler, E., Taussig, C., & Black, K. (1992). Early childhood intervention: A promising preventative for juvenile delinquency. *American Psychologist, 47,* 997–1006.

*Special thanks to Maeda Galinsky and Jan Schopler at the School of Social Work, University of North Carolina at Chapel Hill, and Robert Lewis at the Utah Department of Human Services for making valuable comments on early versions of this article. This research was supported, in part, by a grant (Contract No. 294411) from the Utah State Department of Human Services. Portions of this report were presented at the 71st*

*Annual Meeting of the American Orthopsychiatric Association, April 1994, Alexandria, VA.*

---

*This chapter was originally published in the July 1996 issue of* Social Work, *Vol. 41, pp. 347–361.*

# 10 Nonconvulsive Seizure Disorders: Importance and Implications for School Social Workers

Diane Kistner and Kevin L. DeWeaver

**M**ore than 30 types of seizures have been identified (University of Minnesota, 1993), some of which, if not treated, can cause a host of problems for a child having seizures as well as for parents, teachers, and other students. The less well known nonconvulsive seizure types often are not recognized or are misdiagnosed. School social workers who know what to look for can make an invaluable contribution by recognizing when problem behaviors may be caused by seizures. Although families can be devastated by the societal stigma and high treatment costs associated with a diagnosis of seizures, failure to diagnose the condition early can have serious physical, educational, and psychosocial consequences that place a child at risk for a lifetime of diminished functioning.

In this article, we present features and symptoms of nonconvulsive seizures to aid in early recognition. We provide an observation record suitable for use by school staff and parents to help secure an accurate diagnosis and evaluate the efficacy of medical and social work interventions. Appropriate postdiagnostic interventions are then suggested to help prevent children with seizure disorders from being disabled by their condition.

Seizure disorders (also referred to as "the epilepsies" or "epilepsy") are far more common than many people realize. Conservative estimates place their incidence in children at one in 50, and a little less than half of those children experience partial (affecting part of the brain) nonconvulsive seizures (personal communication with J. Hall, Director of Education, Georgia Chapter, Epilepsy Foundation of America, September 20, 1995). A *seizure* is defined as "a brief, excessive surge of electrical activity in the brain that causes a change in how a person feels, senses things, or behaves" (Devinsky, 1994, p. 18). Simply speaking, a nonconvulsive seizure is one that does not cause convulsive jerking (Freeman, Vining, & Pillas, 1990). Both convulsive and nonconvulsive seizures, neither of which is contagious, can be caused by metabolic disorders, illnesses such as meningitis or measles, congenital or developmental defects, substance abuse, lead poisoning, or head injuries sustained during normal activities such as bike riding or in abusive environments (Beit-Jones & Kapust, 1986; Devinsky, 1994; Freeman et al., 1990; Hauser & Hesdorffer, 1990; Teicher, Glod, Surrey, & Swett, 1993).

Some seizures cause symptoms now readily recognized by teachers and school social workers, such as convulsions in a tonic-clonic (formerly termed "grand mal") seizure or staring in a nonconvulsive absence (pronounced *ab-sóntz*) seizure (formerly termed "petit mal") (Devinsky, 1994). Many nonconvulsive seizure types, however, are not recognized as such because their symptoms are similar to those of emotional disturbances, behavior disorders, or even major psychiatric illnesses (Beit-Jones & Kapust, 1986; Benson, Miller, & Signer, 1986; Busick & Gorman, 1986; Devinsky, 1994; Devinsky, Putnam, Grafman, Bromfield, & Theodore, 1989; Mesulam, 1981; Schenk & Bear, 1981). Untreated, nonconvulsive seizures can cause troublesome episodic behaviors that frighten or confuse children, making the classroom difficult to control and stressful for everyone.

## DISABILITY ISSUES

Fortunately, with treatment—usually with an anticonvulsant drug—seizures can be controlled in many cases and in time may go into remission or be outgrown (Hauser & Hesdorffer, 1990). Congress has recognized, however, that epilepsy is a developmental disability that substantially limits one or more major life activities, even when seizures are controlled by medication (Epilepsy Foundation of America, 1992a). In a surveillance report issued by the Centers for Disease Control and Prevention (CDC), childhood seizure disorders were found to be "a significant public health problem and one of the major developmental disabilities among children" ("CDC Notes Need," 1994, p. 1).

Even with good seizure control, children with seizure disorders typically experience high levels of anxiety that may cause them to fail to perform up to their abilities. Goldin and Margolin (1975), contrasting epilepsy with constantly present orthopedic or speech disabilities, aptly described seizures as being like a "physical and psychosocial 'Sword of Damocles'" (p. 67); a child with a seizure disorder may function normally, but no one can predict when or if a seizure might occur. Psychosocial difficulties, often in evidence when a child has seizures, can heighten this anxiety and lower self-esteem, thus negatively affecting the child's ability to learn.

If having a seizure disorder affects a child's educational performance, he or she may be entitled to, and greatly benefit from, special education and related services (Epilepsy Foundation of America, 1992c). Only a small percentage of children with seizure disorders require special education. Most are best served by mainstream classes and should not be restricted from full participation in normal childhood activities (Devinsky, 1994; Lannon, 1991).

## LITERATURE REVIEW

The impact of developmental disabilities on children and families has been rigorously studied by social workers, educators, psychologists, and others; however, few articles in the social work literature have focused on seizure disorders. The importance of early intervention—as early as infancy (Saunders, 1995)—with children with developmental disabilities has been stressed by many authors. Unfortunately, because of misinformation and failure to ascribe their emotional and behavioral symptoms to seizures, many children having nonconvulsive seizures do not benefit from early intervention.

Appolone and Gibson (1980) explained that a seizure disorder is a medical illness with psychosocial ramifications that are often more disabling than the seizures. Freeman et al. (1990) noted that for centuries epilepsy has been a psychosocial disease caused by factors not intrinsic to the disorder itself. The negative reactions, misunderstanding, and rejection of others constantly aggravate the person's emotional and behavioral condition and can even increase the frequency of seizures (Devinsky, 1994; Freeman et al., 1990). For these reasons, educating families, the child's peers, and the community is one of the most vital components of school social work intervention (Beit-Jones & Kapust, 1986; Fraser, 1983) and is essential to the successful integration of children with seizure disorders into mainstream classrooms.

Addressing school social workers in particular, Black (1979) noted that epilepsy is an important disorder on which to focus because of the wide range of symptoms and levels of intellectual and physical abilities represented in children with seizure disorders. She stressed the importance of going beyond individual needs, stating that the "problem complex" presented by a diagnosis of epilepsy requires school social workers to adopt multiple roles in intervening with children with seizure disorders, their families, medical personnel, and the community.

While acknowledging the role of the family and significant others in contributing to learned helplessness in people diagnosed with seizure disorders, several authors have focused on clinical work with adults (Appolone & Gibson, 1980; Lessman & Mollick, 1978). This population is considered particularly difficult to work with because sick-role behaviors have often become entrenched by adulthood, even if a person's seizure disorder is under good control or has been outgrown (Appolone & Gibson, 1980; Lessman & Mollick, 1978). Authors addressing and recommending interventions with children with seizure disorders have taken a more general approach, either providing a brief overview of various seizure symptoms (Black, 1979; Smith, 1978) or examining the impact of epilepsy on the family system (Appolone, 1978; Atkins, 1989; Feeman & Hagen, 1990; Romeis, 1980).

Only a few social workers (Beit-Jones & Kapust, 1986) have specifically addressed nonconvulsive seizure disorders and the need to differentiate them from other disorders—most notably psychiatric illnesses—with which they are often confused. Drawing on the then-current literature on temporal lobe epilepsy (that is, partial seizures), Beit-Jones and Kapust discussed traits and behaviors indicative of a hypothesized interictal (between-seizure) syndrome, now termed "Geschwind's syndrome," which has since been determined to occur in a very small percentage of people with temporal lobe epilepsy (LaPlante, 1993). It is not uncommon, however, for people having nonconvulsive seizures to experience the following symptoms between seizures: confusion; fatigue; anxiety; irritation; depression; or mood, personality, or behavior changes (Devinsky, 1994; Epilepsy Foundation of America, 1992d; Fraser, 1983). These changes, combined with the dissociative episodes that people with seizure disorders sometimes experience, have led a number of researchers (Benson et al., 1986; Devinsky et al., 1989; Mesulam, 1981; Schenk & Bear, 1981) to explore a possible link between dissociative disorders (dissociative identity disorder in particular) and seizures.

The most vigorous research on nonconvulsive seizure disorders appears in the psychiatric, neurological, and neuropsychological literature. Unfortunately, because of high caseloads, few school social workers have time to keep abreast of rapid developments in these fields. The Epilepsy Foundation of America (1-800-EFA-1000) disseminates succinct, well-written pamphlets, books, and videotapes targeted to educators, health professionals, parents, and children that school social workers may find particularly useful in helping identify and appropriately treat children with nonconvulsive seizure disorders.

## RECOGNIZING NONCONVULSIVE SEIZURES

The ability to recognize a nonconvulsive seizure comes from understanding where these seizures originate and how they affect brain function. Partial seizures affect functioning that is controlled by the part or parts of the brain through which they spread, with the left hemisphere controlling the right side of the body and vice versa (Devinsky, 1994; Freeman et al., 1990). It is not unusual for two or more types to be present in one individual (University of Minnesota, 1993). A child's seizure pattern and symptoms are as unique as a fingerprint.

Absence seizures, a special type of nonconvulsive seizure that may be more readily recognized by school personnel, occur predominantly in children, are generalized (involve both brain hemispheres), and usually last less than 10 seconds (Devinsky, 1994). Consciousness is impaired during the seizure. The child appears to be staring and may start blinking or chewing or make brief aimless movements with the hands or limbs (Epilepsy Foundation of America, 1992e). Although each seizure is short-lived and the child returns to immediate alertness when it is over, a child may have many absence seizures during the day that, combined, greatly interfere with comprehension and learning ability (Freeman et al., 1990).

According to Devinsky (1994), partial nonconvulsive seizures originate in and usually stay confined to one part of the brain, although they can secondarily generalize to cause a convulsive seizure. Partial seizures can last several minutes and are often followed by confusion and decreased ability to remember, understand language, or do schoolwork. If confronted or restrained after the seizure, the child may react with negative behaviors such as verbal or physical aggression. During the seizure, the child may lash out instinctively if grabbed or held down.

The most seizure-prone brain regions are the temporal lobes, which control speech, emotion, sensory perceptions, autonomic functions, and memory storage, and the frontal lobes, which are involved with alertness, awareness, memory, personality, and anxiety (Freeman et al., 1990). The temporal and frontal lobes have many connections, and seizures arising in either of these areas can quickly spread to the other. Seizures less frequently occur in or spread to the occipital lobe, which registers vision, or the parietal lobe, which governs the ability to make connections.

Two categories of partial seizures exist—simple and complex. The basic difference between the two is whether consciousness remains intact or is impaired during the seizure (Epilepsy Foundation of America, 1994). A simple partial seizure, which is consciously experienced and usually (but not always) remembered, can precede a complex partial seizure and serve as an aura, or warning, that consciousness is about to be altered (Devinsky, 1994; Epilepsy Foundation of America, 1994).

Simple partial seizures can cause any of a bewildering array of bizarre symptoms and experiences, as described by Devinsky (1994):

> The symptoms include bodily sensations and discomforts; powerful emotions such as fear, anxiety, depression, or embarrassment for no apparent reason; feeling as if the mind and body are separating; strange thoughts suddenly racing through the mind; seeing objects and people get larger or smaller or appear distorted; seeing things that are not there (visual hallucinations); smelling things that are not there (olfactory hallucinations); and hearing things that are not there (auditory hallucinations). (p. 190)

Psychic symptoms of this type of seizure include disturbing memory flashbacks or frequent disconcerting feelings of déjà vu (something or someone unfamiliar seems familiar) or jamais vu (something or someone familiar seems unfamiliar) (Freeman et al., 1990). Time distortions, out-of-body experiences, sudden nausea, or stomach pain may occur (Epilepsy Foundation of America, 1994). Simple partial seizures can be frightening to a child.

Complex partial seizures affect a larger area of the brain and therefore impair consciousness (Epilepsy Foundation of America, 1994). The child may appear to be conscious, but he or she will be in an altered state of consciousness, an almost trancelike state (Epilepsy Foundation of America, 1994). During a complex partial seizure, the child loses contact with his or her surroundings and may wander around as though sleepwalking, pick at clothing, mumble, make chewing movements, cry out, speak the same words over and over, or run away in apparent fear. If engaged in activity, movements are usually disorganized, confused, and unfocused, but others may find it hard to believe that the child does not know what he or she is doing (Epilepsy Foundation of America, 1994).

A child having a nonconvulsive seizure will not have all of the above symptoms; instead, he or she will likely have a unique constellation or pattern of symptoms that tends to be the same and to occur in the same order each time (Epilepsy Foundation of America, 1994). This pattern, however, may change over time (Devinsky, 1994), which complicates assessment. A repetitive pattern of behavior; attendant unresponsiveness to instruction; and confusion, lack of awareness, or memory loss following the behavior should raise the school social worker's index of suspicion that the behavior may be attributable to a nonconvulsive seizure disorder.

Although symptoms and behaviors exhibited during and immediately after nonconvulsive seizures may seem bizarre to the child and others, it is important that the school social worker help them understand that seizures are caused by a disorder of brain function and do not indicate that the child is mentally ill (Devinsky, 1994). Some partial seizures, however, are mistaken for psychosis;

this mistake is unfortunate because antipsychotic medications typically exacerbate seizures, making the "psychiatric illness" worse (Beit-Jones & Kapust, 1986; Busick & Gorman, 1986). Even experienced clinicians can fail to consider a seizure disorder when making psychiatric diagnoses (Farber, Schmaltz, Voile, & Hecht, 1986), ignore seizures as an important diagnostic symptom (Elizur & Minuchin, 1992), or generalize the prevalence of psychiatric symptoms in patients with seizure disorders in mental hospitals or psychiatric clinics to the general population, where incidence of psychiatric illness in those having seizures is low (Stevens, 1988).

Many children with seizure disorders will reach adulthood with psychiatric complications because of misdiagnosis or delayed diagnosis and treatment as well as other people's attitudes arising from misunderstanding of their disorder ("CDC Notes Need," 1994; Devinsky, 1994; Parker, 1988). As the following case suggests, differential diagnosis can be a complex endeavor made even more difficult when seizures occur during stressful periods or mimic or co-occur with other disorders. It is important to note that with or without co-occurrence and whether or not environmental stressors are part of the equation, failure to appropriately treat an underlying seizure disorder is likely to result in failure of interventions aimed at ameliorating emotional or behavioral symptoms.

## CASE EXAMPLE

Ed entered middle school during a stressful period of family disintegration and divorce. Although he was a gifted child, he began doing poorly in his classes. Ed told his mother that his teachers would write information on the board but not give him time to read it before they erased it. Frustrated, he said they refused to answer his questions, saying they had already been over the material and he should know it. Ed's teachers were also frustrated. They complained that Ed was acting out so much that it was impossible to teach. "Trying to get attention," he would slide out of his seat, sing in a babyish voice, twist his clothes into knots, scribble on himself, or repeat nonsensical phrases over and over. On several occasions, Ed suddenly became greatly distressed and ran out of the school building. Ed insisted he did not remember doing these things.

Even more disturbing was Ed's increasing depression. He began to look pale and exhausted and often told his mother he wanted to die. In one parent–teacher conference, Ed's teachers agreed that he was seriously disturbed. One said the regular public school was not the place for him. Another just shook her head and said he was obviously hallucinating. In an effort to be helpful, the guidance counselor—because of funding cuts, a school social worker was not available—gave Ed's mother a list of area psychotherapists.

Ed's mother began to wonder whether her son might have a seizure disorder similar to her own. She had not been diagnosed until she was middle-aged, even though her neurologist told her she probably had been born with the disorder. Before receiving proper treatment, she had periodically experienced odd, disturbing hallucinations followed by dissociative episodes, dazed confusion, and depression. She remembered as a child being tied to her school desk with a jump rope without knowing why and "coming to" in the hall or in the principal's office where she was paddled for "impossible behavior" that she could not recall. When Ed's mother asked his teachers whether they thought his behavior might be a result of seizures, they said no, because they had never seen him shaking or staring.

Ed finally was diagnosed as having attention deficit disorder and co-occurring simple and complex partial seizures. After he began taking an anticonvulsant medication, he improved somewhat; without the support of school personnel, however, stabilizing Ed on his medication proved impossible. It was not until a social worker helped Ed's teachers understand the nature of his seizures and his need for stress reduction and their support that Ed really began to improve. He then began to make high grades and to exhibit considerable artistic talent.

## IMPLICATIONS FOR SCHOOL SOCIAL WORK PRACTICE

Without the mother's recognition that his bizarre behavior was caused by seizures exacerbated by stress and inadequate sleep, Ed's case would not have had such a positive outcome. Unfortunately, teachers and other school personnel are not the only ones who sometimes fail to recognize the symptoms of nonconvulsive seizure disorders. The American Psychiatric Association's (1994) *Diagnostic and Statistical Manual of Mental Disorders* is rife with cautions about the need to differentiate seizure disorders or specific seizure types—most notably complex partial seizures—from major psychiatric illnesses. Despite similar cautions, one DSM-III–based study (Farber et al., 1986) found that of 78 clinical psychologists surveyed for their ability to differentiate temporal lobe epilepsy from five other psychiatric disorders, only 5 percent were accurate in their diagnosis. The clinicians' area of specialty or years of experience did not significantly increase their diagnostic accuracy. School social workers are in an excellent position to effect positive outcomes for children with nonconvulsive seizure disorders by ensuring that their condition is recognized, medically diagnosed, and appropriately treated.

### Prediagnostic Interventions

Helping secure a diagnosis for the child suspected of having nonconvulsive seizures is the first important step in managing this complex and often chronic condition. As previously discussed, nonconvulsive seizures can cause changes in a child's cognition, mood, or behavior between seizures that might suggest another disorder. An actual seizure, however, can be differentiated from other alterations in consciousness or behavior by "abrupt onset; altered or lost awareness (if not a simple partial seizure); brief duration; rapid recovery; and recurrent stereotypic episodes" (Epilepsy Foundation of America, 1992d, p. 3).

Involving teachers, social workers, and caregivers in objective observation and recording of emotional, behavioral, and cognitive symptoms using an observation record, such as the one in Figure 10-1 (see also Epilepsy Foundation of America, 1992b, 1992d, 1992e), can yield important clues that help the diagnosing physician (often but not necessarily a neurologist) determine whether alterations in consciousness or behavior are the result of seizures.

*Figure 10-1*

## Observation Record to Aid in Differential Diagnosis of Seizure Disorder and Evaluation of Effectiveness of Medical and Psychosocial Interventions

Child's name and age _____

Time, place, and date _____

Name of observer and relationship _____

Possible behavioral, cognitive, and emotional symptoms a child may exhibit before, during, or after a seizure are listed below. Carefully observe the child, recording stage 1 (before seizure), 2 (during seizure), or 3 (after seizure) beside observed symptoms. If the same symptom occurs at different stages, record more than one number beside that symptom. If a stage or symptom category is not directly observed, leave it blank. Specify any unlisted symptoms under "Other."

### List of Symptoms

| Behavioral Symptoms | Cognitive Symptoms | Emotional Symptoms |
|---|---|---|
| ___ Agitated | ___ Alert | ___ Angry |
| ___ Behaves normally | ___ Awake but unresponsive | ___ Anxious |
| ___ Combative | ___ Confused | ___ Depressed |
| ___ Fatigued | ___ Exhibits memory loss | ___ Excited |
| ___ Hyperactive | ___ Talks illogically | ___ Fearful |
| ___ Slowed | ___ Unaware of surroundings | ___ Happy |
| ___ Withdrawn | ___ Unconscious | ___ Irritated |
| ___ Other | ___ Other | ___ Other |

### Observer's Anecdotal Description of Seizure Events

Describe the sequence of events during the seizure, especially what happened first and how long the seizure lasted. Note the side of the body involved, if applicable, plus any suspected triggers (such as flashing lights, temperature changes, hyperventilation, illness, sleep deprivation, or stress). How long after the seizure did it take the child to return to normal functioning?

### Child's Subjective Description of Seizure Events

Speaking in a calm tone of voice, ask the child to describe any physical sensations, feelings, or experiences he or she can remember having before, then during, and then after the seizure. Try to determine to what degree consciousness was altered and at what stage. For example, test for memory loss by making a comment or pointing out an object to the child during the seizure, then seeing if the child can remember it after the seizure is over.

Because a seizure may not occur in the physician's office or during a routine electroencephalogram to detect the presence of seizure discharges, observation records can be of great diagnostic value (Epilepsy Foundation of America, 1992b). Careful records can help pinpoint the specific seizure type and region of the brain affected by the seizure, which helps the physician match the seizure type to the anticonvulsant medication most likely to be effective in controlling the child's seizures (Epilepsy Foundation of America, 1992b, 1992d, 1992e).

## Postdiagnostic Interventions

The four roles identified by Black (1979) for school social workers intervening with students with disabilities are appropriate and necessary when working with children diagnosed with nonconvulsive seizure disorders: (1) casework, (2) education, (3) coordination and liaison services with medical institutions, and (4) advocacy. DeWeaver and Rose (1987) noted the value of an ecological approach to working with children with a developmental disability. They emphasized the importance of optimizing interdisciplinary teamwork, especially in the development of individualized education plans; sustaining strong case management, linkage, and brokering efforts; and increasing knowledge and skill in the disabilities domain. In a monograph targeted to neurologists and other allied health professionals working with clients with seizure disorders, the Epilepsy Foundation of America (1992b) emphasized that "the treatment team must include an individual who is knowledgeable about the medical, social, and psychological management of those with epilepsy and who maintains close ties to local resources" (p. 9).

In working with children with nonconvulsive seizure disorders, the discharge of school social work responsibilities under the Education for All Handicapped Children Act of 1975 (P.L. 94-142) will result in the acquisition of knowledge and skills that the school social worker needs to become a valued member of both the educational planning and clinical management teams. These responsibilities include preparing a social or developmental history, counseling with the child and family, working with problems in the child's living situation that affect his or her school adjustment, and mobilizing school and community resources so the child can derive maximum benefits from his or her educational program (DeWeaver & Rose, 1987).

Enhancing self-determination of the client system in the environmental context is especially important if the child with a nonconvulsive seizure disorder is to live up to his or her potential. The school social worker must help families adjust to the diagnosis of seizures, which often involves engaging them in educational and self-help activities and teaching them how to network and find information—in effect, how to be their own case managers. Seizure disorders, which are costly to manage, create financial hardships for families. If left untreated, however, they can be even more costly in human terms.

Counseling is often required, at least in the beginning, to ensure that the child, the parents, and significant others understand their pivotal role as part of the treatment team. Medication must be taken regularly, continuously monitored, and periodically adjusted or changed, all of which can cause the child to feel sick and powerless. All seizure types and the medications used to treat them can cause memory and other learning deficits that must be addressed (Devinsky, 1994; Parker, 1988). Depending on the severity of the disorder, application for disability status may need to be pursued and special education and long-term care decisions made. The school social worker can empower the family by teaching them what they can do to help manage seizures. Ensuring that the child takes medication as prescribed and gets sufficient rest and exercise, reducing stress, and developing a positive and nonpathologizing attitude about the child's condition are as important as medical care in seizure control.

Funding for social services is often insufficient; this makes the family's active involvement in seizure management more critical. Franklin and Streeter (1995) suggested ways that public schools and human services can be linked to maximize resources and effectiveness of social work interventions. One possible avenue for networking is that seizure disorders can co-occur with and complicate treatment for other conditions including mental retardation, cerebral palsy, dyslexia, attention deficit disorders, and learning disabilities (Barkley, 1990; Devinsky, 1994; Freeman et al., 1990; Lannon, 1991). Content on nonconvulsive seizure disorders can sometimes be easily added to existing disability education programming.

In schools that do not have a school social worker, a visiting social worker can help coordinate in-service teacher training in seizure recognition and first aid, support for children with seizure disorders and their families, family involvement in self-help and advocacy efforts, and educational programs directed at the community. As a starting point, many local Epilepsy Foundation of America affiliates offer free training, speakers, and other assistance to schools within their service range and can be invaluable allies to school social workers. As the social worker's knowledge of the potentially remediable causes of seizures increases, and as interdisciplinary alliances are forged, efforts can also eventually be targeted toward prevention of nonconvulsive seizure disorders.

Given the societal stigma associated with seizure disorders, many parents feel guilt and shame at having a child with a seizure disorder and try to hide the condition from others. The goal for the parents ultimately is acceptance. In addition, the school social worker can help the child and family members understand that they can be instrumental in reducing stigma by educating themselves and others about seizures and refusing to give in to feelings of shame. A prevalent myth that seizure disorders cause mental retardation or mental illness must be dispelled. The school social worker can reassure families that some of the world's most accomplished writers, artists, politicians, physicians, attorneys, and scientists have had seizure disorders (Devinsky, 1994; LaPlante, 1993; Smith, 1978).

## CONCLUSION

Failure to recognize and secure treatment for children with nonconvulsive seizure disorders can have tragic lifelong consequences. Some evidence exists that over time, uncontrolled seizures may cause structural changes in the brain that sensitize the affected brain tissue and make a person more likely to have more seizures (Devinsky, 1994; Kramer, 1993; "Panel Offers Clues," 1995); therefore, timely diagnosis and intervention are critical. After diagnosis, ongoing education, networking, and strong case management and advocacy efforts can help prevent the debilitating physical, educational, and psychosocial complications that children with seizure disorders often face. Appropriate school social work interventions based on current information will help prevent children with nonconvulsive seizure disorders from becoming debilitated by their condition and will provide a means of assisting teachers and administrators in maintaining a classroom atmosphere that is conducive to learning for all children.

## REFERENCES

American Psychiatric Association. (1994). *Diagnostic and statistical manual of mental disorders* (4th ed.). Washington, DC: Author.

Appolone, C. (1978). Preventive social work intervention with families of children with epilepsy. *Social Work and Health Care, 4*, 139–148.

Appolone, C., & Gibson, P. (1980). Group work with young adult epilepsy patients. *Social Work in Health Care, 6*, 23–32.

Atkins, S. (1989). Siblings of handicapped children. *Child and Adolescent Social Work, 6*, 271–282.

Barkley, R. A. (1990). *Attention deficit hyperactivity disorder: A handbook for diagnosis and treatment.* New York: Guilford Press.

Beit-Jones, M. S., & Kapust, L. R. (1986). Temporal lobe epilepsy: Social and psychological considerations. *Social Work in Health Care, 11*, 17–33.

Benson, D. F., Miller, B. L., & Signer, S. R. (1986). Dual personality associated with epilepsy. *Archives of Neurology, 43*, 471–474.

Black, R. B. (1979). Epilepsy: Multiple roles for school social workers. *School Social Work Quarterly, 1*, 5–15.

Busick, B. S., & Gorman, M. (1986). *Ill, not insane.* Boulder, CO: New Idea Press.

CDC notes need, plans to develop epilepsy program. (1994, December). *Epilepsy USA*, pp. 1, 5.

Devinsky, O. (1994). *A guide to understanding and living with epilepsy.* Philadelphia: F. A. Davis.

Devinsky, O., Putnam, F., Grafman, J., Bromfield, E., & Theodore, W. H. (1989). Dissociative states and epilepsy. *Neurology, 39*, 835–840.

DeWeaver, K. L., & Rose, S. R. (1987). School social work with developmentally disabled pupils: Past, present, and future. *School Social Work Journal, 11*, 47–58.

Education for All Handicapped Children Act of 1975, P.L. 94-142, 89 Stat. 773.

Elizur, J., & Minuchin, S. (1992). *Institutionalizing madness: Families, therapy, and society.* New York: Basic Books.

Epilepsy Foundation of America. (1992a). *The Americans with Disabilities Act: Questions and answers about provisions affecting persons with seizure disorders* [Pamphlet]. Landover, MD: Author.

Epilepsy Foundation of America. (1992b). *The comprehensive clinical management of the epilepsies* (2nd ed.) [Monograph]. Landover, MD: Author.

Epilepsy Foundation of America. (1992c). *Epilepsy: Legal rights, legal issues* [Pamphlet]. Landover, MD: Author.

Epilepsy Foundation of America. (1992d). *How to recognize and classify seizures and epilepsy* (2nd ed.) [Monograph]. Landover, MD: Author.

Epilepsy Foundation of America. (1992e). *Seizure recognition and observation: A guide for allied health professionals* (2nd ed.) [Monograph]. Landover, MD: Author.

Epilepsy Foundation of America. (1994). *All about partial seizures* [Pamphlet]. Landover, MD: Author.

Farber, L. G., Schmaltz, L. W., Voile, F. O., & Hecht, P. (1986). Temporal lobe epilepsy: Diagnostic accuracy. *International Journal of Clinical Neuropsychology, 8*, 76–79.

Feeman, D. J., & Hagen, J. W. (1990). Effects of childhood chronic illness on families. *Social Work in Health Care, 14*, 37–53.

Franklin, C., & Streeter, C. L. (1995). School reform: Linking public schools with human services. *Social Work, 40*, 773–782.

Fraser, R. T. (1983). A needs review in epilepsy rehabilitation: Toward solutions in the 1980s. *Rehabilitation Literature, 44*, 264–269.

Freeman, J. M., Vining, E.P.G., & Pillas, D. J. (1990). *Seizures and epilepsy in childhood: A guide for parents.* Baltimore: Johns Hopkins University Press.

Goldin, G. J., & Margolin, R. J. (1975). The psychosocial aspects of epilepsy. In G. Wright (Ed.), *Epilepsy rehabilitation* (pp. 66–80). Boston: Little, Brown.

Hauser, W. A., & Hesdorffer, D. C. (1990). *Facts about epilepsy* [Pamphlet]. Landover, MD: Epilepsy Foundation of America.

Kramer, P. D. (1993). *Listening to Prozac*. New York: Penguin Books.

Lannon, S. (1991). *Families with epilepsy: Psychosocial aspects* [Pamphlet]. Morris Plains, NJ: Warner-Lambert.

LaPlante, E. (1993). *Seized: Temporal lobe epilepsy as a medical, historical, and artistic phenomenon*. New York: HarperCollins.

Lessman, S. E., & Mollick, L. R. (1978). Group treatment of epileptics. *Health & Social Work, 3,* 105–121.

Mesulam, M. M. (1981). Dissociative states with abnormal temporal lobe EEG. *Archives of Neurology, 38,* 176–181.

Panel offers clues to memory problems. (1995, January–February). *Epilepsy USA,* pp. 7, 10.

Parker, W. A. (1988). Epilepsy. In E. T. Herfindal, D. R. Gourley, & L. L. Hart (Eds.), *Clinical pharmacy and therapeutics* (4th ed., pp. 570–592). Baltimore: Williams & Wilkins.

Romeis, J. C. (1980). The role of grandparents in adjustment to epilepsy. *Social Work in Health Care, 6,* 37–43.

Saunders, E. J. (1995). Services for infants and toddlers with disabilities: IDEA, Part H. *Health & Social Work, 20,* 39–45.

Schenk, L., & Bear, D. (1981). Multiple personality and related dissociative phenomena in patients with temporal lobe epilepsy. *American Journal of Psychiatry, 138,* 1311–1316.

Smith, L. L. (1978). Social work with epileptic patients. *Health & Social Work, 3,* 157–174.

Stevens, J. R. (1988). Psychiatric aspects of epilepsy. *Journal of Clinical Psychiatry, 49*(Suppl.), 49–57.

Teicher, M. H., Glod, C. A., Surrey, J., & Swett, C. (1993). Early childhood abuse and limbic system ratings in adult psychiatric patients. *Journal of Neuropsychiatry and Clinical Neuroscience, 5,* 301–306.

University of Minnesota. (1993). *Epilepsy: Medical aspects* [Brochure]. Minneapolis: Author.

*This chapter was originally published in the April 1997 issue of* Social Work in Education, *Vol. 19, pp. 73–85.*

# Part II

# SKILLS AND INTERVENTIONS FOR PRACTICE WITH FAMILIES

# Part II: Skills and Interventions for Practice with Families

School social workers spend a tremendous amount of time helping and serving parents and families of students. In their unique role as family–school–community liaisons, school social workers have many opportunities to help families by enhancing their social and community functioning and increasing their knowledge so that they can effectively engage with school systems. This section presents nine chapters covering essential and timely topics on how to work with family systems. Chapters provide a variety of skills for addressing problems of children and families as they are confronted with the challenges of life and interactions with public school systems. Included are helpful skills for working with culturally diverse families. Cultural diversity has become a specialized practice area in which social workers are believed to have considerable expertise. These chapters provide both general skills for working with culturally diverse children of color and their families, as well as more specific skills for working with particular students of color such as Chinese American children.

Linkages between families and schools are important matters for schools to address. Techniques for assessing these connections are presented in a practice-friendly manner using the case study or case example method. These case examples are useful for understanding how to apply various assessment methods in their own practice. Attendance issues remain a major topic confronting school social workers. Strategies for setting up home-based programs for improving attendance of elementary school children are described in some detail. Literature on interventions and programs for families of preschool children has not been sufficiently developed. Specific methods for empowering families of preschool children and descriptions of how to operate a program for these families are described.

Clinical and therapeutic techniques are presented that help school social workers make effective family interventions in school settings. Prevention of adolescent pregnancy, HIV infection, and AIDS is of considerable concern to schools. The most up-to-date knowledge and skills for how to intervene with adolescent pregnancy are presented. Of special interest is information that links sexual abuse with adolescent pregnancy and that describes the skills for running prevention programs aimed at sexually abused teenagers. Finally, school-linked programs are becoming important vehicles of service in many schools and communities. Skills for setting up school-linked, family resource centers are presented in the context of reaching out to impoverished communities.

# Engaging Effectively with Culturally Diverse Families and Children

Frances S. Caple, Ramon M. Salcido, and John di Cecco

Despite the creation of numerous programs to help children achieve success, the public school system has fallen short of meeting this goal for all children. Culturally sensitive supports and interventions are receiving increased attention as key factors in the formulation of effective strategies for achieving the National Educational Goals (Goals 2000: Educate America Act, P.L. 103-227). As increasing numbers of culturally diverse children enter schools, they will encounter students and professionals who are not of their cultural background. This situation is especially evident in the Los Angeles Unified School District, where students and staff are identified in seven major racial or ethnic groups. The 633,000 students enrolled in 1994 included 66.6 percent Hispanics, 14.4 percent African Americans, 11.6 percent whites, 4.8 percent Asian Americans, 1.9 percent Filipinos, 0.4 percent Pacific Islanders, and 0.3 percent American Indians. Further stratification within each group creates even greater diversity among cultural backgrounds, and these students were greeted with even more diversity as they received services from the 30,100 professional staff who were 57.6 percent white, 16.3 percent African American, 16.3 percent Hispanic, 7.6 percent Asian American, 1.3 percent Filipino, 0.7 percent American Indian, and 0.1 percent Pacific Islander (Los Angeles Unified School District, 1995). The needs of these children, the unique and rich perspectives they bring to schools, and the dynamic forces with which they interact will determine the mass educational and social outcomes of the 21st century. Many of these children will experience problems deriving from fragmented and destabilizing service delivery systems (Gardner, 1990), insensitive staff, and in some cases a school environment that is nonsympathetic and rejecting.

Brown (1981) argued that one reason school social workers should be involved with minority[1] children and their families is based on the experiences of such

---

[1]The authors are aware of and acknowledge certain merit in the current debate concerning the use of the term "minority" when used particularly to describe people of color. The term, as used in this article, does not refer to relative size of the group with which a family is identified or how they are valued. Rather, as sociologists use the term, minority families are those that have historically been in a subordinate position with regard to social and economic power, privilege, and prestige as compared with the dominant majority (Longres, 1991). This subordination results most typically "as a consequence of their race, ancestry and/or other characteristics" the dominant groups hold in low esteem (Taylor, 1994, p. 1). The authors prefer the term "culturally diverse" for purposes of this article given that a wide range of family and child issues can be conceptualized within such a term.

families in a racist society. The literature on social work intervention with minority clients identifies strategies to combat oppression (Devore & Schlesinger, 1987; Hopps, 1982), use indigenous practice methods (Humm-Delgado & Delgado, 1986; Mokuau, 1991), emphasize cultural sensitivity (Green, 1982), and provide a comprehensive plan for assessment and treatment (Ho, 1992). These models of practice tend to emphasize the importance of culture and cultural differences. Although these approaches are of great value in understanding cross-cultural intervention, they offer limited knowledge about effective interaction skills with diverse students, parents, and communities in a school context. School social workers need to develop cross-cultural knowledge and intervention skills to assist culturally diverse parents in pursuing educational and functional goals for their children.

This article describes a cross-cultural practice model for use in school settings, recognizing the important role the school community plays in successfully preparing children to assume adult roles and engage in advanced learning. In addition, the use of interpreters is examined as one example of how such cross-cultural practice can be conducted effectively. We define the client system as the pupil and parent unit, recognizing the extended familial and community context as important to this discussion of engagement and assessment of students from diverse racial and ethnic groups.

## PREPARING FOR PRACTICE COMPETENCE

Their education has systematically provided social workers with basic knowledge for effective engagement with clients. There is less assurance that social work education has systematically included knowledge for effective practice with culturally diverse families and children. For example, in a recent informal survey conducted by the authors, participants in a continuing education session revealed that people completing social work programs more than five years ago had virtually no course content that highlighted cultural issues and needs. Furthermore, Allen-Meares (1992) emphasized that school social workers need a cross-cultural perspective for practice, but she noted the lack of adequate attention to such a perspective in the educational preparation of social workers and other school personnel. Given that school social workers assume various roles such as direct service provider and collaborator–consultant to other school personnel, there is some urgency to the need to explore means of intervening with culturally diverse families and children.

One of the critical markers of the beginning phase of social work treatment is that it lays the foundation for all treatment that follows. Therefore, it is vital that the professional entering the engagement period be competent in receiving and processing all that the client brings to the situation. Along with the generic knowledge and skills needed for engaging with any client, the practitioner must formulate one or more perspectives for practice, using specific knowledge, skills, and beliefs about particular characteristics of clients, their problems, and the environments in which they are striving to exist. Perspective building thus assumes a major part of the worker's mental preparation before engaging with clients. For example, a worker may formulate a perspective for crisis intervention after receiving a referral in which the presenting problem is stated in relation to a client's recent personal loss. A different perspective would be taken if the loss occurred years before.

Similarly, then, whether consciously acknowledged or not, the practitioner typically formulates a perspective for working with culturally diverse clients. The contents of these perspectives are drawn not only from specialized knowledge and skills but also from the values and beliefs of the social worker. Although generally there is some balance among these elements, in the absence of adequate knowledge or a way of organizing acquired knowledge, the practitioner may resort to formulating unbalanced, value-based, or biased perspectives.

## UNDERSTANDING CULTURE THROUGH PERSPECTIVE BUILDING

Social workers seeking competence in cross-cultural practice soon realize the impossibility of acquiring specific knowledge about every racially, ethnically, or otherwise culturally diverse client. We have identified four principles as essential for developing a generic perspective for culturally competent practice: (1) there is no single American culture, (2) members of each cultural group are diverse, (3) acculturation is a dynamic process, and (4) diversity is to be acknowledged and valued.

### There Is No Single American Culture

Despite the myth that has persisted in this regard, in reality American society is composed of multicultural environments based on one or more of the following: race, ethnicity, socioeconomic class, national or regional origin, sexual orientation, age, physical and mental ability, and gender. Cultural referents based on racial and ethnic differences are the ones most frequently highlighted and subjected to heated debate; differences may be recognized and discussed with somewhat less emotion when comparing the customs, beliefs, and attitudes of, for example, Northerners and Southerners or urban and rural dwellers.

### Members of Each Cultural Group Are Diverse

There is no single profile that fits all members of any specific cultural group. Over the past two decades, social workers and other mental health professionals have sought to learn quickly core cultural elements of particular racial or ethnic groups. As a result, some or all of several conference and classroom presentations and written publications have contained specific descriptions of "typical" realities of African Americans, Hispanic/Latino populations, Asian Americans, and occasionally American Indians (Green, 1982; Taylor, 1994). More recently, some authors have pointed out concerns about the tendency of social services providers to stereotype clients on the basis of a generalized picture of people from particular racial and ethnic groups and have included some useful discussion of diversity within various groups (Boyd-Franklin, 1989; Browne & Broderick, 1994; Castex, 1994; Fong & Mokuau, 1994).

Although general material is helpful in broadening one's knowledge of a cultural group, Solomon (1976) noted a limited use for such material in forming initial hypotheses about a client's situation. For example, a social worker who is helping a Latino family may hypothesize the following: "If in most Latino families the father is the dominant member and spokesperson, this may be true in the family with whom I am sitting right now." This hypothesis provides only a starting point and cannot be substituted for the practitioner's actual engagement activity, which must be direct exploration of this particular family's reality.

Given that in the social work treatment process there can be no reliance on the worker's acquired knowledge of how Americans behave or how members of a given ethnic group behave, the most direct and accurate source of data concerning cultural realities is the client. The social worker must be willing to assume the role of social worker–learner (Green, 1982). Specifically, the social worker must begin immediately to explore directly with the client, within the context of the client's cultural values and lifestyles, the meaning of life events and presenting problems, any history of past or current oppression, and the client's relative acculturation to the dominant culture.

## Acculturation Is a Dynamic Process

*Acculturation* is a dynamic "process of adopting the cultural traits or social patterns of another group, esp. a dominant one" (*Random House Webster's College Dictionary*, 1992, p. 10). A common conceptualization of acculturation considers only the client's status in this regard. Actually, all members of a multicultural society, including social workers, are subject to some degree of acculturation as they commingle and interact with other members of the society. In the most general terms, this phenomenon is observable as native-born Americans eat foods indigenous to other countries and as immigrants from those countries seek out American cuisine or as hairstyles, clothing, music, dance, and selected rituals are adopted from one group by members of another. The understanding and appreciation of such cultural exchanges are vital for the promotion of professional competence in cross-cultural practice.

To some extent, all children engage in a process of acculturation throughout their school years. Although some family cultures are similar to that of the school, each child will make some adaptive shifts from one system to the other. Thus, it is not uncommon for families to report a different set of child behaviors at home than reported by school personnel. In addition, immigrant children may be at a different level of acculturation to dominant American culture than their parents, and this fact may require special attention in the engagement and ongoing treatment process.

Most schoolchildren will make such shifts between family and school cultures without much difficulty; the child perceives the norms of the school and behaves accordingly. The greater the incongruity between the personal culture of the individual and the culture of the system in which interaction occurs, the more dynamic the process of acculturation becomes. The potential for conflicts is particularly high when the cultural imperatives of one group are ignored or openly dismissed as irrelevant in person–environment transactions. The social worker should be prepared to recognize, assess, and negotiate resolution of such conflicts. One approach to conflict resolution would include the facilitation of an accurate perception of cultural differences and the open sharing of cultural beliefs and norms by all parties engaged in the social work process.

## Diversity Is to Be Acknowledged and Valued

The distinct diversity of each client system, and of the various groups to which clients belong, is to be acknowledged and valued as providing real and potential sources of strength for the client's overall functioning and well-being. This principle is consistent with the core social work value and practice of assuming a nonjudgmental attitude toward clients. In the professional relationship the social worker assumes a nonjudgmental attitude by genuinely demonstrating acceptance, especially in the engagement phase but throughout the treatment process as well.

In every culture there exist some expectations and codes of behavior around areas of discipline, time, health, and religious beliefs. A worker's understanding of what these values are, where they fall on a value continuum of traditional to modern, and how they interface with behavioral expectations of the education system regarding children's learning are key elements of cross-cultural practice in school settings.

People from diverse racial and ethnic groups have experienced different forms of oppression and racism in their interactions with the majority culture. Placing these concerns into a cross-cultural perspective involves exploring the client's historical experiences with the majority culture and, if applicable, with migration and immigration. This history may include movement both within the United States and across foreign borders.

If the social worker has difficulty understanding the cultural reality described by the client, a cultural consultant may be helpful. This consultant would be an objective individual who is knowledgeable about the meaning of nuances of the client's specific cultural communication. Equally important is the worker's alertness to the likelihood that his or her own value systems and interpretations of life events may interfere with the effective engagement of the client.

Observations have been made that the greater the similarity between "the cognitive and affective characteristics of the client and the worker, the greater the chance for effective communication" (Green, 1982, p. 54). Likewise, the greater the similarity between the client's and the social worker's value systems, the greater the chance of effective service delivery (Longres, 1991). An early and ongoing task of the social worker is the assessment of the worker–client situation to identify cultural similarities and differences and provide clues for potential conflicts. Conflicts may arise because of positively or negatively biased behaviors or attitudes toward the client. Ongoing self-awareness checks with a professional consultant can be useful. A worker's ethnocentrism—the attitude that "my values and beliefs are more noble than those of the client and are worthy of emulation"—will not promote worker competence and effectiveness. The worker's personal work should focus on increasing openness and acceptance of the client's reality as potentially useful to the client's resolution of present problems.

## A FRAMEWORK FOR CROSS–CULTURAL PRACTICE

Several models of social work practice and "the ethnic reality" have been reviewed and discussed by Devore and Schlesinger (1987). We find that the ecosystems perspective, as currently used in social work practice, provides the overarching framework most compatible with Devore and Schlesinger's view of cultural practice in school settings. The ecosystems perspective recognizes that there are specific enduring and transient relationships between and among individuals, families, other groups, institutions, and society at large and that transactions between or among these systems have profound effects on human behavior and functioning. Because the nature of these transactions is reciprocal, practice in school settings should address the problems created by person–environment interactions by assessing the entire ecosystem and intervening at the most appropriate points in the system to effect desired change. To address person–environment problems, the practitioner can use culturally sensitive interactions based on the perspective developed as described earlier and by identifying and using appropriate problem-solving techniques (Germain, 1973, 1991; Meyer, 1983; Zastrow & Kirst-Ashman, 1994). The effectiveness of problem solving depends on the worker's understanding of and sensitivity to the client's cultural beliefs, lifestyle, and social support systems.

The worker who uses the ecosystems framework assumes various roles—enabler, facilitator, coordinator, mediator, and teacher—as she or he moves across system boundaries in dealing with the transactions between the client system and the school ecosystem. A primary emphasis of treatment is to empower the client system (pupils and their families) and intervene in other parts of the ecosystem that create barriers to empowerment. The social worker emphasizes activities based on the cultural strengths of the client system. The focus of treatment ultimately is to improve the goodness of fit between the client and others in the ecosystem, including the social worker. Therefore, interventions may be directed toward the family, specific members of the family, the teacher, or others in the ecosystem.

## Basic Skills for Cross-Cultural Practice

Several authors have identified the importance of determining and applying specific skills in cross-cultural practice (for example, Gallegos, 1984; Green, 1982; Lum, 1986). The core skills proposed here for working with diverse clients are synthesized from cross-cultural models, social work skills, and practice wisdom.

*Common Basic Skills.* In the beginning stages of intervention it is recommended that social workers take basic steps to establish an initial positive relationship. A major problem in most public schools is the lack of positive, cooperative relationships among students, staff, parents, and administration (Curiel, 1991). In building positive interactions, basic etiquette should be observed to convey respect, including making proper introductions, asking how the client wants to be addressed, and using common courtesies. The practitioner should spend a few minutes getting acquainted with the clients in a relaxed manner. Ivey (1977) stressed the importance of establishing and maintaining eye contact at this stage. These initial interpersonal exchanges contribute to the client's perception of the practitioner as helper.

Interaction between practitioner and client may also be influenced by the parents' perceptions of the roles of the worker. In the countries of origin of some immigrant clients, the social work role is not known, and some of these clients may view the practitioner as a government agent. Therefore, the task of the practitioner is to explain his or her professional role and the function of the services he or she can provide. Sue and Sue (1990) emphasized the importance of credibility when working with Asian clients. To strengthen the client's confidence in the worker's abilities, workers should display all degrees and other items indicating professional competence on the walls of their offices and should present their professional title to the client.

*Relationship-Building Skills.* The building of the worker–client relationship is the next task after observing courtesy protocols. Our observation in working with parents is that minority parents often feel powerless to express their needs to professionals if they feel the practitioner will not "hear" them. Thus, an important part of establishing rapport is being an effective listener and demonstrating attention and interest in the client's communications. The practitioner's use of facilitation skills can demonstrate to clients a desire to truly listen. Chamberlain et al. (1985) defined *facilitation* as short utterances used by the practitioner to prompt the client to continue talking. Ivey and Authier (1978) suggested nodding the head, using phrases such as "mm hmm" and "tell me more," and repeating one or two words spoken by the client as approaches to promote a continuing conversation. These behaviors convey interest and acceptance.

*Communication Skills.* Effective cross-cultural practice requires effectiveness not only in listening and facilitation, but also in spoken communication. Ivey and Authier (1978) proposed that one way the effective practitioner can engage in culturally appropriate behavior is by generating an infinite array of selective communication skills including open- and closed-ended questions, paraphrasing, reflection of feelings, and summarization. Ivey's (1977) work on cross-cultural skill development (microcounseling) set the groundwork for developing universal cross-cultural communication skills. After using paraphrasing, reflection of feelings, and summarization, the practitioner then repeats the information he or she has gathered and specifically asks the client if the information is accurate. In our model, we conceptualize this validation step as a "cultural check."

*Understanding the Client's Definition of the Problem.* Definitions of problems are culture specific and complex. Sue and Zane (1987) argued that defining a problem is a culturally bound activity. Members of a particular cultural group may not agree with the definition of a problem provided by members of the dominant culture (Gold & Bogo, 1992). Green (1982) noted that it is critical to recognize how the client views the problem. Pedersen (1988) explained that each person perceives the world from his or her own cultural point of view, and one skill practitioners can use is to perceive the problem from the client's cultural point of view. The nature of the client's worldviews and values interacts with the behavioral norms that the client has adopted (Mokuau & Shimizu, 1991).

The problems or issues discussed need to be well identified and conceptualized by the client. The school social worker should ask parents or family units what the problem means to them, their family, and their culture. Various cultures have developed their own indigenous models of service, help-seeking behaviors, and belief systems. The school social worker must have or seek knowledge of the array of culturally specific imperatives and responses available in a particular school's ecosystem to understand the client's cultural definition of the problem. These cultural perceptions may then lead to a decision to work with the entire extended family, respected community leaders, and other natural helpers (Morales & Salcido, 1995).

## Working with Interpreters

There are instances in cross-cultural practice when the social worker needs an interpreter to manage communication across language and cultural systems. Because language is the major mechanism for conveying cultural contents and meanings, special attention must always be given to the client's use of language. Even when English is the native language of both the worker and the client, there may be subtle or clear confusion due to regional origins, age, or racial differences. For example, teenagers' use of language may need some "interpretation" in the social work practice situation.

An interpreter is most necessary when the client speaks the worker's language either insufficiently or not at all. Agencies who used interpreters for non-English-speaking clients demonstrated success (Kline, Acosta, Austin, & Johnson, 1980), although in contrast to the clients' high satisfaction ratings, the workers reported feeling ineffective and concerned that they did not accurately convey an understanding of the clients and that the clients would not return for future services. These divergent worker and client perceptions suggest that the interpretation process must convey not only words, but also other types of information to establish relationships among worker, client, and interpreter. Communication of subtle affect and signals for key relationship guideposts such as respect, deference, or attention are subject to a wide range of cultural expression. Body language, despite the popular belief in its universality, may in fact convey quite different meanings in various cultures and is just one of many factors that may contribute to confusion in the interpretation process. Glasser (1983) and Owan et al. (1985) recommended that social workers be sensitive to issues of power and subordination when using interpreters and pointed out that the class and social status of the interpreter and the client may negatively interact in the interpretive process.

*Interpretive Approaches.* Baker (1981) identified two contrasting interpretive approaches he called the verbatim style and the independent intervention. With verbatim style, or instantaneous interpretation, words are translated as closely as possible, and the participation of the interpreter in the content of the interview is kept to a minimum. With independent intervention, on the other hand, the interpreter is a cultural bridge enabling the worker to understand the client's behavior, body language, and perceptions. Allowing the interpreter to take a more active role in the interview process may be productive provided he or she understands the social work process and the purpose of the interview.

Interpretation is more cumbersome when cultural and linguistic differences are greatest. Interpretation of European languages with similar speech forms and worldviews is not as difficult as interpretation between English and Hmong, for example. Because language reflects cultural ideas and worldviews, it is unhelpful to translate verbatim the Hmong phrase "Our ancestors are rejoicing at the rising of the sun and the tea being poured by my mother's sister," which means "You have gained our trust and acceptance as you understand our world and the importance of our forefathers. It's great to see you and you are welcome as a member of our family." In addition, Owan et al. (1985) noted that confidentiality is an unfamiliar concept in many Southeast Asian cultures. In such cultures, talking publicly about taboo subjects might be considered deviant by both client and interpreter. It would be assumed that all public agencies would then know the client's personal business and family history, placing him or her in a dangerous and vulnerable position. Clearly, the interpreter needs considerable skill to convey meaning across both linguistic and cultural systems.

*Preparing for the Interview.* Planning for interpretation (Freed, 1988) is akin to developing a team approach; both social worker and interpreter must understand the purpose and focus of the social work interview and agree on the type of interpretation to be provided. The worker should conduct a briefing with the interpreter before the interview to assess attitudes and characteristics of the interpreter that may affect the interview process. Orienting the interpreter as to the interview's purpose and preparing him or her for content that may be sexual, graphic, or emotionally laden will help him or her function while the clinician directs difficult interviews. Marcos (1979) observed interpreters who compensated for disordered thought and inappropriate affect of clients in client mental status examinations to make their interpretation appear adequate and thereby please the clinicians. Because these interpreters lacked understanding of the purpose of the interview and the nature of the social work process, they were unable to focus on and convey critical information in the interpretation process.

*After the Interview.* After each interview, the social worker should debrief the interpreter to elicit subtle information about the client that may not have emerged during the interpretation process. For example, the interpreter should report if the client did not always make sense or spoke with a particular accent or articulation problem. The interpreter may reveal confusion regarding inappropriate affect, ambivalence, or blunted expression of mood or emotion. The interpreter's observations regarding aspects of the client's language such as baby talk, poor syntax, or difficulty with expression also assist the clinician in formulating a more developed assessment of the client. Using the interpreter as a cultural guide helps the social worker place the client's behaviors in a cultural context. The interpreter can help the social worker understand the norms, expectations, and values of the culture so that the worker can assess the client's functioning in his or her ethnic or cultural community.

*Scarcity of Skilled Interpreters.* Unfortunately, skilled interpreters with ideal characteristics are not always available. When a member of the client's social network, such as a child, neighbor, or relative, is asked to interpret, the social worker must think carefully about the effect on the social and familial functioning of the client. Interviews requiring a minimum of distortion, intense emotional material, or an investigative function are likely to fail if conducted with a family member or friend as the interpreter. Agencies should develop contacts with interpreters in ethnic communities as a development activity to serve targeted linguistic populations.

## CONCLUSION

Cross-cultural social work is anchored in a definition of culture that acknowledges the many dimensions that affect the engagement process with children and families. There is no single American culture, nor is there a single profile that fits all members of any specific cultural group. Knowledge of cultural groups, however, is useful in both engaging with and assessing the unique cultural perspective of clients. To understand the client's worldview, the social worker must consider the client's immigration or migration history and his or her history of interaction with the dominant culture and other powerful groups. School social workers who apply this framework will then view person–environment transactions from a more culturally sensitive standpoint. Understanding of self, including cultural consultation for self-awareness checks, is a necessary adjunct to successful work across cultural systems. Competent practice with culturally diverse clients is an ongoing process of developing self-awareness; increasing one's generic and specific knowledge about cultural groups and their interactions; and sharpening practice skills that facilitate communication and understanding among client, school, and social worker.

## REFERENCES

Allen-Meares, P. (1992). Prevention and cross-cultural perspective: Preparing school social workers for the 21st century. *Social Work in Education, 14,* 3–5.
Baker, N. G. (1981). Social work through an interpreter. *Social Work, 26,* 391–397.
Boyd-Franklin, N. (1989). *Black families in therapy: A multisystems approach.* New York: Guilford Press.
Brown, J. A. (1981). Parent education groups for Mexican-Americans. *Social Work in Education, 3,* 22–31.
Browne, C., & Broderick, A. (1994). Asian and Pacific Island elders: Issues for social work practice and education. *Social Work, 39,* 252–259.
Castex, G. (1994). Providing services to Hispanic/Latino populations: Profiles in diversity. *Social Work, 39,* 288–296.
Chamberlain, P., Davis, J. P., Forgatch, M. S., Frey, J., Patterson, G. R., Ray, J., Rothchild, A., & Trombley, J. (1985). *The therapy process code: A multidimensional system for observing therapist and client interactions.* Eugene: Oregon Social Learning Center.
Curiel, H. (1991). Strengthening family and school bonds in promoting Hispanic children's school performance. In M. Sotomayor (Ed.), *Empowering Hispanic families: A critical issue for the 90's* (pp. 75–95). Milwaukee: Family Service America.
Devore, W., & Schlesinger, E. (1987). *Ethnic-sensitive social work practice* (2nd ed.). Columbus, OH: Merrill.
Fong, R., & Mokuau, N. (1994). Not simply "Asian Americans": Periodical literature review on Asians and Pacific Islanders. *Social Work, 39,* 298–305.
Freed, A. O. (1988). Interviewing through an interpreter. *Social Work, 33,* 315–319.
Gallegos, J. (1984). The ethnic competence model for social work education. In B. W. White (Ed.), *Color in a white society* (pp. 1–9). Silver Spring, MD: National Association of Social Workers.
Gardner, S. (1990, Winter). Failure by fragmentation. *California Tomorrow,* pp. 3–9.
Germain, C. B. (1973). An ecological perspective in casework practice. *Social Casework, 54,* 323–333.

Germain, C. B. (1991). *Human behavior in the social environment: An ecological view.* New York: Columbia University Press.

Glasser, I. (1983). Guidelines for using an interpreter in social work. *Child Welfare, 62,* 468–470.

Goals 2000: Educate America Act, P.L. 103-227, 108 Stat. 125 (1994).

Gold, N., & Bogo, M. (1992). Social work research in a multicultural society: Challenges and approaches. *Journal of Multicultural Social Work, 2*(4), 7–22.

Green, J. (1982). *Cultural awareness in the human services.* Englewood Cliffs, NJ: Prentice Hall.

Ho, M. K. (1992). *Minority children and adolescents in therapy.* Newbury Park, CA: Sage Publications.

Hopps, J. (1982). Oppression based on color [Special issue: Social work and people of color]. *Social Work, 27,* 3–5.

Humm-Delgado, D., & Delgado, M. (1986). Gaining community entree to assess service needs of Hispanics. *Social Casework, 67*(2), 80–89.

Ivey, A. (1977). Cultural expertise: Toward systematic outcome criteria in counseling and psychological education. *Personnel and Guidance Journal, 55,* 296–302.

Ivey, A., & Authier, J. (1978). *Micro counseling.* Springfield, IL: Charles C Thomas.

Kline, F., Acosta, F., Austin, W., & Johnson, R. (1980). The misunderstood Spanish-speaking patient. *American Journal of Psychiatry, 137,* 1530–1633.

Longres, J. (1991). Toward a status model of ethnic-sensitive practice. *Journal of Multicultural Social Work, 1*(1), 41–56.

Los Angeles Unified School District. (1995). *Fall ethnic survey report, Los Angeles Unified School District* (Publication No. 123). Los Angeles: Author.

Lum, D. (1986). *Social work practice and people of color: Process-stage approach.* Monterey, CA: Brooks/Cole.

Marcos, L. (1979). Effects of interpreters on the evaluation of psychopathology in non-English speaking patients. *American Journal of Psychiatry, 136,* 171–174.

Meyer, C. H. (Ed.). (1983). *Clinical social work in the eco-systems perspective.* New York: Columbia University Press.

Mokuau, N. (Ed.). (1991). *Handbook of social services for Asian and Pacific Islanders.* New York: Greenwood Press.

Mokuau, N., & Shimizu, D. (1991). Conceptual framework for social services for Asian and Pacific Islander Americans. In N. Mokuau (Ed.), *Handbook of social services for Asian and Pacific Islanders* (pp. 21–36). New York: Greenwood Press.

Morales, A. T., & Salcido, R. (1995). Social work practice with Mexican Americans. In A. T. Morales & B. W. Shaefor (Eds.), *Social work: A profession of many faces* (7th ed., pp. 527–552). Boston: Allyn & Bacon.

Owan, T. C., Bliatout, B., Lin, K.-M., Liu, W., Nguyen, T. D., & Wong, H. Z. (Eds.). (1985). *Southeast Asian mental health: Treatment, prevention, services, training, and research.* Washington, DC: U.S. Department of Health and Human Services.

Pedersen, R. (1988). *A handbook for developing multicultural awareness.* Alexandria, VA: American Association for Counseling and Development.

*Random House Webster's college dictionary.* (1992). New York: Random House.

Solomon, B. (1976). *Black empowerment: Social work in oppressed communities.* New York: Columbia University Press.

Sue, D., & Sue, D. (1990). *Counseling the culturally different.* New York: John Wiley & Sons.

Sue, S., & Zane, N. (1987). The role of culture and cultural techniques in psychotherapy. *American Psychologist, 42,* 37–45.

Taylor, R. (1994). Minority families in America: An introduction. In R. L. Taylor (Ed.), *Minority families in the United States: A multicultural perspective* (pp. 1–16). Englewood Cliffs, NJ: Prentice Hall.

Zastrow, C., & Kirst-Ashman, K. (1994). *Understanding human behavior and the social environment* (3rd ed.). Chicago: Nelson-Hall.

*A version of this chapter was presented at NASW's Annual Meeting of the Profession, October 1994, Nashville, TN.*

*This chapter was originally published in the July 1995 issue of* Social Work in Education, *Vol. 17, pp. 159–170.*

# 12 Techniques for Assessing Family–School Connections

Carolyn B. Pryor

In March 1994 President Clinton signed into law the Goals 2000: Educate America Act (P.L. 103-227). This act added an important goal to the list adopted by President Bush and the nation's governors in 1990: Every school will promote partnerships that increase parental involvement and participation in promoting the social, emotional, and academic growth of children.

Adoption of this goal came after years of research on the effects of parent involvement on children's education, which has documented repeatedly that parental involvement is critically important in helping children do better in school (Henderson, 1987), go to better schools (Henderson, 1988), stay in school (Coleman, 1987; Hamby, 1992; LeCompte & Dworkin, 1991), and lead drug-free lives (Favorini & Pryor, 1994). Studies have also shown that there are many barriers to the attainment of ideal parent involvement (Chavkin, 1989a, 1989b; Chavkin & Williams, 1989; U.S. Department of Health and Human Services, 1991) that with properly designed programs can sometimes be overcome.

School social workers have a vital interest in these National Educational Goals. Their long history as family–school liaisons provides them with needed knowledge and skills. Social workers have traditionally based their work on a careful assessment of their clients' needs. When the target of intervention becomes the relationships between schools and families, social workers need to use techniques for analyzing the connections between these systems—the attitudes, exchanges, linkages, and alliances that affect the bonds between families and schools.

This article reviews several assessment techniques that a parent involvement team or school improvement committee could implement. Its purpose is to encourage and equip school social workers to serve as leaders in the assessment of family–school connections. Such assessments can lead to effective family involvement projects and better educational experiences for high-risk children and youths.

## METHOD OF INVESTIGATION

Between 1992 and 1994, a colleague and I received a U.S. Department of Education School Personnel Training Grant to initiate Parent Alliances for Student Services (PASS), a program to train teams of school personnel from six high-need school districts to increase parent and community involvement on behalf of high-risk youths. The districts selected were an inner-city alternative school, two urban districts, a highly mobile semirural district, and two rural districts. To evaluate this project, we measured parent involvement and student characteristics before and after the training took place. We also provided training to the partici-pating teams on how to conduct a needs assessment in their school districts, how to use the results to plan innovative parent involvement programs to help youths at risk of dropping out or abusing substances, and how to reassess family–school connections to determine if planned innovations were having a positive impact. These teams consisted of parents, teachers, pupil personnel staff, and administra-tors. Graduate social work students worked with us and the school personnel "partners" to study assessment techniques and develop our own tools for mea-suring family–school connections.

## ASSESSMENT TECHNIQUES

We investigated the following eight methods of assessing family–school rela-tionships: (1) informal observation and discussion; (2) examination of preexist-ing data; (3) review of places, policies, and programs; (4) focus group discus-sion; (5) mailed survey; (6) survey at school; (7) telephone survey; and (8) radio call-in. Each method was evaluated in terms of time, cost, direct and indirect benefits, limitations, resources, and practical tips.

### Informal Observation and Discussion

On the basis of their experiences as they carry out their day-to-day activities, school social workers get strong impressions of how parents feel about the school and how school personnel feel about parents and communicate to them. Their careful observations give them valuable ideas about what is going on in a com-munity. Getting parents and staff who are most knowledgeable about family–school relationships together to pool their ideas about the relationships between families and the school is an important first step in assessing family–school con-nections. What is known and unknown can be identified, and some well-grounded hypotheses can be generated about key factors influencing family–school relations.

In the PASS program, the first year of the two-year program was devoted to training and assessment. Teams attended training sessions jointly, shared their initial impressions about family–school relationships in their districts, received information on assessment techniques, and then planned further assessment activities. Some districts found that preconceived ideas about how to help high-risk youths were built on faulty assumptions and took a very different approach after conducting the family–school assessment.

The informal observation and discussion technique is cost-effective and easy to conduct. No additional funds or skills are needed—only time to come to-gether and talk. In some situations, reasonable new programs can be developed. However, simply relying on impressions is risky because faulty conclusions may be made about parents and the community as a whole. It is a valuable begin-ning technique but needs to be supplemented with others.

### Examination of Pre-existing Data

In preparing for any new program, it is important for the planners to think ahead about how to evaluate the program's success. School social workers can work with other school personnel to identify available data that could be relevant to program goals. These data can provide a baseline, which can be examined again after a new program has been implemented. By creatively using existing data, the cost of elaborate data collection methods can be eliminated (Gabriel & Brinkerhoff, 1990).

Many schools now include the number of parents attending parent–teacher conferences in their Annual Education Report. Additional statistics that school social workers might want to examine are the number of parents using a homework hot line, the number of parents and other adults from the community serving as volunteers in the school, and the number of books on parenting issues in the school library and the frequency with which they are checked out.

If data are not available on items of interest, the social worker could encourage school personnel to start collecting it. Simply asking teachers to keep track of relevant behaviors may increase their awareness of the importance of the activity. For example, if teachers are asked to report how many times each month they telephoned parents to report good news on their child and how many times they called with a negative report, teachers may be motivated to start making "good news" calls.

### Review of Places, Policies, and Programs

To thoroughly assess family–school connections, several important questions need to be answered (some questions are adapted from Allen-Meares, Washington, & Welsh, 1986, pp. 219–220):

- How are parents greeted when they call or visit the school?
- Is there a room set aside in the school building for parents' use that gives them a sense of belonging?
- Does the school state explicitly in all major documents that parents play a key role in the educational process?
- Is there a staff member with explicit responsibility and resources for developing parental involvement?
- What roles are performed by parents throughout the school?
- Which and what combination of linking mechanisms does the school use to communicate with parents (for example, newsletters, principal coffee klatches, "welcome wagons" for new families, and so forth)?
- When parent participation is expected, is adequate concern shown for their needs (including child care, transportation, and convenient time and location)? The needs that form the basis for Glasser's (1984) control theory— fun, freedom, belonging, power, and survival—should be kept in mind as well. Beverages and snacks can help make meetings more enjoyable. In low-income neighborhoods, it may be important to pay parents a stipend for coming to meetings. Door prizes and other rewards have been successfully used for families in some school programs.
- What percentage of parents participate in the following school activities: parent–teacher conferences, disciplinary meetings with administrators, prevention task force, advisory board, athletic events, parent education classes, school board, curriculum committee, school–community organizations,

school and class visitation, fundraising, prevention-focused student activities?

- How representative are the parents who participate in school activities of the parents as a whole? What special efforts, if any, are made to get underrepresented students' parents to participate? What is being done to sensitize staff to the needs and concerns of the underrepresented students and parents?
- How are other community individuals and groups brought into the activities of the school? How do they use the building? Are they invited to be represented at school meetings?
- What are the diverse family and community values regarding education and the school?

The process of gathering this information may help school personnel become more aware of the structures and situations that help or hinder parent involvement. This type of assessment can be done with a team or committee of current staff and parent volunteers without additional cost. It can also be useful for team development. However, this quantitative data will not give investigators the reasons for the behaviors measured. Other techniques are needed for this.

## Focus Group Discussion

Focus groups have become a popular way for determining consumers' reactions to products and can be valuable in any assessment process (Morgan, 1988; Stewart & Shamdasani, 1990). Focus groups bring together small groups of people representing a population of concern to the investigators to give their opinions and reactions to topics and questions. Schools have tried focus groups for various purposes with mixed results. Focus groups work best when the groups are relatively homogeneous. They produce more information, insights, and ideas than individual interviews. Levels of participation in the groups can be improved by scheduling them at a time and place convenient for parents. Providing food, child care, and transportation also encourages participation.

Although conducting focus groups requires some expenditures, this technique sends the message that the district really wants parent input. Also, parents appreciate the opportunity to be heard. Regional Education Service Agencies (RESAs) may have personnel available to help local districts with this process and guidelines for effective use of focus groups. Newsprint, audiotapes, and videotapes provide information that can be analyzed. Those who participate also find it very interesting to learn the views of their peers.

Among the questions that could be asked in parent focus groups are the following: How do parents feel about the roles they are given to play in their children's education? about school programs to prevent the misuse of alcohol and other drugs? about the chances of their children getting the education they need? What do they perceive as barriers to greater parental involvement?

Focus groups could also be used effectively with teachers and students. Teachers could be asked what they see as barriers to greater parent involvement and what would they like to have done about these barriers? Students can also share their views about how greater family involvement in their education could be obtained and how they feel about that involvement.

Focus groups take time and require some output for incentives, but we found that the participants really liked the experience. The recorded dialogue's content can be analyzed in retrospect by objective investigators.

A problem with focus groups is that despite elaborate preparations by the school, frequently only 15 percent to 25 percent of the parents who say they will come to a focus group session show up. One of our trainers reported that when she tried doing focus groups, 19 parents said they would come. Dinner was provided, but only three parents showed up. On another occasion, 400 parents were expected for a conference, but 15 showed up. This can be disheartening and can reinforce negative stereotypes of parents. It is important to anticipate the turnout problem. Leaders need to have a way to manage a full turnout but avoid embarrassment if a small percentage show up.

## Mailed Survey

Mailing a survey to the home can work reasonably well. Several techniques can be used to increase the response rate, such as second and third mailings to those who have not responded. Processing and analyzing the data can be time consuming and expensive, but support may be available from universities or RESAs. Useful and well-developed surveys are available from the Center on Families, Communities, Schools and Children's Learning of the Johns Hopkins University (Epstein, Connors, & Salinas, 1992) and the San Diego County Office of Education (Chrispeels, Boruta, & Daugherty, 1988). The National Committee for Citizens in Education has developed a manual, *Taking Stock* (Berla, Garlington, & Henderson, 1992), designed to help school personnel learn what parents and families, teachers and community members, the principal, and other school staff think about the relationship between a school and its families. They also provide instructions to help a group of volunteers get together, tally the results, and come up with an action plan. The questions are slanted to make respondents aware of the value of parent involvement.

One advantage to a mailed survey is that uniform measures and procedures can be implemented and results can be reported with scientific accuracy. Another advantage is that the results can be compared with studies done in other schools and communities. If the school population is large, a random sample and sound research methods can give a good estimate of parents' attitudes and behaviors while containing costs.

## Survey at School

Sending a survey home with students works effectively when surveys are brightly and attractively packaged and when students see direct personal benefits if surveys are filled out and returned (personal communication with Alice McCarthy, president, Bridge Communications, Birmingham, MI, May 1993). Another dollar-saving option is to have parents who attend school events fill out a survey. However, if the parents who come to school are not representative of the relevant parent population, the results will be of limited value. Surveys of teachers and students, of course, can most efficiently be done in school. Ensuring the confidentiality of their responses is essential to obtain valid information.

An extensive set of questions about school–community relations that we found useful for developing a teacher questionnaire is found in *Open Schools, Healthy Schools* (Hoy, Tarter, & Kottkamp, 1991). The authors of this thought-provoking book are concerned that too much openness to the community interferes with the mission of the school.

### Telephone Survey

School personnel report that having a trained person telephone parents to find out their views provides helpful information. A random selection of parents to be phoned can be used. In our project, we developed separate questionnaires for parents, students, and teachers and mailed them to homes. We then had a parent call and invite parents who did not return the survey to a focus group session, where they had another opportunity to fill out the survey. Some parents who neither mailed back the survey nor came to the focus groups were contacted by phone and interviewed. We found that interviewing by phone is a time-efficient and cost-effective technique. It is probably a more effective way to reach insecure parents or parents with reading problems than a mailed survey. However, if a number of parents do not have phones or listed phone numbers, there could be a problem. In comparison to focus groups, interviewees do not get the benefit of hearing what others have to say. This limitation can be offset by making the results of the survey available to all participants.

### Radio Call-In

The school district of Saginaw, Michigan, uses radio announcements effectively to inform the public of its Parent Resource Center. The center director, Pari Mikalski, suggested that a radio call-in talk show could be a catchy way to do an assessment of how parents and community members feel about the school. Because talk shows are so popular now, why not use this technique to reach busy people and develop a dialogue about the need for student services in schools? We did not try this idea but believe it is creative and has potential. It could serve as a stimulus for greater involvement and scientific assessment.

## DATA ANALYSIS

Once data have been collected, they have to be processed and analyzed. A team approach to data analysis and interpretation of findings is important. RESA staff, community leaders, and university faculty are desirable assistants and consultants. They will have access to computer programs that can help with the analysis of quantitative and qualitative data. School social workers and school administrators can work with research experts to meaningfully interpret the findings.

A conceptual model can be valuable in analyzing and presenting the results. Compher's (1982) clinically based triadic assessment of parent, child, and school interaction, which describes patterns of passive entanglement, aggressive entanglement, and adaptive response, provides a useful framework. Once an analysis of possible causes and effects of attitudes and behavior of family, child, school, and community have been mapped out, interventions to improve connections and interaction can be planned.

To interpret the data collected, it is also valuable to conduct an analysis of neighborhood and community characteristics. Melaville and Blank (1993) described the neighborhood analysis in their useful book *Together We Can: A Guide for Crafting a Profamily System of Education and Human Services*. They stated that a neighborhood analysis should consider the following:

- history, racial, and ethnic composition
- cultural and language diversity
- primary risk factors of its children and families
- neighborhood assets
- locations of services
- key community leaders or potential advocates.

## HELPFUL REPORTS

Findings from other schools may shed light on what is happening in a given district. Some interesting reports are in a book edited by Chavkin (1993), *Families and Schools in a Pluralistic Society*. For example, Dauber and Epstein (1993) reported that parents' level of involvement is directly linked to specific school practices, and Chavkin and Williams (1993) reported that parents and educators concur on the importance of parent involvement in education. In another recent publication, Connors and Epstein (1994) reported the results of their surveys of high school students, parents, and teachers. They found a shared vision of partnership, similarity in goals, a strong desire on the part of parents for information they can use at home to assist with their child's education, and student desire for well-designed and implemented family involvement practices.

A well-written report of carefully collected findings can not only help schools plan effectively, but also be shared with others and add to the knowledge and resources available to all people working to improve America's schools.

## ROLES FOR SOCIAL WORKERS

School social workers can perform many valuable roles in the assessment process. The task of assessing family–school connections will be most effective when conducted as a team effort. Social workers can use skills as leaders and administrators to bring key people together to work on the task. Social workers are links to parents. They can be helpful in getting parents who have not previously participated in school governance involved. Social workers are also nonjudgmental communicators and listeners. Parents, youths, and teachers who have not been heard in the school may respond well to school social workers' efforts to elicit their ideas and make their voices heard. Social workers can organize parent volunteers, contact other parents, and analyze findings. They can be resource brokers by linking the school with resources for assessing needs related to parent partnerships, such as the U.S. Department of Education, experts on assessment at RESAs, and university faculty from related disciplines.

Social workers can be trainers of focus group facilitators or even serve as facilitators themselves. They also have an important role to play as reporters, making the findings known to people in positions to bring about change. And social workers can serve as advocates by working to ensure that no families are denied opportunities to participate as partners with schools.

## OUTCOMES AND DISCUSSION

A sound assessment of family–school connections can identify strengths and needs and lead to appropriate and well-received intervention programs. In the PASS program, several highly effective family involvement projects resulted. An inner-city alternative school hired parents as aides to ride school buses and gave parents stipends to attend classes on parenting issues. One urban district trained a record number of parents to be drug education leaders. Another large urban district expanded its Parent Resource Center programs to include families of middle-school students and provided parenting classes led by school social workers for every elementary school. A semirural district started a Jump Start program for incoming middle-school students and their families, a community newspaper column on family–school issues, and classes for "grandparents as parents." A rural school discontinued lumping high-risk middle-school students onto a single track, and instead staff interviewed parents in their homes to determine their students' learning styles and ideal classroom program. Parents were also given scholarships to participate in field trips with students. Another rural district hired a parent to coordinate parent involvement and substance abuse prevention activities designed to address concerns of students and parents.

All six teams of school personnel that participated in the PASS program felt energized by the experience. The time spent together and planning as teams in an educational program, the money available through the program to support innovations, and the inspiration provided by others' success contributed to the implementation of effective parent–school activities. However, assessment was a vital part of the overall process.

## CONCLUSION

Because of the complexity of the subject and the importance of the task, it is best to use a combination of techniques to assess family–school connections. These techniques can bring a variety of perspectives to the task. Financial resources will dictate how extensive an assessment can be. The amount of time and effort put into the assessment should be proportional to the anticipated total cost of improvement projects. Quality assessments have a price, which, unfortunately, the public may not be willing to pay. However, a talented and dedicated team can produce sound results within a modest budget.

School social workers have many skills that can help schools attain greater parental involvement. By broadening and strengthening their skills in social study and diagnosis, they can become experts in assessing family–school–community relationships. Quality assessments will help ensure quality parent involvement programs, improved schools, and a better education for all children.

## REFERENCES

Allen-Meares, P., Washington, R. O., & Welsh, B. L. (1986). *Social work services in schools.* Englewood Cliffs, NJ: Prentice Hall.

Berla, N., Garlington, J., & Henderson, A. T. (1992). *Taking stock: The inventory of family, community and school support for student achievement.* Washington, DC: National Committee for Citizens in Education.

Chavkin, N. F. (1989a, Summer). Debunking the myth about minority parents. *Educational Horizons,* pp. 119–123.

Chavkin, N. F. (1989b). A multicultural perspective on parent involvement: Implications for policy and practice. *Education, 109,* 276–285.

Chavkin, N. F. (Ed.). (1993). *Families and schools in a pluralistic society.* New York: State University of New York Press.

Chavkin, N. F., & Williams, D. L., Jr. (1989). Low-income parents' attitudes toward parent involvement in education. *Journal of Sociology & Social Welfare, 16,* 17–28.

Chavkin, N. F., & Williams, D. L., Jr. (1993). Minority parents and the elementary school: Attitudes and practices. In N. F. Chavkin (Ed.), *Families and schools in a pluralistic society* (pp. 73–83). New York: State University of New York Press.

Chrispeels, J., Boruta, M., & Daugherty, M. (1988). *Communicating with parents.* San Diego, CA: San Diego County Office of Education.

Coleman, J. S. (1987). *Public and private high schools: The impact of communities.* New York: Basic Books.

Compher, J. (1982). Parent–school–child systems: Triadic assessment and intervention. *Social Casework, 63,* 415–423.

Connors, L. J., & Epstein, J. L. (1994, August). *Taking stock: Views of teachers, parents, and students on school, family, and community partnerships in high schools* (Report No. 25). Baltimore: Johns Hopkins University, Center on Families, Communities, Schools and Children's Learning.

Dauber, S. L., & Epstein, J. L. (1993). Parents' attitudes and practices of involvement in inner-city elementary and middle schools. In N. F. Chavkin (Ed.), *Families and schools in a pluralistic society* (pp. 53–71). New York: State University of New York Press.

Epstein, J., Connors, L. J., & Salinas, K. C. (1992). *Surveys of school and family partnerships: Questions for teachers, parents and students.* Baltimore: Johns Hopkins University, Center on Families, Communities, Schools and Children's Learning, Dissemination Office.

Favorini, A., & Pryor, C. (1994). Family–school alliances: A centerpiece strategy for alcohol and drug prevention programs. *Social Work in Education, 16,* 155–170.

Gabriel, R. M., & Brinkerhoff, C. (1990). *Developing a community profile: A handbook for using pre-existing data in prevention planning.* Portland, OR: Northwest Regional Educational Laboratory.

Glasser, W. (1984). *Control theory.* New York: Harper & Row.

Goals 2000: Educate America Act, P.L. 103-227, 108 Stat. 125 (1994).

Hamby, J. V. (1992). The school–family link: A key to dropout prevention. In L. Kaplan (Ed.), *Education and the family* (pp. 54–68). Boston: Allyn & Bacon.

Henderson, A. (1987). *The evidence continues to grow: Parent involvement improves student achievement: An annotated bibliography.* Washington, DC: National Committee for Citizens in Education.

Henderson, A. (1988). Parents are a school's best friends. *Phi Delta Kappan, 69,* 149–153.

Hoy, W. K., Tarter, C. J., & Kottkamp, R. B. (1991). *Open schools, healthy schools: Measuring organizational climate.* Newbury Park, CA: Sage Publications.

LeCompte, M. D., & Dworkin, A. G. (1991). *Giving up on school: Student dropouts and teacher burnouts.* Newbury Park, CA: Corwin Press.

Melaville, A. I., & Blank, M. J., with Asayesh, G. (1993). *Together we can: A guide for crafting a profamily system of education and human services.* Washington, DC: U.S. Government Printing Office.

Morgan, D. L. (1988). *Focus groups as qualitative research.* Newbury Park, CA: Sage Publications.

Stewart, D. W., & Shamdasani, P. N. (1990). *Focus groups: Theory and practice.* Newbury Park, CA: Sage Publications.

U.S. Department of Health and Human Services. (1991). *Parent training is prevention: Preventing alcohol and other drug problems among youth in the family.* Washington, DC: U.S. Government Printing Office.

*A technical report describing the PASS project and its outcomes in detail is available from the author. A video for use in promoting effective parent involvement on behalf of high-risk youths and a companion training manual are also available from the author at reproduction and mailing costs.*

*This chapter was originally published in the April 1996 issue of* Social Work in Education, *Vol. 18, pp. 85–93.*

# 13 Socialization Issues for Chinese American Children and Families

Rowena Fong and David Y. H. Wu

The United States is an increasingly multicultural country. In every region the influx of immigrants and refugees from Latin America, the Caribbean, Asia, and the Pacific; the rapidly increasing rate of interracial marriages; and the constant movement of people within the country bring together many varieties of people who had little or no contact in the past. This multicultural reality makes the task of the social worker and the social work educator more complicated. Understanding culture and social environments is a prerequisite for culturally competent practice in schools, services, and communities.

In social work education, there is a strong emphasis on the need to understand human behavior in the context of social environments (Brooks, 1986; Germain, 1991; Sze, Keller, & Keller, 1979). Typically, the focus is on examining biophysical, psychological, social, economic, and cultural components of human behavior; issues in human development from child socialization to gerontology; and other key ecological factors such as class, gender, and ethnicity. School social workers must be sensitive to issues in ethnic diversity such as race, oppression, and discrimination at the macro level and ethnically different families at the micro level (Longres, 1990; Zastrow & Kirst-Ashman, 1994). Some multicultural content has been emphasized in the areas of recent immigrants and refugee resettlement issues (Longres, 1990).

However, what is lacking is the exploration of any single culture and the impact of varying political and social environments on that culture. There is some analytical and comparative breadth but hardly any depth, particularly on any single ethnic group, in the area of multiculturalism and understanding human behavior in the social environment (Ishisaka & Takagi, 1981).

When examining issues related to culturally competent practice, criticism has been directed against social workers and other practitioners for not integrating macro-level issues with micro-level issues (Brooks, 1986; Fong, in press; Fong & Mokuau, 1994). Lacking is the understanding of individual functioning that comes in part from understanding the values that operate on a macro societal level, particularly with respect to non-European ethnic groups (Devore & Schlesinger, 1987; Furuto, Biswas, Chung, Murase, & Ross-Sheriff, 1992; Lum, 1996).

Some recent literature has called for detailed treatment of separate ethnic groups (Fong & Mokuau, 1994; Uba, 1994). However, little has yet been written on the changing environmental effect of different social environments on a single ethnic group. Some efforts have been made in the social work education literature on human behavior in the social environment (HBSE) to include discussion and examples of ethnic groups at the macro and mezzo levels (Germain, 1991; Longres, 1990; Pillari, 1988; Zastrow & Kirst-Ashman, 1994). However, no single ethnic group is covered in much depth, and the subgroups within ethnic groups are not examined.

It is important to acknowledge that not all ethnicities are homogeneous and that within a single group there may be differences, some contributed by the social and political environments. The HBSE literature needs to go beyond generalizations about dealing with ethnically diverse clients to provide social workers with sufficient information about each ethnic group so that they can become competent to serve that ethnic population.

This article focuses on one American ethnic group, the Chinese. The Chinese are one of the fastest growing non-European ethnic populations in the United States and represent the largest percentage of the Asian American population— 22.6 percent (Uba, 1994; U.S. Bureau of the Census, 1990). Chinese culture provides a good example of the effect of social and environmental differences on human behavior. There are several kinds of Chinese Americans. For example, families that immigrated from the People's Republic of China (PRC) before 1979 typically have several children. More recent immigrants from the PRC, because of the introduction of the single-child policy in 1979, usually have just one child; nuclear and extended family dynamics are different, and "spoiling" may be an issue (Fong, 1990). Other Chinese families come from Hong Kong, Taiwan, or Singapore. Still others have lived in the United States for four or five generations.

There are commonalities among all these groups of Chinese Americans, but there are also distinct differences in their cultural and social environments. As the Chinese immigrant population increases in the United States, it is important for social workers to know about their original cultural environments to understand the effect of these environments on client behaviors and to apply culturally competent practices when dealing with Chinese American children and families. One important issue that Chinese American cultures present to social workers in schools or in social services agencies is the socialization of children.

## SOCIALIZATION OF CHILDREN

Socialization is the process by which an individual learns "'proper' (as defined by the society) ways of acting in a culture" (Zastrow & Bowker, 1984, p. 25). Analyses of socialization usually focus on the goals of socialization, the agents, the process, and the outcomes. This article considers the four main socialization environments that have shaped members of the Chinese American population: traditional China, the People's Republic of China, the PRC in the era of communist decline, and Chinese American communities. There are other environments for socialization, such as Taiwan and Singapore, but the four in this article indicate the range of Chinese socialization environments. Social workers need to know the common characteristics of Chinese Americans and also the ways these four Chinese populations differ from one another. With respect to each population, this article describes the goals of parents in the socialization of children, the primary agents of socialization, the process of socialization, and the desired outcomes of socialization. Finally, the article considers the practice implications of macro-level environment impact on micro-level behavior and the need for further attention in social work education.

## Traditional China

Chinese culture has been dominated by Confucianism, which emphasizes principles of interpersonal relationships. The most important is filial piety. Filial piety dictates how children behave toward parents, how younger people behave toward elders, and how family members behave toward one another (Hsu, 1981; Shon & Ja, 1982). The expectations set up by filial piety affect parent socialization of children.

*Goals.* The goals of socialization in the traditional Chinese orientation are somewhat different according to gender and sibling order. However, general goals are to socialize children to bring honor to the family name, to be respectful to the elder generation, and to be obedient and responsible to the parents' household (Fong, 1990; Wolf, 1978). Boys are socialized to bear the family name and to be heads of their extended families. The eldest son, particularly, is groomed to follow in the footsteps of the father or grandfather, whoever was more prestigious. Sons are socialized to do great things for the sake of the family name. Daughters are socialized to be virtuous women and to marry well. Traditionally, girls were of greatest value if they knew how to cook, bear sons, and serve their mothers-in-law well (Andors, 1983; Croll, 1978).

*Agents.* In the traditional Chinese family, the mother is the main socialization agent. She is responsible for training and raising well-behaved children who have proper Chinese etiquette *(you limao)*. Extended family members—sisters-in-law, aunts, and grandmothers—are also included in the circle of social reinforcers. The women socialize boys and girls. When the boys reach their teenage years, the men take over the socializing duties (Wolf, 1978). According to this traditional orientation, young men need to know the ways of the world and the expectations of male duties of honoring male ancestors, defending the family name, and providing economic security for three generations: their own, their parents', and their grandparents'. Many traditional Chinese households, even in modern cities with mixed cultures such as Singapore and Hong Kong, contain three or more generations in one living unit or close by one another.

*Process.* The process of socialization is dictated by Chinese cultural norms and behaviors. Traditional Chinese parents teach the children through moralizing and shaming (Shon & Ja, 1982; Wolf, 1978). Mothers explain to their children the expected behaviors, such as being polite to Chinese relatives and addressing them by the name of their social position in the family—for example, First Elder Paternal Aunt. However, if the children fail to follow this behavior, they are publicly shamed by the parent, who will chastise them for not having proper Chinese manners *(ni mei you limao)*. In private the child will receive further criticism from other female family members, depending on the degree of the offense. If the offense is great, such as making derogatory remarks about an older person in front of that person, thus causing that person to lose face, the child or youth will be not only criticized but also possibly beaten and given a long, loud, moralizing lecture on how the child has endangered the harmony between families (Hsu, 1981; Wolf, 1978).

*Desired Outcome.* The result of socializing children in the traditional orientation is to make them behave properly so that they will respect elders, show proper manners toward adults, and avoid making comments that cause their own family or another family to lose face. The majority of these traditional values of socialization of Chinese children are evident in the families who come from social and political environments that still uphold these values, such as Hong Kong, Taiwan, Singapore, or Malaysia, where Confucianism still has a major effect. These traditional values may be found even in the United States, where first-generation Chinese adults reside with the family and still have an effect on child-rearing values and practices.

Social workers need to keep the traditional child-rearing model in mind when working with clients whose problems include adolescent conflicts with identity because of loyalty issues or problems with achievement because of authority dilemmas among bilingual children (Hsu, 1981; Sue & Chin, 1983).

## People's Republic of China, 1949 to 1979

Traditional values were strongly challenged when Confucianism was officially replaced with communism. After the Communist Revolution of 1949, under a rapidly developing socialist value system, Confucianist values of putting the family first and being concerned about the family's face were replaced by the expectation of primary loyalty to the state (Parish & Whyte, 1978; Yang, 1959). Chinese people who grew up in this period and have since come to the United States are likely to show the effects of this state-oriented value system, along with (and sometimes with internal conflict with) the remnants of the Confucian value system. Chinese culture under communism was guided by the state's dictates for the relationships between people. The motherland and the achievement of socialism were supposed to come before the family. The slogan "serve the people" was the cornerstone philosophy for nationwide reform, and it was a hallmark slogan of child socialization (Chin, 1988; Cleverly, 1985). The state was an overpowering entity, superior to parents and family and able to trump all their desires. In raising their children, parents were supposed to adopt the goals of the state (Kessen, 1975).

*Goals.* Unlike those of traditional China, the child-rearing goals of the People's Republic did not officially differ by gender; they were supposedly the same for boys and girls. These goals included becoming good communist cadres or young pioneers, putting the needs of the state first, being cooperative in work or play, being a responsible and contributing group member, and helping the playmate or classmate with no expectation of return or obligation (Kessen, 1975; Sidel, 1982).

*Agents.* The main socialization agents for children were the schools, because parents were expected to contribute to the state by working (Cleverly, 1985; Gamberg, 1977; Unger, 1982). Teachers played a major role in teaching boys and girls how to be cooperative and productive group members. Individual desires were not encouraged. Parents reinforced the teaching of the schools at home.

Extended family members did not play as significant a role, because there was no longer the expectation that all family members would be under one roof. Family members were assigned jobs in any part of China where they were most needed by the state. Neighbors became surrogate family members and helped reinforce the rules and expectations of the schools, which were dictated by state policies and socialist values.

*Process.* Socializing children in the PRC relied heavily on role modeling and group pressure. Teachers were the role models in the classroom. Sometimes legendary figures—communist heroes (or heroines) such as Lei Fung, who literally worked himself to death serving the people—were used as examples of how children should behave (Heng & Shapiro, 1983; Schurmann, 1968; Wilkinson, 1973). If a child disobeyed, the teacher would use the peer group to put pressure on the individual child to conform, for example, by having the whole class wait for the misbehaving individual to sit quietly before the class could eat lunch or go out for recess. In the home, social reinforcers such as parents repeating the teacher's words or threatening to tell the teachers were combined with shaming, moralizing, and inducing guilt (Fong, 1990).

*Desired Outcome.* The desired outcome of socializing children in the PRC was to produce obedient, productive, cooperative, state-oriented group members. Boys and girls were to be socialized equally in goals, process, and outcome. Socialization to these goals began at an early age and continued even through adulthood, with the expectation that the needs of the state would always come first.

*Remnants of Traditional Values.* The older Chinese value system did not suddenly disappear. There remained a strong undercurrent of family orientation despite all the emphasis on loyalty to the state. And the roles of men and women did not immediately become equal, despite official ideology (Andors, 1983; Croll, 1978; Johnson, 1983). Yet it is remarkable how thoroughly the communist regime suppressed traditional values and substituted new ones using fairly coercive methods during the Anti-Rightist Campaign of 1957–58 and the Cultural Revolution of 1966–76 (Heng & Shapiro, 1983; G. Yuan, 1987). Some traditional values, such as obedience and conformity, remained, only to be transferred from family to state. Other values, such as putting family first, were pushed beneath the surface and did not reappear until after 1979.

## People's Republic of China, 1979 to Present

Putting the needs of the state before oneself and family began to be challenged after 1979 when two things happened. First, the state began to retreat from socialist principles of economics and social organization, and second, it instituted a single-child policy (Croll, Davin, & Kane, 1985). To try to hold the population at 1 billion people, in 1979 the Chinese government limited most married couples to having one child. In this period of rapid social and economic change, with state support systems crumbling, parents with only one child began to put their needs or the child's needs ahead of the state's (L. Yuan, 1987; Zhang, 1986). The single-child policy has been better implemented in urban than rural areas and has been revised to include exceptions for members of various ethnic groups, parents who themselves are only children, and parents whose only child has a disability (Chen, 1985; Croll et al., 1985).

*Goals.* The single-child policy has had a dramatic effect on the socialization of children. The communist goals of socializing children to be productive, cooperative, state-oriented group members have been challenged by the existence of only children. Single children today are the focal point of two parents and four grandparents, who tend to focus on the child, not the state.

The goals of only-child parents are not always the same as the state's goals of raising productive workers and party members (Fong, 1990). Parents are concerned about their own welfare and whether the only child will respect them and care for them in their old age (state support for elderly people is very limited) (Chan, 1993). As a result, parents tend to indulge the child, with the indirect goal that, when the child is an adult, he or she will in return indulge and care for the parents in their old age (Tobin, Wu, & Davidson, 1989). This indulgence is exacerbated by the lack of opportunity for parents to socialize the child to be cooperative, because there are no other siblings in the home with whom to interact.

*Agents.* Teachers are no longer the primary socialization agents in one-child China. Even though they still work, parents play a greater role in socializing their only child. Parents sometimes disagree with the manner in which the teachers are socializing their child (Fong, 1990; Tobin et al., 1989). If the grandparents live in the vicinity of the grandchild, they will also take part in socializing the child, often contributing to spoiling the child by buying sweets and material goods. This may cause conflicts between parents and grandparents or, more commonly, between schools and grandparents (Fong, 1990).

*Process.* The process of socializing the only child is more complex when teachers and parents or grandparents disagree on the goals. Disagreement on goals often leads to criticism of the process. Teachers are criticized for not giving enough individual attention to the children, who are used to receiving lots of attention at home. The teacher's expectation for the only child to conform in groups is challenged by the parental argument that the individual gifts and talents of the only child cannot be realized if he or she must conform to the group. Teachers find themselves defending themselves to parents rather than receiving support from parents (Fong, 1990; Vaughan, 1993).

*Desired Outcome.* The outcome of socializing only children in the PRC is twofold: (1) Teachers often still want only children to become productive, cooperative young pioneers, and (2) parents want their only children to achieve their potential, be happy, and take care of the parents in the parents' old age (Fong, 1990). In the single-child PRC, traditional values and socialist state values are clashing. Recent immigrants to the United States from the People's Republic of China may bring this clash of values with them. Social workers in schools and in social services agencies may see Chinese parents from China torn between wanting the best for their only child, which may border on spoiling (Fong, 1990); wanting the only child to care for them in their old age; and wanting the child to adjust to the United States and become independent and self-sufficient. All of this may at times produce tension and conflict.

## Chinese American Communities

The socialization of Chinese children in the United States depends on the time and place of the family's arrival in this country. From the time Chinese immigrants first arrived in the United States in the 1850s to the aftermath of World War II, Chinese Americans experienced much discrimination but kept up the traditional values of honoring and respecting elders, keeping the family name unblemished, and marrying to have sons for worshipping the ancestors (Fong, 1992; Takaki, 1989). The family socialized children with traditional Chinese values, counting not on extended family members but on people from the same clan or village to help socialize the child and to maintain Chinese values in this country. As generations passed, kinship networks built up in the United States similar to those in China. Since World War II, however, there has been a decline in anti-Chinese discrimination and a decided trend in the American-born generations toward American norms such as the nuclear family and individual achievement.

Socialization of Chinese children has also been affected by place. U.S. cities that had large Chinese populations, such as San Francisco, New York, Chicago, Seattle, and Boston, had Chinatowns where traditional Chinese values were expected. In a survey of San Francisco's Chinatown, 60 percent of residents reported that it was very important for Chinese children to learn the language and culture (Loo, 1991).

*Goals.* The goals of socializing Chinese children in the United States were a mix of the American values of independence, self-realization, assertiveness, and equality between the sexes and the Chinese values of harmony, respect, male dominance, and obedience to authority figures. This situation sometimes causes Chinese American children to experience frustration, alienation, and situations of self-doubt and low self-esteem (Huang & Ying, 1990; Sue & Chin, 1983).

*Agents.* The agents for socializing children depended on the degree of acculturation to the United States. First- and second-generation families may have depended more on extended family members, whereas third- or fourth-generation Chinese Americans included neighbors or day care centers and after-school programs to help socialize the children. Within the structured school settings, Chinese children were also likely to be influenced by peers and the media, which were likely to introduce the child to adjustment- and socialization-related issues such as divorce, blended family situations, and violence in the home.

*Process.* The process of socializing Chinese children in the United States has also depended largely on the degree of acculturation among family members. First- and second-generation immigrants were more likely to maintain Chinese methods of shaming the child for not conforming or not obeying. By contrast, third- or fourth-generation Chinese Americans may resort more to the American way of talking to the child and establishing rewards and consequences or removal of privileges as means to socialize the child.

*Desired Outcome.* The outcomes of socializing a Chinese child in the United States are to develop and encourage the child to be self-confident, self-realized, and a high achiever according to American standards. But these standards depend on the degree of acculturation of the family and child to American society. Uba (1994) asserted, "It seems that as succeeding generations of Asian Americans become acculturated, their child-rearing practices become more like those of most American families" (p. 13).

The more acculturated the family, the more tension there may be for some families in integrating values of American independence and Chinese mutual dependence or American equality and Chinese hierarchical sexism. Hsu (1981) summarized the conflict between American and Chinese parent–child interactions as follows: "The important thing to Americans is what parents do for their children; to Chinese, what children do for their parents" (p. 80).

## IMPLICATIONS FOR CULTURALLY SENSITIVE SOCIAL WORK

Knowledge of the differing environments for socializing Chinese and Chinese American children has several practice implications for social workers:

- There are many varieties of Chinese Americans from many social environments.
- Immigrants and refugees may have different perspectives.
- There are some Chinese cultural norms common to all environments.
- There are differences in expectations of child socialization across different populations.

### Diversity among Chinese Americans

It is important for social workers, counselors, and teachers to recognize the differences among the various Chinese clients they may encounter. There is enormous diversity and complexity within the population called Chinese Americans, as suggested by the four socialization models laid out in the first half of this article. School social workers need to study the history of China and the perceptions that Chinese people have of themselves to work effectively with this population.

China is as large in land area as Europe and much larger in population; it possesses a similar variety of cultural groups. Although China's government has for many centuries tried to blend the country's many peoples, the blending has not been complete (Fong & Spickard, 1994; Gladney, 1991). In modern Chinese countries (including Taiwan) both the government and intellectuals have spent a great deal of time and energy trying to forge an image of a unified, homogenous Chinese people (in race and culture) and nation-state (Wu, 1991). The reality is far from this image. Ethnic prejudice and discrimination by one Chinese group against another are common practices in Chinese social life, especially in major cities where migrant communities, such as merchant groups or craftsmen, are formed.

Almost all Chinese citizens use a common written language, but there are many distinct regional dialects. Similarly, there are many regional variations on national patterns of child socialization. There is a strong Chinese national identity, but regional and ethnic subidentities are also strong (Honig, 1992; Wu, 1991). For example, there is a subtle difference between people from Cantonese-speaking southern China and people from Mandarin-speaking northern China. For a school social worker to refer a Cantonese-speaking family to a Mandarin-speaking counselor is about as helpful as sending a German-speaking family to an Italian-speaking counselor.

## Immigrants and Refugees

It is also important to distinguish between immigrants and refugees. According to Longres (1990), immigrants "take up stakes, more or less voluntarily, in one national society and migrate to another land, where they become part of a new national society" (p. 101). By contrast, refugees are people who have no choice and leave their homelands involuntarily under coercion with no guarantee of ethnic or cultural survival (Timberland & Cook, 1984; Trueba, Jacobs, & Kirton, 1990). This distinction is important because what people have experienced before coming to the United States and under what circumstances they have come greatly affect their adjustment to their new social environment.

Immigrants have experienced many sorts of difficulty but generally have plans and hopes that compensate for their pains. Refugees have experienced much trauma in leaving their country in addition to settling into a new life; they often have to deal with extremely stressful issues, such as separating from or trying to locate family members (Huang, 1990; Land, Nishimoto, & Chau, 1988).

Immigrants from coastal urban centers with strong capitalist economies and changing social structures and relationships bring with them a legacy of social striving and instability; most recent Chinese immigrants have come from such rapidly changing places. By contrast, immigrants who come in much smaller numbers from rural stable provinces are less likely to be skilled in the highly competitive ways of capitalist economies, and their families are more likely to approximate traditional norms.

Recent Chinese immigrants from Hong Kong are different yet again. More of them speak at least some English because of a century and a half of British colonialism. Many Hong Kong immigrants are fleeing the chaos they anticipate will overtake their homeland after reversion to rule by the People's Republic. Hirayama and Cetingok (1988) observed that social workers can empower Asian immigrants by supplying them with "power resources," defined as information about "money, housing, health care, and education" (p. 44). As social workers and educators in schools interact with Chinese American children and families, it is essential that they know the distinctions between native-born and immigrant, between immigrant and refugee, between immigrants from Hong Kong and from the People's Republic, and between people from different parts of the PRC and other parts of the Chinese world.

## Similar Cultural Norms

Despite the diversity among the different kinds of Chinese Americans, there are certain commonalities based on Chinese cultural norms; in all types of Chinese environments there are some similarities in beliefs about valuing children, placing the family first, and fulfilling obligations. Chinese people in all environments place a high value on children and put great burdens and expectations on them.

Each Chinese society has always placed a high value on the family system and the need for children to perpetuate the family line and bring honor to its name. In Chinese families the role of the individual is established in the context of the family. A social worker who singles out an individual—adult or child—may cause discomfort if the value of family has been ingrained (Ho, 1992; Lee, 1982; Shon & Ja, 1982). The family, not the individual, is the proper unit of analysis and treatment in dealing with Chinese clients. For example, if school social workers have encountered unsuccessful individualized education plans, it is highly recommended that they review the plan to be sure that all family members, especially elderly grandparents, were consulted in the planning. Otherwise, it is not uncommon for the Chinese family to refuse treatment or only partially participate because an elderly family member feared that treatment as planned would cause the family to lose face or be shamed in the community or that the family would feel too obligated to the school social worker in accomplishing such an ambitious plan. Family expectations can be a burden, but the family serves as protector from outside threats and as a source of wisdom. Lee cited the Chinese family as being of "central importance in providing the necessary resources for growth and the definition of social expectations and responsibilities" (p. 536).

## Different Socialization Expectations

Chinese socialization of children differs significantly because of the different goals, agents, processes, and outcomes in the different environments. Recent immigrant parents who have socialized their children in a communist environment may have adjustments to make for themselves and their children in a democratic environment. They may feel pressure to speak up for themselves and for their children, and they may chafe at the U.S. acceptance of children asserting themselves even with their parents. Social work educators need to teach practitioners and even the Chinese parents themselves the differences in expectations between environments and to urge them to maintain respect for both. To discount one or the other environment may cause confusion and alienation.

Another example is the difference in expectations of socialization agents, exemplified in the possibilities and challenges faced by mothers, the primary socializers in the various environments. In traditional China and pre-1979 PRC, women were expected to have many children, particularly sons, to honor the ancestors and carry on the family name. However, in the United States there is a problem related to family size and mothers' activities. In the United States, as the cost of raising the family increases and the career aspirations of the wife become greater, the expectation of many children is not as heavily enforced. The value of having children continues to work on people's emotions, but there is also pressure for women to become more educated and marketable to add to the family's financial resources. This necessity exerts a practical downward pressure on family size, which conflicts with the ideal of a large family.

There is also the question of obligation to the family and responsibility for parents' welfare. Traditionally, the family comes first and under communism the state comes first. In the United States the obligation to family is conditional, depending on the degree of adherence to traditional values. These different attitudes toward responsibility to the family have an effect on the socialization of the child. If a school social worker is worried about the negative self-esteem a Chinese child may have or might be developing, the social worker can guide the traditional family to use positive praise instead of belittlement or shame but also explain how this praise can improve the child's academic achievement and thus bring honor to the family. Chinese parents are willing to change behaviors if it will help improve their perceptions of themselves and their families, because public reputation is culturally important.

## CONCLUSION

The kinds of topics and questions that have driven this analysis of Chinese American socialization ought to be used by social workers and social work educators to analyze other ethnic populations in the United States. Social work education needs to pay more attention to the effect of changing environments on a single culture. It also needs to emphasize that social workers learn to inquire about the original backgrounds of the ethnically diverse families they serve. This process should focus on macro-level issues, which include the history of immigration, refugee migration, and residence in the United States; the social and political environment of the country from which the family emigrated; and the traditional cultural values of that country and the ways they have been affected by interaction with American values. In particular, social workers need to learn how the political environment of the country of origin (and the United States) has an effect on the social behavior of the client.

When social workers try to understand the effect of the social environment on the socialization of Chinese children, they should ask the following: In what country was the client born and raised? During what historical period was the client born, and what were the political and social events happening that would affect the social environment? What are the socialization goals of the family, and how have they been affected by the social environment of the country in which they lived? What is the socialization process? Are there tensions in the process as a result of the change in social environments? How do socialization outcomes reflect the effect of the social environment from which the family came and the one in which the family is now living? By asking such questions, the social worker can be more sure of addressing culturally competent practice, a much needed service as the United States becomes a more multicultural society.

## REFERENCES

Andors, P. (1983). *The unfinished revolution of Chinese women, 1949–1980.* Bloomington: Indiana University Press.

Brooks, W. (1986). Human behavior/social environment: Past and present, future or folly? *Journal of Social Work Education, 23*(1), 18–24.

Chan, C. (1993). *The myth of neighborhood mutual help.* Hong Kong: Hong Kong University Press.

Chen, X. (1985). The one-child policy, modernization, and the extended family. *Journal of Marriage and the Family, 47,* 193–202.

Chin, A. (1988). *Children of China: Voices from recent years.* New York: Alfred A. Knopf.

Cleverly, J. (1985). *The schooling of China: Tradition and modernity in Chinese schooling.* Boston: George Allen & Unwin.

Croll, E. (1978). *Feminism and socialism in China.* New York: Schocken Books.

Croll, E., Davin, D., & Kane, P. (1985). *China's one child family policy.* New York: St. Martin's Press.

Devore, W., & Schlesinger, E. (1987). *Ethnic-sensitive social work practice* (2nd ed.). Columbus, OH: Charles E. Merrill.

Fong, R. (1990). *China's single child policy: The impact on family and schools.* Unpublished doctoral dissertation, Harvard University, Cambridge, MA.

Fong, R. (1992). History of Asian Americans. In S. Furuto, R. Biswas, D. Chung, K. Murase, & F. Ross-Sheriff (Eds.), *Social work practice with Asian Americans* (pp. 3–26). Newbury Park, CA: Sage Publications.

Fong, R. (in press). Child welfare practice with Chinese families: Assessment issues for immigrants from the People's Republic of China. *Journal of Family Social Work.*

Fong, R., & Mokuau, N. (1994). Not simply "Asian Americans": Periodical literature review on Asians and Pacific Islanders. *Social Work, 39,* 298–305.

Fong, R., & Spickard, P. (1994). Ethnic relations in the People's Republic of China: Images and social distance. *Journal of Northeast Asian Studies, 13,* 26–48.

Furuto, S., Biswas, R., Chung, D., Murase, K., & Ross-Sheriff, F. (Eds.). (1992). *Social work practice with Asian Americans.* Newbury Park, CA: Sage Publications.

Gamberg, R. (1977). *Red and expert: Education in the People's Republic of China.* New York: Schocken Books.

Germain, C. (1991). *Human behavior in the social environment: An ecological view.* New York: Columbia University Press.

Gladney, D. (1991). *Muslim Chinese: Ethnic nationalism in the People's Republic.* Cambridge, MA: Harvard University, Council on East Asian Studies.

Heng, L., & Shapiro, J. (1983). *Son of the revolution.* New York: Vintage Books.

Hirayama, H., & Cetingok, M. (1988). Empowerment: A social work approach for Asian immigrants. *Social Casework, 69,* 41–47.

Ho, M. K. (1992). *Minority children and adolescents in therapy.* Newbury Park, CA: Sage Publications.

Honig, E. (1992). *Creating Chinese ethnicity: Subei people in Shanghai, 1850–1980.* New Haven, CT: Yale University Press.

Hsu, F. (1981). *Americans and Chinese: Passages to differences* (3rd ed.). Honolulu: University of Hawaii Press.

Huang, L. (1990). Southeast Asian refugee children and adolescents. In J. T. Gibbs, L. Huang, & Associates (Eds.), *Children of color: Psychological interventions with minority youth* (pp. 278–321). San Francisco: Jossey-Bass.

Huang, L., & Ying, Y. (1990). Chinese American children and adolescents. In J. T. Gibbs, L. Huang, & Associates (Eds.), *Children of color: Psychological interventions with minority youth* (pp. 30–66). San Francisco: Jossey-Bass.

Ishisaka, A., & Takagi, C. (1981). Toward professional pluralism: The Pacific/Asian American case. *Journal of Social Work Education, 17*(1), 44–52.

Johnson, A. (1983). *Women, the family, and peasant revolution in China.* Chicago: University of Chicago Press.

Kessen, W. (Ed.). (1975). *Childhood in China.* New Haven, CT: Yale University Press.

Land, H., Nishimoto, R., & Chau, K. (1988). Interventive and preventive services for Vietnamese Chinese refugees. *Social Service Review, 62,* 468–484.

Lee, E. (1982). A social systems approach to assessment and treatment of Chinese American families. In M. McGoldrick, J. Pearce, & J. Giordano (Eds.), *Ethnicity and family therapy* (pp. 527–551). New York: Guilford Press.

Longres, J. (1990). *Human behavior in the social environment.* Itasca, IL: F. E. Peacock.

Loo, C. (1991). *Chinatown: Most time, hard time.* New York: Praeger.

Lum, D. (1996). *Social work practice and people of color: A process-stage approach* (3rd ed.). Pacific Grove, CA: Brooks/Cole.

Parish, K. W., & Whyte, M. (1978). *Village and family in contemporary China.* Chicago: University of Chicago Press.

Pillari, V. (1988). *Human behavior in the social environment*. Pacific Grove, CA: Brooks/Cole.

Schurmann, F. (1968). *Ideology and organization in communist China* (2nd ed.). Berkeley: University of California Press.

Shon, S., & Ja, D. (1982). Asian families. In M. McGoldrick, J. Pearce, & J. Giordano (Eds.), *Ethnicity and family therapy* (pp. 208–228). New York: Guilford Press.

Sidel, R. (1982). *Women and childcare in China* (rev. ed.). New York: Penguin Books.

Sue, S., & Chin, R. (1983). The mental health of Chinese American children: Stressors and resources. In G. Powell (Ed.), *The psychosocial development of minority group children* (pp. 385–400). New York: Brunner/Mazel.

Sze, W., Keller, R., & Keller, D. (1979). A comparative study of two different teaching and curricular arrangements in human behavior and social environment. *Journal of Social Work Education, 15,* 103–109.

Takaki, R. (1989). *Strangers from a different shore*. Boston: Little, Brown.

Timberland, E., & Cook, K. (1984). Social work and the Vietnamese refugee. *Social Work, 29,* 108–114.

Tobin, J., Wu, D., & Davidson, D. (1989). *Preschool in three cultures*. New Haven, CT: Yale University Press.

Trueba, H., Jacobs, L., & Kirton, E. (1990). *Cultural conflict and adaptation*. New York: Palmer Press.

Uba, L. (1994). *Asian Americans: Personality patterns, identity, and mental health*. New York: Guilford Press.

Unger, J. (1982). *Education under Mao*. New York: Columbia University Press.

U.S. Bureau of the Census. (1990). *Social and economic characteristics, race, and Hispanic origin*. Washington, DC: U.S. Department of Commerce.

Vaughan, J. (1993, Summer). Early childhood education in China. *Childhood Education*, pp. 196–200.

Wilkinson, E. (1973). *Lei Feng: The people's comic book*. New York: Doubleday.

Wolf, M. (1978). Child training and the Chinese family. In A. Wolf (Ed.), *Studies in Chinese society* (pp. 221–246). Stanford, CA: Stanford University Press.

Wu, D. (1991). The construction of Chinese and non-Chinese identities. *Daedalus, 20,* 159–180.

Yang, C. K. (1959). *Chinese communist society: The family and the village*. Cambridge: Massachusetts Institute of Technology.

Yuan, G. (1987). *Born red: A chronicle of the Cultural Revolution*. Stanford, CA: Stanford University Press.

Yuan, L. (1987, June). China's little emperors: Women of China. *Beijing*, pp. 5–6.

Zastrow, C., & Bowker, L. (1984). *Social problems*. Chicago: Nelson-Hall.

Zastrow, C., & Kirst-Ashman, K. (1994). *Understanding human behavior and the social environment* (3rd ed.). Chicago: Nelson-Hall.

Zhang, Y. (1986). My dear baby. In New World Press (Ed.), *Mommy, daddy, and me* (pp. 5–7). Beijing, China: Foreign Language Press.

*This chapter was originally published in the April 1996 issue of* Social Work in Education, *Vol. 18, pp. 71–83.*

# 14 Early Intervention to Improve Attendance in Elementary School for At-Risk Children: A Pilot Program

Janet Ford and Richard D. Sutphen

Educators and administrators in public schools have identified pupil nonattendance or truancy as a major problem. Nonattendance has potential negative consequences for students, families, schools, and society. Nonattenders generally fall behind their peers in academic achievement and the development of social competence. Their parents face pressure from the school and may even receive fines or jail time for failure to comply with compulsory attendance laws. Budgets for most school districts are based on average daily attendance rates, so high absenteeism can result in loss of school funds. Nonattendance is associated with a lack of preparation to enter the workforce and higher rates of unemployment, poverty, and involvement in the juvenile and adult criminal justice systems (Barth, 1984; Carlson, Clark, Nerad, & Taylor, 1993; McMillan & Reed, 1994; Rohrman, 1992; Zigler, Taussig, & Black, 1992).

Most recent literature on programs designed to reduce absenteeism in schools focuses on middle-school or early adolescent truants and on school administrators' efforts to remediate the problem (McMillan & Reed, 1994; Rohrman, 1992; Waltzer, 1984; Wheeler, 1992). The literature suggests that interventions to reduce attendance problems must combine strategies that address the problems of individual students, the students' family and home situations, and the school's relationship with the students (Levine, 1984). Strategies for reducing absenteeism include developing incentives for students to attend or making coming to school more rewarding for students; increasing communication with parents or other adult figures in the students' lives and encouraging their involvement in the students' educational experience; and helping families identify and deal with problems that may be contributing to the students' low attendance, either through direct intervention or by linking them to assessment and support services.

Many of the problems and intervention strategies reviewed in the recent literature can be identified and implemented at the elementary school level, where at-risk students and their families would be engaged at an early stage of problem development. Middle and high school attendance programs can be described as remedial, reactive, corrective efforts to bring about change where there is a recognized problem (Lofquist, 1993). Elementary school intervention programs have the potential to prevent the onset of truancy or to address attendance

154

problems before they become entrenched. Children who like school and find support there are less likely to become low academic achievers or dropouts (McMillan & Reed, 1994) and are also less likely to engage in antisocial or delinquent behaviors (Zigler et al., 1992). Working to help a child establish a positive relationship with the school system in the earliest grades would seem to be more feasible than working to rectify a negative relationship when the child becomes an adolescent.

School social workers can be key players in elementary school programs. They are in a prime position to assess individual students' situations, work directly with students and parents, and coordinate academic and social services resources for individual students and their families (Carlson et al., 1993). They can also assist in the development and implementation of effective schoolwide programs to promote and reward attendance.

This article describes the development of an attendance incentive program within an elementary school setting. The program included both a schoolwide attendance promotion and a focus program that developed individual intervention plans for high-risk children identified as having excessive absences.

## PROGRAM DEVELOPMENT AND IMPLEMENTATION

Three bachelor's-level social work students were given practicum placements in the elementary school to initiate and implement the attendance program. There were two parts to the attendance program: a schoolwide intervention and a focused intervention for students who already had a high number of absences. One social work student was assigned to the schoolwide program, and two students worked with the children at risk for high absenteeism.

### Schoolwide Program

A letter was sent to the parents of all the elementary school students stating the school's mission to encourage perfect attendance among the student body and the school's policy on absences and lateness. It also informed the parents that the schoolwide attendance program was going to be implemented and requested that they support the effort by completing an attached contract authorizing their child's participation in the program.

The intent of the attendance program was to encourage perfect attendance during each nine-week grading period by providing incentives based on schoolwide recognition and other rewards. To initiate the program, posters were placed around the school listing the names of students who had perfect or good attendance the previous school year. Perfect attendance was defined as missing zero days and being late no more than twice. Good attendance was defined as missing no more than two days (excused absences) and being late no more than twice. After the first nine-week grading period was completed, new posters were constructed and placed around the school listing all students with perfect or good attendance for that period. Students with perfect attendance received a certificate acknowledging their accomplishment and a reward. The principal also read their names over the public address system. Students at the good attendance level also received acknowledgments and rewards.

## Focus Program

This aspect of the program was designed for students in the first through third grades who had either missed at least 20 days of school (excused or unexcused) in the previous year and were still attending the elementary school at the beginning of the 1993–94 school year or had accumulated six or more absences in the first nine-week grading period of the 1993–94 school year. The objectives of this aspect of the program were to determine the reasons for the high rates of absenteeism and to provide support and incentives to the children and their families to improve attendance.

At the beginning of the 1993–94 school year, cumulative absentee records from the previous school year were reviewed to identify students who had at least 20 absences for that year. Twenty-three students in the first through third grades met this criterion. At the end of the first nine-week period of the 1993–94 school year, two more students were identified as candidates for the focus program. One student had accumulated six absences during the first nine-week quarter, and the school social worker recommended the other student because of a history of significant absenteeism at a previous school. Several of the students found to be eligible for the program transferred out of the school district during the selection phase.

Thirteen students were included as participants in the focus program, but four of them transferred to other districts during the early phase of the program. Sufficient data for the 1993–94 school year were obtained for only nine of the students included in the focus program. The lack of data reflects two phenomena that made evaluation of this initial effort difficult. One was the high level of residential instability of the families in this particular elementary school. The other was the absence of centralized attendance records for the county school system, which effectively prohibited the tracking of students' attendance from one school to another.

The focus program was designed to be implemented in two phases: first, an intensive intervention to be conducted in the nine-week second quarter of the 1993–94 school year, then a maintenance program to be continued over the 18 weeks of the third and fourth quarters of the school year. Initial assessments were conducted by social work students, who interviewed program participants and their parents either in school or in their homes. A questionnaire elicited information about family demographics, school preparation routines, transportation, parental supervision, home activities when the child was absent, school history, and family and child attachments to school (Table 14-1). An intervention strategy was then implemented following a two-pronged school-based and home-based approach.

*School-Based Interventions.* A school-based program was introduced to promote student attachment to school. Each child was provided with an individual attendance chart (calendar) that was monitored by the social work students. During the intensive phase, the social work students met with each child on a daily basis and gave verbal praise and encouragement for attending school. Each day the child attended, the worker affixed a sticker to the attendance calendar and gave the child a token.

*Table 14-1*

## Reasons for Absences Given by Participants and Contributing Factors (*N* = 9)

| Reasons | Frequency of Response |
|---|---|
| Child (participant) was ill | 7 |
| Mother wanted company | 6 |
| Parent was ill | 4 |
| Siblings were home from school | 4 |
| Parents took participant with them on visit to doctor, relative, and so forth | 4 |
| Family had car or transportation problems | 4 |
| Child didn't feel like going to school | 3 |
| Child was too tired to go to school | 3 |
| Relative was ill | 2 |
| No one was home to see child off to school | 2 |

| Contributing Factors | Frequency of Response |
|---|---|
| No school preparation routines | |
| No set time for homework | 4 |
| No set breakfast routine | 3 |
| No set bedtime; child stays up late | 3 |
| No supervision or assistance in the morning | 3 |
| Transportation or car problems | 4 |
| Family problems | |
| Marital problems | 2 |
| Substance abuse problems | 2 |
| Domestic violence | 1 |
| Parents have disabilities | 1 |
| Parents unemployed | 1 |
| Older sibling in prison | 1 |
| Family has no communication with school | 1 |

Each child also had daily counseling sessions with the social work students, which typically lasted from 15 minutes to an hour. The social work students were instructed to be empathic and caring with the children during these sessions, to encourage the children to verbalize their feelings and concerns, and to watch and listen for physical or verbal expressions. The participating children were asked to identify aspects of school life that they particularly enjoyed, and the social work students were instructed to emphasize these positive connections to school.

If any children were absent for any part of the week, the school social worker discussed with them why they were absent and encouraged their efforts at attendance. At the end of each week, children in the focus program were given "passes to success" by their teachers so that they could meet with the social work students to cash in the tokens they had earned for that week. The value of the prizes (candy, fancy pens or pencils, markers, toys) varied so that better attendance earned a more valuable prize.

At the end of the nine-week intensive intervention period, each child in the program was placed on a maintenance program for the remainder of the school year. During this phase of the program, the social work students met with the children on a weekly rather than daily basis to check attendance charts, award tokens, and provide counseling and encouragement.

*Home-Based Interventions.* The second component of the program was development of individualized family interventions to address specific family problem areas or behaviors that seemed to be impeding the student's school attendance. Many of the participants' absences could be linked to limited or inconsistent parental involvement in school preparation routines: Children did not have fixed homework times or bedtimes; no one was encouraging or helping them wake up in time to get ready for school; or they were left on their own in the morning to eat, dress, and collect their belongings for school. Transportation to school was also identified as contributing to absenteeism. Car problems were mentioned by four children.

Family-based interventions primarily consisted of making home visits or telephoning parents to encourage them to become more attentive to and involved in their children's school activities and responsibilities. Specific problem-solving interventions included helping families establish evening and morning school preparation routines. They also included seeking alternative forms of transportation to school when unreliable transportation was identified as a problem.

Factors such as unstable employment, transient family residency patterns, child-rearing issues, or emotional needs of the parents were also commonly identified problems contributing to high absenteeism. These problems were beyond the scope of direct intervention by the social work students but were addressed in some cases by helping to connect family members to support services to increase financial and emotional stability.

## PROGRAM EVALUATION

### Schoolwide Program

The attendance rates for the entire school were compared for the school years 1992–93 (pre–program implementation) and 1993–94 (program implementation) to determine whether attendance increased, decreased, or stayed the same after the attendance incentive program was introduced. Teachers in the elementary school were also surveyed regarding their perceptions of the program's effect on students.

Schoolwide attendance increased from 94.8 percent in 1992–93 to 95.4 percent in 1993–94. The increase was not statistically significant and could not be conclusively associated with the attendance program. However, feedback from the teachers was very positive. Their responses to survey items are summarized in Table 14-2. Most thought that the program had been effective and wanted it to continue. Some commented that having the schoolwide program as well as the special program was positive because it rewarded all students with good attendance and did not just focus on (and reward) students showing problem behaviors.

### Focus Program

Comparisons of the pre- and post-intervention absences of the nine children in the focus program were positive overall but showed mixed results for the individual

*Table 14-2*

**Results of Teacher Survey (N = 26)**

| Question | Yes n | Yes % | No n | No % | No Response n | No Response % |
|---|---|---|---|---|---|---|
| Was the attendance program effective? | 19 | 73 | 2 | 8 | 5 | 19 |
| Should the program continue? | 24 | 92 | 0 | 0 | 2 | 8 |
| Do you have other students you would refer to the focus group? | 13 | 50 | 12 | 46 | 1 | 4 |
| Do you have students you would refer for problems other than attendance? | 19 | 73 | 0 | 0 | 7 | 27 |
| Would you want a social work student assigned to your classroom? | 13 | 50 | 6 | 23 | 7 | 27 |

children (see Table 14-3). The first quarter was the baseline period, during which no intervention occurred. The second quarter was the intensive phase of the program, when the children were interacting with the social work students on a daily basis. The third and fourth quarters were the maintenance phase of the program, when the children were being monitored and rewarded for good attendance on a weekly basis. As shown in Table 14-3, six children showed a decrease in the number of absences during the intensive phase of the program, but the other three showed an increase from the first (no intervention) to the second (intensive intervention) quarter. Overall, average absences for the group decreased from 7.5 in the first quarter to 5.1 in the second quarter. This was a significant decrease [$t(8) = 2.06$, $p = .037$, one-tailed]. During the maintenance (third and fourth) quarters, average absences increased from the intensive quarter but still remained lower than in the baseline quarter. Three children had more absences than in the baseline quarter, but the other six showed some

*Table 14-3*

**Children's Absences during the Evaluation Period**

| Child | 1st Quarter (Baseline) | 2nd Quarter (Intensive Phase) | 3rd Quarter (Maintenance) | 4th Quarter (Maintenance) |
|---|---|---|---|---|
| 1 | 4.0 | 3.0 | 7.0 | 5.0 |
| 2 | 6.0 | 2.0 | 11.0 | 13.0 |
| 3 | 2.5 | 4.0 | 6.0 | 7.0 |
| 4 | 8.0 | 10.0 | 5.0 | 4.0 |
| 5 | 7.0 | 4.0 | 3.0 | 5.0 |
| 6[a] | 9.0 | 9.5 | 7.0 | 8.3 |
| 7[a] | 8.0 | 4.5 | 5.0 | 4.8 |
| 8 | 10.0 | 2.0 | 2.0 | 3.0 |
| 9 | 13.0 | 7.0 | 5.0 | 3.0 |
| M | 7.5 | 5.1 | 5.7 | 5.9 |
| SD | 3.1 | 3.0 | 2.6 | 3.2 |

[a]These siblings were withdrawn from school at the end of the 3rd quarter; 4th-quarter absences are estimated from 2nd and 3rd quarters.

increase in attendance. As noted in Table 14-3, two children from the same family moved out of the school district after the third quarter; their fourth-quarter absences were estimated from their second- and third-quarter average. Overall, absences increased slightly during the maintenance phase but still remained slightly lower than during the baseline phase of the program. Overall changes were not significant.

## DISCUSSION

Although the results of the evaluation of the focus group proved to be inconclusive overall, the pilot effort to develop and implement an attendance incentive program in the elementary setting described in this article had a number of positive results. First, attendance in the focus group improved significantly during the intensive intervention phase, suggesting that the daily interaction and feedback were effective in reducing absences among the at-risk students. The intervention with weekly interaction appeared less effective at promoting good attendance, but further study is needed to determine if other factors, such as time of year or maturation of participants, influenced the outcomes.

Second, the project gave the social workers a better understanding of the issues related to early school nonattendance. None of the children in the focus group expressed a fear or dislike of school; eight of the nine participants indicated that they liked school "a lot." Most of the reasons given for their absences were related to parents being unable or unwilling to provide supervision, guidance, or discipline to the children. It was apparent that many of the issues and problems contributing to the children's excessive nonattendance could not be resolved with microlevel, short-term interventions. School social worker interventions to address the problem of nonattendance must work in coordination with a variety of other community resources and services. However, many of the children appeared to benefit from the individual assistance, support, and encouragement in maintaining a positive connection to the educational system.

Third, the project helped promote better communication and cooperation between the teachers and social workers at the school. Most of the teachers at the school rated the schoolwide program as being successful, and at least half of the teachers surveyed were willing to refer other students to the focus group for attendance or other problems. Many of the teachers indicated that although attendance was not a problem for most of their students, they would welcome the chance to refer students for other social work services such as social skills training, basic needs, and home visits to facilitate home–school communication. The feedback from teachers was helpful in planning the next phase of the focus group program to expand the effort to address problems in addition to nonattendance.

Finally, the project provided expanded learning opportunities for social work students in a practicum setting. Participation in a pilot effort gave the students the experience of helping plan, develop, and implement a new program in a school setting. They received hands-on administrative as well as direct service experience and were able to examine and address the problems of absenteeism at the individual, family, and school levels.

## CONCLUSION

The results of the pilot effort paved the way for an expanded program that continues to address absenteeism but also attempts to promote positive attachments to school in a more general manner. The target population has expanded beyond high-absentee students to include children with other needs including social skills training, anger management, and academic assistance. Social work student involvement has also increased to four BSW students and one MSW student/supervisor who have made a two-semester commitment to the program. More assessment of child–school–family interaction is being conducted, and more family- as well as individual-based interventions are being developed to help children succeed in school. The expanded effort has been well received by the school personnel and students. Evaluation of the expanded effort is ongoing.

This pilot program and its evaluation were limited in size and scope. Further studies that include larger samples and more variables are needed. If issues and problems contributing to at-risk children's lack of attachment to school are to be addressed, assessments and interventions conducted by school social workers must reach beyond the individual child and school focus to include family members and other significant influences on these students. Interventions involving several different services, resources, and systems may be necessary. This type of multimodal approach may best be initiated, coordinated, documented, and evaluated by a school setting through the efforts of school social workers. School social workers can be key players in the delivery of broad-based support services to children at risk.

## REFERENCES

Barth, R. P. (1984). Reducing nonattendance in elementary schools. *Social Work in Education, 6,* 151–165.

Carlson, S., Clark, J. P., Nerad, D., & Taylor, J. (1993). School social work with children at risk and their families. *School Social Work Journal, 17*(2), 45–46.

Levine, R. S. (1984). An assessment tool for early intervention in cases of truancy. *Social Work in Education, 6,* 133–150.

Lofquist, W. A. (1993). *The technology of prevention workbook.* Tucson, AZ: Associates for Youth Development Publications.

McMillan, J. H., & Reed, D. F. (1994). At-risk students and resiliency: Factors contributing to academic success. *Clearing House, 67,* 137–140.

Rohrman, D. (1992, April). Combating truancy in our schools—A community effort. *NASSP Bulletin,* pp. 40–45.

Waltzer, F. (1984). Using a behavioral group approach with chronic truants. *Social Work in Education, 6,* 193–200.

Wheeler, P. (1992, April). Promoting parent involvement in secondary schools. *NASSP Bulletin,* pp. 28–35.

Zigler, E., Taussig, C., & Black, K. (1992). Early childhood intervention. *American Psychologist, 47,* 997–1006.

*This chapter was originally published in the April 1996 issue of* Social Work in Education, *Vol. 18, pp. 95–102.*

# 15 Supporting and Empowering Families through Cooperative Preschool Education

Katherine M. Dunlap

> If you've made up your mind you can do anything,
> You are absolutely right.
> The human mind doesn't care what you plant—success or failure—
> But it will return what you plant.
> A great pleasure in life is doing what people say you cannot do.
> —*Archie Allen, Parent*

Preschool education began in the United States during the middle of the 19th century, but it first became popular and prevalent during the 1960s, when it was considered the most effective weapon in the War on Poverty. Head Start, a national compensatory education project, was and is the largest and most visible preschool education program; however, many innovative early intervention projects were established in the 1960s. Educators and researchers hoped that early childhood education could eradicate the social problems associated with poverty (Zigler & Berman, 1983).

Research proliferated in the fertile political environment of that era. Henniger (1979) compiled a bibliography of more than 1,300 titles produced from 1970 to 1978 and published in diverse periodicals ranging from popular works to academic journals. Inquiries focused on children and longitudinal studies consistently describe lasting, positive benefits of preschool education for youths (Berrueta-Clement, Schweinhart, Barnett, Epstein, & Weikart, 1984; Bronfenbrenner, 1974; Consortium for Longitudinal Studies, 1983). In most programs, parents were required to attend didactic training sessions. Over time, parent training evolved into family support (Kagan, Powell, Weissbourd, & Zigler, 1987); however, there have been few attempts to evaluate the impact of parental involvement on adults (Weiss & Jacobs, 1988; Weissbourd & Kagan, 1989). This article describes a compelling preschool education program that succeeds in helping parents attain and maintain self-sufficiency.

## EMPOWERING FAMILIES

### Empowerment as a Process

Recent efforts to reform the welfare system have popularized the word "empowerment." Banks claim to "empower" people to borrow money. Schools report they "empower" parents to attend teacher conferences. Although both consumers and parents benefit from these services, they are not examples of empowerment. Banks lend money to earn money, and schools involve parents to elicit their help. In social work terms, "empowerment" means helping people help themselves (Simon, 1994). True empowerment enables people to discover, develop, and use the power within themselves, and it also promotes self-sufficiency (Rappaport, 1987).

There are two components of empowerment. The first is the acquisition of power. Most middle-class and professional people acquire power as a function of role, status, or resources, whereas others must learn how to obtain power. The second component is the use of power. Powerful people wield power. Martin Luther King Jr. explained this element in his last address to the Southern Christian Leadership Conference in 1967: "The problem of transforming the ghetto, therefore, is a problem of power. . . . Now power properly understood is nothing but the ability to achieve purpose. It is the strength required to bring about social, political, and economic change" (quoted in Washington, 1986, p. 246).

The term "empowerment" captures both elements by incorporating a psychological and a behavioral state. The former involves the perception of competence and ability; the latter enables people to pursue activities that promote change and convey power (Mondros & Wilson, 1994).

## Evolution of Family Support

Empowerment has long been an ancillary goal of preschool education. Early programs—rooted in the cultural deficit model of poverty—plucked children from their families and plunged them into compensatory education (Valentine & Stark, 1979). Adult sessions focused on parent training and home economics. Usually middle-class workers presented didactic instruction without regard for the interests or needs of adults. Research indicates that preschool education has distinct benefits for children (Becher, 1986; Honig, 1982); however, few studies have examined changes in adults who participate in these programs, and no conclusions can be drawn from them (Goodson & Hess, 1975).

Bronfenbrenner (1974) spurred a re-examination of family issues, and family support programs gradually replaced parent training. Family support provides emotional sustenance and instrumental assistance in addition to education and information. Programs maintain an ecological focus wherein the parent is both a recipient and a provider of services (Zigler & Weiss, 1985). Furthermore, they empower by building on strengths rather than deficits (Weissbourd & Kagan, 1989).

The transition toward empowering content is a defining element in an effective program. As Martin Luther King Jr. once explained, "It's all right to tell a man to lift himself by his own bootstraps, but is a cruel jest to say to a bootless man that he ought to lift himself by his own bootstraps" (quoted in Washington, 1986, p. 271). King continued, "We must utilize the community action groups and training centers now proliferating in some slum areas to create not only merely an electorate, but a conscious, alert and informed people who know their direction and whose collective wisdom and vitality commands respect" (p. 312).

Evaluations of family support have also been sparse, for funding has been limited and there are substantial difficulties related to design (Zigler & Black, 1989). Research suggests that empowerment is a long-term process of adult learning and development typically accomplished through a series of small steps (Kieffer, 1984). Furthermore, empowerment programs can have a long-term impact on family patterns, including economic self-sufficiency, educational attainment, quality of life, psychological well-being, and limitations on family size (Parker, Peotrkowski, & Peay, 1987; Seitz, 1987). However, dropout rates from voluntary programs often exceed 50 percent (Cochran, 1988), and required attendance is a controversial issue.

Many unanswered questions remain, including not only which family support programs work, but also how, when, where, why, and for whom (Weiss & Jacobs, 1988). Such information is critical, for it can help social workers break the bonds of poverty and dependency that have snared disadvantaged families. Given the current political climate of decreasing public support for families, empowerment is a necessary, albeit challenging, goal for parents with small children (Cochran, 1987). This article describes the key elements of a family support program that promotes empowerment and thus self-sufficiency for disadvantaged caregivers.

## METHOD

### Research Questions

This study was designed to explore two primary questions: To what extent does required adult participation in a cooperative preschool foster empowerment among adults? What program elements promote the empowerment of caregivers? *Empowerment* is defined as a process of adult development that enables parents to sustain self-sufficiency and gain mastery over their affairs.

### Setting

Weiss and Jacobs (1988) divided early intervention programs into two types: flagships and fleet projects. Flagships are a few dozen university-supported research projects. Fleet programs are small, fledgling, community-based operations. This research was conducted in a ship of the fleet—a private, academic preschool in a major southern city. The preschool is housed in an inner-city church across the street from the city's second-oldest public housing project. It is operated by five part-time staff and a volunteer board representing a variety of professional fields and the neighborhood. The annual budget of about $75,000 is raised by the board. With children, teachers use High/Scope, a curriculum developed by the Perry Preschool Project (Weikart, Rogers, Adcock, & McClelland, 1971).

### Research Design

Naturalistic inquiry was chosen as the method of design for several reasons (Jorgensen, 1989). First, little is known about the effect of preschool involvement on caregivers. (The term "caregiver" is used because many participants were extended family members—including grandmothers, aunts, and even an uncle.) Second, there are substantial differences between the views of outsiders—even planners and teachers—and those of insiders (the caregivers). Third, the phenomenon is not easily accessible and has not been captured by traditional research. Finally, appropriate quantitative measures have not yet been developed (Fetterman, 1988).

A qualitative study permits important dimensions to emerge without presupposing critical elements; therefore, internal validity is a major strength. Limitations include time constraints, the need for extensive field notes, a dearth of standards for data analysis, and distortion due to observer bias. A rigorous research design addressed these limitations by extending exposure to the field and by soliciting independent corroboration.

Although this preschool program is unique, it is not atypical. All elements—setting, participants, and staff—are common to cities across the United States. This article describes these features in a way that promotes reliability and facilitates confirmation (Laosa, 1991).

## Procedure

The study was conducted in several phases. After an exhaustive literature analysis, the author spent 18 months as a participant observer, attending all events involving adults. At the end of the second year, the author conducted focus groups with 15 active caregivers and conducted home visits with nine people who had completed the program in previous years. These nine had been identified by staff as successful. Each was asked to name other graduates who were also successful. The participants' list matched the staff list exactly, ensuring confidence that the sample accurately represents the population of successful program graduates.

## Data Analysis

Field notes and verbatim transcripts were analyzed using the techniques recommended by Miles and Huberman (1984). The process was divided into discrete steps: Data were organized by question and tested against working hypotheses. Then data were reorganized by themes, and discrepancies were examined. Finally, data were compiled on a person–event matrix. Data from key informants, supplemental sources, written records, and oral histories were triangulated with field notes to ensure validity (Patton, 1990). Participants, community leaders, and staff corroborated each step.

## Sample

The target community was a public housing site riddled with illegal drug use and criminal activity. At the beginning of the school year, all residents with small children were invited to participate. There were no fees, because all were living below the poverty level; instead, caregivers were required to help in the classroom, attend weekly parent meetings, and assist with homework.

In the fall of 1992, 18 families enrolled their children. At the end of the school year, 15 families, all African American, were still active; the sample comprised these 15 families. All mothers were adolescents when their first child was born, although their current ages ranged from 22 to 33 years. Seven mothers had three children each; the number of children per family ranged from one to five. One caregiver was an uncle. Seven of them had participated in this program in previous years.

Levels of participation differed, and three groups emerged. About one-third of the adults consistently exceeded minimum requirements and assumed leadership roles. Another third met minimum requirements but tended to be captious. The final third demonstrated erratic involvement, rarely fulfilling monthly obligations without assistance.

## RESULTS

Before the empowerment process could begin, the preschool had to meet two challenges: The first was to attract caregivers. The second was to sustain their interest and engage them in an appropriate curriculum.

### Attracting Caregivers

At the beginning of the school year, all caregivers stated that they felt isolated. Most knew virtually no one else in a neighborhood of 1,000 people. Familiar with the history of community violence, all were afraid to let their children play outside. They sequestered themselves in small apartments behind locked doors. Andrea's situation was typical: She could provide no names as emergency contacts. Another participant, Jennifer, said, "There would be some mornings we would just lay in bed all day." Although other day care facilities were available, parents chose this site for convenience and location, explaining that it was important to be able to walk to school if there were an emergency.

Initially, caregivers were reluctant participants. None wanted to attend the weekly parents' meetings, and many were afraid to speak before the group. When Shontay was welcomed, she spat, "I don't want to be here. I don't like people. I am not a sociable person." Nevertheless, caregivers recognized the importance of preschool education and saw immediate benefits for their children. Fay explained, "I knew she needed some sort of advance before she really started school." Ann agreed: "I felt it would help her out as she was growing." Hope, one of the most reserved mothers, described her son's reaction: "He done learn a lot. He opened up—he was real shy. He wouldn't talk to nobody. I mean nobody! And it didn't take but two days and he started opening up!"

Seeing their children blossom encouraged the caregivers. Dana added, "When my daughter came home the first day, she did not want to go to sleep. She was so anxious to get up and go to school the next day, and she loved it so much that she motivated me." Marlette echoed this sentiment: "Bobby liked school. He would wake me on Saturday and say, 'Mama, I'm going to school!'" Andrea concurred: "Even when Dionne is sick, he be crying to go to school." Martha summarized the situation: "You know, if you place your children somewhere and they seem to be happy there, it will make you feel like being there too."

From these and similar comments, it was clear that parents chose this preschool option because it was convenient. Although they did not relish the cooperative requirements, they initially stayed because they observed immediate, positive benefits for their children.

## Sustaining Interest

Given their initial discomfort, caregivers were asked what sustained their interest and facilitated the transition from isolation to affiliation. All found that the structure provided a welcome respite from boredom and fear. The parents' room was open daily for camaraderie, crafts, and spontaneous activities, and parents were encouraged to go along on field trips. One caregiver, Judy, participated in activities such as meetings, luncheons, fund-raisers, field trips, gymnastics classes, and music lessons with the children. In the classroom, Judy told stories, read, organized games, and supervised the housekeeping center. Kim recalled, "I loved that preschool. I was over there every day before I started school myself."

Adult activities promoted membership, an important prelude to empowerment (Gutierrez, 1990). Maggie noted, "It took me a while to get adjusted because I was like petrified and terrified. I don't want to come in here and start up a conversation and somebody be talk[ing] me down. But you know, once I started coming over and got to know everybody. . ." Lily finished the sentence: "It was A-OK! You felt you was home."

## Promoting Change

A key element of empowerment is the tenet that individuals understand their own needs better than others are able to understand them (Cochran & Woolever, 1983). This tenet is followed by the corollary that people should have the power to act on their understanding (Pinderhughes, 1983).

The adult program embraced these tenets by incorporating the plan–act–reflect strategies of the High/Scope curriculum. Caregivers planned their own events, including service schedules and topics for required meetings. After each activity, they reflected on their experiences, and their conclusions guided their plans for the next event.

*Classroom Service.* Through mandatory classroom service, caregivers learned about normal behavior for preschool children, practiced educational activities, developed social skills, and gained parenting and job skills. Most adults enjoyed working in the classroom. Angela, a regular helper, found the experience rewarding: "I feel like when I go into the classroom, if I can just teach one child to do something that day, that boosts up my self-esteem." Jackie explained, "You have an opportunity to work with the kids as if you are part of the staff." Meg added, "It gives you pride."

Some mothers vehemently disliked the service component. Shontay was afraid she could not control her temper in a setting that prohibited corporal punishment: "I'm the type of person I will not bite my tongue. I'll beat her butt right in front of the classroom. And then if someone say something, I'll be ready to jump on them!" Dana had similar comments: "I just cannot go into the classroom. I went one time and left. It is not because I am not interested in my daughter. I don't have the patience for so many kids. I found myself wanting to scream at another person's child."

In general, caregivers who avoided the classroom did not know how to manage groups of small children clamoring for adult attention. They were uncomfortable because they did not know how to redirect or discipline children effectively. As a result, staff developed additional training units to teach reticent caregivers to function more comfortably and effectively in the classroom.

*Required Meetings.* In addition to classroom service, adults attended 20 required meetings during the year. Each meeting included rituals, a business session, a formal program, and time for discussion. These four elements were designed to foster membership and growth.

Rituals and motivational parables provided structure and promoted affiliation. Staff opened sessions with a ritual called "Positive Comments." Each adult was asked to say something positive to the person on the right. Staff modeled the interaction for the participants. At first, caregivers had difficulty responding, and this exercise gave them a chance to practice social skills in a nonthreatening environment. By spring, caregivers could lead the exercise, an honor that encouraged and rewarded new behavior.

Business sessions provided an opportunity for caregivers to shape policies, as the following incident illustrates: At the conclusion of each meeting, a drawing was held to select a door prize for an adult in attendance. Because prizes were chosen from donations to the preschool, the supply of adult gifts was limited. In March, Joanne received a child's toy. Disappointed, she confronted staff at the next meeting. Joanne had practiced her speech and delivered it assertively:

> I want to talk about what happened last week. You know, all the other times when we be getting a door prize, they be for the parent. I been waiting and waiting for my name to be pulled, and it never was. And then last week, someone finally pulled my name, and I was so excited! I wanted something for me! But [the leader] said I had to choose between two toys. . . . The parent gift should be for the parent, not for the kids. This should be my turn.

At first, staff seemed defensive as they explained that educational toys help children learn. The group supported Joanne, and staff began to negotiate. Finally, the director proposed a compromise, and she empowered caregivers by giving them the final decision.

Formal programs emerged from the needs of group members, who suggested meeting topics. For example, when someone complained about the breakfast menu, the coordinator asked a nutritionist to address the next session. Her recommendations were not what caregivers wanted to hear—they thought children should eat sausage and eggs every morning! But they accepted her ideas; negotiated tasty, nutritious meals with the cook; and agreed to post weekly menus so that children who did not like a selection could eat at home.

Like the participants, most speakers were African American. Those from the professional community spoke on topics such as personal safety or drug abuse prevention. Middle-class citizens recounted their own struggles to escape poverty. These guests brought evidence that caregivers could escape welfare dependency. As role models, they demonstrated how caregivers could accomplish their goals without violating their cultural heritage (Gutierrez, 1990). A physical therapist illustrated this process. After discussing the need for personal responsibility, mutual aid, and community action, she stressed their strong, African American heritage: "In the Fellowship Hall, I was looking at pictures of black leaders who have gone before and paved the way: Sojourner Truth, Harriet Tubman, Martin Luther King Jr. . . . And the leaders of the future are here: Andrea, Jessica, Lily, Joanne, Dana." When the mothers heard their names, they became excited. "That's me!" they buzzed as they exchanged glances. They were inspired by recognition and affirmation.

Adults listened to the speakers carefully, for most had never conversed with middle-class African American women outside of the welfare office. One speaker exhorted, "You each need a BMW—a black male working!" Caregivers were shocked by the implication that they deserved security and support from their partners. They ruminated on this speech all year, using the slogan "BMW" to chastise and inspire each other. They were touched by women who understood their plight, and they accepted much of the advice, finding "It works—if you really try."

Discussion periods promoted friendship and mutual understanding (Swick & Graves, 1993). Kim commented, "I learned that you can trust other people when you have a problem that is too big for one person to solve." Martha agreed: "Before, I was comfortable just sitting home and being left alone. I really didn't want to be bothered with nobody. Then I started going [to preschool], and I started enjoying myself so good. And I found out that I wanted to be around other people. I found out I could enjoy life a lot better just being around other people."

Discussions also promoted group solidarity, introduced new ways of thinking and coping, and encouraged development of new skills. Jennifer elaborated: "[Discussions] helped me be more responsible and have a better attitude toward my children. Talking with the parents, it seemed like we all had the same problems we were trying to accomplish."

***Preschool Governance.*** A board of directors was ultimately responsible for operation of the preschool. Each year, two caregivers were selected by their peers to serve as voting members of the board. Every cohort criticized something. Parent representatives brought concerns to the board, where they were explored and resolved, generally in favor of caregivers. The experience of interacting with the board affirmed caregivers and taught them to negotiate with the establishment.

***Other Activities.*** The preschool celebrated five holidays with parties that featured games, awards, and a meal prepared by caregivers. Cooking provided an important focus. Although many caregivers could not identify a measuring spoon, they could prepare traditional Southern dishes. They were proud of this skill and often used the kitchen for spontaneous lunches as well as scheduled events. Because they took cooking so seriously, they refused to leave the kitchen when they became mad at each other. Instead, they learned to discuss differences and settle arguments among themselves. Andrea recalled, "We were like a family in the kitchen, wasn't we!" Lily agreed: "It's like we were in a family reunion." For many, the preschool constituted their only family.

Caregivers were encouraged to contribute ideas, which staff helped them implement. For example, Terry wanted to start a lending library. Staff solicited more than 500 books. Terry and others organized them and developed a lending system still in existence five years later.

## Staff Roles and Attitudes

The success of a family support program depends not on program content but on staff ability to deliver that content. According to Weissbourd and Kagan (1989), community workers can be particularly effective because they share the culture of the participants. They serve as models of people who have successfully mastered the system—often against great odds. Because they are familiar with the community, they can extend networks, broker services, and identify families in need. Halpern and Larner (1988) found that successful lay helpers are flexible, sensitive, and secure. In a setting that empowers, the professional serves as collaborator, facilitator, and colleague rather than as expert or adviser (Gutierrez, 1990; Rappaport, 1987). Effective staff establish relationships marked by intimacy and reciprocity, but not necessarily by peer relations (Wasik, Bryant, & Lyons, 1990). Slaughter added that staff attitudes must include self-respect, enthusiasm, the belief that people can and do change in positive ways, a desire to be part of that change, and a commitment to the program (as cited in Weiss & Jacobs, 1988).

Trained by a master's-level social worker, the staff at the preschool exemplified these traits. Jennifer described their dedication: "There is nothing [the staff] don't care about. They pay attention to everything. They can be talking to five people, but they pay attention." Marline expanded, "[The cook] know who don't like eggs and who don't like grits." Joanne concluded, "That is important. When the person who is feeding your child cares, she cares."

Bronfenbrenner (1979) and Edelman (1986) maintained that children need a stable caregiver. The same principle appears to apply to parents. Like their children, the caregivers needed a stable mentor with whom they could laugh, cry, tease, fight, rebel, reconcile, love, and try new behaviors with impunity. The family coordinator was working toward a BSW degree, and this foundation helped her understand her role as a balance between intimacy and distance. She inspired confidence, encouraged reluctant learners, opened opportunities, welcomed feedback, preserved dignity, affirmed success, and facilitated changes that made the preschool more responsive to the needs and interests of the participants. She was not daunted by angry words or hostile actions. Caregivers appreciated this persistence of the staff, as Kim explained:

> [She] keep saying, "Kim, go back to school!" I said, "I'm not going back to school!" She said, "Yes, you are. I am going to see that you go back to school." Every day, [she] would come to my door and say, "Kim, I know you are in there. Come out." She will come in and look at me until I say, "Okay." So I didn't have no other choice but to go back to school.

Carol elaborated on a similar experience: "She really pushed me. It made me feel confidence in myself because she told me I could do it." Nancy added, "She said, 'If you don't come, I am going to come and get you. I am going to wake you up. You are going to get over here [to preschool].' If it hadn't been for her, I would still be home sleeping, and that's the truth."

To maximize limited resources, staff eventually realized that they would have to limit their involvement with those caregivers who consistently failed to meet obligations. Staff did not intend to "cream" (that is, select those most likely to succeed) (Etzioni, 1994), but they found it necessary to monitor demands and avoid decisions that favored one person. This policy, a derivative of functional social work (Hasenfeld, 1987), enabled staff to concentrate on those ready to benefit. Interestingly, several caregivers who terminated their participation in the program during the year resumed full participation later, and some tried the program multiple times before becoming securely attached to the preschool.

## IMPLICATIONS FOR PRACTICE

Before the preschool experience, these 24 caregivers were involved in almost no activities outside their apartments. They espoused no goals, for they believed that they were incapable of changing their lives. After participating in a family support program at a cooperative preschool, these same people consistently demonstrated evidence of empowerment. All used more effective parenting skills. All were employed or attending school, and all expressed confidence in their own capacities.

Initially caregivers were willing to attend because the preschool was beneficial for their children. The opportunity for affiliation and affirmation sustained adult interest. Group meetings, which consistently emerged from participant needs, provided role models who inspired, taught diverse skills, and encouraged new behaviors, including the ability to work toward goals. Staff fostered change by providing stable support and a structure that demanded shared responsibility.

This study begins to define program elements that create a successful family support program within a cooperative preschool. It suggests that schools and educational institutions can be part of the continuing effort to break the cycle of poverty by incorporating strategies that empower families. By definition, programs that promote self-sufficiency must be open to those who need them—often caregivers with few skills and little hope. Because lasting change takes time, educational institutions must maintain their commitment for many years. Nevertheless, empowering programs can be cost-effective, for they create a more effective learning environment for children, and they also bolster the fabric of a fragile society.

The cardinal social work values respecting worth, dignity, and self-determination are essential to such programs. For example, this study suggests that parents want to be able to reach their young children in times of trouble. Social workers operationalize these cardinal values by helping parents have access to schools that are geographically removed from their neighborhoods. Bus or taxi vouchers are most effective, for they transfer control to parents. Providing a ride to school minimizes self-determination, for control resides with the driver.

People who are isolated are vulnerable; therefore, membership is a prelude to empowerment. When caregivers know that their children are happy, they are more willing to try new behaviors themselves, and they enjoy participating in stimulating, rewarding activities that foster affiliation. Adult attention can be sustained by using the plan–act–reflect approach, a strategy that fosters friendship and charts program content.

In parent training programs, instructors used programmed curricula or developed agendas weeks and months in advance. This strategy is inappropriate in family support programs. The most effective curricula emerge from the needs and goals of the group. Social workers facilitate content as participants identify and request it. Delimited planning pressures social workers to begin the school year with a strong network of resources—people who understand the program's aims and who are willing to contribute when asked. Within the community, social workers must advocate for family support, and they must eradicate red tape to broker services in a timely manner.

The critical element in cooperative education is not curriculum but staff. Family support programs are more expensive than parent training, because staff must be skilled in educational practices as well as social work methods. Family coordinators must possess the knowledge and skills needed for practice with individuals and groups. They must remain undaunted by hostility or rejection, and they must recognize the teachable moments embedded in everyday activities.

In addition to direct practice activities, social workers can coordinate the efforts of teachers and team members who may not fully grasp the empowerment process. When community workers provide family support, a master's-level social worker can add advanced content during weekly planning meetings. These meetings will be most productive if parent representatives are included. A dedicated staff can break many barriers if they have the freedom to create programs that couple the goals of the institution with the dreams of the participants.

In some settings, there may be concern about the service requirement. Participation is a privilege, not an entitlement, and parents must demonstrate their commitment by contributing service hours. Classroom participation is often a bother for teachers, who must supervise untrained, sometimes reluctant, volunteers. However, classroom service has substantial benefits for caregivers: They gain information about normal development and school-readiness skills, learn effective methods of discipline, and increase their own self-esteem. The decision to require participation reflects current political ideology, but it is rooted in functional social work principles. Mandated service uses agency limits to teach personal responsibility, a prerequisite of family empowerment.

## REFERENCES

Becher, R. M. (1986). Parent involvement: A review of research and principles of successful practice. In L. G. Katz (Ed.), *Current topics in early childhood education* (Vol. 6, pp. 85–122). Norwood, NJ: Ablex.

Berrueta-Clement, J. R., Schweinhart, L. J., Barnett, W. S., Epstein, A. S., & Weikart, D. P. (1984). *Changed lives: The effects of the Perry Preschool Program on youths through age 19* (Monograph No. 8 of the High/Scope Educational Research Foundation). Ypsilanti, MI: High/Scope Press.

Bronfenbrenner, U. (1974). *A report on longitudinal evaluations of preschool programs: Vol. 2. Is early intervention effective?* (DHEW Publication No. OHD 76-30024). Washington, DC: U.S. Government Printing Office.

Bronfenbrenner, U. (1979). *The ecology of human development: Experiments by nature and design.* Cambridge, MA: Harvard University Press.

Cochran, M. (1987). The parental empowerment process: Building on family strengths. *Equity and Choice, 4,* 9–23.

Cochran, M. (1988). Between cause and effect: The ecology of program impacts. In A. R. Pence (Ed.), *Ecological research with children and families: From concepts to methodology* (pp. 143–169). New York: Teachers College Press.

Cochran, M., & Woolever, F. (1983). Beyond the deficit model: The empowerment of parents with information and informal supports. In I. E. Sigel & L. M. Laosa (Eds.), *Changing families* (pp. 225–245). New York: Plenum Press.

Consortium for Longitudinal Studies. (1983). *As the twig is bent—Lasting effects of preschool programs.* Hillsdale, NJ: Lawrence Erlbaum.

Edelman, M. W. (1986). *Families in peril: An agenda for social change.* Cambridge, MA: Harvard University Press.

Etzioni, A. (1994, July). Incorrigible: Bringing social hope and political rhetoric into instructive contact with what it means to be human. *Atlantic Monthly,* pp. 14, 16.

Fetterman, D. M. (1988). Qualitative approaches to evaluating education. *Educational Researcher, 17*(8), 17–23.

Goodson, B. D., & Hess, R. D. (1975). *Parents as teachers of young children: An evaluative review of some contemporary concepts and programs* (Report No. PS 009 247). Washington, DC: U.S. Department of Health, Education, and Welfare. (ERIC Document Reproduction Service No. ED 136 967)

Gutierrez, L. M. (1990). Working with women of color: An empowerment perspective. *Social Work, 35,* 149–153.

Halpern, R., & Larner, M. (1988). The design of family support programs in high-risk communities: Lessons from the Child Survival/Fair Start Initiative. In D. R. Powell (Ed.), *Parent education as early childhood intervention: Emerging directions in theory, research, and practice* (pp. 181–207). Norwood, NJ: Ablex.

Hasenfeld, Y. (1987). Power in social work practice. *Social Service Review, 61,* 469–483.

Henniger, M. L. (Compiler). (1979). *Parent involvement in education: A bibliography* (Report No. PS 010 780). Washington, DC: National Institute of Education. (ERIC Document Reproduction Service No. ED 174 352)

Honig, A. S. (1982). Parent involvement in early childhood education. In B. Spodek (Ed.), *Handbook of research in early childhood education* (pp. 426–455). New York: Free Press.

Jorgensen, D. L. (1989). *Participant observation: A methodology for human studies* (Vol. 15, Applied Social Research Methods Series). Newbury Park, CA: Sage Publications.

Kagan, S. L., Powell, D. R., Weissbourd, B., & Zigler, E. F. (Eds.). (1987). *America's family support programs.* New Haven, CT: Yale University Press.

Kieffer, C. H. (1984). Citizen empowerment: A developmental perspective. *Prevention in Human Services, 3*(2–3), 9–36.

Laosa, L. M. (1991). The cultural context of construct validity and the ethics of generalizability. *Early Childhood Research Quarterly, 6,* 313–323.

Miles, M. B., & Huberman, A. M. (1984). *Qualitative data analysis: A sourcebook of new methods.* Beverly Hills, CA: Sage Publications.

Mondros, J. B., & Wilson, S. M. (1994). *Organizing for power and empowerment.* New York: Longman.

Parker, F. L., Peotrkowski, C. S., & Peay, L. (1987). Head Start as a social support for mothers: The psychological benefits of involvement. *American Journal of Orthopsychiatry, 57,* 220–233.

Patton, M. Q. (1990). *Qualitative evaluation and research methods* (2nd ed.). Newbury Park, CA: Sage Publications.

Pinderhughes, E. B. (1983). Empowerment for our clients and for ourselves. *Social Casework, 64,* 331–338.

Rappaport, J. (1987). Terms of empowerment/Exemplars of prevention: Toward a theory for community psychology. *American Journal of Community Psychology, 15,* 121–148.

Seitz, V. (1987). Outcome evaluation of family support programs: Research design alternatives to true experiments. In S. L. Kagan, D. R. Powell, H. Weissbourd, & E. F. Zigler (Eds.), *America's family support programs* (pp. 329–342). New Haven, CT: Yale University Press.

Simon, B. L. (1994). *The empowerment tradition in American social work: A history.* New York: Columbia University Press.

Swick, K. J., & Graves, S. B. (1993). *Empowering at-risk families during the early childhood years.* Washington, DC: National Education Association.

Valentine, J., & Stark, E. (1979). The social context of parent involvement in Head Start. In E. Zigler & J. Valentine (Eds.), *Project Head Start: A legacy of the War on Poverty* (pp. 291–313). New York: Free Press.

Washington, J. M. (Ed.). (1986). *A testament of hope: The essential writings of Martin Luther King Jr.* San Francisco: Harper & Row.

Wasik, B. H., Bryant, D. M., & Lyons, C. M. (1990). *Home visiting: Procedures for helping families.* Newbury Park, CA: Sage Publications.

Weikart, D. P., Rogers, L., Adcock, C., & McClelland, D. (1971). *The cognitively oriented curriculum: A framework for preschool teachers.* Urbana: University of Illinois.

Weiss, H. B., & Jacobs, F. H. (Eds.). (1988). *Evaluating family programs.* New York: Aldine de Gruyter.

Weissbourd, B., & Kagan, S. L. (1989). Family support programs: Catalysts for change. *American Journal of Orthopsychiatry, 59,* 20–31.

Zigler, E. F., & Berman, W. (1983). Discerning the future of early childhood intervention. *American Psychologist, 38,* 894–906.

Zigler, E. F., & Black, K. B. (1989). America's family support movement: Strengths and limitations. *American Journal of Orthopsychiatry, 59,* 6–19.

Zigler, E. F., & Weiss, H. B. (1985). Family support systems: An ecological approach to child development. In R. N. Rapoport (Ed.), *Children, youth and families: The action–research relationship* (pp. 166–205). New York: Cambridge University Press.

*An earlier version of this chapter was presented at the Annual Program Meeting of the Council on Social Work Education, March 1995, San Diego. This chapter is extracted from the doctoral dissertation "Family Empowerment: One Outcome of Parental Participation in Cooperative Preschool Education," accepted by the Mandel School of Applied Social Sciences, Case Western Reserve University, Cleveland, in October 1993.*

*This chapter was originally published in the October 1996 issue of* Social Work in Education, *Vol. 18, pp. 210–221.*

# 16 School Social Workers as Family Therapists: A Dialectical–Systemic–Constructivist Model

Gilbert J. Greene, Dorothy Harper Jones, Cara Frappier, Martha Klein, and Barbara Culton

Students with problems in behavior or academic performance are a major concern of school social workers. Because the functioning of a child's family is integral to his or her success or failure in school (Allen-Meares, Washington, & Welsh, 1986), it is important to involve the family in prevention and remediation of a child's problems in school (Allen-Meares et al., 1986; Pennekamp & Freeman, 1988; Winters & Maluccio, 1988). School social workers have long provided individual and group services to students in the school setting, but their involvement with families is usually limited to supportive educational services. When a family needs therapeutic services, school social workers usually refer them to agencies in the community for family intervention because school social workers' heavy caseloads leave them little time to provide ongoing family therapy (Wattenberg & Kagle, 1986).

Referrals to agencies outside the school setting are often not successful because client families often do not follow through with them (Gonzalez-Ramos, 1990). Families have indicated that they would be much more willing to follow through on recommended family therapy if it were provided in the educational setting (Gonzalez-Ramos, 1990). School social workers can build on this willingness and on their relationships with families to provide needed family therapy on site in the school.

Examination of the school social work literature resulted in only two articles that specifically advocated that school social workers routinely provide family therapy on site in the school setting (Christian, Henderson, Morse, & Wilson, 1983; Millard, 1990). Millard did not provide a specific model of delivery for school social workers to use in providing family therapy. Christian et al. discussed use of the Bowen Family Systems Theory in providing family therapy in the school setting, but they did not operationalize this within the realities of everyday practice.

This article describes a model for school social worker–provided family therapy that the authors, two of whom have over 20 years' experience each in providing family therapy as school social workers, have found to be workable and effective. The model is the result of our monthly teamwork over a four-year period.

## THEORETICAL RATIONALE

The conventional wisdom that therapeutic sessions should be provided on a weekly basis may preclude school social workers from providing family therapy. The model discussed in this article advocates monthly family therapy sessions on the basis of the theoretical concepts of developmental dialectics, systems theory, and constructivism.

### Developmental Dialectics

Furthering a client's psychological and emotional development is a major purpose of counseling and psychotherapy (Ivey, 1986). For personal development to occur, the individual needs to experience both support and challenge (novelty) from the environment (Riegal, 1976). Development, therefore, involves the individual's experience of the contradictions of stability and change at the same time (Riegal, 1976). Resolving such contradictions results in development (change); this is a dialectical process (Liddle, 1984). The basis of dialectics is "thesis" (the current homeostatic situation) encountering "antithesis" (novelty), resulting in "synthesis" (development). In turn, the synthesis becomes a new thesis, and development continues in a spiraling process (Ivey, 1986).

For an intervention to be dialectical, it must address both stability and change (Keeney, 1987). According to Omer (1991), "Dialectical interventions are treatment strategies that embody two antithetical moves in such a way that as the pendulum swings from one to the other, change forces are mobilized and resistances neutralized" (p. 565).

*Thesis.* Thesis in family therapy is the homeostatic situation in which the family is stuck. Thesis involves the client's assumptions (rules) about change. A common dynamic of families with a problematic child is that they are continually using the same ineffective problem-solving tactics without getting positive results and have run out of ideas for change. For example, often parents assume that giving children advice will improve their behavior. If the worker gives the parent advice on how to be a better parent (parent education), then the therapist is still operating in accordance with the client's rules for change. By providing parent education, the worker is using thesis to deal with thesis; the worker is offering ideas about change in accordance with the client's rules for change, which frequently are ineffective. Consequently, the worker does not offer the client any novelty from the environment, and the stability (homeostasis) of the client's problematic situation is reinforced rather than changed. Such attempts are referred to as "first-order change" (Dowd & Pace, 1989).

*Antithesis.* Antithesis involves "second-order change," which goes beyond the existing rules (assumptions) of the client system (Watzlawick, Weakland, & Fisch, 1974). The catalyst for going beyond the existing rules is the introduction of novelty to the client's environment. An intervention will be experienced as novel when it is a catalyst for family members to question an aspect of their assumptive world. Accommodation to novelty leads to growth and development (synthesis) (Dowd & Pace, 1989; Ivey, 1986). Because second-order change interventions go beyond the client's existing rules, they can initially seem to be illogical, impractical, and temporarily destabilizing to client equilibrium.

One frequently used second-order change intervention is "reframing." Reframing usually involves tentatively giving a plausible positive meaning to the "facts" of the problematic situation that has been defined negatively by the family (Watzlawick et al., 1974). For example, a child's acting out can be reframed as an attempt to mobilize a depressed parent. The notion that problems and symptoms might "help" or "protect" others in the family has been discussed in the literature (Jackson & Haley, 1968; Keeney, Ross, & Silverstein, 1983; Selvini-Palazzoli, Cecchin, Prata, & Boscolo, 1978). The use of such alternative, plausible reframing can introduce novelty to the client's worldview.

Another type of second-order change intervention involves the use of "restraint from change," which can be classified as "soft" or "hard" (Rohrbaugh, Tennen, Press, & White, 1981). In a soft restraint-from-change intervention, the worker can suggest in the early stages of therapy that perhaps the client "should probably not change for now" or at least "go slowly trying to make changes." A more potent, or hard, restraint-from-change intervention involves suggesting to the client that he or she might want to exhibit the problem or an aspect of the problem at a different time in a different place with more frequency or intensity. When using a restraint-from-change intervention, the worker needs to provide the client with a plausible rationale that usually includes a positive reframing.

*Synthesis.* To help the client achieve synthesis (growth and development), the social worker should provide him or her with at least two choices: (1) a specific request for change (that is, better parenting skills, rational beliefs, relaxation training) and (2) restraint from change (a request for no change in the problem for the time being). Essentially, the clinician gives the client two simultaneous messages—(1) Change, and here's how, and (2) Don't change, and here's why—but prescribes neither. In keeping with Weeks's (1977) view, a therapist with a dialectical approach will help the client develop as many options as possible. The development of options is empowering because it allows the client to create new responses and to be self-determining (Weeks, 1977).

## Systems Theory

According to Levine and Fitzgerald (1992), "A system is a functional whole composed of a set of component parts (subsystems, units) that, when coupled together, generate a level of organization that is fundamentally different from the level of organization represented in any individual or subset of the component parts" (p. vii). Systems are goal oriented and self-correcting.

*Feedback.* To be self-correcting, a system must be able to process feedback (Bateson, 1971). Processing feedback involves "utilizing the results of one's communication to help shape one's subsequent communication" (Keeney & Silverstein, 1986, p. 15). Clients in family therapy can use feedback processes to monitor reactions of people in the environment to their behaviors and communications and then make adjustments for future behavior and communication.

The components of a system are interconnected; change in one part of a system can result in change in the other parts of the system and in the overall structure of the system itself (Anderson & Carter, 1990). The introduction of novelty from the environment—"news of difference" or "a difference that makes a difference"—

can result in change in a part or parts of the system (Bateson, 1979; Keeney, 1983). There is, however, usually a delay between the time the system experiences the novelty and the consequent changes (Levine, Van Sell, & Rubin, 1992; Senge, 1990).

*Overcorrection.* The initial response of a system to novel feedback is to over-correct (Senge, 1990). Overcorrecting can cause systems to oscillate. In families this change may be experienced by members as instability and crisis. Some period of time is necessary for change to work its way around a system (Levine et al., 1992; Selvini-Palazzoli, 1980; Senge, 1990). If the initial intervention with a family is followed up too quickly by another one to head off the crisis and instability resulting from the novelty, the initial intervention's effectiveness could be short-circuited. Consequently, the original presenting problematic homeostasis is often maintained, resulting in a therapeutic impasse; at such times clients are accused of being "resistant."

## Constructivism

According to the constructivist approach to social work practice (Gallant, 1993; Greene, Jensen, & Jones, 1996) and family therapy (Hoffman, 1988), a person's sense of reality is "socially constructed" through interactions with others (Hoffman, 1988). From these interactions an individual develops meanings, interpretations, and assumptions about themselves, other people, and the world (Dowd & Pace, 1989; Goolishian & Winderman, 1988). The individual is an active participant in this meaning-making process rather than the passive recipient of stimulus–response input.

A social worker working from a constructivist perspective must join with the family to create a therapeutic system in which the clinician is both participant and observer (Becvar & Becvar, 1993). Within the therapeutic system, the social worker and family interact to co-construct a new reality that excludes the presenting problem. For co-construction to occur, the worker–family relationship must be collaborative and nonhierarchical (Hoffman, 1988).

A constructivist approach to therapy also holds that client systems are self-organizing and cannot be changed in a predetermined direction by someone outside the system (Hoffman, 1988). Because the school social worker cannot control the outcome, all he or she can do in working with a family system is "give it a bump and watch it jump" (Hoffman, 1985, p. 388). The bump in a constructivist approach is the novelty introduced into the family system from the worker's ideas and hypotheses about stability and change.

## MODEL FOR SCHOOL SOCIAL WORKER–PROVIDED FAMILY THERAPY

Drawing on developmental dialectics and systems theory, the model of school social worker–provided family therapy developed by the authors emphasizes two features: (1) meeting with the family once a month and (2) giving a dialectical message to the family toward the end of each session.

Monthly sessions allow enough time for an intervention to work its way around the system between sessions, thus reducing client resistance (Selvini-Palazzoli, 1980). Monthly sessions also allow a school social worker to accommodate many more families. In addition, meeting monthly increases the likelihood that the entire family, as well as other professionals involved with the family, can be brought together. If families are unwilling to follow through on referrals to community agencies, then monthly sessions with the school social worker ensure continuity in the provision of some therapeutic services.

In organizing clinical work, we have adapted the six-step approach of the Mental Research Institute (MRI) (Nardone & Watzlawick, 1993):

1. Join the client system.
2. Define the problem from the client's perspective.
3. Define the goal from the client's perspective.
4. Identify the attempted solutions (first-order change).
5. Develop and implement appropriate interventions.
6. Terminate.

In addition, each session follows a four-step approach similar to that of the Milan systemic approach to family therapy (Tomm, 1984): (1) family interview, (2) intersession break, (3) intervention, and (4) end of the session. (Step 5 of the MRI approach is implemented during the intersession break and delivery of the intervention.)

**Step 1: Family Interview**

At the initial session, all family members (at least all those living in the same household) are asked to be present; this in itself may be a novel experience. However, because change in one part of a system can lead to change in the rest of the system, treatment can still be effective with only parts of the family system present.

*Joining.* The initial session focuses on joining with the family, defining the problem, identifying the family members' first-order change attempts to solve the presenting problem, and establishing the consequent outcome goal. Joining the family system is analogous to developing a trusting and collaborative relationship (Minuchin & Fishman, 1981). Joining is critical to the first session but continues throughout the clinical work. Numerous behaviors and skills of the social worker are involved in joining, among them empathy, support, acceptance, tracking, matching and mirroring, and using the family's language.

*Defining Problems and Outcome Goal.* Defining the presenting problem, identifying the attempted solutions, and establishing the outcome goal should be done as concretely, specifically, and behaviorally as possible in terms of who, what, when, where, how, and how often. The problem and goal should be placed on a 10-point Likert scale ranging from 1= worst possible scenario to 10 = most desirable outcome. Identifying the attempted solutions involves tracking the interactional patterns and sequences that reinforce the problem—that is, what the parents have been doing to try to eliminate the child's problematic behavior and how these attempts at first-order change maintain the problem.

In the MRI approach, the "solution is the problem," so interventions should focus first on changes in the attempted solutions, which ultimately will lead to changes in the presenting problem. Usually the worker begins each subsequent session by asking family members where they are on the problem–goal scale and what they have been doing to get there. Using the scale not only is a mechanism for evaluating progress, but also is an intervention itself (Greene, 1989; Walter & Peller, 1992).

*Constructing the Genogram.* Also during the first session, the worker, in collaboration with the family, starts developing a three-generation genogram (see McGoldrick & Gerson, 1985). The genogram displays for the family a more expansive view of their reality; it includes strengths as well as unresolved issues such as death, divorce, disability, unemployment, physical and sexual child abuse, and substance abuse. The genogram is usually constructed on large newsprint and posted in the interview room for every session.

Genogram construction is emphasized in the first two sessions and continues throughout the clinical work as new information about the family is discovered. We agree with Walsh and McGoldrick (1991) that frequently unresolved grief is involved in the development and maintenance of presenting problems and at some point must be addressed for treatment to be successful. The information gathered from the family is a source of feedback, ideas, and hypotheses. In addition, the information and ideas gathered from this process often provide the basis for the messages (interventions) given to the family at the end of the session.

*Using Circular Questioning.* Critical to the interview stage, as well as to the rest of treatment, is the use of circular questioning (see Fleuridas, Nelson, & Rosenthal, 1986). Circular questioning involves having each family member give his or her perception of a single issue; family members see how others view the dynamics (patterns of interactions, alliances, and so forth) in the family. Circular questioning can indirectly expand the family members' thinking about the problem from monadic and linear to systemic and nonlinear. Such questioning allows all family members to become aware that each plays a part in the maintenance of the problem and, thus, its eventual resolution. Family members usually hear some news of difference and experience some novelty.

*Identifying Exceptions.* Also during the interview stage of every session, the therapist can use forms of questioning typically found in solution-focused (Walter & Peller, 1992) and narrative approaches (White & Epston, 1990) to clinical work. These questions, which seek to identify exceptions (Walter & Peller, 1992) or "unique outcomes" (White & Epston, 1990) to the problem, are designed to discover strengths and competencies clients use during those times when the presenting problem is manifested not at all or in lesser degrees of frequency or intensity. Such questions can be used in conjunction with others later in the sessions (O'Hanlon & Weiner-Davis, 1989).

## Step 2: Intersession Break

An important component of this family therapy model is the intersession break. The original use of the break involved the clinician leaving the family and consulting with colleagues who had been observing the session from behind a one-way mirror (Tomm, 1984). During the break these colleagues shared impressions and together formulated the message that would be given to the family at the end of the session.

Taking such a break is helpful for several reasons. A family system is a powerful emotional entity, especially when it is large or when the problem is longstanding, multigenerational, or crisis driven. The power of the family's influence is decreased by the worker's physical separation; this separation allows the school social worker to hypothesize about the family's dynamics more objectively. Another benefit of taking the break is the family's increased receptivity to the message–intervention that follows (de Shazer et al., 1986). This heightened receptivity may be an artifact of waiting for and anticipating the school social worker's comments.

In addition, a break can especially help the school social worker when working alone resist the family's pull into their view of the problem. Such loss of objectivity may contribute to maintaining the family's problematic homeostasis and developing a therapeutic impasse.

## Step 3: Intervention

*Tray of Hors D'oeuvres Message.* After the school social worker and the family return to the interview room following the break, the worker should first compliment the family in some way (Wall, Kleckner, Amendt, & Bryant, 1989). Compliments are feedback to the family and can take the form of comments about their strengths, successes, or exceptions and unique outcomes or they can take the form of positive reframing. Many families come to treatment expecting to be judged and criticized and anticipating the need to defend themselves. The worker's compliments strengthen the joining process, facilitate client cooperation rather than defensiveness and resistance, and increase the family members' receptivity to the session-ending message. Whenever possible, it is best to use the family's own language when giving compliments or delivering messages.

The worker then communicates to the family a message (intervention) in the form of feedback and ideas about their problematic situation and how to change it. We have referred to this form of intervention as presenting the family a "tray of hors d'oeuvres" (a term borrowed from the annals of family therapy, original sources unknown). In presenting the feedback and ideas, the school social worker qualifies them as hypotheses, educated guesses, or food for thought for them to consider between the present session and the next.

The message should include specific ideas for first-order and second-order change, for example, ways to handle the problem differently or the suggestion not to change for now. Providing options increases the possibility that one or more family members will experience a change in perception that will lead ultimately to change in the way the system views itself and thus the way it acts in the future. At the same time the worker does not want to rush through the message. The worker should deliver the message slowly and deliberately using frequent pauses; this can also enhance the family's receptivity to the message. The worker may find it helpful to repeat the message or parts of it several times but in slightly different ways.

*Empowering Messages.* When giving a restraint-from-change message and a reframing message, it is important that the ideas behind them are plausible to both the family and the social worker. The social worker can only hypothesize about what is going on with the family. The dialectical messages in essence involve the social worker openly sharing with the family his or her hypotheses but structuring them in a way that the family does not feel criticized or blamed.

The idea of presenting the family with several messages or ways of viewing its system and relationship to the problem is based on the notion that there is no one right way for a family system to make desired changes. The school social worker cannot know with certainty what it was about the therapeutic process that provoked change; consequently, the most therapeutically prudent moves for intervention involve discovering options with the family for moving out of their vicious cycle. Interventions presented in this way can be empowering because when families change, they do so on the basis of their own decisions and expertise, not those of the school social worker.

## Step 4: End of the Session

After presenting the tray of hors d'oeuvres, the school social worker should schedule the next appointment. The worker should then quickly end the session to prevent the family from asking a lot of questions about the message and analyzing its meaning. Such discussion can reduce the therapeutic effectiveness of the message.

## Case Example

At the time of the interview, the Allen family (a composite of several cases seen by school social workers) consisted of the father, Jim, 37; the mother, Jo, 35; and their son, Ken, 7. Ken was in the second grade and had been acting out at school and at home. The parents reported that Ken had been fairly well behaved until about two years ago.

At school Ken talked to other students when he should not, talked back to the teachers, hit and kicked other students, and would not stay in his seat. At home he was generally oppositional. He talked back to his parents, went into the street, and would not respond to discipline.

During the first session both parents admitted that they had very different parenting styles: Jim was very stern and firm, whereas Jo gave Ken many warnings before giving a consequence and did not consistently follow through. Jo stated that she was aware that she tried to compensate for Jim's harsh style of discipline by being overly lenient with Ken. Jo and Jim stated that they had tried to talk about their differences in parenting, but the discussions resulted in arguments, with each one defending his or her parenting style. Consequently, the parents had given up trying to parent together. At the end of the first session the school social worker gave them the following message:

> First, I would like to tell you that I am very impressed with the fact that you both are aware that you have very different parenting styles. The fact that you have very different approaches to parenting could be a contributing factor in Ken's behavior problems. Having parents who have different expectations and consequences can be confusing to children. When children are confused they can get anxious, and when they are anxious they often misbehave. As you know, children at Ken's age are prone to act out their feelings rather than talk about them.

It would be very tempting for me at this point to tell you to work on developing a joint approach to parenting. However, I think that for now you might want to go very slowly about changing. You have been parenting this way for some time. It's just that many times I have seen families get very impatient to change and end up changing too much too quickly, and sometimes this can at least temporarily backfire. So you might just want to think about change between now and our next session.

However, one technique some parents have found helpful for starters is the odd day–even day approach. With this approach one of you is the parent in charge on odd days and the other one is the parent in charge on even days. When it is your day to be in charge, then you have all the responsibility for parenting—you make all the decisions and are responsible for enforcing the rules and for disciplining Ken if he breaks the rules. When it is not your day, then you have a vacation from parenting. For example, if Ken comes to you to ask permission to go somewhere and it is not your day to parent, then you must refer Ken to the other parent, who will then make the decision. A flip of a coin can decide who goes first in being the in-charge parent.

Now I'm not telling you to do the odd day–even day technique; it is just something some parents I have worked with have found to be helpful. Whether you do it or not is up to you. All that I have mentioned is just food for thought at this time. Again, it might be best at this time to just think about change for now.

When the Allens returned for the second session the parents reported that they tried the odd day–even day approach a few times and would have done it more but usually forgot to do it. However, most of the time during the past month they used their usual approaches to parenting Ken. Jim and Jo did report that Ken was behaving a little better, but he was still getting into a lot of trouble at school and was still very oppositional at home. Also during this session it came out that Jim's father had died a little over two years earlier. Jim said that his father's death was very difficult for him, and he had yet to visit his father's grave. As he was saying this, Jim became teary eyed. At the end of the second session, the school social worker gave the following message to the family:

I want to commend you for doing some experimenting with trying the odd day–even day technique. Even though many parents have found it effective, many others will not even give it a try. At least you did, and that shows a lot of commitment and courage on your part.

Again, Jo and Jim, it is tempting for me to instruct you in improving your parenting skills so that you are working together as parents. It is also tempting for me to instruct you to do the odd day–even day technique even more in this coming month. But what I am aware of is that Ken's problem behaviors started about the time of the death of your father, Jim. It appears, Jim, that you are still grieving your father's death. Along with grief comes a lot of sadness, which is normal. Sometimes, however, a parent's grief may go unresolved over an extended period of time, and he or she will then become depressed. When that happens, often one of the children in the family will start to act out as a way of helping the parent deal with his or her depression. Often children would rather see a parent angry, even if it is at the child, than depressed. It may be that Ken, by getting into a lot of trouble at home and school, is trying to help you, Jim, deal with your sadness and depression about your father's death. You get angry at Ken when he is misbehaving, and when you are angry you are less likely to be depressed. Ken's misbehaving then might mobilize you, Jim, out of your depression.

Ken, if there is any truth to what I am saying, then you might find yourself not wanting to become too well behaved too quickly, at least until you feel reassured that your father no longer needs you to help him with his sadness about your grandfather's death. Now I am not saying that this is true, only that it might apply to your situation. What I am saying is only food for thought for you as a family at this time.

At the next session, Jim reported that he visited his father's grave. In addition, the parents reported that during the past month Ken's behavior was the worst it had ever been at school; he had started fights with classmates two days in a row. Jo and Jim stated that they realized they needed to do something drastically different in their parenting. They stated that they were willing to do anything to help Ken improve his behavior.

Frequently the child's problem temporarily worsens when the parents start making changes in their parenting. The changes in parenting and the worsening of the child's behavior indicate that there has been a loosening up in the family system and, thus, an increased responsiveness to therapeutic first-order change interventions dealing with improving communication and increasing consistency in parenting. Therefore, during the third session, much of the time was spent with the parents doing an enactment to negotiate a consistent, united front as parents (Minuchin & Fishman, 1981).

## Postsession Letter

Sending families letters noting the positive changes, successes, solutions, strengths, and resources discussed in the previous session can enhance the use of monthly sessions. The therapeutic effect of such letters has been estimated to be equivalent to five sessions (White, cited in Friedman, 1993). These letters can be short and quickly composed based on the worker's notes. Ideally, the family should receive the letter one to two weeks after a session. The following is an example of one such letter (see White & Epston, 1990, and Friedman, 1993, for other examples):

Dear Jim, Jo, and Ken,
As I have done previously, I want to share with you some things I noted at our last meeting. I want to commend you, Jim and Jo, for making good strides toward overcoming "inconsistent parenting." Jo, you did an excellent job of supporting Jim's decision about discipline for Ken when he was carelessly throwing rocks in your backyard. Jim, you were very receptive to Jo's support in that situation and expressed your appreciation to her. I was impressed with your awareness that Jo can at times discard her "Mary Poppins" demeanor and back you up as a parent.

I also want to commend you, Jo, for your commitment to Jim to take the words "you always" and "you never" out of your vocabulary when you speak with him about his behavior toward you.

I want to congratulate you, Ken, for being willing and able to learn from your parents when they gave you consequences for the rock-throwing incident. You could see that your Mom and Dad had good points about what you did, and you accepted the consequences without putting up a big fuss.

It appears that you are on track toward your goals as a family. Keep up the good work, and I look forward to our next meeting.

The model discussed in this article uses letters noting only the family's positive changes, successes, solutions, strengths, and resources; letters containing paradoxical messages to families (Selvini-Palazzoli et al., 1978) are not used.

**Interprofessional Collaboration**

Frequently, school social workers see children and families when the presenting problem is long-standing and crisis driven. In those instances many helpers and agencies may be involved, including school principals, teachers, and counselors; community mental health centers; police; courts and juvenile probation officers; and residential treatment facilities. Often these involved parties have idiosyncratic definitions of the problem and are working at cross-purposes, resulting in therapeutic impasse and maintenance of the problem.

When there are multiple helpers, school social workers should first contact the relevant parties either through telephone calls or letters to coordinate the services and make sure everyone is working together. If these communications are unsuccessful in breaking the therapeutic impasse, the next step is to get these other professionals directly involved with the school social worker in the clinical work with the family, in keeping with a basic rule of systems theory articulated by Bateson (1971): "If you want to understand some phenomenon or appearance, you must consider that phenomenon within the context of all *completed* circuits [feedback loops] which are relevant to it" (p. 244).

With the family's permission, the worker should ask other significant professionals to attend at least one session and to participate in whatever way they feel comfortable, as either cotherapists or observers. The observations of these professionals can be added to the tray of hors d'oeuvres offered to the family in the message stage of the session. Such interprofessional work is consistent with the family–larger system perspective (Imber-Black, 1991) and the "problem-determined systems approach" (Anderson, Goolishian, & Winderman, 1986; Goolishian & Winderman, 1988) to working with multiproblem families as well as the growing thrust of interprofessional collaboration in education (Dryfoos, 1994).

## DISCUSSION

The authors believe that the use of the techniques discussed in this article is necessary but not sufficient for family therapy to be effective on a monthly basis. The primary intent of this article is not to present school social workers with a recipe for using techniques in family treatment but to suggest a way of thinking—dialectical–systemic–constructivist—about organizing treatment and presenting families with new ideas for solving problems and finding solutions.

By suggesting, not prescribing, to families several ideas about doing things differently and the same, the school social worker provides novelty and choices, thus increasing the likelihood that families will make, rather than resist, systemic change in their own way when they are ready. For such a dialectical approach to be effective, the worker must be willing to give the novel ideas time to work their way around the entire family system. The dialectical–systemic–constructivist integrative model presented in this article therefore emphasizes a therapy of ideas rather than techniques.

The monthly family therapy model presented in this article is just part of the continuum of school social work services. Family therapy–oriented school social workers must still respond to teacher referrals and attempt to resolve the presenting problem as quickly as possible. In responding to such referrals, school social workers will continue to work with teachers to develop plans for dealing with a child's problematic behavior in the classroom. Monthly family therapy is usually provided only after the family has not followed through on referrals to outside agencies and resources and after other interventions, provided either in the school or by outside sources, have failed. Consequently, school social workers provide this model of family therapy only as determined by the needs of the case. Throughout the course of monthly family therapy, the school social worker and teacher will continue to consult with each other about the progress of the child and family.

The use of this model can be cost-effective because the school social worker is able to provide services to more children and families. Often there are other school-aged children in the family affected by its dysfunction. Monthly family therapy should benefit these other children by preventing or resolving identified problems. In addition, when the family has new crises, a school social worker can more quickly rejoin the family and successfully intervene with them because of their treatment history.

The two authors of this article who are school social workers found that it became easier to provide family therapy within the context of their jobs if the school personnel with whom they worked also knew how to think in terms of family systems. When initially providing family therapy in the schools, these workers made presentations to principals, teachers, secretarial staff, and school bus drivers on the basics of family systems dynamics and family therapy. The school personnel have continued to be supportive of monthly family therapy.

## CONCLUSION

School social workers are often presented with the dilemma of what to do with cases in which in-school interventions and referrals to community resources for family therapy have been unsuccessful. Despite the various demands of their jobs, school social workers need some ways to intervene successfully in such cases. The model presented here provides school social workers with a method of intervening with problematic children and their families.

The dialectical–systemic–constructivist model is integrative, allowing for systematic borrowing from other therapeutic approaches. Integration of therapeutic approaches is becoming increasingly prevalent in family therapy (Case & Robinson, 1990). Although this article discusses the use of several specific techniques, others preferred by individual school social workers can also be integrated into this model. The authors believe that school social workers who have a consistent way of thinking will be more flexible and creative in using the techniques they already know and open to learning and using new ones. Beyond consistently thinking dialectically–systemically–constructivistically, school social workers will be limited only by their belief in the ability of families to use their own strengths, to be self-determining, and to cure themselves.

The authors and several school social workers they have trained have found this model to be effective with a variety of schoolchildren and their families. Thus far, however, the evidence of this model's effectiveness is anecdotal and qualitative. This dialectical–systemic–constructivist model of school social worker–provided family therapy now needs to be more systematically evaluated. The multiple baseline single-subject research design would be useful in evaluating this model across different families, kinds of problems, school social workers, and school sites.

## REFERENCES

Allen-Meares, P., Washington, R. O., & Welsh, B. L. (1986). *Social work services in schools.* Englewood Cliffs, NJ: Prentice Hall.

Anderson, H., Goolishian, H., & Winderman, L. (1986). Problem-determined systems: Toward transformation in family therapy. *Journal of Strategic and Systemic Therapies, 5,* 14–19.

Anderson, R. E., & Carter, I. (1990). *Human behavior in the social environment: A social systems approach* (4th ed.). New York: Aldine de Gruyter.

Bateson, G. (1971). A systems approach. *International Journal of Psychiatry, 9,* 242–244.

Bateson, G. (1979). *Mind and nature: A necessary unity.* New York: E. P. Dutton.

Becvar, D. S., & Becvar, R. J. (1993). *Family therapy: A systemic integration.* Boston: Allyn & Bacon.

Case, E. M., & Robinson, N. S. (1990). Toward integration: The changing world of family therapy. *American Journal of Family Therapy, 18,* 153–160.

Christian, A. A., Henderson, J., Morse, B. A., & Wilson, N. C. (1983). A family-focused treatment program for emotionally disturbed students. *Social Work in Education, 5,* 165–177.

de Shazer, S., Berg, I. K., Lipchik, E., Nunnally, E., Molnar, A., Gingerich, W., & Weiner-Davis, M. (1986). Brief therapy: Focused solution development. *Family Process, 25,* 207–221.

Dowd, E. T., & Pace, T. M. (1989). The relativity of reality: Second-order change in psychotherapy. In A. Freeman, K. M. Simon, L. E. Beutler, & H. Arkowitz (Eds.), *Comprehensive handbook of cognitive therapy* (pp. 213–226). New York: Plenum Press.

Dryfoos, J. G. (1994). *Full-service schools: A revolution in health and social services for children, youth, and families.* San Francisco: Jossey-Bass.

Fleuridas, C., Nelson, T. S., & Rosenthal, D. M. (1986). The evolution of circular questions: Training family therapists. *Journal of Marital and Family Therapy, 12,* 113–127.

Friedman, S. (Ed.). (1993). *The new language of change: Constructive collaboration in psychotherapy.* New York: Guilford Press.

Gallant, J. P. (1993). New ideas for the school social worker in the counseling of children and families. *Social Work in Education, 15,* 119–128.

Gonzalez-Ramos, G. (1990). Examining the myth of Hispanic families' resistance to treatment: Using the school as a site for services. *Social Work in Education, 12,* 261–274.

Goolishian, H. A., & Winderman, L. (1988). Constructivism, autopoiesis and problem-determined systems. *Irish Journal of Psychology, 9,* 130–143.

Greene, G. J. (1989). Using the written contract for evaluating and enhancing practice effectiveness. *Journal of Independent Social Work, 4,* 135–155.

Greene, G. J., Jensen, C., & Jones, D. H. (1996). A constructivist perspective on clinical social work practice with ethnically diverse clients. *Social Work, 41,* 172–180.

Hoffman, L. (1985). Beyond power and control: Toward a "second order" family systems therapy. *Family Systems Medicine, 4,* 381–396.

Hoffman, L. (1988). A constructivist position for family therapy. *Irish Journal of Psychology, 9,* 110–129.

Imber-Black, E. (1991). A family–larger-system perspective. In A. S. Gurman & D. P. Kniskern (Eds.), *Handbook of family therapy* (Vol. 2, pp. 583–605). New York: Brunner/Mazel.

Ivey, A. E. (1986). *Developmental therapy.* San Francisco: Jossey-Bass.

Jackson, D. D., & Haley, J. (1968). Transference revisited. In D. D. Jackson (Ed.), *Therapy, communication, and change: Human communication* (Vol. 2, pp. 115–128). Palo Alto, CA: Science and Behavior Books.

Keeney, B. P. (1983). *Aesthetics of change.* New York: Guilford Press.

Keeney, B. P. (1987). The construction of therapeutic realities. *Psychotherapy, 24,* 469–476.

Keeney, B. P., Ross, J., & Silverstein, O. (1983). Mind in bodies: The treatment of a family presenting a migraine headache. *Family Systems Medicine, 1,* 61–77.

Keeney, B. P., & Silverstein, O. (1986). *The therapeutic voice of Olga Silverstein.* New York: Guilford Press.

Levine, R. L., & Fitzgerald, H. E. (Eds.). (1992). *Analysis of dynamic psychological systems: Vol. 1. Basic approaches to general systems, dynamic systems, and cybernetics.* New York: Plenum Press.

Levine, R. L., Van Sell, M., & Rubin, B. (1992). System dynamics and the analysis of feedback processes in social and behavioral systems. In R. L. Levine & H. E. Fitzgerald (Eds.), *Analysis of dynamic psychological systems: Vol. 1. Basic approaches to general systems, dynamic systems, and cybernetics* (pp. 145–266). New York: Plenum Press.

Liddle, H. A. (1984). Toward a dialectical–contextual–coevolutionary translation of structural–strategic family therapy. *Journal of Strategic and Systemic Therapies, 4,* 66–79.

McGoldrick, M., & Gerson, R. (1985). *Genograms in family assessment.* New York: W. W. Norton.

Millard, T. L. (1990). School-based social work and family therapy. *Adolescence, 25,* 401–408.

Minuchin, S., & Fishman, H. C. (1981). *Family therapy techniques.* Cambridge, MA: Harvard University Press.

Nardone, G., & Watzlawick, P. (1993). *The art of change: Strategic therapy and hypnotherapy without trance.* San Francisco: Jossey-Bass.

O'Hanlon, W. H., & Weiner-Davis, M. (1989). *In search of solutions: A new direction in psycho-therapy.* New York: W. W. Norton.

Omer, H. (1991). Dialectical interventions and the structure of strategy. *Psychotherapy, 28,* 563–571.

Pennekamp, M., & Freeman, E. M. (1988). Toward a partnership perspective: Schools, families, and school social worker. *Social Work in Education, 10,* 246–259.

Riegal, K. F. (1976). The dialectics of human development. *American Psychologist, 31,* 689–700.

Rohrbaugh, M., Tennen, H., Press, S., & White, L. (1981). Compliance, defiance and therapeutic paradox: Guidelines for strategic use of paradoxical interventions. *American Journal of Orthopsychiatry, 51,* 454–467.

Selvini-Palazzoli, M. S. (1980). Why a long interval between sessions? The therapeutic control of the family–therapist suprasystem. In M. Andolfi & I. Zwerling (Eds.), *Dimensions of family therapy* (pp. 161–169). New York: Guilford Press.

Selvini-Palazzoli, M., Cecchin, G., Prata, G., & Boscolo, L. (1978). *Paradox and counterparadox.* New York: Jason Aronson.

Senge, P. M. (1990). *The fifth discipline: The art and practice of the learning organization.* New York: Doubleday.

Tomm, K. (1984). One perspective on the Milan systemic approach: Part II. Description of session format, interviewing style and interventions. *Journal of Marital and Family Therapy, 10,* 253–271.

Wall, M. D., Kleckner, T., Amendt, J. H., & Bryant, R. (1989). Therapeutic compliments: Setting the stage for successful therapy. *Journal of Marital and Family Therapy, 15,* 159–167.

Walsh, F., & McGoldrick, M. (1991). Loss and the family: A systemic perspective. In F. Walsh & M. McGoldrick (Eds.), *Living beyond loss: Death in the family* (pp. 1–29). New York: W. W. Norton.

Walter, J. L., & Peller, J. E. (1992). *Becoming solution-focused in brief therapy.* New York: Brunner/Mazel.

Wattenberg, S. H., & Kagle, J. D. (1986). School social work referrals for family therapy. *Social Work in Education, 8,* 231–242.

Watzlawick, P., Weakland, J. H., & Fisch, R. (1974). *Change: Principles of problem formation and problem resolution.* New York: W. W. Norton.

Weeks, G. R. (1977). Toward a dialectical approach to intervention. *Human Development, 20,* 277–292.

White, M., & Epston, D. (1990). *Narrative means to therapeutic ends.* New York: W. W. Norton.

Winters, W., & Maluccio, A. (1988). School, family, and community: Working together to promote social competence. *Social Work in Education, 10,* 207–217.

*The work reported in this chapter was supported in part by a State of Michigan Department of Education Special Education Enhancement Grant, 1993–1994. The authors thank Thomas Koepke, PhD, director, Division of Special Education, Ingham Intermediate School District, Mason, MI, for his consistent support.*

*This chapter was originally published in the October 1996 issue of* Social Work in Education, *Vol. 18, pp. 222–236.*

# 17 The Link between Childhood Maltreatment and Teenage Pregnancy

Carolyn A. Smith

C hild maltreatment, encompassing child abuse and neglect of various types, is encountered by social workers in a variety of settings (Allen-Meares, 1995). Mounting evidence now suggests that in addition to its immediate effect on children, maltreatment is associated with a range of problems in older children and adolescents, including substance use and delinquency (Howing, Wodarski, Kurtz, & Gaudin, 1993; Smith & Thornberry, 1995; Widom, 1994). Although studies following maltreated children have not in general found evidence linking maltreatment with subsequent teenage pregnancy, a small body of retrospective research with pregnant teenagers suggests that high proportions have histories of abuse (Boyer & Fine, 1992; Butler & Burton, 1990). In view of the level of concern about outcomes for teenage parents and their children (Furstenberg, Brooks-Gunn, & Morgan, 1987; Hayes, 1987), it is important to identify risk factors associated with teenage pregnancy. Maltreatment may be a particularly important risk factor for intervention policy, because such a history may increase the risk of disrupted parenting in the next generation (Kinard & Klerman, 1989; Widom, 1994).

This study reviews the evidence linking maltreatment and teenage pregnancy from a longitudinal study of urban teenagers and their families. Because sociodemographic factors such as age, family structure, and family disadvantage are linked with both maltreatment and teenage pregnancy, these are controlled in the statistical analyses to evaluate the independent contribution of maltreatment to teenage pregnancy. This research also investigates the role of possible mediating factors. The discussion focuses on implications for intervention in developmental chains that may place young women with a maltreatment history at risk for pregnancy.

## PRIOR RESEARCH

There are two possible models of the relationship between child maltreatment and later outcomes (Starr, MacLean, & Keating, 1991). The first is a specific effects model, which posits that a particular type of maltreatment is translated into specific behavioral and psychological outcomes. For example, a link has been posited between childhood sexual abuse and teenage pregnancy, focusing on the notion of traumatic sexualization that accompanies sexual abuse, leading to sexual preoccupation, sexual behavior, and more serious manifestations such as sexual aggression and sex offending (Friedrich, 1993; Widom, 1994). Recent developmental theory and life-span perspectives are moving away from specific effects models such as this. Maltreatment is increasingly viewed as a manifestation of more general patterns of disrupted parenting that may affect several aspects of development, leading to a broad range of developmental consequences in later life (Cicchetti, 1989; Wolfe & McGee, 1991). Negative developmental consequences also depend on the presence of various other factors in the social context.

Research on the link between maltreatment and teenage pregnancy has, however, been confined mainly to an exploration of a specific and direct link between childhood sexual abuse and teenage pregnancy. For example, Boyer and Fine (1992) found that 53 percent of the 535 pregnant teenagers from school and community programs surveyed reported an experience of sexual molestation, with half of those experiences involving a family member. In another study, 62 percent of 445 teenage parents attending a community program reported coercive sexual experiences, one-third of these at the hands of a family member (Gershenson et al., 1989). Butler and Burton (1990) found that 54 percent of the teenage mothers interviewed reported a previous sexually abusive experience.

Despite the apparently high prevalence of coercive sexual experiences among teenage mothers, there are a number of problems with these studies. Reports of coercive sexual experiences were not measured consistently and were not limited to family abuse alone. Variables were all self-reported, and data were gathered retrospectively rather than prospectively, raising the possibility of biased measurement. In addition, these studies used small samples not representative of the population in general, did not investigate the role of confounding factors such as family disadvantage, and did not investigate the presence of other forms of maltreatment.

Interestingly, some studies that focused on the link between sexual abuse and teenage pregnancy also collected data indicating the presence of other maltreatment in the early lives of teenage mothers. Boyer and Fine (1992) found that 36 percent of the pregnant teenagers in their sample reported emotional abuse while they were growing up, and 64 percent reported evidence of physical abuse and neglect. Stevens-Simon and McAnarney (1994) reported that 33 percent of 127 pregnant teenagers in their study reported either physical abuse or sexual abuse. Moreover, two studies have also linked physical abuse with sexual risk-taking behavior in general (Cunningham, Stiffman, Dore, & Earls, 1994; Luster & Small, 1994).

Researchers have also noted that multiple types of maltreatment coexist in the same families (Barnett, Manly, & Cicchetti, 1993). Psychological maltreatment has serious and relatively unresearched effects that may overlap with other maltreatment categories (Briere & Runtz, 1990). Furthermore, carefully designed studies of the impact of maltreatment have found that different kinds of maltreatment have similar effects. For example, neglect has consequences for criminality that are at least as serious as the consequences of physical abuse (Widom, 1989). This implies that one should look more broadly at the range of maltreatment experiences that may be associated with teenage pregnancy and search for a range of linkages.

## Spurious Links

An important issue underlying any discussion of the connection between maltreatment and teenage pregnancy is the association of contextual factors with both issues. Parents who are poor, those with less education, female heads of household, and parents of color are more likely to have official records of maltreatment according to a number of studies (Garbarino & Plantz, 1986; Trickett, Aber, Carlson, & Cicchetti, 1991; Zuravin, 1988). Pregnant teenagers also are more likely to come from homes marked by poverty and lack of education (Franklin, 1988; Hayes, 1987; Hogan & Kitagawa, 1985). Pregnancy rates are consistently higher among African American teenagers and to some extent among Hispanic teenagers (Hayes, 1987; Miller & Moore, 1990), and children from single-parent homes consistently have higher pregnancy rates than children from homes in which both biological parents are present (Stephan & Stephan, 1989; Wu & Martinson, 1993). The contribution of these contextual factors to both maltreatment and teenage pregnancy indicates that the link between maltreatment and teenage pregnancy may in fact be spurious unless the impact of these factors can be controlled.

## Mediating Mechanisms

Assuming the link is nonspurious, research suggests several indirect links between maltreatment and teenage pregnancy. Maltreatment in children has been associated with effects on behavioral, socioemotional, and cognitive development (Howing et al., 1993; Wolfe, 1987). Children who have been maltreated tend to do more poorly in school, exhibit more disruptive behavior, lack the social skills that would lead to inclusion in conventional peer groups, and show increased levels of depression and low self-esteem (Aber, Allen, Carlson, & Cicchetti, 1989; Howing et al., 1993).

Few studies have followed maltreated children into adolescence. However, it is likely that the combination of poor school performance, lack of close relationships with conventional friends, lack of supportive adults, and negative self-concept may promote a risk scenario in which adolescents experiment with a number of adultlike behaviors including early sexual activity, substance use, and disengagement from home and school (Dryfoos, 1991; Jessor, Donovan, & Costa, 1991). This is particularly the case when factors such as economic and educational disadvantage also are present, as is often the case for urban teenagers of color. A number of negative outcomes in adolescence have in fact been linked with earlier experiences of maltreatment (see Widom, 1994, for a comprehensive review). At the same time, looking backward at the life course from studies of teenage parents, developmental disruptions in the domains of family, peers, school, and personal attitudes and behavior are consistently associated with teenage pregnancy (Hayes, 1987; Rosenheim & Testa, 1992).

## Questions for Analysis

In summary, few studies have directly explored the relationship between maltreatment in childhood and subsequent teenage pregnancy, and none have investigated this issue using a sample not selected on the basis of maltreatment or pregnancy. Although small nonrandom studies link pregnancy with earlier sexual abuse, scattered findings suggest that a range of maltreatment experiences may have an impact on teenage pregnancy. Common factors in the family ecology of maltreated children and pregnant teenagers such as poverty need to be controlled in any investigation of their association. Research on both maltreatment and teenage pregnancy suggests a number of factors that may mediate any relationship between maltreatment and pregnancy. On the basis of this review, questions for analysis include the following:

1. Is a history of maltreatment associated with higher rates of school-age pregnancy among urban adolescent girls?
2. What forms of maltreatment are linked with teenage pregnancy?
3. Is there a relationship between maltreatment and teenage pregnancy controlling for confounding factors such as age, poverty, family structure, and race?
4. What are some of the factors involved in the link between childhood maltreatment and becoming pregnant as a teenager?

## METHOD

### Sample

The data for this analysis are from the Rochester Youth Development Study (RYDS), a multiwave panel study designed to examine the development of delinquent behavior and drug use among urban adolescents. The sample was drawn from the population of approximately 4,000 seventh- and eighth-grade public school students in Rochester, New York, a midsized city. To generate a target panel of 1,000 students, 1,334 eligible students were sampled based on an estimated nonparticipation rate of approximately 25 percent. Students were considered ineligible if they moved out of Rochester before wave 1 cases were fielded, if neither English nor Spanish was spoken in their home, if a sibling was in the sample, or if they were older than the expected age for the cohort.

To obtain a sample in which there would be sufficient variability in delinquency, students were selected into the study in proportion to the adult arrest rate of their census tract of residence. In city census tracts with the highest adult arrest rates, all eligible students were asked to participate in the study; in the remaining census tracts, students were selected at a rate proportionate to the tract's contribution to the city's arrest rate. Once the number of students to be selected from a tract was determined, the student population in the tract was stratified by grade (7 or 8) and gender, and students were selected from those strata at random. Detailed discussions of the sampling plan and retention can be found elsewhere (Thornberry, Bjerregaard, & Miles, 1993). Because the probability of selection is known, cases can be weighted by this probability to represent all seventh and eighth graders attending Rochester public schools. All data, including descriptive statistics, are weighted in the analyses presented here.

In the final panel of 1,000, male teenagers ($n = 729$) are overrepresented by approximately three to one (73 percent to 27 percent). The urban sample and sampling strategy resulted in a high proportion of teenagers of color: African

Americans constituted 68 percent of the total sample, 15 percent were white, and 17 percent were Hispanic. Of the 271 females in the final panel, 249 are included in this study.

## Procedure

Structured interviews with the adolescent and a parent or guardian were conducted by trained RYDS staff at six-month intervals (waves) between spring 1988 and fall 1992. Student interviews were completed primarily in school settings, which ensured privacy; if the adolescent could not be contacted in school, he or she was interviewed at home or in an institutional setting if required. Parent interviews were conducted in the home; in 85 percent of the cases the primary caretaker was the natural mother. Hispanic parents were interviewed by bilingual interviewers using a Spanish interview when necessary. Interviews with parents and adolescents lasted about an hour. Data were also collected from a variety of Rochester agencies such as schools and social services.

## Measurement

The present analysis is based on a self-report of pregnancy in any of interview waves 4 through 9; a measure of maltreatment taken from county child protective services records; and information on background, peer, family, school, and individual factors from wave 2 adolescent and parent interviews.

*Pregnancy.* Participants were designated as pregnant in the analysis (coded as 1) if they answered positively in any interview in waves 4 (when the average age was 14.8 years) through 9 (when the average age was 17.3 years) to a question asking whether they had become pregnant in the six-month interval between interviews. To ensure that they were exposed to pregnancy risk, teenagers were included in the analysis only if they were interviewed at least once after they were 16. Because participants were of school age during this period, "teenage pregnancy" in this study refers to school-age pregnancy.

*Maltreatment.* The measure of maltreatment is based on data obtained from the child protective services records of the Monroe County Department of Social Services, the county of residence for all participants at the start of the RYDS project. In this analysis, only substantiated incidents of abuse or maltreatment occurring before the participant's 12th birthday were included to control for the temporal order of maltreatment and pregnancy. This restriction provides for a very conservative test of the link between maltreatment and teenage pregnancy, because this analysis excludes cases of teenage maltreatment, which may be more common among female teenagers (Garbarino, 1989). It is important to note that we were not able to assess whether participants classified as not maltreated by this procedure may in fact have experienced nonreported maltreatment during their childhood years. The possible inclusion of maltreated participants in the nonmaltreated group introduces a further conservative bias to the investigation of the hypothesized relationship between maltreatment and pregnancy.

Details on the maltreatment incidents were coded from case records according to the well-validated classification system developed by Cicchetti (Barnett et al., 1993). In the classification scheme, maltreatment incidents are coded as including one or more of six types of maltreatment: sexual abuse, physical abuse, emotional maltreatment, physical neglect, lack of supervision, and moral–legal–educational maltreatment. In preliminary analyses it was established that maltreated participants had experienced a range of different types of maltreatment. The most common types of maltreatment included emotional abuse, physical neglect, and lack of supervision. However, because more than half of the 35 maltreated participants were exposed to multiple types of maltreatment, it became unmeaningful to compare pregnancy rates across maltreatment subtypes. For example, among the five sexually abused participants, four became pregnant as teenagers; however, three were also exposed to other forms of maltreatment. Therefore, it cannot be determined from these data whether sexually abused adolescents were at particular risk for pregnancy. However, it is possible to explore the impact of exposure to multiple types of maltreatment. Measures of maltreatment used in this analysis include ever maltreated (maltreatment is coded as 1, no maltreatment as 0) and multiple maltreatment (with exposure to multiple types of maltreatment coded as 2, a single type of maltreatment as 1, and no maltreatment as 0).

*Control Variables.* A number of sociodemographic variables were held constant in the analysis, because these factors have been shown to relate to both maltreatment and pregnancy. White and Hispanic were dummy variables, with African American as the comparison group. If the family received welfare benefits as reported by the primary caretaker in wave 1 or wave 2, this variable was coded as 1 as a proxy for poverty income, because federally defined poverty guidelines are the threshold for receiving Aid to Families with Dependent Children. Family structure was a dummy variable, with 1 indicating households in which the biological parents were in the home at the start of the study in comparison to other types of family structures. Parent education was a dummy variable, with 1 indicating that the parent respondent reported that he or she had completed high school.

*Mediating Variables.* Another set of measures were taken from the major domains that influence adolescent behavior and that may link maltreatment and teenage pregnancy, including school, family, peer, and individual variables. School variables included school aspirations, a four-point variable indicating the importance the child places on going to college, and a cognitive measure, school performance, measured by the California Achievement Test percentile reading score from school records in grades 7 or 8. Involvement with parents was an 11-item scale measuring the adolescent's perception of involvement with parents, including communication with parents about life issues and time spent with parents inside and outside the home. Delinquent friends was a measure of the extent to which the participant's group of friends were involved in a list of eight delinquent activities, with high scores indicating more involvement by friends in delinquency. Measures of individual factors included a seven-item depression scale adapted from the Center for Epidemiologic Studies–Depressed Mood Scale (CES–D) (Radloff, 1977), with higher scores indicating greater depression, and a self-report prevalence measure of early substance use, with 1 indicating that the teenager reported the use of alcohol or any illegal drug in the wave 2 interview. Finally, early sexual intercourse indicated that the teenager was involved in sexual activity at age 14 or younger, another marker for early at-risk behavior.

## RESULTS

Maltreatment was present in the backgrounds of 35 of the 249 teenagers, a maltreatment prevalence of 14 percent (Table 17-1). Higher rates of maltreatment were found among teenagers in families receiving government assistance or welfare: 19 percent of the 134 families on welfare had children with maltreatment records, compared with only 6 percent of the 96 families not on welfare. Significantly higher maltreatment rates were found among teenagers without both biological parents present compared with those with both parents present (17 percent of 180 versus 4 percent of 64). There were no significant differences in maltreatment by level of education of the primary caretaker. However, there were significant differences in maltreatment level by race and ethnicity, although the number of white and Hispanic teenage girls in the study was small. The prevalence of maltreatment among the 16 white families was 33 percent, among the 33 Hispanic families 5 percent, and among the 200 African American families 13 percent.

A total of 111 of the 249 participants became pregnant while of school age, a pregnancy prevalence rate of 45 percent (Table 17-2). This high prevalence rate was probably related to the urban sample and the high proportion of adolescents of color, among whom pregnancy rates were higher in other studies (Miller

Table 17-1

**Prevalence of Maltreatment in Female Teenagers, by Demographic Characteristics**

| Characteristic | % Maltreated | | n |
| --- | --- | --- | --- |
| | Yes | No | |
| Total sample | 14 | 86 | 249 |
| Welfare recipient | | | |
| Yes | 19 | 81 | 134 |
| No | 6 | 94* | 96 |
| Parent education | | | |
| Not a high school graduate | 13 | 87 | 137 |
| High school graduate | 14 | 86 | 111 |
| Family structure | | | |
| Other | 17 | 83 | 180 |
| Both biological parents present | 4 | 96* | 64 |
| Race and ethnicity | | | |
| White | 33 | 67* | 16 |
| Hispanic | 5 | 95 | 33 |
| African American | 13 | 87 | 200 |

*$p < .05$, one-tailed.

*Table 17-2*
**Prevalence of Pregnancy, by Demographic Characteristics**

|  | % Pregnant | | |
| Characteristic | Yes | No | *n* |
| --- | --- | --- | --- |
| Total sample | 45 | 55 | 249 |
| Welfare recipient |  |  |  |
| Yes | 49 | 51 | 134 |
| No | 35 | 65* | 96 |
| Parent education |  |  |  |
| Not a high school graduate | 50 | 50 | 137 |
| High school graduate | 37 | 63* | 111 |
| Family structure |  |  |  |
| Other | 47 | 53 | 180 |
| Both biological parents present | 33 | 67* | 64 |
| Race and ethnicity |  |  |  |
| White | 27 | 73 | 16 |
| Hispanic | 37 | 63 | 33 |
| African American | 47 | 53 | 200 |

*$p < .05$, one-tailed.

& Moore, 1990; Rosenheim & Testa, 1992). Pregnancy rates were significantly higher among teenagers with parents receiving welfare—49 percent of the girls in the 134 families receiving welfare became pregnant, compared with 35 percent in the 96 families not receiving welfare. Pregnancy rates were also significantly higher among children of caretakers without a high school education (50 percent of the 137 nongraduates, compared with 37 percent of the 111 graduates) and among families without two biological parents present (47 percent of 180 families versus 33 percent of 64). Differences in pregnancy prevalence by race and ethnicity were not significant, although trends were in line with current research, with higher pregnancy rates among African American and Hispanic teenagers (Miller & Moore, 1990).

With this information as a backdrop, the next and primary issue for analysis was the prevalence of teenage pregnancy among maltreated and nonmaltreated participants (Table 17-3). In the total sample, 62 percent of the 35 maltreated participants became pregnant, compared with 40 percent of the nonmaltreated group of 214, a significant difference. Thus, initial data support a link between maltreatment and pregnancy in a representative sample of urban adolescent girls.

The analysis next investigated whether experiencing multiple types of maltreatment exposed teenage girls to greater pregnancy risk. Whereas the pregnancy rate for those exposed to only one type of maltreatment ($n = 19$) was 56 percent, the pregnancy rate among those exposed to at least two types of maltreatment ($n = 21$) rises to 66 percent (Table 17-3). Differences among the three groups are significant. This finding suggests that in addition to maltreatment

Table 17-3

**Prevalence of Pregnancy, by Maltreatment Status**

|  | % Pregnant | | |
|---|---|---|---|
| Status | Yes | No | *n* |
| Ever maltreated | | | |
| Not maltreated | 40 | 60* | 214 |
| Maltreated | 62 | 38 | 35 |
| Multiple maltreatment | | | |
| Not maltreated | 40 | 60* | 209 |
| One type only | 56 | 44 | 19 |
| More than one type | 66 | 34 | 21 |

*p < .05, one-tailed.

per se, it may be the range of developmental domains affected by maltreatment that is associated with pregnancy risk.

The third issue for analysis is whether the connection between maltreatment and teenage pregnancy is spurious owing to the presence of other factors that are related to both maltreatment and pregnancy. Because the dependent variable, teenage pregnancy, is dichotomous, multivariate logistic regression analysis was used to examine the main effects of maltreatment net of background factors. Logistic regression coefficients, their significance, and the odds ratios associated with each variable are presented in Table 17-4. The sign of the logistic

Table 17-4

**Results from Logistic Regression Equations Predicting Pregnancy**

| | Model 1 (*n* = 209) | | Model 2 (*n* = 209) | |
|---|---|---|---|---|
| Measure | Logistic Coefficient | Odds Ratio | Logistic Coefficient | Odds Ratio |
| Maltreatment | 1.01* | 2.76 | .94 | 2.55 |
| Welfare | .34 | 1.41 | .22 | 1.24 |
| Parent education | −.75* | .47 | −.78* | .46 |
| Family structure | −.18 | .83 | −.17 | .84 |
| Hispanic | −.54 | .58 | −.20 | .82 |
| White | −2.04* | .13 | −1.36 | .26 |
| Involvement with parents | | | −.21 | .81 |
| Delinquent friends | | | −.30 | .74 |
| School performance | | | −.03** | .97 |
| School aspirations | | | −.95* | .38 |
| Early substance use | | | 1.17* | 3.23 |
| Depression | | | .39 | 1.47 |
| Early sexual intercourse | | | .97** | 2.65 |
| Constant | −.04 | | 4.3 | |
| Log likelihood | 255.0, NS | | 209.2, NS | |
| Model chi-square | 20.6$^a$** | | 66.5$^b$** | |

NOTE: NS = not significant.
$^a$df = 6. $^b$df = 13.
*p < .05. **p < .01.

coefficients—positive or negative—can be interpreted like that of ordinary least squares coefficients as indicating increases or decreases in the dependent variable, with a one-unit change in each independent variable (Morgan & Teachman, 1988). However, the dependent variable in this procedure was the logarithm of the odds of becoming pregnant. Odds ratios represent expected changes in the log odds of pregnancy net of other variables in the model. It should be noted that the sample for the multivariate analyses is 209, reduced by 40 cases due to missing data on independent variables.

In model 1 the logistic regression coefficient for maltreatment was significant, indicating that maltreatment affected the prevalence of school-age pregnancy even when the control variables were held constant. The odds ratio suggests that maltreated teenagers were 2.76 times more likely to become pregnant than nonmaltreated teenagers. These results underline the importance of maltreatment as a risk factor for teenage pregnancy, even controlling for possible confounding variables. The odds of pregnancy were also enhanced for participants of color and those from homes in which the primary caretaker had not completed high school, findings in line with research on teenage pregnancy. Family structure and family welfare dependence were not associated with pregnancy.

The final issue for analysis is the investigation of factors that mediate the observed relationship between maltreatment and teenage pregnancy (model 2 in Table 17-4). Pregnancy was regressed on maltreatment; the control variables mentioned earlier; and seven variables hypothesized to link maltreatment and pregnancy, including school aspirations and performance, involvement with parents, delinquent friends, depression, early substance use, and early sexual intercourse (age 14 or younger). Model 2 fits the data well, as the model statistics indicate.

When potential intervening factors were entered into the equation, the coefficient for maltreatment became insignificant, suggesting that some of the variance in pregnancy previously explained by maltreatment was accounted for by these factors. Among the control variables, parent education was still related to teenage pregnancy. Additional factors predicting teenage pregnancy include low school aspirations, poor school performance, early substance use, and early sexual intercourse. Receipt of welfare, family structure, involvement with parents, delinquent friends, and depression were not related to pregnancy, nor was race or ethnicity.

In further analysis not reported here, maltreatment was entered as a three-category variable, with both single and multiple types of maltreatment, and contrasted with the nonmaltreated category. Results indicate that teenagers exposed to multiple types of maltreatment were more likely than nonmaltreated teenagers to become pregnant, whereas teenagers exposed to only one type of maltreatment were not significantly more likely than nonmaltreated teenagers to become pregnant. The relationship of other predictors remained substantially the same. This finding underlines the need to assess the extensiveness of maltreatment in evaluating its impact on later developmental outcomes.

A range of issues, including school, family, and individual behaviors, influence teenage pregnancy. Family issues include maltreatment and lack of parent education, behavioral issues include early substance use and early sexual intercourse, and school issues include low aspirations and low performance. Although it is not clear from these data what psychological processes may be implicated, findings are consistent with research on maltreated children, which suggests that a range of developmental consequences may follow maltreatment, including lack of competence in school and problem behaviors. Longer-term consequences of these issues may include teenage pregnancy.

## DISCUSSION

This study addresses four issues. The first is an assessment of the relationship between being maltreated as a child and becoming pregnant as an adolescent. There is a significant bivariate association between maltreatment and school-age pregnancy, indicating that maltreatment is a risk factor for teenage pregnancy in this urban sample. Although past research on pregnant and parenting teenagers has suggested that abuse may be disproportionately present in their background, this study confirms this link with longitudinal data on a sample of young urban women not preselected on the basis of pregnancy.

The second issue is the relationship between sexual abuse and teenage pregnancy. It is not possible to tell, given the small number of sexually abused participants in the sample and their exposure to other forms of maltreatment, whether sexual abuse played a particularly prominent role in later pregnancy. The data in general suggest that it is exposure to a range of maltreatment experiences, rather than any specific type, that constitutes a risk for pregnancy. This finding is consistent with the growing body of longitudinal research that suggests that maltreatment has a wide-ranging and accumulating developmental impact (Cicchetti, 1989) and with implications from these data that a greater breadth of maltreatment experience is associated with a higher rate of problem outcomes, including pregnancy.

The third issue is whether any link found between pregnancy and maltreatment might be considered spurious, given the common factors associated with both maltreatment and pregnancy. In this study maltreatment is a significant predictor of teenage pregnancy in a multivariate analysis, even when controls are introduced for possible confounding variables.

The final issue is to elucidate some of the linkages in the nonspurious relationship found between maltreatment and teenage pregnancy. Findings suggest that maltreatment may affect pregnancy through increased educational disadvantage, increased substance use, and early search for sexual intimacy. The data suggest that maltreated teenagers who become pregnant are those who in early adolescence fall into the category of high-risk youths engaging in a constellation of activities that generally place them at risk for poor outcomes. Whereas some research has suggested that sex-related and other problem behaviors are less likely to co-occur for young women in comparison to their male counterparts (Ensminger, 1990), teenage girls who have been maltreated may be at higher risk for multiple problem behaviors. It is also important to note that some maltreated teenagers do not become pregnant. The data suggest some issues that may protect them, including containing and limiting maltreatment, promoting school success, and avoiding other risk behaviors.

Some limitations of the study need to be considered before discussing the implications of these findings. First, although the sample is representative of an urban population, the sample selection process resulted in too few white and Hispanic teenagers to look at differences in the maltreatment–pregnancy relationship by race or ethnicity. It is not possible to dismiss the notion that cultural and protective factors may operate differently for different groups.

Although the sample was representative, it included too few maltreatment cases for analysis of specific maltreatment subtypes, and this affects exploration of the effects of sexual abuse. However, sexual abuse is less common than other types of maltreatment such as neglect, and the finding that a range of maltreatment experiences enhances risk of pregnancy opens the door to wider-ranging exploration of developmental pathways and linkages. Other types of maltreatment may also be more amenable to intervention.

Finally, the primary focus of the main study limited the variables available for analysis. Factors that have been related to teenage pregnancy in other research and that may also be related to maltreatment include other experiences of victimization and extensive teenage pregnancy in the peer group and neighborhood. The study does, however, incorporate measures from different life domains and perspectives.

## INTERVENTION IMPLICATIONS

### Intervening with Maltreating Families

Continued efforts to prevent and curtail maltreatment are important as a first-line strategy in preventing later developmental problems in affected children. A range of strategies has been invoked, although their success is hard to evaluate (Allen-Meares, 1995). The range of developmental ramifications of maltreatment suggests that intervention in families in which maltreatment has occurred needs to address a wide range of targets, necessitating a "coordinated range of community-based services for children and families in crisis" (Howing et al., 1993, p. 135). These include services that reduce environmental stress, improve parent support, and prevent and modify harmful parenting (Wolfe, 1987; Wolfe, Edwards, Manion, & Koverola, 1988). These findings also suggest the importance of improving parent educational opportunities, because their lack of education increases the odds of teenage pregnancy in the next generation. Those who work with maltreated children and their families need to be aware of the fact that long-term consequences of prolonged and extensive maltreatment may play out in a variety of arenas during adolescence (Widom, 1994). On the positive side, when intervention and services are helpful in reducing subsequent maltreatment risk, children can demonstrate resilience and recovery.

### Promoting Resilience to Maltreatment

The data indicate that not all maltreated teenagers become pregnant. Although little is known about how to insulate maltreated children from pregnancy risk, a broad literature is emerging that suggests factors connected to general resilience among at-risk children, including supportive adults, opportunities, and personal skills (Rutter, 1987). Interventions that seek to prevent early substance use and premature sexual involvement may be influential in helping adolescents avoid pregnancy and other developmental hazards (for example, Kirby, 1994; Ooms, 1995).

These findings augment other studies that point to the general role of educational success in adolescent resilience (Smith, Lizotte, Thornberry, & Krohn, 1995; Winfield, 1991). School achievement is promoted by diverse strategies, including compensatory preschool programs (Karweit, 1989), family involvement, and school organizational structures that link developmental and learning needs of disadvantaged children (Clancy, 1995). Remediating school problems later in the school experience is more challenging, although "turnaround" can be achieved even for high-risk adolescents (Gregory, 1995).

## Preventing Pregnancy and Sexual Exploitation

Maltreatment as a form of victimization and devaluation may lead to other experiences of victimization and exploitation, including in sexual situations. Some recent studies suggest that many early sexual experiences are nonvoluntary or involve much older men or both (Moore, Nord, & Peterson, 1989; Small & Kearns, 1993). This is becoming recognized as a policy concern and may call for legal remedies (Miller, 1995).

Pregnant teenagers in this study were more likely to have initiated sexual relations during their early development, when they were unlikely to be able to manage sexual choices competently. Others have noted that the environment and norms of young urban men may encourage their predatory behavior with young women (Anderson, 1993). This issue suggests implications for educational intervention with young men and women and their parents. Teenagers need "multi-pronged, coordinated prevention strategies" (Ooms, 1995, p. 252), and some progress has been made in developing programs that have demonstrated effectiveness (Kirby, 1994).

Maltreated children and their caretakers need to be educated specifically about enhanced risk during adolescence and offered help in communicating with each other about issues such as the importance of careful sexual decision making and contraception. It is also important to make treatment available to address victimization experiences among high-risk groups (for example, in institutional settings), lest interventions with troubled teenagers ignore and thus perpetuate experiences of victimization (Bowers, 1990; Dembo et al., 1987).

## Providing Assessment and Services for Maltreated Pregnant Teenagers

The enhanced risk of pregnancy for maltreated teenagers raises concerns about the implications of having a maltreatment history for teenage mothers' parenting. Research suggests that teenage parents may be at greater risk for maltreating their children, not specifically on the grounds of age or unmarried status, but to the extent that they experience additional risk factors including lack of education, poverty, disrupted family life, and involvement in problem behavior (Kinard & Klerman, 1989; Zuravin, 1988). To the extent that pregnant teenagers may also have been maltreated, used illegal substances, and failed to complete their education, they may be among those who are at particular risk for maltreating their own children. Current welfare reform proposals to cut back on government assistance to childbearing teenagers seems particularly ill advised in this context.

An additional risk factor for teenage parents may be the selection of unstable and antisocial partners whose behavior may perpetuate victimization (Rutter, 1989). These factors underline the need to assess maltreatment and domestic abuse history among pregnant teenagers and target broad-based early preventive services to those most at risk.

## CONCLUSION

The most significant issue raised by these preliminary findings is that young urban teenage women who have been maltreated may be at higher risk for becoming teenage parents. Further research is needed to establish the processes that inhibit or facilitate this outcome so researchers can continue to develop intervention approaches that are responsive to the needs of teenagers and to the welfare of the next generation of children.

## REFERENCES

Aber, J. L., Allen, J. P., Carlson, V., & Cicchetti, D. (1989). The effects of maltreatment on development during early childhood. In D. Cicchetti & V. Carlson (Eds.), *Child maltreatment: Theory and research on the causes and consequences of child abuse and neglect* (pp. 579–619). New York: Cambridge University Press.

Allen-Meares, P. (1995). *Social work with children and adolescents*. White Plains, NY: Longman.

Anderson, E. (1993). Sex codes among inner-city youth. In R. J. Lerman & T. J. Ooms (Eds.), *Young unwed fathers: Changing roles and emerging policies* (pp. 74–98). Philadelphia: Temple University Press.

Barnett, D., Manly, J. T., & Cicchetti, D. (1993). Defining child maltreatment: The interface between policy and research. In D. Cicchetti & S. L. Toth (Eds.), *Child abuse, child development, and social policy* (pp. 7–73). Norwood, NJ: Ablex.

Bowers, L. B. (1990). Traumas precipitating female delinquency: Implications for assessment, practice and policy. *Child and Adolescent Social Work, 7,* 389–402.

Boyer, D., & Fine, D. (1992). Sexual abuse as a factor in adolescent pregnancy and child maltreatment. *Family Planning Perspectives, 24,* 4–11.

Briere, J., & Runtz, M. (1990). Differential adult symptomatology associated with three types of child abuse histories. *Child Abuse & Neglect, 14,* 357–364.

Butler, J., & Burton, L. (1990). Rethinking teenage childbearing: Is sexual abuse a missing link? *Family Relations, 39,* 73–80.

Cicchetti, D. (1989). How research on child development has informed the study of child development: Perspectives from developmental psychopathology. In D. Cicchetti & V. Carlson (Eds.), *Child maltreatment: Theory and research on the causes and consequences of child abuse and neglect* (pp. 377–431). New York: Cambridge University Press.

Clancy, J. (1995). Ecological school social work: The reality and the vision. *Social Work in Education, 17,* 40–47.

Cunningham, R. M., Stiffman, A. R., Dore, P., & Earls, F. (1994). The association of physical and sexual abuse with HIV risk behaviors in adolescence and young adulthood: Implications for public health. *Child Abuse & Neglect, 18,* 233–245.

Dembo, R., Dertke, M., La Voie, L., Borders, S., Washburn, M., & Schmeidler, J. (1987). Physical abuse, sexual victimization and illicit drug use: A structural analysis among high-risk adolescents. *Journal of Adolescence, 10,* 10–33.

Dryfoos, J. G. (1991). *Adolescents at risk: Prevalence and prevention*. New York: Oxford University Press.

Ensminger, M. (1990). Sexual activity and problem behavior among black urban adolescents. *Child Development, 61,* 2032–2046.

Franklin, D. L. (1988). Race, class and adolescent pregnancy: An ecological analysis. *American Journal of Orthopsychiatry, 58,* 339–354.

Friedrich, W. N. (1993). Sexual victimization and sexual behavior in children: A review of recent literature. *Child Abuse & Neglect, 17,* 59–66.

Furstenberg, F. F., Brooks-Gunn, J., & Morgan, S. P. (1987). *Adolescent mothers in later life.* Cambridge, England: Cambridge University Press.

Garbarino, J. (1989). Troubled youth, troubled families: The dynamics of adolescent maltreatment. In D. Cicchetti & V. Carlson (Eds.), *Child maltreatment: Theory and research on the causes and consequences of child abuse and neglect* (pp. 685–706). New York: Cambridge University Press.

Garbarino, J., & Plantz, M. C. (1986). Child abuse and juvenile delinquency: What are the links? In J. Garbarino, C. Schellenbach, & J. Sebes (Eds.), *Troubled youth, troubled families* (pp. 27–39). New York: Aldine de Gruyter.

Gershenson, H. P., Misick, J. S., Ruch-Ross, H. S., Magee, V., Kamina-Rubino, K., & Rosenberg, D. (1989). The prevalence of coercive sexual experience among teenage mothers. *Journal of Interpersonal Violence, 4,* 204–219.

Gregory, L. W. (1995). The "turnaround" process: Factors influencing the school success of urban youth. *Journal of Adolescent Research, 10,* 136–154.

Hayes, C. D. (1987). *Risking the future* (Vol. 1). Washington, DC: National Academy Press.

Hogan, D., & Kitagawa, E. (1985). The impact of social status, family structure, and neighborhood on the fertility of black adolescents. *American Journal of Sociology, 90,* 825–855.

Howing, P. T., Wodarski, J. S., Kurtz, P. D., & Gaudin, P. D. (1993). *Maltreatment and the school-age child: Developmental outcomes and system issues.* New York: Haworth Press.

Jessor, R., Donovan, J. E., & Costa, F. M. (1991). *Beyond adolescence: Problem behavior and young adult development.* Cambridge, England: Cambridge University Press.

Karweit, N. L. (1989). Effective preschool programs for students at risk. In R. E. Salvin, N. L. Karweit, & N. A. Madden (Eds.), *Effective programs for students at risk* (pp. 75–102). Boston: Allyn & Bacon.

Kinard, E. R., & Klerman, L. V. (1989). Teenage parenting and child abuse: Are they related? *American Journal of Orthopsychiatry, 50,* 41–44.

Kirby, D. (1994). Sexuality and HIV education programs in schools. In J. Garrison, M. D. Smith, & D. J. Besharov (Eds.), *Sex education in the schools* (pp. 1–41). Menlo Park, CA: Kaiser Family Foundation.

Luster, T., & Small, S. A. (1994). Factors associated with sexual risk-taking behaviors among adolescents. *Journal of Marriage and the Family, 56,* 622–632.

Miller, B. C. (1995). Risk factors for adolescent non-marital childbearing. In *Report to Congress on out-of-wedlock childbearing* (Publication No. 95-1257, pp. 217–227). Hyattsville, MD: U.S. Department of Health and Human Services.

Miller, B. C., & Moore, K. A. (1990). Adolescent sexual behavior, pregnancy and parenting: Research through the 1980's. *Journal of Marriage and the Family, 53,* 1025–1044.

Moore, K. A., Nord, C. W., & Peterson, J. L. (1989). Non-voluntary sexual activity among adolescents. *Family Planning Perspectives, 20,* 128–136.

Morgan, S. P., & Teachman, J. D. (1988). Logistic regression: Description, examples and comparisons. *Journal of Marriage and the Family, 50,* 929–936.

Ooms, T. (1995). Strategies to reduce nonmarital childbearing. In *Report to Congress on out-of-wedlock childbearing* (Publication No. 95-1257, pp. 241–261). Hyattsville, MD: U.S. Department of Health and Human Services.

Radloff, L. S. (1977). The CES–D Scale: A self-report depression scale for research in the general population. *Applied Psychological Measurement, 1,* 385–401.

Rosenheim, M. K., & Testa, M. F. (Eds.). (1992). *Early parenthood and coming of age in the 1990's.* Hillsdale, NJ: Lawrence Erlbaum.

Rutter, M. (1987). Psychosocial resilience and protective mechanisms. *American Journal of Orthopsychiatry, 57,* 316–331.

Rutter, M. (1989). Intergenerational continuities and discontinuities in serious parenting difficulties. In D. Cicchetti & V. Carlson (Eds.), *Child maltreatment: Theory and research on the causes and consequences of child abuse and neglect* (pp. 317–349). New York: Cambridge University Press.

Small, S. A., & Kearns, D. (1993). Unwanted sexual activity among peers during early and middle adolescence: Incidence and risk factors. *Journal of Marriage and the Family, 55,* 941–952.

Smith, C. A., Lizotte, A. J., Thornberry, T. P., & Krohn, M. D. (1995). Resilient youth: Identifying factors that prevent high-risk youth from engaging in delinquency and drug use. In J. Hagen (Ed.), *Delinquency and disrepute in the life course* (pp. 217–247). Greenwich, CT: JAI Press.

Smith, C. A., & Thornberry, T. P. (1995). The relationship between childhood maltreatment and adolescent involvement in delinquency. *Criminology, 33,* 451–481.

Starr, R. H., MacLean, D. J., & Keating, D. P. (1991). Life span developmental outcomes of child maltreatment. In R. H. Starr & D. Wolfe (Eds.), *The effects of child abuse and neglect* (pp. 1–32). New York: Guilford Press.

Stephan, C. W., & Stephan, W. G. (1989). Family configuration in relation to the sexual behavior of adolescents. *Family Planning Perspectives, 21,* 499–506.

Stevens-Simon, C., & McAnarney, E. R. (1994). Childhood victimization: Relationship to adolescent pregnancy outcomes. *Child Abuse & Neglect, 18,* 569–575.

Thornberry, T. P., Bjerregaard, B., & Miles, W. (1993). The consequences of respondent attrition in panel studies: A simulation based on the Rochester Youth Development Study. *Journal of Quantitative Criminology, 9,* 127–158.

Trickett, P. K., Aber, J. L., Carlson, V., & Cicchetti, D. (1991). The relationship of socioeconomic status to the etiology and development sequelae of physical child abuse. *Developmental Psychology, 27,* 148–158.

Widom, C. S. (1989). Child abuse, neglect, and violent criminal behavior. *Criminology, 27,* 251–271.

Widom, C. S. (1994). Childhood victimization and adolescent problem behavior. In M. E. Lamb & R. Ketterlinus (Eds.), *Adolescent problem behaviors* (pp. 127–164). Hillsdale, NJ: Lawrence Erlbaum.

Winfield, L. F. (1991). Resilience, schooling and development in African American youth. *Education and Urban Society, 24,* 5–13.

Wolfe, D. A. (1987). *Child abuse: Implications for child development and psychopathology.* Beverly Hills, CA: Sage Publications.

Wolfe, D., Edwards, B., Manion, I., & Koverola, C. (1988). Early intervention for parents at risk of child abuse and neglect: A preliminary investigation. *Journal of Consulting and Clinical Psychology, 56,* 40–47.

Wolfe, D. A., & McGee, R. (1991). Assessment of emotional status among maltreated children. In R. H. Starr, Jr., & D. A. Wolfe (Eds.), *The effects of child abuse and neglect: Issues and research* (pp. 257–277). New York: Guilford Press.

Wu, L. W., & Martinson, B. C. (1993). Family structure and the risk of a premarital birth. *American Sociological Review, 58,* 210–232.

Zuravin, S. J. (1988). Child maltreatment and teenage first births: A relationship mediated by chronic sociodemographic stress. *American Journal of Orthopsychiatry, 58,* 91–103.

*This chapter was prepared under Grant No. 86-JN-CX-0007 (S-3) from the Office of Juvenile Justice and Delinquency Prevention, Office of Justice Programs, U.S. Department of Justice; Grant No. 5 R01 DA05512-02 from the National Institute on Drug Abuse; Grant No. SES-8912274 from the National Science Foundation; and Drescher Leave Award 320-9670-0 from the State University of New York. Points of view or opinions in this article are those of the author and do not necessarily represent the official position or policies of the funding agencies. I gratefully acknowledge the helpful comments made by Jan Hagen, Terence Thornberry, and Cathy Spatz-Widom on earlier versions of this chapter. I also thank Pam Porter for her editorial help and Patty Glynn for her assistance with computer analysis.*

*This chapter was originally published in the September 1996 issue of* Social Work Research, *Vol. 20, pp. 131–141.*

# 18 Factors Associated with Early Sexual Activity among Urban Adolescents

Carolyn A. Smith

A dolescent sexuality presents multiple challenges for social work, involving complex developmental processes as well as cultural, social, and family issues (Allen-Meares, 1995). Although Americans as a nation continue to be ambivalent about sexuality and how teenagers should express it, it is clear that sexual activity is "migrating down" to very young adolescents (Hahn, 1995), placing them at risk for contracting AIDS and other sexually transmitted diseases (STDs) and for becoming pregnant (Irwin & Shafer, 1992). The well-being of children born to young teenagers also is at stake (Hayes, 1987).

The potential for problem outcomes of early sexual activity is enhanced for teenagers of color because of the disproportionate economic and community stresses they face (Battle, 1987; Ladner, 1987). To shed further light on appropriate social work responses, this study uses lifespan and ecological frameworks to investigate the origins and effects of early sexual activity among urban adolescents.

## LIFESPAN PERSPECTIVE

The lifespan perspective emphasizes age-related dynamics in the life course, including, for example, the impact of particular life stages such as adolescence and important stage-related events such as the transition to sexual activity. Events that occur "off-time" can be associated with disruptions in normal developmental sequences, leading to potential difficulty in later development (Elder, 1985).

Sexual exploration is part of the normal lifecycle experience. Currently, by the end of high school, the majority of adolescents experience sexual intercourse (Irwin & Shafer, 1992; Kahn, Kalsbeek, & Hofferth, 1988). Sexual activity during adolescence may, however, be more or less out of phase and problematic depending on the age involved. Early adolescence, ages 11 to 15, is a critical period of the life course given the wide-ranging sexual, emotional, social, and cognitive changes that occur (Hahn, 1995; Simmons & Blyth, 1987). Teenagers of color face additional developmental challenges in this phase because they are developing their own cultural identity while confronting the culture and values of the majority and coping with its barriers and prejudices (Spencer & Dornbusch, 1990). In general, adolescents in this phase are less likely to display the developmental readiness to engage in sensible sexual decision making (Hamburg, 1986; Petersen & Crockett, 1992).

Although few studies have specifically explored sexual behavior in representative samples of young teenagers, available evidence does suggest worse consequences at earlier ages. Young teenagers are more likely to engage in sporadic and unplanned sexual activity (Chilman, 1986), are less likely to use contraception (Zabin, Hirsch, Smith, & Hardy, 1984), and are more likely to risk pregnancy and STDs (Sonenstein, Pleck, & Ku, 1989). Older adolescents generally are more sexually active, and earlier studies have shown that the majority of adolescents made the transition to intercourse after age 15 (Kahn et al., 1988; Miller & Moore, 1990). However, sexual activity at young ages is increasing (Hahn, 1995). Although rates of early sexual activity are increasing among all groups of teenagers, rates are higher among young urban African American and Hispanic teenagers (Fennelly, 1988; Forste & Heaton, 1988).

## ECOLOGICAL PERSPECTIVE

The ecological perspective holds that people are active participants in nested and overlapping systems that influence developmental outcomes (Bronfenbrenner, 1986; Garbarino, 1992). This perspective has been used to explore the life contexts that influence teenage sexuality (Franklin, 1988; Small & Luster, 1994). For heuristic simplicity, influences on sexual behavior are grouped into distal contexts that set the stage for development, such as neighborhood and sociodemographic characteristics, and proximal contexts that impinge on adolescents directly, including family, school, and individual influences.

Recent research has stressed the influential role of neighborhoods on teenage sexuality. Research using data from the National Survey of Family Growth on girls ages 15 to 19 (Brewster, 1994; Brewster, Billy, & Grady, 1993) found that differences in neighborhood characteristics, including employment, income, race, and education, accounted for part of the race difference in rates of sexual activity, although individual and family risk factors were also important. Hogan and Kitagawa (1985) also found that neighborhood risk measured at the census tract level was associated with fertility of young African American women, as were family and educational factors. Findings from a national survey of boys ages 15 to 19 suggested that lack of economic resources and job opportunities at the neighborhood level was associated with sexual activity (Ku, Sonenstein, & Pleck, 1993).

Sociodemographic background, including race, income, and family structure, consistently has been associated with teenage sexuality. Race and minority status have been linked with differences in both male and female sexuality and fertility, including the earlier onset of sexual activity (for example, Furstenberg, Morgan, Moore, & Peterson, 1987; Ku et al., 1993; Moore, Simms, & Betsey, 1986). Household income, as well as race and age, was significantly associated with sexual activity in girls ages 15 to 19 in the National Survey of Young Women (Bingham, Miller, & Adams, 1990). Findings from a national labor market survey of boys and girls ages 14 to 21 (Day, 1992) suggested that family socioeconomic status, as well as family structure, school composition, and urban location, affects the transition to sexual activity. Studies also consistently suggest that more precocious sexual activity exists in families headed by single parents, although there is little data on young men (Hogan & Kitagawa, 1985; Stephan & Stephan, 1989).

Family functioning has been linked with teenage sexuality (Fox, 1981). Studies that focus only on family variables suggest that rates of teenage sexual intercourse are lower in families with higher levels of family attachment, involvement, and supervision (Hayes, 1987; Hovell et al., 1994; Miller, Olson, & Wallace, 1986). Multivariate studies have found mixed results for family influences. In some studies supervision was associated with reduced sexual activity and risk of pregnancy (Hogan & Kitagawa, 1985; Small & Luster, 1994). However, one longitudinal study found that parental social control had little impact among younger teenagers (Udry & Billy, 1987). Another study linked child maltreatment, a marker for severe parental disruption, with teenage sexual activity (Small & Luster, 1994).

School factors, including grades and educational aspirations, have been linked to teenage sexual activity. Educational plans and performance were related to adolescent sexual activity in a predominantly white high school sample (Miller & Sneesby, 1988). An earlier longitudinal study of predominantly white teenagers found that higher expectations for academic achievement were associated with later sexual initiation, in addition to personality and family factors (Jessor, Costa, Jessor, & Donovan, 1983). A more recent longitudinal study of white teenagers suggested that educational variables are better predictors of early sexual activity for girls (Ohannessian & Crockett, 1993). Studies of African American adolescents also suggest an important role for educational variables (Gibbs, 1986).

Individual factors also are linked with teenage sexual behavior, although there are mixed findings about variables from this context. Depression, often associated with low self-worth, has been linked to teenage sexual activity, particularly for girls (Abrahamse, Morrison, & Waite, 1988; Whitbeck, Hoyt, Miller, & Kao, 1992). Whitbeck et al. found that depression stemming from lack of family support was related to sexual activity. Use of alcohol and drugs has been consistently associated with teenage sexuality (Elliott & Morse, 1989; Ensminger, 1990), and possible reasons are that substance use is a marker for precocious independence (Jessor et al., 1983), a facilitator of disinhibition (Day, 1992; Rosenbaum & Kandel, 1990), and a link to other sexually advanced peers (Whitbeck et al., 1992).

Although these studies shed light on the range of contexts that influence adolescent sexuality, there are significant limitations. Explaining racial differences in sexuality and fertility has been a dominant theme, whereas few studies have examined the contexts that are important for groups of adolescents in similar urban environments. In addition, few studies have focused on differences in risk factors between boys and girls, although there appear to be differences in the determinants and patterns of sexual activity by gender. The most important limitation is that no representative studies focus on the early adolescent life phase.

## METHOD

### Study Questions

This study responds to the limitations of earlier studies by focusing on the following research questions: What is the prevalence of sexual intercourse in a representative sample of urban teenagers of color ages 15 and younger? Comparing those who initiate sexual activity at ages 15 and younger with those who initiate sexual activity at ages older than 15, is early initiation associated with higher-risk sexual behavior? Which life contexts are more closely linked with early sexual activity among these adolescents, and are there differences between genders?

## Sample

The target panel of 1,000 adolescents was drawn from a population of about 4,000 seventh and eighth graders attending public schools in an eastern city during the 1987–88 school year. The purpose of the overall project from which the data were drawn was to investigate the causes and correlates of delinquency and drug use. To include a sufficient number of students likely to be involved in these behaviors, the sample overrepresented young men (75 percent to 25 percent). In addition, the sample was stratified based on 1986 census tract arrest rates. Students were selected in proportion to their tract's contribution to the arrest rate: 1,334 students were selected in this way, based on an estimated nonresponse rate of 25 percent, to reach the target of 1,000 students.

Because each student's chance of selection into the sample was known, a weighting strategy was used to adjust the sample back to a random sample of urban schoolchildren. The weights correct for the overrepresentation of young men and students from the census tracts with high arrest rates by assigning a proportionally higher weighting to young women and students from census tracts with fewer arrests (Thornberry, Bjerregaard, & Miles, 1993). All data were weighted.

Data were from a nine-wave panel study of urban adolescents begun in 1987. Each adolescent and a primary caretaker, usually the mother, were interviewed at six-month intervals. Wave 1 was conducted in spring 1988 when the average age of the students was 13.5 years; wave 9 was conducted in spring 1992 when the average age was 17.4 years. Structured interviews with teenagers were completed primarily in the schools, and interviews with parents were conducted in the home. Hispanic parents were interviewed by bilingual interviewers in Spanish where necessary. The interviews lasted about an hour. Agencies such as schools, police, and social services provided additional information.

Longitudinal data were available for a subsample of 803 African American and Hispanic teenagers. To maximize the number of students in the analysis, students were retained if they were interviewed at least once after wave 7 (that is, after they had reached age 16). The sample included 566 boys (443 African American and 123 Hispanic) and 237 girls (205 African American and 32 Hispanic). The Hispanic teenagers were primarily of Puerto Rican ancestry. Retention rates were 88 percent at wave 9, and the project established that data are not biased by differential attrition (Thornberry et al., 1993). Sample numbers vary due to missing data on some variables.

## Measures

Measures include variables relating to sexuality and fertility, as well as important aspects of the life contexts linked with sexual behavior summarized earlier.

Life context measures were taken from parent and teenager interviews during wave 2, school records, county protective services records, and 1980 census data. Measures relating to sexuality and fertility came from teenager interviews in waves 2 through 9. In addition to standard measures, some measures were specific to or adapted for this study (Farnworth, Thornberry, Lizotte, & Krohn, 1992; Huizinga, Loeber, & Thornberry, 1994).

*Sexual Behavior.* Questions about sexuality and fertility began in wave 2. Students were asked whether they had been sexually active since their last interview, an interval of about six months. Sex at age 15 or younger was scored as 1. Because age refers to the student's age at the interview when intercourse was first reported, age may be overestimated by up to six months. The age cutoff was selected because of the identification of the early-adolescent age range as a distinctive developmental phase (Hahn, 1995; Hamburg, 1986; Mincy, 1994). A number of teenagers, particularly boys, reported they were sexually active at wave 2, so the temporal order of sexual debut and other variables is unknown.

To identify students whose sexual behavior was considered more risky, frequency distributions of variables including frequency of intercourse and number of partners were examined for each gender separately. "Multiple partners" was a dichotomous variable derived from the top quartile of the frequency distribution of the maximum number of partners reported in any single interview wave. High frequency of sexual intercourse was a dichotomous variable derived from the number of times students reported having had intercourse, summed across waves. Students in the top quartile of the frequency distribution had a score of 1 on this variable. Students scoring 1 on regular condom use reported in waves 6 through 9 that condoms were always used during intercourse in the waves in which they were sexually active. "Ever pregnant" was a dichotomous variable, with 1 indicating a yes answer to any question about being pregnant or making a girl pregnant. "Had a child" meant that the student answered yes to any questions about having a child. The last two questions were asked for girls in waves 4 through 9 and for boys in waves 5 through 9. That information on sexuality was collected at several waves and from different respondents makes it possible to check the accuracy of some data. For example, there was a 95 percent agreement with parents' reports of teenagers' childbearing (Thornberry, Smith, & Howard, in press).

*Contexts Influencing Sexual Activity.* Measures of neighborhood and sociodemographic status were taken from data gathered at waves 1 or 2, with the exception of neighborhood poverty, a census measure indicating the percentage of households living in poverty in the census tract where the family lived at the start of the study. Parents who reported receiving welfare, a proxy for family poverty-level income, were coded 1 on this variable. Students who reported that they were living with both biological parents were coded as 1; other household types were coded 0. Hispanic race was coded as 1, with 0 as the reference category for African American.

Measures that have been linked to sexual activity include family, school, and individual variables. Family variables measured include an 11-item scale of parent attachment adapted from the Parent Attitudes Toward Child Scale (Hudson,

1982). Higher scores indicated greater attachment (Cronbach's alpha = .87). Child maltreatment was a dichotomous variable, with 1 indicating that the student had a substantiated report of neglect or abuse before age 12 on file with social services. The coding procedure for these data was elaborate, and interrater reliability was assessed as 88 percent (Smith & Thornberry, 1995). Supervision was a four-item scale developed for the Rochester Youth Development Study (RYDS) (see Krohn, Stern, Thornberry, & Jang, 1992), with higher scores indicating teenagers' perceptions of higher supervision (Cronbach's alpha = .56).

Measures used to assess the school context include school aspirations, a four-point variable indicating the importance of college to the teenager, and the reading achievement score from the California Achievement Test from school records in grade 7 or 8. Higher scores indicated higher ambition and school success.

Measures of individual factors included a seven-item depression scale abbreviated from a standardized self-report depression inventory (Radloff, 1977), with higher scores indicating more depressive symptoms (Cronbach's alpha = .72). Early substance use was measured from students' self-reports, with 1 indicating any use of alcohol or illegal drugs at wave 2. The validity of the drug measure was suggested by the correspondence of RYDS substance use rates with national estimates (Elliott, Huizinga, & Menard, 1989).

## RESULTS

About three-quarters of the teenage boys (72.2 percent) and almost half of the girls (46.7 percent) reported onset of sexual activity at age 15 or younger (Table 18-1). Less than one-fifth (17.5 percent) of the boys initiated intercourse at age 16 or older, and 10.3 percent remained sexually inexperienced. Of the girls, 29.7 percent became sexually active after age 16, and 23.6 percent were still inactive during the study. Although these prevalence figures are high compared with other studies, they are consistent with more recent estimates of sexual activity, particularly among teenagers of color (Furstenberg, Brooks-Gunn, & Morgan, 1987; Rosenbaum & Kandel, 1990).

*Table 18-1*

**Reported Age When Sexual Activity Was Initiated**

| Age | Boys (N = 566) (%) | Girls (N = 237) (%) |
|---|---|---|
| Age 15 or younger | 72.2 | 46.7 |
| Age 13 or younger | 8.6 | 6.8 |
| Age 14 | 27.3 | 17.7 |
| Age 15 | 36.3 | 22.2 |
| Age 16 or older | 17.5 | 29.7 |
| No sex reported[a] | 10.3 | 23.6 |

NOTES: Distribution is truncated because some students were younger than 13 at the start of the study (mean age at wave 1 = 13.5 years). By wave 9, some students were still 16 (mean age = 17.4 years).

[a]Includes students interviewed at least once after age 16 who did not report sexual intercourse during any wave in which they were interviewed.

Boys who had sex at a young age were significantly less likely than later initiators to use a condom regularly and were more likely to have multiple partners (Table 18-2). The boys who became sexually active early were not significantly more likely to have a high frequency of sex. Findings are similar for girls, with the exception that those who initiated sexual activity early were also significantly more likely to have frequent sex. The boys who became sexually active at young ages were more likely to report causing a pregnancy and were more likely to have a child than boys who became sexually active later. For the girls, the younger group was more likely to become pregnant than the older group. Of most concern, 54 percent of the girls who initiated sexual intercourse at ages 15 or younger had a child during the course of the study, compared to 18 percent of those who waited until after age 16.

Because the dependent variable is dichotomous, logistic regression was used to examine which of the factors described earlier had the most impact on early sexual activity (Table 18-3). The change in the probability of early sexual activity associated with an increase of one unit in each of the significant independent variables is reported. Significance was calculated on the basis of one-tailed tests, because the direction of the relationships was predicted. A discussion of translating logistic regression coefficients into probabilities can be found in Peterson (1985). Changes in probability were calculated at the mean of the dependent variable, which was .72 for boys and .47 for girls. The model fits the data well; the chi-square improvement in prediction over chance for boys was 58.2 ($p < .0001$) and for girls, 57.8 ($p < .0001$).

For the boys, two distal factors and four proximal factors were associated with early sexual activity. Coming from a home without two biological parents present increased the probability of early intercourse by .08, and being Hispanic was related to a probability of early sexual activity that was .12 lower than for African Americans, the reference category. Proximal characteristics included lower parent attachment, child maltreatment, lower supervision, and substance use. Having parents who were less strongly attached increased the probability of intercourse by .08, as did the perception by students that they were weakly supervised. Being maltreated increased the probability of early sexual activity by .14. Substance use was associated with a .17 increase in the probability of early sexual activity.

*Table 18-2*

**Relationship of Early versus Later Sexual Activity to Other Risk Behaviors**

| Behavior | Boys (%) | | Girls (%) | |
|---|---|---|---|---|
| | ≤Age 15 | Age 16+ | ≤Age 15 | Age 16+ |
| Regular condom use | 28 | 45* | 19 | 34* |
| Multiple partners | 25 | 16* | 28 | 8* |
| High frequency of sexual intercourse | 26 | 20 | 30 | 16* |
| Ever pregnant or ever impregnated | 40 | 27* | 67 | 42* |
| Had a child | 20 | 11* | 54 | 18* |

*Chi-square, $p < .05$.

*Table 18-3*

**Results from Logistic Regression Equations Predicting Early Sexual Activity**

| Variable | Boys (N = 511) | | | Girls (N = 212) | | |
|---|---|---|---|---|---|---|
| | Parameter Estimate | SE | Changes in Probability | Parameter Estimate | SE | Changes in Probability |
| Neighborhood poverty | -.27 | .25 | | -.14 | .41 | |
| Family receives welfare | -.23 | .24 | | -.02 | .36 | |
| Both parents in home | -.45* | .23 | -.08 | -1.27** | .42 | -.29 |
| Parent attachment | -.45* | .26 | -.08 | -.61* | .36 | -.15 |
| Child maltreatment | .86** | .37 | .14 | .55 | .52 | |
| Supervision | -.47* | .28 | -.08 | -.62 | .51 | |
| School aspirations | .11 | .17 | | -.47* | .27 | -.12 |
| Reading score | -.06 | .05 | | -.04 | .08 | |
| Depression | .32 | .25 | | .73** | .37 | .18 |
| Substance use | 1.12** | .28 | .17 | 1.16** | .37 | .27 |
| Hispanic | -.69** | .25 | -.12 | -.84 | .50 | |
| Chi-square improvement | 58.20*** | | | 57.82*** | | |

*$p < .05$. **$p < .01$. ***$p < .0001$.

Several contexts in the teenage ecology were unrelated to early sexual activity for the boys. Neighborhood poverty and receiving welfare were not related. (To explore the issue further, in an analysis not reported here, other neighborhood and socioeconomic variables were substituted into the equation. None were significant on a bivariate or multivariate level. The same held true for the school variables.) School achievement and aspirations also were unrelated, as was depression. The strongest predictors for boys were maltreatment and substance use.

For the girls there were substantial similarities in the interrelationships of contexts and sexual behavior. Neighborhood poverty and receipt of welfare were unrelated to early sexual activity. Having two biological parents in the home was significantly related to the postponement of sexual activity, decreasing the probability of sexual involvement by .29. Weak parent attachment was associated with a .15 increase in the probability of early sexual activity. The lack of relationship between sexual activity and supervision for girls is surprising and in contrast to findings from other research, although we did not measure one important aspect of supervision—supervision of dating relationships (Hogan & Kitagawa, 1985).

Having low aspirations for school achievement predicted early sexual activity. For girls who aspired to attend college, the probability of early sexual activity dropped by .12, suggesting that girls who see an educational future for themselves are much less likely to get involved in sexual relationships in early adolescence (Abrahamse et al., 1988).

Depression had an impact on girls' early sexual activity, with each one-unit increase in depression increasing the probability by .18. Depression may be related to lack of optimism about future options, which also may be a factor in the use of substances to deal with stress (Dryfoos, 1991). As with boys, substance use was associated with a high probability of early intercourse, a .27 increase in probability for girls.

Hispanic ethnicity was not significantly associated with later sexual activity among girls, although significance might be found with a larger female sample. It may be that different cultural factors operate for Hispanic adolescents, for example, extra emphasis on protecting young girls (Fennelly, 1988; Ho, 1992). Unfortunately, we were not able to look further at this issue because of the small subsample of Hispanic girls.

Predictors of early sexual activity common to both boys and girls were not having both parents in the home, lack of parent attachment, and substance use. That single-parent households were associated with early sexual activity is consistent with other research and has been interpreted in several ways. Family instability and conflict, as well as instability in living arrangements and economic base, have been linked to early sexual activity (Burton, 1995; Wu, 1996). A link between nonbiological family structures and early sexuality has been suggested by research in poor urban areas, where there is an increased acceptance of adolescent childbearing (Abrahamse et al., 1988; Burton, 1995; Hogan & Kitagawa, 1985), as well as many mothers who were themselves teenage parents (Ensminger, 1990). An ethnographic study suggested that boys are more likely to be sexually responsible with girls who have fathers in the home (Anderson, 1993).

For both genders, having parents who are disengaged from their children and cannot offer support and guidance through a challenging life phase has been linked to early sexual activity. Stress may take a different toll on teenage boys, who may show more overt risk behaviors in contrast to the internalizing symptoms more characteristic of teenage girls (Colton, Gore, & Aseltine, 1991). Although possibly equally sensitive to severe family stresses such as maltreatment, boys are more likely to respond with overt risk behaviors (Kavanagh & Hops, 1994). The presence of substance use as a predictor for early sexual activity for both genders coincides with other research linking early sexual experimentation with a broader spectrum of problem behaviors (Colton et al., 1991; Ensminger, 1990). These behaviors have been linked with pressure for precocious maturity that is linked with the restricted life options of many inner-city teenagers (Abrahamse et al., 1988; Ladner, 1987).

## DISCUSSION

About three-quarters of the boys and almost half of the girls in this study were sexually active at ages when management of the circumstances and consequences of sexual activity is developmentally problematic. A few years' difference in the age when teenagers begin having sexual intercourse can make a substantial difference in their ability to manage this complex behavior. In addition, being older allows for the development of cognitive and social skills that can protect adolescents from the potential negative outcomes of sexual activity (Hamburg, 1986).

The findings strongly suggest that sexual activity at young ages is more problematic than sexual activity initiated in later adolescence. Teenagers who initiated intercourse early were more likely to engage in unprotected sex and to have multiple partners, risk markers for exposure to STDs. Teenage boys were more likely to have sexual intercourse early, thus prolonging their exposure to disease. Teenage girls who initiated sex earlier were substantially more likely to become pregnant in addition to risking STDs; in fact, more than half of those who had sex early became teenage parents. This problem poses enormous challenges for young parents whose own health, education, and economic situations may be severely compromised and whose children also bear the consequences (Furstenberg, Morgan, et al., 1987).

Although several aspects of the ecology of teenagers were implicated in this study, the impact of more distal factors such as neighborhood was less for both sexes than studies of older adolescents have shown. In early adolescence, it may be that distal factors including neighborhood and family poverty exert more impact through proximate contexts such as the family, for example, through family stress and disrupted parenting (Conger & Elder, 1994; Stern & Smith, 1995). Also, all teenagers in this study were of color, living in urban areas, and attending city public schools, thus limiting somewhat the variability in living environments. The consistent and strong impact of substance use on early sexual activity is also probably related to the urban ecology. Overt drug use and drug sales are a feature of degraded urban neighborhoods where institutional and other supports for family life have evaporated and where pressures are high for teenagers to become involved with substance use as well as sexual intercourse (Bowser, Fullilove, & Fullilove, 1990).

In contrast to the more distal ecology, factors closer to home and to the individual do affect early sexual activity. Along with substance use, aspects of parenting were identified as important in predicting early sexual activity. For girls, school aspirations and depression also were important.

## IMPLICATIONS FOR PRACTICE

Sexual activity is common among young urban teenagers and is likely to have serious consequences in their life course. This fact suggests a compelling need for social workers and agencies involved with the health and well-being of younger teenagers to consider their role in intervention. The framework of the study suggests sensitivity to developmental stage and to the contexts that affect teenage sexuality.

In the current urban context, teenagers may find themselves in a climate where seemingly "everyone is doing it." However, even in situations of overwhelming peer pressure, not all young teenagers are engaging in risky behavior; more than half the younger girls and more than a quarter of the younger boys in this study were not having sex. This finding has important implications for further assessment of factors that protect these teenagers and for involvement of such teenagers in peer programs. For example, social workers in schools and community service centers can take advantage of programs that use peer leaders to model social and resistance skills. These programs have been successful in decreasing substance use, and their use is promising for sexual behavior (Durlak, 1995).

A two-pronged strategy to promote safety in sexual activity seems unavoidable. The first message, more heavily pitched to younger teenagers, would promote abstaining from sexual activity. The second message, aimed at older teenagers, would promote contraception and safe sex for sexually active teenagers. Some promising programs include both objectives (for example, Allen-Meares, 1995; Kirby, 1994; Postrado & Nicholson, 1992; Schinke, Gilchrist, & Small, 1979). In a recent evaluation of published studies that aimed to influence sexual behaviors, Kirby concluded that successful programs have several common features: They have a clear and specific focus on reducing risk-taking behaviors, they apply social learning principles to behavior change, they have an active skills-oriented approach to increasing safe-sex practices, they attend to social and media influences, and they explicitly reinforce norms against early sex and risky sex. Teenagers who are already having sex can be encouraged to use new skills to evaluate their choices and alternatives, to become effective communicators, and to control their sexual expression (Murray, 1994).

Social workers can extend their efforts to develop skills-building programs based on sexual problem solving and decision making. Partnerships with educators and health professionals are important in tailoring programs to those with immature cognitive skills. For example, Zabin, Hirsch, Smith, Street, and Hardy (1986) developed a successful program for inner-city teenagers that both delayed the onset of sexual intercourse among young girls and reduced pregnancy rates. In this program, nurses and social workers delivered multiple services from a reproductive health clinic based near inner-city schools. Schools are important sites for such programs, because young teenagers generally attend school (Durlak, 1995; Kirby, 1994), which implies a strong role for school social workers.

One criterion for successful programs found in Kirby's (1994) review was staff training. Familiarity with the ecology of teenagers—their media input, their communities, and their ethnic and cultural backgrounds—is a key component in effective programming (Allen-Meares, 1995; Gibbs, 1986). For example, one successful urban program included components to enhance cultural identity and build support networks as well as to teach skills (Schinke, Holden, & Moncher, 1989). Other programs targeted to urban Latino and African American teenagers at risk for AIDS have been successful in changing sex behaviors, including condom use and fewer partners (Jemmott, Jemmott, & Fong, 1992; Walter & Vaughn, 1993).

Because parents are the major socializing agents for children and family factors are clearly interwoven with early sexual behavior, more effort should be devoted to helping parents become effective sex educators (Murray, 1994). It is particularly important that social workers are sensitive to cultural conceptions about sexuality and teenage parenthood (Ho, 1992). Parents need assistance with helping teenagers discuss and develop mature sexual behavior. In particular, the fear that open acknowledgment of sexuality and provision of information about sex and contraception will increase sexual activity and curiosity needs to be exposed as unfounded (Kirby, 1994). Parents also may need to acknowledge to teenagers that there are benefits to sex at the appropriate life stage and to provide alternative models and guideposts for mature adulthood. Parents, as well as social workers, need opportunities for skills development to address sexual issues with teenagers in a credible and responsive way. Local churches and community organizations can be important resources (Allen-Meares, 1989; Edelman, 1987).

To the extent that the family environment plays a role in adolescent sexual behavior, efforts to involve and support families are important, for example, in managing family stress and modeling responsible sexual behavior (Kirby, 1994). In view of the relationship between child maltreatment and early male adolescent sexuality, those who work with maltreated children and their families should pay close attention to the possibility that long-term consequences may play out in a variety of arenas during adolescence (Widom, 1994). It is not clear to what extent early sexual activity may involve coercion and abuse, and this area needs more research (Moore, Nord, & Peterson, 1989).

Greater efforts to reach young men need to be made, because their high level of sexual activity affects their partners as well as themselves but is unlikely to be matched by a sense of consequences for and effects on both genders. Urban communities have characteristics that may enhance or inhibit the development of young men. The environment and peer culture can work against their adaptive development and responsible sexuality (Anderson, 1993). Community programs that provide positive, enjoyable, age-appropriate experiences for predominantly fatherless boys can enhance positive development (Pittman & Zeldin, 1994). Social workers can use macro practice strategies and nonclinical roles to identify the spectrum of community resources, recognize gaps, and network to develop more comprehensive support systems (Freeman, 1989; Pittman & Zeldin, 1994).

Because the risk of early pregnancy and other negative outcomes of sexual activity is lower for girls with high educational aspirations and positive attitudes toward school, interventions that help teenagers improve school experiences and skills and that plan for the future are likely to reduce early sexual activity and its consequences (Edelman, 1987). School social workers are well positioned to enhance the community–school and family–school linkages that encourage school involvement and skills building (Clancy, 1995).

The findings from this study concur with research that points to the interlinking of risk factors in the lives of adolescents, as well as the interlinking of problem behaviors (Ooms, 1995). Early sexual activity and substance use are clearly linked, supporting the call for multipronged prevention strategies incorporating a holistic view of adolescents. Both school-based prevention centers and multiservice youth centers are appearing across the country in urban communities. These centers have a wide mission, including family counseling, recreation, substance abuse counseling, and health and sex education (Durlak, 1995; Ooms, 1995). Programs that attend to both substance use and sexual activity among young teenagers are particularly crucial, because these factors are associated not only with the risk of pregnancy, but also with parenting problems in the next generation (Starr, MacLean, & Keating, 1991). The challenge for social workers is to promote better communication and coordination among service providers.

This study underlines the need to focus on young sexually active adolescents as a distinctive risk group. Because early sexual activity is interwoven with many developmental issues and contexts, no single intervention model or strategy is likely to be effective. Social workers are uniquely poised to address the many facets of this issue across systems, in collaboration with teenagers and their families, and in collaboration with professionals in other disciplines.

## REFERENCES

Abrahamse, A. F., Morrison, P. A., & Waite, L. J. (1988). Teenagers willing to consider single parenthood: Who is at greatest risk? *Family Planning Perspectives, 20*, 13–18.
Allen-Meares, P. (1989). Adolescent sexuality and premature parenthood: Role of the black church in prevention. *Journal of Social Work and Human Sexuality, 8*, 133–142.
Allen-Meares, P. (1995). *Social work with children and adolescents.* White Plains, NY: Longman.
Anderson, E. (1993). Sex codes and family life among poor inner-city youths. In R. I. Lerman & T. J. Ooms (Eds.), *Young unwed fathers: Changing roles and emerging policies* (pp. 74–98). Philadelphia: Temple University Press.
Battle, S. (Ed.). (1987). *The black adolescent parent.* New York: Haworth Press.
Bingham, C. R., Miller, B. C., & Adams, G. R. (1990). Correlates of age at first sexual intercourse in a national sample of young women. *Journal of Adolescent Research, 5*, 18–33.
Bowser, B. P., Fullilove, M. T., & Fullilove, R. E. (1990). African American youth and AIDS high risk behavior: The social context and barriers to prevention. *Youth and Society, 22*, 54–66.
Brewster, K. L. (1994). Race differences in sexual activity among adolescent women: The role of neighborhood characteristics. *American Sociological Review, 59*, 408–424.

Brewster, K. L., Billy, J.O.G., & Grady, W. R. (1993). Social context and adolescent behavior: The impact of community on transition to sexual activity. *Social Forces, 71,* 713–740.

Bronfenbrenner, U. (1986). Ecology of the family as a context for human development. *Developmental Psychology, 22,* 723–742.

Burton, L. M. (1995). Family structure and non-marital fertility: Perspectives from ethnographic research. In K. A. Moore (Ed.), *Report to Congress on out-of-wedlock childbearing* (pp. 147–165). Hyattsville, MD: U.S. Department of Health and Human Services.

Chilman, C. S. (1986). Some psychosocial aspects of adolescent sexual and contraceptive behaviors in a changing American society. In J. Lancaster & B. Hamburg (Eds.), *School-age pregnancy and parenthood: Biosocial dimensions* (pp. 191–218). New York: Aldine de Gruyter.

Clancy, J. (1995). Ecological school social work: The reality and the vision. *Social Work in Education, 17,* 40–47.

Colton, M. E., Gore, S., & Aseltine, R. H., Jr. (1991). The patterning of distress and disorder in a community sample of high school aged youth. In M. E. Colton & S. Gore (Eds.), *Adolescent stress: Causes and consequences* (pp. 157–180). New York: Aldine de Gruyter.

Conger, R. D., & Elder, G. H., Jr. (1994). *Families in troubled times.* New York: Aldine de Gruyter.

Day, R. D. (1992). The transition to first intercourse among racially and culturally diverse youth. *Journal of Marriage and the Family, 54,* 749–762.

Dryfoos, J. (1991). *Adolescents at risk: Prevalence and prevention.* New York: Oxford University Press.

Durlak, J. A. (1995). *School-based prevention programs for children and adolescents.* Thousand Oaks, CA: Sage Publications.

Edelman, M. W. (1987). Preventing adolescent pregnancy: A new role for social work services. *Urban Education, 22,* 496–509.

Elder, G. H., Jr. (1985). Perspectives on the life course. In G. H. Elder, Jr. (Ed.), *Life course dynamics: Transitions and trajectories* (pp. 23–49). Ithaca, NY: Cornell University Press.

Elliott, D. B., Huizinga, D., & Menard, S. (1989). *Multiple problem youth: Delinquency, substance use, and mental health problems.* New York: Springer-Verlag.

Elliott, D. B., & Morse, B. J. (1989). Delinquency and drug use as risk factors in teenage sexual activity. *Youth and Society, 21,* 32–60.

Ensminger, M. (1990). Sexual activity and problem behavior among black urban adolescents. *Child Development, 61,* 2032–2046.

Farnworth, M., Thornberry, T. P., Lizotte, A. J., & Krohn, M. D. (1992). *Data sources and measurement* (Tech. Rep. No. 2, Rochester Youth Development Study). Albany: State University of New York, Hindelang Criminal Justice Research Center.

Fennelly, K. (1988). *El embarazo precoz: Childbearing among Hispanic teenagers in the United States.* New York: Dowers Printing.

Forste, R. T., & Heaton, T. B. (1988). Initiation of sexual activity among female adolescents. *Youth and Society, 19,* 250–268.

Fox, G. L. (1981). The family's role in adolescent sexual behavior. In T. Ooms (Ed.), *Teenage pregnancy in a family context* (pp. 73–130). Philadelphia: Temple University Press.

Franklin, D. L. (1988). Race, class and adolescent pregnancy: An ecological analysis. *American Journal of Orthopsychiatry, 58,* 339–354.

Freeman, E. M. (1989). Adolescent fathers in urban communities: Exploring their needs and role in preventing pregnancy. *Journal of Social Work and Human Sexuality, 8,* 113–132.

Furstenberg, F., Brooks-Gunn, J., & Morgan, S. P. (1987). *Adolescent mothers in later life.* Cambridge, MA: Cambridge University Press.

Furstenberg, F. F., Jr., Morgan, S. P., Moore, K., & Peterson, J. L. (1987). Race differences in the timing of adolescent intercourse. *American Sociological Review, 52,* 511–518.

Garbarino, J. (1992). *Children and families in the social environment* (2nd ed.). New York: Aldine de Gruyter.

Gibbs, F. (1986). Psychosocial correlates of sexual attitudes and behaviors in urban adolescent females: Implications for intervention. *Journal of Social Work and Human Sexuality, 5,* 81–97.

Hahn, A. B. (1995). *America's middle child: Making age count in the development of a national youth policy.* Waltham, MA: Brandeis University.

Hamburg, B. A. (1986). Subsets of adolescent mothers: Developmental, biomedical, and psychosocial issues. In J. Lancaster & B. Hamburg (Eds.), *School-age pregnancy and parenthood: Biosocial dimensions* (pp. 115–146). New York: Aldine de Gruyter.

Hayes, C. D. (1987). *Risking the future* (Vol. 1). Washington, DC: National Academy Press.

Ho, M. K. (1992). *Minority children and adolescents in therapy.* Newbury Park, CA: Sage Publications.

Hogan, D., & Kitagawa, E. (1985). The impact of social status, family structure, and neighborhood on the fertility of black adolescents. *American Journal of Sociology, 90,* 825–855.

Hovell, M., Sipan, C., Blumberg, E., Atkins, C., Hofstetter, R., & Kreitner, S. (1994). Family influences on Latino and Anglo adolescent sexual behavior. *Journal of Marriage and the Family, 56,* 973–986.

Hudson, W. (1982). *The clinical measurement package: A field manual.* Homewood, IL: Dorsey Press.

Huizinga, D., Loeber, R., & Thornberry, T. P. (Eds.). (1994). *Urban delinquency and substance abuse: Initial findings* (prepared for the Office of Juvenile Justice and Delinquency Prevention). Washington, DC: U.S. Department of Justice.

Irwin, C. E., Jr., & Shafer, M. A. (1992). Adolescent sexuality: Negative outcomes of a normative behavior. In D. E. Rodgers & E. Ginzberg (Eds.), *Adolescents at risk: Medical and social perspectives* (pp. 35–79). Boulder, CO: Westview Press.

Jemmott, J. B. III, Jemmott, L. S., & Fong, G. T. (1992). Reductions in HIV risk-associated sexual behaviors among black male adolescents: Effects of an AIDS prevention intervention. *American Journal of Public Health, 82,* 372–377.

Jessor, R., Costa, F., Jessor, S. L., & Donovan, J. (1983). Time of first intercourse: A prospective study. *Journal of Personality and Social Psychology, 44,* 608–626.

Kahn, J., Kalsbeek, W., & Hofferth, S. (1988). National estimates of teenage sexual activity: Evaluating the comparability of three national surveys. *Demography, 25,* 189–204.

Kavanagh, K., & Hops, H. (1994). Good girls? Bad boys? Gender and development as contexts for diagnosis and treatment. In T. H. Ollendick & R. J. Prinz (Eds.), *Advances in clinical child psychology* (Vol. 16, pp. 45–79). New York: Plenum Press.

Kirby, D. (1994). Sexuality and HIV education programs in schools. In D. Kirby (Ed.), *Sex education in the schools* (pp. 1–41). Menlo Park, CA: Kaiser Family Foundation.

Krohn, M. D., Stern, S. B., Thornberry, T. P., & Jang, S. J. (1992). The measurement of family process variables: An examination of adolescent and parent perceptions of family life on delinquent behavior. *Journal of Quantitative Criminology, 8,* 287–315.

Ku, L., Sonenstein, F. L., & Pleck, J. (1993). Neighborhood, family and work: Influences on the premarital behaviors of adolescent males. *Social Forces, 72,* 479–503.

Ladner, J. (1987). Black teenage pregnancy: A problem for educators. *Journal of Negro Education, 56,* 53–63.

Miller, B. C., & Moore, K. A. (1990). Adolescent sexual behavior, pregnancy and parenting: Research through the 1980's. *Journal of Marriage and the Family, 52,* 1025–1044.

Miller, B. C., Olson, T. D., & Wallace, C. M. (1986). Parental discipline and control attempts in relation to adolescent sexual attitudes and behavior. *Journal of Marriage and the Family, 48,* 513–525.

Miller, B. C., & Sneesby, K. R. (1988). Educational correlates of adolescents' sexual attitudes and behavior. *Journal of Youth and Adolescence, 17,* 521–530.

Mincy, R. B. (1994). Introduction. In R. B. Mincy (Ed.), *Nurturing young black males: Challenges to agencies, programs, and social policy* (pp. 7–21). Washington, DC: Urban Institute Press.

Moore, K. A., Nord, C. W., & Peterson, J. L. (1989). Non-voluntary sexual activity among adolescents. *Family Planning Perspectives, 21,* 110–114.

Moore, K. A., Simms, M. C., & Betsey, C. L. (1986). *Choice and circumstances: Racial differences in adolescent sexuality and fertility.* New Brunswick, NJ: Transaction Books.

Murray, V. M. (1994). Adolescent sexuality. In S. J. Price, P. C. Henry, & S. M. Gavazzi (Eds.), *Vision 2010: Families and adolescents* (pp. 18–19). Minneapolis: National Council in Family Relations.

Ohannessian, C. M., & Crockett, L. J. (1993). A longitudinal investigation of the relationship between educational investment and adolescent sexual activity. *Journal of Adolescent Research*, *8*, 167–192.

Ooms, T. (1995). Strategies to reduce non-marital childbearing. In K. A. Moore (Ed.), *Report to Congress on out-of-wedlock childbearing* (pp. 241–265). Hyattsville, MD: U.S. Department of Health and Human Services.

Petersen, A. C., & Crockett, L. A. (1992). Adolescent sexuality, pregnancy, and child rearing: Developmental perspectives. In M. K. Rosenheim & M. F. Testa (Eds.), *Early parenthood and coming of age in the 1990's* (pp. 34–45). New Brunswick, NJ: Lawrence Erlbaum.

Peterson, T. (1985). A comment on presenting results from logit and probit models. *American Sociological Review*, *50*, 130–131.

Pittman, K., & Zeldin, S. (1994). From deterrence to development: Shifting the focus of youth programs for African American males. In R. B. Mincy (Ed.), *Nurturing young black males: Challenges to agencies, programs, and social policy* (pp. 45–58). Washington, DC: Urban Institute Press.

Postrado, L. T., & Nicholson, H. J. (1992). Effectiveness in delaying the initiation of sexual intercourse in girls ages 12–13. *Youth and Society*, *23*, 356–379.

Radloff, L. S. (1977). The CES–D Scale: A self-report depression scale for research in the general population. *Applied Psychological Measurement*, *1*, 385–401.

Rosenbaum, E., & Kandel, D. (1990). Early onset of adolescent sexual behavior and drug involvement. *Journal of Marriage and the Family*, *52*, 783–798.

Schinke, S. P., Gilchrist, L., & Small, R. (1979). Preventing unwanted adolescent pregnancy. *American Journal of Orthopsychiatry*, *49*, 56–81.

Schinke, S. P., Holden, G. W., & Moncher, M. S. (1989). Preventing HIV infection among black and Hispanic adolescents. *Journal of Social Work and Human Sexuality*, *8*, 63–73.

Simmons, R. G., & Blyth, D. (1987). *Moving into adolescence: The impact of pubertal change and school context*. New York: Aldine de Gruyter.

Small, S. A., & Luster, T. (1994). Adolescent sexual activity: An ecological risk-factor approach. *Journal of Marriage and the Family*, *56*, 181–192.

Smith, C., & Thornberry, T. P. (1995). The relationship between childhood maltreatment and adolescent involvement in delinquency. *Criminology*, *86*, 37–58.

Sonenstein, F. L., Pleck, J. H., & Ku, L. C. (1989). Sexual activity, condom use and AIDS awareness among adolescent males. *Family Planning Perspectives*, *21*, 152–158.

Spencer, M. B., & Dornbusch, S. M. (1990). Challenges in studying minority youth. In S. S. Feldman & G. R. Elliott (Eds.), *At the threshold: The developing adolescent* (pp. 123–146). Cambridge, MA: Harvard University Press.

Starr, R. H., MacLean, D. J., & Keating, D. P. (1991). Life span developmental outcomes of child maltreatment. In R. H. Starr & D. Wolfe (Eds.), *The effects of child abuse and neglect* (pp. 1–32). New York: Guilford Press.

Stephan, C. W., & Stephan, W. G. (1989). Family configuration in relation to the sexual behavior of adolescents. *Family Planning Perspectives*, *21*, 499–506.

Stern, S., & Smith, C. A. (1995). Family processes and delinquency in an ecological context. *Social Service Review*, *69*, 703–731.

Thornberry, T. P., Bjerregaard, B., & Miles, W. (1993). The consequences of respondent attrition in panel studies: A simulation based on the Rochester Youth Development Study. *Journal of Quantitative Criminology*, *9*, 127–158.

Thornberry, T. P., Smith, C., & Howard, G. J. (in press). Risk factors for teenage fatherhood. *Journal of Marriage and the Family*.

Udry, J. R., & Billy, J.O.G. (1987). Initiation of coitus in early adolescence. *American Sociological Review*, *52*, 841–855.

Walter, H. J., & Vaughn, R. D. (1993). AIDS risk reduction among a multiethnic sample of urban high school students. *JAMA*, *270*, 725–730.

Whitbeck, L., Hoyt, D., Miller, M., & Kao, M. (1992). Parental support, depressed affect, and sexual experience among adolescents. *Youth and Society*, *24*, 166–177.

Widom, C. S. (1994). Childhood victimization and risk for adolescent problem behavior. In M. E. Lamb & R. Ketterlinus (Eds.), *Adolescent problem behaviors* (pp. 127–164). New York: Lawrence Erlbaum.

Wu, L. (1996). Effects of family instability, income, and income instability on the risk of a premarital birth. *American Sociological Review, 61,* 386–406.

Zabin, L. S., Hirsch, M., Smith, E., & Hardy, J. (1984). Adolescent sexual attitudes and behavior: Are they consistent? *Family Planning Perspectives, 16,* 181–185.

Zabin, L. S., Hirsch, M. B., Smith, E. A., Street, R., & Hardy, J. B. (1986). Evaluation of a pregnancy prevention program for urban teenagers. *Family Planning Perspectives, 18,* 119–126.

*This chapter was originally published in the July 1997 issue of* Social Work, *Vol. 42, pp. 334–346.*

# 19 Outcomes of Mandated Preventive Services Programs for Homeless and Truant Children: A Follow-up Study

Diane Tirado-Lampert and James A. Twaite

Homelessness is associated with a broad range of negative outcomes for children, including poor health, truancy, impaired cognitive functioning, and behavioral problems (Bassuk & Rosenberg, 1988, 1990; Bassuk, Rubin, & Lauriat, 1986; Gewirtzman & Fodor, 1987; Molnar, Rath, & Klein, 1990). It has been estimated that fewer than half of homeless school-aged children go to school at all (Maza & Hall, 1987). Moreover, regulations on permanent residency in many school districts bar homeless children from both the school nearest their former home and the school serving the neighborhood where they are temporarily residing (Edelman & Mihaly, 1989).

Homeless children who attend school are far more likely than other children to experience difficulties. Bassuk et al. (1986) reported that homeless children who attended school experienced irregular attendance, disproportionately high rates of failure and retention, and high probability of placement in special classes. Bassuk and Rosenberg (1988, 1990) compared a sample of homeless children with a matched group of low-income children with homes. They found that the homeless children scored significantly lower than the children with homes on measures of socioemotional and cognitive functioning.

Gewirtzman and Fodor (1987) reported that homeless children were unusually likely to manifest behavioral problems ranging from extreme aggressiveness in some children to extreme withdrawal in others. These researchers also described homeless children as frequently listless, apathetic, and tearful. Ziesemer, Marcoux, and Marwell (1994) reported that one-fourth to one-half of the homeless children in their sample were sufficiently disturbed as to need further psychiatric assessment. These reports make it clear that the condition of homelessness represents a significant risk factor for children, increasing the likelihood of school failure and involvement with the judicial system.

## RESEARCH ON PREVENTION PROGRAMS

In view of this risk, programs for homeless children aimed at preventing truancy and problem behavior appear to be warranted. Mandated preventive services (MPS) are a vehicle for the delivery of such programs. Several published reports have described MPS programs designed to improve educational outcomes (Padilla & Lindholm, 1984), to prevent behavior difficulties (Johnson &

Breckenridge, 1982), and to promote the involvement of parents in the education of their children (Blum & Phillips, 1982). However, none of these studies
has considered the factors that predict positive outcomes for families participating in such programs. The study reported in this article was designed to identify such factors.

Studies of prevention programs have emphasized the importance of parental
involvement in the treatment process. Brim (1959) suggested that the parent–
child relationship is the most important predictor of positive behavioral outcomes for children, and he argued that parent education could have a favorable
effect on parenting skills. Johnson and Breckenridge (1982) demonstrated that a
program aimed at teaching mothers to identify and respond to their children's
emotional states was effective in reducing destructive, overactive, and atten-
tion-seeking behavior. Bolton, Charlton, and Guy (1985) identified poor parenting
skills as a risk factor for children and recommended parent education to prevent negative emotional outcomes.

Although these studies suggest that parental factors are crucial to children's
behavioral, emotional, and academic outcomes, studies reported to date have
not focused specifically on MPS programs, and they have not demonstrated
significant relationships between parental involvement in the MPS program and
the child's adjustment following termination from the MPS program. The study
reported here examined the following predictors of successful outcomes: parental attendance at the MPS clinical sessions; intensity of parental involvement in
the MPS program; parental understanding of the child's pathology; and the extent to which the parents provided their child with appropriate structure, stimulation, and warmth. In addition, the severity of the child's pathology on entry
into the MPS program was assessed. These predictors were correlated with two
outcome measures: (1) family compliance with the termination plan and (2) the
child's adjustment six months following MPS termination.

## STUDY SETTING

This study focused on two MPS programs run by the Yonkers Youth Connection
(YYC), a multiservice nonresidential program for high-risk adolescents in
Westchester County, New York. The programs were the Mandated Preventive
Services Homeless Families Project and the Mandated Preventive Services Tru-
ancy Diversion Program. Referrals are made to these programs by the Yonkers
Board of Education, the Department of Probation, and the Department of Social
Services.

The Homeless Families Project provides intensive casework counseling to
families of adolescents between the ages of 10 and 18. The adolescents in the
program are "persons in need of supervision" (PINS), abused and neglected
children, and runaways. The PINS designation is determined by the family court
on the basis of family conflict, truancy, use of drugs or alcohol, or involvement
with the criminal justice system. At the time of referral to the Homeless Families
Project, the adolescents reside with their families in temporary housing, generally in a local motel that is occupied almost entirely by clients of the Department
of Social Services. One of the functions of the Homeless Families Project is to

assist families in securing permanent housing, and obtaining such housing is a criterion for termination from the MPS program.

The Truancy Diversion Program focuses on children and adolescents between the ages of six and 18 who have been truant from school or have manifested problem behaviors in school or the community.

Both programs involve caseworker contacts with children and parents, parent skills training, transportation, and advocacy support services. Services are typically authorized for a six-month period, after which cases are evaluated for termination from the MPS program. The decision to terminate involvement in the MPS program is made in a case conference on the basis of recommendations from the caseworker in consultation with officials at the Board of Education or the Department of Probation. On termination from the MPS program, clients are referred to another appropriate agency for follow-up services. Caseworkers at the YYC maintain contact with the clients' subsequent social workers to monitor compliance with the MPS program termination plan.

## METHODS

### Sample

A random sample of 100 cases was drawn from the case records of children who were referred out of one of the two MPS programs between 1989 and 1994. The sample size of 100 was determined on the basis of a power analysis. The sample size of 100 yields a power of .92 for a test of the significance of a Pearson correlation, assuming a medium effect size (population correlation = .30) and a two-tailed hypothesis test at the .05 level. The power of the same test at the .01 level is .76.

The children in the sample ranged in age from 10 to 16 at the time they were referred to the MPS program; the mean age was 13.4 years. The majority of the children (54 of 100) lived in a mother-only household. Only 20 of the children lived with both parents. Forty-two of the children were black, 35 were Hispanic, 19 were white, and four were from other ethnic groups. The largest number ($n$ = 37) were referred for being aggressive, 31 were categorized as both aggressive and emotionally disturbed, and 25 were diagnosed as emotionally disturbed only. Seven of the children were referred for other reasons.

### Measures

Data were obtained from two sources. On each of the five predictors, data were obtained from family case records, and on each of the two dependent variables, data were obtained from a follow-up telephone contact with a staff member at the program to which the child was referred after termination from the MPS program.

The case records for the MPS program contain detailed information on each child and his or her parents, including clinical assessments and educational reports; 30-day, 90-day, and six-month utilization case reviews describing the activities and progress of both child and parents; monthly reports of formal case conferences on each family; periodic reports from any specialist working with the child (for example, a psychologist); and a termination report that describes the progress made during the MPS program and the termination plan, including the agency to which the case was referred.

On the basis of data in the case records, we devised a rating form that contained scales to measure each of the independent variables. For example, the severity of the child's pathology on entering the MPS program was assessed by rating the following:

- anxious, fearful behavior
- isolated, remote behavior
- impulsiveness
- aggressive, acting-out behavior.

Each child was rated in each of these four areas on a four-point Likert-type rating scale ranging from 1 = no pathology in the area to 4 = extreme pathology in the area. The ratings were summed to obtain an overall measure of pathology.

Within 30 days of referral to MPS, the parents were similarly rated by the caseworker on the extent to which they met the needs of their child in the areas of structure, stimulation, and warmth. In each of these areas, the rating scale was as follows: 1 = does not provide at all, 2 = provides to some degree but not adequately, 3 = provides adequately, and 4 = provides to an excessive degree. These ratings were recoded so that a rating of 3 (adequate) counted 3 points and a rating of 4 (excessive) counted 2 points, the same as inadequate provision. The ratings in these three areas were summed to obtain a total score for appropriate parenting behavior.

The intensity of the parents' involvement in the MPS program was measured on the basis of ratings of the parents' investment in the relationship with the clinical social worker and the parents' use of the suggestions made by the social worker. In each of these areas, rating options ranged from 1 = not at all to 4 = a great deal. The two items were summed to obtain a single measure of intensity of involvement. A single item was used to rate the parents' understanding of the child's pathology. The rating options were 1 = not at all, 2 = a little, 3 = moderately, and 4 = very well.

One additional independent variable, parental attendance, was drawn from the material in the case records. Because attendance is recorded for each session and absences are noted, this is an objective measure. A proportional attendance measure was obtained by dividing the number of sessions attended by the sum of sessions attended plus absences.

## Validity of Scales

The validity of these rating scales is supported by the following steps taken during their development: The areas were selected on the basis of a careful review of 50 case records. In each case record, data were available on which to base each rating. The areas selected were reviewed with colleagues both within the YYC and outside the agency. A total of five social workers familiar with the MPS program commented on the validity of the items and indicated that the scales were relevant. For each rating scale, the principal investigator developed a set of illustrative case record excerpts to serve as guidelines in assigning ratings. As a final step in the validation process, two clinicians other than the principal investigator independently applied the rating scales to 20 case records selected at random from the program files. Both of these clinicians reported that they were able to complete the ratings for every case on the basis of the material in the records and the guidelines provided.

### Reliability of Ratings

Before rating all of the cases for the study, the reliability of the ratings was assessed by calculating the kappa coefficients between the independent ratings of the two clinicians. Kappas were calculated for the overall scores on severity of the child's pathology, parental structure, parental stimulation, parental warmth, intensity of parental involvement, and parental understanding of child's pathology. These kappa coefficients ranged from .90 to .96.

### Scoring

Once the reliability of the rating scales had been established, the 100 case records used for the study were divided randomly into two sets of 50 each. One set was scored by each of two clinical social workers who had been trained in the use of the rating scales but who were blind to the purpose of the study. The use of trained blind raters was designed to reduce the possibility of contamination of results due to experimenter bias.

### Case Follow-up Contact

After termination of families from the MPS program, cases are routinely followed up by MPS staff, who contact the agency to which the family has been referred. To assess the family's compliance with the termination plan and the child's adjustment six months after MPS termination, the principal investigator contacted the family's social worker at the new agency. She asked the worker to rate the family's compliance on a scale from 0 to 10, where 0 = complete noncompliance and 10 = full compliance. The worker was also asked to rate the child's adjustment six months after the family's termination with the MPS program, considering social, emotional, and academic adjustment. The rating scale ranged from 0 = maladjustment severe enough to require institutionalization to 10 = perfect adjustment.

### RESULTS

Descriptive statistics on the predictors and the criterion variables are presented in Table 19-1. Attendance ranged from 25 percent of scheduled sessions to 100 percent, with a mean of 78 percent. Intensity of involvement in the relationship with the social worker and use of the worker's suggestions were measured on a scale ranging from 1 = not at all to 4 = a great deal for both areas. The mean score was 2.80, closest to the moderate rating of 3.00. Ratings of parental understanding of the child's pathology also ranged from 1.00 to 4.00, but the mean was 2.48, approximately midway between a rating of little understanding (2) and a rating of moderate understanding (3).

Ratings of parents' ability to provide structure, stimulation, and warmth (adequacy of parenting) ranged from 1.33 to 3.00. The mean score was 2.38, suggesting

Table 19-1

**Descriptive Statistics on Predictors and Criterion Variables for Families in MPS Programs**

| Variable | N | Minimum | Maximum | M | SD |
|---|---|---|---|---|---|
| Predictor | | | | | |
| Parental attendance | 99 | .25 | 1.00 | .78 | .15 |
| Intensity of parental involvement | 100 | 1.00 | 4.00 | 2.80 | .77 |
| Parental understanding of child's pathology | 100 | 1.00 | 4.00 | 2.48 | .75 |
| Adequacy of parenting | 100 | 1.33 | 3.00 | 2.38 | .44 |
| Child's pathology at entry | 100 | 1.00 | 3.67 | 2.12 | .61 |
| Criterion | | | | | |
| Compliance with termination plan | 100 | 0.00 | 9.00 | 5.59 | 2.13 |
| Child's adjustment six months after termination | 100 | 0.00 | 8.00 | 5.69 | 2.15 |

NOTES: MPS = mandated preventive services; N = number of valid cases on the scale.

moderately positive perceptions of adequacy of parenting. Ratings of the child's pathology ranged from 1.00 to 3.67, with a mean of 2.12. Thus, the case folders generally indicated that the children's pathologies were closer to mild than to moderate.

Ratings on both criterion measures had means between 5 and 6 on scales having theoretical ranges of 0 to 10. Thus, it appears that social workers in the programs to which families were referred following the MPS program viewed compliance and adjustment as moderate. The standard deviation on each of these measures was above 2.0, indicating substantial variability in ratings.

## Correlations

Preliminary analyses were carried out to determine whether the predictor variables were related significantly to the background variables of age at the time of referral, who the child lived with, and ethnic group. Pearson correlations were calculated between age at the time of referral and each of the predictors. None of these correlations was significant. One-way multivariate analyses of variance (MANOVAs) were used to determine whether any of the predictors were related significantly to who the child lived with (collapsed to with mother and father, and other) and ethnic group (white, black, and Hispanic). Neither of these MANOVAs was significant. On the basis of these analyses, we concluded that there was no need to control for these variables in evaluating the relationships among the predictor variables and the criterion variables of compliance with the termination plan and child's adjustment six months following termination.

The data indicate moderate to strong intercorrelations among the predictors, ranging in absolute value from .41 to .75 (for all correlations, $p < .001$) (Table 19-2). The correlation between the two criterion measures was .90 ($p < .001$), indicating that these two measures are virtually identical. Correlations between the predictors were all significant, ranging in absolute value from .30 ($p < .01$) to .51 ($p < .001$). Thus, all the predictors assessed were related moderately to MPS outcomes.

Table 19-2

## Correlations among Predictors and Criterion Variables (N = 100)

| Variable | Intensity of Parental Involvement | Parental Understanding of Child's Pathology | Adequacy of Parenting | Child's Pathology at Entry | Compliance with Termination Plan | Child's Adjustment Six Months after Termination |
|---|---|---|---|---|---|---|
| Parental attendance[a] | .66** | .55** | .58** | -.42** | .51** | .47** |
| Intensity of parental involvement | | .75** | .70** | -.41** | .51** | .42** |
| Parental understanding of child's pathology | | | .73** | -.46** | .46** | .42** |
| Adequacy of parenting | | | | -.42** | .51** | .47** |
| Child's pathology at entry | | | | | -.30* | -.35** |
| Compliance with termination plan | | | | | | .90** |
| Child's adjustment six months after termination | | | | | | |

[a]For correlations with attendance, $N = 99$.
*$p < .01$. **$p < .001$.

## Multiple Regression

A multiple regression analysis was used to identify the optimal set of parental variables for predicting favorable outcomes. In view of the high correlation between the two criterion variables, these were summed to obtain a single dependent variable. Because of the moderate to strong correlations among the predictors, the problem of multicollinearity was addressed by using a hierarchical stepwise regression with rather stringent entry criteria.

Child's pathology at entry to the MPS program was entered first to control for initial pathology. Then the parental predictors were evaluated for entry in a stepwise manner, using a probability to enter of .05. The results of this analysis are presented in Table 19-3. After controlling for the rated initial severity of the child's pathology, the adequacy of parental structure, stimulation, and warmth explained significant additional variability in MPS outcome ($t = 4.44$, $p < .001$). The proportion of variability explained rose from 12 percent to 27 percent with the addition of the parental adequacy measure. None of the remaining parental predictors would have been significant if included at step 3.

## DISCUSSION AND IMPLICATIONS FOR PROGRAMS FOR HOMELESS FAMILIES

The findings provide further empirical support for the argument that parental variables are important predictors of favorable outcomes for MPS programs. All the parental predictors were related significantly and moderately to each outcome measure, particularly a rating of the parent's ability to provide adequate structure, stimulation, and warmth, which is probably more a function of individual differences among parents than a product of learning during the program. However, the parental predictors also included factors that do appear to be program related, such as parental understanding of the nature of the child's pathology, which may well have improved because of parent education, parental attendance, and the degree to which parents indicated that they were invested in the MPS program.

Table 19-3

**Regression of MPS Program Outcome on Child's Rated Pathology and Parental Variables**

| Variable | Step | $R$ | $R^2$ | $t$ (Entry) | $\beta$ | $t$ (Final) |
|---|---|---|---|---|---|---|
| Child's pathology | 1 | .35 | .12 | −3.63** | −.16 | −1.62 |
| Adequacy of parenting | 2 | .52 | .27 | 4.44** | .43 | 4.44** |

| **Variables Not Included in Equation** | | | |
|---|---|---|---|
| Variable | $\beta$ In | Partial | $t$ |
| Parental attendance | .18 | .17 | 1.66 |
| Parental understanding | .19 | .13 | 1.33 |
| Parental investment | .24 | .19 | 1.92 |

NOTE: MPS = mandated preventive services.
**$p < .001$.

These findings support the view expressed by Blum and Phillips (1982) and by the New York State Department of Social Services (1992) that parental participation in MPS programs is a crucial factor in determining the success of these programs. The study reported here is the first to provide empirical evidence of the relationship between the intensity of parental involvement and the effectiveness of the MPS program.

This evidence supports the view that MPS programs should be structured to maximize parental involvement, implying the value of such MPS program features as transportation and child care for younger children while parents attend program activities. The programs under study include these program components.

Moreover, these MPS programs run a series of social and recreational activities and events, including field trips, cookouts, and coffee hours. The families participating in these MPS programs expressed satisfaction with these activities, which bring enjoyment into lives that may be otherwise devoid of entertainment. The activities increase attendance and develop a familylike atmosphere within the program. It is logical to assume that parents will learn more from their caseworkers in this type of atmosphere than they would in a less rewarding and more formal one.

The generally positive ratings social workers assigned to compliance with the termination plan and the child's psychosocial adjustment six months after MPS termination provide support for continued or expanded funding for MPS programs. It is likely that the funds invested in these children in the MPS program will more than pay for themselves in the future economic contributions of these children and in savings to the welfare, court, and prison systems. Additional research on MPS programs is recommended in the form of longer-term follow-up studies of children completing such programs. Ideally, such research would follow program participants into adulthood.

## REFERENCES

Bassuk, E. L., & Rosenberg, L. (1988). Why does family homelessness occur? A case control study. *American Journal of Public Health, 78,* 783–787.

Bassuk, E. L., & Rosenberg, L. (1990). Psychosocial characteristics of homeless children and children with homes. *Pediatrics, 85,* 257–286.

Bassuk, E. L., Rubin, L., & Lauriat, A. S. (1986). Characteristics of sheltered homeless families. *American Journal of Public Health, 76,* 1097–1101.

Blum, B. B., & Phillips, N. P. (1982). *Preventive services in New York State: A status report.* Albany: New York State Department of Social Services.

Bolton, F. G., Jr., Charlton, J. R., & Guy, D. S. (1985). Preventive screening of adolescent mothers and infants: Critical variables in assessing risk for child maltreatment. *Journal of Primary Prevention, 5,* 169–187.

Brim, O. G. (1959). *Education for child rearing.* New York: Russell Sage Foundation.

Edelman, M. W., & Mihaly, L. (1989). Homeless families and the housing crisis in the U.S. *Children and Youth Services Review, 11,* 91–108.

Gewirtzman, R., & Fodor, I. (1987). The homeless child of school age: From welfare hotel to classroom. *Child Welfare, 66,* 237–245.

Johnson, D. L., & Breckenridge, J. N. (1982). The Houston Parent–Child Development Center and the primary prevention of behavior problems in young children. *American Journal of Community Psychology, 10,* 305–316.

Maza, P. L., & Hall, J. A. (1987). *Study of homeless children and families: Preliminary findings.* Washington, DC: Child Welfare League of America and Traveler's Aid International.

Molnar, J. M., Rath, W. R., & Klein, T. P. (1990). Constantly compromised: The impact of homelessness on children. *Journal of Social Issues, 46*(4), 109–124.

New York State Department of Social Services. (1992, April). *Families in the child welfare system: Foster care and preventive services in the nineties.* New York: Author.

Padilla, A. M., & Lindholm, K. J. (1984). Hispanic behavioral science research: Recommendations for future research. *Hispanic Journal of Behavioral Sciences, 6,* 13–32.

Ziesemer, C., Marcoux, L., & Marwell, B. E. (1994). Homeless children: Are they different from other low-income children? *Social Work, 39,* 658–668.

*This chapter was originally published in the January 1997 issue of* Social Work, *Vol. 42, pp. 11–18.*

# Part III

# SKILLS FOR PRACTICE WITH GROUPS AND CLASSROOMS

# Part III: Skills for Practice with Groups and Classrooms

School social workers often use group interventions because they are developmentally appropriate for children and youths and because they enable practitioners to reach greater numbers of children than more traditional methods. There are other reasons for this pattern, including the universality of the concerns that cause most children and youths to be referred for services and the important role that peer influence can play in helping address and resolve those concerns. This section is, therefore, focused on a variety of group methods, ranging from the performing arts to violence prevention to counseling and mutual-support groups to classroom groups for students and staff development groups for teachers. Although some group services described in this section are for students at risk for school failure, often the services are focused on helping students manage various related transitions, whether developmentally based or caused by external conditions. Thus, these chapters can help school social workers normalize the students' needs that have led to referrals for these services, as well as the students' use of such services.

These chapters are informative for school social workers for other reasons. They discuss many social, political, and educational issues related to students' needs for services and provide an understanding of the broader context surrounding those needs. Many authors discuss issues related to the overdiagnosis of attention deficit hyperactivity disorder, the impact of high unemployment and drug use in impoverished neighborhoods, and the overrepresentation of youths of color in the juvenile justice system as part of the context for deciding how group process should be designed for the students involved. Some authors also point out how past efforts to provide group services for students, for example, those involved in violence, may have failed because they did not consider such social, cultural, and systems factors.

Equally important, these authors include descriptions of their group interventions, their efforts to monitor the effects of those interventions, and the outcomes in terms of changes in individual students and in their peer networks. Most school social workers are aware of how important it is to influence these networks so that changes can occur through group work and be maintained over time. Finally, many chapters illustrate one of the primary benefits of group work—the role and effects of the mutual group empowerment process and the facilitative interventions by school social workers that provide opportunities for that process to occur.

# 20 Social Work with Groups and the Performing Arts in the Schools

Flavio Francisco Marsiglia and Marjorie Witt Johnson

The Social Work with Groups and the Performing Arts (SWGPA) model is part of an ongoing reconceptualization effort being undertaken and documented by the authors. This culturally grounded approach to social work with groups aims to create environments in which the whole child is acknowledged, supported, and empowered.

The developmental approach strongly influenced the conceptualization of the SWGPA model. This approach studies the relationship between culture and human development. The main exponent of this school of thought is Lev Vygotsky (1979). He focused on the historically shaped and culturally transmitted psychology of human beings. Vygotsky maintained that humans are active, vigorous participants in their own existence and that at each stage of development children acquire the means by which they can competently affect their world and themselves.

Vygotsky spoke of auxiliary stimuli as components of a process experienced by humans for active adaptation. *Auxiliary stimuli* include the tools of the culture in which the child was born (practices, beliefs, and traditions), the language of those who raise the child, and the ingenious means produced by the child, including the use of his or her own body for self-expression. In the course of development, according to this approach, psychological systems arise that unite separate functions into new combinations and complexes. For example, the acquisition of a second language at home gives the child an understanding of certain culturally grounded concepts and a unique symbology that distinguish him or her from other children. Because historical conditions—which to a large extent determine the opportunities for human experience—are constantly changing, universal schemes do not exist that adequately represent the dynamic relationship between the external and the internal aspects of development of the child (Freire, 1995).

The use of the developmental approach enhances the group process and the individuality of group members. Guided by the principles of the developmental approach, the SWGPA model aims to provide children and youths with opportunities to constructively connect or reconnect with themselves, their peers, and their elders. It becomes a creative approach to accomplish what Brazilian educator Paulo Freire (1994) called "stepping back." Students realize that they have some ownership over their lives and that they can together work toward creating a new reality for themselves. Interventions guided by this approach assist students in becoming better dreamers. To learn to dream better and to create better realities strengthens the student's sense of self (Marsiglia & Zorita, 1996). The performing arts are a tool for individual and collective discovery and celebration.

## SWGPA MODEL

The SWGPA model uses creative modern dance or other performing arts through which students express themselves in their own spontaneous and unique ways. Dance or other performing arts are introduced from the beginning of the group formation as an asset to the group process. Thus, group participation includes verbal communication and communication through body movement or other creative expression. For the purpose of this article, modern dance is presented as the art form of choice; however, other creative art forms are equally suitable (Johnson & Marsiglia, 1994).

Modern dance is a means of expressing the experiences of human life and people's reactions to the social scene through routine movements. The holistic activity of creative dance exposes the student to movement, exploration, and problem-solving situations. When guided by a culturally competent leader, group participation helps students become aware of their own culture. Wilson and Ryland (1949) stated the following about the potential of modern dance: "Creative modern dance . . . is primarily a means for the communication of ideas, thoughts, feelings and emotions; a communication through movement of the experiences of human life of people's reaction to the modern scene" (p. 257).

The SWGPA model follows this tradition and adds the group work process as an empowering activity. Students are encouraged to explore who and what they are through modern dance fundamentals, such as rhythm and music, movement, and dance composition or choreography. Group process and dance relate to each other in a reciprocal way. The dance helps lower the barriers among members in the group—it is a holistic icebreaker. Students can interact in the group using means of self-expression that go beyond verbal communication. The main role of the social worker is to facilitate the group process and to help develop a theme (a cofacilitator can do the choreographic work). For example, if some group members are feeling rejected at school, rejection may become the theme for a new choreography. As group members develop a new choreography, they start to take control of their own situations. The final product may be a choreographic piece called "Inclusion."

The SWGPA model was pilot tested at a junior high school in a multiethnic neighborhood of a major midwestern city. The project was called "New Choreography from Folk Dance and Oral Traditions." The school population was very diverse. Fifty-two percent of the students were African American. The next largest group, white students (26 percent), were mostly Appalachian natives and recent Central European immigrants. Fourteen percent were Latino, most of Puerto Rican descent, and 8 percent were Asian, including students of Vietnamese, Cambodian, Laotian, Filipino, and Chinese origin. This article describes the project and uses selected ethnographic data—gathered through participant observation, intensive interviewing, and a review of group progress notes—to illustrate how the performing arts and the group process were integrated in a schoolwide project. The names used are fictitious to protect the students' anonymity.

The performing arts and the social work with group process complemented each other. To achieve this syncretism, the social work with group development stages were followed by the different groups formed. All groups were interconnected through the overall project's organizational structure. The groups followed these stages: (1) preplanning, (2) group formation, (3) beginning stage, (4) middle and working stage, and (5) mastery and termination process (Toseland & Rivas, 1995).

## Preplanning

The group workers and other school personnel negotiated the specifics concerning the structure of the groups, as well as the time, meeting places, and the purpose of the groups. They discussed students' needs and the type of dance or other art form to be used. Together they made decisions about how the group's and individual members' progress was to be assessed and shared with the referral source. The group workers identified cofacilitators and other performing arts resources to be used in the groups.

During this first stage, a multidisciplinary, multilingual, and multicultural project staff was recruited. The project team agreed that the purpose of the project was to serve the psychosocial and educational needs of the students using their diverse cultures as a resource and a strength for success. Teachers and other school staff received intensive training on how to infuse the students' different cultures into the curriculum. Teachers, administrators, and social workers were trained simultaneously, learning how to work together across disciplines. Oral histories from the different cultures were documented and shared among students, teachers, social workers, and other community members before the groups were formed.

## Group Formation

Reasons to start the group were openly discussed among the students, teachers, and the group workers. The social workers assisted group members in formulating a purpose and goals. The project was organized into an after-school component as well as a regular school day curriculum component. All group sessions took place after school hours; however, group activities were prepared, followed up, and reinforced in the classroom. Some students volunteered to be in a group; other students were recruited or referred by their classmates, teachers, the principal, or social workers. Reasons for referrals varied. As Alicia's case illustrates, shyness was a reason commonly identified by teachers. Alicia was a Puerto Rican student who participated little in class and was labeled as "shy" by several teachers. In a group session she described how she became involved:

> The teachers went around and asked if we wanted to be in the dance group. I wanted to be in the Hispanic dance group so I went and tried out, and I was accepted. Everybody in my family knows how to dance. This is my first year dancing even though I am in the eighth grade. I was nervous when we first came out but calmed down because I felt inside of me the best. My friends in

the group were talking to me back and forth helping me out. Many things make me feel different, and dancing happens to be one of them.

In Alicia's case, dancing became the key to feeling part of a group and part of the school. She found the right medium to open up and communicate more freely. In group discussions she was able to integrate, universalize, and celebrate her progress.

Jose, also a Puerto Rican student, was also selected to be part of the Hispanic dance group. In one of the first group sessions he narrated how he felt about it:

I really felt great about being selected to be in this group. I got to meet other people and to perform in front of the school. My parents felt proud of me because I told them I would be dancing and . . . this type of music. I also dance at home when my family has a party. I have a seven-year-old brother, and he is getting as good as I am at dancing. We have everything at school, African dancers, Mexican dancers, Puerto Rican dancers. It's great!

Jose connected his participation in the group with culture and family. Through his participation in group program activities, he integrated the home–culture dimension of his life in the school. In the group sessions he often verbalized the sense of pride he shared with others through dance.

## Beginning Stage

In their early sessions, group members articulated dance steps and movement and the value of being together as a group. The leaders identified the roles of authority and leadership. Subgroups as well as unique interaction styles began to form. Dance or other performing art forms were used to inspire, motivate, and heal. Students began to express emotionally laden topics, which they often acted out in negative ways, in a different form and forum. The students created their own stage where they processed situations and issues that were of real significance to them. They gained from each other by building on each other's experiences, problems, points of view, strengths, and weaknesses.

Group participants began to discover a lot about themselves and others. That was the case with Tom, who was one of two Appalachian young men who participated in one of the New Choreography groups. He interviewed several group members as a means of finding material for new choreographies. He seemed especially proud of his interview with an African American group member. He commented, "We learned about African American ancestry together in the New Choreography group." As Tom's case exemplifies, during this stage, students of different backgrounds started to get to know each other better and gained respect for each other's cultures.

## Middle and Working Stage

During this stage, planning and problem solving occurred and cohesiveness developed. As the group members organized and began to share things, they started to take risks. They began to share values, concerns, and problems from their daily lives. They also became vulnerable and curious about a new art form. Dance offered a nonthreatening medium in the hands of a skilled facilitator. Struggling group members were helped to grow by learning concrete dance skills, by obtaining support, and by receiving affirmation from the facilitator as well as the mutuality of the group members. As the group members related their lives to the choreography, expressions of feelings took a concrete form. As members danced together, they worked out problems or emerging conflicts. As conflicts were managed and problems discussed, group cohesiveness was strengthened. The group workers used knowledge, skills, and self-awareness to help each other.

Through folk dance, oral histories, new choreographies, and the visual arts, students were exposed to hands-on activities in learning about and celebrating their cultures. As a group, the students engaged in discussions and integrated, processed, and personalized each other's experiences. Classroom projects in the different content areas and a family and community participation component were ongoing throughout the project.

During the working stage, definitions of art were challenged and expanded by the group members. Martin's case illustrates how this expansion took place. Martin was an African American student with a special talent for writing and performing raps; however, he was always getting in trouble at school. The group supported him in further developing his rapping skills. He was invited to perform at a downtown hotel by the assistant superintendent. Martin commented,

> Basically, the raps are about accomplishments of black people and black music yesterday and today. I get most of the information for the raps from my head. I know all about music from just being around. The superintendent told me basically what he wanted the rap to be about for the special program at the downtown hotel. He wrote his information on paper, and I went from there. The rap was about a guy named William E. Smith who was a painter. He painted a bunch of pictures about poverty. Now he is old and finally became famous. The social worker gave me a book to read about the painter. So I used the notes and the book to create the rap.

Martin also interviewed students from other cultures while looking for new materials for his rap. He took the initiative of asking a Puerto Rican classmate to act as interpreter for an interview with a Mexican group member who was not yet proficient in English. Although the participants were somewhat apprehensive at first, the interview was successful, and all three young men became close. Program activities pushed the boundaries of ethnicity and language and allowed students to communicate—in many cases for the first time—across cultural boundaries. The groups prepared the students for these experiences and served as sounding boards after they took place.

### Mastery and Termination Process

The final creative modern dance piece illuminated most groups' termination process. The individual group members experienced joy in their accomplishments. Collectively, the members experienced the exhilaration of the group as a whole as the dancers received praise from those who viewed their performances. The mastery phase set in motion the needed process of termination. At this stage of the group process, members and facilitators assessed themselves as individuals and as a group. The group members reviewed their accomplishments and began to plan for the future. The workers prepared the individual members and the group as a whole for a smooth termination. Branler and Roman (1984) suggested that by evaluating gains, identifying growth, and acknowledging loss during the termination phase, the worker can enable a letting-go process to begin and encourage members to build other supportive networks. Finally, some members grew to a sense that the groups no longer met their needs. Termination was facilitated by participating in school calendar closing events that were agreed on when the groups formed. Termination in many cases meant acceptance into the broader group called "school."

Anthony's experience speaks about reconnecting. Anthony was an overweight African American student who had serious behavioral problems in the classroom and was not liked by his peers. He became a dancer with one of the New Choreography groups. After six months of participation in the group, he received a standing ovation from his fellow students in a schoolwide talent show. The language of dance broke the walls of isolation that trapped this student. By mastering dance skills and through group discussions with the other dancers, he started to accept his body and himself, and his peers began to accept him.

## DISCUSSION AND IMPLICATIONS

The SWGPA model challenges traditional school social work practice models and provides an alternative approach to group therapy by integrating the performing arts and group work into a service delivery system. Dance and other performing arts are used to inspire, motivate, and heal students, families, and communities. Group members gain by building on each other's strengths. The SWGPA helps school social workers facilitate students' involvement in their own development as creators of their own destiny. The SWGPA makes empowerment possible and tangible at the school building.

A schoolwide application of the SWGPA model is recommended; however, starting on a smaller scale may be preferable in schools where conditions are not optimal. Awareness and skills-building training are key components of either approach. In addition, the administration, faculty, social workers, students, and their families need to be a part of the process from its inception. Existing resources need to be shared in a cost-effective manner to be most effective.

The students' comments illustrated the high levels of energy generated by the pilot program. From data gathered through intensive interviews with teachers and other school personnel, the program appears to have re-energized many faculty members as well. Program activities appeared to have helped some adults change their views and attitudes toward some students. Although outcome data were collected and analyzed about these issues, the lack of a control group makes it impossible to attribute identified improvements to the project. Further research is needed to assess the impact the program had on individual students and on the school community as a whole. The available exploratory data justify such a future endeavor.

## REFERENCES

Branler, S., & Roman, C. (1984). *Group work skills and strategies for effective interventions.* New York: Haworth Press.

Freire, P. (1994). *Pedagogy of hope.* New York: Continuum.

Freire, P. (1995). *Pedagogy of the oppressed.* New York: Continuum.

Johnson, M. W., & Marsiglia, F. F. (1994, October). *Group work and the performing arts in the school setting.* Paper presented at the 16th Annual Symposium of the Association for the Advancement of Social Work with Groups, Hartford, CT.

Marsiglia, F. F., & Zorita, P. (1996). Narratives as a means to support Latino/a students in higher education. *Reflections, 2,* 54–62.

Toseland, R. W., & Rivas, R. (1995). *An introduction to group work practice* (2nd ed.). Boston: Allyn & Bacon.

Vygotsky, L. (1979). *Mind in society: The development of higher psychological processes.* Cambridge, MA: Harvard University Press.

Wilson, G., & Ryland, G. (1949). *Social group work practice.* Cambridge, MA: Harvard University Press.

*This chapter was originally published in the January 1997 issue of* Social Work in Education, *Vol. 19, pp. 53–59.*

# 21 Assessment and Prevention of Aggressive Behavior among Youths of Color: Integrating Cultural and Social Factors

Jorge Delva

Findings of a recent study conducted by the National Council on Crime and Delinquency on violent crimes show that the number of violent crimes committed by juveniles between 1982 and 1992 grew from 17.2 percent to 17.5 percent, an increase of merely three-tenths of a percent (Jones & Krisberg, 1994). However, the same study suggested that although the total number of incidents may not have changed dramatically, the lethality of these incidents (for example, gang-related deaths and suicides) seems to be higher than a decade ago. The destructive effects of these incidents, particularly in the school environment, are felt by students, parents, and teachers alike regardless of race and socioeconomic status. However, the combination of particular environmental conditions (for example, poverty, unemployment, and drugs) and institutional racism create school environments where students of color are twice as likely to be victims of violence than white students (Quarles, 1989). In fact, students of color not only are more likely to be victims of crime but also are overrepresented in the juvenile justice system (Jones & Krisberg, 1994). Consequently, measures to identify youths at risk of engaging in violent behaviors, particularly youths of color, are seriously needed.

This article discusses how school social workers can incorporate cultural and social factors in the assessment and prevention of youths' aggressive behavior in the school setting. The integration of cultural and ethnic idiosyncracies in the prevention of aggression is important; these components have been largely neglected in explaining the behavior of youths from ethnic minority groups. This article proposes that preventive efforts can be effective only when social workers examine the assumptions, prejudices, and behaviors that they and the social structure (for example, school personnel, school board, community) use in dealing with youths from oppressed populations.

## HOW YOUTHS LEARN TO BE AGGRESSIVE

For the purposes of this article, *aggressive behaviors* are defined as physical and verbal behaviors that a youth or group of youths exhibit in an attempt to injure others. Examples of such behaviors range from schoolyard fighting to killing. Risk factors associated with the development of these behaviors include family instability (for example, marital discord or divorce), family psychopathology and criminal behavior, poor discipline practices, lack of parental supervision, academic problems, and a range of other environmental factors (for example, high teacher–student ratio, poor working conditions for youths) (Kazdin, 1991).

Most studies suggest that aggressive behaviors are learned at a very early age, are stable over time, and are quite resistant to treatment (Paterson, DeBaryshe, & Ramsey, 1989). Behavioral models suggest that aggressive responses are primarily learned from parents, siblings, and peers who reinforce and reward aggressive types of problem solving (Bjorkqvist & Osterman, 1992). Other studies on youths' aggressive behaviors indicate that aggressive responses are in part due to frustration and an improper perception of situations (Delva, 1992). These studies suggest that youths have learned to respond to situations aggressively without the proper observation of the perceived offense and without the ability to think of alternatives.

Unfortunately, the risks and causal factors predicting aggression among youths often are characteristics attributed to members of minority groups. It is not uncommon to hear people speak of these factors as if they were cultural characteristics common to all the members of a particular ethnic group—for example, "*They* don't have any self-control" (Bibus, 1992). Support for these false beliefs is found in crime statistics that show an overrepresentation of people of color (Stark, 1993). In view of these false beliefs, it is of utmost importance for social workers to be critical of four areas: stereotyping, historical factors, simplistic explanations for behavior, and the cultural bases of aggression.

## SOCIAL WORKER SELF-EVALUATION

Social workers must be critical of the overrepresentation of people of color in crime statistics. Studies have shown that on average, people of color who commit crimes are more likely to be arrested and to receive longer sentences than white people who commit crimes (Cuervo, Lees, & Lacey, 1984; Stark, 1993). Thus, the beliefs that most violent crimes are committed primarily by people of color are examples of myths that must be challenged with adequate data. The percentage of people of color who commit crimes is small and should not be taken as representing the behavior of the whole group.

Social workers must recognize that accurate knowledge about different cultures or ethnic groups is clearly lacking. Examples of political and historical factors that hinder the intellectual and moral education of young people of color abound (Schostak, 1986). For example, the educational system and the communications system, primarily television, fail to inform people of the diversity of cultures and when they do so, they often offer only a stereotypical portrayal. This educational failure is but a shadow of the legacy of years of segregation and oppression of people of color by a white-dominated society (Jaynes & Robin, 1989).

Social workers must also be aware of the tendency of individuals to explain behaviors, particularly aggression, in simplistic ways. Several models have been developed to explain aggressive behavior: genetic, behavioral, cognitive, sociological, economic, and psychoanalytic (Blanchard & Blanchard, 1984). None of these factors solely explains aggressive behavior. It is likely that a combination of these factors, interacting in ways still unknown to researchers, can explain aggression in humans.

Social workers face the dilemma of recognizing when aggressive behaviors are skills learned to survive in a hostile environment (for example, a high-crime community). Under these circumstances, any attempts to change the youth's behavior will be met with strong resistance unless alternative environments are provided such as housing in a different neighborhood and significant after-school activities.

In summary, the intervention process must begin with the worker's critical and rigorous evaluation of his or her values and beliefs about the youth of color with whom he or she is intervening. The worker's perceptions will largely influence the information sought from the youth during the assessment period and will influence the selection of the intervention. The importance of self-awareness has long been recognized in the social work field and cannot be emphasized enough when working with young people of color.

## CONDUCTING A CULTURALLY INFORMED ASSESSMENT

The complexity and multifaceted nature of aggression requires that a thorough assessment be conducted. In assessing aggressive behavior, it is important that the assessment methods and instruments chosen identify the type, frequency, and intensity of the behaviors. The assessment of aggressive behavior also should include the antecedents, places where behaviors occur, and the consequences. The best method for obtaining this information is through direct observation of the youth's interaction with peers, teachers, and parents. Different measures are available to record the extent to which aggressive behavior and related problems occur.

In addition to clinical utility, it is important that these measures have adequate validity (that they actually measure the concept they say they measure) and reliability (that the measure is consistent). For example, the Child Behavior Checklist (CBCL) (Achenbach, 1991) is a widely used instrument to assess social competence and academic and adaptive functioning of youths between the ages of four and 18. Other measures commonly used to assess youths' behaviors in schools include the Teacher Self-Control Rating Scale (TSCRS) (Humphrey, 1982) and the Personality Inventory for Children (Rapport, 1993). Although these measures have excellent validity and reliability scores, the adequacy of these measures with young people of color remains to be shown. Thus, in the assessment process it is necessary that the measures be reviewed for their appropriateness for the specific youth. In the absence of culturally adequate measures, the worker will have to use his or her discretion. For example, some questions may need to be translated, others may need to be read to the child, and in some cases the wording of some questions may need to be changed. Ideally, changes in the scales will be minimal, as these changes will affect the psychometric properties of the scales. In general, the information obtained from these assessment instruments should be viewed within the sociocultural perspective of the youth.

In addition to measuring aggression, it is important for the social worker to gain a complete understanding of the youth's lifestyle and worldview by assessing other areas of the youth's life. These areas include family functioning, academic achievement, and cultural practices (for example, extent of collective orientation, importance of saving face, degree of familial interdependence, and spiritual beliefs).

Proctor and Davis (1994) indicated that the helper, who is usually from the mainstream group, generally has little understanding of the experiences of people of color and often has a difficult time recognizing that such differences can affect the relationship. The social worker who has knowledge of the youth's culture will have an advantage in gaining trust and forming a bond. Increased trust has been associated with better treatment outcomes (Corey, 1991). This additional knowledge may inform the worker whether the behaviors, values, motivations, and coping styles learned within the family setting vary significantly from the values of the mainstream society. For instance, whereas Anglo-American culture values "independence, individualism, competition, materialism, and directedness, other cultures value traditions, interdependence, cooperation, group welfare, and indirectedness" (Hanson, 1992, p. 84). Thus, the types of reinforcement, support, and self-validation that the youth receives from his or her peers and teachers are dependent to the extent that the youth's values and behaviors are appreciated and that the family's practices are viewed as congruent with society's.

An assessment of the youth's sense of belonging and safety in the classroom, school, and larger community is essential. It is important to know whether the youth feels he or she holds a place in society, because many of them feel, and many are, marginalized.

Historically, people of color have had a relentless struggle to gain a respectful and safe place in society. The social worker needs to be aware of the historical, economic, and political forces that have affected the various ethnic groups in the United States. Some of these forces include the experience of disempowerment, ostracism, forced assimilation in an often hostile environment, and employment and housing discrimination (Allen-Meares, Washington, & Welsh, 1986; Gibbs, 1988). It is crucial for the social worker to know the extent to which the youth has been affected by these experiences. For example, holding a place in the classroom, school, community, and society means that the youth is accepted and enjoys affection and respect. On the other hand, the forces mentioned earlier can lead to a lack of acceptance and respect not only from mainstream society but also from the youths themselves as they internalize these feelings, which has long-lasting effects (West, 1993). Consequently, assessment of the experiences the youth and his or her family have had with the dominant culture is needed.

The intent of this sort of assessment is a recognition that racism, discrimination, and prejudice are intricate parts of the world of the youth, including his or her family and ethnic group. Simple probing questions such as "Have you ever felt that you could not do something because of your skin color or ethnic background?" and "Has anyone ever stopped you from doing something because of your skin color or ethnic background?" can elicit valuable information about the youth's experiences with discrimination and racism. Some youths, especially younger ones, may have an easier time providing answers about someone they know, such as a parent or sibling, who has been treated poorly or denied access to some activity because of skin color or ethnic background. The worker should be careful not to dismiss the youths' experiences with discrimination as being exaggerated or nonexistent. On the other hand, some youths may not recognize the effects of racism. Youths who make derogatory statements about their physical characteristics (for example: "I want to make my afro hair straight," "My lips are too big") or who deny their background (for example, "I am European," when in fact the individual was born in the Caribbean to a black father and a white French mother and has never been to Europe) show signs of being affected by racism but may not be aware of their internalization of such attitudes.

It is equally important to recognize that individuals who are members of certain ethnic groups are heterogeneous and that not everyone in the group will have experienced discrimination. Therefore, the intent of conducting an assessment of the experiences of the youth of color with regard to the mainstream group or other ethnic or racial groups is not to create a witch-hunt but to allow those youths who have experienced these forces to share them and to find validation so that healing can begin (Cose, 1993). In addition, an assessment of these experiences will allow the social worker to determine whether there is a link between them and the youth's aggression.

Social workers' strengths lie in their comprehensive view of human nature. The responsibility to know of each other's cultures was stated quite eloquently by Ewalt (1994), who said, "We have an obligation, to the best of our ability, to know the facts of discrimination as it still exists, whether in the degradation of inner-city life or in the indignities still endured by middle-class and upper-class people of color" (p. 246).

Once the social worker thinks that adequate information has been obtained to develop a treatment plan, he or she needs to develop the intervention that will best meet the needs of the youth; he or she can then implement a multisystem intervention.

## MULTISYSTEM INTERVENTIONS FOR AGGRESSIVE YOUTHS

Many interventions have been developed to curb aggressive behavior among youths. These interventions include individual and group psychotherapy, cognitive and behavioral therapy, pharmacotherapy, family therapy, and communitywide interventions. A multisystem intervention involving individual, group, and family counseling; youth advocacy; education of teachers; and referral to services can prevent youths' acting out from developing into problematic aggressive behaviors.

The effectiveness of a cognitive–behavioral intervention is enhanced by the social worker's understanding of social and cultural issues. The cognitive–behavioral component of the intervention, illustrated by a case study, is based on the work of Strain (1981) and Weissberg and Gesten (1982). The criteria for the selection of the intervention are the documented effectiveness of the intervention in reducing aggressive behavior and its applicability to the school and classroom settings. The latter criterion is particularly important for school social workers. The first part of the case study describes a cognitive–behavioral intervention used to decrease the aggressive behavior of an 11-year-old African American–Hispanic female. The second part describes how knowledge about the client's cultural and social background was integrated into the intervention. Although the two components are discussed separately, in practice, the culturally informed social worker will find that these parts are intertwined.

## CASE STUDY

### Cognitive–Behavioral Intervention

Alicia, an 11-year-old African American–Hispanic female, was referred to the school counselor because of her aggressive behavior toward her peers and teachers in school. At school, her behavior was difficult to control. She argued with teachers, disrupted the class, and befriended a group of girls who belonged to a gang. The assessment process began with gathering baseline data about Alicia's aggressive and nonaggressive behaviors. Alicia's teachers completed the TSCRS, and her primary teacher completed the CBCL. In addition, for two weeks, the school social worker kept a daily log of the frequency and type of Alicia's aggressive and nonaggressive interactions. Furthermore, the social worker met with Alicia's teachers to obtain information on the teachers' perceptions of Alicia, including possible prejudicial or stereotypical attitudes they may have held toward her.

The baseline data provided the necessary information to plan the intervention. The first part of the intervention involved teaching Alicia to distinguish between appropriate and inappropriate behaviors. A series of steps were taught to her to deal with conflict. First, Alicia was taught to define the problem and to identify the feelings generated by the situation. Then, she learned to delay her aggressive responses by telling herself to "stop and think." Then she was encouraged to think of as many alternative responses as possible and to consider possible consequences of her actions. Alicia learned these steps through modeling by her worker, who also provided her with cues and reinforcement. After repeatedly practicing these steps in the counseling office, the worker encouraged Alicia to implement these behaviors (define the problem, identify how she feels, stop and think) on the playground. A self-evaluation component (the youth asks herself, "How did I do?") was included to encourage Alicia to reflect on her performance with her newly acquired skills.

At the beginning of the day, Alicia received a set of points that could be lost if she behaved aggressively on the playground. If she displayed constructive (nonaggressive) behavior, she was praised and was allowed to keep the points. At the end of the day, these points were exchanged for a set of privileges that varied from movie passes to attendance at her favorite school functions.

Alicia's peers were also used as contingencies to reinforce appropriate behavior. For example, if Alicia met the target behavior by the end of the day, a group activity was made available to the entire class of peers. In this case, her classmates, especially her friends, were motivated to assist Alicia in acquiring and maintaining appropriate behaviors. However, knowing that the child's household has a significant effect on the child's behavior, the social worker reached out to Alicia's mother and opened a door to opportunities for a more comprehensive intervention.

## Sociocultural Understanding

The social worker contacted Alicia's mother to gather information about family interaction, extent of acculturation and social support, and economic conditions. Alicia's mother worked full-time as a babysitter and consequently was unable to attend the school meeting. Alicia's mother spoke very little English, but the social worker obtained some information about the household with the help of a bilingual (Spanish) teacher. Alicia was born in the United States. Her mother was from Central America and had married an African American soldier stationed in her country; they were separated when they moved to this country. Alicia and her mother did not have any relatives in the United States but had made some friends, also Spanish-speaking, through their attendance at church. Alicia had an older brother who had had some problems with the law. Realizing that Alicia's family was experiencing much stress, the social worker arranged for a home visit.

The goal of the home visit was to conduct a thorough assessment of the family's conditions. In her visit, the worker found that although Alicia's mother spoke little English, she could communicate adequately if everyone spoke slowly. The worker's caring attitude as well as interest conveyed to the family by her verbal and nonverbal behaviors allowed Alicia's mother to relax and be willing to share personal things. It was apparent that Alicia's mother was depressed, felt lonely in this country, and missed her family very much. She also seemed genuinely concerned about her children's behaviors but did not know what to do. She wanted her children to get at least a high school education so that they could have better job opportunities than she had had. However, she also said that she knew her children had to be aggressive "to watch their backs because most people do not like blacks and Hispanics." Also, Alicia's mother shared that her daughter was embarrassed to say where her mother was from, that Alicia did not want to learn Spanish because other children made fun of her, and that twice during the year she had asked if it was possible to wash her black color off to be more white like Barbie.

Although Alicia's mother refused a referral to the local social services agency where they had bilingual staff, she wrote down the agency's number in case she needed to call about her son. Also, she agreed to have the worker send descriptive information in Spanish about this agency. The worker asked Alicia's mother if she would prefer to have a Spanish-speaking social worker but also stated that she would very much like to continue working with her and helping her daughter. Alicia's mother indicated that for now she had no problems with the present worker, who was an African American. Alicia's mother indicated that she was willing to cooperate with the school to improve her daughter's behaviors. However, she could not come to the school because of her job, so she agreed to periodic telephone calls and future home visits if "the worker don't mind." The telephone conversations and home visits would provide the worker with the opportunity to build a closer therapeutic relationship with this family.

At school, the worker held a meeting with Alicia's teachers to suggest that they praise her a bit more and to alert them about the alleged put-downs that Alicia might be experiencing in school as a result of her skin color. In addition, the worker created an all-girls group that met weekly to talk about different issues facing women growing up in the 1990s (for example, future career plans, boys, drugs, going to intermediate school). In these meetings, discussions about standards of beauty and racial issues (for example, how "black is beautiful," how Hispanics are beautiful, how people can get along) were conducted. The worker used appropriate self-disclosure about her own experiences of being African American to encourage the youths to share their own worldviews. After six months, the social worker collected the same data that initially had been gathered to obtain a profile of Alicia's aggressive behavior at school. Results of the comparison of these data with the initial baseline validated what Alicia had reported to the group and what the worker had already observed; Alicia's aggressive behaviors had considerably decreased, and her school experience was more fulfilling. At the end of the year, Alicia continued participating in band, had slightly better grades, and intended to register in a Spanish class.

The success of this intervention was related to the worker's successful use of the self and the skillful integration of various roles, such as broker and counselor, in targeting different but interconnected systems—family, peers, and teachers. This intervention shows that it is possible to develop a successful helping relationship between individuals from two different ethnic or racial groups. The successful engagement of Alicia's mother was probably related to the worker's sensitivity to the issues facing this family. The worker validated the experiences of shame, distrust, and isolation experienced by Alicia and her mother by offering a referral to an agency that provided bilingual counseling services, by offering to send information about the agency in Spanish, by providing Alicia's mother with the choice of selecting another worker, and by developing a strategy to increase Alicia's self-esteem in addressing the issues that concerned Alicia's mother.

## CONCLUSION

The simplistic nature of interventions normally used with people of color is supported by the findings of McMahon and Allen-Meares's (1992) content analysis of several social work journals. Their review led them to conclude that "In general, the majority of articles surveyed attempted to understand minorities acontextually, that is, without reference to the real social processes, such as racism and poverty, that shape people's lives" (p. 537). Their conclusion underscores the fact that efforts at preventing aggressive behaviors, among youths in general and youths of color in particular, must target the different environments that an individual interacts with as well as be sensitive to the individual's cultural and social experiences. If self-esteem, self-worth, competence, social skills, hope in a better future, and pride in our communities are to be modeled, developed, and struggled for, then social workers must make a serious commitment to the study of factors that contribute to both individual empowerment and social justice. To this end, aggressive cross-cultural education is needed to rid the population of bigotry and to prepare students, teachers, and social workers to meet the needs of the ever-increasing multicultural population (Allen-Meares, 1992).

Although referring to the racism found among schoolteachers, Schostak's (1986) words also speak to the social work profession: "Being involved wittingly or unwittingly in the institutional processes which reproduce discrimination is itself a political act with political consequences" (p. 110). Social workers need to be critical of the roles they play in a racist society. Social work's relentless commitment to social justice is the key factor in bringing about the necessary changes.

## REFERENCES

Achenbach, T. M. (1991). *Integrative guide for the 1991 CBCL/4–18, YSR, and TRF profiles.* Burlington: University of Vermont, Department of Psychiatry.

Allen-Meares, P. (1992). Prevention and cross-cultural perspective: Preparing school social workers for the 21st century [Editorial]. *Social Work in Education, 14,* 3–5.

Allen-Meares, P., Washington, P. O., & Welsh, B. L. (1986). *Social work services in schools.* Englewood Cliffs, NJ: Prentice Hall.

Bibus, A. A. III. (1992). Family metaphors in three plays by August Wilson: A source of deeper cultural sensitivity. *Social Work in Education, 14,* 15–23.

Bjorkqvist, K., & Osterman, K. (1992). Parental influence on children's self-estimated aggressiveness. *Aggressive Behavior, 18,* 411–423.

Blanchard, R. J., & Blanchard, D. C. (Eds.). (1984). *Advances in the study of aggression* (Vol. 1). Orlando, FL: Academic Press.

Corey, G. (1991). *Theory and practice of counseling and psychotherapy.* Pacific Grove, CA: Brooks/ Cole.

Cose, E. (1993). *The rage of a privileged class.* Scranton, PA: HarperCollins.

Cuervo, A. G., Lees, J., & Lacey, R. (1984). *Toward better and safer schools.* Alexandria, VA: National School Boards Association.

Delva, J. (1992). *Aikido principles of breathing, harmonious movements, and philosophy: An Eastern approach to reducing children's aggressive behavior.* Unpublished master's thesis, University of Hawaii, Honolulu.

Ewalt, P. (1994). On not knowing [Editorial]. *Social Work, 39,* 245–246.

Gibbs, T. J. (Ed.). (1988). *Young, black, and male in America: An endangered species.* Dover, MA: Auburn House.

Hanson, M. (1992). Families with Anglo-European roots. In E. Lynch & M. Hanson (Eds.), *Developing cross-cultural competence: A guide for working with young children and their families* (pp. 65–84). Baltimore: Paul H. Brookes.

Humphrey, L. (1982). Children's and teachers' perspectives on children's self-control: The development of two rating scales. *Journal of Consulting and Clinical Psychology, 50,* 624–633.

Jaynes, G. D., & Robin, W. M., Jr. (1989). *A common destiny: Blacks and American society.* Washington, DC: National Academy Press.

Jones, M., & Krisberg, B. (1994). *Images and reality: Juvenile crime, youth violence and public policy.* San Francisco: National Council on Crime and Delinquency.

Kazdin, A. (1991). Aggressive behavior and conduct disorder. In T. Kratochwill & R. Morris (Eds.), *The practice of child therapy* (pp. 174–221). New York: Pergamon Press.

McMahon, A., & Allen-Meares, P. (1992). Is social work racist? A content analysis of recent literature. *Social Work, 37,* 533–539.

Paterson, G. R., DeBaryshe, B. B., & Ramsey, E. (1989). A developmental perspective on antisocial behavior. *American Psychologist, 44,* 329–335.

Proctor, E., & Davis, L. (1994). The challenge of racial difference: Skills for clinical practice. *Social Work, 39,* 314–323.

Quarles, C. (1989). *School violence: A survival guide for school staff.* Washington, DC: National Education Association.

Rapport, M. (1993). Attention deficit hyperactivity disorder. In T. Ollendick & M. Hersen (Eds.), *Handbook of child and adolescent assessment* (pp. 269–291). Boston: Allyn & Bacon.

Schostak, J. F. (1986). *Schooling the violent imagination.* New York: Routledge & Kegan Paul.

Stark, E. (1993). The myth of black violence [Comments on Currents]. *Social Work, 38,* 485–490.

Strain, P. S. (Ed.). (1981). *The utilization of classroom peers as behavior change agents.* New York: Plenum Press.

Weissberg, R., & Gesten, E. (1982). Considerations for developing effective school-based social problem-solving (SPS) training programs. *School Psychology Review, 11,* 46–63.

West, C. (1993). *Race matters.* Boston: Beacon Press.

---

*This chapter was originally published in the April 1995 issue of* Social Work in Education, *Vol. 17, pp. 83–91.*

# 22

# A Model for School Social Work Facilitation of Teacher Self-Efficacy and Empowerment

Rosemary O'Connor and Wynne S. Korr

lthough the crisis in teacher motivation has been identified as the "single greatest impediment to school improvement" (Ashton & Webb, 1986, p. 1), school social workers have just begun to consider what they can do to empower teachers and improve their motivation and *self-efficacy*, defined in this article as a teacher's perception of his or her ability to handle classroom problems. Promoting collegiality and combating feelings of helplessness and powerlessness can reduce demoralization and improve motivation and self-efficacy. As Germain (1991) pointed out, "If the school's effectiveness with vulnerable children and their parents is to be increased, social work practice must include work with teachers who have been rendered powerless by conditions under which they teach" (p. 93).

Urban schools can be particularly stressful environments. Teachers are often faced with children who come to school ill equipped physically and emotionally to learn. Teachers may also feel they have no input into policies that affect their work. The feelings and behavior of teachers who perceive that they do not have a positive effect on students may adversely affect student achievement.

This article describes a model for school social work involvement in teacher staff development to improve empowerment and self-efficacy and presents findings from a study done in two urban schools. In the model the social worker serves as a facilitator of a peer-coaching program that promotes teacher sharing and advice giving.

## TEACHER EMPOWERMENT AND SELF–EFFICACY

Germain, addressing educational reform and empowerment-based social work practice, stated that "the concept of power, including powerlessness and empowerment, has particular relevance for . . . school social work" (1991, p. 88). She identified the school social worker's role in the empowerment of children, parents, and teachers:

> School social workers should engage in a continuous analysis of the process of disempowerment and exclusion in the school. They should facilitate adults' and children's rediscovery and further development of their own capacities for problem solving, decision making, and effective action in the processes of learning, teaching, and other school activities. They should generate linkages to needed resources [and] mobilize and support human relatedness, competence, self-direction, and self-esteem as components of personal power. (p. 89)

Self-efficacy, as conceptualized by Bandura (1986), relates to an individual's ability to examine alternatives and implement a course of action (for example, a teacher's consideration of and response to classroom problems). Empowerment without self-efficacy is unlikely. "Self-efficacy involves a generative capability in which cognitive, social, and behavioral skills must be organized into integrated courses of action to serve innumerable purposes. Success is often attained only after generating and testing alternative forms of behavior and strategies. Self-doubters are quick to abort this process if their initial efforts prove deficient" (p. 391).

Research has shown the relationship between teacher self-efficacy and student outcomes. Meijer and Foster's (1988) study of 230 primary teachers in the Netherlands found that teacher self-efficacy was a significant predictor of teachers' ratings of the seriousness of a student's problems and their referral of the student as at-risk for academic failure. Ashton and Webb (1986) reported that higher teacher self-efficacy resulted in higher student achievement. McLaughlin and Berman (1977) found that teacher self-efficacy was significantly related to student achievement in reading.

## MODEL FOR SCHOOL SOCIAL WORK INTERVENTION

In the model described in this article, the school social worker helps facilitate changes in teachers' beliefs in their capability to address students' needs. The social worker works toward this objective by organizing a teacher staff development program based on peer coaching. Peer coaching involves teacher observation of a colleague's instruction in the classroom followed by structured feedback and discussion in an atmosphere of companionship, collegiality, and confidentiality rather than criticism (Showers, 1985). School social workers are not in a position of authority relative to teachers; therefore, they are not seen as evaluators or judges of teachers. Like consultants, social workers are in a coordinate relationship with teachers in which "the teacher is viewed as a fully competent professional who retains full authority and responsibility for the student. . . . the consultant does not act as a teacher, supervisor, or therapist because these roles imply some degree of authority over the consultee that the consultant does not have" (Sabatino, 1991, p. 263). By linking teachers in a nonjudgmental setting, social workers can empower teachers and help combat their feelings of isolation and helplessness.

Social workers can also encourage problem solving, mediate in problem situations, and help prevent problems. Teachers' problems may involve the need for knowledge, skills, self-confidence, and objectivity (Sabatino, 1991). The intervention presented here addresses the first two problems through information-sharing sessions and the second two through peer coaching and group meetings.

In addition to the roles already described, the school social workers assist in all phases of implementing the teacher staff development program. Before beginning the information-sharing sessions in this study, the social worker solicited requests for information about teaching approaches and recruited speakers for each major issue identified by the teachers. Three one-hour sessions were conducted, and teachers received research material on each topic before the session.

The social worker organized peer coaching by facilitating the matching of teachers, changing the pairing group if necessary, and arranging for coverage of the teachers' classes during the peer-coaching sessions. Each of the four sessions began with a 15-minute conference in which the teachers shared information about class objectives and composition. Classroom observation lasted 30 minutes and was reciprocal (partners observed each other's class). The social worker facilitated a 15-minute conference after the observation to ensure that the norms of confidentiality and nonjudgmental feedback were observed.

The social worker facilitated three one-hour group meetings on problem solving that were alternated with the information-sharing sessions. Experts who had spoken at information-sharing sessions also attended the meetings. New teachers presented case examples that involved a problem in the classroom and engaged in problem solving with the more experienced teachers. In the final meeting, all teachers shared concerns, feelings, and perceptions and identified problem areas and plans for solutions.

## METHOD

The model, tested in two Chicago elementary schools serving a low-income, Hispanic neighborhood, was developed and implemented in conjunction with a larger study of interventions to decrease referrals of students for special education services. The first author, an experienced school social worker, was engaged by that project to develop and implement the peer-coaching model.

### Research Questions

The major research questions included the following: Did teachers' self-perceptions of efficacy improve after participating in the staff development program? Did program participants have better self-perceptions of efficacy than members of a comparison group? Did program participants solicit more advice from peers? Did program participants offer advice more frequently? Did program participants share more of their experiences with peers?

### Study Design

The research included both quantitative and qualitative elements. To test gains in self-efficacy, a pretest–posttest design with a comparison group was used. Content analysis was done of the transcripts of the audiotaped group meetings. Information was also obtained from interviews with and questionnaires completed by program participants.

### Research Instruments

An 11-item self-efficacy scale developed by Meijer and Foster (1988) was used to measure teachers' perceptions of how capable they are in affecting student learning and reducing problem behaviors. Meijer and Foster reported an alpha value of .63 for this scale.

Six questions were asked of both participants and comparison group members before and after the staff development program to obtain information about teacher advice giving and sharing (Figure 22-1).

*Figure 22-1*

## Interview Questions about Teacher Advice Giving and Sharing

1. Do you ask your fellow teachers for advice about classroom practices?
    a. If yes, about what do you ask for advice?
    b. How often does this occur?
    c. From whom do you seek advice?
    d. In what setting does this occur?
    e. If no, do you ask someone else? Who?
2. From whom would you like to obtain advice about classroom practices?
3. Do your fellow teachers ask you for advice about classroom practices?
    a. About what do fellow teachers ask you for advice?
    b. How often are you asked for advice?
4. Do you share with your colleagues/peers your experiences working with children (specific children)?
    a. How often do you share with your colleagues/peers your experiences working with children (specific children)?
    b. Does this collegial interaction affect how you feel about yourself professionally? In what ways?
5. Do you feel isolated? Supported?
6. What one thing would help you feel better about your teaching or about being a teacher?

Group meetings were audiotaped, transcribed, and coded by two independent raters. Frequency counts were obtained on advice and sharing.

### Sample

The sample included 20 teachers from two schools located four blocks apart (see Table 22-1 for teacher characteristics). Ten teachers participated in the peer-coaching

*Table 22-1*

## Teacher Characteristics

| Characteristic | Treatment Group (N = 10) | Comparison Group (N = 10) |
|---|---|---|
| Gender | | |
| Men | 1 | 5 |
| Women | 9 | 5 |
| Race | | |
| African American | 1 | 4 |
| Hispanic | 3 | 2 |
| White | 6 | 4 |
| Number of years teaching | | |
| 0–5 | 3 | 5 |
| 6–10 | 2 | 2 |
| 11–15 | 1 | 2 |
| 16 or more | 4 | 1 |
| Bilingual | | |
| Yes | 8 | 4 |
| No | 2 | 6 |

program. The 10 teachers in the comparison group had other after-school duties that made it impossible for them to participate in the program. In one school, of 15 teachers, five were in the peer-coaching program and four were in the comparison group. In the other school, of 33 teachers, five were in the program and six in the comparison group. Data are presented on the nine in each group who responded to both pretest and posttest questionnaires and interviews.

## FINDINGS

### Self-Efficacy

Participants in the program and comparison groups differed significantly in self-efficacy (one-tailed Dunnett's posthoc comparison of means, $p \leq .05$) (see Table 22-2), but these differences came from the comparison group's drop in self-efficacy scores at posttest rather than from an increase in participants' self-efficacy scores. We speculate that the intervention may have helped prevent a similar drop in scores in the program participants. The comparison group's higher scores at pretest may be because more men were in that group, and the men had higher self-efficacy scores.

### Seeking and Giving Advice

The pretest and posttest interviews were coded for the amount of advice seeking and sharing (see Tables 22-3, 22-4, and 22-5). Two independent raters coded 25 percent of the interviews on the frequency of advice and sharing and had complete agreement in their coding. The program participants increased their frequency of asking for advice, giving advice, and sharing experiences from pretest to posttest.

Examination of the interview data sheds additional light on the sharing process. For example, one program participant said she frequently sought advice on classroom practices, even if it did not always go well: "I asked a couple of teachers . . . and in one instance I was sorry I asked and in another instance it was nice to get feedback." In contrast, a teacher in the comparison group said that seeking advice seldom happened: "We talk vaguely but as far as specifics, no."

Program participants shifted from offering advice to sharing experiences over the course of the three group meetings. At the first meeting the teachers were

*Table 22-2*

**Mean Pretest and Posttest Self-Efficacy Scores, by Gender**

| Gender | Treatment Group (N = 9) | | Comparison Group (N = 9) | |
| --- | --- | --- | --- | --- |
| | Pretest | Posttest | Pretest | Posttest |
| Men | 36.0 | 38.0 | 33.4 | 33.0 |
| Women | 31.6 | 32.3 | 32.5 | 29.5 |
| All | 32.1 | 33.0 | 35.6 | 31.5 |
| *SD* | 2.15 | 3.08 | 4.09 | 5.03 |

NOTES: $p \leq .05$. Scores are based on the Meijer and Foster (1988) self-efficacy scale.

Table 22-3

## Percentage of Teachers Asking for Advice about Classroom Practices

| Frequency | Treatment Group | | Comparison Group | |
|---|---|---|---|---|
| | Pretest | Posttest | Pretest | Posttest |
| Daily | 11 | 44 | 11 | 0 |
| 1–2 times per week | 78 | 56 | 56 | 56 |
| Once per month | 11 | 0 | 22 | 22 |
| 1–2 times per year | 0 | 0 | 0 | 11 |
| Never | 0 | 0 | 11 | 11 |

reluctant to offer advice and asked more than 45 clarifying questions before the first suggestion was made. One teacher observed, "Teachers have respect for knowing their own situation, and they have enough respect for other people so that they don't go around offering advice."

In the first two meetings in which the new teachers presented cases, the more experienced teachers modeled a method of problem solving that placed the problems in a broader context than the classroom. At the first meeting one teacher spoke about her case in ways that related only to the student or to herself: "I can't get him to do work. I can't get him to turn in work. . . . He's lazy and immature." Others asked questions and offered advice that went beyond the teacher and student into other environments: "Do you ever see this child on the playground?" "How does he do in gym?" The response was, "Well, he's had to 'sit out' several times because he didn't have the right shoes." One teacher described how she works with the parents of a similar child: "I sit down with one or both parents, and we talk about the kid and how he is at home, and I tell them how he is at school. I usually ask if he has any responsibilities at home, and if he doesn't then I suggest . . . something that he needs to do consistently every day because I think that carries over into school." At the second meeting a teacher spoke about a student's problems with handwriting and spelling. One teacher asked, "Are her eyes OK?" The first teacher did not know and agreed to find out.

At the second meeting the discussion went beyond individual cases to the feelings teachers had as they understood more about their students' problems

Table 22-4

## Percentage of Teachers Being Asked for Advice about Classroom Practices

| Frequency | Treatment Group | | Comparison Group | |
|---|---|---|---|---|
| | Pretest | Posttest | Pretest | Posttest |
| Daily | 12.5 | 50 | 25 | 12.5 |
| 1–2 times per week | 25 | 50 | 25 | 37.5 |
| Once per month | 50 | 0 | 37.5 | 25 |
| 1–2 times per year | 12.5 | 0 | 0 | 0 |
| Never | 0 | 0 | 12.5 | 25 |

Table 22-5

**Percentage of Teachers Sharing Their Experiences Working with Children**

| | Treatment Group | | Comparison Group | |
|---|---|---|---|---|
| Frequency | Pretest | Posttest | Pretest | Posttest |
| Daily | 12.5 | 50 | 25 | 12.5 |
| 1–2 times per week | 25 | 50 | 25 | 37.5 |
| Once per month | 50 | 0 | 37.5 | 25 |
| 1–2 times per year | 12.5 | 0 | 0 | 0 |
| Never | 0 | 0 | 12.5 | 25 |

at home: "We are dealing with an awful lot of factors in a school like this. . . . I sometimes feel overwhelmed." Teachers also began to explore problems in the school and solutions to them: "I think . . . the best solution as far as trying to deal with all of this is something which is out of our hands, which is decreasing the class size or giving the teachers an aide so that they can get around." The teachers began to make references to systemwide change efforts: "I think with school reform, too, that might be something; to implement a longer day. . . . I think that having a time when everyone has to be here [after school] might foster talking about students or talking about things to help each other."

In the final meeting the teachers agreed to work together on systemic problems: "We're not going to get directions from downtown. . . . [We] have the staff and people with the ability to sit down and really think through our bilingual program and come up with a program . . . to meet the needs of our students. That's what I would really like to be part of, because I think we have the resources here at this school to do that. We don't have to continue the way we're doing it."

## IMPLICATIONS FOR RESEARCH

Given that this preliminary study of the teacher efficacy and empowerment model reduced teacher isolation by increasing advice giving and sharing, replication on a larger scale is warranted. Future studies should use larger samples and be conducted in multiple sites with more than one school social worker. Variables such as gender and race should be examined to assess their differential effects. Research should also assess the impact of the intervention on student behavior and performance.

## IMPLICATIONS FOR SCHOOL SOCIAL WORKERS

This model helps school social workers "generate linkages to needed resources [and] mobilize and support human relatedness, competencies, self-direction, and self-esteem" (Germain, 1991, p. 89). School social workers have expertise in relationship building and working in all parts of the educational community and can help create linkages across grade levels and even buildings to facilitate the connections needed to initiate a teacher empowerment and self-efficacy program. Because institutional support and sanction of such a program is necessary for successful implementation, school social workers will need to seek administrative or school board support to obtain funding for teacher substitutes during the program's peer-coaching sessions. The social worker could also contact local universities or colleges to arrange for coverage of classes by students enrolled in teacher education programs.

## REFERENCES

Ashton, P., & Webb, R. (1986). *Making a difference.* New York: Longman.

Bandura, A. (1986). *Social foundations of thought and action.* Englewood Cliffs, NJ: Prentice Hall.

Germain, C. B. (1991). Educational reform, power and practice in the 1990s. In R. Constable, J. P. Flynn, & S. McDonald (Eds.), *School social work: Practice and research perspectives* (2nd ed., pp. 87–95). Chicago: Lyceum Books.

McLaughlin, M., & Berman, P. (1977). Retooling staff development in a period of retrenchment. *Educational Leadership, 35*(2), 191–194.

Meijer, C. J., & Foster, S. F. (1988). The effect of teacher self-efficacy on referral chance. *Journal of Special Education, 22,* 378–385.

Sabatino, C. (1991). School social work consultation: Theory, practice, and research. In R. Constable, J. P. Flynn, & S. McDonald (Eds.), *School social work: Practice and research perspectives* (2nd ed., pp. 257–272). Chicago: Lyceum Books.

Showers, B. (1985). Teachers coaching teachers. *Educational Leadership, 42*(7), 43–48.

*This chapter was originally published in the January 1996 issue of* Social Work in Education, *Vol. 18, pp. 45–51.*

# 23 Group Work with High-Risk Urban Youths on Probation

Harriet Goodman and William Ford

In recent years, rehabilitation has been out of favor in the criminal justice community, although both recidivism and incarceration have increased. Expanding numbers of violent young offenders have placed a burden on the courts, jails, and prisons in many large urban centers. As a result, young first-offense felons can plea bargain and receive probation sentences instead of going to prison. Along with the systemic pressures to use community corrections for first offenders, recent criminal justice research has found that rehabilitation approaches are more effective than punitive measures in reducing rearrest (Andrews, 1989; Boone, 1994; Gendreau, 1993; Matthews, Boone, & Fogg, 1994; O'Leary & Clear, 1984).

Whereas "punishing smarter" programs such as shock incarceration or boot camp actually increase rates of recidivism, offender rehabilitation programs with specific characteristics can result in the reduction of criminal activity (Fabiano, 1991a, 1991b; Gendreau, 1993; Petersilla, 1990). Interventions that have proved the most effective are intensive, behavioral, and focused on the highest risk offenders (Andrews, 1989). When they follow principles of effective rehabilitation interventions, sentences of probation have the potential to reduce recidivism. Community corrections programs can be more efficient and effective than incarceration.

This article describes an innovative group work project designed for a large urban probation department. The project targets 16- to 20-year-old African American and Latino young men on probation who are at high risk of rearrest. The purpose is to teach young probationers how to protect their physical safety and avoid rearrest by adopting prosocial thinking and actions. The department adopted this approach to test the potential of cognitive–behavioral group work to reduce rearrest rates among young men on probation.

The project design translates the criminal justice literature into specific interventions that rely heavily on cognitive restructuring. Recent theoretical models for social cognitive approaches (Gilcrist, Schinke, Bolbo, & Snow, 1986; Nurius, 1989, 1994; Shilling, El-Bassel, Hadden, & Gilbert, 1995), particularly in working with involuntary clients (Brown & Caddick, 1993; Ivanoff, Blythe, & Tripodi, 1994), provided the rationale for collaboration between the probation department and social work faculty.

## DESCRIPTION OF PROJECT AND PARTICIPANTS

The group work project was customized to reflect the issues that commonly confront urban youths of color. Many of these young men are routinely exposed to criminal activity and violence associated with drug use, random shootings, easy access to handguns, and intrafamily violence. Loss permeates their lives. They quickly develop a sense of nihilism and alienation that gives ready justification for violent acts.

The cognitive–behavioral group intervention described in this article is called SAFE-T; it provides a rehabilitation modality for use in probation supervision. The acronym SAFE-T stands for *self*, *a*wareness, *f*eelings, *e*ducation, and *t*asks; it links the ideas of thinking and action.

## Participants

Group members are 16- to 20-year-old African American and Latino youths who are serving probation terms of five years for crimes such as drug dealing, robbery, and assault. Twelve to 15 members are assigned to each group, and probationers' commitments to school, training, substance abuse treatment, or employment are accommodated.

## Group Leaders

Group sessions are led by probation officers who receive intensive training in group work methods. In addition, the officers learn about the ever-changing and colorful language of the young men. In preparation for their groups, officers listen to the latest rap music and watch movies and television programs marketed at urban youths.

## Group Sessions

The 32 sessions of the SAFE-T groups are divided into four modules of eight 105-minute meetings, each including a 15-minute break. Each module consists of meetings twice a week on two consecutive days for four weeks. The modules move from a highly predetermined structure, during which the probationers have restricted opportunity for personal participation, to progressively more open sessions. The sessions begin with less intimate content and move to more intimate topics.

Attendance at the group sessions is mandated as a condition of probation. Pre-established rules determine attendance and basic norms and expectations for group participation. Participants are not permitted to make up sessions in other groups, and once assigned to a specific group, they are required to remain members of their assigned group through completion of the four modules.

Each session has a consistent pattern of activities: a "ritual beginning," a "ritual ending," and an informal break with light snacks. Homework is assigned at the end of each session, and group members are required to report on homework assignments at the beginning of each group meeting. A completion ceremony, when the probation officers and department officials publicly recognize individual participants' progress, marks the end of the fourth and finale module.

## Mnemonic Devices

Wallet-sized cards with mnemonic reminders of session content are distributed to group members. Group leaders give the probationers small wallets to carry these cards in a private way. Probationers are expected to carry their wallets at all times and to refer to the mnemonic cards in dangerous situations. The cards serve as thinking guides for probationers. These mnemonic devices are useful because they teach participants to take time to reflect on options and consider the consequences of their behaviors before they act.

### Role Playing

Role playing provides an opportunity for rehearsal and application of session content. At first the group works with prepared role-play examples. Later, as the group develops its own culture and cohesiveness, members generate their own examples. The integration of the personal experiences of the young men into the content of the group exercises is critical to the development of a program that captures the realities of their day-to-day experiences.

## GROUP WORK WITH YOUNG OFFENDERS

The groups focus on teaching members specific skills; these skills enable them to accomplish the tasks required to achieve personal goals. Each probationer who participates in the group identifies a short-term goal with the probation officer. Goals include registration in a graduate equivalency degree program, reduction of intrafamily violence, or location of a job-training program.

Through skills-building techniques, members learn to organize daily schedules, follow routines, and develop tools for prosocial interpersonal skills. Group content enhances thinking and problem-solving skills; the probation officers introduce exercises for practice and rehearsal of those skills. Antisocial thinking frequently emerges in the group. When this occurs, the probation officer, and eventually other group members, challenge thinking that would place a probationer at risk and derail him from meeting his life goals.

### Cognitive Strategies

Cognitive tools and group methods are introduced throughout the SAFE-T group sessions in a carefully paced fashion, building on the increasing capacity of members to meet the six objectives of the group model: (1) to be a part of a group; (2) to take responsibility for actions in the group; (3) to take responsibility between group sessions for completing tasks and assignments; (4) to learn problem-solving techniques using cognitive tools; (5) to apply the tools in situations that pose a high risk for violent behavior; and (6) to help others inside and outside the group.

The SAFE-T group is an arena for correcting thinking that triggers and then justifies violent behavior. The methods used translate cognitive strategies into activities that are consonant with the life experiences and language of contemporary urban youths. They reflect the particular experiences and cultural symbols of their generation and their communities.

The group program was designed for probationers who had committed violent acts and who had been victims of violence. Although the probationers participated in acts of violence, they were also constantly vulnerable to it. As they learned that their personal safety was constantly at risk, they often rationalized their own violence as a justifiable means of survival, thus denying their criminality.

Therefore, their violent acts were not only behaviors but a pervasive construct of their thinking. Within the perceived security of the group, sharing past criminal and antisocial acts is a way for group members to come to terms with the faulty thinking that made them vulnerable to peer pressure, to committing crimes, and to engaging in violence.

## Case Example

The following case illustrates the ubiquitous presence of violence in the lives of urban youths and how it increases the potential for rearrest and compromises their personal safety. Officer Smith, an African American probation officer, met with a group of probationers twice a week for six weeks. Midway through the second module, Officer Smith introduced the important problem of peer pressure. Group members then discussed how to deal with peer pressure.

*Narratives.* During the beginning of the meeting, members reported on their homework assignment, which was to write about examples from their lives when friends had placed them at risk of violence and arrest. Chris began by saying that he was on probation because he followed his friends: "All the times I got in trouble is because I was following friends. But I can remember times that I did not follow my friends; that's what I wrote about." Chris looked at the worker and away from the other group members. He mentioned that once his friends wanted him to smoke a "wollah," a street term for a marijuana cigar laced with cocaine. Chris said that he knew that he had done some stupid things in his life, but he emphatically said, "I ain't doing no crack!"

Anthony told of an incident when he was hanging out with his friends. They wanted to steal a car, which he had done with them in the past. Looking at the group, Anthony said, "Well, you know when you sometimes get a funny feeling that you should not do something. Well, that is how I felt at the time, so I told them I wasn't down [going to follow them]. They start riffing [pressuring through belittling], but I told them, 'no.'"

The "funny feeling" served as a trigger that Anthony had learned to identify in early SAFE-T sessions. It is an internal warning to stop and think about alternatives and their consequences before acting. Learning to recognize feeling cues is an essential component of the SAFE-T program. Once the probationers can identify these feelings, they are able then to make conscious choices on the basis of prosocial thinking skills that they develop through rehearsals and exercises in the group setting.

Officer Smith reinforced the positive actions that the two members reported, acknowledging that going against friends was difficult. However, the tone of the experiences the members reported suggested the fragility of their resistance to peer pressure. Later in the session, another member described ignoring a similar "feeling" and ultimately being arrested.

The probationers became more willing to reveal participation in illegal activities later in the session as they became more comfortable. Chris said, "Yo, Smith, you know that there are times in the past that I didn't make the right choice." He told about the incident for which he was arrested, convicted, and placed on probation. He was out with friends, and they were driving a van that carried drugs. Chris and his friends were delivering the drugs from the main dealer to some sellers in the neighborhood. While he was in the van, Chris had a strong feeling that he should not be in the van with his friends. "Those cops had us on the sidewalk on our knees for at least two hours while they searched the van. When they found the drugs, they started hitting us and asking where the gun was. They said that they got a report that we had a gun, and they starting pushing us to the ground. We had no gun."

At this point, the worker noticed the change of tone in the group from quiet discussions to loud assertions of how violent the police are in the neighborhood and became very self-conscious, because he was also a peace officer. He asked the group members what they thought about what Chris described. John said, "I can't tell you how many times that has happened to me. We can be just hanging in front of the building, and the cops will just keep rolling past us. You know what we do then? We all pull our 'hoodies' [hoods of sweatshirts] up and give them something to follow. Yo, what I like is when they come over to ask what we are doing, and then they start searching us and don't find nothing." Sean reinforced John in the same mocking fashion, "Yo, the same thing happens to me when I'm in school. The cops are always harassing the blacks!"

*Role Playing.* The officer used the group members' discussions of their interactions with the police as the basis for a role play. The role play is an opportunity to analyze behavior within the context of the cognitive skills the members have learned. He asked the group members to show him how they saw the police harassing them. Group members selected roles as either youths or police and acted out a "typical" scenario. In this one, the police were yelling and screaming at the youths to move on. The young men were searched and even pushed by the end of the role play.

After the role play, the officer had two tasks. First, he had to validate group members' feelings of rage and helplessness when they are subjected to blatant discrimination. Then he had to find ways for them to channel these feelings into thinking to promote actions that precluded their vulnerability to danger from the police.

The worker asked the members who played the police in the role play to describe how they felt in one word. Juan volunteered, "Powerful!" Ronald said, "Good." Officer Smith then asked the members who played the young men to respond to their feelings in the role play. Robert exclaimed, "Mad! Yo, Smith, I just feel like I want to punch those cops out! Why they got to be bothering us?" Robert had consistently expressed a great deal of anger toward the police in the group because of an incident when the police had robbed him. To protect himself the next time, he bought a gun. He was arrested for possession of this gun. Allan said that he felt "pissed off." Sean followed this by saying "frustrated." The worker affirmed how upsetting these feelings were and how overwhelming they could be in situations with the police. Robert, with a slight smile on his face, said to Officer Smith, "At least the police can't harass you, because you are one of them."

*Shared Experiences.* The worker then told the group that it was reasonable to question how much they could trust him, because he had a good deal in common with police officers: He could send them to prison for violating the conditions of probation. He continued the discussion by asking why they assumed that because he was a peace officer he did not have experiences like theirs in his life. He told the members about a recent event when the police stopped his car:

> The police officer derisively asked how I could possibly get the money to have a red sports car. Two police officers asked me to place my hands behind my back and lean against the car, while they frisked me. Only after that did I have the opportunity to give identification as a probation officer. The police officers then sheepishly told me to be cool and forget the whole thing, and they sped off.

Robert said, "Shit, it was good you had your badge."

*Reinforcement.* The officer had to continuously correct thinking errors that the members used to justify antisocial actions. The racism that the young men experienced could not become an excuse for actions that might provoke arrest. Role playing not only allows the young men to "rehearse," it also exposes faulty thinking by the actors. However, the most powerful aspect of this session involved Officer Smith's willingness to describe his own encounter with racist behavior by the police. It gave him an unanticipated opportunity to model prosocial behavior in a provocative situation.

Sean contributed with a tone of desperation, "But when you live in a racist system it don't matter. If they want you in jail, they find a way to put you in." The officer asked the group for reactions. Robert answered, "Naw, I mean he's right, but I know that I don't have to always talk back to the cops, and sometimes I don't. Smith, I don't know what you want." Officer Smith said he was offering the members of the group an option for how they could handle very difficult situations differently. They could withstand group pressure, even with the obstacles they faced.

## DISCUSSION

The SAFE-T groups emerged after several years of intensive work with young men on probation. It is a hybridized practice formulation using an interactionist–mutual aid approach (Gitterman & Shulman, 1994; Rose & Edelson, 1987; Schwartz, 1976) with the systematic introduction of cognitive–behavioral strategies (Brown & Caddick, 1993; Persons, 1989; Schuyler, 1991). Such a strategy is not incompatible or inappropriate for the problems associated with violence-prone adolescents at risk of victimizing others and who themselves are victims of urban and domestic violence (Dryfoos, 1994).

The group experience is an opportunity to develop skills to survive in an urban environment that is rife with violence. The cognitive strategies the young men learn in the group have the potential to keep them safe from future encounters with the criminal justice system. The shared perceptions that the youths have about the system help them integrate new ways of thinking.

Although the court mandates participation, the coercive power of the probation officer–group worker soon gives way to the reciprocal activities that underlie emerging contractual and normative power. *Contractual power* refers to the group worker's ability to engage the members in activities through mutual agreement; this is particularly important in the early phases of the group's development. Normative power, perhaps the most important source of power that the officer has with the group, arises out of the group members' emotional and instrumental identification with the workers' feelings, ideas, and actions. The consistency and constancy of the group leader's presence and expectations for the group are crucial.

The group leader serves as a viable model to young people of color of alternative ways to think about and respond to the interrelated phenomena of violence, racism, and authority in their communities. The leader and the youths establish group norms that they can carry over to their lives in neighborhoods. The experience serves as a laboratory and catalyst for the young men's more prosocial activities outside the group.

The group leader is most effective if he or she perseveres at the following: shortening the social distance between the leader and the group while clarifying the boundaries of authority and responsibility; encouraging the exploration of the mutual "unknownness" from which all human beings suffer because of differences in race, class, gender, sexual orientation, ethnicity, age, disability, and so forth; and recognizing the pervasiveness and grim consequences of institutional racism in the daily lives of people of color (Gitterman & Schaeffer, 1972), particularly as young people of color experience it in the form of police harassment and brutality.

But young people must learn not to use the oppression they experience from the police and others to justify antisocial and violent activity. The group members must learn to apply skills to manage the rage they feel as a consequence of their experiences with institutional racism so they do not get involved in unproductive activities such as crime, domestic violence, and substance abuse.

The group members' examinations of their perceptions of the group leader allow for a deepened understanding of the ideas of authority and race in their lives. In one sense, the race or ethnicity of the group leader does not preclude the need for group members to examine how differences and similarities in race are confounded by the fact that the probation officer–group leader has ultimate authority over their freedom to be in the community. The group leader must have the personal assurance to allow group members to explore questions of the worker's race and his or her authority over them. Discussion of race and authority shortens the social distance between members and the worker. The group worker's ability to maintain appropriate boundaries with members takes considerable delicacy and skill.

Acknowledging the mutual unknownness that exists between people with significant differences in race, socioeconomic status, gender, and education is the sine qua non of skill with groups. In work with young people, workers must exhibit knowledge of and respect for their language and the metaphors they use to define their individuality. Furthermore, the group leader and the group must develop mutual respect for each other's values.

Cognitive–behavioral tools provide the vital structure for group members to manage their lives and begin to think their way out of highly dangerous situations as they become less dependent on the demands placed on them by peers to engage in criminal activities. They begin to see how antisocial activities are tied to a false sense of pride and to derive positive pride from prosocial activities, which may include completing school or working rather than abusing drugs or hanging out.

Preliminary comparisons between youths who participated in the SAFE-T groups and those who received traditional probation supervision suggest a marked reduction in rearrest rates for the SAFE-T group participants. The number of young men who have participated in the intervention is small. But the department will continue to use this intervention with larger numbers of young men sentenced to probation. At the same time, it will engage a third party to conduct a comprehensive, longitudinal evaluation of the intervention to learn the extent of its effectiveness over time.

## CONCLUSION

Social work's historical connection with probation has diminished in recent decades. However, collaboration between criminal justice agencies and social workers creates a synergy in addressing problems common to both disciplines. The primary mission for probation is to ensure community safety. However, social work and criminal justice agencies share a commitment to helping youths establish productive lives. Community corrections programs have the potential to help reduce violence in urban settings. Social group work as a part of a rehabilitation approach with criminal justice clients offers an excellent opportunity to engage hard-to-reach young people.

## REFERENCES

Andrews, D. A. (1989). Recidivism is predictable and can be influenced: Using risk assessments to reduce recidivism. *Forum on Corrections Research, 2,* 11–17.

Boone, H. N. (1994, Winter). An examination of recidivism and other outcome measures. *American Probation and Parole Association Perspectives,* pp. 12–18.

Brown, A., & Caddick, B. (Eds.). (1993). *Group work with offenders.* London: Whiting & Birch.

Dryfoos, J. (1994). *Full-service schools: A revolution in health and social services for children, youth, and families.* San Francisco: Jossey-Bass.

Fabiano, E. A. (1991a, August). Canada's cognitive skills program corrects offenders' faulty thinking. *Corrections Today,* pp. 104–108.

Fabiano, E. A. (1991b). How education can be correctional and how corrections can be educational. *Journal of Correctional Education, 42,* 100–106.

Gendreau, P. (1993, November). *The principles of effective intervention with offenders.* Paper presented at the conference of the International Association of Residential and Community Alternatives, Philadelphia.

Gilcrist, L. D., Schinke, S. P., Bolbo, J. K., & Snow, W. H. (1986). Self-control skills for preventing smoking. *Addictive Behaviors, 11,* 169–174.

Gitterman, A., & Schaeffer, A. (1972). The white professional and the black client. *Social Work, 17,* 280–291.

Gitterman, A., & Shulman, L. (Eds.). (1994). *Mutual aid groups and the lifecycle.* New York: Columbia University Press.

Ivanoff, A., Blythe, B. J., & Tripodi, T. (1994). *Involuntary clients in social work practice: A research-based approach.* New York: Aldine de Gruyter.

Matthews, T., Boone, H. N., & Fogg, V. (1994, Winter). Alternative outcome measures: The concept. *American Probation and Parole Association Perspectives,* pp. 11–12.

Nurius, P. S. (1989). Form and function of the self-concept: A social cognitive update. *Social Casework, 70,* 285–294.

Nurius, P. S. (1994). Assessing and changing self-concept: Guidelines from the memory system. *Social Work, 39,* 221–229.

O'Leary, V., & Clear, T. R. (1984). *Directions for community corrections in the 1990s.* Washington, DC: National Institute of Corrections.

Persons, J. B. (1989). *Cognitive therapy in practice: A case formulation approach.* New York: W. W. Norton.

Petersilla, J. (1990, March). When probation becomes more dreaded than prison. *Federal Probation,* pp. 23–27.

Rose, S. D., & Edelson, J. L. (1987). *Working with children and adolescents in groups.* San Francisco: Jossey-Bass.

Schuyler, D. (1991). *A practical guide to cognitive therapy.* New York: W. W. Norton.

Schwartz, W. (1976). Between client and system: The mediating function. In R. W. Roberts & H. Northen (Eds.), *Theories of social work with groups* (pp. 171–197). New York: Columbia University Press.

Shilling, R. F., El-Bassel, N., Hadden, B., & Gilbert, L. (1995). Skills training groups to reduce HIV transmission and drug use among methadone patients. *Social Work, 40,* 91–101.

*This chapter was originally published in the July 1996 issue of* Social Work, *Vol. 41, pp. 375–381.*

# 24 Group Support for Teenagers with Attention Deficit Hyperactivity Disorder

David F. Timmer

Attention deficit hyperactivity disorder (ADHD) "is the most prevalent diagnosis in North American epidemiological studies and the most frequent referral problem to many clinical programs" (Cunningham, 1993, p. 4). Therefore, school social workers must become as informed as possible about its causes, its effects on children, and its treatment. This article describes the group process experiences of children who have ADHD and presents an accumulation of lessons learned from a support group for teenagers with ADHD.

## BACKGROUND

The president of Children with Attention Deficit Disorders (CHADD) provided the impetus for the support group by expressing an interest in assisting teenagers with ADHD through a support group. The association was already conducting such a group for adults who had children with attention deficit disorders. The local CHADD chapter offered to share their high school location to promote participation from those parents' children. The theory was that a teenagers' meeting held in conjunction with the parents' meeting would generate interest, convenience, and the participation needed to compose a group. The theory followed the assumptions of family systems theory that "therapy is more effective and more rapid when more family members are involved" (Haley, 1991, p. 13).

Studies by Sayger (1987), Walker (1985), and Horn and Sayger (1990) have shown that effective family therapeutic involvement helps reduce a variety of problematic behaviors exhibited by those with a diagnosis of ADHD. Walker, for example, found that family involvement resulted in a 48 percent reduction in aggressive, disruptive behaviors at school. In addition, most medical professionals prescribing medication also support therapy as part of a comprehensive multimodal approach.

After a location was chosen, the monthly CHADD newsletter to parents announced the intention to form a group for their children. The announcement stated that the support group was open to any interested parties between ages 13 and 18 who were diagnosed with ADHD. When others learned of this group, their curiosity was piqued and they sought information. Some called from as far away as Connecticut seeking information and making suggestions (for example, about the structure, composition, and frequency of meetings).

The approaches for working with children with attention deficit disorders through support groups were derived from Barkley's (1981, 1990) course notes and the author's family therapist certification training and experience with guidance-based school support groups. From his experience with support groups based on these theoretical approaches, the author learned several important lessons.

## LESSONS LEARNED

### Age Range

The 13-to-18 age range chosen was too wide. The developmental abilities of the various ages (for example, in thinking abstractly rather than concretely) varied too greatly. Most of the group members thought in a concrete operational framework "dominated by external events" and their own individual reality—most were unable to assume the viewpoint of others (Ivey, 1986). Barkley (1990) reinforced this notion, emphasizing that age ranges of two years or less improve the likelihood that children with ADHD are functioning at similar levels of cognitive development and social experience. Restricting the age range for the author's group may have resulted in stronger group cohesiveness, because discussion would have been relevant and understandable to more participants.

### Format

The focus of the group was built around specific topics to promote structure and foster personal growth: family, self-esteem, feelings, behavior change, communication, conflict, friendship, anger, and problem solving. Preformulated questions related to these topics provided a structural impetus and addressed common social skills deficits of ADHD and socially rejected children. This format was followed into the ninth month, after which the group was able to function without reliance on preformulated questions to carry on discussions. Participants cautiously began to talk about problems and concerns for themselves and no longer needed the prescribed topics to provide structure. Yalom (1975) found that "a group goes through an initial stage of orientation, characterized by a search for structure and goals and a great dependency on the leader" (p. 302).

However, once the format changed, individual developmental differences became glaringly apparent. Older participants tended to be more verbal and, as a result, dominated group time. The facilitator's attempts to divide time evenly to include those who were less verbal in the group process were unsuccessful. Few of the less verbal participants knew how to take advantage of the opportunity to express themselves. Many group members became distracted after the discussion topics for the group were eliminated. Those who were ambivalent about participating in this group were lost when this less structured format was used.

Barkley (1990) warned facilitators that they must guard against becoming too unstructured. He advised them to make sure sessions remained highly structured and interesting as well as fast paced, thus ensuring that ADHD group participants remained actively involved in the group process. Less direction for the group benefited them less overall. Dependence on their volunteering to keep ideas and conversation flowing did not work because of the reluctance of some to participate.

## Frequency and Length of Meetings

Furthermore, cohesiveness for group members was not reached because of the infrequency of the meetings. In 10 months the group met 10 times. Once-a-month meetings did not provide enough sessions to engender a solid bond of trust. Once-a-week meetings would have been much more advantageous in helping create and maintain unity. Because the teenager support meeting was held concurrently with the adult support meeting, both meetings lasted 90 minutes. This was a mistake. For the teenagers, 45 to 60 minutes was adequate time to captivate interest, to allow sufficient participation, and to prevent restlessness.

## Therapy

Even though the original intention was to run a support group only, the facilitator frequently performed therapy. When a facilitator listens, is nonjudgmental, asks carefully neutral questions, and refrains from giving advice, he or she is leading a support group. Such an approach was nearly impossible with the ADHD group. Attempts to simply "facilitate" conversation did not work. Most of the time, the group was off-task (that is, talking out of turn, asking irrelevant questions, making faces, arguing, getting out of their seats). Therefore, a nondirective approach was unsupportive. A direct approach was necessary to keep some semblance of control. It is important to realize that therapy does have a role in a support group for teenagers with ADHD.

## Other Diagnoses

Many teenagers who have been diagnosed with ADHD have concurrent conduct or oppositional–defiant disorders. According to Barkley (1990), by adolescence 40 percent to 60 percent of those diagnosed with ADHD also have a diagnosis of conduct disorder. Of the regular group of about 10 participants, nearly half had another diagnosis besides ADHD. Consequently, most were resentful of authority, represented by the facilitator. Some almost seemed proud of the precarious positions they found themselves in at school and in the community. They boasted about it to challenge the facilitator. At nearly every meeting, the participants gloated about who had managed to get into the most trouble.

To neutralize this pattern, the facilitator questioned group members to elicit thought about the consequences of their actions and thinking and to engage them in some sort of formal thinking (that is, examining their thoughts, feelings, and actions).

## More Than One Facilitator

An extremely helpful factor in the sixth session was the addition of another social worker to help facilitate. This person assisted in keeping others focused and also helped note some of the group process. Having a cofacilitator was not only helpful, but also critical for better group functioning.

## RECOMMENDATIONS

An essential element for these support groups is the early statement and initiation of consequences for unacceptable behavior and incentives for cooperation to help prevent those who are opposed to participating from disrupting others and setting a negative precedent. Incentives and punishments should be coordinated with parents; for example, a meeting of parent, teenager, and facilitator to discuss a rating card that the facilitator will complete after each session might encourage the teenager to participate and the parent to monitor participation.

A screening process would also be beneficial. The facilitator could conduct a standardized interview with each parent and participant to gather a brief social and medical history, including questions pertaining to previous group and other counseling experiences. Excellent devices for measuring results of group work can be accomplished with pre- and postgroup rating scales. Two scales that independently address behavioral and family change can be quickly and conveniently administered: The Revised Behavior Problem Checklist (Quay & Peterson, 1983) documents the effects of group work related to attention problems, conduct disorders, aggression, and anxiety, and FACES III (Olson, Portner, & Lavee, 1985) is a standardized questionnaire that examines the dimensions of family cohesion and adaptability. Using these tests, a facilitator could become familiar with each participant before the group began. As Barkley (1981) stated, "No adult is more likely to have the wealth of knowledge about, history of interactions with, or sheer time spent with a child than a parent" (p. 88). After the tests, parent, facilitator, and teenager could review the group contract and openly discuss expectations and consequences. Acceptance of each candidate into the group would be based on the willingness of each student to accept the rules.

A final recommendation is that once the group sessions begin, no new members should be allowed to join randomly. Late-entering members can be extremely disruptive. Perhaps taking new members at the start of and halfway through the school year might be acceptable. This would enable the facilitator to minimize efforts spent explaining, organizing, and encouraging.

## CONCLUSION

The support group for teenagers with ADHD met for an entire school year. Two months into the next school year, the group was discontinued. Despite some flaws in the planning process, group members benefited overall. Most participants enjoyed the support program. One of the boys in the group, for example, voluntarily brought his best friend to the meeting. Both came regularly, as did about eight others who formed the core group. The participants who returned weekly benefited from the group in the following ways: They engaged in discussion about their families, school, and community, and they worked on conflict resolution, communication skills, and exercises designed to elicit feelings. Teenagers were able to participate in a group with peers who had ADHD and to foster healthy self-esteem by learning to think about themselves in a positive way.

We hoped that this group would be found to be less aggressive and disruptive at school like the posttherapy subjects in Walker's (1985) study. Five of the 12 families who participated in the support group were contacted two years later. Encouraging feedback was gathered at the interviews. All five reported that their children had graduated from high school or were going to graduate.

All parents reported improved behavior and compliance with community rules. A key factor in this success was the parents' commitment to involving their teenagers in a multimodal treatment program.

## REFERENCES

Barkley, R. A. (1981). *Hyperactive children: A handbook for diagnosis and treatment*. New York: Guilford Press.

Barkley, R. A. (1990). *Attention deficit disorder: A handbook for diagnosis and treatment*. New York: Guilford Press.

Cunningham, C. E. (1993). Increasing the availability and accessibility of services for ADHD children. *ADHD Report, 1*(5), 4–5.

Haley, J. (1991). *Problem-solving therapy* (2nd ed.). San Francisco: Jossey-Bass.

Horn, A., & Sayger, T. (1990). *Treating conduct and oppositional defiant disorders in children*. New York: Pergamon Press.

Ivey, A. E. (1986). *Developmental therapy*. San Francisco: Jossey-Bass.

Olson, D. H., Portner, J., & Lavee, Y. (1985). *FACES III*. St. Paul: University of Minnesota.

Quay, H. C., & Peterson, D. R. (1983). *Revised Behavior Problem Checklist*. Coral Gables, FL: University of Miami.

Sayger, T. V. (1987). Behavioral systems family counseling: Treatment program for families with disruptive children. *Contemporary Education, 58*, 160–166.

Walker, J. M. (1985). A study of the effectiveness of social learning family therapy for reducing aggressive behavior in boys. *Dissertation Abstracts International, 45*(9), 3088-B.

Yalom, I. D. (1975). *The theory and practice of group psychotherapy* (2nd ed.). New York: Basic Books.

*This chapter was originally published in the July 1995 issue of* Social Work in Education, *Vol. 17, pp. 194–198.*

# 25 Honoring Children's Narratives: Practice Strategies

Edith M. Freeman

These are both perilous and good times for children. The state of the art in medicine, education, technology, and other areas continues to improve at astounding rates with many anticipated and unanticipated consequences. Social conditions have changed as well, exposing children to a wider variety of both positive and harmful situations. In addition, through the media most children receive detailed information about the harmful experiences of other children as well as the many opportunities open to them on a daily basis. As a consequence, parents and helping professionals have noted that some children have experienced information overload. They have been bombarded, for example, with the threat of war, especially nuclear war; natural disasters such as hurricanes and earthquakes; and the deaths of other children in the bombing of an Oklahoma City federal building and the burning of the Branch Davidian compound in Waco, Texas. The recent media attention to parents who have killed their children, like Susan Smith in South Carolina, has heightened the fears of some children even more.

## NARRATIVES AS A CHILDREN'S COPING METHOD

Children need ways to understand and cope with this rapidly changing environment that seems more and more hostile. Even positive experiences with change can be perilous for children if age-appropriate avenues for perspective taking are not available. Storytelling is one natural avenue of expression for children. Their narratives can tell us much about what they are experiencing and how they are coping with those experiences.

With the increasing emphasis on naturalistic inquiry in the social sciences, there has been a renewed interest in the use of narratives by social workers and other helping professionals. Questions have been raised, and a debate has ensued, about the definition and use of narratives, especially in regard to children (Gardner, 1994). Many authors have expressed fears about the possibility of adults misusing or influencing children's narratives and about the legal ramifications of using children's narratives in child custody and sexual abuse cases (Bender, 1994; Gardner, 1994; Rhue & Lynn, 1991).

The narrative of 14-year-old Anne Frank in *Anne Frank: The Diary of a Young Girl* (Frank, 1952) is a moving reminder, however, of the broader historical role of children's narratives. On July 15, 1944, only three weeks before her Jewish family's hiding place in the Netherlands was discovered and they were sent to a

German concentration camp where she died seven months later, Anne wrote the following passage:

> "For in its innermost depths youth is lonelier than old age." I read this saying in some book and I've always remembered it, and found it to be true. Is it true then that grownups have a more difficult time here than we do? No, I know it isn't. Older people have formed their opinions about everything, and don't waver before they act. It's twice as hard for us young ones to hold our ground, and maintain our opinions, in a time when all ideals are being shattered and destroyed, when people are showing their worst side, and do not know whether to believe in truth and right and God. . . . It's really a wonder that I haven't dropped all my ideals, because they seem so absurd and impossible to carry out. Yet I keep them, because in spite of everything I still believe that people are really good at heart. (Frank, 1952, p. 278)

## DEFINING NARRATIVES AND STORYTELLING

Anne Frank's narrative and those of other children are defined as individual written or verbal accounts "of the relationship among self-relevant events across time, a way of connecting coherently the events of our own lives" (Laird, 1989, p. 429). These narratives often reveal the impact of relationships with adults, social institutions, technological advances, and historical–social events on children's lives. Storytelling is a process of telling the narrative to others, or a way of creating the self (Laird, 1989). In creating and retelling a narrative, children and adults begin to see themselves in a particular light based on the heroic or nonheroic descriptions of their coping and problem-solving behaviors in the narrative. Thus, narratives, and the process of retelling them, can influence future behaviors and perceptions about life by providing a mirror image or reflection of "the way things are and the ways things can be" (Freeman, 1992, p. 54).

## INDIVIDUAL AND GROUP PRACTICE STRATEGIES

Some current examples of children's narratives reflect issues that are similar to those in the diary of Anne Frank, such as narratives of children from military families who were affected by the 1990–91 Persian Gulf Conflict. It is clear from the Holocaust and from the Vietnam War that the effects of those traumatic experiences did not end with the individuals who were directly involved. Intergenerational consequences such as posttraumatic stress disorder have been documented in children and other family members (Eth & Pynoos, 1985; Figley, 1985). I believe that the children of Persian Gulf veterans may be vulnerable to such consequences, and it is possible that many of them have not had either permission or opportunity to tell their stories. Those who have not may need to tell their stories over and over again, because new experiences can trigger unresolved fears; memories of information overload; or the opposite, stress from family secrets related to the conflict.

### Types of Narratives

Positive narratives focus on family celebrations; ethnic or cultural traditions; empowerment experiences involving the development of new skills or completion of a major task; field trips; resolution of a sibling, peer, or parent–child conflict; substance abuse recovery; or the planned termination of participation in peer counseling groups or individual sessions. Positive narratives can be shared in magic circle exercises in the classroom and in school newsletters, local newspaper and television programs, school awards ceremonies, displays at shopping centers, holiday celebrations, and storytelling festivals.

Negative narratives include unresolved peer or family conflicts, illness and hospitalization, parental separation or divorce, migration to a new country, a special education placement, reintegration into the regular classroom, and child abuse. A narrative that involves negative events may have a positive focus, as illustrated by the passage from Anne Frank's diary. Or the reverse can be true.

## Examples of Narratives

The following examples help clarify important issues for different groups of children in school social workers' caseloads. A 12-year-old boy wrote about his first field trip to a town his mother had always dreamed about visiting, pointing out to a community center social worker what he learned:

> This was my first time in [the city] . . . my first trip anyplace. First time riding the train, first time in a hotel. My mama's dream was about going to [this city] so she let me go. I had fun, we did some activities like . . . swimming, the [Botanical] gardens. The zoo was fun to [sic] when they let us go on our own. I learned about reproduction and camafloge [sic], etc. And we got along just a little bit. Two boys had a fight at the Science Center, but I still had fun. The trip was very nice and it gave me time to think and listen. I learned to ignore some people at times. How to make new friends. I would like to do this again.

An eight-year-old girl dictated the following description of her drawing to a school social worker. In it she describes her eyewitness account of a man's suicide in front of a religious mural in her housing project after he killed three people:

> This is a picture about me, V, and my brother, E, getting wet on a hot day, while my little brother is watching us from the window, laughing. This is my house. The houses are red. The houses are big.
>
> Something happened at my house that I don't want to talk about. A man went in my house, he went upstairs, opened the balcony door and jumped to two other houses. He came back to our house, kicked the balcony door and shot a few times on the wall where Mary and Jesus are and then shot himself. He was shooting at Jesus and Mary because the police officers were hiding in back of some cars. By accident he shot a white car and the police officers told us to get out of the house, but I went back upstairs to get my brother because he was asleep. Then, we went to grandma's house because a police officer told us it was going to be too much for my brothers and I because they had to investigate.

## Analysis of Narratives

These examples illustrate how telling or writing narratives can teach children to connect events with their reactions to those events. Narratives can also be used to teach children about the association between their behaviors and related consequences and the connection between their behaviors and those of significant others. Kottman and Stiles (1990) emphasized the importance of this learning because "initially they [children] understand the connection between their purpose, their behavior, and the consequences of their behavior . . . only after the behavior has occurred" (p. 148). Some narratives allow children to get closer to these connections in a less threatening way by adding a pretend or "what if" quality (Krietemeyer & Heiney, 1992). Self-validation, reconciliation, and healing, along with problem solving, are more likely to occur when this type of reflective process has taken place at the child's level.

Children are helped to reflect when key individuals listen actively and "hear" the narrative. Listening should occur at three levels:

1. the facts of the narrative (event component)
2. the meaning the storyteller makes of these facts (evaluative component)
3. the storyteller's worldview or belief system (explanatory component).

Barriers to active listening include the assumptions that not talking about the negative events or relationships will cause the pain to go away or that positive or neutral narratives are less important in a child's life.

In addition, school social workers and other adults may fear remembering their own narratives, memories, and unresolved fears that they "put away" many years before. Professional issues also may be a factor, for example, the legal and ethical debates surrounding issues such as the false memory syndrome (Gardner, 1994). These barriers encourage adults to silence rather than honor children's narratives.

## Group Opportunities to Hear and Respond to Narratives

School social workers can honor children's narratives in several ways. They should identify the many opportunities available for helping children tell and retell their narratives. One opportunity is cofacilitation activities with teachers and other school personnel using positive narratives as an initial step for later eliciting the more painful negative narratives. Nontraditional forms of collaboration with the physical education teacher, the school nurse, or a teacher's aide might offer the most creative opportunities and topics for eliciting children's positive or negative narratives. Another opportunity is peer group, family, and individual counseling sessions provided by the school social worker or a community professional. Group and family counseling can normalize the telling and sharing of narratives among children and between children and family members.

Listening actively and helping children record their narratives is an important part of the group individual counseling process. The social worker could use the typical assessment questions and forms as a follow-up or supplement to children's narratives rather than as a way of structuring the sessions. Tape-recording the narrative, having the child dictate it to the worker for a personal book, or using drama therapy to act out the narrative are creative ways to record the story. Restorying techniques such as mutual storytelling, in which a more adaptive ending is provided by the school social worker to a child's maladaptive narrative, can also be used in counseling. Or a child can be asked to complete the ending of a stimulus completion story provided by the social worker or to give a new ending to his or her own story (Freeman, 1992; Kottman & Stiles, 1990). The use of children's narratives can be combined with therapeutic play and artwork as well with children in peer groups.

## CONCLUSION

Now that children have returned to schools this autumn, school social workers can use these techniques to discover the old and new narratives of some of the children in their schools. Children are likely to develop greater trust in social workers and other adults when their narratives are honored, when they can share the narratives and gain help in resolving or coping with their situations. A focus on narratives about unresolved experiences is important, but helping children talk about positive narratives or the healing process of reconciling negative narratives can make them more hopeful about the future, thereby helping them empower themselves and enrich their environments.

## REFERENCES

Bender, W. N. (1994). Joint custody: The option of choice. *Journal of Divorce and Remarriage, 21*, 115–131.

Eth, S., & Pynoos, R. S. (1985). *Post-traumatic stress disorder in children*. Washington, DC: American Psychiatric Press.

Figley, C. R. (1985). *Trauma and its wake*. New York: Brunner/Mazel.

Frank, O. H. (1952). *Anne Frank: The diary of a young girl*. New York: Modern Library.

Freeman, E. M. (1992). The use of storytelling techniques with young African American males: Implications for substance abuse prevention. *Journal of Intergroup Relations, 19*, 53–72.

Gardner, R. A. (1994). Differentiating between true and false sex abuse accusations in child-custody disputes. *Journal of Divorce and Remarriage, 21*, 1–20.

Kottman, T., & Stiles, K. (1990). The mutual storytelling technique: An Adlerian application in child therapy. *Individual Psychology Journal of Adlerian Theory, Research, and Practice, 46*, 148–156.

Krietemeyer, B. C., & Heiney, S. P. (1992). Storytelling as a therapeutic technique in a group for school-age oncology patients. *CHC, 21*, 14–20.

Laird, J. (1989). Women and stories: Restorying women's self-constructions. In M. McGoldrick, C. Anderson, & F. Walsh (Eds.), *Women in families: A framework for family therapy* (pp. 427–450). New York: W. W. Norton.

Rhue, J., & Lynn, S. (1991). Storytelling, hypnosis, and the treatment of sexually abused children. *International Journal of Clinical and Experimental Hypnosis, 39*, 198–214.

*This chapter was originally published in the October 1995 issue of* Social Work in Education, *Vol. 17, pp. 202–206.*

# 26 School Violence: A Blueprint for Elementary School Interventions

Ron A. Astor

School violence is an increasing concern in U.S. society. In recent years, opinion surveys and the media have focused the attention of the public and politicians on school violence (Bureau of Justice Statistics, 1991a, 1991b; Center to Prevent Handgun Violence, 1993; Gallup Organization & Phi Delta Kappan, 1991; Metropolitan Life Insurance Company & Harris Poll, 1993; Washington State Department of Health, 1993). Multiple private, state, and federal grant funding sources have targeted school violence as a priority for new projects (for example, Carnegie Foundation of New York, U.S. Department of Education, Hitachi Foundation, William T. Grant Foundation). Within academia a consensus is growing that violence intervention programs should be geared toward younger children before they become involved with "serious" acts of violence (American Psychological Association, 1993; Furlong & Smith, 1994; Garbarino, Dubrow, Kostelny, & Pardo, 1992; Goldstein & Huff, 1993; Larson, 1994a, 1994b; Morrison, Furlong, & Morrison, 1994; Stephens, 1994).

However, at present, violence prevention programs in elementary schools are not widespread in most school districts. School social workers could be instrumental in disseminating empirically based information and advocating for the creation of elementary school violence intervention programs. This article proposes that violence prevention programs should begin at a very young age and should include all children, staff, and teachers in school settings. The article reviews research relevant to violence in elementary schools; provides a definition of violence and a rationale for schoolwide social work violence interventions with young children that reflect the research findings; and outlines how school social workers can collect needed empirical data, create violence prevention programs, and influence policy concerning school violence.

## BACKGROUND: EARLY PRECURSORS TO SEVERE VIOLENCE IN ADOLESCENCE

In recent years there has been an explosion of research on elementary school violence. With few exceptions (for example, Wodarski & Hedrick, 1987), this research has not been integrated into the social work literature. The findings from this research may have implications for how school social workers define their approach to school violence.

For many years there has been a general sentiment that aggressive behaviors exhibited in childhood are not strongly associated with aggression in adolescence or with violence in adulthood (see Farrington, 1991; Huesmann, Eron, Lefkowitz, & Walder, 1984; Olweus, 1991; and Patterson, 1982, for critiques of these assumptions). However, in the past 15 to 20 years the empirical literature has accumulated many well-designed, large-scale, longitudinal studies that show a strong association between high aggression exhibited in childhood and high aggression in adolescence and adulthood. This does not mean that every aggressive child will become an aggressive adolescent or adult, but aggressive children are far more likely to demonstrate severe forms of aggression later in life. Primary and secondary interventions aimed at young children have the potential to change this trajectory.

Overall, longitudinal studies have consistently found that high aggression at a young age is stable throughout development (Eron, 1987; Farrington, 1991; Huesmann et al., 1984; Olweus, 1991; Patterson, 1982). In these studies aggression in elementary school is usually measured by the number of aggressive acts, classroom peer ratings, and teacher ratings of aggression when compared with children in their own age group. For example, all children and teachers in a school or classroom may be asked to anonymously nominate one or a few children who get into the most fights. The children with the highest number of peer nominations, highest ratings of aggression by teachers, and highest number of fights—the most reliable measures of later adolescent and adult aggression— are considered "highly aggressive" for their age groups.

Researchers have suggested that high levels of aggression are as stable as IQ measures across development (Farrington, 1991; Olweus, 1984). Without early intervention, aggressive young children who exhibit chronic and aggressive bullying behaviors have a high likelihood of remaining aggressive as adolescents and adults. Nevertheless, high aggression in the early grades is manifested differently than in adolescence. For example, in elementary school an aggressive child may exhibit violence by a high frequency of fights, aggressive bullying, and pushing. Eron (1987), Farrington (1991), and Olweus (1991) found strong associations between these behaviors and more extreme forms of violence later in life.

Eron's (1987) 22-year longitudinal study of 638 children found that (independent of economic status and intelligence) children exhibiting these behaviors at age eight were significantly more likely than their less aggressive classmates to have been involved with the juvenile justice system by age 19. By age 30 the aggressive group was four times more likely to have been convicted of serious crimes (and also had higher rates of drunk driving, spouse abuse, and poor educational achievement). Patterson (1982) analyzed data from Eron's study and found that of the third graders rated in the 95th percentile on aggression, 100 percent were above the 50th percentile for aggression 10 years later. For third graders rated at the 90th percentile for aggression, 88 percent were above the mean 10 years later, and for children at the 85th percentile, 79 percent were above the mean 10 years later. Of these highly aggressive eight-year-olds, 32 percent to 38 percent stayed at the same high percentiles (85th, 90th, or 95th) 10 years later.

Using peer nomination, Olweus (1991), in a longitudinal study of 900 children, found that 60 percent of the children nominated as bullies in early grades had at least one serious legal conviction by age 24 (40 percent had three or more convictions, compared to only 10 percent of the nonaggressive children). Farrington's (1991) longitudinal study of 411 boys found that 59 percent of the children identified as aggressive between ages eight and 10 were also identified by teachers as highly aggressive at ages 12 to 14. Forty-nine percent were considered highly aggressive at age 32 (for example, by self-report, listed number of self-initiated recent fights, use of deadly weapons), and 57 percent had at least one serious conviction. Cairns and Cairns (1991) found similar results in their longitudinal study. If we consider early severe aggressive behaviors that involve the juvenile justice system, the stability rates are even higher. Patterson, Capaldi, and Bank (1991) suggested that for these children, high frequency of early violence is related to severity of violence and criminal outcomes in adolescence and adulthood.

Cairns and Cairns (1991) found that although children's early aggression is highly predictive of later aggression, every aggressive child in their study had at least one year of very low aggression during their school years, perhaps because the child received extra support from someone in the school environment (teacher, coach, social worker, or other peer). This study suggests that it is not only the children's aggression that is stable; it is probable that negative interactions, rejection, and isolation in children's social environments are also extremely stable throughout development. Thus, social support models of intervention must be long term.

This research has several implications for school social workers interested in creating primary and secondary prevention programs. First, intervention programs should target entire grades or school social settings to avoid the stigma of "pull out" programs that select only the most aggressive children. Students, teachers, parents, administrators, and school personnel should all be viewed as key players in reducing the overall level of violence in schools. Second, interventions for the overall group and very aggressive children should begin at a young age, possibly kindergarten or first grade. The interventions should be structured to mirror supports needed for healthy child development, including professional supervision and monitoring of young children, active work to reduce social isolation and rejection in aggressive children, and development of ways to ensure that each child has active and caring adults who will monitor his or her academic and social progress throughout the early school years. Initiating interventions in middle school may not be effective for children who exhibited high levels of aggression in elementary school.

Third, social workers in schools can play a central role in creating an awareness of violence in the lower grades. Educating significant adults about the outcomes of longitudinal studies may encourage more concern about frequent fistfights, pushing, and more minor forms of assault. Some teachers, administrators, and parents may not be aware of the relationship between persistent early bullying and violence in later life. Finally, research on the stability and development of violence calls into question society's reservation of the word "violence" for severe acts more likely to first appear only in adolescence.

## DEFINING "VIOLENCE"

The definition of violence affects a school's response to physical conflict between young children. The term generally is reserved for severe forms of physical harm, so many do not perceive violence to be a serious problem before adolescence. Consequently, research and interventions are targeted primarily at adolescent children. However, the word "violence" can usefully be applied to situations other than severe conflict given the empirical data regarding the development and stability of violence.

Social workers should consider adopting the definition of violence presented by Straus, Gelles, and Steinmetz (1980): Violence is "an act carried out with the intention, or a perceived intention, of causing physical pain or injury to another person. The physical pain can range from a slight pain such as a slap, to murder. The basis for 'intent to hurt' may range from a concern for the child's safety (such as when a child is spanked for running into the street) to hostility so intense that the death of the other person is desired" (p. 20). This definition of violence is consistent with the developmental and bullying research because it includes the milder forms of aggression, including high frequency of fights, aggressive bullying, and pushing, exhibited in elementary school. Straus et al.'s definition encompasses the description of *bully* given by Olweus (1991) as a person who repeatedly and over time exposes others to negative actions. Olweus stated, "It is a negative action when someone intentionally inflicts or attempts to inflict injury or discomfort upon another—basically what is implied in the definition of aggressive behavior" (p. 413).

Data from the bullying literature are relevant to a discussion of violence because much of early violence is manifested through physically aggressive bullying. Although bullying is a broader concept than violence, peer physical aggression involved in bullying appears to be the most stable component through development. The data and reality of bullying and peer-oriented school violence are so similar that most researchers use data from physical bullying, childhood violence, and school violence interchangeably. Unfortunately, most developmental researchers do not report that virtually all the data collected on childhood violence and bullies are collected in school settings. Consequently, in most instances the data on bullies and childhood development of violence are documenting interpersonal peer violence in school settings.

Straus et al.'s (1980) definition of violence focuses on interpersonal violence. However, the term "school violence" may also include acts of vandalism, arson, and theft, which do not necessarily include interpersonal violence (see Furlong & Morrison, 1994, for an example). Even so, many national surveys have shown that interpersonal violence on school grounds is a serious concern for administrators, teachers, parents, students, and communities. Consequently, this article addresses physical violence between individuals or between groups in the school social environment.

Widespread adoption of this definition of violence could reduce the tolerance schools (and society) have for less severe forms of violence between children. In many ways, the current task of defining "violence" in elementary schools is similar to the task social workers had during the 1970s and 1980s in defining and creating awareness about domestic violence. If significant adults do not perceive minor forms of physical contact to be violence, they may not respond to them with an array of consequences that curtail these forms of violence (Olweus, 1987).

## ESTIMATING THE SCOPE OF THE PROBLEM

Using the term "violence" exclusively in severe situations has an impact on the collection of data needed to address elementary school violence on a broad scale. The United States lacks reliable data on elementary school violence because most national surveys on violence have not included elementary schools (Bureau of Justice Statistics, 1991a, 1991b; Center to Prevent Handgun Violence, 1993). The few surveys that included elementary schools did not examine or attempt to estimate the extent of specific behaviors at different grades. For example, the National Center for Educational Statistics (1991, 1992) asked principals and teachers if "physical conflict among students" was "a problem" in their school. In that study 32 percent of elementary school teachers and 23 percent of elementary school principals said that physical conflict among students was a moderate or serious problem. However, the study did not provide a definition of "physical conflict" or ask for an estimation of the frequency of physical conflict, so the extent of violence in elementary schools cannot be determined. Teachers and principals may have wide-ranging definitions of what types of physical conflict are a problem. Future research should ask for a frequency estimation of specific behaviors and then ask if these behaviors are a "problem." This would provide an estimate of elementary school violence and the tolerance level teachers and principals have for specific behaviors. An accurate estimate of early violence could be used to educate the public, the educational system, and policymakers.

Other countries' approach to elementary school violence may serve as a model for the United States. Scandinavian researchers have collected data on the prevalence of bullies and victims of bullies in elementary schools (see Olweus, 1991, for a comprehensive review). On the basis of the European data, Olweus (1987) estimated that the bully–victim problem in U.S. schools (grades 1 through 9) may affect 15 percent of U.S. children. If this approximation is accurate, 4.8 million American children are affected, approximately 2.7 million children of them victims and 2.1 million of them bullies.

However, it is probable that these estimations severely underestimate the scope of the problem in the United States. In one study of Chicago's South Side (Bell & Jenkins, 1993), 21 percent of children ages seven to 15 reported starting a fight once or twice a week. In addition, 78 percent of the children had witnessed a beating, 30 percent a stabbing, and 26 percent a shooting. It is probable that the United States has a larger elementary school violence problem than Scandinavian countries, and the continued use of the Scandinavian data to estimate the scope of school violence in the United States may be misleading to policymakers and the general public. In addition, comparative national data are needed on rural, suburban, and economic variables to avoid stereotyping school violence as an exclusively inner-city issue.

To improve data collection, some changes are needed in reporting laws. Several states (for example, California, Connecticut, Hawaii, and South Carolina) and school districts have mandated the reporting of elementary school violence. Unfortunately, these data often are not available for researchers or practitioners who want to design interventions. In California, schools have been reporting these data since 1984, but funds have not been appropriated to compile, analyze, or publish the data. Reporting laws should specify the violent behaviors likely to occur in elementary schools as reportable. It is extremely important that the laws assure specific schools or school districts that the data they report will not be used to punish the schools; schools may underreport violence because they fear negative consequences from politicians or embarrassing news coverage. Social workers should encourage a research-based reporting system that guarantees that schools cannot be identified or punished for accurate reporting (such a system exists in California) and that provides access to data that would facilitate the creation of more effective programs.

## ISSUES IN VIOLENCE PREVENTION INTERVENTION
### Using the Social Network of the School
Historically, U.S. schools have not developed violence prevention interventions that are part of the social structure or normal functioning of the school. More often, solutions to the problem have centered on social structures external to the school. When interventions take place on school grounds, they usually do not actively include school personnel or become integrated into the daily functioning of the school. This separation of schools and violence-related interventions results from conceptions of what causes violence. Most theoretical orientations perceive violence as a behavioral or cognitive deficit independent of social settings. Therefore, interventions emerging from these orientations focus not on changing the school setting, but rather on cognitive changes in or social consequences for the violent individual.

Politicians and the general public commonly perceive school violence as a disciplinary or law enforcement problem aimed almost exclusively at adolescents. Interventions that reflect this perspective include expulsions, suspensions, prison sentences, probation, lowering of the age of treatment as an adult by the courts, increases in security and metal detectors, legal consequences for the parents, and other "get tough" policies. A basic assumption of this approach is that punishment will at best deter violent offenders and at minimum remove criminals (albeit young criminals) from the school or society. However, some research suggests that the "revolving door" of the juvenile justice system may actually increase children's chances of becoming violent criminals (Patterson et al., 1991). These interventions alone do not address prevention from a developmental or social work perspective. Also, these consequences do not address early violent behaviors such as fights that are more common in elementary schools.

From a psychological perspective, violence is commonly perceived as a social skills deficit problem (Akhtar & Bradley, 1991; Camp, 1977; Hollin, 1993; Kendall, Ronan, & Epps, 1991; Larson, 1994b; Pepler, King, & Byrd, 1991; Spivak & Shure, 1974; Wodarski & Hedrick, 1987). This perspective advocates teaching children a variety of social skills that they presumably have not received through the normal acquisition process. Consequently, interventions originally developed for outpatient mental health clinics have been transplanted into school settings.

Empirical evaluations of social skills programs suggest that they are marginally effective or ineffective in reducing violence (Bandura, 1986; Coie, Underwood, & Lochman, 1991; Rose-Kransor, 1991). A consistent finding is that aggressive children tend to learn the social skills in role plays (they may have already had them) but choose not to implement them (called a "production deficit") in real social situations. Several studies suggest that motivation is a factor (Bandura, 1986; Camp, 1977; Coie, Underwood, & Lochman, 1991). Nevertheless, these and other traditional models of "therapy" (Berman, 1984) for aggressive children persist in some school settings. Frequently, these efforts do not fully account for or use the social ecology and complexity of the school (for example, classroom, peer dynamics, teacher–child relationships). For example, research shows that most peer violence occurs in hallways, during recess and lunch, and before or after school. Consequently, if fights tend to occur primarily in school contexts in which the adult–student ratio is low, it may be possible to reduce fights by increasing the teacher–child ratio during transition periods, recess, and lunch and before and after school on the playground (Olweus, 1987). School social workers developing violence prevention programs need to be sure that the programs are integrated into the social fabric of the school.

Most people acknowledge that schools play a significant role in children's social and cognitive development. There is an impressive body of research showing that for some children schools are "protective settings" that counteract other social influences (Garbarino et al., 1992). However, in contrast to other "setting" forms of violence, such as family violence, school violence has received scant theoretical and empirical attention despite evidence that school violence is a serious problem with social elements that set it apart from other forms of violence. As early as 1978 the *Safe School Report to Congress* stated, "young teenagers in the cities run a greater risk of violence in schools than elsewhere" (U.S. Department of Education, 1978, p. iii). Nevertheless, in the United States there have not been strong empirical efforts to conceptualize the uniqueness of school violence or the school's role in facilitating or stemming violent behavior.

### Promising European Interventions

The projects of Dan Olweus (see Olweus, 1991, for a review) are perhaps the most comprehensive school-based studies of interventions relevant to school violence. Olweus has been researching the phenomenon of bullies and victims of bullies for more than 20 years. His empirical studies examined a variety of important questions such as the following: How much do teachers and parents know about bullying, and what do they do about it? What are the typical profiles of bullies and victims of bullies? What are the differences between boys and girls? What is the scope of bully and victim problems at each grade level? Are there differences between city and rural bullying problems? What happens to bullies as they grow older? The results of these inquiries challenge many common myths about violence in schools. For example, "the size of the class or school appears to be of negligible importance for the relative frequency or level of bully/victim problems in schools" (Olweus, 1991, p. 422), although of course the absolute number of bullies is greater in larger classes and larger schools. Another study (described briefly by Olweus, 1987) suggested that bullying could be reduced by significantly increasing the number of supervising adults (who are willing to intervene) during recess and lunch.

In the early 1980s Olweus conducted a school-based violence intervention program that included 42 elementary and junior high schools in Norway (see Olweus, 1987, 1991, for a full description and discussion of the program components and evaluation). The educational interventions were time limited (eight to 20 months), and they systematically targeted school variables (rather than cognitive or skills variables) through the training of all the people in the school setting—teachers, principals, support staff, parents, and students. The program included multiple-level schoolwide interventions that attempted to change school culture regarding violence. The interventions stemmed from "a fundamental democratic principle: Every individual should have the right to be spared oppression and repeated, intentional humiliation, in school as in society at large" (Olweus, 1991, p. 427). This allowed school personnel to take responsibility for securing the rights of the children in the school. The four goals of the program included (1) to increase awareness of the violence problem and knowledge about it, (2) to achieve active involvement on the part of parents and teachers, (3) to develop clear school rules and procedures against bullying behavior, and (4) to provide support and protection for the victims (Olweus, 1991). The interventions were designed to use the existing school social environments. School psychologists and social workers helped plan and coordinate schoolwide training, and social workers consulted with teachers and parent groups and were involved in the most serious cases, but overall the principals, teachers, parents, students, and school staff implemented the program.

Components of the program were conceptualized at the school level, the classroom level, and the individual level. At the school level interventions included a schoolwide conference day on bully and victim problems; better supervision at recess; more attractive school playgrounds, halls, and classrooms (involving children and staff to improve surroundings); the regular use of teacher–home telephone contact; frequent meetings between staff and parents; the creation and maintenance of teacher groups for the development of a safe school climate; and the creation of "parent circles" that studied and discussed the problem in each school.

At the classroom level interventions included detailed rules against bullying and procedures for praise, clarification, and sanctions; regular whole-classroom meetings for all the children to discuss issues regarding bullies and victims; cooperative learning with academic subjects; frequent parent–child–teacher meetings both at school and at home; efforts to involve all children in common positive activities when the class is successful in dealing with bullies or supporting victims; role playing; and the use of children's literature in academic subjects that allow children to discuss bullies and victims.

At the individual level the interventions included serious talks with and consequences for bullies and victims, inclusion of parents of bullies and victims in an action plan, teacher use of creativity and imagination to help bullies and victims, training and recruitment of neutral students to mediate conflict, a brochure for parents with advice on how to proceed if their child is a persistent victim or bully, ongoing discussion groups with parents of victims and bullies as a support, and reassignment to another school or classroom if the problems do not decrease.

The preliminary results of the project are impressive. The 42 schools involved in the project experienced a 50 percent reduction in bullying problems for two years following the project (further follow-up analyses may show that the effect lasts longer). There was also a decrease in theft, vandalism, and truancy and an increase in student satisfaction with school life (particularly recess and lunch). Teachers also had favorable reactions to the program. Olweus (1987) concluded,

> It is definitely possible to dramatically reduce bully/victim problems in school and other problem behaviors with a suitable intervention program. Thus, whether these problems will be tackled or not no longer depends on whether we have the knowledge necessary to achieve desirable changes. It is much more a matter of our willingness to involve ourselves and to use the existing knowledge to counteract these problems. (p. 11)

Researchers from Australia (Slee, 1993), Ireland (O'Moore & Hillery, 1989), and England (Sharp & Smith, 1991) have also begun studying the bullying phenomenon.

These intervention strategies provide potential models for projects and research in U.S. elementary schools. Furthermore, they are consistent with the empowerment and ecological perspectives of social work. It is unknown whether these interventions would produce the same results in American schools, and it is not clear to what degree components of the program need to be changed when adapting it to the United States. Definitional and awareness issues regarding schools and their role in stemming violence are the major obstacles social workers need to address in implementing such programs in this country.

On the basis of European experiences, the following principles should guide the adaptation and creation of new social work school violence programs in the United States:

- Schools have the ability to reduce violence on school grounds. Often teachers and administrators claim that dealing with violence is outside the domain of the school. Clearly, though, research suggests that it is possible to reduce violence within schools.
- Violence can most effectively be reduced by introducing changes in the settings where children live (school, community, and home) and in the adults who spend the most time with children (teachers and parents).
- Programs attempting to reduce school violence should focus on the entire school and its subsystems. Without schoolwide awareness, interventions aimed primarily at aggressive children will probably not have a long-term effect. Furthermore, reducing the overall frequency of violent events creates a better school atmosphere, reduces administrator and teacher burnout, and reduces the number of severe events on campus.
- School personnel's willingness and knowledge of how to create a nonviolent educational environment reduce the school's sense of helplessness and have long-lasting effects that spill over into other areas (such as truancy and academics).

## Related Research with Implications for Violence Prevention

*Supervision and Monitoring.* U.S. society has not taken responsibility for the supervision of large numbers of children. Parents, schools, and community organizations appear to agree that children should be supervised. Among politicians there seems to be a growing consensus that schools can be central players in offering enrichment programs and monitoring large numbers of young children who otherwise may drift toward crime and violence.

Nevertheless, the current systems of support for overburdened families and children at risk are inadequate (Dryfoos, 1990, 1994; Garbarino et al., 1992). Children who are not monitored or supervised in a consistent way have a greater chance of becoming violent (Dryfoos, 1994; Patterson et al., 1991). It is fair to assert that elementary-age children should be monitored by a caring adult in a safe environment all the time. Unfortunately, many young children are unsupervised during significant segments of the day and evening (also during school hours, particularly on the playground and during lunch when adult–child ratios are low). Several societal factors contribute to this phenomenon, including cutbacks in after-school and park recreation programs, the increase in single working parents, low family income, and lack of knowledge regarding supervision. Many model community programs based on the monitoring and supervision premise claim success in preventing and reducing violence in schools. However, there are few large-scale or well-designed studies to demonstrate their effectiveness (Dryfoos, 1990; Lovell & Pope, 1993).

Social workers can play a pivotal role in creating awareness in teachers, parents, administrators, and the community about the importance of adult monitoring and supervision of children at all times. Social workers could organize parents, the school, and community groups to create school-based monitoring systems before, during, and after school. The creation of sports clubs, arts programs, drama groups, homework tutoring centers, and youth groups on school grounds could be very effective in reducing school violence if all children in the school are included. The creation of parent and community baby-sitting cooperatives on school grounds or in neighborhoods surrounding the schools could be effective. Youth programs supervised by volunteers, parents, and college students could also provide longer monitoring hours. These programs should maintain a relatively high adult–student ratio, and adults should be trained how to monitor (Olweus, 1991). Programs that recruit adults to secure the safety of children during trips to and from school are needed in some settings.

An orientation toward client support has traditionally been the strength of social work interventions. Currently, many monitoring and supervision programs claim dramatic success in reducing a whole array of risk problems (Dryfoos, 1990, 1994), but very little research and formal evaluation with controls are available on these programs. Social workers could begin directing small-scale systematic efforts to document the effectiveness of these community and context-oriented programs in a few schools. These programs may have a greater impact on national and state policies if social workers are able to empirically demonstrate short-term and long-term effects. From a research perspective, outcome data should include grades, test scores, and other academic indicators. Educators frequently mention that it is not possible to learn without feeling safe, but this assertion needs to be supported by data demonstrating overall academic gains when the school system is considered safer by teachers and children. At present, these types of data are not available.

From a secondary prevention approach, aggressive children are more challenging to teach and parent (Patterson, 1982; Patterson et al., 1991). Teachers and parents may have similar difficulties in controlling aggressive children. Parents and teachers in high-violence neighborhoods need monitoring systems and a unique array of monitoring skills to help children avoid violent behavior (Goldstein, 1992). Patterson (1982) was effective in reducing violence in children by training parents. Perhaps a similar model could be implemented with teachers and parents together to facilitate making the school and home environments more philosophically consistent. Although most meetings occur on school grounds, some discussions could be scheduled in the children's homes. In my experience, home meetings have been effective in coordinating a monitoring strategy between the school and parents.

Developmentally, children could be followed by selecting an adult in the school to be a "home teacher" or "advisor" who becomes familiar with the children and follows small groups of children through elementary and middle school. School-based youth groups and sports programs could also follow children through the elementary grades to create a more effective social monitoring system, a sense of community, and a positive feeling of belonging within the peer group. School staff stability and involvement in children's lives would be key components for a successful program. Having a significant and caring group of adults follow children through development may reduce some children's sense of alienation and drift into violence. The development of school-based monitoring systems is crucial for children in high-violence neighborhoods and settings where caretakers are overburdened (Dryfoos, 1994; Garbarino et al., 1992).

*Aggressive Children.* Aggressive children perceive themselves as victims in situations of social conflict. Many young aggressive children state that they are picked on or disliked. Teachers and administrators may view such statements made by aggressive children as disingenuous. However, research suggests that aggressive children have frequent victim experiences on school grounds and that aggressive children become part of a cyclical social process in which they are perpetrators and victims in family and school situations (Patterson, 1982; Patterson et al., 1991). A coercive pattern begins at home between the child and the parents and continues in school with peer groups and teachers. Other research supports the hypothesis that aggressive children are victims as well as perpetrators in school: Aggressive children are more often rejected by their nonviolent classmates (Cairns & Cairns, 1991; Coie, Dodge, Terry, & Wright, 1991), the objects of provocation by peers (Patterson, 1982), and disliked by teachers (Cairns & Cairns, 1991; Coie, Dodge, et al., 1991). Research also suggests that young aggressive children drift toward an aggressive peer group for social support (Cairns & Cairns, 1991); they may choose to affiliate with an aggressive peer group because of social isolation and rejection by other peers.

Aggressive children perceive social situations similarly to nonaggressive children when the intent of the perpetrator is straightforward. However, aggressive children are more likely than nonaggressive children to attribute hostile intent when the intent of the other child is ambiguous (Dodge, 1980, 1985, 1986, 1991; Dodge, Pettit, McClaskey, & Brown, 1986). Astor (1994) found that violent children as young as first grade are more likely to approve of violence for provocations such as name-calling, stealing, lying, and hitting because they perceive these provocations as "injustices." Violent children may believe that the school is an unjust setting and that the rule systems are inconsistently applied or biased against them because of their aggressive reputations. They have particular difficulties understanding why it is not all right to hit in response to name-calling and other provocations they believe are just as bad or worse than hitting (Astor, 1994).

School personnel should consider the following when creating school policies and constructing a school-based system of justice:

- Violent children may truly be victims as well as perpetrators. They may have long histories of being assaulted on school grounds and in other settings.
- Violent children tend to perceive adults as unfair, inconsistent, and ineffective at stopping injustices committed against them. They attribute hostile intent to others in situations in which the intent is not clear.
- Rules and consequences on school grounds should weight physical harm worse than psychological harm. Nevertheless, serious consequences should be designed to address provocations causing psychological harm. This may reduce children's need to hit as a form of justice.
- Integrating aggressive children positively into the school social system may help change their negative social stigma and break the cycle of victim–perpetrator. Ways for children to be integrated include being a principal's assistant; being trained and assisting in yard monitoring; tutoring younger children; and being involved in other positive, high-status events visible to teachers and peers.

Most importantly, a clear multilevel system of justice needs to be agreed on and articulated to all school subsystems. Issues such as due process, consequences, victims' rights and support, innocence until proved guilty, and peer responsibility to help victims and deter perpetrators should be included (Olweus, 1991). Frequently, discipline policies are not known or implemented consistently to all parties involved.

## CONCLUSION

School social workers can become leaders in the campaign to reduce elementary school violence. They will need to promote deeper awareness of the strong relationship between early violence and later adolescent violence and to advocate for the collection of data on elementary school violence at the district, state, and national levels. The European school-based epidemiological and intervention studies should be replicated in the United States. Finally, social workers should be active in the development of interventions that use the entire school social system and empower school staff to respond to student experiences with peer violence. If successful, the reduction of aggression in children could lead to a reduction in adolescent and adult aggression rates.

Some may question the monetary cost of these propositions. Currently, society is spending disproportionate and increasing resources on detention facilities and on the juvenile justice system. Unfortunately, many in this society do not believe in the effectiveness of prevention programs. If a redistribution of funds to early prevention is desired, then social workers must empirically demonstrate the success of such programs. Finally, reducing monetary costs is important but not social work's main purpose. School social workers should promote programs that are likely to succeed and that address the pain endured by many children. Demonstrating the effectiveness of early violence intervention programs may encourage this society to examine its willingness to intervene.

## REFERENCES

Akhtar, N., & Bradley, J. (1991). Social information-processing deficits of aggressive children: Present findings and implications for social skills training. *Clinical Psychology Review, 11,* 621–644.

American Psychological Association. (1993). *Violence and youth: Psychology's response* (Vol. 1). Washington, DC: Author.

Astor, R. A. (1994). Children's moral reasoning about family and peer violence: The role of provocation and retribution. *Child Development, 65,* 1054–1067.

Bandura, A. (1986). *Social foundations of thought and action: A social–cognitive theory.* Englewood Cliffs, NJ: Prentice Hall.

Bell, C. C., & Jenkins, E. J. (1993). Community violence and children on Chicago's Southside. *Psychiatry: Interpersonal and Biological Processes, 56,* 46–54.

Berman, S. (1984). The relationship of aggressive behavior and violence to psychic reorganization in adolescence. In C. R. Keith (Ed.), *The aggressive adolescent: Clinical perspectives* (pp. 3–16). New York: Macmillan.

Bureau of Justice Statistics. (1991a). *School crime: A national crime victimization survey report.* Washington, DC: U.S. Department of Justice.

Bureau of Justice Statistics. (1991b). *Teenage victims: A national crime victimization survey report.* Washington, DC: U.S. Department of Justice.

Cairns, R. B., & Cairns, B. D. (1991). Social cognition and social networks: A developmental perspective. In D. J. Pepler & K. H. Rubin (Eds.), *The development and treatment of childhood aggression* (pp. 249–278). Hillsdale, NJ: Lawrence Erlbaum.

Camp, B. W. (1977). Verbal mediation in young aggressive boys. *Journal of Abnormal Psychology, 86,* 145–153.

Center to Prevent Handgun Violence. (1993). *Kids carrying guns: Loopholes in state and federal firearms laws.* Washington, DC: Author.

Coie, J. D., Dodge, K. A., Terry, R., & Wright, V. (1991). The role of aggression in peer relations: An analysis of aggression episodes in boys' play groups. *Child Development, 62,* 812–862.

Coie, J. D., Underwood, M., & Lochman, J. E. (1991). Programmatic intervention with aggressive children in the school setting. In D. J. Pepler & K. H. Rubin (Eds.), *The development and treatment of childhood aggression* (pp. 389–407). Hillsdale, NJ: Lawrence Erlbaum.

Dodge, K. A. (1980). Social cognition and children's aggressive behavior. *Child Development, 51,* 162–172.

Dodge, K. A. (1985). Attributional bias in aggressive children. In P. C. Kendall (Ed.), *Advances in cognitive–behavioral research and therapy* (Vol. 4). New York: Academic Press.

Dodge, K. A. (1986). A social information-processing model of social competence in children. In F. Perlmutter (Ed.), *Minnesota Symposium on Child Psychology* (Vol. 18, pp. 77–125). Hillsdale, NJ: Lawrence Erlbaum.

Dodge, K. A. (1991). The structure and function of reactive and proactive aggression. In D. J. Pepler & K. H. Rubin (Eds.), *The development and treatment of childhood aggression* (pp. 201–218). Hillsdale, NJ: Lawrence Erlbaum.

Dodge, K. A., Pettit, G. S., McClaskey, C. L., & Brown, M. M. (1986). Social competence in children. *Monographs of the Society for Research in Child Development, 51* (Serial No. 213).

Dryfoos, J. (1990). *Adolescents at risk: Prevalence and prevention*. New York: Oxford University Press.

Dryfoos, J. (1994). *Full-service schools: A revolution in health and social services for children, youth, and families*. San Francisco: Jossey-Bass.

Eron, L. D. (1987). Aggression through the ages. In *School safety: Special issue on bullies* (pp. 12–17). Malibu, CA: Pepperdine University, National School Safety Center.

Farrington, D. P. (1991). Childhood aggression and adult violence: Early precursors and later life outcomes. In D. J. Pepler & K. H. Rubin (Eds.), *The development and treatment of childhood aggression* (pp. 5–31). Hillsdale, NJ: Lawrence Erlbaum.

Furlong, M. J., & Morrison, G. M. (1994). School violence and safety in perspective. *School Psychology Review, 23*, 139–150.

Furlong, M. J., & Smith, D. C. (Eds.). (1994). *Anger, hostility, and aggression: Assessment, prevention, and intervention strategies for youth*. Brandon, VT: Clinical Psychology.

Gallup Organization & Phi Delta Kappan. (1991). *23rd annual Gallup Poll of the public's attitude toward the public schools*. Princeton, NJ: Author.

Garbarino, J., Dubrow, N., Kostelny, K., & Pardo, C. (1992). *Children in danger: Coping with the consequences of community violence*. San Francisco: Jossey-Bass.

Goldstein, A. P. (1992, May 4). *School violence: Its community context and potential solutions*. Congressional testimony presented to the Subcommittee on Elementary, Secondary and Vocational Education, Committee on Education and Labor, Washington, DC.

Goldstein, A. P., & Huff, C. R. (Eds.). (1993). *The gang intervention handbook*. Champaign, IL: Research Press.

Hollin, C. R. (1993). Cognitive–behavioral interventions. In A. P. Goldstein & C. R. Huff (Eds.), *The gang intervention handbook* (pp. 55–85). Champaign, IL: Research Press.

Huesmann, R., Eron, L. D., Lefkowitz, M. M., & Walder, L. O. (1984). Stability of aggression over time and generations. *Developmental Psychology, 20*, 1120–1134.

Kendall, P. C., Ronan, K. R., & Epps, J. (1991). Aggression in children/adolescents: Cognitive–behavioral treatment perspectives. In D. J. Pepler & K. H. Rubin (Eds.), *The development and treatment of childhood aggression* (pp. 341–360). Hillsdale, NJ: Lawrence Erlbaum.

Larson, J. (1994a). Cognitive–behavioral treatment of anger-induced aggression in the school setting. In M. J. Furlong & D. C. Smith (Eds.), *Anger, hostility, and aggression: Assessment, prevention, and intervention strategies for youth* (pp. 393–440). Brandon, VT: Clinical Psychology.

Larson, J. (1994b). Violence prevention in the schools: A review of selected programs and procedures. *School Psychology Review, 23*, 151–164.

Lovell, R., & Pope, C. E. (1993). Recreational interventions. In A. P. Goldstein & C. R. Huff (Eds.), *The gang intervention handbook* (pp. 319–332). Champaign, IL: Research Press.

Metropolitan Life Insurance Company & Harris Poll. (1993). *The Metropolitan Life survey of the American teacher, 1993*. New York: Author.

Morrison, G. M., Furlong, M. J., & Morrison, R. L. (1994). School violence to school safety: Reframing the issue for school psychologists. *School Psychology Review, 23*, 236–256.

National Center for Educational Statistics. (1991). *Public school teacher survey on safe, disciplined, and drug-free schools*. Washington, DC: U.S. Department of Education.

National Center for Educational Statistics. (1992). *Public school principal survey on safe, disciplined, and drug-free schools*. Washington, DC: U.S. Department of Education.

Olweus, D. (1984). Aggressors and their victims: Bullying at school. In N. Frude & H. Gault (Eds.), *Disruptive behavior in schools* (pp. 57–76). New York: John Wiley & Sons.

Olweus, D. (1987). Schoolyard bullying intervention. In *School safety: Special issue on bullies* (pp. 4–11). Malibu, CA: Pepperdine University, National School Safety Center.

Olweus, D. (1991). Bully/victim problems among schoolchildren: Basic facts and effects of a school-based intervention program. In D. J. Pepler & K. H. Rubin (Eds.), *The development and treatment of childhood aggression* (pp. 411–448). Hillsdale, NJ: Lawrence Erlbaum.

O'Moore, A. M., & Hillery, B. (1989). Bullying in Dublin schools. *Irish Journal of Psychology, 10*, 426–441.

Patterson, G. R. (1982). *A social learning approach to family intervention.* Eugene, OR: Castilia.

Patterson, G. R., Capaldi, D., & Bank, L. (1991). An early starter model for predicting delinquency. In D. J. Pepler & K. H. Rubin (Eds.), *The development and treatment of childhood aggression* (pp. 139–168). Hillsdale, NJ: Lawrence Erlbaum.

Pepler, D. J., King, G., & Byrd, W. (1991). A social–cognitively based social skills training program for aggressive children. In D. J. Pepler & K. H. Rubin (Eds.), *The development and treatment of childhood aggression* (pp. 361–379). Hillsdale, NJ: Lawrence Erlbaum.

Rose-Kransor, L. (1991). Commentary: Social–cognitive treatment programs. In D. J. Pepler & K. H. Rubin (Eds.), *The development and treatment of childhood aggression* (pp. 380–386). Hillsdale, NJ: Lawrence Erlbaum.

Sharp, S., & Smith, P. (1991). Bullying in U.K. schools: The DES Sheffield Bullying Project. *Early Childhood Development and Care, 77,* 47–55.

Slee, P. T. (1993). Bullying: A preliminary investigation of its nature and the effects of social cognition. *Early Childhood Development and Care, 87,* 47–57.

Spivak, G., & Shure, M. B. (1974). *Social adjustment in young children.* San Francisco: Jossey-Bass.

Stephens, R. D. (1994). Planning for safer and better schools: School violence prevention and intervention strategies. *School Psychology Review, 23,* 204–215.

Straus, M., Gelles, R., & Steinmetz, S. K. (1980). *Behind closed doors: Violence in the American family.* New York: Anchor Press/Doubleday.

U.S. Department of Education. (1978). *Violent schools–safe schools: The safe school report to Congress.* Washington, DC: U.S. Government Printing Office.

Washington State Department of Health. (1993). *Washington State survey of adolescent health behaviors, 1988–1992.* Olympia: Author.

Wodarski, J. S., & Hedrick, M. (1987). Violent children: A practice paradigm. *Social Work in Education, 10,* 28–42.

## RESOURCES

Center for the Study and Prevention of Violence, University of Colorado at Boulder, Institute of Behavioral Science, Campus Box 422, Boulder, CO 80309.

National School Safety Center, 4165 Thousand Oaks Boulevard, Suite 290, Westlake Village, CA 91362.

---

*This chapter was originally published in the April 1995 issue of* Social Work in Education, *Vol. 17, pp. 101–115.*

# 27 The Many Faces of Violence: Policy and Practice Implications

Edith M. Freeman

It is easier to ignore violence in schools and communities when it feels distant and impersonal. But violence often becomes personal when it assumes a familiar voice and face, when it involves someone we know. Then it is more difficult to ignore or distance oneself from the violence. For children and youths, experiencing and then attempting to cope with violence can be even more devastating than for adults. Although often resilient in many ways, children tend to have fewer life experiences to help them understand such events and fewer resources for coping with them (Paterson, DeBaryshe, & Ramsey, 1989). The short- and long-term effects on their mental health and school adjustment may be readily observable, or they can be masked.

## PROCESS AND GROUP SERVICES

In one instance, a school social worker was facilitating an anger management group when he noticed that one member, Manuel, was more withdrawn than usual. Manuel was a gang member who often presented a "macho" appearance in the group. When Kenneth, the group facilitator, asked why he was so quiet, Manuel mentioned in a detached way that a friend of his had been killed that weekend.

A series of patient, exploratory questions by Kenneth slowly revealed the source of Manuel's detachment and a vivid picture of what had happened that weekend. Manuel had been sitting in the backseat of a car talking with two other boys; the boy who was killed was sitting in the driver's seat. The youth who did the shooting walked up to the back door of the car next to Manuel, leaned in, and pointed a gun through the window at the driver. As he aimed the gun, his arm was directly in front of Manuel's face. When the boy quickly pulled the trigger three times, Manuel felt the vibrations so hard that he thought he had also been shot.

Manuel could not say how he reacted to or felt about the experience. He had nightmares that weekend but said the killing did not bother him because "it [violence] happens all the time." Kenneth believed Manuel was so traumatized by the killing that he was still in shock, causing him to deny how horrible the experience had been. One could predict that after the shock wore off, Manuel and the other witnesses might see the violence as very real, personal, and impossible to ignore. Over time, they could develop symptoms of posttraumatic stress disorder, such as hypervigilence and paranoia. These are natural initial reactions to violence that can become dysfunctional coping patterns if they continue over time (Eth & Pynoos, 1985; Newman, 1987).

Other possible reactions are a more long-term detachment or depression, escalating aggression and school failure, or suicide attempts in children as young as 10 years old (Kazdin, 1991; Norman & Mishara, 1992). As for Manuel's peers in the anger management group and Kenneth, this act of violence had a very familiar voice and face. They experienced the killing through Manuel's "in the moment" recounting with an intensity and realness that could not be ignored. The focus of this and later sessions was on exploring the effects of the incident, how to cope with the effects, and handling other positive and negative aspects of their daily lives.

## COLLECTIVE DENIAL

Unfortunately, the type of killing that Manuel experienced has been labeled "urban violence" by many people and, therefore, considered unlikely to occur in the average school or neighborhood. The labels "random" and "urban" violence reflect society's denial that violence is more predictable, widespread, and resolvable than is generally assumed. This denial has encouraged a narrow focus on inner-city, poor, and minority communities; violence in rural, suburban, middle-income, affluent, and predominantly or all white communities has been ignored.

The narrow focus has prevented schools from developing more widespread and comprehensive approaches to addressing the problem. Efforts are necessary at all levels including the family, school, workplace, and community and the state, national, and international levels. Like many others, school social workers can provide assistance in their specialized areas by educating and helping people address and prevent violence and getting involved in efforts to develop school and community policies related to the problem.

## MULTISYSTEMS PREVENTIVE EDUCATION

First, we all need to learn as a natural part of early ongoing education that a continuum of violence exists, including intense verbal conflict or abuse (name-calling, put-downs, jokes about racial or ethnic and gender stereotypes, and power-dominated arguments), intimidation and bullying (threats, extortion, and other physically aggressive behavior), robbery, assault and battery, sexual assault, and the taking of a life (murder and suicide) (Blanchard & Blanchard, 1984; Finkelhor, Gelles, Hotaling, & Strauss, 1983; Paterson et al., 1989).

The common pattern in these behaviors is the threat of or actual harm done to other people, whether the harm is verbal or physical or committed with a part of the body or another type of weapon. Education should emphasize that all violence is dangerous, that it escalates when it is not resolved effectively, and that it is value- and power-driven (*Attorney General's Task Force Report on Family Violence*, 1984). In individuals, violence escalates when the person commits more dangerous types of violence or when the number of situations, people, or episodes involved increases. Violence escalates in a similar manner in communities, nationally, and internationally when it is condoned or not addressed effectively. The wars in Bosnia and Chechnya are recent examples of escalating and unchecked violence.

Education about violence for children's groups and peer networks should emphasize that people can learn about violence both directly and indirectly from an early age (Blanchard & Blanchard, 1984). Most people understand that children learn about aggression from directly observing acts of violence, whether the violence is toward them or some other person, and whether it is observed in their personal environment or in the media. Education also can help to clarify how violence is taught indirectly and why that form of learning is so powerful. For example, children learn indirectly when adults ignore violence because it seems distant and unrelated to their daily lives, condone violence toward or by someone they view as inferior or unimportant, collaborate by profiting from money derived from acts of violence (for example, money laundering from illegal weapons or drug sales), or commit acts of violence while giving conflicting antiviolence messages.

School social workers can use such knowledge about violence to develop educational programs for other school social workers, school staff, children and youths, and community members in school and community settings. They can serve on school crisis teams and community task forces to provide many of the direct and indirect services for coping with violence and violence reduction (Fairchild, 1986; Freeman & Pennekamp, 1988). These practice activities are a blend of micro and macro interventions, consistent with the ecological perspective.

## POLICY IMPLICATIONS

A second arena for violence reduction and prevention is policy. Service on school and community policy-making committees is the most critical contribution school social workers can make (Figueira-McDonough, 1993). They can help develop "zero tolerance" policies about violence and safety and then participate in hearings designed to enforce the policies or to monitor whether administrators implement them fairly and equitably. Finally, they can help identify school and community risk factors that initiate or reinforce violence and work toward addressing those conditions through the reform or development of related policies.

## REFERENCES

*Attorney General's Task Force Report on Family Violence: Final Report.* (1984, September). Washington, DC: U.S. Government Printing Office.

Blanchard, R. J., & Blanchard, D. C. (Eds.). (1984). *Advances in the study of aggression* (Vol. 1). Orlando, FL: Academic Press.

Eth, S., & Pynoos, R. S. (1985). *Post-traumatic stress disorder in children.* Washington, DC: American Psychiatric Press.

Fairchild, T. N. (1986). *Crisis intervention for school-based helpers.* Springfield, IL: Charles C Thomas.

Figueira-McDonough, J. (1993). Policy practice: The neglected side of social work intervention. *Social Work, 38,* 179–188.

Finkelhor, D., Gelles, R., Hotaling, G., & Strauss, R. (1983). *The dark side of families: Current family violence research.* Beverly Hills, CA: Sage Publications.

Freeman, E. M., & Pennekamp, M. (1988). *Social work practice: Toward a child, family, school, community perspective.* Springfield, IL: Charles C Thomas.

Kazdin, A. (1991). Aggressive behavior and conduct disorder. In T. Kratochwill & R. Morris (Eds.), *The practice of child therapy* (pp. 174–221). New York: Pergamon Press.

Newman, J. (1987). Differential diagnosis in posttraumatic stress disorder. In T. Williams (Ed.), *Posttraumatic stress disorders* (pp. 19–33). Cincinnati: Disabled American Veterans.

Norman, C. L., & Mishara, B. L. (1992). The development of the concept of suicide in children. *Omega, 25,* 198–205.

Paterson, G. R., DeBaryshe, B. B., & Ramsey, E. (1989). A developmental perspective on antisocial behavior. *American Psychologist, 44,* 329–335.

*This chapter was originally published in the April 1995 issue of* Social Work in Education, *Vol. 17, pp. 67–69.*

# 28 Traumatic Event Debriefing: Service Delivery Designs and the Role of Social Work

Janet L. Bell

Traumatic events are powerful and overwhelming incidents that lie outside the range of usual human experience. Such incidents are capable of producing severe stress reactions in any human being, regardless of the person's normal abilities to cope successfully (Figley, 1985, 1986). Stress reactions may last days, weeks, or even longer. If the traumatic stress is not treated quickly and adequately, posttraumatic stress can result in permanent impairment (Mitchell & Bray, 1990; van der Kolk, 1987).

## TYPES OF TRAUMATIC EVENTS AND STRESS SYMPTOMATOLOGY

Three types of catastrophic events have been found to result in traumatic stress: (1) natural catastrophes such as hurricanes, lightning-caused fires, tornadoes, or earthquakes; (2) accidental catastrophes such as malfunctioning airplanes or vehicles resulting in fatalities; and (3) human-induced catastrophes such as war, assault, robbery, sabotage, hostage-taking, arson, or murder. Individuals exposed to any of these catastrophes are at risk for developing traumatic stress reactions. However, for people subjected to human-induced catastrophes, the assault on basic life assumptions or normal expectancies is particularly devastating (Figley, 1985; Ochberg, 1988; van der Kolk, 1987).

Stress reactions fall within four symptom clusters (Gist & Lubin, 1989; Mitchell & Bray, 1990; van der Kolk, 1987): (1) physiological (for example, diarrhea, sleep disturbance, and trembling); (2) behavioral (for example, hypervigilance; withdrawal; or excessive changes in activity, communication, or interaction); (3) cognitive (for example, poor thinking or concentrating, confusion, flashbacks, and upsetting dreams or images); and (4) emotional (for example, profound depression, fear, anxiety, guilt, anger, or withdrawal). Without intervention during the first hours or days after the trauma (the acute stage), even those individuals who initially appear to have coped well may, without warning, experience these symptoms as particular sights, sounds, smells, or tactile stimuli evoke terrifying memories of the traumatic event. Such individuals are at risk of developing posttraumatic stress disorder (PTSD) as the symptoms become debilitating and prevent them from returning to their pretrauma level of functioning.

## USE OF TRAUMATIC EVENT DEBRIEFINGS WITH GROUPS

A debriefing is a powerful crisis intervention method designed for groups of three or more individuals who together have experienced a traumatic event.

Traumatic event debriefings (TEDs) help reduce symptoms and accelerate the recovery process (Bohl, 1990; Kennedy-Ewing, 1989; McMaines, 1986; Mitchell & Bray, 1990). To decrease the possibility of PTSD, prompt intervention is imperative. TEDs are typically conducted 24 to 72 hours after the individuals have been exposed to the traumatic event (Barnett-Queen & Bergman, 1988; Mitchell & Bray, 1990). Gilliland and James (1988) warned that "what occurs during the immediate aftermath of the crisis event determines whether or not the crisis will become a disease reservoir that will be transformed into a chronic and long-term state" (p. 4).

## EVOLUTION OF DEBRIEFING–TYPE TRAUMATIC STRESS INTERVENTIONS

The study of 20th-century wartime experiences and subsequent readjustment to civilian life of military personnel has contributed extensively to the existing base of knowledge about traumatic stress. Significant findings include

- the discovery that providing soldiers with immediate psychological intervention close to the front lines increased the likelihood of their recovering sufficiently to return to duty
- the 1980 identification and delineation of PTSD in the *Diagnostic and Statistical Manual of Mental Disorders, Third Edition* (American Psychiatric Association, 1980), which evolved from post-Vietnam-era treatment of combat veterans' traumatic stress reactions (Figley, 1985, 1986; Wilson, Harel, & Kahana, 1988)
- Veterans Administration use of "rap therapy" as a form of group intervention for combat veterans with PTSD symptoms (Figley, 1986; Goodwin, n.d.; Wilson et al., 1988).

Other traumatized populations also have received increased systematic study since the mid-1970s. These include rape victims (Bard & Ellison, 1974; Vernonen & Best, 1983), victims of the Holocaust (Danieli, 1988; Wilson et al., 1988), airplane crash survivors and victims' next of kin (Foreman, 1990; Parr, 1991), victims of natural disasters (Gist & Lubin, 1989; Wee, 1991), schoolchildren terrorized by armed gunmen (Terr, 1979, 1983), and police involved in line-of-duty shootings (Bohl, 1990; Britt, 1990; Mantell, 1986; McMaines, 1986).

Another significant contribution was made by Mitchell (1983), a firefighter paramedic, who developed critical incident stress management teams and the seven-phase debriefing method for emergency service providers who experience a traumatic event in the performance of their duty. As of September 1994, there are 300 national and 50 international teams providing psychological and educational support for emergency service providers.

Debriefing-type interventions have been used primarily for the following groups: those exposed to wartime trauma, emergency service workers, children involved in school-related traumatic events, and aircraft crash survivors and families of victims. Debriefings for these groups have been beneficial in ameliorating the effects of the trauma and in hastening recovery.

However, this vital psychological and educational intervention also must reach a wider population who are at risk for traumatic stress: those involved in catastrophic work-related events. Such events, which are regularly reported by the media, cover a wide range of work-related trauma: industrial accidents, bank and store employees robbed and sometimes taken hostage, a substance-abusing train engineer responsible for a derailment resulting in death and trauma to commuters, psychiatric personnel assaulted by patients, jury and court personnel subjected to horrific evidence, prison guards injured by inmates, journalists exposed to gruesome sights while covering a story, and personnel shocked by the suicide of a fellow employee. Each event puts its victims at risk for PTSD.

## TRAUMATIC EVENT DEBRIEFING (TED)

After a traumatic event, a debriefing team's coordinators are contacted by the affected organization and, in concert with the team's clinical director, determine the number of debriefers necessary (usually two to four). This writer recommends that the debriefing consist of fewer than 25 attendees and two to six TED team members because a group of more than 30 individuals is likely to be too large for optimal therapeutic value. One way to avoid too large a group is to conduct two separate debriefings. The debriefing itself takes approximately two to three hours.

The seven phases of a debriefing, which are discussed in detail by Mitchell and Bray (1990), are summarized here. Attendees, seated in a circle with the debriefers, are asked specific open-ended questions designed to take them from a cognitive level to an emotional level, then back to a cognitive level by the close of the debriefing. Going around the circle, the TED team gives each individual ample time to reflect on and answer specific questions in detail. If an individual does not wish to speak, his or her decision is respected. However, he or she is encouraged to join in whenever he or she feels ready. Some individuals may initially be reluctant to speak, but experience shows that they typically later join in the process.

The debriefing team members, or the attendees themselves, often inject thoughts during the process, thereby helping to create a less formal atmosphere and stimulating further sharing. The members of the debriefing team might seek clarification through light probing, sometimes reframe statements, and frequently offer validation. In addition, attendees may offer praise for actions taken by fellow attendees at the scene or express reassurance and comfort for the pain being expressed. In this way, the debriefing becomes a major cathartic experience for the attendees, making it necessary for TED team members to be comfortable with a wide variety of strong emotional responses.

## SEVEN PHASES OF THE TRAUMATIC EVENT DEBRIEFING

A designated social work team member is responsible for facilitating the debriefing and begins by briefly explaining the purpose of the debriefing process. Attendees are reassured, for the first of many times, that the wide variety of symptoms they may be experiencing are normal reactions by normal people to an abnormal event (Frankl, 1974; Mitchell & Bray, 1990; Wilson et al., 1988). During the first phase the debriefing team is introduced and the rules are established:

- Confidentiality is maintained (what is said in the room stays in the room).
- Only those individuals involved in this particular traumatic event may attend (no fellow workers or family).

- You do not have to speak but are encouraged to do so.
- Speak only for yourself.
- Although this is not an investigation, it is possible attendees could be subpoenaed if one developed. Attendees should therefore not reveal potentially damaging details regarding the event or actions of personnel.
- No breaks are taken during the debriefing. If an attendee must leave, a team member will leave with him or her to ensure that everything is OK.
- Pagers are turned off.
- All personnel have equal status during the debriefing (no rank).
- Attendees are encouraged to ask questions during the debriefing.
- Team members will be available at the close of the debriefing to talk with attendees individually during the refreshment time.

The second phase of the debriefing is the fact phase. Each person explains what happened during the traumatic event from his or her perspective. The details and varying perspectives presented during this phase recreate the event for everyone. This provides the easiest and least threatening way for the attendees to begin discussing the event.

The third phase is the thought phase. Attendees are asked to describe their initial thoughts at the time of the incident. This phase begins to elicit more-personal aspects of the event for the participants and starts the transition to a more emotional level.

During the fourth phase, the reaction phase, the attendees address what, for them, was the worst part of the incident. Emotional responses that may have started in the thought phase usually become intensified. Typical responses are crying, anger, and expressions of frustration and guilt.

The fifth phase, or symptom phase, provides a transition from a predominantly emotional level of processing back to a more cognitive level. Here, the attendees describe their physical, cognitive, behavioral, and emotional reactions.

In the sixth, or teaching phase, the debriefing team describes in detail the four clusters of stress symptoms commonly experienced by individuals subsequent to a traumatic event. Again, attendees are reminded that these are normal reactions by normal people to abnormal events. They are reassured that with the passage of time their symptoms will very likely taper off. Verbal and written instructions are distributed describing stress reduction techniques. Lists of mental health providers (all of whom have the requisite specialized training and experience in traumatic stress) are provided for attendees who may desire further help. Attendees are now back at a cognitive level.

The seventh, or re-entry phase, brings the debriefing to an end. Time is allowed for one last comment or closing statement by each attendee and team member. Refreshments are made available, and attendees are encouraged to stay and chat with the team and one another.

The socialization at the end of the re-entry phase provides the attendees a transition between the debriefing process and the resumption of their individual lives. This writer has observed that despite the lengthy and emotionally intense debriefing, almost all participants remain to chat informally. One explanation for this may be that the attendees are already beginning to feel better and simply want to extend their good feelings. Before the debriefing team members return to their own homes or work, it is vital that they themselves be debriefed. In this process, the team discusses what went well, what could and should be done differently, and how individually they are coping with the emotions stirred by the debriefing.

## THREE TEAM DESIGNS FOR SERVICE DELIVERY

The ecological system's person-in-situation perspective ensures that the delivery of services will be rooted in the realities and needs of the target population (Compton & Galaway, 1989). This writer has developed three different teams for the delivery of debriefings based on experience with individuals exposed to a traumatic event, as clinical director of two teams, and as a consultant for team training. Each team is consonant with the environment in which it operates and the population it serves. Ecological issues considered in team development include characteristics of the workplace (for example, the organization's size and mission and the availability and suitability of prospective team members), the auspices under which the team would be asked to conduct the debriefing (for example, a store owner, a personnel director, the chief of an emergency service provider organization, a factory vice president, a human services organization, or a disaster relief organization), and difficulties in developing the debriefing team and various ways these can be addressed (for example, volunteers, employee assistance contract, private contractor, or exchange of volunteers from one organization to a similar one).

There are three service delivery designs that use three different types of TED team: (1) the in-house team, (2) the contract team, and (3) the humanitarian–civic team. With these three designs serving as a template, an organization can select the team that is most appropriate for its needs. For each team the minimum critical number of social workers is three, although five or more are preferable. Fewer than three social workers can easily become overtaxed.

### In-House Traumatic Event Debriefing

There are two primary kinds of organizations in which an in-house TED team comprising existing staff members can best be used. One is a host organization that employs social workers to deliver clinical services to their clients (for example, a hospital or criminal justice organization). The other is an organization that employs social workers for on-site employee assistance programs. Such organizations are often large industrial facilities such as telephone companies, but they also can be service providers such as civil service agencies. In both types of settings, the team is employed to serve an identified client population or other employees at a host setting that is not a social services organization.

In-house TED teams should include "peers" (non–social work employees), who contribute to the debriefing process in three principal ways. First, through participation peers often feel that they are contributing to the greater good. The entire work force feels supported by knowing they are represented by at least one of "their own." Second, individuals often believe that only a peer can understand what it was like to experience the traumatic event (for example, to be assaulted by a psychiatric patient, to be injured on the line, to be knifed by a prisoner). Finally, the safety and unconditional support peers provide are invaluable during the debriefing process, and often later, by providing a basis for an informal support network within the work environment. The ratio of social workers to peers is generally in the range of 1:3 to 1:5. Although the peers assist with the debriefing process, it is always a clinical social worker who is the team leader during a debriefing.

*In-House Team Example.* Northville Regional Psychiatric Hospital, the largest psychiatric hospital in Michigan, requested training for an in-house debriefing team. The team consisted of 30 volunteer mental health professionals (nurses, social workers, and psychologists) and peer members (aides, security personnel, secretaries, union stewards, and management personnel) and represented all three shifts. The most common basis for a debriefing referral was assaults on personnel by patients. Personnel who attended debriefings reported them to be beneficial in reducing their level of stress and also expressed appreciation that the administration recognized their need for assistance after a traumatic event. Research on cost-effectiveness and participant satisfaction is presently being conducted. The team has regular meetings and continuing education presentations. In addition, this in-house team formed a partnership with the state disaster response team to assist in times of major catastrophes (for example, airplane crashes or natural disasters). An unexpected ripple effect of the in-house team has been the development of more cordial and trusting relationships between team members representing unions and management.

## Contract Traumatic Event Debriefing

There may be times, however, when a large organization may need to contract with an outside team for a TED. If there is a large-scale traumatic event, such as a plant explosion or a fire injuring many employees, it may be too massive and overpowering a situation for the in-house team or "too close to home"—involving relatives, close friends, or associates of team employees. In these situations contracting with an outside team to do the debriefing becomes necessary.

The contract team can best be used with two types of organizations: (1) businesses and industries for which clinical social workers are not on-site or number fewer than three (for example, banks or convenience stores) and (2) social work institutions (for example, social work departments and family services agencies). In these situations, this author recommends that the affected organization contract with social workers in clinical practices or employee assistance programs who have received comprehensive training and are skilled in conducting debriefings. This writer concurs with Mitchell (1983) in recommending not using team members on a debriefing for individuals who work side-by-side. The situation of some employees debriefing other employees and then returning immediately to their usual work relationships can create unnecessary and complicated role confusion. Instead, organizations are advised to enter into an agreement with a social services agency in another county or region whereby TEDs could be exchanged as the need developed, perhaps excluding the need for financial remuneration or, if such an arrangement is not feasible, to contract for debriefings.

*Contract Team Example.* This writer has trained both employee assistance program and family services agency personnel in disaster psychology and traumatic event debriefings. These organizations report that the most frequent requests for debriefings have been for traumatic events such as bank robberies, industrial accidents, and the suicide of a fellow employee and for personnel such as a hospital's rescue helicopter crew and emergency department employees.

## Humanitarian–Civic Traumatic Event Debriefing

The humanitarian–civic design uses a voluntary philanthropic debriefing team, typically drawing members from a wide geographic area. Such teams usually work in concert with emergency service workers or disaster response teams on a county, state, national, or international level.

The humanitarian–civic design is consistent with the Mitchell critical incident stress method teams that serve emergency service providers (Mitchell & Bray, 1990). Similarly, other teams may be organized that offer debriefings, free of charge, for victims of large-scale disasters. Examples are state and county American Red Cross disaster mental health teams. Humanitarian–civic teams may or may not include peers.

*Humanitarian–Civic Team Example.* During the past five years, the Capitol Area–Critical Incident Stress Management Team, of which this writer is the clinical director, has conducted 51 debriefings for emergency service providers in a tricounty area. The majority of the debriefings have been for firefighters, emergency medical service personnel, and ambulance service groups. The number of participants has ranged from three to 54. Most of the traumatic events have involved the death of or mutilating injuries to children and young adults in vehicle accidents. There also have been debriefings for a mass murder, four suicides, two line-of-duty deaths, and the death of a seven-member family in a house fire.

## SOCIAL WORKERS' UNIQUE QUALIFICATIONS

Among mental health professionals, social workers have unique qualifications of perspective, skills, and training (derived from their educational program leading to the master's degree in social work) that make them the profession of choice to develop and lead debriefing teams.

### Providing Mental Health Services within the Community

TEDs do not take place in a therapist's office. Instead, they are conducted at a facility close to where the victims live or work. This concept of providing services in the client's own environment is familiar to social workers experienced in outreach and home visits. In addition, both historically and today, social workers are the major providers of community mental health services.

### Systems and Person-in-Environment Perspective

Social work expertise is focused at the juncture of the person and his or her environment. Social workers traditionally view clients as a part of various systems and use that perspective for assessment and treatment. This social–environmental perspective is essential for understanding the impact of the particular environment in which the trauma was experienced; identifying the variety of other environments in which the victim functions and the potential impact of those environments on the victim's recovery; gaining a clear understanding of the implications that the shared traumatic experience might have for the victims (for example, with respect to anger and confrontation, building alliances, and social support); and determining the impact of the trauma and its potential for psychological risk on secondary victims—family, coworkers, and emergency service providers.

## Crisis Intervention and Group Work Practice Methods

Crisis intervention skills and group work practice models are fundamental to the debriefing process. Crisis theory and its attendant practice methodology are core psychological interventions used by clinical social workers in numerous settings. In addition, the social worker recognizes the role and importance of the group as a powerful system to facilitate the healing process (for example, in correcting cognitive errors, modeling behaviors, and giving support).

## Role of the Educator

Since the days of Jane Addams, social workers have striven to empower their clients by providing the tools for informed decision making through education and information sharing. The educational component of the debriefing is key to helping victims understand the wide variety of stress symptoms, become familiar with various stress reduction techniques, and become capable of replacing maladaptive coping strategies with constructive and effective ones.

## Community Organization

Community organization has been a basic element in the master of social work (MSW) degree. The theories, strategies, and principles learned in community organization are critical to the development of debriefing teams. Particularly important are an understanding of the social units of formal organizations and primary groups and how to foster their participation, facilitation of community relations and interorganizational linkages, awareness of local grassroots development and training programs and the use of indigenous leadership, familiarity with the role of public education as advanced through community information programs and self-help and voluntary cooperative enterprises, and training in policy and program development with evaluation of program outcomes.

Each of the areas of social work expertise detailed above is an essential prerequisite for both the development of debriefing teams and the conduct of TEDs. However, because traumatic event debriefing is a new method of intervention, social workers have not received this specialized training through their MSW programs. This additional training is imperative before social workers can develop teams or conduct debriefings.

Humanitarian–civic team training, designed originally for emergency service providers by Mitchell (1983), is offered through the International Critical Incident Stress Foundation in Ellicott City, Maryland. Training in acute traumatic stress debriefing and the three team designs was also offered by the Michigan chapter of the National Association of Social Workers (NASW) at their annual program meeting in 1991 and through their Special Programs in Continuing Education (SPICE) workshop in 1992. Similar training needs to be made available to all NASW chapters so that interested clinical social workers can use this effective intervention.

## CONCLUSION

Social workers constitute the profession of choice to bring traumatic stress intervention to those in the workplace. Social workers, with their unique perspective, training, and practice methodologies, can identify where in the community teams are most needed and which debriefing design is most appropriate. Then, by developing and leading debriefings, social workers can help those exposed to traumatic events ameliorate their stress symptoms and hasten their recovery process. Although the traumatic event will never be erased from the victim's memory, the debriefing can help change his or her perception from that of victim to survivor, making possible the resumption of life-enriching activities and relationships.

## REFERENCES

American Psychiatric Association. (1980). *Diagnostic and statistical manual of mental disorders* (3rd ed.). Washington, DC: Author.

Bard, M., & Ellison, K. (1974). Crisis intervention and investigation of forcible rape. *Police Chief, 41,* 68–73.

Barnett-Queen, T., & Bergman, L. H. (1988, August). Post-trauma response programs. *Fire Engineering,* pp. 89–91.

Bohl, N. (1990). The effectiveness of brief psychological interventions in police officers after critical incidents. In J. T. Reese, J. M. Horn, & C. Dunning (Eds.), *Critical incidents in policing* (pp. 51–61). Washington, DC: U.S. Government Printing Office.

Britt, J. M. (1990). U.S. Secret Service critical incident peer support team. In J. T. Reese, J. M. Horn, & C. Dunning (Eds.), *Critical incidents in policing* (pp. 89–97). Washington, DC: U.S. Government Printing Office.

Compton, B. A., & Galaway, B. (1989). *Social work processes* (4th ed.). Belmont, CA: Wadsworth.

Danieli, Y. (1988). Treating survivors and children of survivors of the Nazi Holocaust. In F. M. Ochberg (Ed.), *Post-traumatic therapy and victims of violence* (pp. 278–294). New York: Brunner/Mazel.

Figley, C. R. (1985). *Trauma and its wake: Vol. 1. The study and treatment of post-traumatic stress disorder.* New York: Brunner/Mazel.

Figley, C. R. (1986). *Trauma and its wake: Vol. 2. Theory, research, and intervention.* New York: Brunner/Mazel.

Foreman, W. C. (1990). Police stress response to a civilian aircraft disaster. In J. T. Reese, J. M. Horn, & C. Dunning (Eds.), *Critical incidents in policing* (pp. 131–147). Washington, DC: U.S. Government Printing Office.

Frankl, V. E. (1974). *Man's search for meaning* (rev. ed.). New York: Pocket Books.

Gilliland, B. E., & James, R. K. (1988). *Crisis intervention strategies.* Monterey, CA: Brooks/Cole.

Gist, R., & Lubin, B. (1989). *Psychosocial aspects of disaster.* New York: John Wiley & Sons.

Goodwin, J. (n.d.). *Readjustment problems among Vietnam veterans: The etiology of combat-related post-traumatic stress disorders.* Cincinnati: Disabled American Veterans.

Kennedy-Ewing, L. (1989, May 5). *Research findings on critical incident stress debriefings.* Paper presented at the Surviving Emergency Stress Conference, Baltimore.

Mantell, M. R. (1986). San Ysidro: When the badge turns blue. In J. T. Reese & H. A. Goldstein (Eds.), *Psychological services for law enforcement.* Washington, DC: U.S. Government Printing Office.

McMaines, M. J. (1986). Post shooting trauma: Demographics of professional support. In J. T. Reese & H. A. Goldstein (Eds.), *Psychological services for law enforcement.* Washington, DC: U.S. Government Printing Office.

Mitchell, J. T. (1983). When disaster strikes: The critical incident stress debriefing process. *Journal of Emergency Medical Services, 1*(8), 36–39.

Mitchell, J. T., & Bray, G. (1990). *Emergency services stress: Guidelines for preserving the health and careers of emergency services personnel.* Englewood Cliffs, NJ: Prentice Hall.

Ochberg, F. M. (1988). *Post-traumatic therapy and victims of violence.* New York: Brunner/Mazel.

Parr, B. (1991, April 13). *Lockerbie Scotland air crash.* Paper presented at the First World Congress on Stress, Trauma and Coping in the Emergency Services Professions, Baltimore.

Terr, L. (1979). Children of Chowchilla: Study of psychic trauma. *Psychoanalytic Study of the Child, 34,* 547–623.

Terr, L. (1983). Chowchilla revisited: The effects of psychic trauma four years after a school bus kidnapping. *American Journal of Psychiatry, 140,* 1543–1550.

van der Kolk, B. (1987). *Psychological trauma.* Washington, DC: American Psychiatric Press.

Vernonen, L., & Best, C. (1983). Assessment and treatment of rape-induced fear and anxiety. *Clinical Psychologist, 36*(43), 99–101.

Wee, D. (1991, April 12). *San Francisco earthquake and other disasters.* Paper presented at the First World Congress on Stress, Trauma and Coping in the Emergency Services Professions, Baltimore.

Wilson, J. P., Harel, Z., & Kahana, B. (Eds.). (1988). *Human adaptation to extreme stress: From the Holocaust to Vietnam.* New York: Plenum Press.

*This chapter was originally published in the January 1995 issue of* Social Work, *Vol. 40, pp. 36–43.*

Part IV

# Skills and Interventions in Community Practice

# Part IV: Skills and Interventions in Community Practice

The current emphasis on school-linked, full-service schools is but one movement within a larger trend toward renewed interest in community practice by the social work profession as a whole. Perhaps it has become more clear that a focus on individual and family self-sufficiency limits the resources available for change and the possibilities for change as well. The focus on mutual responsibility and community capacity building, in contrast, provides a broader and richer pool of leadership and political action resources that are necessary for improving educational and other services to children and families.

In this section, chapters focus on some of the various subtrends within the larger "back to community" movement. Some examples are the use of kinship networks and other community resources for family support and out-of-home placements in public child welfare, and multicultural organizing and coalition building, along with comprehensive and integrated school-based services for homeless, truant, substance-abusing, and traumatized students. The unique skills and interventions necessary for these mezzo-focused systems changes are described, and school social work roles are analyzed in relation to the roles of other professionals who deliver, coordinate, or facilitate this multisystem work on behalf of students and families.

Also, the complicated policy changes needed to support these multisystem strategies are described at the organizational and community level. Thus, these chapters describe how school social workers should shift from an education-centered perspective that views services, such as transportation, health, mental health, economic, and other resources, as related or secondary services in schools. A more community-centered perspective views such services as primary components of a school–community continuum of resources designed to achieve maximum accessibility for the residents. These resources are necessary for maintaining students in schools and for helping communities build their capacities for well-being and growth.

# 29 Everything I Know about Consultation: Implications for Community Practice

Edith M. Freeman

A recent professional experience reminded me of the importance of capacity-building and empowerment in school–community practice. The experience reinforced everything I thought I knew about consultation and planned change while also challenging my beliefs and values about how one can facilitate the process best. Concepts such as capacity-building, empowerment, self-sufficiency, and parent–community involvement have become somewhat trite in the past few years. Their overuse has obscured their true meaning, making it difficult to move from the underlying philosophy to action in daily practice (Conger & Kanungo, 1988; Swift, 1984). The lessons or practice wisdom surrounding the concepts have become elusive as well. Therefore, I was grateful for a consultation opportunity that helped me remember these important lessons about community practice.

## BACKGROUND

A child psychiatrist called a colleague and asked for the name of someone who could provide consultation to a community planning group in San Pedro, California. The group had received a one-year Healthy Start planning grant from the state and was in the process of applying for an implementation grant from the same funder. Their activities had been focused on developing a community-based planning coalition to design an integrated services program in an elementary school. Their goal was to maintain the high level of school, social services, and community involvement necessary during the planning stage (Behrman, 1992; Malaville, Blan, & Assayes, 1993) through the next stage of implementing and staffing the program.

The planning group represented a multicultural community consisting of white people, African Americans, recent Portugese and Asian immigrants, and a majority of immigrant and first-generation Hispanics–Latinos. The group membership included parents and other community residents, the school principal, a bilingual school social worker, a teacher aide, a Department of Children's Services worker, a public health nurse, and a child psychiatrist who was in private practice, as well as others.

In my initial telephone discussion with the child psychiatrist, he clarified how I might assist the group. They were interested in my knowledge and experience in school practice and community planning. He urged me to come two hours early for the group's next meeting at the school so that I could observe the Halloween celebration. He thought this would help me understand the relationship between the school, which already had a few on-site health and social services, and the surrounding multicultural community.

Later, I was glad he had made the suggestion. The celebration consisted of a class-by-class parade of students and teachers from all grades in costumes. A larger multicultural crowd than I expected cheered for each group of paraders. The parade ended with the awarding of prizes for the best costume at each grade level. All this activity suggested that the school was attempting to be inclusive in terms of age and development, ethnicity, and parent–community involvement. The prizes were provided by community businesses, and some of the owners had joined the onlookers. Observing this event reminded me that it is important to allow a school or community group to direct the consultant's attention to what makes them unique and what is important to them (Kahn & Bender, 1985).

## MEMBERS' COLLECTIVE STORYTELLING

Later during the meeting, members of the planning group shared some of the key events from the past year and their different conclusions about what had been accomplished. Such storytelling always has a purpose. If the consultant listens actively, he or she can gain insight into the school's or community's common history, strengths, and goals. Their stories showed that they had pooled their existing resources effectively (Katz, 1984), including their expertise in community mobilization and involvement, bilingual education and services, grant writing, information and referral, and collaboration among line staff from the organizations involved in the planning coalition.

## AGENDA SETTING

Given their successful history in planning during the past year, I tried to guide the discussion toward what they hoped to achieve next to help them assess their readiness to change as a group and the level of group consensus about their new goals. They wanted to obtain administrative buy-ins from the heads of agencies they hoped to involve in designing and implementing the integrated services program. They knew they needed more than a memorandum of agreement from each administrator in support of the concept to make the project successful (Pentz, 1986).

At that point, one of the community residents asked why I was at the meeting and what I could do for them. His questions stopped the interaction. In retrospect, I realize that questions about the consultant's authority and expertise are a gift because they provide an opportunity to speak directly to the skeptics about whether the consultant is needed and can be helpful. My response was that I was not certain yet whether I could be helpful to them. I acknowledged the strengths and key resources identified from their previous discussion. With these resources, it was clear that they knew what they wanted to do. Perhaps I could act as a catalyst for their ideas. I reframed their ambivalence about whether I could be helpful as a positive sign of the group's self-sufficiency (Solomon, 1987).

In that moment, my status shifted from that of an expert consultant to a consultant who could help them use their own expertise (Mattessich & Monsay, 1993).

## COMMUNITY PLANNING

As the discussion shifted to how they could accomplish their goals, the group decided to invite the agency directors to a luncheon meeting to share information about the group's progress and what it needed from the administrators. I had presented some alternative ways to engage the directors. They noted that the directors often sent designees to such functions, so one of my suggestions was that each of them be responsible for directly contacting specific directors. They also agreed to tell directors that if they sent a designee, it should be someone who could make decisions about resources. Providing advice in the form of alternatives and consequences instead of "shoulds" and "oughts" allowed the group to stay in control and to continue to empower themselves.

## OUTCOME EVALUATION

The planning group evaluated the luncheon meeting as successful. All of the directors attended the meeting and responded positively to the well-planned agenda by agreeing to provide certain resources and to participate in additional planning and implementation of the integrated services program. The group had assigned me a role in presenting part of the agenda consistent with what they assessed as one of my strengths; this assignment was evidence that the consultation was working because they chose how to use my expertise.

Finally, at the end of the luncheon meeting (we had reached the number of sessions we had contracted for), I indicated I could be available for future sessions if a need existed. I was clearly ambivalent about ending our sessions, yet I felt the group would be successful in being awarded the implementation grant. My reaction reminded me that a consultant is by nature a temporary role designed to facilitate problem solving, empowerment, and self-discovery but is not meant to last indefinitely (Zischka & Fox, 1985).

## CONCLUSION

This emphasis on self-discovery and empowerment in consultation is generalizable to other forms of school–community practice, including direct services to children and families as well as school staff. Linking the underlying philosophy with practice activities should be a continuing challenge to us all. This is clearly not an easy task, but we need to be reminded of the charge periodically.

## REFERENCES

Behrman, R. E. (1992). *The future of children: School-linked services center for the future of children.* Los Altos, CA: Lucille Packard Foundation.

Conger, J., & Kanungo, R. (1988). The empowerment process: Integrating theory and practice. *Academy of Management Review, 13,* 478–482.

Kahn, A., & Bender, E. I. (1985). Self-help groups as a crucible for people empowerment in the context of social development. *Social Development Issues, 9,* 4–13.

Katz, R. F. (1984). Empowerment and synergy: Expanding the community's healing resources. *Prevention in Human Services, 3,* 201–226.

Malaville, A. I., Blan, M. J., & Assayes, G. (1993). *Together we can: A guide for crafting a profamily system of education and human services.* Washington, DC: U.S. Government Printing Office.

Mattessich, P. W., & Monsay, B. R. (1993). *Collaboration: What makes it work?* St. Paul, MN: Amherst Wilder Foundation.

Pentz, M. A. (1986). Community organization and school liaisons: How to get programs started. *Journal of School Health, 56,* 382–388.

Solomon, B. (1987). Empowerment: Social work in oppressed communities. *Journal of Social Work Practice, 2,* 79–91.

Swift, C. (1984). Empowerment: An antidote for folly. In J. Rappaport & C. Swift (Eds.), *Studies in empowerment: Steps toward understanding and action* (pp. 5–21). New York: Haworth Press.

Zischka, P. C., & Fox, R. (1985). Consultation as a function of school social work. *Social Work in Education, 7,* 69–79.

*This chapter was originally published in the January 1995 issue of* Social Work in Education, *Vol. 17, pp. 3–5.*

# 30 School Social Workers Are a Critical Part of the Link

Cynthia G. Franklin and Paula Allen-Meares

The progressive legacy of John Dewey is alive and well in today's educational reform movements. These initiatives unite school personnel and other professionals to create schools that offer a full array of human services (Allen-Meares, Washington, & Welsh, 1996).

School-linked services programs may require a redefinition of the roles of the pupil services team, including school social workers. However, when change occurs there is a tendency to resist such efforts. It is important to keep in mind the different ways in which linking education, health, and human services can be viewed.

## INTEGRATED SERVICES MOVEMENT

### Human Services Reform

Linking services can be associated with a broader reform movement to restructure human services systems. We refer to the linking of human services as a "movement" because it involves reform initiatives in, for example, mental health, children's services, education, and health care (Bruner, 1991; Cibulka & Kritek, 1996; Franklin & Streeter, 1995; Melaville & Blank, 1993; Morrill, 1992). Such initiatives are currently being funded in several states (see Franklin & Streeter, 1995; Gomby & Larson, 1992; Hare, 1995; Melaville & Blank, 1991, 1993).

Central to the movement is the belief that the systems of care, including school systems, can be improved through engineering new systems in which practitioners from various disciplines become partners to meet human needs. Currently, human services systems are isolated from each other, making it difficult for them to collaborate effectively and leaving them ill equipped to educate, socialize, and intervene in the lives of those whom they serve. Children, in particular, have been a focus of concern. The movement has emerged partially as a response to childhood poverty (Hare, 1995). Services integration has been depicted as a child welfare movement offering family-centered reforms (Hooper-Briar & Lawson, 1994; Kirst, 1991; Melaville & Blank, 1993). Problems confronting the systems serving children and families include fragmentation, over-professionalization, and bureaucratic complexity (Hare, 1995; Larson, Gomby, Shiono, Lewit, & Behrman, 1992; Morrill, 1992).

The terms "school-linked services," "comprehensive services," "full-service schools," "services integration," "wraparound services," "one-stop shopping," "colocated services," and "interprofessional collaboration" have been associated with the integrationist movement. These terms originate in different sectors and converge in philosophy concerning the need for collaboration and services integration (Dryfoos, 1994; Kahn & Kammerman, 1992; Melaville & Blank, 1993). For example, the terms "services integration" and "wraparound services" are found frequently in the social services and mental health literature, and the terms "interprofessional collaboration," "full-service schools," and "comprehensive schools" are encountered in the education literature. "School-linked services" has become a well-known generic term that encompasses integration efforts that involve educational systems (Pennekamp, 1992). Larson et al. (1992) defined *school-linked services* as a

> part of a larger movement for more integration of education, health and social services for children. . . . In the school-linked approach to integrating services for children, (a) services are provided to children and their families through a collaboration among schools, health care providers, and social services agencies; (b) the schools are among the central participants in the planning and governing of the collaborative effort; and (c) the services are provided at, or are coordinated by personnel located at, the school or a site near the school. (p. 7)

Integration takes on several meanings in the literature. For some, "integration" refers to the total restructuring of human services, including educational systems, to create an improved services delivery system. To others, however, the term means only initiatives to formulate partnerships and interprofessional collaborations to provide more effective and efficient human services (Franklin & Streeter, 1995). Increased access to services, reduced costs, and greater efficiency and effectiveness in services delivery are major reasons cited for integration. Whether these goals are accomplished, however, remains an empirical question; sufficient research has not been conducted that would conclusively support the effectiveness of school-linked services programs (Gomby & Larson, 1992).

## Models and School Social Worker Roles

Proponents of the services integration movement refer to the school as a central hub for human services delivery because it allows the maximum access to children. There are, however, a variety of models and different methods for carrying out integrated services delivery (Chaskin & Richman, 1992). Some proponents believe that human services can collaborate more effectively if services are housed in the same location, such as a large shopping mall (Franklin & Streeter, 1995; Melaville & Blank, 1991). In fact, because of concerns such as confidentiality, the school is not always viewed as the best location for the services. Others feel strongly that the school is an ideal location. Dryfoos (1994), for example, wrote about the full-services school that offers every conceivable human service, including individualized instruction, social skills training, health screening and services, mental health services, family welfare services, parent education and literacy, child care, laundry facilities, legal aid, and crisis intervention. Regardless of the model implemented, these initiatives are usually beyond the current efforts provided by the pupil services team and greatly affect the roles of human services personnel who are already employed in the school.

Effects of school-linked services on school social workers are not completely known. School social workers should approach the school-linked services movement as an opportunity—a time to demonstrate knowledge of service delivery systems that when combined can yield positive outcomes for at-risk children. However, some practitioners may fear being replaced or may be concerned about the political difficulties involved in a collaboration of many disciplines and professions. Other barriers are organizational and philosophical in nature. To collaborate, organizations and individuals must be willing to make changes to accommodate the others involved. Resolving these difficulties takes extra effort in mediation and conflict negotiation (Franklin & Streeter, 1995). School social workers can use their practice expertise to help professionals resolve political, organizational, and philosophical differences. In this way, school social workers can become leaders in developing successful school-linked services programs.

In fact, there are numerous roles for school social workers in school-linked services. Case management will be needed to track students involved in the myriad services. Community organization skills will be needed to help form collaborative relationships among the service providers. Social services coordination will be needed if all of the services are on the school campus. More expertise, education, and support will be needed in areas of cultural diversity. To some extent, all of these are traditional administrative and community roles and tasks carried out by school social workers (Allen-Meares, 1994).

However, Markward (1993) found that traditional clinical services were the focal point of school social workers in one school district. In schools fostering school-linked programs, the roles involving community practice will likely increase as the service providers move to the school campus and require the full-time attention of the pupil services team, which will be bombarded with a diversity of programs and professionals. This situation may require that clinical and counseling services be offered in greater frequency by clinical social workers and other therapists working as a part of mental health teams. This may lessen but not necessarily eliminate the need for such services to be provided by school social workers. Certainly it will increase the need for school social workers to coordinate the clinically oriented school-linked programs.

## Gaining Momentum

The school-linked services movement presently has sufficient momentum that it is not likely to be stopped by a few dissenting voices. In addition, the movement will likely become increasingly intertwined with managed behavioral health care and new ways to fund health and human services. For example, more Medicaid funding may be available to fund human services on school campuses. Both public and private human services contractors are gaining access to public funds to provide services to children and families (Franklin & Johnson, 1996). Because education is important to the long-term outcomes of children, these services are including contingencies for school improvement as part of designated outcomes for contracts. This will likely lead to a greater investment in schools by human services providers and advance further the need for partnerships with schools.

## REFERENCES

Allen-Meares, P. (1994). Social work services in schools: A national study of entry-level tasks. *Social Work, 39,* 560–565.

Allen-Meares, P., Washington, R. O., & Welsh, B. L. (1996). *Social work services in schools* (2nd ed.). Boston: Allyn & Bacon.

Bruner, C. (1991). *Thinking collaboratively: Ten questions and answers to help policy makers improve children's services.* Washington, DC: Educational and Human Services Consortium.

Chaskin, R. J., & Richman, H. A. (1992). Concerns about school-linked services: Institution-based versus community-based models. *Future of Children, 2,* 107–117.

Cibulka, J., & Kritek, W. (Eds.). (1996). *Coordination among schools, families and communities.* Albany, NY: SUNY Press.

Dryfoos, J. G. (1994). *Full-service schools: A revolution in health and social services for children, youth, and families.* San Francisco: Jossey-Bass.

Franklin, C., & Johnson, C. (1996). Family social work practice: Onward to therapy and policy. *Journal of Family Social Work, 1*(3), 33–47.

Franklin, C., & Streeter, C. L. (1995). School reform: Linking public schools with human services. *Social Work, 40,* 773–782.

Gomby, D. S., & Larson, C. S. (1992). Evaluation of school-linked services. *Future of Children, 2,* 68–84.

Hare, I. (1995). School-linked services. In R. L. Edwards (Ed.-in-Chief), *Encyclopedia of social work* (19th ed., Vol. 3, pp. 2100–2109). Washington, DC: NASW Press.

Hooper-Briar, K., & Lawson, H. A. (1994). *Serving children, youth and families through interprofessional collaboration and services integration: A framework for action.* Oxford, OH: Miami University, Danforth Foundation and Institute for Educational Renewal.

Kahn, A. J., & Kammerman, S. B. (1992). *Integrating services integration: An overview of initiatives, issues and possibilities.* New York: Columbia University, School of Public Health, National Center for Children in Poverty.

Kirst, M. W. (1991). Improving children's services. *Phi Delta Kappan, 72,* 615–618.

Larson, C. S., Gomby, D. S., Shiono, S., Lewit, E. M., & Behrman, R. E. (1992). School-linked services: Analysis. *Future of Children, 2,* 6–18.

Markward, M. J. (1993). Assessing the effectiveness of social work practice in a school–community partnership: An illuminative approach. *Early Child Development and Care, 86,* 105–121.

Melaville, A. I., & Blank, M. J. (1991). *What it takes: Structuring interagency partnerships to connect children and families to comprehensive services.* Washington, DC: Education and Human Services Consortium. (ERIC Document Reproduction Service No. ED 330 748)

Melaville, A. I., & Blank, M. J. (1993). *Together we can: A guide to crafting a profamily system of education and human services.* Washington, DC: U.S. Department of Education and U.S. Department of Health and Human Services.

Morrill, W. A. (1992). Overview of service delivery to children. *Future of Children, 2,* 32–43.

Pennekamp, M. (1992). Toward school-linked and school-based human services for children and families [Trends & Issues]. *Social Work in Education, 14,* 125–130.

*This chapter was originally published in the July 1997 issue of* Social Work in Education, *Vol. 19, pp. 131–135.*

# 31 Children in Protective Services: The Missing Educational Link for Children in Kinship Networks

Barbara Rittner and Arlene Sacks

S chool social workers and child protective services (CPS) workers can collaborate to improve the social and educational functioning of abused and neglected children living in kinship networks. Chavkin (1989) identified school social workers in evolving and expanding arenas of practice as liaisons between schools and the families of abused and neglected children. Such workers intervene to empower families by linking them to networks within the community; by locating services that reduce economic and social stressors; and by offering crisis intervention, advocacy, counseling, and mentoring services (Chavkin, 1989; Nystrom, 1989).

This chapter reviews the literature on the role of school social workers in enhancing services to children in out-of-home placements; describes a study on the impact of children in care's school experiences on their academic and social outcomes; and discusses the implications for school social workers, related in particular to Individuals with Disabilities Education Act policy.

## LITERATURE REVIEW

Although there is broad acceptance of the need for school social workers to be more engaged with maltreated children, the primary focus tends to be on services to children under CPS supervision who are in foster care. Recent articles suggest that schools can bring about greater permanency, consistency, and stability in abused and neglected children's lives, particularly when their efforts are coordinated by school social workers (Chavkin, 1989; Gustavsson, 1991; Radin, 1989). Gustavsson, for example, identified a myriad of services that school social workers can provide to foster care children in response to their vulnerability to unstable and unsure living arrangements. However, little attention has been paid to children under CPS supervision who are cared for in kinship networks. In fact, the literature did not identify any models for school-based CPS programs for children cared for in kinship networks. Like many foster care children, some children under CPS supervision experience unstable living arrangements because they are moved around in their kinship networks. Few school-based programs specifically identify them as targets of intervention.

As a result of the passage of the Adoption Assistance and Child Welfare Act of 1980 (P.L. 96-272), the movement in child welfare has been away from placing children in foster care and toward keeping them with their families, primarily through family preservation programs (Fanshel, 1992; Testa, 1992). In Illinois, for example, relative care of abused and neglected children increased 120 percent from 1986 to 1990, a trend also noted nationwide (Testa, 1992). A widespread impression has developed that permanency planning through family preservation programs results in fewer children experiencing the unstable and impermanent placements associated with foster care, a perception not necessarily supported in the literature (Feldman, 1991). It has not been adequately examined whether children under CPS supervision residing in kinship care are being shuttled between relatives and parents in an effort to keep the children out of foster care. Equally unknown are the potential emotional repercussions of such multiple living arrangements. It is apparent, however, that for many children, kinship care results in the same disruptions of peer and teacher relationships and losses of community supports and affiliations experienced by foster care children.

Unfortunately, particularly in large metropolitan areas, a move of even a small distance can result in a change in school assignment. For CPS-supervised children, new placements in kinship networks often result in school changes as well. A powerful new role for school social workers is as advocates for these children as they struggle for constancy in their lives.

Recent studies indicate that abused and neglected children are, in general, socially and economically disenfranchised (Hutchison, 1993), making it more difficult for them to gain access to school and community resources (Chavkin, 1989; Radin, 1989). Children who suffer one form of abuse are likely to be victims of other types of abuse and are more likely to be living with a substance-abusing caretaker (Festinger, 1983; Hutchison, 1993; Murphy et al., 1991; U.S. Department of Health and Human Services, 1990, 1992). Although there is no indication that they are any more likely to be abused or neglected, minority children are more heavily represented in the CPS system, are more likely to be placed with relatives or in foster care by CPS workers, and are likely to receive services over longer periods (Close, 1983; DiLeonardi, 1980; English, 1990; Hansen, Conaway, & Christopher, 1990; Korbin, 1980; Payne, 1989; Rosenthal, 1988).

There is ample evidence that abuse can result in major incapacitating problems in childhood and throughout life (Alfaro, 1983; Main & George, 1985; Terr, 1991). Numerous studies have found that abused children are more socially immature, have more maladaptive social skills, are more aggressive, are more prone to temper tantrums and delinquency, are more easily distracted, and are more likely to be enuretic than nonabused children (Cicchetti, Toth, & Hennessy, 1989; Egeland, Sroufe, & Erickson, 1983; Martin & Beezley, 1977; Mash, Johnston, & Kovitz, 1983; Tharinger & Vevier, 1987; Wolfe & Mosk, 1983). It is therefore not surprising that these children are reported as having poorer school adjustment histories than their nonabused counterparts (Berrick & Barth, 1991; Caffaro-Rouget, Lang, & van Santen, 1989; Friedrich & Einbender, 1983; Hansen et al., 1990; Howing, Wodarski, Kurtz, Gaudin, & Herbst, 1990; Walker & Downey, 1990). Maltreated children are less ready to take on the tasks of school and have lower academic performance as a result of cognitive delays (Aber & Allen, 1987; Howing et al., 1990). These children are also more likely to exhibit maladaptive behaviors that provoke punitive responses from teachers and other adults (Fantuzzo et al., 1988; Howing et al., 1990).

## ONE COUNTY'S EXPERIENCE

To examine some of these concerns, an exploratory study was conducted in an ethnically diverse, metropolitan southeastern Florida county. We analyzed placement and school referral patterns of 447 children under CPS supervision and in the care of kinship networks that included parents, parents living with relatives, and relatives alone. Of 500 preselected cases, a total of 200 open and 247 closed case records (205 were closed out of the system and 42 were referred to foster care after a minimum of six months in kinship care) were located and read. These children, reported to CPS because of abuse and neglect, had not been placed in foster care but remained in the care of parents or relatives. All the cases had been open for a minimum of six months of continuous CPS supervision. The cases represented 11.7 percent of CPS cases in the county that involved kinship care and that were open or recently closed at the time of the study. The systematic selection using a $k$th selection process from unit listings was geographically stratified to ensure representation of countywide socioeconomic differences.

Using a pretested instrument, data were collected from all information sources found in the case records, including narratives, abuse complaint reports, court documents, clinical evaluations, correspondence, and computerized client information forms. We also gathered information from the case records on the number of placements the children experienced while under CPS supervision and the number of lifetime caretakers. Special attention was given to evidence of referrals of children by CPS or by schools for mental health services and for assessment by special educational programs as a result of identified emotional or behavioral problems. Data were categorized into five separate recording spans: (1) point of initial intake, (2) through six months after intake, (3) seven to 12 months after intake, (4) 13 to 18 months after intake, and (5) longer than 18 months after intake.

In addition, to examine the relationships between CPS and the local school system, we used a semistructured interview schedule to determine the perceptions of 10 CPS workers (representing a 10 percent convenience sample) about school-based programs and possible barriers to using school-based services. The interview asked two questions about school referrals: (1) Have you ever referred a child to the school system for services, and what was your experience doing so? and (2) If you never referred a child to the school system, why haven't you?

## FINDINGS

### Sociocultural Characteristics

The mean age of the children at intake was 4.4 years (*SD*, 5.0 years; range, 0 to 17 years); most were younger than six years ($n = 267$, 59.7 percent). Ethnically, the children sampled were identified as African American ($n = 266$, 59.5 percent), white ($n = 72$, 16.2 percent), Caribbean Hispanic ($n = 63$, 14.1 percent), Central

American ($n$ = 24, 5.4 percent), Haitian ($n$ = 10, 2.2 percent), South American ($n$ = 7, 1.6 percent), and multiethnic ($n$ = 3, 0.7 percent). In two cases, ethnicity could not be determined (0.4 percent).

The children came predominantly from poor homes. At intake, 106 principal caretakers had no clear or reliable source of income, 103 (primarily single mothers) received Aid to Families with Dependent Children, 52 received various types of disability payments, and only 56 were employed. In 130 cases, income sources were not indicated. None of the adults in the survey were receiving unemployment or workers' compensation, although 16 mothers (3.6 percent) were receiving Supplemental Security Income because of chronic mental illness. (The authors did not collect data on the backgrounds and placement changes of children in traditional foster care in the community, so comparisons cannot be made between those children and the children included in this study.)

Table 31-1 describes living arrangements for the children at the time they came under CPS supervision and at the last recorded entry in the case record. At intake most children either were substance-exposed newborns in hospitals or were cared for by single mothers ($\chi^2$ = 91.595, $df$ = 5, $p$ < .0001). Differences in living arrangements between intake and the time of the study reflect the discharge of substance-exposed newborns from hospitals, decreased frequency of mothers residing with unrelated men, increased caretaking by fathers, and placements into the foster care system. This table reflects the tendency of CPS workers to place substance-exposed newborns, neglected children, and sexually abused children with relatives after intake. Mothers were encouraged to live alone or

*Table 31-1*

## Comparison of Living Arrangements at Intake and at Time of Study

| Caretaker | Intake Living Arrangement ($N$ = 447) | | Current Living Arrangement ($N$ = 425) | | Change (%) |
|---|---|---|---|---|---|
| | $n$ | % | $n$ | % | |
| Hospital (substance-exposed newborns) | 147 | 32.9 | NA | NA | |
| Parent | | | | | |
| Mother only | 127 | 28.4 | 107 | 25.2 | −15.5 |
| Father only | 7 | 1.6 | 10 | 2.4 | 42.8 |
| Both parents | 38 | 8.5 | 42 | 9.9 | 10.5 |
| Mother and unrelated man | 47 | 10.5 | 12 | 2.8 | −74.5 |
| Parent and stepparent | 24 | 5.4 | 17 | 4.0 | −29.2 |
| Mother and relative | 22 | 4.9 | 49 | 11.5 | 122.7 |
| Father and relative | 0 | 0 | 10 | 2.4 | NA |
| Kinship network | | | | | |
| Maternal relative | 17 | 3.8 | 108 | 25.4 | 535.3 |
| Paternal relative | 5 | 1.1 | 26 | 6.1 | 420.0 |
| Other | 13[a] | 2.9 | 44[b] | 10.4 | 238.5 |

Notes: For the current living arrangement, 22 of the original 447 children could not be located. NA = not applicable.

[a]Includes 13 children living with godparents and other nonlegal relatives.

[b]Includes 42 children referred to foster care and two children living with godparents.

reside with relatives to regain custody of their children and were discouraged from living with unrelated men. Some substance-exposed newborns were placed with paternal relatives, especially if their mothers were still active drug users and estranged from their own families. Ongoing pressure was applied to some relatives to agree to permanent transfer of custody (which would require a termination of parental rights), though none agreed. Therefore, all 134 children residing with relatives alone remained under supervision until they were reunited with their parents.

## Changes in Caretakers and Residences

Children were moved around in their kinship networks. The number of lifetime caretakers for 425 children whose placement histories were known ranged from one to 10, with 35.6 percent having one caretaker, 40.0 percent having two caretakers, and 24.4 percent having three or more caretakers. In 22 cases, it proved impossible to track the number of caretakers because the case record was incomplete. The mean lifetime number of caretakers for all children was 2.01. When shelter placements were included, children older than three years averaged 2.39 changes during their lifetime, compared with 2.16 changes for children younger than three years. The substance-exposed newborns placed with maternal relatives tended to have the most stable living arrangements, whereas older children at intake tended to have more placements.

Data on children who experienced changes in both caretakers and residences during the 18 months of supervision after the intake decision indicate that during the first six months of supervision, 145 children (32.4 percent of the total sample) experienced changes in both caretakers and residences. CPS workers, in an effort to ensure the safety of these children, moved them from the homes of their parents to the homes of relatives and back again. These children were those identified as at greatest risk of repeated abuse or ongoing neglect and, therefore, most likely to experience problems in school as well. After seven to 12 months of supervision, 58 more children (16.6 percent of 349) experienced such changes, and after 13 to 18 months of supervision, 38 more children (14.4 percent of 263) experienced the same. (Data reported at the point of intake are not presented because disproportionately high frequencies of temporary and short-term shelter care would skew results, and data reported after the 18th month are not presented because of differential recording periods.) Placements with relatives were considered temporary by CPS workers. Case plans focused on obtaining treatment and resources that would enable parents to have their children returned to them. In fact, cases were not closed by CPS until children were returned to the parents or placed in foster care. Therefore, children would continue to be moved in kinship networks until they were reunited with parents, regardless of safety factors, school placements, or attachments formed.

## Mental Health System Referrals

Screening children for mental health problems was not a mandated CPS service in this community and usually occurred only when children were sexually abused or when behavioral problems at home or in the community were severe.

The case records indicated that CPS did not notify the school system when children were referred for mental health services. Likewise, the records contained no documentation indicating that the schools notified CPS when they assessed children for placement in programs for severely emotionally disturbed children or other special school settings.

A total of 71 of the children were referred by CPS to mental health centers during the first six months of service. Of these, 11 children were placed on waiting lists, 49 received counseling, six families refused services, and five referrals had no follow-up information. By the end of the first year of continuous CPS services, 77 of the children had been referred to community-based mental health providers. Of these, 11 were still on waiting lists. Four additional families refused services, and two had no follow-up information. After the first year of CPS supervision, 25 children were still in counseling.

## School System Referrals

During the first 18 months of services, only 30 of the children were referred by CPS workers to the school system for diagnostic testing and evaluation for possible placement in special classroom or preschool settings. All of these referrals were still pending one year later. Ten of these referrals (under the Child Find provisions) were to an early childhood diagnostic school-based center used to screen children who might be autistic or otherwise developmentally delayed. (Child Find is a federally funded program implemented by each state to identify children who may be at risk for poor school advancement and provide a full range of services for them in school settings.) An additional 54 children were referred to a multidisciplinary early childhood development program connected to a large teaching hospital but unconnected to the school system. These children were primarily substance-exposed newborns recruited by the hospital at the point of birth for a multiyear study on the long-term effects of cocaine exposure.

## Worker Perceptions of CPS Services

In semistructured interviews with six CPS workers who had more than two years of experience, the workers expressed frustration with trying to place children in school-based programs. They felt that insurmountable obstacles and barriers prevented access to school-based services for CPS children. Most admitted that they rarely made referrals because of long waiting lists and cumbersome procedures that had to be traversed to get children tested and placed. Furthermore, there was no mechanism for paperwork to follow children transferred from one school to another if the prescreening had not been completed, thus requiring CPS workers to reinitiate paperwork in each new school setting. Because waiting lists often exceeded six months, experienced workers felt that children identified as at risk were likely to be relocated in kinship networks or into foster home placements before being served. Furthermore, they felt that schools were unwilling to assign a high priority to these children, despite clear evidence that children with abuse histories were likely to have many problems in school.

Many CPS workers expressed strong feelings that middle- and upper-income children, especially nonminority children, were more likely to receive the limited services available to emotionally acting out children. Poor children, particularly those in foster care or under CPS supervision, were perceived as disenfranchised. Because many children under CPS supervision are poor, such perceptions can become reflexive.

When the four workers with less than two years of experience were asked if they had ever tried to obtain school-based services for children, most admitted they had not, but "knew about the problems." The problems they identified were generally those cited by experienced workers. Neither new nor experienced workers identified infants, toddlers, or preschool-age children as eligible for any school-based services and tended to refer these children for day care instead.

Because they saw that formal policies and procedures developed at administrative levels were absent, CPS workers felt that school referrals were a "waste of time," and time was an important consideration given that assigned caseloads exceeded 70 children and actual caseloads approached 100 when additional children from uncovered caseloads (caseloads with an unfilled caseworker position attached to it) were assigned. Finally, most CPS workers felt that they did not have time to screen children for possible mental health problems and had not been trained to do so; they nonetheless felt they could identify children exhibiting severe emotional problems at home or in shelter care. In general, the CPS workers lacked knowledge of the range of services available under the Individuals with Disabilities Education Act (IDEA, P.L. 101-476), including those for preschool-age children, and few knew that the schools could be an important resource for all maltreated children, including preschoolers, toddlers, and infants.

## IMPLICATIONS FOR SCHOOL SOCIAL WORKERS

The findings in this study suggest that some abused and neglected children who are cared for by kinship networks under CPS supervision experience unstable living arrangements. Like children placed in foster care, some of these children come from uncaring, dangerous, or violent environments or from neglectful homes, precipitating their entry into protective supervision, and they remain vulnerable to repeated abuse and neglect while under supervision (Festinger, 1983). However, unlike foster care children, children cared for in kinship networks under CPS supervision are not identified as such in the school systems unless specific mechanisms are in place.

School social workers need to work on behalf of children placed in kinship networks by CPS toward developing coordinated services between school systems and CPS programs. Assessing risk and intervening to ameliorate threats to the ongoing safety of children are the mandated functions of most CPS programs. This role is a limited but vital and highly complex one. School social workers, on the other hand, can facilitate the provision of a complex array of services for at-risk children and their families. Unfortunately, school social workers may not be aware that a child is under CPS supervision unless that child is living in a foster home or the school initiated the abuse complaint (Berrick & Barth, 1991).

It is incumbent on CPS programs and school systems to structure, coordinate, and formalize cooperative agreements to address the social, educational, and psychological needs of maltreated children. Such agreements can be accomplished under the provisions of IDEA, which expanded the Education for All Handicapped Children Act of 1975 (P.L. 94-142) and the Education of the Handicapped Act Amendments of 1986 (P.L. 99-457) to emphasize "people first" language (instead of disability), extended educational programs to infants and toddlers at risk of developmental and cognitive delays, provided transition service plans in individualized educational plans (IEPs) beginning at age 16 for youths, and made available social work services to eligible children and their families.

## MODEL FOR SCHOOL–CPS PARTNERSHIP

IDEA offers both schools and CPS a mechanism to develop a partnership to serve maltreated children. Representatives of both systems can become allies in coordinating continuity of services for free, appropriate public education in the least restrictive environment to ameliorate the potential developmental and academic delays prevalent in maltreated children.

Under a model based on the provisions of IDEA, CPS workers would first identify maltreated children placed in kinship networks to school social workers, who would serve as liaisons for prescreening services under IDEA. School social workers would function as service brokers for these children through the prescreening and screening processes. If the prescreening and screening evaluations indicate the presence of risk factors, especially abuse or substance exposure, school social workers would coordinate and monitor appropriate special education and related services, including transportation, health, mental health, and social work services; occupational services; economic services; and service continuity as the children moved in kinship networks. CPS workers would advise school liaison social workers of permanency plans to ensure that decisions regarding school settings coincide with placements in kinship networks. Early interventions are consistent with the intent of IDEA, P.L. 94-142, and P.L. 99-457 to prevent or reverse developmental delays in cognitive as well as psychological functioning. Costs associated with the development of demonstration programs for coordinated services are covered under grants provisions of Title V of IDEA, which authorizes funding for the establishment of such partnerships.

To address the specific needs of infants and toddlers (birth to age 36 months), multidisciplinary teams would be developed, with school social workers acting as central referral coordinators across agencies in accordance with the Early Intervention Program (Part H) of IDEA. Initial prescreenings would be arranged by school social workers with appropriate members of the interdisciplinary team. School social workers would ensure the flow of information among team members, including information about the type of maltreatment reported to CPS and about short-term and long-term placement plans for the children. Interdisciplinary teams may include educators; CPS workers; mental health practitioners;

nutritionists; physicians; addictions counselors; and physical, speech, hearing, and occupational therapists, as appropriate.

Infants and toddlers could be monitored in their homes or referred for more intensive services on the basis of needs assessments at prescreenings and screenings. For some children, the provision of stable, nurturing caretakers may be identified as necessary to alleviate the problems associated with histories of multiple placements and caretakers. School social workers would be the coordinators of the Individual Family Service Plan (IFSP) for each infant and toddler identified as needing services under IDEA.

Preschoolers under CPS supervision would be prescreened for social and cognitive developmental problems and other possible risk factors. School social workers would function as liaisons to CPS to identify and track the children. Furthermore, school social workers could ensure that at-risk children in need of services were placed in programs that enhanced school placement stability. School social workers could play an instrumental role in coordinating input from families and CPS for development of the IFSP. In conjunction with parents or relatives and CPS, school social workers could develop transportation services that enable children to continue in a given program even if the child was moved in the kinship network.

IDEA also provides for a range of programs and services for school-age children. School social workers would coordinate multidisciplinary teams that included CPS workers to assess these children for educational, social, and emotional problems. As active members of the mandated IEP team—often as leaders—school social workers would ensure that IEPs coordinate services without duplication and explore the psychological as well as the educational needs of the children.

Under the provisions in IDEA, school social workers can enhance the efficacy of school settings as potential points of constancy in the otherwise unstable lives of maltreated children. School social workers can work with schools, families, and CPS workers to assist in shaping plans that use schools as focal points for responding to the special needs of children under CPS supervision. Their efforts would also ensure these children the possibility of experiencing some uniformity of environment and personnel, affording them a greater opportunity to form relationships with school social workers, teachers, and other school personnel, relationships more enduring than their unstable home lives would otherwise offer.

Future studies should examine other strategies to exercise the flexibility of bureaucratic boundaries and to increase the delivery of services that address the problems of CPS-supervised children and their families proactively, rather than reflexively. Once both systems become part of multisystem, multidisciplinary teams developing comprehensive rather than piecemeal plans, maltreated children should begin to receive more effective services to ameliorate their negative life and social services experiences. Clearly, such coordination of services would do much to enable both systems to plan effectively for the use of limited resources, to eliminate duplication of services, and to streamline procedurally encumbered programs.

## REFERENCES

Aber, J. L., & Allen, J. P. (1987). The effects of maltreatment on young children's socio-emotional development: An attachment theory perspective. *Developmental Psychology, 23*, 406–414.

Adoption Assistance and Child Welfare Act of 1980, P.L. 96-272, 94 Stat. 500.

Alfaro, J. D. (1983). Report on the relationship between child abuse and neglect: Later socially deviant behavior. In R. J. Hanger & Y. E. Walker (Eds.), *Exploring the relationship between child abuse and delinquency* (pp. 175–219). Montclair, NJ: Allanheld, Osmun.

Berrick, J. D., & Barth, R. P. (1991). The role of the school social worker in child abuse prevention. *Social Work in Education, 13*, 195–202.

Caffaro-Rouget, A., Lang, R. A., & van Santen, V. (1989). The impact of child sexual abuse on victims' adjustment. *Annals of Sex Research, 2*, 29–47.

Chavkin, N. F. (1989). Linking schools and parents. *Social Work in Education, 11*, 149–159.

Cicchetti, D., Toth, S. L., & Hennessy, K. (1989). Research on the consequences of child maltreatment and its application to educational settings. *Topics in Early Childhood Special Education, 9*(2), 33–55.

Close, M. M. (1983). Child welfare and people of color: Denial of equal access. *Social Work Research & Abstracts, 19*(4), 13–20.

DiLeonardi, J. W. (1980). Decision making in protective services. *Child Welfare, 49*, 358–364.

Education for All Handicapped Children Act of 1975, P.L. 94-142, 89 Stat. 773.

Education of the Handicapped Act Amendments of 1986, P.L. 99-457, 100 Stat. 1145.

Egeland, B., Sroufe, L. A., & Erickson, M. (1983). The developmental consequences of different patterns of maltreatment. *Child Abuse and Neglect, 7*, 459–469.

English, D. (1990). *Cultural issues related to assessment of child abuse and neglect* (Fourth national roundtable of CPS risk assessment: Summary of highlights). Washington, DC: American Public Welfare Association.

Fanshel, D. (1992). Foster care as a two-tiered system. *Children and Youth Services Review, 14*, 49–60.

Fantuzzo, J. W., Jurecic, L., Stovall, A., Hightower, A. D., Goins, C., & Schachtel, D. (1988). Effects of adult and peer initiations on the social behavior of withdrawn, maltreated preschool children. *Journal of Continuing and Clinical Psychology, 56*, 34–39.

Feldman, L. H. (1991). Evaluating the impact of intensive family preservation services in New Jersey. In K. Wells & D. E. Biegel (Eds.), *Family preservation services: Research and evaluation* (pp. 47–71). San Francisco: Sage Publications.

Festinger, T. (1983). *No one ever asked.* New York: Columbia University Press.

Friedrich, W. N., & Einbender, A. J. (1983). The abused child: A psychological review. *Journal of Clinical Child Psychology, 12*, 244–256.

Gustavsson, N. S. (1991). The school and the maltreated child in foster care: The role for the school social worker. *Social Work in Education, 13*, 224–236.

Hansen, D. J., Conaway, L. P., & Christopher, J. S. (1990). Victims of child abuse. In R. T. Ammerman & M. Hansen (Eds.), *Treatment of family violence.* New York: Wiley-Interscience.

Howing, P. T., Wodarski, J. S., Kurtz, P. D., Gaudin, J. M., & Herbst, E. N. (1990). Child abuse and delinquency: The empirical and theoretical links. *Social Work, 35*, 244–249.

Hutchison, E. D. (1993). Mandatory reporting laws: Child protective case finding gone awry? *Social Work, 38*, 56–63.

Individuals with Disabilities Education Act, P.L. 101-476, 104 Stat. 1142.

Korbin, J. E. (1980). The cross-cultural context of child abuse and neglect. In C. Kempe & R. E. Helfer (Eds.), *The battered child* (3rd ed., pp. 21–35). Chicago: University of Chicago Press.

Main, M., & George, C. (1985). Responses of abused and disadvantaged toddlers to distress in agemates: A study in the daycare setting. *Developmental Psychology, 21*, 407–412.

Martin, H. P., & Beezley, P. (1977). Behavioral observations of abused children. *Developmental Medicine and Child Neurology, 19*, 373–387.

Mash, E. J., Johnston, C., & Kovitz, K. (1983). A comparison of the mother–child interactions of physically abused children during play and task situations. *Journal of Clinical Child Psychology, 12*, 337–346.

Murphy, J. M., Jellinek, M., Quinn, D., Smith, G., Poitrast, F. G., & Goshko, M. (1991). Substance abuse and serious child mistreatment: Prevalence, risk, and outcome in a court sample. *Child Abuse and Neglect, 15,* 197–211.

Nystrom, J. F. (1989). Empowerment model for delivery of social work services in public schools. *Social Work in Education, 11,* 160–170.

Payne, M. A. (1989). Use and abuse of corporal punishment: A Caribbean view. *Child Abuse and Neglect, 13,* 389–401.

Radin, N. (1989). School social work practice: Past, present, and future trends. *Social Work in Education, 11,* 213–215.

Rosenthal, J. A. (1988). Patterns of reported child abuse and neglect. *Child Abuse and Neglect, 12,* 263–271.

Terr, L. (1991). Childhood trauma: An outline and overview. *American Journal of Psychiatry, 148,* 10–20.

Testa, M. F. (1992). Conditions of risk for substitute care. *Children and Youth Services Review, 14,* 27–36.

Tharinger, D. J., & Vevier, E. (1987). Child sexual abuse: A review and intervention framework for the teacher. *Journal of Research and Development in Education, 20*(4), 12–24.

U.S. Department of Health and Human Services. (1990). *Technical amendment to the study findings—National incidence and prevalence of child abuse and neglect: 1988.* Washington, DC: Center on Child Abuse and Neglect.

U.S. Department of Health and Human Services. (1992). *Child abuse and neglect: A shared community concern.* Washington, DC: Center on Child Abuse and Neglect.

Walker, E. F., & Downey, G. (1990). The effects of familial risk factors on social–cognitive abilities in children. *Child Psychiatry and Human Development, 20,* 253–267.

Wolfe, D. A., & Mosk, M. D. (1983). Behavioral comparisons of children from abusive and distressed families. *Journal of Consulting and Clinical Psychology, 51,* 702–708.

---

*This chapter was originally published in the January 1995 issue of* Social Work in Education, *Vol. 17, pp. 7–17.*

# 32 Maintaining Positive School Relationships: The Role of the Social Worker vis-à-vis Full-Service Schools

Jill Duerr Berrick and Mark Duerr

School staff are increasingly faced with students who mirror the social concerns of their communities, bringing problems of child abuse and neglect, homelessness, poor health, and family poverty to school campuses across the country (Bond & Compas, 1989). Children raised in these difficult and stressful environments may be unprepared to manage the daily educational tasks required within the school. Young children in particular are often unable to focus on the academic and social demands of schools.

Increasingly, educators have turned to full-service schools to address this challenge (Dryfoos, 1993; Healthy Kids, Healthy California, 1991; Klopf, Shedlin, & Zanet, 1988; Social Development Research Group, 1990). Rather than focusing solely on children's academic achievement, programs are developing that also foster children's health, mental health, and social development. In many cases, these programs are funded by private foundation support; however, in recent years several states—for example, Florida, New Jersey, New York, and California—have initiated demonstration projects to test the concept (see Dryfoos, 1993, for a discussion of various state demonstration models). These programs are usually offered to schools with particularly large groups of high-risk children (defined by the percentage of low-income or Chapter 1–eligible children) and offer an array of services.

Some services are narrowly targeted to children who display specific types of problems or at-risk behavior. These services might include group sessions for gang-involved children; individual counseling for substance-using youths (Botvin & Dusenbury, 1989), children of alcoholic parents (McElligatt, 1986), or children of divorcing parents (Strauss & McGann, 1987); child and parent services to reduce nonattendance at school (Barth, 1984; Levine, 1984); or mental health services for children with emotional or behavioral problems (Newton-Logsdon & Armstrong, 1993). Other programs are more broad based and offer case management, advocacy, in-home teaching and demonstration, counseling, transportation, and child care for children and their families suffering from a variety of problems.

Full-service school programs are often based on a collaborative model between school districts and community-based organizations (CBOs). The introduction of social and mental health workers into the school environment is intended to enhance the school environment for children and school staff. Under optimal conditions, teachers and CBO staff work together to design customized service plans for children that will increase attendance; enhance academic performance; and, as the backdrop for these outcomes, address the social or psychological problems that may be interrupting children's focus on school activities. CBO staff are also used as consultants to teaching staff (Allen-Meares, 1977) to stimulate new ideas for managing children's classroom behavior.

The social workers and paraprofessional "friendly visitors" who largely staff CBOs must actively cultivate and then work to sustain their relationships with school staff. Although teachers and social workers often have similar long-term goals for children, their philosophical approach, training, and short-term goals may clash (Pennekamp, 1992). Several steps should be kept in mind as social workers attempt to establish full-service programs to reduce the likelihood of tension and increase the success of their efforts.

## LESSONS FROM THE LEARN PROGRAM

This article describes a few basic steps that should be considered in the early phases of program development. These principles have evolved from a four-year study that examined the establishment of full-service programs in 35 elementary schools across California through the state-sponsored LEARN (Local Efforts to Address and Reduce Neglect) program (Duerr Evaluation Resources, 1993).

LEARN operates in nine sites across California. The program is designed to reduce physical neglect among children as manifested by hunger, inappropriate clothing, inadequate hygiene, insufficient or inappropriate supervision, and too little sleep; to lessen school absences; and to ultimately reduce formal child welfare intervention among these children's families. It is also directed toward increasing parenting skills and improving family functioning. The core service is voluntary in-home assistance, which includes assessment of family problems, referral to other community agencies and resources, and direct intervention with neglect-related problems in the home. All projects also provide intervention at school with client children through group or one-on-one self-esteem or skills-building sessions, parent support or education groups, and parent or family counseling. On average, clients receive 14 hours of in-home assistance and referral services, 10 hours of service to children, seven hours of parent group intervention, and three hours of counseling—a total of 34 hours over about 20 to 30 weeks.

Two programs operate under the auspices of the local county Department of Social Services, three are operated by community-based nonprofit organizations, and two are managed by local school districts. Although these programs are operated under distinct auspices, differences in program implementation are not significant. All projects rely on a combination of professional social workers and therapists and paraprofessional "home visitors." Each also employs about three full-time equivalent staff who work in an average of four schools. On average, each project completes services with 35 families a year and offers services to 15 more who do not complete services (because they move or drop out of the program).

Families are eligible for the program if they are not currently involved with the child welfare system and if they have a child ages five to eight (kindergarten through third grade) who exhibits signs of physical neglect. Teachers are the primary referral source into the program. Staff in the LEARN program not only provide individual services to families but also offer advice and consultation to school staff.

The program was conducted as a four-year demonstration. In the first year of operation, program staff were given the opportunity to develop their skills and to work out the many details of program implementation. In the second and third years, an experimental study of the effectiveness of program services was conducted using the following three levels of program evaluation: (1) an experimental study with random assignment to target and control groups; (2) a pretest and posttest of family functioning with target group families only; and (3) an extensive process evaluation that included numerous and lengthy site visits, focus groups with teachers and LEARN staff, and interviews with school principals and district officials. The practice wisdom that emerged from this study is drawn from the third tier of the evaluation. Results from the first two tiers of the study can be obtained elsewhere (Duerr Evaluation Resources, 1993).

## PRINCIPLES OF ACTION FOR SCHOOL SOCIAL WORKERS AND CBO STAFF

The principles enumerated below apply best when an outside CBO is working with a local school to develop their full-service program. Many of the principles, however, are equally relevant for school social workers employed by the school district but whose role is viewed as distinct from other school staff.

### Fit into the Existing Structure

The CBO staff must become part of the existing social and organizational structure of the school setting. School dynamics vary greatly, even within districts. The attitudes, training, and vision of the school principal and staff are probably the most important part of what drives a school's identity, and an agency must, for the most part, try to fit within this existing web of personalities and values. Agencies that try to come in and change this web probably will not succeed. The first link in developing this new relationship is the CBO's rapport with the principal. If the principal is not enthusiastic about an agency's work from the start, or if he or she does not see how the agency's services can be incorporated into the existing operational paradigm, then CBO staff are unlikely to be able to develop and implement the project with any appreciable success. The principal will be integral in paving the way for the project's success with school staff only if he or she develops ownership of the project. One strategy to help involve principals is to actively pursue their participation in the selection of project staff who will work in their schools. In short, agencies should attempt to work only in those schools in which the staff enthusiastically greet them and are willing to integrate the program into their full vision of school services. As a corollary, if a school seems willing to integrate the program at first but then puts up major barriers, CBO staff may wish to consider dropping the school and working with another. Experience has shown that it can take up to a year or longer to win over reluctant school personnel, time that may be better spent building a positive relationship elsewhere with a willing school staff.

## Communicate, Communicate, Communicate

Although school staff may initially be reluctant to attend meetings, regular conferences must occur to establish the goals and objectives of the service program. Although especially important during the early phases of program implementation, these meetings must be sustained over the course of the year. Regularly scheduled meetings facilitate referrals, assist in the development of service plans, and provide an opportunity for school staff to become involved in the personal circumstances of children beyond the school's walls. For schools with multiple outside agencies working on-site, regular meetings are essential to clearly establish roles and responsibilities of all child-serving professionals. Clarity about individual responsibilities will reduce duplication among families and will also reduce confusion among school staff, who may be unclear about the service possibilities afforded to their students.

## Be Realistic about Services to Be Provided

Once a program has started in a school, it is not uncommon for agencies to build false expectations among teachers about how many children will be served. In our study one social worker felt she had to promise a great deal to make the project appealing to the teachers, but then she spent nearly a year explaining why her staff could not accept a wider range or higher number of students. Agency staff should explain what they can do for a school site, but they should also be very specific about what they cannot accomplish. Once teachers have an expectation that cannot be met, it is very difficult and time consuming to regain their confidence.

## Be Clear about Who You Can Serve

At the heart of school participation in a project that relies on teacher referral is generating sufficient but not overwhelming numbers of referrals. Teachers are more likely to refer children when they are clear about who can be served, when they have an instrument to aid them in screening children, and when they are confident that the CBO staff will begin working with a referred child within a reasonable time after referral. If thresholds for service are set too low, agency staff can receive hundreds of referrals, many of which will be inappropriate for service. For example, an agency may suggest that they can serve any at-risk child. If teachers interpret this message broadly, they will refer most children in their classrooms. Yet a relatively small school-based program will be unable to serve most children in a school site.

## Make Yourself Known

Outside agencies working within the school system must prove that they are an integral part of the school service paradigm by maintaining regular contact with the principal and teachers. This can best by accomplished by following five general guidelines:

1. Staff should be visible at the school site so that they are seen as accessible by teachers. It is preferable that staff have some type of work space at the school and be available during hours when teachers might be free, especially in the first 45 minutes after the school day ends.
2. If an agency is attempting to work in more than one school, only one staff member should be assigned to each school. This avoids confusion among teachers about who to contact and makes it easier to develop closer ties with agency staff.
3. CBO staff should attempt to join school personnel at social gatherings, at lunch hours, and at staff meetings so that they come to be seen as part of the school team.
4. When a child is referred to the program, staff should provide written feedback to teachers within a specified time (within a few days, if possible) about the status of the child's referral. Teachers should also know when the staff member will begin work with the child's family. Teachers rely heavily on the written word. Comments exchanged in the halls may be of value in the moment but may also be forgotten in the rush of other activities. Leaving a paper trail of brief progress notes is an effective means of keeping teachers current about the status of served children and may provide a symbolic gesture about the presence of the program, necessary to keep the program current in teachers' minds.
5. Once a family is involved in the service, the teacher should be notified. If the family cannot be engaged after some period of time, the teacher should receive written notification and should be informed about the types of efforts staff have made to engage the family. Teachers should also be asked for their suggestions. They might wish to play a role in engaging the family, thereby becoming a more active member of the service team. Once the family is involved in service, teachers should continue to be consulted and encouraged to develop an individualized service plan for monitoring and encouraging the child's gains within the classroom.

## FUTURE OF FULL-SERVICE SCHOOLS

To accomplish the goals set forth for the development of full-service schools, a new identity for school staff and mental health and social services professionals will need to emerge. Teaching staff, whose primary identity has been locked into the sole role of educator, must change to accommodate a fuller identity as child-serving professionals. Similarly, mental health and social services professionals, whose primary role since the establishment of social work and psychotherapy has been that of the therapeutic professional, must change to see themselves as part of an educational community whose mission is to see children grow and thrive both intellectually and interpersonally. If all professionals remain focused on their mission in the context of children and families, their work toward developing a coordinated approach will indeed grow easier over time.

With a change in philosophical orientation, full-service schools may be initiated more easily, but their sustained implementation may be problematic. Although the idea is gaining favor as a theoretical construct, its execution is rarely straightforward. School, mental health, and social services professionals may share a number of common goals for children, but the daily practicalities of service provision often are overlooked by the lofty aspirations of agency staff. Unless the practical considerations outlined earlier are understood, little will be accomplished in advancing the mission of coordinated services. More important, once an agency has won the support of school staff, the far more complex and challenging work of delivering effective services to children and families must begin.

## REFERENCES

Allen-Meares, P. (1977). Analysis of tasks in school social work. *Social Work, 22*, 196–201.

Barth, R. P. (1984). Reducing nonattendance in elementary schools. *Social Work in Education, 6*, 151–166.

Bond, L. A., & Compas, B. E. (Eds.). (1989). *Primary prevention and promotion in the schools.* Newbury Park, CA: Sage Publications.

Botvin, G. J., & Dusenbury, L. (1989). Substance abuse prevention and the promotion of competence. In L. A. Bond & B. E. Compas (Eds.), *Primary prevention and promotion in the schools* (pp. 146–178). Newbury Park, CA: Sage Publications.

Dryfoos, J. G. (1993). *Full-service schools: A revolution in health and social services for children, youth, and families.* San Francisco: Jossey-Bass.

Duerr Evaluation Resources. (1993). *Third year evaluation report: Local efforts to address and reduce neglect.* Chico, CA: Author. (Available from Duerr Evaluation Resources, 5 Governor's Lane, Chico, CA 95926)

Healthy Kids, Healthy California. (1991). *Not schools alone.* Sacramento: California Department of Education.

Klopf, G., Shedlin, A., & Zanet, E. (1988). *The school as locus for advocacy for all children.* New York: Elementary School Center.

Levine, R. S. (1984). An assessment tool for early intervention in cases of truancy. *Social Work in Education, 6*, 133–150.

McElligatt, K. (1986). Identifying and treating children of alcoholic parents. *Social Work in Education, 8*, 55–70.

Newton-Logsdon, G., & Armstrong, M. I. (1993). School-based mental health services. *Social Work in Education, 15*, 187–191.

Pennekamp, M. (1992). Toward school-linked and school-based human services for children and families. *Social Work in Education, 14*, 125–130.

Social Development Research Group. (1990). *Together! Planning guide.* Seattle: University of Washington, School of Social Work, Cooperative Education and Washington State University.

Strauss, J. B., & McGann, J. (1987). Building a network for children of divorce. *Social Work in Education, 9*, 96–105.

*The authors are coprincipal investigators of the LEARN evaluation described here. Funding for this study was provided by the California Department of Social Services, Office of Child Abuse Prevention.*

*This chapter was originally published in the January 1996 issue of* Social Work in Education, *Vol. 18, pp. 53–58.*

# 33 Homeless Children and Their Families: Delivery of Educational and Social Services through School Systems and Communities

Jack C. Wall

The role of school social workers in facilitating a positive and relevant educational experience for the rapidly growing population of homeless children is central. Since the 1980s children have represented the fastest growing population of homeless individuals in the United States (Molnar & Rath, 1990). In 1989 approximately 38 percent of all homeless individuals were children (Molnar & Rath, 1990). The families of homeless children generally are headed by young single mothers who dropped out of school and do not possess marketable job skills (Gewirtzman & Fodor, 1987). In addition, homeless families from African American and Latino backgrounds are overrepresented in the homeless population (Gewirtzman & Fodor, 1987; Rescorla, Parker, & Stolley, 1991).

While families are homeless, they may reside in several temporary facilities located in various communities, or they may live on the streets (National Coalition for the Homeless, 1987). Because of this state of transience, children often do not attend school or have high rates of absenteeism (Eddowes & Hranitz, 1989). Homeless children generally have a variety of academic problems related to their transience and the difficulties associated with frequent absences from school (Eddowes & Hranitz, 1989; Gewirtzman & Fodor, 1887; Molnar & Rath, 1990). Many homeless children have moderate to severe learning, emotional, and behavioral problems and require specialized programs to help them in their learning (Bassuk & Rubin, 1987; Molnar & Rath, 1990; Rescorla et al., 1991).

The unique and numerous complexities related to assisting these children and supporting their families require innovative strategies of intervention. In particular, a collaborative approach both within and outside of the school system needs to be developed to address the myriad institutional, communal, familial, and personal issues that interfere with attempts to prevent and ameliorate homelessness. This article discusses the personal, familial, social, and institutional factors that significantly affect the lives of these children and their families. In addition, delivery systems both within and outside of schools and the particular roles and functions of school social workers are explored.

## FACTORS AFFECTING HOMELESS CHILDREN

Several major environmental, psychosocial, and institutional factors negatively affect the ability of homeless children to receive educational and social services.

## Environmental Factors

A significant aspect of children's developing a sense of continuity in their lives involves the communities in which their families are embedded (Wall, 1993). Continued relationships with neighborhood families, institutions, and other social groups offer children a sense of belonging to a wider community. In addition, both individuals and institutions in communities frequently reflect the ethos and values of the families that reside in a particular area (Anderson & Carter, 1990; Fellin, 1987). These external sources of validation and support provide children with additional figures for identification.

Becoming homeless symbolizes not only a loss of residence, but also a severing of many significant familial, social, and institutional relationships (Wall, 1993). Frequent disruptions have a profound effect on homeless children. Many cannot continue to attend their original schools once their families lose their homes, because residency requirements preclude their continued enrollment. In addition, families generally move several times during their period of homelessness, which necessitates enrolling in new schools subsequent to each move. These persistent interruptions can preclude the establishment of significant ties between school systems and homeless children and their parents.

## Psychosocial Factors

*Lack of Continuity.* The inability of parents to provide adequate living arrangements for their children challenges children's fundamental assumptions about themselves as individuals and about their parents' abilities to fulfill basic parental functions. Becoming homeless undermines two fundamental needs of children—a sense of continuity and a belief that parents will provide the physical, social, and emotional resources required for their survival, growth, and development (Wall, 1993). Child development theories and research consistently indicate that continuity is a major factor in children's development of trust in the world and themselves and of a cohesive, stable identity (Erikson, 1980; Mahler, Pine, & Bergman, 1975).

A primary parental function is to provide an environment that creates and maintains a sense of continuity within the family. Continuity ordinarily is achieved through predictable family structures, values, routines, rituals, and family history (Carter & McGoldrick, 1989; Minuchin, 1974). Young children's early senses of identity develop, in part, through experiencing their families' unique repeated patterns of interaction, behaviors, and relationships (Minuchin, 1974).

*Separation and Loss.* Children identify separation and loss as predominant themes related to being homeless (Timberlake, 1993; Timberlake & Sabatino, 1994; Walsh, 1992). Timberlake indicated that concerns about basic survival needs related to caretaking, nurturance, and security and protection dominate homeless children's perceptions of being homeless. Preoccupation with such fundamental requirements for survival and feelings of loss and separation often compromise homeless children's critical developmental tasks such as learning new skills; developing a sense of competence and mastery; and creating positive, ongoing adult or peer relationships (Bassuk & Rubin, 1987; Timberlake, 1993; Tower, 1992; Walsh, 1992).

*Coping Mechanisms.* The effects of deleterious influences vary within this population (Bassuk & Rubin, 1987; Rescorla et al., 1991; Timberlake, 1993; Timberlake & Sabatino, 1994; Walsh, 1992). Timberlake found that approximately 25 percent of the children in her study had successful coping mechanisms they used to counteract the damaging effects of homelessness. These children seemed to perceive themselves as competent both to deal with the stresses of their living arrangements and to maintain a high level of academic achievement despite their disordered lives. This cohort of children obviously possessed more effective coping mechanisms and greater skills in using resources in the environment than the rest of the sample, who were managing less well in a homeless situation. It is important, therefore, to understand that the homeless population is composed of diverse subgroups of children who have differing capabilities and needs. This diversity requires social workers to develop individualized plans for helping these children according to their particular strengths and weaknesses.

Children's differential capacities to manage their stressful living situations are influenced by their parents' abilities to cope effectively with being homeless. Van Ry (1992) identified two primary categories of homeless families—maintainers and improvers. She argued that maintainers left their homes when events they could not control occurred—generally eviction, rejection (being told by extended family members and friends to leave their homes), and abandonment by spouses or partners.

Improvers usually initiated moves to improve their lives by seeking employment in other communities, to safeguard their children from abuse, and to escape domestic violence. Although both types of families were determined to improve their lives, maintainers tended to be more reactive to situations, whereas improvers appeared to take a proactive stance to address undesirable conditions.

It may be assumed that the differences between these two major categories of homeless families influence children's development of particular coping mechanisms. The actual circumstances that led to being homeless, the meaning parents attribute to the situation, and the coping strategies they use to deal with stress may influence the children's perceptions and management of the crisis.

## Institutional Factors

Institutional obstacles often impede successful relationships between school systems and homeless families. The National Coalition for the Homeless (1987) identified seven major institutional barriers that prevent schools from adequately addressing the needs of homeless children and families:

1. residency requirements
2. restricted access to schools
3. space limitations in schools
4. lack of transportation between shelters and schools
5. lack of readily available academic records
6. special education requirements
7. guardianship requirements.

In addition, homeless children face another institutional barrier to education—stereotyping and prejudice.

*Residency Requirements.* Most schools require children to reside in the community that the school system serves. Loss of residence and subsequent relocation therefore generally renders children ineligible to attend their former community schools. Lacking a domicile also traditionally precludes homeless children from being able to register to attend school.

In recognition of this common residency requirement, Congress passed the Stewart B. McKinney Homeless Assistance Act (P.L. 100-77) in 1987. A major mandate of this law is that children have the right of access to an education regardless of their homelessness. Many schools, however, do not comply with this law. The necessary structures and services to meet the educational and psychosocial needs of these children and families have not been established.

*Restricted Access to Schools.* Many families can stay at motels for only a limited time because of policy mandates of social welfare agencies; consequently, children may not be in a particular school district long enough to meet residency requirements. In addition, disagreements between school districts about how residency is determined frequently occur. These disagreements can result in homeless children not attending school in either district.

*Space Limitations.* Some schools already are overcrowded, making it difficult for school systems to accommodate homeless children.

*Lack of Transportation.* Another major obstacle to attending school is lack of transportation between shelters and school systems (Johnson, 1992; National Coalition for the Homeless, 1987). Even when school systems supply transportation to maintain homeless children in their schools, travel may involve long and circuitous routes, creating additional strain in their already stressful lives (Johnson, 1992).

*Lack of Academic Records.* Frequently, obtaining records from schools that homeless children previously attended is time consuming and results in delayed registration of these children at the new school. Records from previous schools may be incomplete, further delaying these children's entrance into schools. The parents' level of stress, preoccupation with finding temporary or permanent housing, and frequent inability to deal effectively with bureaucracies make it extremely arduous for them to provide the necessary documents to enroll their children in school in a timely fashion.

*Need for Special Education.* The sizable numbers of homeless children needing special education services present difficulties for many school systems. Entrance into such programs usually requires comprehensive and often lengthy evaluations and procedures to ensure an appropriate educational placement. Despite the desirability and usefulness of these processes, homeless children's transience renders standard assessment methods ineffective. Thus, homeless children often receive inadequate educational services because they cannot obtain timely assessments and rapid implementation of education plans (National Coalition for the Homeless, 1987; Tower, 1992).

*Guardianship Requirements.* Because many homeless children often reside with extended family or friends who do not have legal custody of them, there is no one with the authority to act on the children's behalf. As a result it is difficult to register these children at a new school, enroll them in special education programs, or obtain appropriate social services.

*Stereotypes and Prejudice.* Administrators, faculty, and staff frequently hold prejudicial attitudes and stereotyped notions about homeless families (Gewirtzman & Fodor, 1987; Gonzalez, 1992). Such attitudes prevent the children and their parents from feeling welcomed and valued as important participants in the system and consequently discourage their attendance at school. In addition, these children frequently join classrooms in which patterns of interaction, friendships, and group norms already are established among classmates and between students and their teachers. Because homeless children are by definition transient, the psychological investment of teachers and classmates in them is often difficult to create (Walsh, 1992).

## SCHOOL SYSTEMS AND HOMELESS CHILDREN

Educational systems may mitigate the myriad negative aspects in the lives of homeless children. Studies reveal that many of these children perceive school as an important factor in helping them cope with their living situations (Timberlake, 1993; Timberlake & Sabatino, 1994; Walsh, 1992). Walsh found that some homeless children considered schools steady, secure, and safe environments. She argued that schools can offer these children a place relatively free of worry, can create opportunities for relationships with caring teachers, and can help children develop their own strengths and interests.

Schools also provide a distraction from the often chaotic world of shelters and the street. The predictable routines and sets of consequences ordinarily provided in schools serve to combat the pervasive disorder related to homelessness (Walsh, 1992). In addition, opportunities for feeling competent can occur as these children master new skills and form positive relationships with peers, teachers, and school support staff (Walsh, 1992).

Even though many homeless children do not remain in the same school after dislocation from their homes, the familiarity of a school environment may offer some continuity and predictability in their lives. In addition to providing continuity, school personnel, particularly social workers, can offer a variety of experiences and services that help alleviate the numerous negative effects related to being homeless.

## COLLABORATIVE SCHOOL–COMMUNITY MODEL FOR EFFECTIVE SERVICE DELIVERY

In spite of the obstacles that homeless children face in obtaining an education, schools continue to be ideal settings for developing and coordinating the array of educational and social services these children require. Because schools are a universal part of children's and families' lives, providing services in these systems can be less stigmatizing than services in private and public institutions that are identified with offering such assistance (Gewirtzman & Fodor, 1987).

Providing comprehensive services to homeless children and families can be done most effectively through a collaborative model encompassing professionals both within and outside the school system. School systems have increasingly recognized the importance of developing interdisciplinary teams to provide effective and comprehensive educational and social services to children and their families. This process encourages interdisciplinary cooperation, which potentially ensures that the needs of the whole child and family are considered and addressed.

Although collaborative approaches exist in many schools, communities also need to develop similar structures among all human services delivery systems and other institutions that offer assistance to children and families. It is assumed that establishing viable collaborative structures and relationships among institutions enables them to more successfully meet the diverse needs of various populations.

Swan and Morgan (1993) defined *collaboration* as "efforts to unite organizations and people for the purpose of achieving common goals that could not be accomplished by any single organization or individual acting alone" (p. 19). They further contended that successful collaborative efforts among institutions generally subscribe to the following premises:

- Each service delivery system recognizes that one agency alone cannot provide all of the complex and often diverse needs of clients.
- Limited resources and categorical foci of programs require agencies to coordinate efforts to avoid unnecessary duplication and service gaps.
- The service delivery system must consist of varied options to address the continuum of clients' needs.
- Agencies must provide support and assistance to one another.
- A structured system of interagency cooperation must exist (Swan & Morgan, 1993).

Through collaborative structures, common goals are articulated clearly and agency resources such as time, personnel, materials, funds, and facilities are committed equitably and efficiently. Although shared decision making exists, each agency maintains control of its own contributions and does not experience any loss of power in relationship to other institutions involved in the collaborative effort (Swan & Morgan, 1993).

Jordan and Hernandez (1990) argued that collaboration among organizations functions most effectively when there is a set of planning principles and procedures rather than a prescribed structure for defining specific kinds of services. These planning principles include clearly defined target populations, development of systemwide goals with measurable external objectives and outcomes, establishment of treatment services and standards, creation of interagency coalitions, and a system for monitoring procedures and client outcome evaluation.

Given the concrete educational and social services required to enable homeless families to resolve their difficulties, many institutions must be actively involved. Concrete services such as obtaining temporary housing, clothing, free school meals, medical care, transportation, and before- and after-school programs; facilitating the process of registering in schools; and obtaining funds for school supplies and fees, tutoring services, recreational opportunities, and other significant services are important (Gonzalez, 1992; Johnson, 1992). Ideally, interagency relationships should exist among schools and health, mental health, and child welfare agencies; recreation centers, homeless shelters, housing authorities, and churches; job training and educational programs for adults; the courts; and volunteer organizations. Such coordinated efforts among institutions can result in the experience of less internal stress in organizations, because avenues to accessing the necessary resources needed by such families will already be in place.

A collaborative model also potentially provides an effective structure for coordinating a proactive approach to preventing families from becoming homeless. Social workers in schools can be instrumental in helping agencies create and implement preventive services. It is imperative, therefore, that social workers in school systems advocate actively in their communities for the development of both preventive and remedial approaches (Moroz & Segal, 1990).

## Role of the School System

School systems can be an important point of entry into an array of necessary services. Schools that are part of a collaborative structure within and outside the educational system will experience greater success in assessing and intervening in the problems of homeless children and their families because coordinated services can address more effectively the diverse needs of this very vulnerable population.

Urban schools, in particular, confront complex emotional and social problems. Many programs have been established that effectively and efficiently coordinate available resources on-site at schools. Because of the continued decline of many inner cities, schools often are the only major institution involved in the lives of many low-income and disenfranchised children and families.

Schools must address these complex issues in conjunction with their primary mission of educating children. Individual systems cannot manage alone the multiplicity of problems that confront homeless children and their families. Coordinating interagency efforts primarily through schools can maximize the usefulness of services by providing them in an environment that is familiar and thereby potentially more acceptable to children and parents.

## Role of School Social Workers

Germain and Gitterman (1980) argued that a unique aspect of social work practice is its expertise in working effectively with multiple systems. School social workers, therefore, can play an important role in creating, implementing, and maintaining a collaborative model, because they possess both the knowledge and skills necessary for intervening at individual, familial, institutional, and community levels. School social workers are the most likely to understand the many factors that affect the lives of homeless children and their families.

School social workers, in particular, are well situated to develop relationships with a variety of other social services agencies and health care facilities. Such extensive networking possibilities afford social workers the unique opportunity to bring diverse groups of organizations together to develop more effective collaborative efforts among them. Social workers can also help forge a collaborative structure through their understanding of team dynamics, institutional cultures, issues related to developing organizational policies, effective negotiating processes, and conflict resolution approaches.

In addition, social workers can readily identify the gaps in services that exist in their communities. Therefore, they can provide information to members of the collaborative structure that enables them to determine the most effective and cost-efficient way to address the unmet needs of the clients. Such a process ensures both more comprehensive delivery of services and the avoidance of unnecessary duplication of programs in communities.

Because many families perceive school systems as unsupportive, hostile, and uncaring because of earlier experiences with such institutions, social workers and other school personnel often face the challenge of engaging parents and children who are suspicious and distrustful of them. Social workers are accustomed to overcoming the obstacles that families frequently use to thwart successful engagement with the school system. Social workers initially can play a key role in orienting both parents and children to the school personnel, the philosophy of the school, and the array of services available within and outside the school (Gonzalez, 1992). In addition, advocating and networking through a collaborative structure for essential concrete services increases the likelihood of engendering positive relationships with these families.

Traditional services such as individual, family, and group treatments or a combination of these approaches can be used effectively once positive relationships are established between social workers and homeless families. Other treatment approaches such as socioeducational programs also may be used either as primary interventions or as adjuncts to traditional services.

## Educational Planning and Services

Ensuring that homeless children receive appropriate educational services is obviously important. Many of these children have problems associated either with learning disabilities or with inconsistent attendance at school. Schools must provide abbreviated assessments and rapid implementation of remedial services to provide meaningful assistance to these children (Tower, 1992). Social workers can facilitate a more timely process by developing, in conjunction with other relevant personnel, a more streamlined process of evaluation.

Even homeless children who do not require special educational services or remedial assistance encounter difficulty in completing their homework assignments. Many shelters for homeless people do not provide environments conducive to studying and completing homework. Schools need to develop on-site opportunities (for example, study halls, before- or after-school tutoring) for children to finish their assignments (Tower, 1992).

*Working with Teachers.* Many homeless children experience a great amount of shame and anxiety; they are often fearful that teachers and other children will ridicule and reject them. Facilitating the integration of homeless children into classrooms requires teachers to educate and sensitize other students about the common issues and feelings related to being without a permanent home (Tower, 1992). Social workers can help with this process by using group work approaches, either with or without teachers present, to facilitate the integration of homeless children into classrooms. They can identify and dispel misperceptions, prejudices, and myths about homeless children and their families.

Teachers have the most daily contact with homeless students in their classrooms; therefore, they are confronted consistently with developing a realistic level of educational expectations and achievable academic standards. Teachers also have to address the dynamics of the classroom and help homeless children and other students cooperate with one another. Teachers must be extremely sensitive and creative in managing this complex process. Social workers can facilitate teachers' efforts by validating the inherent challenges related to educating this population and providing information specific to the unique complexities of each homeless child and family so that teachers have a comprehensive understanding of each child's situation (Gewirtzman & Fodor, 1987; Tower, 1992). Social workers can keep teachers informed about the various services being offered homeless children and their families and any changes occurring in the lives of students and their parents.

Teachers can facilitate the learning process by tailoring the kind and amount of schoolwork so that homeless children can complete their assignments successfully during regular class time (Gewirtzman & Fodor, 1987; Gonzalez, 1992; Tower, 1992). Social workers can help them develop tailored, realistic academic assignments that can be done in a relatively short time and that will provide some sense of accomplishment and pride (Gewirtzman & Fodor, 1987).

*Working with Support Staff.* Support staff also require some information and education about issues related to homeless children and their families. Anxious or hostile homeless parents are more likely to follow through with registering their children in schools that demonstrate a positive attitude toward them from the earliest contact. Because support staff frequently have the initial contact with these parents, it is essential that they respond in a welcoming manner and facilitate connection with appropriate administrators and other relevant professionals within the educational system (Gewirtzman & Fodor, 1987; Gonzalez, 1992).

Social workers can offer support staff opportunities to discuss their concerns, issues, and attitudes toward homeless children and their families and provide useful strategies for relating effectively with this population. Consultations and training can be offered to support staff through individual or group meetings.

## CONCLUSION

School social workers perform essential roles and functions in addressing the concerns of homeless children and their families. Identifying, assessing, and developing strategies for intervening at individual, familial, institutional, and community levels afford social workers opportunities to develop comprehensive educational and social services for these children and their families. In addition, school social workers need to be acutely aware of institutional barriers that thwart the access of homeless children to quality education and essential social services. Challenging the rationale of these institutional barriers as well as creating policies and service delivery systems that are more conducive to assisting these children and their families is an important function of school social workers. Because social workers possess the knowledge and skills related to understanding and intervening at the multiple levels impinging on the lives of homeless children and their families, it is incumbent on these professionals to be actively involved in the development and provision of services to this exceptionally vulnerable and oppressed population.

## REFERENCES

Anderson, R. E., & Carter, I. (1990). *Human behavior in the social environment: A social-systems approach.* New York: Aldine de Gruyter.

Bassuk, E., & Rubin, L. (1987). Homeless children: A neglected population. *American Journal of Orthopsychiatry, 57,* 279–286.

Carter, B., & McGoldrick, M. (1989). Overview: The changing family life cycle. In B. Carter & M. McGoldrick (Eds.), *The changing family life cycle* (pp. 3–28). Boston: Allyn & Bacon.

Eddowes, E., & Hranitz, J. (1989). Educating children of the homeless. *Childhood Education, 65,* 197–200.

Erikson, E. H. (1980). *Identity and the life cycle.* New York: W. W. Norton.

Fellin, P. (1987). *The community and the social worker.* Itasca, IL: F. E. Peacock.

Germain, C. B., & Gitterman, A. (1980). *The life model of social work practice.* New York: Columbia University Press.

Gewirtzman, R., & Fodor, I. (1987). The homeless child at school: From welfare hotel to classroom. *Child Welfare, 66,* 237–245.

Gonzalez, M. (1992). Education climate for the homeless: Cultivating the family and school relationship. In J. H. Stronge (Ed.), *Educating homeless children and adolescents: Evaluating practice policy and practice* (pp. 194–211). Newbury Park, CA: Sage Publications.

Johnson, J. (1992). Educational support services for homeless children and youth. In J. H. Stronge (Ed.), *Educating homeless children and adolescents: Evaluating practice policy and practice* (pp. 153–176). Newbury Park, CA: Sage Publications.

Jordan, D. D., & Hernandez, M. (1990). The Ventura Planning Model: A proposal for mental health reform. *Journal of Mental Health Administration, 17*(1), 26–47.

Mahler, M. S., Pine, F., & Bergman, A. (1975). *The psychological birth of the human infant.* New York: Basic Books.

Minuchin, S. (1974). *Families and family therapy.* Cambridge, MA: Harvard University Press.

Molnar, J. M., & Rath, W. R. (1990). Constantly compromised: The impact of homelessness on children. *Journal of Social Issues, 46*(4), 109–124.

Moroz, K., & Segal, E. (1990). Homeless children: Intervention strategies for school social workers. *Social Work in Education, 12,* 134–143.

National Coalition for the Homeless. (1987). *Broken lives: Denial of education to homeless children.* Washington, DC: Author.

Rescorla, L., Parker, R., & Stolley, P. (1991). Ability, achievement and adjustment in homeless children. *American Journal of Orthopsychiatry, 61,* 210–220.

Stewart B. McKinney Homeless Assistance Act, P.L. 100-77, 101 Stat. 482 (1987).

Swan, W. W., & Morgan, J. (1993). *Collaborating for comprehensive services for young children and their families.* Baltimore: Paul H. Brookes.

Timberlake, E. M. (1993, May). *Homeless mothers and children.* Paper presented at the Annual Spring Institute of the School of Social Work of Loyola University of Chicago and the Chicago Institute of Clinical Social Work, Chicago.

Timberlake, E. M., & Sabatino, C. A. (1994). Homeless children: Impact of school attendance on self-esteem and loneliness. *Social Work in Education, 16,* 9–20.

Tower, C. (1992). The psychosocial context: Supporting education for homeless children and youth. In J. H. Stronge (Ed.), *Educating homeless children and adolescents: Evaluating practice policy and practice* (pp. 42–61). Newbury Park, CA: Sage Publications.

Van Ry, M. (1992). The context of family: Implications for educating homeless children. In J. H. Stronge (Ed.), *Educating homeless children and adolescents: Evaluating practice policy and practice* (pp. 62–76). Newbury Park, CA: Sage Publications.

Wall, J. (1993, May). *Remarks on Dr. Timberlake's presentation.* Paper presented at the Annual Spring Institute of the School of Social Work of Loyola University of Chicago and the Chicago Institute of Clinical Social Work, Chicago.

Walsh, M. (1992). *Moving to nowhere: Children's stories of homelessness.* Westport, CT: Greenwood Press.

*An earlier version of this chapter was presented at the Annual Spring Institute of the School of Social Work, Loyola University of Chicago, and the Chicago Institute of Clinical Social Work, May 1993, Chicago.*

*This chapter was originally published in the July 1996 issue of* Social Work in Education, *Vol. 18, pp. 135–144.*

# 34

# Using a Lawyer–Doctor Education Team for Substance Abuse Prevention in a Middle School

Lynne E. Orens, Lori J. Brady, and John E. McIntosh, Jr.

**D**espite the presence of substance abuse prevention programs in many public and private forums such as schools, churches, community centers, and health maintenance organizations, young people continue to turn to drugs and alcohol to cope with the stressors associated with the biological, cognitive, and social changes of adolescence (Beman, 1995). There is increasing evidence that children are willing to experiment with drugs and alcohol at a younger age. In the annual National High School Senior Survey on Drug Abuse funded by the National Institute on Drug Abuse (1991–1992), eighth graders reported increases from 1991 to 1992 in nearly every category of the survey, including frequency and types of drug use and availability of drugs. In 1992 eighth graders were significantly less likely than those in 1991 to see cocaine and crack as dangerous. Although this study has been issued every year since 1975, the researchers have been collecting data on eighth graders only since 1991.

In Fairfax County, Virginia, which has one of the highest per capita incomes in the United States, 120 of the school system's 57,225 middle and high school students were recommended for expulsion for drug and alcohol violations during the 1995–96 school year. Of these students, 52 (43 percent) were seventh and eighth graders (Fairfax County Public Schools, 1997). In the 1994–95 school year, 66 students were recommended for expulsion for these offenses; 15 (23 percent) were seventh and eighth graders. Although the number is very small, it nevertheless supports the need for education and prevention programs for these students. The Drug-Free Schools and Communities Act Amendments of 1989 (P.L. 101-226) requires schools to implement at least information programs to prevent substance abuse by students (Chang, 1993).

School-based education has attempted to affect drug use through factors at two levels: personal and social competence (Goodstadt, 1989). Personal competence includes possession of information about drugs and decision-making and problem-solving skills. One of the most effective ways to help young people make decisions about their choices in life is to help them understand that there are logical consequences to those decisions. By providing them with information about the medical and legal consequences of using drugs and alcohol, it is hoped that teenagers will be better able to make decisions that can help avoid life-altering situations.

It is important to provide this information in a meaningful and timely way. Early middle school is the most logical time and place for substance abuse prevention education to be provided. Doctors and lawyers, with their specific experiences and knowledge in dealing with the issues, are effective professionals to deliver the information. This article describes the local implementation of a nationwide substance abuse prevention program linking the public middle school setting with a doctor–lawyer team to help educate students about the consequences of substance abuse.

## LAWYER/DOCTOR EDUCATION TEAM COMMUNITY PROJECT

In 1993 the Lawyer/Doctor Education Team Project was developed by the American Bar Association's (ABA's) Special Committee on Youth Education for Citizenship and the American Medical Association's (AMA's) Department of Substance Abuse. Both organizations studied the many problems associated with the use of alcohol and drugs and found that many of the young people who had suffered adverse legal and medical effects of substance abuse were not aware of the possibility they would occur (McIntosh, 1995). The ABA and the AMA felt that their respective professions were qualified to carry out six tasks of effective prevention: (1) to affect policy, (2) to encourage the involvement of influential community members, (3) to provide authoritative and practical information, (4) to promote healthy lifestyles, (5) to strengthen social competence and peer resistance skills, and (6) to act as positive role models. The project called for doctors and lawyers to form teams with educators and leaders in youth-serving organizations in local communities and to lead discussions designed to educate students, parents, and teachers about the legal and medical consequences of substance abuse.

## IMPLEMENTING THE SCHOOL–COMMUNITY PROJECT IN FAIRFAX COUNTY

In spring 1993 the Fairfax County Bar Association, through its Medical/Legal Committee, initiated contact with the Fairfax County Public Schools Office of Alcohol and Other Drugs to explore how to implement the program in the schools. The office referred the committee to a school social worker assigned to one county middle school to initiate a pilot program. The middle school already had an active substance abuse awareness program that included a club for students called KIDDS (Keep Involved, Don't Do Substances), which continues to meet. For the past 11 years, faculty members have worn KIDDS T-shirts on the first Friday of each month. Eight medical–legal presentations were made between November 1993 and January 1994 to more than 600 students. By the end of the 1995–96 school year, the program had expanded to four middle schools in the county. The program expanded to seven middle schools during the 1996–97 school year.

A progress report issued by the Lawyer/Doctor Education Team Project in March 1994 indicated that the program had been implemented in 17 states in a variety of communities (ABA & AMA, 1994). Although some programs formed alliances with juvenile justice programs or community centers and some targeted fourth through sixth graders, most of the programs were school based and presented for seventh and eighth graders. Some states, such as Maryland, have teamed with civic organizations who have lent support and funding for ongoing community awareness in the form of videotapes and other resource materials. Other programs, such as one in Delaware, have a community service component in which students work with community-based organizations to design a drug awareness learning project.

## Presentations

The Medical/Legal Committee recruited volunteer doctors and lawyers who were qualified to address the issues involved and who had the interpersonal skills necessary to communicate effectively with middle school students. The committee solicited recommendations in the legal community from judges, juvenile criminal law practitioners, and former prosecutors. In the medical community, the committee recruited emergency room physicians, family practitioners, and addiction specialists. Both professional groups showed enthusiastic support for the program, and a good volunteer base was established. The ABA, in cooperation with the AMA, prepared a videotape to show how lawyer–doctor teams can interact effectively with young people, as well as a resource packet of lesson plans, fact sheets, posters, and other material to help with the presentations.

The first group of volunteers, four lawyers and five doctors, was given discussion outlines from the program called *Talking Points,* pamphlets published by both organizations (ABA & AMA, n.d.-a, n.d.-b) for their respective professionals. Both outlines describe the purpose of the presentations. The lawyers' outline defines a "juvenile," describes the penalties governing illegal use of drugs and alcohol and driving under the influence, explains how these laws affect juveniles, and discusses how offenses are recorded and how they can affect a young person in the future. The doctors' outline defines specific medical concerns and statistics about substance abuse and how these concerns relate to adolescent drug and alcohol use, separates facts about using drugs and alcohol from common misbeliefs, highlights issues of peer pressure, identifies signs that addiction may be present, and explains where students can go for help.

Both professionals are advised to speak to student groups at an age-appropriate level, without "talking down" or preaching to them. They are advised to include activities that will encourage interaction with the students and that will challenge students' understanding.

## School Personnel

To ensure the success of the program, the social worker enlisted support from each school principal and served as the program's coordinator and liaison between the faculty and the teams. The next step was engaging the teaching staff, who ultimately implement the program. It was decided in the pilot school to implement the program through the social studies curriculum and to work with the teachers of seventh graders. Dates and times were coordinated with the teachers to accommodate a presentation that would allow time for questions and answers as well as creative interactions between the students and speakers.

Once the dates and times were established, the lawyer coordinating the teams arranged for presenters. The school social worker contacted the presenters to determine needs such as overhead projectors, special seating, and so forth. An attempt was made to find a space to accommodate a large number of students while maintaining an atmosphere that enabled students to ask questions and feel involved in the discussion. In some instances, index cards were made available for students who did not feel comfortable asking questions in the large group. Students were able to write their questions anonymously for the presenters' response.

The teachers prepared the students for the presentations by emphasizing the mature content of the material and the professional team's expertise with the subject matter. They also tried to prepare the students for some of the graphic pictures that they would see or stories they would hear.

## Content

Although each presenter used the outline created by his or her professional organization, the presentations were diverse. Some of the presenters included role-playing a variety of situations with the students. Students were asked to consider themselves as members of a jury in a court case of a defendant charged with vehicular manslaughter while driving under the influence. A lively discussion followed about how the students would vote as jurors. A slide presentation of pictures of accident victims in the emergency room was interspersed with statistics on the effects of increasing amounts of beer consumed over time. The medical effects of specific substances on various organs of the human body was a powerful presentation tool.

Many of the presenters used personal examples to help students connect factual information to real-life situations. Lawyers' presentations used court cases to illustrate the legal consequences of situations such as serving beer to minors at a party. They addressed questions such as who can be arrested and why, what happens after the arrest is made, and how this affects the future driver's license of a student who is age 15 at the time of the arrest. Some discussions offered students alternatives to managing potentially compromising situations with friends and illegal substances.

Presentations raised specific concerns for students who were coping with substance abusers in their family. At times students indicated more personal experiences and concerns, especially about the medical consequences of alcohol abuse. To help those who wanted to share personal concerns, students were advised to contact the school social worker or guidance counselor for a private meeting.

## Program Evaluation

After the presentations, teachers asked the students to summarize in writing two legal consequences and two medical consequences of substance abuse, what they thought of the program, and what they would like to know about substance abuse that was not presented. Because each session was different in content and style of the presenter, it helped to make certain that the most important facts and ideas from the presentation were summarized.

Overall, the students' comments were very positive. Many wrote that they learned new information about what drugs can do to the body. In one program, students reported learning that a small amount of alcohol can impair judgment, that alcohol can have effects on babies born to women who drink, and that there are a variety of chemicals in tobacco. They were surprised to learn of the legal repercussions that can prevent them from entering certain professions and from obtaining a driver's license. Students also were surprised that lawyers will charge a large fee to represent them in court. They enjoyed the personal stories, as well as some of the personalities of the presenters. In thank-you notes to the presenters, some students revealed personal concerns about how to get their parents to stop drinking or smoking. They expressed feeling motivated to stand up to peer pressure and hoped that their friends who smoked and drank would stop as a result of hearing the information. Perhaps most telling was a quote from one student, who wrote, "I thought things like that happened to other people, not to people my age."

The teachers are asked to evaluate the program with a simple form that ranks the relevance and effectiveness of the presentation and its format. They are also asked to comment on the most and least helpful aspects of the presentation. The teachers have welcomed the opportunity to have other professionals help them educate the students. They expressed the positive value of the program, feeling that students benefited from the knowledge imparted and from the contact with professionals who deal with real-life situations daily. They also expressed concern and dismay about how much the students knew about various drugs.

After the presentations, the school social worker wrote thank-you letters to the presenters that included feedback from the students and teachers about the value of the program. This feedback has been helpful to the doctors and lawyers in preparing for future presentations.

## IMPLICATIONS FOR SOCIAL WORK PRACTICE

The role of school social workers encompasses a variety of interventions in dealing with the increasing problems of substance abuse. These interventions include work with individual students, with groups of children of substance abusers, and with staff to educate them about the warning signs of substance abuse. One of the most important functions of school social workers is linking students and families to community-based programs. Involvement in the Lawyer/Doctor Education Team Project is a logical extension of this role.

As Cobia, Center, Buckhalt, and Meadows (1995) pointed out, it is more difficult, and possibly unrealistic, for any one professional to possess the expertise to solve problems alone. Communication and cooperation with those in other professions is needed if the scope of intervention is to match the scope of the needs of students. Schools alone cannot assume responsibility for all the problems that prevent youths from succeeding. Bringing together all the services needed by at-risk students is historically the function of school social workers.

## REFERENCES

American Bar Association, & American Medical Association. (1994). *Lawyer/Doctor Education Team Project: Progress report.* Chicago: Authors.

American Bar Association, & American Medical Association. (n.d.-a). *Lawyer/Doctor Education Team Project: Talking points for doctors.* Chicago: Authors.

American Bar Association, & American Medical Association. (n.d.-b). *Lawyer/Doctor Education Team Project: Talking points for lawyers.* Chicago: Authors.

Beman, D. S. (1995). Risk factors leading to adolescent substance abuse. *Adolescence, 30,* 201–208.

Chang, V. N. (1993). Prevent and empower: A student-to-student strategy with alcohol abuse. *Social Work in Education, 15,* 207–213.

Cobia, D. C., Center, H., Buckhalt, J. A., & Meadows, M. E. (1995). An interprofessional model for serving youth at risk for substance abuse: The team case study. *Journal of Drug Education, 25,* 99–109.

Drug-Free Schools and Communities Act Amendments of 1989, P.L. 101-226, 103 Stat. 1928.

Fairfax County Public Schools, Management Information Services. (1997). [Data on expulsions]. Fairfax, VA: Author.

Goodstadt, M. S. (1989). Substance abuse curricula vs. school drug policies. *Journal of School Health, 59,* 246–250.

McIntosh, J. (1995, May). Seventh graders relate to "real consequences" presented in foundation's drug education program. *Fairfax Bar Journal,* p. 1.

National Institute on Drug Abuse. (1991–1992). *Monitoring the Future study.* Washington, DC: Author.

---

*This chapter was originally published in the July 1997 issue of* Social Work in Education, *Vol. 19, pp. 203–208.*

# 35 The School's and Community's Role in the Prevention of Youth Suicide

Brenda Robinson Ward

The statistics on suicidal behavior among youths are staggering. Suicide is the second leading cause of death for young people ages 15 to 24, second only to accidental deaths (Fairchild, 1986; Peach & Reddick, 1991; Smaby, Peterson, Bergman, Bacig, & Swearingen, 1990). Additionally, the Suicide Prevention Center of Los Angeles estimated that 50 percent of reported accidental deaths among children are, in fact, suicides (Stefanowski-Harding, 1990). Research has shown that between 1960 and 1986, the suicide rate among youths ages 15 to 19 increased 142 percent (Allberg & Chu, 1990). Suicide attempts are increasing at an even greater rate than completed suicides. For every completed adolescent suicide, there are 50 to 100 attempts (Kalafat, 1990). Suicidal behavior is occurring at increasingly younger ages as well. For children under the age of 12, there are 200 reported suicides each year in the United States (Stiles & Kottman, 1990).

## SCHOOL'S ROLE IN PREVENTION

Suicide by youths "is a societal problem with tremendous implications for the schools" (Poland, 1989, p. 1). School personnel have the opportunity to take leadership roles in addressing the issue of youth suicide. School staff interact daily with students and can closely observe students for changes in behavior, can understand the stressful situations students encounter, and can respond to direct or subtle cries for help (Leenaars & Wenckstern, 1991).

The schools, however, have been reluctant to develop and implement formal intervention programs: "At present, most suicide intervention programs in the schools are developed in the aftermath of a crisis, and there is a tendency to allow such programs to remain dormant much of the time" (Poland, 1989, p. 1). Three considerations justify the schools' involvement before a crisis: (1) schools have a responsibility to help students become productive citizens, (2) schools have a responsibility to identify and help resolve problems that interfere with the learning process, and (3) schools have crucial opportunities and resources to observe and assist youths who may be at risk for suicide (Leenaars & Wenckstern, 1991).

Schools must take the lead and develop suicide intervention plans. Social workers can function as key personnel in such plans. In a recent study, 60 school counselors in six southeastern states reported that a home–school–community network was needed to address the youth suicide issue (Peach & Reddick, 1991).

Which school staff member is better prepared to address an issue in this context than the school social worker?

## THEORETICAL BASE

In recent years, there has been "a gradual shift away from the bandage, after-the-fact approach to mental health" intervention (Wodarski, 1988, p. 6). Programs aimed at *prevention*, defined as discouraging a problematic behavior before it actually happens or before it becomes a problem, are becoming the key to successful intervention (Wodarski, 1988). A systems approach is essential in preventing youth suicides: "If the present course is to be changed, effort is needed from all segments of the community, including teenagers and their families, schools, churches, community organizations and medical personnel as well as mental health professionals and volunteers" (Governor's Advocacy Council on Children and Youth, 1985, p. 219). According to McLaughlin and Vacha (1992), a common element across all school-based programs for at-risk youths is early intervention or prevention.

According to the Committee for Economic Development, providing prevention services to at-risk youths is an "excellent investment . . . that can be postponed only at a great cost to society" (Schorr & Schorr, 1989, p. 273). Prevention programs have demonstrated their effectiveness in many ways. For example, according to Schorr and Schorr (1989), "good prenatal care reduces low birthweight" and expensive in-hospital care; "good family and social services reduce the need for . . . out-of-home placement of children"; and positive "pre-school experiences and a good start in elementary school [can] reduce the need for special education services and improve other social outcomes" (pp. 271–272).

## TEAMWORK AND COLLABORATION

The school social worker can be most effective by working as a member of a school-based suicide intervention team. As members of the team, the school social worker and the school counselor may have overlapping roles. The individual responsibilities of the two professionals may vary from school to school, depending on the specific expertise each brings to the team. However, the most successful suicide intervention program will be the one in which these two professionals, with equally important skills, relax professional boundaries and strive for teamwork.

"Children who hurt, hurt all over. Children who fail, fail at everything they do. Risk is pervasive" (Frymier, 1992, p. 258). School personnel must work together, as well as with families and community organizations, to address the many needs of children in our schools.

A team approach also helps "to ease the burdens of this work" (Leenaars & Wenckstern, 1991, p. 223). Team intervention offers collegial support, feedback, and opportunities for resource sharing. Teamwork should include all school staff. Student services staff, to whom others turn in times of crisis, can be trained in this specialty area and assisted to supplement their already available skills and techniques, making their contributions to a suicide intervention team particularly effective (Johnson & Maile, 1987).

The school administration's function is to create policy, sanction activities, and demonstrate active support of the program. Classroom teachers can address a range of topics related to suicide prevention, such as peer relationships and adolescent stresses, and can "note academic performance, general behavior, and interaction with peers" (Johnson & Maile, 1987, p. 226). Art, music, and physical education teachers can provide the opportunity for expression of feelings and physical activity for a positive release of negative emotions. Library staff can "acquire suitable materials relevant to students' problem areas and can provide a quiet place to work" (Johnson & Maile, 1987, p. 226). Support staff (such as cafeteria and custodial staff and bus drivers) can note eating changes, observe social interactions, and help provide a supportive milieu. Student services staff can monitor internal support networks and maintain relationships with students, their families, and the outside helping networks—a role of particular importance to school social workers (Johnson & Maile, 1987). It is imperative that all school staff be included in training sessions and encouraged to give input to the team.

## SCHOOL–COMMUNITY PROGRAM DEVELOPMENT

Several important preliminary steps must be taken as a part of program development. The first is to gain administrative support: "The key to whether a suicide intervention program is implemented in a school is whether the top administrators support the program" (Poland, 1989, p. 60). Administrative support is "crucial to gaining community support, promoting staff support, forming an effective assessment team, gaining access to . . . resources, and promoting a school atmosphere conducive to a successful program" (Cultice, 1992, p. 69). The school social worker can seek the administration's support by demonstrating the need for the services through collection of statistics from municipal, county, state, and national sources. Local mental health centers, medical centers, law enforcement organizations, social services agencies, and coroners' offices can provide data about youth suicide in the area.

A community crisis intervention committee can be established to assist with program development: "Since youth crisis is a community problem, no one individual or agency can deal effectively with the issue. A collaborative effort is essential" (Cultice, 1992, p. 69). Committee members should include educators, administrators, student services staff, mental health and social services staff, law enforcement personnel, public health workers, clergy, and an attorney. In addition, community agencies and the media should be informed about the program and its purpose (Cultice, 1992). The school social worker can be very active in this initial process by keeping the administration informed, assisting with the development of the committee, and participating as a committee member. In addition, a comprehensive program should address the issues of prevention, intervention, and "postvention" (Cultice, 1992; Leenaars & Wenckstern, 1991) and should include evaluation as its final component.

### Community Prevention: School-Based Services for All Youths

Prevention includes activities that help youths, families, and the community to prevent suicides, "to identify those youth who are at-risk for suicide," and "to develop an awareness of and a plan of action for coping with the issues sur-rounding youth suicide" (Cultice, 1992, p. 71).

Prevention activities should begin in kindergarten and continue through high school. The need to begin intervention early is evident. By conservative esti-mates, 10 percent of first graders and 50 percent of third graders have at least a basic understanding of suicide (Normand & Mishara, 1992). Research has shown that early intervention can effectively identify and assist at-risk children. The emphasis in the earlier grades should be on strengthening the child's "ability to cope with the interpersonal and academic demands of school" (Munn, McAlpine, & Taylor, 1989, p. 372). Specific intervention strategies "include improving so-cial interaction, cooperation, concentration, achievement, and self-esteem" (p. 372). The school social worker in a team effort with the school counselor can provide the intervention directly or serve as a consultant to teachers, volun-teers, and others providing the intervention in the early grades.

*In-service Training.* The social worker–counselor team can play a major role in another aspect of prevention by providing in-service training to other school personnel. Critical areas for staff development include early identification of risk, interpersonal communication skills, and enhancement of self-concept and coping skills (Fairchild, 1986). The school social worker–counselor team can teach teachers and other staff to recognize signs of suicide potential and inform them of the referral process to school-based helpers. The team can assist teachers with communication skills and discipline approaches that will enable them to relate more effectively to students. Teachers and other staff can learn ways to boost self-concept in the classroom and to include decision making and problem solv-ing as part of a student's daily routine, thus enhancing coping skills (Fairchild, 1986).

*Family–Peer–Community Involvement.* Families play an important role in suicidal students' crises and need to be involved in prevention and intervention training. Workshops designed to help parents improve their parenting skills can be offered. The primary purpose of such programs is to "provide informa-tion regarding how to . . . effectively manage and communicate with [their] children" (Fairchild, 1986, p. 327).

In addition to parent education, programs with specific suicide-related con-tent should be used to inform students directly about suicide: "These programs often combine emotional development content that deals with life factors such as depression, loss, and substance abuse, and suicide content that is significantly related to these other problems" (Leenaars & Wenckstern, 1991, p. 88). Students can be taught the warning signs of suicide and appropriate interventions, such as what to do if a friend talks about suicide and how to use the resources avail-able at the school. Because most students tend to discuss suicidal thoughts first with a peer rather than an adult, this student training is an essential part of the prevention program. The school social worker–counselor team can present this part of the program directly to the students or can provide consultation to the classroom teacher as needed. School social workers can also be instrumental in coordinating a peer support network to ensure that a receptive and attentive group is ready to appropriately respond to suicidal ideation.

Parent organizations, mental health clinics, other community agencies, and the media can be tremendous resources to schools in both implementing and maintaining a suicide prevention program: "The school district should assume a leadership role to call youth suicide to the attention of the community" (Poland, 1989, p. 97). The support of the community can be a crucial asset to the prevention program. As the program is coordinated with people and agencies in the community, the school can develop a community support network with other professionals. The result is that students' needs are better served and prevention is more effective. The school social worker can act as liaison to ensure that agencies work together.

## Intervention: Specific Services for At-Risk Youths

The second element of a comprehensive suicide prevention program is intervention "to interfere with the chain of events that may lead to suicide" (Cultice, 1992, p. 71). Intervention consists of "those coordinated services and activities that are directed toward all youth, but especially those youth who are identified as at-risk for suicide" (p. 71). Intervention aims to identify the problem early so that an appropriate response is immediately available. Intervention includes establishing effective and appropriate referral links with community resources and ensuring follow-up with students, parents, and outside helping resources (Leenaars & Wenckstern, 1991).

*Clues to Potential Suicide.* Most suicidal people are ambivalent about dying and often provide clues to others about their intentions: "Researchers have been able to conclude that many people who committed suicide spoke to teachers, doctors, or professionals a relatively short time before their deaths" (Crespi, 1990, p. 257). Clues can be verbal, behavioral, situational, and syndromatic (Fairchild, 1986). Verbal clues often have a theme of loneliness, despair, and helplessness (Cohen, 1991).

Any sudden change in typical behavior is significant. Giving away possessions, making a will, and distancing from others are behavioral clues to possible suicidal intent (Fairchild, 1986). The most significant behavioral clue is a previous attempt. A past suicide attempt greatly increases the current risk for suicide.

Situational clues include family problems, expulsion from school, death of a loved one, the end of a relationship, and legal troubles. "Depression is one of the most common syndromatic clues" (Fairchild, 1986, p. 331). Depression may be expressed in many ways, including but not limited to feelings of unhappiness and worthlessness, irritability, changes in sleep and eating patterns, social withdrawal, and other significant changes in behavior.

It is important to note that in some cases no clues are evident. Even in these circumstances, however, the initial ambivalence is present and can be used to foster effective intervention.

*Other Risk Factors.* Although there is no single predictor of suicide, other risk factors that should be considered are drug and alcohol use (Felts, Chenier, & Barnes, 1992; Kalafat, 1990; Kandel, Raveis, & Davies, 1991; Kirkpatrick-Smith & Rich, 1991–1992), a history of impulsive and aggressive behavior (Kalafat, 1990), identification as gifted (Weisse, 1990) or learning disabled (Kalafat, 1990), perfectionism (Kalafat, 1990), and incidence of suicide in the family (Kalafat, 1990). School social worker–counselor teams can provide other school personnel with in-service training about clues and risk factors. By having this knowledge, school personnel will be able to identify students who need to be referred for further assessment.

*Assessment of Potential Suicidal Behavior.* The school social worker can be instrumental in ensuring that the student receives an assessment by a qualified professional trained in the mental health field. The social worker, of course, may possess the appropriate training and may conduct the initial assessment. An assessment to determine the suicide risk includes discovering what events occurred in the student's life that are contributing to a state of crisis. Helpers must ask questions that will clarify the student's psychological state (Fairchild, 1986). One pertinent question is whether the student has had any thoughts about harming himself or herself. Asking the question does not plant the idea, as some believe; in fact, many youths are relieved to be able to discuss their suicidal thoughts in an open and honest manner. The helper must attempt to discover coping skills that the student has used successfully in the past and that may be useful again. The helper also must identify individuals who are important to the student. These significant others can provide critical support during a crisis.

Social and personal resources must also be assessed. The more resources available to the student, the more successful the crisis intervention (Fairchild, 1986). Psychiatric and medical status must be assessed because previous psychiatric care or medical problems can increase the risk of suicide.

And finally, questions about a suicide plan must be asked. The suicide plan details the student's ways and means of committing suicide (Fairchild, 1986): "The intensity of the . . . student's distress is reflected in . . . [the] plan" (p. 339). The four criteria that need careful consideration are method, specificity, availability, and lethality. In general, the more realistic and specific the plan, the more available the means, and the more lethal the method, the higher the risk for suicide (Fairchild, 1986).

*Crisis Counseling and Community Referral.* Following assessment, the social worker implements additional crisis intervention activities if necessary, including initial crisis counseling and referral. The counseling focuses on the immediate prevention of self-harm and stabilization of the student's present level of coping. The helper involves the student in discussion and exploration of feelings and identification of sources of the crisis and its effects on the student. "Employing a problem-solving strategy assists students in coping with their present crises effectively and teaches them a process that they can employ in future situations" (Fairchild, 1986, p. 351). The school social worker can facilitate student participation in this process by being encouraging and by reinforcing the student's positive behavior.

A referral to another community professional is indicated when the assessment reveals that suicide potential is high. The school social worker can act as liaison with other community agencies, such as a mental health clinic, to facilitate the referral. It is important that the referral process be developed before a crisis so that it flows smoothly during an actual crisis. It is imperative that the helper who initiates the referral "remain involved until contact is made and a relationship is established between [the] suicidal student and the resource person [or] agency" (Fairchild, 1986, p. 359).

   *Confidentiality: A Legal and Ethical Bind.* When providing suicide intervention, the social worker must face the important issue of confidentiality. According to the *NASW Code of Ethics* (National Association of Social Workers, 1994), "The social worker should respect the privacy of clients and hold in confidence all information obtained in the course of professional service" (p. 1). The potential exceptions to the helper's ability to maintain confidentiality must be clearly understood by both the helper and the student at the outset. One such exception occurs when the student's condition indicates impending danger of self-harm. Helpers must breach confidentiality in this case to protect the health and safety of the student. When it becomes necessary, the disclosure should be limited only to those who have a need to know: a school administrator, student services team, the parents of the student, and other mental health professionals who will provide additional help (Zirkel, 1992).

   The disclosure of confidential information is an ethical and legal issue. Ethically, the helper has an obligation to maintain the student's privacy and to prevent harm to the student whenever possible. However, to keep suicide intent confidential does not meet the ethical requirement, because harm or even death may occur.

   Legally, the helper "may be vulnerable to suit for breaching confidentiality" (Sheeley & Herlihy, 1989, p. 94). Alternatively, if a student is injured or commits suicide and the social worker could have prevented it, there is also the potential for liability. "Courts, [however], have consistently . . . ruled that disclosure of confidential communications by other mental health . . . [professionals] is justifiable if . . . made in the best interest of the client" (p. 94). "Recognizing that ethics and law are overlapping, not coterminous, we cannot be confident about keeping all confidences" (Zirkel, 1992, p. 734).

## Postvention: School–Community Services after a Completed Suicide

"Postvention" refers to those coordinated services and activities that assist youths, their family and friends, other students, and the community in coping with the aftermath of a student's suicide (Cultice, 1992). Survivors' reactions to suicide range from normal adaptive to maladaptive coping responses (Fairchild, 1986): "The focus of postvention activities is to enable survivors to honestly discuss the suicide, explore their feelings of shock, grief, anger, guilt, and learn how to cope with the loss" (pp. 363–364). School social worker–counselor teams can play an active role in providing direct intervention to survivors, particularly the other students in the school. Solid preparation before a crisis occurs, good communication, a caring staff, and honesty are elements of a good postvention program (Barish, 1991). "Under no circumstances should suicide be treated as glorious, heroic, or noble" (p. 100). Asking students to reflect on alternatives to suicide is a positive approach to life, not death.

   The Centers for Disease Control and Prevention recommend that schools provide a "timely flow of accurate and appropriate information" to the media following a suicide (Leenaars & Wenckstern, 1991, p. 217). A media spokesperson for the schools, preferably from the social worker–counselor team, should, with administrative support, provide the needed information to media sources. This ensures that someone who thoroughly understands the program can accurately portray and emphasize the positive aspects of the program (Leenaars & Wenckstern, 1991).

It is important for all helpers to be debriefed after a suicide. The school social worker should arrange an outside source to provide this service. Debriefing provides an opportunity for staff to talk about the suicide with other professionals, giving the helpers an outlet for their stresses and validating their feelings, thereby reducing the negative effects on the helpers themselves.

### Program Evaluation

Evaluation of the program is the final component of the overall plan. It is recommended that the program be evaluated five to six months after implementation (Cultice, 1992). Specifically, the effectiveness of the program's interventions with at-risk students and the effectiveness of the prototype used in meeting the needs of the youths should be evaluated. Conventional indications of effectiveness may be reflected by an "increase in . . . referrals of at-risk youth" to school or community helpers, "the operation of the program . . . [within] the projected time [frame], personnel and cost estimates, and a broadened comprehension of the symptoms, causes, and prevention of youth suicide on the part of school staff, parents, . . . and the public at large" (Cultice, 1992, p. 71).

In addition to outcome measures, evaluation should focus on the materials and processes used in the program (Leenaars & Wenckstern, 1991). The school social worker–counselor team should use both quantitative and qualitative methods to gain the most comprehensive results. The team should ensure that evaluation is an ongoing process.

## CONCLUSION

A comprehensive program including suicide prevention, intervention, and postvention offered in schools is crucial for addressing the increase in youth suicide. School staff's ability and availability to identify and respond to at-risk behavior is integral to effective suicide intervention: "Suicide prevention is everyone's responsibility. Every school district needs a comprehensive suicide intervention program that is coordinated with community resources" (Poland, 1989, p. 189). A school-based intervention program with community involvement enables professionals and others to share the responsibility for assisting students at risk for suicide.

School student services professionals must work closely together in a team approach to meet the varied needs of their students. Without such an approach, it is unlikely that a suicide intervention program will be successful: "Partnerships are borne of collective self-interest and a shared professional agenda" (Gibelman, 1993, p. 51).

A coordinated approach can encourage funding and convince school boards, parent groups, and community organizations of the necessity of confronting, within the school setting, suicidal and other high-risk behaviors (Smaby et al., 1990). School social workers have the expertise to offer, and they must establish and maintain key team member roles in comprehensive suicide intervention programs.

## REFERENCES

Allberg, W. R., & Chu, L. (1990). Understanding adolescent suicide: Correlates in a developmental perspective. *School Counselor, 37,* 343–350.

Barish, S. (1991, November). Responding to adolescent suicide: A multi-faceted plan. *NASSP Bulletin,* pp. 98–103.

Cohen, Y. (1991). Gender identity conflicts in adolescents as motivation for suicide. *Adolescence, 26,* 19–29.

Crespi, T. D. (1990). Approaching adolescent suicide: Queries and signposts. *School Counselor, 37,* 256–259.

Cultice, W. W. (1992, April). Establishing an effective crisis intervention program. *NASSP Bulletin,* pp. 68–72.

Fairchild, T. N. (1986). *Crisis intervention for school-based helpers.* Springfield, IL: Charles C Thomas.

Felts, W. M., Chenier, T., & Barnes, R. (1992). Drug use and suicide ideation and behaviors among North Carolina public school students. *American Journal of Public Health, 82,* 870–872.

Frymier, J. (1992). Children who hurt, children who fail. *Phi Delta Kappan, 74,* 257–259.

Gibelman, M. (1993). School social workers, counselors, and psychologists in collaboration: A shared agenda. *Social Work in Education, 15,* 45–53.

Governor's Advocacy Council on Children and Youth. (1985). *Excerpts from "Teenage Suicide: The Final Cry."* Raleigh, NC: Author.

Johnson, S. W., & Maile, L. J. (1987). *Suicide and the schools: A handbook for prevention, intervention, and rehabilitation.* Springfield, IL: Charles C Thomas.

Kalafat, J. (1990). Adolescent suicide and the implications for school response programs. *School Counselor, 37,* 359–369.

Kandel, D. B., Raveis, V. H., & Davies, M. (1991). Suicidal ideation in adolescence: Depression, substance abuse, and other risk factors. *Journal of Youth and Adolescence, 20,* 289–308.

Kirkpatrick-Smith, J., & Rich, A. R. (1991–1992). Psychological vulnerability and substance abuse as predictors of suicide ideation among adolescents. *Omega, 24(1),* 21–32.

Leenaars, A. A., & Wenckstern, S. (1991). *Suicide prevention in schools.* New York: Hemisphere.

McLaughlin, T. F., & Vacha, E. F. (1992). Schools programs for at-risk children and youth: A review. *Education and Treatment of Children, 15,* 255–267.

Munn, J., McAlpine, A. H., & Taylor, L. (1989). The kindergarten intervention program: Development of an early mental health program using trained volunteers. *School Counselor, 36,* 371–375.

National Association of Social Workers. (1994). *NASW code of ethics.* Washington, DC: Author.

Normand, C. L., & Mishara, B. L. (1992). The development of the concept of suicide in children. *Omega, 25(3),* 183–203.

Peach, L., & Reddick, T. L. (1991). Counselors can make a difference in preventing adolescent suicide. *School Counselor, 38,* 107–110.

Poland, S. (1989). *Suicide intervention in the schools.* New York: Guilford Press.

Schorr, L. B., & Schorr, D. (1989). *Within our reach: Breaking the cycle of disadvantage.* New York: Anchor Books.

Sheeley, V. L., & Herlihy, B. (1989). Counseling suicidal teens: A duty to warn and protect. *School Counselor, 37,* 89–97.

Smaby, M. H., Peterson, T. L., Bergman, P. E., Bacig, K. L., & Swearingen, S. (1990). School-based community intervention: The school counselor as lead consultant for suicide prevention and intervention programs. *School Counselor, 37,* 370–377.

Stefanowski-Harding, S. (1990). Child suicide: A review of the literature and implications for school counselors. *School Counselor, 37*, 328–336.

Stiles, K., & Kottman, T. (1990). Mutual storytelling: An intervention for depressed and suicidal children. *School Counselor, 37*, 337–342.

Weisse, D. E. (1990). Gifted adolescents and suicide. *School Counselor, 37*, 351–358.

Wodarski, J. S. (1988). Preventive health services for adolescents: A practice paradigm. *Social Work in Education, 11*, 5–20.

Zirkel, P. A. (1992, May). Confident about confidences? *Phi Delta Kappan, 73*, 732–734.

*This chapter was originally published in the April 1995 issue of* Social Work in Education, *Vol. 17, pp. 92–100.*

Part V

# SKILLS AND INTERVENTIONS WITH LARGER SYSTEMS AND POLICY DEVELOPMENT AND REFORM

# Part V: Skills and Interventions with Larger Systems and Policy Development and Reform

S chools are embedded in the larger social context of our society. In this cultural context there are important community discourses and practices, institutional and governmental structures, public policies, and continuous policy reforms. These larger systems issues affect public schools, their clients, and the practices of school social workers. This section presents some of the most current policy and reform issues affecting public schools and school social workers. All nine chapters have in common a focus on intervention and provide information and skills that can aid school social workers as they confront new policies, reforms, and larger systems issues. Consequently, information in this section may empower school social workers as they join initiatives in a spectrum of reform movements aimed at improving services to children and families.

New policy development in the area of HIV/AIDS education is also of significance to school social workers. This section provides updates from research and helpful lessons to follow in one's own practice in regard to HIV/AIDS education. Perhaps one of the most important pieces of legislation to face schools in many years is the Individuals with Disabilities Education Act (IDEA). Critical information about IDEA as it relates to school social work services is provided. Managed care's focus on fiscal accountability and containing the costs of medical and mental health services has changed the way mental health and social services are funded and practiced. Managed care has restructured Medicaid, making it possible for a variety of practitioners to receive funding for their services in different contexts. School practices are not exempt from the influences of the managed care service delivery system and may benefit from knowledge of the effects of managed care on clients and school social workers, along with the practice implications for poor children and families.

The school-linked services movement is a significant school reform aimed at integrating education, health, and social services. Information is provided on different models available for operating school-linked services systems, and the skills and resources of school social workers that will aid in the development and operation of these programs are highlighted. Information and skills for writing grants and obtaining funding for the development of school-linked services programs are also presented in detail, including helpful tools and guides. Policies and legislation affecting special education and the mental health treatment of children in schools remain an important concern of schools and a significant focus of many school social workers. Information is provided for combining mental health treatment with education for preschool children and for addressing controversies about appropriate versus least-restrictive educational policies for children with educational disabilities. Finally, recent policies and reforms directly affect the professional status and practices of school social workers, their job descriptions, and their roles in schools. One challenge confronting every school social worker is the regulation of school social work practice. Another issue concerns the status of the profession within public schools in the United States. The review of these issues updates school social workers on salient and timely issues facing the profession.

# 36 HIV/AIDS Policy Development and Reform: Lessons from Practice, Research, and Education

Edith M. Freeman, Marion Halim, and K. Jean Peterson

Students who are affected directly or indirectly by HIV/AIDS are not always visible in American schools. We know they are there and can even estimate their numbers, but we cannot see them as we pass them in the halls or as we reach out to serve other students whose problems are more identifiable. Often, out of compassion, we speculate about how HIV/AIDS may be affecting the lives of these students. But in reality, their subjective experiences, struggles, needs, hopes, and dreams are largely unknown to us.

Their invisibility will make it difficult for children and youths with HIV/AIDS to be acknowledged by policymakers and other decision makers as a constituency whose needs should or must be considered. Consequently, it is unlikely that these children and youths will develop the broad range of advocates necessary for influencing HIV/AIDS policy at organizational, local, state, and national levels. Lessons can be learned from the experiences of gay men, who have organized themselves into a constituency with a diverse range of political activists who advocate for their needs in key medical, psychosocial, economic, and research areas (Koetting, 1996).

Children and youths affected by HIV/AIDS must rely on others for such leadership, which to date has not been fully developed. Barriers in the school and community have gained periodic media attention, as in the cases of Ryan White, who was initially barred from attending school, and the two brothers in Florida whose family home was burned because they were HIV positive. However, the loss of policy supports that can assist in problem solving and coping as well as systems change has not received the same media attention. For example, social supports provided by the Ryan White CARE (Comprehensive AIDS Resources Emergency) Act of 1990 and Medicaid were lost through Congress's recent cost-containment policies and social program reforms (Freeman, 1996; NASW, Office of Government Relations, 1996; Wiener, Fair, & Garcia, 1995). A closer examination of some of the lessons learned about HIV/AIDS policy is timely, in part because of the invisibility of the problem in schools, but also because of the regressive policy reforms being enacted. The lessons are from social work practice, research, and preservice education.

## LESSONS LEARNED FROM SOCIAL WORK PRACTICE

### Case Example

The lessons learned from social work practice open a window into the subjective environment and realities of students affected by HIV/AIDS that are not

371

visible from important, although impersonal, statistics about the problem. This window reveals the world of Sam, age 9, who is a third-grade African American student and HIV positive. Sam lives with his grandparents after being placed in a series of foster homes. His mother died earlier this year from complications related to AIDS, which she contracted during many years of drug use. Sam has never known his father.

The school social worker became aware of Sam's health status from a casual conversation between his teacher and her colleagues in the teachers' lounge. The teacher had not informed the social worker about Sam, "because everyone knew what the end result would be for Sam." In observing Sam in class, the social worker noted that he appeared to be withdrawn and afraid to speak or move from his seat. His classmates acted as though he was not there. Later Sam told the social worker that the students' reactions did not bother him; he felt the less attention he received, the better off he was. Sam said his life was fine until he became very ill and had to spend three weeks in the hospital, where he was told he was HIV positive. At recess Sam played alone or simply sat and watched the other children play. Sometimes he cried when he thought no one was watching him. His teacher did not ignore him, nor did she give him much attention. Sam said that if there was something he did not understand, he hesitated to ask the teacher because he was fearful that she would not come close enough for him to understand her answers or that she would reject him. Over time, Sam asked his teacher for help less often.

## Policy Development and Reform

Sam's situation illustrates one of the most basic needs of students affected by HIV/AIDS: the need for a friend or other supporter who will interact with them in a personal manner and touch them and with whom they can regularly share their fears and dreams. Schools should have organizational policies that help meet this basic need. Policies that require a combination of supports for newly enrolled students can be adjusted to meet the needs of students who have chronic illnesses such as AIDS or who have family members with such conditions. Schools should involve groups of peers in helping students with a chronic illness such as AIDS or peer problems succeed in class and in unstructured activities outside the classroom.

Another lesson is related to teachers. Policies that mandate HIV/AIDS education for teachers, other school staff, and students can reduce stigma and provide a supportive atmosphere conducive to learning. The type of stigma Sam experienced leads to exclusion of and, in some cases, violence against those affected by the problem (Koetting, 1996). Districtwide policies are needed to provide supports to family members who are caring for affected students or who have HIV/AIDS themselves. Sam's grandparents need education and a support group for managing loss and grief related to their daughter's death, Sam's diagnosis and health regimen, and their own lifestyle changes (Dane & Miller, 1992; Freeman, 1990; Land & Harangody, 1990).

The school social worker has a pivotal role in terms of organizational policy. He or she should be the link between the school and family, which in Sam's case involves helping the grandparents work closely with the school. This role in-cludes coordinating services provided by the school and supports provided by community agencies such as the hospital, mental health center, and local public child welfare agency.

A more critical lesson learned, however, is related to confidentiality. Discussion of Sam's situation in the teachers' lounge is an obvious breach of confidentiality. The school social worker can help the school team determine who should have such information, how to monitor whether confidentiality is being observed in the handling of students' records and in verbal communications, and what to do in situations in which confidentiality is not being observed. Schools need a policy also for addressing issues such as how to handle medical emergencies involving students with HIV/AIDS.

## LESSONS LEARNED FROM RESEARCH: PRACTICE AND POLICY IMPLICATIONS

To fill their role related to organizational policy, school social workers need up-to-date knowledge about medical and psychosocial issues related to HIV/AIDS. However, in a recent survey concerning social workers' knowledge about AIDS, Peterson (1991) found that none of the respondents who were school social workers believed they had a professional reason for being knowledgeable about HIV/AIDS. Increasingly, school social workers will be confronted with situations such as Sam's and expected to be knowledgeable and skilled in regard to HIV/AIDS. Clarification of these knowledge areas and the lessons to be learned for effective policy development is essential.

### Prevention of HIV

A major focus of the research literature is on the prevention of HIV infection among children and adolescents. This emphasis on primary prevention is consistent with the *NASW Standards for School Social Work Services* (NASW, 1992) and the *NASW Code of Ethics* (NASW, 1996). Research has shown the importance of maintaining a focus on children and youths as a major part of the prevention effort for HIV/AIDS.

Although less than 1 percent of the total AIDS cases diagnosed in the United States have been in adolescents, the average length of time between HIV infection and a diagnosis of AIDS is 10 years. In June 1996 the Centers for Disease Control and Prevention (CDC) reported that 17.9 percent of all AIDS cases (98,028 cases through June 1996) were among people ages 20 to 29. Most of these young adults were infected with HIV during adolescence (CDC, 1996).

Sex education in the schools has been a primary focus of HIV prevention efforts, but there has been controversy over both the content of the curriculum and the methods of instruction. Although there is general agreement among those who support sex education that it needs to start early, policy for many current programs has required a focus on abstinence only. However, the majority of adolescents are sexually active by the time they graduate from high school, raising serious questions about the efficacy of the abstinence-only approach (Schinke, Orlandi, Forgey, Rugg, & Douglas, 1992). A combination of individual, peer, family, and other environmental factors affect decisions about whether to become sexually active (Chilman, 1989) and should be the focus of prevention efforts.

## Students with HIV/AIDS

Children younger than 13 are categorized as pediatric cases, and the vast majority (90 percent) were infected through mother-to-child transmission (CDC, 1996). In contrast, adolescents (ages 13 to 19) are infected through different routes of transmission. Forty-one percent of teenage boys were exposed through hemophilia, and 33 percent were exposed through sex with other males. Fifty-five percent of adolescent girls were exposed through heterosexual contact with an HIV-infected partner. In June 1996 the CDC reported 7,296 cases of pediatric AIDS and 2,574 cases of AIDS in adolescents. These figures represent only those children and adolescents diagnosed with AIDS. Many more school-age children like Sam receive medical care for HIV infection but have not yet progressed to an AIDS diagnosis. However, the issues they face are similar to those facing children with an AIDS diagnosis.

Wiener, Fair, and Granowsky (1995) discussed AIDS issues facing school-age children. Children and youths with HIV/AIDS confront, based on their level of understanding, the likelihood of their own early deaths. The issues for latency-age children cannot be separated from the attitudes and feelings of their parents, who may model for their children attitudes of denial and a taboo against discussing HIV/AIDS openly. Many parents feel ambivalent about discussing the diagnosis of AIDS with their children because of fear and guilt. Fear is often associated with the realistic concern that knowledge of this diagnosis will result in abandonment by family and friends. Guilt comes from either having exposed the child to HIV through high-risk behaviors or, with hemophilia, having possibly given the child the injection that exposed him or her to HIV. Even before they are informed, children like Sam are aware that something serious is happening to them. Helping parents and other caretakers handle the fear and guilt is the first step toward helping the child. As the diagnosis becomes known, school social workers will need to be available to work with the child and to educate and answer questions from the child with AIDS and his or her peers, caretakers, teachers, and other school staff.

Adolescents with AIDS are concerned with how their illness will affect their relationships with peers: "These anxieties can lead to poor school performance, depression, isolation, resentment, and acting-out behaviors" (Wiener, Fair, & Granowsky, 1995, p. 111). School social workers are in an optimal position to help adolescents address these issues.

## Healthy Children in Families Affected by AIDS

Perhaps the largest and least understood group of students affected by the AIDS epidemic are those who have parents or siblings diagnosed with AIDS but who are not themselves infected with HIV. It is unclear how many children fall into this category, but some estimate that HIV-infected mothers will leave 125,000 to 150,000 children orphaned by 1998 (Fair, Spencer, Wiener, & Riekert, 1995). This figure is probably an underestimate, because women of childbearing age are one of the fastest growing groups of people infected with HIV. In addition, this estimate does not include children whose fathers or siblings have AIDS. Healthy children living in families affected by AIDS have issues similar to children facing the death of a parent, but these issues are exacerbated by the stigma and secrecy surrounding AIDS.

That these children are often lost or invisible as the focus is placed on those who are ill is reflected in the scarcity of available data about the numbers or psychosocial needs of these children. These children may be asked to assume additional responsibilities in the home and to carry the burden of secrecy and stigma. Fanos and Wiener (1994) found that many latency-age children whose siblings had AIDS reported an inability to concentrate in school, resulting in school failure. Adolescents may experience more problems in school as they cope with increasing responsibilities at home, and they may attempt to escape feelings of isolation, guilt, and grief by engaging in activities that place them at high risk for contracting HIV. Of particular concern is engagement in sexual activity to obtain the security and intimacy they have lost at home (Fair et al., 1995).

**Policy Development**

The research specifies how school social workers can be active in the development of local, state, and national policy that supports practice related to HIV/AIDS. First, because AIDS education policies requiring a focus on abstinence only and involving only students have largely been ineffective, these policies should be broadened to include other alternatives to abstinence and to include parents and other family members, school staff, and the community (Schinke et al., 1992). In addition, because many people ages 20 to 29 were infected during adolescence, prevention policies should be aimed at all children and youths. Such expanded prevention efforts may require a shift in resource priorities and the development of a merged funding mechanism between the state departments of education, health, mental health, and child welfare to support primary prevention (Freeman, 1996; Segal, 1992). School social workers can advocate for and help develop, implement, and monitor such policies.

Second, school social workers should become familiar with existing policies on other services provided by the different departments (Aguirre, 1995). For example, services need to support child welfare policies that ensure continuity for children who are orphaned because of AIDS. Familiarity with public health and local policies on HIV can help school social workers provide accurate information to families considering certain decisions related to AIDS (Wiener, Fair, & Garcia, 1995). This knowledge is essential also for school social workers in providing education programs for students, school staff, and families. HIV services policies developed at national, state, and local levels are not likely to include school social workers as mandated services unless school social workers become more knowledgeable about HIV/AIDS.

## LESSONS LEARNED FROM PRESERVICE EDUCATION

The school social worker in Sam's school had to clarify her knowledge gaps as well as what she knew about his health status and the impact of HIV infection on his school performance and peer and family relationships. The process of identifying assets and gaps in knowledge is similar to what occurs in the formal preservice teaching-learning process.

## The Education Process

School social work and other practice courses, as well as the field practicum, are ideal situations in which the teaching-learning process about HIV/AIDS can be facilitated. In one example, an MSW student in a school placement raised questions in class about a request he had received from a principal. Susan, a 17-year-old white student, had attempted to kill herself. The principal asked the school social work student to meet with Susan when she returned to school to assess her risk for another attempt. The class discussion soon centered around whether the principal's request was appropriate for the school social worker and if it was indeed possible to assess the suicide potential of a student like Susan.

In his meeting with Susan, the student learned that as a young child Susan had been sexually abused by her stepfather and that she was found to be HIV positive after a hospital admission for what she thought was a nonresponsive case of mononucleosis. The family, which had been waiting in dread after learning of the stepfather's death from AIDS two years before, was now in a crisis about Susan's suicide attempt and diagnosis. In addition, the principal and the rest of the school were moving toward a crisis as more people in the school and community became aware of Susan's suicide attempt.

The process of exploring the practice implications of Susan's situation was helpful in identifying class members' concerns as learners. Although many of their concerns were expressed directly, some of them were stated in terms of what school staff, other parents, and Susan's peers might focus on. For example, they thought that school staff and other parents would be overly concerned about the possibility of contagion in school and the source of Susan's HIV infection. These concerns reflected a lack of knowledge by the school social work students and the school staff about how HIV is transmitted and the insensitivity of asking how a person came to be infected.

Some of the students talked about the difficulty of using an ecological perspective, because it would be easy to become overwhelmed by the number of systems involved and their current crisis reactions. The students were concerned about the risk of burnout in such cases and how confidentiality and issues of loss, grief, and shame should be handled.

## Policy Implications

These class reactions reflect implicit lessons about HIV/AIDS policy in the teaching-learning process. First, children and youths affected by HIV are often invisible in their schools, and when their issues surface they are often masked by other symptoms such as suicide attempts, chronic infections, absenteeism, social isolation, depression, and anxiety (Wiener, Fair, & Garcia, 1995). This fact reinforces the need for national, state, and local policy to support HIV/AIDS education of school social work students as well as for all students in school- and health-related fields (Lloyd, 1995). The graduate students in Susan's example desired education about current medical information about HIV/AIDS; confidentiality; helping children, youths, and family members cope and problem solve; loss and grief issues; education of school staff; developing parental guardianship plans; and related community resources.

Susan's example also indicates the need for policies that encourage schools and community agencies to coordinate and integrate their services to families affected by HIV/AIDS (Aguirre, 1995). Advocacy by school social workers may be needed to help overcome schools' turf issues and the tendency to resist services integration and reduction of fragmentation in HIV/AIDS services: "Despite concerted efforts, services have not always been effectively coordinated, and insufficient attention has been given to supporting interorganizational relationships" (Lloyd, 1995, p. 1277).

## CONCLUSION

Because of concerns expressed about contagion and staff burnout, a policy is needed within schools that provides opportunities for staff support groups, especially in schools with students with HIV/AIDS or with family members with the syndrome. Staff support groups can prevent case hardening (Lloyd, 1995) and improve stress management among staff and students (Taylor-Brown, 1995); they can also help staff manage the types of school and community crisis reactions experienced in Susan's situation. School social workers and other school staff need a safe, confidential environment in which to discuss their fears, even irrational ones, and to address attitudes and knowledge gaps that can lessen the effectiveness of their work with children and youths.

## REFERENCES

Aguirre, L. M. (1995). California's efforts toward school-linked, integrated, comprehensive services. *Social Work in Education, 17,* 217–225.

Centers for Disease Control and Prevention. (1996). U.S. HIV and AIDS cases reported through June 1996. *HIV/AIDS Surveillance Report, 8,* 11–12.

Chilman, C. S. (1989). Some major issues regarding adolescent sexuality and childrearing in the United States. *Adolescent Sexuality, 8,* 3–26.

Dane, B. O., & Miller, S. O. (1992). *AIDS: Intervening with hidden grievers.* Westbury, CT: Auburn House.

Fair, C. D., Spencer, E. D., Wiener, L., & Riekert, S. (1995). Healthy children in families affected by AIDS: Epidemiological and psychosocial considerations. *Child and Adolescent Social Work Journal, 12,* 165–181.

Fanos, J., & Wiener, L. (1994). Tomorrow's survivors: Siblings of HIV-infected children. *Journal of Developmental and Behavioral Pediatrics, 15,* 43–48.

Freeman, E. M. (1990). The black family's life cycle: Operationalizing a strengths perspective. In S.M.L. Logan, E. M. Freeman, & R. G. McRoy (Eds.), *Social work practice with black families: A culturally specific perspective* (pp. 55–72). New York: Longman.

Freeman, E. M. (1996). President Clinton and the 104th Congress: The nightmare on Capitol Hill [Editorial]. *Social Work in Education, 18,* 67–70.

Koetting, M. E. (1996). A group design for HIV-negative gay men. *Social Work, 41,* 407–416.

Land, H., & Harangody, G. (1990). A support group for partners of persons with AIDS. *Families in Society, 7,* 471–481.

Lloyd, G. A. (1995). HIV/AIDS overview. In R. L. Edwards (Ed.-in-Chief), *Encyclopedia of social work* (19th ed., Vol. 2, pp. 1257–1290). Washington, DC: NASW Press.

National Association of Social Workers. (1992). *NASW standards for school social work services*. Washington, DC: Author.

National Association of Social Workers. (1996). *NASW code of ethics*. Washington, DC: Author.

National Association of Social Workers, Office of Government Relations. (1996, March 4). *Social workers urged to respond to governors' proposals on welfare and Medicaid* (Government Relations Alert). Washington, DC: Author.

Peterson, K. J. (1991). Social workers' knowledge about AIDS: A national survey. *Social Work, 36*, 31–37.

Ryan White CARE Act of 1990, P.L. 101-381, 104 Stat. 576.

Schinke, S. P., Orlandi, M. A., Forgey, M. A., Rugg, D. L., & Douglas, K. A. (1992). Multicomponent, school-based strategies to prevent HIV infection and sexually transmitted diseases among adolescents: Theory and research into practice. *Research on Social Work Practice, 2*, 364–379.

Segal, E. A. (1992). Multineed children in the social services system [Trends & Issues]. *Social Work in Education, 14*, 190–198.

Taylor-Brown, S. (1995). HIV/AIDS: Direct practice. In R. L. Edwards (Ed.-in-Chief), *Encyclopedia of social work* (19th ed., Vol. 2, pp. 1291–1305). Washington, DC: NASW Press.

Wiener, L., Fair, C., & Garcia, A. (1995). HIV/AIDS: Pediatric. In R. L. Edwards (Ed.-in-Chief), *Encyclopedia of social work* (19th ed., Vol. 2, pp. 1314–1324). Washington, DC: NASW Press.

Wiener, L. S., Fair, C., & Granowsky, R. T. (1995). HIV infection in infants, children, and adolescents: Implications for social work practice. In V. J. Lynch, G. A. Lloyd, & M. F. Fimbres (Eds.), *The changing face of AIDS: Implications for social work practice* (pp. 105–121). Westport, CT: Auburn House.

---

*This chapter was originally published in the January 1997 issue of* Social Work in Education, *Vol. 19, pp. 2–8.*

# 37 Medicaid Managed Care and Urban Poor People: Implications for Social Work

Janet D. Perloff

**M**anaged care is rapidly becoming the predominant method of financing and delivering health care to Medicaid recipients. The shift from Medicaid fee-for-service arrangements to managed care has important implications for the health care available to low-income and uninsured people living in U.S. cities. It also presents significant new challenges to the financial viability of urban "safety-net" providers—that is, the public hospitals, academic medical centers, community health centers, local health department clinics, school-based clinics, and other community-based health care providers that traditionally serve residents of low-income urban communities.

Social workers in direct practice and management positions in urban hospitals, clinics, and managed care plans, as well as in policy development and advocacy positions, have many opportunities to influence the transition to Medicaid managed care in cities. This article aims to help equip social workers for broad-scale implementation of Medicaid managed care by describing its theoretical basis and development; presenting reasons for its apparent popularity; and analyzing its likely effects on access to care, the long-term viability of urban safety-net providers, and social workers with Medicaid clients. Steps are identified by which social workers can support clients in the transition to Medicaid managed care and work for the preservation of access to care for disadvantaged urban populations.

## MEDICAID MANAGED CARE

### Theoretical Basis

Enrollment of Medicaid recipients in managed care reflects the widely held belief that managed care can improve health care access while also promoting cost containment and federal and state budget control (Edinburg & Cottler, 1995; Keigher, 1995). Medicaid managed care seeks to bring increasing numbers of recipients into health care delivery systems that are subject to "the new economics of managed care" (Shortell, Gillies, & Anderson, 1994, p. 48), which is based on the fact that care is provided to a defined number of enrollees at a fixed rate per member per month. Under capitation-based health care, all revenues are earned "up front" when contracts are negotiated. All system components—including hospitals, clinics, imaging centers, and primary care physicians' offices—are transformed from revenue centers to cost centers; these cost centers need to be managed within the capitation-based budget. In theory, these arrangements create incentives for keeping people well and, when they become sick, for treating them at the most cost-effective location on the continuum of care and in the most cost-effective manner. These arrangements also create incentives to underserve patients.

## Types

Medicaid managed care plans vary in the strength of their incentives for cost containment. Three major types of Medicaid managed care plans are (1) fee-for-service case management, under which the state pays a health care provider a monthly case management fee to perform gatekeeping and service coordination for each person enrolled; (2) fully capitated systems, under which the state pays a managed care plan, usually some form of health maintenance organization (HMO), a preset, or capitated, rate for each person enrolled, and the plan is then at risk for paying the costs of providing a comprehensive package of services to its enrollees, usually including inpatient, specialty, and primary care; and (3) partially capitated systems, under which the state pays a managed care plan a capitated rate for each person enrolled, but the plan assumes risk for the costs of providing a more limited package of services, usually excluding some specialty and inpatient care but including at least primary care services (Perkins & Rivera, 1995). Fully capitated systems contain the strongest incentives for cost containment; therefore, states are placing the greatest emphasis on developing and enrolling Medicaid recipients in fully capitated plans. As a result, fully capitated systems are the fastest growing type of Medicaid managed care, covering an estimated 63 percent of all Medicaid managed care enrollees in June 1994 (Lewin-VHI, 1995).

## Growth

Recent increases in the number of Medicaid recipients enrolled in managed care have been dramatic. In 1983, 750,000 Medicaid recipients—3 percent of the Medicaid population—were enrolled in managed care. In 1994, about 7.8 million recipients—23 percent of all Medicaid recipients—were enrolled in managed care. Between 1993 and 1994 Medicaid managed care enrollment grew 63 percent, from 4.8 million to 7.8 million recipients (Kaiser Commission on the Future of Medicaid, 1995).

Currently, the populations being enrolled in Medicaid managed care are primarily children and adults receiving Aid to Families with Dependent Children and other low-income pregnant women and children. Historically, elderly and disabled Medicaid recipients have been excluded from Medicaid managed care because of their complex service needs, technical challenges in setting appropriate capitation payments, and difficulties finding plans willing to serve these populations. However, the high cost of the care of these Medicaid recipients has increased state interest in serving elderly and disabled people through managed care arrangements (Lewin-VHI, 1995). Some states have also begun to enroll special subpopulations of Medicaid patients in managed care, including patients with AIDS, substance abuse problems, and serious and persistent mental illness (Kaiser Commission on the Future of Medicaid, 1995; State of New York, 1995).

The pervasiveness of Medicaid managed care is indicated by the fact that as of June 1994, all states except Alaska, Connecticut, Maine, Nebraska, Oklahoma, Vermont, and Wyoming had some form of Medicaid managed care program (Kaiser Commission on the Future of Medicaid, 1995). In many states, Medicaid recipients voluntarily enroll in a managed care plan. However, mandatory Medicaid managed care programs are more attractive because they are more likely to yield cost savings (U.S. General Accounting Office [GAO], 1993). Many states are presently requesting and receiving federal approval to implement mandatory Medicaid managed care plans, and indications are that mandatory enrollment of Medicaid recipients in managed care plans will grow exponentially over the next several years (Holahan, Coughlin, Ku, Lipson, & Rajan, 1995; Kaiser Commission on the Future of Medicaid, 1995; Lewin-VHI, 1995).

## EMPIRICAL EVIDENCE AND IMPLEMENTATION ISSUES

States are enthusiastic about the promise of Medicaid managed care for improving access, costs, quality, and health outcomes. However, the empirical evidence about Medicaid managed care is equivocal. Several recent reviews of empirical studies concluded that some versions of Medicaid managed care bring improvements in utilization, costs, and access over traditional fee-for-service arrangements (Fox & McManus, 1992; Hurley, Freund, & Paul, 1993; Lewin-VHI, 1995), but others concluded that the available evidence does not support many of the claims about cost savings, improved access, or improved quality (Freund & Lewit, 1993; Rowland, Rosenbaum, Simon, & Chait, 1995).

In the absence of definitive empirical evidence about its impact, Medicaid managed care is perhaps best viewed with a mixture of optimism and caution. Four questions are central to whether state Medicaid managed care initiatives can achieve their full potential: (1) Are managed care plans adequately prepared to meet the unique, pressing, and often complex health care needs of urban poor people? (2) Is the supply and distribution of primary care in cities adequate to ensure that Medicaid recipients enrolled in managed care will be able to find care? (3) What is the future of the health care providers who have traditionally served low-income urban residents? and (4) Will Medicaid recipients be adequately prepared to choose among managed care plans and to protect themselves against managed care's potential for aggressive enrollment and underservice?

### Health Care Needs of Urban Poor People

Cities have high incidence rates for health problems such as low-birthweight babies and infant deaths, measles, tuberculosis, AIDS, and sexually transmitted diseases. Many of these problems, particularly those affecting low-income women and children, are concentrated in the most socioeconomically disadvantaged urban communities (Fossett & Perloff, 1995). These urban residents live in states that are the most eager to enroll in Medicaid managed care plans.

Little empirical evidence exists about the impact of Medicaid managed care on service utilization and health outcomes of high-risk populations. Research is needed to fully assess the effects of managed care on urban Medicaid recipients and to develop systems of care that produce the best health and mental health outcomes for these clients. However, the available empirical literature provides reasons to be cautious about the likely impact of Medicaid managed care on service utilization patterns and health outcomes for high-risk, multiproblem, chronically ill, and more expensive patients (Fossett & Perloff, 1995). Most managed care organizations are accustomed to serving employed, low-risk populations and have little experience with providing support services such as outreach, case management, transportation, and other psychosocial services that are beneficial to high-risk populations. In addition, because managed care organizations, especially those participating in full capitation programs, face strong financial incentives to limit utilization, patients enrolled in these plans may encounter difficulties obtaining the full range of health and related social services. As a result, patients needing these services have frequently not fared well in managed care arrangements (Schlesinger, 1986, 1989).

## Urban Primary Care Supply and Distribution

There are reasons to be cautious about whether the supply and distribution of primary care in low-income urban neighborhoods will be adequate to meet the needs of Medicaid recipients (Rosenthal, 1993). Most of the nation's metropolitan areas are richly supplied with doctors and hospitals, but embedded in them are areas that lack health care resources adequate to serve the needs of their residents (Fossett & Perloff, 1995; Ginzburg, Berliner, & Ostow, 1993). This maldistribution originates, in part, because private physicians and other health care providers tend to select locations that enable them to attract a large and profitable clientele. As a result of the limited profit-making potential of poor neighborhoods, these areas have historically had very few private health care providers such as office-based physicians or private community hospitals.

The shortage of physicians is aggravated by the fact that many physicians in metropolitan areas do not accept Medicaid patients or limit the number of Medicaid patients they treat (Perloff, Kletke, & Fossett, 1995; Perloff, Kletke, Fossett, & Banks, 1995). The lack of private providers is made worse by some providers' personal inclinations to avoid crime, AIDS, and racial and ethnic diversity, as well as to avoid the challenges posed by patients beset with complex and often unyielding social problems (Physician Payment Review Commission, 1993).

Because many low-income urban neighborhoods already lack an adequate supply of health care providers, there is ample reason to be pessimistic that Medicaid managed care will improve the quantity and quality of health care available in these neighborhoods (Fossett & Perloff, 1995). In theory, Medicaid managed care tries to use the payment system to improve access to care in underserved communities. States set capitation rates at a level that will improve the attractiveness of the Medicaid population to managed care entities and then use mandatory enrollment to ensure HMOs a large and lucrative Medicaid market. It has been argued that the resulting competition among managed care organizations for contracts to serve Medicaid patients will improve the range of available health care alternatives.

However, managed care plans will face equally strong financial incentives to avoid making large investments in developing the health care provider supply.

States may set capitation rates at levels that make it attractive for managed care plans to enroll Medicaid recipients, but the supply of care providers in many low-income urban neighborhoods will be inadequate to support mass mandatory enrollment. Without sufficiently generous capitation payments or other financial incentives, managed care plans will unlikely foster significant improvements in the underlying supply of care providers.

## Urban Safety-Net Providers

With little access to private physicians and other health care providers, residents of low-income urban communities have come to depend on urban safety-net providers (Fossett & Perloff, 1995). The safety net includes public hospitals and clinics run by cities or counties and also academic medical centers that have historically tended to be in or near urban communities so that physicians, nurses, social workers, and other professionals in training could serve the needs of disadvantaged patients in exchange for rich learning opportunities. The clinics run by county and city health departments, the community health centers funded by federal grants, and the variety of family-planning and other community-based agencies that are supported by a mix of private and public resources have also become important elements in the urban health care safety net.

Safety-net providers offer many features that are valuable to urban poor and uninsured people (Fossett & Perloff, 1995). Providers are often close by, enhancing the probability of their use, and many offer a wider array of enabling services (including outreach, case management, and follow-up) and support services (including transportation, translation, and child care), which are important complements to medical services.

However, managed care organizations will be selective in forming networks, including only those providers who can be successful in keeping down the costs of care. Such network selectivity is likely to result in excluding or drastically reducing the role of the urban safety-net providers in the care of Medicaid patients. Some characteristics typical of safety-net providers may make them less than attractive as network providers for managed care organizations (Fossett & Perloff, 1995). Safety-net providers are often in poor financial condition, undercapitalized, outdated and in disrepair, inefficiently run, lacking in adequate information and management systems, and incompatible with both the mission and the management style of fully capitated health plans. Given the potentially high costs of working with these providers, managed care organizations may not be eager to include them in their managed care network.

Some safety-net providers have benefited from far-sighted and effective leadership and are prepared to be successful in a managed care environment by creating their own managed care plans or securing contracts as providers within the networks of private managed care plans. More typically, however, safety-net providers have had very little experience with managed care. These providers are accustomed to fee-for-service revenues and, in some instances, contributions to their budget from state or local appropriations. For safety-net hospitals, Medicaid's disproportionate share payments, which are made to hospitals that serve more than their share of poor and uninsured people, provide a vital subsidy.

Accustomed to the world of fee-for-service with a subsidy, these providers lack experience in competing for patients; their inexperience places them at a competitive disadvantage.

Recent evidence suggests that Medicaid managed care is shifting patients away from urban safety-net providers, although the consequences of this redistribution of patients are not fully understood (Henneberger, 1994; Peck & Hubbert, 1994; Sack, 1995; Winslow, 1995). However, there is ample reason for concern. Exclusion of safety-net providers from managed care networks has the potential to disrupt existing arrangements that residents of underserved neighborhoods have made to obtain care and to shift these patients into the care of providers less responsive to their unique and often complex needs. In addition, the loss of Medicaid patients to managed care plans represents a significant loss of revenues for safety-net providers. Medicaid revenues are used by these agencies and institutions to subsidize the care they provide to the uninsured population. The loss of these revenues will limit the ability of these agencies to care for uninsured people in the future.

### Recipient Preparedness

Medicaid managed care is a significant departure from the way recipients have received care in the past and will require a reorientation to the health care system (Perloff, 1993). For the first time, Medicaid recipients will be asked to select a health plan and a primary care provider, limit their use to certain providers, and obtain authorization and referrals before using certain services such as emergency rooms or specialists. Medicaid recipients will need a lot of information if they are to make informed choices about both plan and provider and to be fully prepared to use the health care system in new ways.

In addition, state agencies will need to ensure that Medicaid recipients are protected from overly aggressive marketing by managed care plans (Perloff, 1987). Medicaid managed care plans face strong incentives to earn the up-front revenue from recipient enrollment. Very rapid build-up in Medicaid managed care enrollment and practices that may even be fraudulent can therefore be expected as plans maneuver to lock in enrollees (Gottlieb, 1995; Pear, 1995). In addition, without adequate monitoring by state Medicaid agencies, enrollment can rapidly outstrip the capacity of managed care organizations to provide needed services (Fisher, 1995). Finally, state agencies will need to ensure that both quality assurance mechanisms and legal protection are in place to protect Medicaid recipients from managed care's inherent incentives to underserve (Perloff, 1987).

## ROLES FOR SOCIAL WORK

Developments associated with Medicaid managed care will have a significant impact on low-income and uninsured people living in cities and will also pose challenges for institutions traditionally serving this population. Social workers have many opportunities to shape the Medicaid managed care debate and to influence the outcome of these developments.

## Direct Practice and Management

Social workers in direct practice can play an important role in helping clients develop the skills needed to obtain health care in the managed care environment. Social workers in settings in which the Medicaid eligibility of clients is being established will have the important task of informing and educating clients about various choices related to their coverage. This role will be particularly important in states implementing mandatory Medicaid managed care plans because, in most instances, clients failing to choose will automatically be assigned to a health plan and a primary care provider. Although the results of automatic assignment may be acceptable to clients, better choices would seem likely to result with client input.

Given that managed care plans have strong incentives to enroll patients and therefore may market themselves aggressively, social workers should place a high priority on helping clients fully evaluate managed care plans and choose the plan through which they will be best served. Clients may face choices between managed care and fee-for-service plans and from among an array of health plans and providers. Carefully assessing a client's situation and helping him or her fully understand and consider the options will improve the probability that good choices are made. For example, noting the existence of transportation barriers or an excellent relationship with a particular primary care provider will improve the likelihood that these situational factors will influence choice.

Social workers will need to be familiar with the rules of Medicaid managed care in their state to help educate clients about new care-seeking requirements and to ensure that these requirements do not become barriers to appropriate care seeking. Changes in care-seeking rules include the requirement to contact one's selected primary care provider before visiting specialists or emergency rooms and, in some states, the possibility that health care previously obtained from public health clinics or community-based agencies (such as immunizations or family-planning services) must now be obtained from one's managed care plan. Clients may also need support to ensure that they are not being underserved by a plan. Social workers can identify instances of potential underservice, compile data documenting such problems, and intervene with managed care plans and state and local Medicaid agencies on behalf of clients whose rights may have been violated.

The informing, educating, and advocating that may be required of social workers in a managed care environment will sometimes put health care social workers at odds with the goals and values of their employers (Cornelius, 1994; Ross, 1993). Social workers will find themselves advocating additional services for a client in an environment that places a premium on cost minimization. Social workers in supervisory positions in hospitals, clinics, and managed care organizations will need to be prepared to help staff social workers satisfactorily resolve such dilemmas arising from the new economics of managed care. To some extent, such dilemmas are inherent in Medicaid managed care. For this reason, social workers outside of Medicaid managed care will have a particularly important role to play in ensuring optimal health outcomes for clients. Because of their independence from the health care system, social workers in other settings—child welfare agencies, community-based social services agencies, mental health agencies, and schools—may be in the best position to help clients judge whether their health care needs are being met, to recognize aspects of Medicaid managed care that are working, and to identify and work toward remedies for aspects that need improvement.

## Policy Development and Advocacy

As was the case during the recent federal health reform debate, social workers should be actively trying to influence Medicaid managed care policy development. State Medicaid managed care initiatives entail a planning process, submission of applications for waivers to the federal government, and in many cases passage of state legislation. These and subsequent stages in the policy development process present numerous opportunities for public comment, testimony, and advocacy. Social workers and organizations representing the profession can also take part in emerging coalitions of providers, consumers, and other health and welfare advocates who are committed to sound planning and implementation of state Medicaid managed care initiatives, ongoing monitoring of the impact of managed care, and change.

In the attempt to influence the shape of Medicaid managed care, social work should make efforts to ensure that vulnerable populations will have access to health care. Social workers should be strong advocates for the development of state-level information systems that will monitor the ability of managed care plans to meet recipients' needs and that can produce timely indicators of access problems. Social workers should also advocate for policy proposals that will give managed care plans strong incentives to develop new capacity in underserved areas, including advocacy for payment of higher capitation levels to plans that propose to increase capacity in specific ways. In addition, ensuring access will require strong and continuing advocacy for federal and state policies aimed at developing the supply of primary care providers in underserved communities. Existing federal programs such as the Migrant and Community Health Centers Program and the National Health Service Corps should be preserved; creative new state and local capacity development initiatives should be developed and supported.

High priority should also be given to supporting policy proposals that strike a reasonable balance between protecting the financial viability of urban safety-net providers and fostering cost containment through competition in local health care markets. For example, California's proposed mandatory Medicaid managed care initiative, which is being implemented in 1996, recognizes that safety-net providers have little experience with and lack adequate preparation for managed care, that they are extremely vulnerable to the loss of Medicaid and disproportionate share revenue that may result from increased competition, and that they will need insulation and time to adapt if they are to survive and continue to meet the needs of Medicaid recipients and the growing uninsured population (GAO, 1995). Features that would mitigate some of the harsher effects of managed care on safety-net providers (some of which are included in California's and other state Medicaid managed care plans) include requiring or creating strong incentives for the inclusion of providers in managed care networks; providing technical assistance to providers in key areas such as risk-based financing, negotiating contracts, and developing effective information systems; and ensuring that there is an ongoing subsidy for the services these settings provide to the uninsured population. In the absence of such features, Medicaid managed care will pose a serious threat to the future of urban safety-net providers, to social workers practicing in these settings, and to the people they serve.

## REFERENCES

Cornelius, D. (1994). Managed care and social work: Constructing a context and a response. *Social Work in Health Care, 20,* 47–63.

Edinburg, G. M., & Cottler, J. M. (1995). Managed care. In R. L. Edwards (Ed.-in-Chief), *Encyclopedia of social work* (19th ed., Vol. 2, pp. 1635–1642). Washington, DC: NASW Press.

Fisher, I. (1995, August 28). Forced marriage of Medicaid and managed care hits snags. *New York Times,* pp. B1, B5.

Fossett, J., & Perloff, J. (1995). *The "new" health reform and access to care: The problem of the inner city* (Background paper). Washington, DC: Kaiser Commission on the Future of Medicaid.

Fox, H., & McManus, M. (1992). *Medicaid managed care arrangements and their impact on children and adolescents: A briefing report.* Washington, DC: Child and Adolescent Health Policy Center.

Freund, D., & Lewit, E. (1993). Managed care for children and pregnant women: Promises and pitfalls. *Future of Children, 3,* 92–122.

Ginzburg, E., Berliner, H. S., & Ostow, M. (1993). *Changing U.S. health care.* Boulder, CO: Westview Press.

Gottlieb, M. (1995, October 2). A free-for-all in swapping Medicaid for managed care. *New York Times,* p. A1.

Henneberger, M. (1994, June 30). New York hospitals fight to retain Medicaid patients. *New York Times,* p. A1.

Holahan, J., Coughlin, T., Ku, L., Lipson, D. J., & Rajan, S. (1995, Spring). Insuring the poor through Section 1115 Medicaid waivers. *Health Affairs,* pp. 199–216.

Hurley, R., Freund, D., & Paul, J. (1993). *Managed care in Medicaid: Lessons for policy and program design.* Ann Arbor, MI: Health Administration Press.

Kaiser Commission on the Future of Medicaid. (1995, April). *Medicaid and managed care: Policy brief.* Washington, DC: Author.

Keigher, S. (1995). Managed care's silent seduction of America and the new politics of choice [National Health Line]. *Health & Social Work, 20,* 146–151.

Lewin-VHI. (1995, February). *States as payers: Managed care for Medicaid populations.* Washington, DC: National Institute for Health Care Management.

Pear, R. (1995, April 24). Florida struggles to lift Medicaid burden. *New York Times,* p. A2.

Peck, M., & Hubbert, E. D. (1994, July). *Changing the rules: Medicaid managed care and MCH in U.S. cities.* Omaha, NE: CityMatch.

Perkins, J., & Rivera, L. A. (1995, March). EPSDT and managed care: Do plans know what they are getting into? *Clearinghouse Review,* pp. 1248–1260.

Perloff, J. (1987). Safeguards are needed for Medicaid HMOs [Editorial]. *Chicago Sun-Times,* p. 38.

Perloff, J. (1993, April). *Medicaid managed care for women and children: What have we learned?* Paper presented at the National Conference on Managed Care Systems for Mothers and Young Children, Baltimore.

Perloff, J., Kletke, P., & Fossett, J. (1995). Which physicians limit their Medicaid participation and why. *Health Services Research, 30,* 9–26.

Perloff, J., Kletke, P., Fossett, P., & Banks, S. (1995, June). *Medicaid participation among urban primary care physicians.* Paper presented at a meeting of the Association for Health Services Research, Chicago.

Physician Payment Review Commission. (1993). *Annual report to Congress.* Washington, DC: Author.

Rosenthal, E. (1993, October 17). Shortage of doctors in poor areas is seen as barrier to health plans. *New York Times,* p. A1.

Ross, J. (1993). Redefining hospital social work: An embattled professional domain [Editorial]. *Health & Social Work, 18,* 243–247.

Rowland, D., Rosenbaum, S., Simon, L., & Chait, E. (1995, March). *Medicaid and managed care: Lessons from the literature.* Washington, DC: Kaiser Commission on the Future of Medicaid.

Sack, K. (1995, August 20). Public hospitals around the country cut basic service. *New York Times,* pp. A1, A24.

Schlesinger, M. (1986). On the limits of expanding health care reform: Chronic care in prepaid settings. *Milbank Quarterly, 62,* 189–216.

Schlesinger, M. (1989). Striking a balance: Capitation, the mentally ill, and public policy. In D. Mechanic & L. Aiken (Eds.), *Paying for services: Promises and pitfalls of capitation* (pp. 186–214). New York: Jossey-Bass.

Shortell, S. M., Gillies, R. R., & Anderson, D. A. (1994, Winter). The new world of managed care: Creating organized delivery systems. *Health Affairs,* pp. 46–64.

State of New York. (1995, March). *The partnership plan: A public–private initiative ensuring healthcare for needy New Yorkers* [Section 1115 waiver application]. Albany: Author.

U.S. General Accounting Office. (1993). *Medicaid: States turn to managed care to improve access and control costs* (Report No. GAO-HRD-93-86). Washington, DC: Author.

U.S. General Accounting Office. (1995). *Expansion of California's Medicaid managed care program* (Report No. GAO-HEHS-95-87). Washington, DC: Author.

Winslow, R. (1995, April 12). Welfare recipients a hot commodity in managed care now. *Wall Street Journal,* p. A1.

---

*This chapter was originally published in the August 1996 issue of* Health & Social Work, *Vol. 21, pp. 189–195.*

# 38 School Reform: Linking Public Schools with Human Services

Cynthia G. Franklin and Calvin L. Streeter

Public education and social work share a common concern for social problems confronting children and families. Both public schools and human services are being challenged to rethink and redesign their efforts to educate, socialize, and intervene in the problems of children and their families. School reform and the restructuring of human services are individually trying to address the need for systemic changes in the institutions that serve children and families (Kirst, 1991; Liontos, 1991a, 1991b; Stroul & Friedman, 1986). Many proponents of these changes point out that schools are a natural place for human services activities because they provide maximum access to the majority of children and families (Franklin, 1992b; Hahn, Danzberger, & Lefkowitz, 1987; Kirst, 1991; Liontos, 1991a, 1991b; Ornstein, 1992; Payzant, 1992; Pickney, 1985; Streeter & Franklin, 1991).

Current reform efforts are placing renewed emphasis on the linkage of public schools and human services agencies to address significant social problems (Landers, 1993; Levy & Copple, 1989; Mellaville & Blank, 1991; Texas Research League, 1991). However, efforts to define the school's role as a provider of broader human services are not new. Progressive education reformers at the turn of the century wanted schools to include a wide range of human services (Sedlak & Schlossman, 1985). In the vision of the progressive reformers, schools would alleviate poverty and respond to human needs by providing lunch programs, health clinics, and a full range of services to meet the needs of children. In addition to regular classroom instruction, professionals such as social workers and nurses would provide information in areas such as personal health, safety, and sex education (Tyack, 1992). School social workers, known at that time as visiting teachers, were a central element of the comprehensive schools envisioned by the progressive reformers and were seen as a critical link between the school, home, and community (Allen-Meares, Washington, & Welsh, 1986; Costin, 1975).

Although the progressive reformers strongly advocated for comprehensive schools, few programs of this type were developed. Instead, schools chose to turn inward by adopting a reform initiative known as "reorganization." Consistent with the bureaucratic management models of the day, the reorganization movement sought to make schools more efficient by consolidating programs and developing hierarchical integration. By the 1950s most public school systems had become large bureaucracies operating as "closed systems" (Tyack, 1991). During this same time, the school social worker's role as school–home–community liaison was abandoned in favor of a more specialized social casework role (Allen-Meares et al., 1986). Under the social casework model, social workers frequently consulted with teachers to interpret a student's emotional difficulties and to aid in early detection of personality problems (Anderson, 1952). But collaboration with other school personnel or with agencies outside the school was given minimal attention.

Recognizing that schools had become isolated systems that were unresponsive to outsiders, reformers of the 1960s sought to decentralize public schools and reclaim some of the visions of the progressive educators. The alternative school movement emerged as an important part of the reform movement of the 1960s (Franklin, 1992a). Most alternative schools were designed to keep problem youths in school and shared many characteristics with the comprehensive schools envisioned by the progressive reformers of the 1920s (Collins, 1987). They not only focused on the education of at-risk youths but also enlisted the expertise of other professionals to increase the youths' social functioning and behavioral competencies.

Two themes in school reform have emerged throughout this century: one of centralization and control and another of decentralization and turning outward for solutions. There is growing evidence that the current wave of school reform is producing a convergence of these themes (Streeter, Brannen, & Franklin, 1994; Streeter & Franklin, 1993; Tyack, 1991). The linking of public schools with broader human services is occurring as reforms are being aimed at increasing the schools' effectiveness with a diverse student population, decreasing the high school dropout rate, and restructuring to meet the demands of an increasingly competitive global economy (Everett, 1992).

## APPROACHES TO LINKING PUBLIC SCHOOLS WITH HUMAN SERVICES

A review of the literature yields five alternative approaches for linking public schools with human services. Because schools and human services agencies tend to be innovative and pragmatic, these approaches may not represent every approach currently in use. However, we believe they are conceptually distinct in their administration, operations, and the degree of reform required for implementation and can be discussed as separate approaches.

Table 38-1 summarizes the five approaches to linking schools and human services—informal relations, coordination, partnerships, collaboration, and integration. As one moves from left to right across the table, the approaches represent greater levels of change in the current system. For example, informal relations represent little or no change in the system, whereas integration represents major reform of the system consistent with "second-order" change, that is, change in the basic philosophy and organization of a system. Each of the approaches is examined along eight dimensions. These dimensions can be thought of as factors to be considered for effective implementation of reform efforts. Implementation factors are generally quite distinct across the different approaches.

Table 38-1

**Five Approaches to Linking Schools and Human Services and Factors for Successful Implementation**

| Implementation Factors | Approaches to Linking Schools and Human Services | | | | |
|---|---|---|---|---|---|
| | Informal Relations | Coordination | Partnerships | Collaboration | Integration |
| Commitment | Little commitment required | Some commitment to formal linkages required | Some formal commitment required for successful implementation | Major formal commitment from board (sometimes from state) required | A significant formal commitment from both state and local levels required |
| Planning | Minimum, usually done by pupil services team | Some community planning and outreach done by school social worker or pupil services team | Formal, contractual agreements based on district-wide planning | Comprehensive planning with human services | Comprehensive planning from state level with local input; process may be highly politicized |
| Training | In-service training done by pupil services team | Staff, teachers, and pupil services team trained on student needs, service availability, and referral process | Training of all staff on roles and functions of partners | Ongoing and intensive interprofessional education | Ongoing and intensive interprofessional education and interdisciplinary teamwork across levels of the system |
| Leadership patterns | Frontline staff and pupil services team | Frontline staff, school social worker, and student services team. Minimum leadership from administration to coordinate with community services | Frontline staff along with administrative leadership from schools and executive leadership from community | Administrative leadership required along with participation from staff and human services personnel | State-level administrative and political leadership and local administrative leadership from schools and human services |
| Resources | Minimum time spent on services but additional time expended on target groups | School staff, time, space, and a viable community services system | Contracted staff, greater time and space, and a viable community services system | New personnel, time, space for colocation of staff, and a viable community services system | Redefinition and redistribution of resources and shared initiatives required |
| Funding | Minimal funding required | Some additional school funds for pupil services | Additional funding from school and community for new services | Additional funding from school and community to deliver better services to more students | Additional funding required for all systems with greater efficiency derived from restructuring agencies |
| Scope of change | None | Minimal change to structure, linkages remain informal | Some reorganization needed to accommodate auxiliary services | Major restructuring and reinterpretation of goals and resources | Total reform of both the structure and process to produce second-order change |
| Impact | Minimum, fragmentation causes difficulty in service delivery | Some benefits from link with service; provides additional services and solves problems for some students | Good benefits in terms of additional programs and resources and linking to larger community systems | Excellent benefits; new programs and resources developed | Maximum benefit through new and better service systems |

## Informal Relations

Informal relations are what many schools have experienced in the past two decades when working with human services agencies. Most contemporary school reformers would probably not consider this approach to be a legitimate form of linked services. In this approach, relationships between public schools and human services agencies are loosely defined and represent little more than a general awareness that each exists in the community. Links exist only because students and their families are also clients of human services agencies. For example, a student who misses school may bring a note from a health provider, or another may ask to be excused early to attend a counseling session. Schools may also find it necessary to report apparent abuse and neglect to child protective services. In addition, schools have added guidance counselors, special education teachers, and school psychologists who provide needed services and work together as a pupil services team. These professionals may develop informal links with some agencies when the mutual management of students requires them to do so.

Under this approach the school's commitment to maintaining links with human services agencies is limited. Planning is minimal and done by a guidance counselor, the pupil services team, or another designated person. Coordination and follow-up are generally not done and, if done, often lack consistency. Training is limited and is usually accomplished through in-service training or handbooks explaining procedures and requirements. Leadership is through the pupil services team. Usually no additional funding or resources are required other than what is budgeted for special education or pupil services. Although schools may expend a considerable amount of personnel time dealing with the issues of at-risk students, no significant change in the school system is made. Because of fragmentation of services and lack of communication, the informal relations approach often produces only minimal benefits.

## Coordination

The coordination approach involves attempts to rally the resources of community agencies to help students and is usually accomplished by a school social worker who becomes a member of the pupil services team. The school social worker brokers services and develops links with community agencies by acting as a home–school–community liaison and case manager. Coordination helps students by identifying resources in the community and referring students to the community for needed services, monitoring their progress, and helping them with school adjustment problems. This is the traditional approach of school social workers who work with the community and family to remove barriers to a student's learning (Allen-Meares et al., 1986). School social workers may also act to solve crises at the building level, make home visits, and advocate for students.

A major limitation to the coordination approach is that the existing services system is fragmented, and it may not be possible to get needed services from the community. For example, agencies may have eligibility requirements that exclude some children, families may not be able to pay for services, or there may be lengthy waiting lists for services. School social workers may act to remediate the fragmentation in the services system by providing some clinical services in the school or by working with agencies to develop new services. For instance, a school social worker may provide screening for substance abuse or work with an agency to provide these screenings free to students at the school. Unfortunately, school social workers often have large caseloads and may not be able to provide all the services that are needed. If the agencies cannot provide the services, schools face the quandary of how to fill the needs. School social workers usually spend time problem solving and troubleshooting to find solutions to such dilemmas.

The coordination approach requires some commitment by the school. The school social worker, principal, teachers, and pupil services team must plan the logistics of managing student referrals and must resolve issues such as confidentiality between the school and community agencies. Training of teachers and staff concerning the role of the social worker is important so that the worker's role is understood and distinguished from that of other pupil services personnel. Also, social workers can provide training either informally or formally on the needs of at-risk youths, and this training becomes important to the referral and case management process within the school. Frontline staff such as the social worker usually take the leadership role in setting up and administering the coordination of services. Administrative leadership is minimal, although support from the principal and staff is essential. Time, space, and personnel are usually required resources, and schools without a social worker will need to hire one. However, minimum restructuring is required in that coordination of services is mostly carried out in the community and the linkages between the human services agencies and school remain informal.

Some restructuring may be required to allow the social worker flexibility in working with students and making the linkages. For example, students may need to be excused from class to talk with the social worker. The school must enable the social worker to run groups or counsel students and families. Benefits of the coordination approach are that the school will develop more linkages with the family and community, will be better able to respond to the complex social problems that students bring to schools, and will be able to draw on the expertise and resources of the broader network of human services in the community.

## Partnerships

Partnerships represent volunteer or contractual agreements among human services agencies, businesses, volunteer organizations, and public schools. The purpose of these agreements is to provide a support services network for the school. Partnerships usually provide services such as tutoring, school-to-work transition, mentoring, and student assistance programs such as drug and alcohol intervention and other counseling services. The partner is a contracted employee or volunteer service provider of the school district and remains a separate entity from the school program. Although partners interface with the school programs on a daily basis, they maintain their autonomy. In contrast to the coordination approach, in the partnership approach the school social worker becomes a member of the pupil services team and may be an employee of the school district. Partnerships between schools and human services agencies are on the increase and are being advocated as important vehicles of school reform (Levy & Copple, 1989; Miranda, 1993).

Schools are increasingly forming partnerships with human services agencies to provide mental health and social services on site. Some partners are brought onto the school campus, and others are located near the campus to provide maximum accessibility to students and families (Rist, 1992). Student assistance programs, such as the Communities in Schools (CIS) program in Texas, are an example of partnerships formed to help school districts (Office of the Governor, 1992; Texas Research League, 1991). Part of the funding for the CIS program comes from a variety of federal, state, and private sources. Communities and local school districts work together to raise the additional support and funding necessary to establish the CIS program. Once on the school campus, CIS enables social workers and other professionals who work with at-risk students to provide services on site and to link students to services in the community.

Also in Texas, the Hogg Foundation has committed $2 million in funding over five years to establish partnerships in four Texas cities. The program, called Schools of the Future, emphasizes partnerships among health, mental health, and social services agencies to establish school-based services (Holtzman, 1992). Some variation exists among the different partnerships because each was developed to meet the needs of the community it serves. However, all partnerships were designed to link community human services agencies and coordinate services at school sites.

Some reorganization is necessary to accommodate partnerships on a school campus. Allocation of space, time, and personnel for interfacing and coordinating the efforts of the partner with the school program is important. Commitment of the school toward the partner's role is mandatory, and training of all staff on the roles and functions of the partner is critical. Leadership must come from frontline staff who recognize the need for the services, the principal, the superintendent, the parents, and the community. The planning process must be ongoing, and consensus building should be used to determine the partner's role in relationship to the school. Mechanisms of communication and coordination between the partner and the school must be established and maintained over time. Still, competing goals and interests may make it difficult to manage diverse political constituencies. In general, additional funding will be required to establish comprehensive student assistance services.

## Collaboration

Collaborative arrangements are increasingly being established as a means of linking public schools with the human services system (Bruner, 1991; Mellaville & Blank, 1991). According to Bruner, collaborations require schools and human services agencies "to jointly develop and agree to a set of common goals and directions, share responsibility for obtaining those goals, and work together to achieve those goals using the expertise of each collaborator" (p. 6). The fundamental difference between collaboration and coordination and partnerships is that collaboration requires schools and human services agencies to give up some of their autonomy to share resources and pursue common goals. Collaboration begins to move beyond coordination to the actual merging of services.

Collaboration has been recommended as a means of addressing the isolation of schools from human services agencies and as a means of creating new and improved service delivery by pooling resources and efforts (Mattessich & Monsey, 1992; Mellaville & Blank, 1993). For example, a collaborative project in Boston linked public schools with public housing to connect children and families living in public housing with child care services and the public schools (Lassen & Janey, 1991). Collaborations seek to address the cracks between agencies and schools that students fall through and to decrease fragmentation by establishing a continuum of care. Like partnerships, collaborations typically bring broader human services onto or near the school campus so that the school becomes the site for coordination and delivery of social and health services.

In San Diego, several agencies and the school district came together in the New Beginnings Project to plan a shared vision for initiating institutional changes in how services are delivered to children and families (Payzant, 1992). Executive leadership from the Departments of Health and Social Services, Juvenile Court, and the City Manager's Office and several assistant superintendents contributed leadership, support services, and staff time to establish this collaborative effort. Social services staff, known as "family services advocates," are located on or near the school campus to provide case management services. Each agency also contributes additional team members who remain in the agencies and provide services to the students. This comprehensive model provides services at the school site to all children ages five to 12 who attend public school.

Considerable commitment is necessary to establish a successful collaborative program. As discussed by Bruner (1991), "developing interagency collaborations is extremely time-consuming and process intensive" (p. 26). Planning must be comprehensive. Executive leadership generally takes the lead in initial efforts, educating their staff and including them in a consensus-driven process of mutual negotiation among community agencies, local policymakers, parents, and the school. Interprofessional education becomes necessary to help all parties involved understand each other and their individual contributions to student achievement. Training must be intensive and ongoing. Staff time, space, support services, and other in-kind contributions are required. Considerable restructuring must take place for the successful implementation of a collaborative effort between public schools and human services agencies. Some redefinition of goals and operations is required to obtain new shared goals and operating procedures. Excellent benefits may be derived from collaborations; new and improved programs may be established, and schools may gain added support services to assist in the education of children.

## Integration

Integration of public schools and human services agencies combines the reform initiatives of both the public schools and the human services to develop a new comprehensive human services system for children and families. These new systems integrate public education with broader human services and intricately intertwine the delivery of educational services with human services. This is the most radical approach to linking public schools with human services in that it moves beyond collaboration to actually merge the two systems into a single, integrated service delivery system. In the integration approach, agencies at the state and local levels must redefine their operations, procedures, and missions to provide new and better services (Kahn & Kamerman, 1992; U.S. General Accounting Office, 1992). Public schools are brought out of isolation and into the broader network of human services. The functions of schools become nestled with the functions of other human services, such as health, mental health, and social services, to provide a combined educational and human services program.

State-mandated or -supported initiatives often provide the catalyst for the development of integrated service delivery systems. The terms "comprehensive school program," "full-service school," or "one-stop shopping" have been loosely associated with this type of restructuring. A typical outcome of integration is state-mandated or -supported school-based health clinics or human services centers. Such school-based programs provide comprehensive services and are integrated with the schools' academic programs. Integration is on the increase, with 623 school-based health centers being reported in 41 states and the District of Columbia (Schlitt, Rickett, Montgomery, & Lear, 1994).

Integration of public schools and human services has been explored by only a few states. For example, under court mandate Kentucky established the Kentucky Integrated Delivery System (KIDS), a multiagency venture involving the Governor's Cabinet of Human Resources and the Departments of Education, Social Services, Health, and Mental Health and Mental Retardation. KIDS seeks to make the services of social workers, mental health therapists, public health professionals, and other human services workers available on school campuses. No new funds were allocated for the program, although the Department of Education provided a state coordinator and agencies provided money for travel and other in-kind services. As a result, service centers providing comprehensive social and health services have been established at school sites throughout the state (Mellaville & Blank, 1991).

In New Jersey, the Department of Human Services operates the school-based Youth Services Program, which funds 29 "one-stop shopping centers" that provide comprehensive health and social services across the state (Palaich, Whitney, & Paolino, 1991). All centers are located on or near school campuses and provide social, health, mental health, and employment services. In addition to core services, many sites also provide child care, family planning, and transportation. Services are available to all public school students who need them (Mellaville & Blank, 1991).

Total commitment to a new system of education and human services is necessary to successfully develop and implement integration. Planning must be comprehensive and long range. Top-down and bottom-up approaches must be coordinated simultaneously in a statewide effort. Executive leadership from state agencies and policy-making bodies must be united to accomplish the restructuring initiative. Communities and local schools must also be included in the planning and implementation process. This is likely to be a highly politicized effort that will require coalition building and involvement of multiple constituencies. Consensus will be difficult to obtain.

Interprofessional education will be mandatory in local schools and agencies and should be developed in teacher and human services preparation at the university level. Resource commitment can be significant in terms of staff time, space, and in-kind services. New funding may be required, although money may become available through the restructuring of agencies and the elimination of service duplication. Successful integration of school programs and human services agencies requires that both systems be prepared to undergo significant reform in the staffing, operation, and mission of their systems. A considerable transition and adjustment period should be anticipated. Staff will need to be prepared and supported through the transition. However, benefits will be maximized as integrated services systems reduce the fragmentation in children and family services and accomplish comprehensive school programs.

## CORE AREAS OF EXPERTISE

Reforms inherent in the five approaches to linking public schools and human services agencies are consistent with the mission of the social work profession, and it is vital that social workers become proactively involved in these initiatives. Some social work practitioners have been involved in school reform (see, for example, Hooper-Briar & Lawson, 1994), but many reforms linking public schools with human services have occurred within mainstream education, without the involvement of social workers. It is imperative for the social work profession to define its role and expertise in school reform. Current school reform efforts provide an excellent opportunity for social workers to help develop integrative school programs and to work in these new programs. Unfortunately, educators are not always aware of the social work profession's expertise in working with school-linked human services programs. Without social workers' proactive involvement in school reform, educators look to others for the knowledge and skills that will help them develop linkages between the human services and educational systems. Social workers must demonstrate to educators their expertise in providing creative and effective leadership in six core areas of school reform efforts: environmental assessment, mediation, goal attainment, resources assessment, political action, and needs assessment and intervention planning.

### Environmental Assessment

Schools are linked to a changing and dynamic environment. The success of any school reform initiative hinges on the extent to which the environment is supportive of the reform effort. Social workers provide expertise in assessing both internal and external environments. The internal environment is the subjective culture of the school, including its belief system, norms, roles, values, rules, and task definitions (Ornstein, 1992). The values, beliefs, and behaviors of administrators, teachers, students, and parents all play a role in determining what type of reform is possible and how successful it will be. The external environment comprises the multiple constituents who have a real or perceived interest in the public school system. Social workers may use their expertise to help school leaders influence the dominant values and belief systems in the environments through public education campaigns, lobbying, community organization, and group processes.

## Mediation

Successful linking of schools and human services requires a shared vision. In many cases, schools are unaware of the roles and functions of human services agencies. At the same time, community agencies may not be familiar with the structure, process, or mission of public education. An important first step is to identify the common ground between them and to formulate a shared vision of how they can work together to make the school the best it can be. This requires mediation and communication skills, which are core social work practice skills (Schulman, 1992). Social workers may use their skills to identify common goals and objectives of participants and to help each understand the issues, priorities, and perspectives of the other.

## Goal Attainment

Social workers have expertise in setting social goals and attaining those goals. Generalist experience in clinical practice, community organization, social policy, public service, and nonprofit organization management equip them with essential skills to accomplish goal setting in the public arena. The goal of educational reform is to create a stimulating and effective learning environment in which all students can maximize their potential. In pursuit of this goal, every reform effort is driven by a set of specific goals or objectives. It is critical to be clear about the objectives of the reform effort when selecting an approach to linking schools and human services. To some extent these objectives are dictated by the particular set of problems confronting the students and families in the school. Social workers know that in determining the objectives for a particular reform effort, it is important that all significant constituent groups are represented. Participation in this process should be broad based and include not only those with the power to negotiate changes but also representatives of the children and families whose lives will be affected by the reform. These are basic principles of community organization and social planning, and social workers can use this expertise to facilitate commitment to goals and objectives in the early stages of the process.

## Resources Assessment

The level of resources available in the community or in the school is critical because it often sets the parameters of what is possible. Social workers have core skills in the assessment, coordination, and brokering of resources. Resource constraints are almost always an issue in initiating school reform. It is important to view the alternative approaches to linking schools and human services in terms of their ability to use existing resources more efficiently. For example, the colocation of services can make existing resources go further because it is possible to offer services in a single location rather than in several different locations. This approach not only reduces overhead costs for each of the individual programs but also creates much greater access for students and their families.

## Political Action

In many communities, linking schools and human services is controversial and highly politicized. Some parents are concerned about the potential loss of parental control. In addition, some educators are concerned that the traditional mission of the school will be significantly altered by linking schools with human services. Others are concerned that the school will lose control of the students or that the educational process will be compromised by the integration of human services and education. Still others worry about the problem of confidentiality and the stigmatizing of students who seek out services in the school. All of these are serious concerns associated with linking schools and human services, and many of these issues can become politically volatile. Such concerns require expertise in political action and consensus building. Social workers can use their practice skills in political action to help school leaders anticipate controversial issues and significant sources of opposition and to build broad-based support in the community for the reform effort.

## Needs Assessment and Intervention Planning

When considering approaches to link schools and human services, there is a tendency for educational systems to want to find the single method that can be universally applied across all school districts. This way of thinking is flawed. Each school, each district, each community, and each state need to evaluate the various approaches and requirements for successful implementation and determine which approach is best for it. The expertise that social workers have in needs assessment and individualized intervention planning may help schools avoid falling into the trap of looking for a universal solution to their reform efforts. In some communities, linking schools and human services may be central to the reform effort. In others it may assume a less important role in the overall reform effort. What is important is that workers not lose sight of the ultimate goal of any reform effort: to enhance the quality of public schools so that all children can learn and grow in a stimulating and supportive environment.

## CONCLUSION

In the past decade awareness has been growing that many families and children in America are plagued with serious social problems such as teenage pregnancy, substance abuse, behavior disorders, hunger, physical and mental illness, and family violence. The social work profession has expertise that can assist schools in finding ways to transcend the artificial organizational and professional boundaries and pull together the collective expertise of social workers and educators to better address the needs of their mutual clients. These efforts are a critical part of the school reform movement and require the continued commitment of both schools and human services to develop service delivery systems that are both mutually beneficial and effective in meeting the needs of the school's most important clients—children.

## REFERENCES

Allen-Meares, P., Washington, R. O., & Welsh, B. L. (1986). *Social work services in schools.* Englewood Cliffs, NJ: Prentice Hall.

Anderson, J. J. (1952). The specific content of school social work. *Bulletin of the National Association of School Social Workers, 27*, 3–13.

Bruner, C. (1991). *Thinking collaboratively: Ten questions and answers to help policy makers improve children's services.* Washington, DC: Educational and Human Services Consortium.

Collins, R. L. (1987). Parents' views of alternative public school programs: Implications for the use of alternative programs to reduce school dropout rates. *Education and Urban Society, 19,* 290–302.

Costin, L. B. (1975). A historical review of school social work. In D. J. Kurpius & I. Thomas (Eds.), *Social services and the public schools* (pp. 5–32). Bloomington: Indiana University.

Everett, M. (1992). Developing interdisciplinary schools for the 21st century. *Education Digest, 57*(7), 57–59.

Franklin, C. (1992a). Alternative school programs for at-risk youths. *Social Work in Education, 14,* 239–251.

Franklin, C. (1992b). Family and individual patterns in a group of middle-class dropout youths. *Social Work, 37,* 338–344.

Hahn, A., Danzberger, J., & Lefkowitz, B. (1987). *Dropouts in America: Enough is known for action.* Washington, DC: Institute for Educational Leadership.

Holtzman, W. (Ed.). (1992). *School of the future.* Washington, DC, and Austin, TX: American Psychological Association and Hogg Foundation.

Hooper-Briar, K., & Lawson, H. A. (1994). *Serving children, youth, and families through interprofessional collaboration and service integration: A framework for action.* Oxford, OH: Danforth Foundation and Institute for Educational Renewal, Miami University.

Kahn, A. J., & Kamerman, S. B. (1992). *Integrating services integration: An overview of initiatives, issues, and possibilities.* New York: Columbia University School of Public Health, National Center for Children in Poverty.

Kirst, M. W. (1991). Improving children's services. *Phi Delta Kappan, 72,* 615–618.

Landers, S. (1993, February). Schools vital link in service coordination. *NASW News,* p. 5.

Lassen, M. M., & Janey, C. B. (1991). Public school, public housing: A collaboration for education. *Education Digest, 57*(3), 16–20.

Levy, J. E., & Copple, C. (1989). *Joining forces: A report from the first year.* Alexandria, VA: National Association of State Boards of Education. (ERIC Document Reproduction Service No. ED 308 609)

Liontos, L. B. (1991a). *Building relationships between schools and social services* (Report No. 66). Eugene: University of Oregon, College of Education, ERIC Clearinghouse on Educational Management. (ERIC Document Reproduction Service No. EDO-EA-91-8)

Liontos, L. B. (1991b). *Social services and schools: Building collaboration that works.* Eugene: University of Oregon, Oregon School Study Council. (ERIC Document Reproduction Service No. ED 339 111)

Mattessich, P. W., & Monsey, B. R. (1992). *Collaboration: What makes it work.* St. Paul, MN: Amherst H. Wilder Foundation.

Mellaville, A. I., & Blank, M. J. (1991). *What it takes: Structuring interagency partnerships to connect children and families with comprehensive services.* Washington, DC: Education and Human Services Consortium. (ERIC Document Reproduction Service No. ED 330 748)

Mellaville, A. I., & Blank, M. J. (1993). *Together we can: A guide for crafting a profamily system of education and human services.* Washington, DC: U.S. Government Printing Office.

Miranda, D. (1993, February). *Developing partnerships for the 21st century.* Keynote address presented at the National Partners in Education Conference, Fort Worth, TX.

Office of the Governor, Education Policy Division. (1992). *Building communities of learners* (The 1992 Texas Progress Report on the National Education Goals). Austin, TX: Author.

Ornstein, A. C. (1992). The state role in school reform. *Education Digest, 57*(7), 48–51.

Palaich, R. M., Whitney, T. N., & Paolino, A. R. (1991). *Changing delivery systems: Addressing the fragmentation in children and youth services.* Denver: Education Commission of the States.

Payzant, T. W. (1992). New beginnings in San Diego: Developing a strategy for interagency collaboration. *Phi Delta Kappan, 74,* 139–146.

Pickney, H. B. (1985, February). Public education: In search of believers and supporters. *Clearing House, 58*(6), 251–252. (ERIC Document Reproduction Service No. ED 316 545)

Rist, M. C. (1992). One-stop shopping for student social services. *Education Digest, 58*(1), 12–15.

Schlitt, J. J., Rickett, K. D., Montgomery, L. L., & Lear, J. (1994). *State initiatives to support school-based health centers: A national survey.* Washington, DC: Making the Grade.

Schulman, L. (1992). *The skills of helping individuals, families and groups.* Itasca, IL: F. E. Peacock.

Sedlak, M. W., & Schlossman, S. (1985, Fall). Public school and social services reassessing the progressive legacy. *Educational Theory, 35,* 371–383. (ERIC Document Reproduction Service No. ED 324 622)

Streeter, C. L., Brannen, S. J., & Franklin, C. (1994). Education reform in America: The Texas Governor's Conference on Total Quality Management and the National Education Goals. *Social Work in Education, 16,* 193–198.

Streeter, C. L., & Franklin, C. (1991). Psychological and family differences between middle-class and low-income dropouts: A discriminant analysis. *High School Journal, 74,* 211–219.

Streeter, C. L., & Franklin, C. (1993). Site-based management opportunities for social workers in the public school. *Social Work in Education, 15,* 71–81.

Stroul, B. A., & Friedman, R. M. (1986). *A system of care for severely emotionally disturbed children and youth.* Washington, DC: Georgetown University Child Development Center, Child and Adolescent Service System Program Technical Assistance Center.

Texas Research League. (1991, April). Social services in schools: A holistic approach to education. *Achieve!,* pp. 1–8.

Tyack, D. (1991). Public school reform: Policy talk and institutional practice. *American Journal of Education, 99*(1), 1–19.

Tyack, D. (1992). Health and social services in public schools: Historical perspectives. *Future of Children, 2*(1), 19–31.

U.S. General Accounting Office. (1992). *Integrating human services: Linking at-risk families with services more successful than system reform efforts.* Washington, DC: U.S. Government Printing Office.

*A previous version of this chapter was presented at the Texas State Conference for School Social Workers, Partnerships for Quality Education, February 1993, Austin.*

*This chapter was originally published in the November 1995 issue of* Social Work, *Vol. 40, pp. 773–782.*

# 39  Services for Infants and Toddlers with Disabilities: IDEA, Part H

Edward J. Saunders

S ocial workers in health care settings whose primary responsibility is infants and toddlers with disabilities have a new ally in the Individuals with Disabilities Education Act (IDEA). Social workers may know this legislation better as P.L. 99-457, the Education of the Handicapped Act Amendments of 1986. IDEA includes two programs—Part H and Part B—that are designed to increase services to young children with special needs and their families: Part H is the Infants and Toddlers with Disabilities Program, and Part B, Section 619, is the Preschool Grants Program. This article addresses the facets of IDEA, Part H, that social workers in health care settings need to know to better serve infants and toddlers with special health care and educational needs.

It is estimated that 750,000 neonates each year may have or be at risk for developmental disabilities (Haber, 1989). After a brief historical introduction to IDEA, this article defines the valuable role that social workers can play in the identification, referral, and coordination of services for disabled, Part H–eligible children from birth up to age 3.

## HISTORY OF IDEA, PART H

IDEA is an evolutionary piece of federal legislation. Its roots are P.L. 91-230, the Education of the Handicapped Act (EHA), which was passed nearly 25 years ago on April 13, 1970. It was not until 1986, however, that amendments were made to the EHA to guarantee that infants and toddlers with special needs and their families in participating states would receive the services they needed to maximize the children's development. These amendments to the EHA became P.L. 99-457, which passed both houses of Congress unopposed and was signed into law on October 8, 1986. This act was again amended in 1988, 1990, and 1991. In 1990, the original title of the act (EHA) was changed to the Individuals with Disabilities Education Act. Although Part H became Subchapter VIII in the revised legislation, it has retained its more easily recognized designation.

The Part H program mandates a statewide, comprehensive, multidisciplinary service system to address the needs of infants and toddlers who are experiencing developmental delays or a diagnosed physical or mental condition with a high probability of an associated developmental disability in one or more of the following areas: cognitive development, physical development, language and speech development, psychosocial development, and self-help skills. In addition, states may opt to define and serve at-risk children. Commonly cited factors that may put an infant or toddler at risk of developmental delay include low birthweight, respiratory distress as a newborn, lack of oxygen, brain hemorrhage, infection, and prenatal exposure to toxins through maternal substance abuse.

Part H is nearing full implementation in many states. The original legislation provided a five-year phase-in period for states to develop their comprehensive system of service for the affected population. Although IDEA does not mandate states' participation in Part H, powerful financial incentives from the federal government have kept every state in the planning process to date. States have been provided extensions of the five-year period as they struggle with the logistic, interagency, and financial demands of developing a statewide system. To ensure a coordinated approach to service delivery and financing of services, federal regulations of Part H require that states develop interagency agreements that define the financial responsibility of each agency and impanel a state interagency coordinating council to assist the lead agency in implementing the statewide system. Regulations also prohibit the substitution of funds and reduction of benefits once the plan is implemented in each state (U.S. Department of Education, 1993).

As states and federal territories (for example, Guam, Puerto Rico, and the Virgin Islands) began to plan for implementation of P.L. 99-457 and later IDEA, their first obligation was to designate an agency that would provide leadership in the planning and administration of the state's comprehensive system. In 22 states or territories the lead agency is the department of education, in 11 others it is the department of health, in another nine it is the department of human services, and the remaining states use combined departments or departments of mental health or developmental disabilities (Trohanis, 1989).

## INTERAGENCY AND MULTIDISCIPLINARY PLANNING AND SERVICE DELIVERY

One of the most revolutionary facets of IDEA is its mandate for interagency planning and coordination of service delivery to the affected population. Although one agency in each state is designated as the lead agency, there is an expectation that all state agencies with a vested interest in the welfare of young children with special needs and their families will jointly develop procedural guidelines and financing mechanisms for effective, nonduplicative service delivery. In Iowa, for example, the interagency agreement was negotiated among the Department of Education (the lead agency), the Department of Human Services, the Department of Public Health, and the Iowa Child Health Specialty Clinics (a service provider to special needs children).

Providing advice in the planning and implementation process in every state is a state interagency coordinating council. IDEA requires that state councils have no fewer than 15 members and include parents of children with disabilities, public or private service providers, state agency representatives, and one person in personnel preparation. In Iowa, five of 21 council members are parents of children with special needs. Members of these councils are appointed by the governor.

Local interagency coordinating councils have also been formed in most states (at either a regional or county–parish level) to plan and coordinate services for children and families. In Iowa, each of 17 educational regions in the state has a coordinating council. Again, parents, service providers, and policymakers meet to review the needs of the region and plan for the implementation of services for every eligible family.

Social workers in health care settings are often key players in these planning and coordination efforts. Their knowledge of developmental disabilities, family systems, and referral sources and their skills in interdisciplinary teamwork are all equally important. These competencies are reflected in the following eight major roles identified for social workers under IDEA, Part H:

1. assess family capacity to provide basic nurturing needs
2. mobilize and link families to available supports
3. investigate allegations of abuse or neglect
4. assess and provide services related to problems in family functioning (for example, marital relations, parent–child interactions, and child support)
5. advocate for family rights and access to community services
6. serve as case managers
7. consult with other professionals about family issues
8. plan and implement family services such as parent support groups, family therapy, marital counseling, or individual counseling.

Hospital social workers head the list of social workers most likely to have contact with eligible infants and their families (Bailey, 1989).

## SERVICE DELIVERY TO AFFECTED CHILDREN AND FAMILIES

Another revolutionary facet of IDEA is the requirement that parents of children with special needs participate fully in evaluation, assessment, and planning activities. As children with disabilities or at risk for disabilities are identified (many at birth), the hospital or health clinic social worker may play a critical role in informing parents about the mandates of IDEA, Part H, and the state's comprehensive service delivery system.

Although states have some discretion in the range of services provided to eligible children and their families, the comprehensive system of services should include the following: family training, counseling, and home visits; special instruction; speech pathology and audiology; occupational therapy; physical therapy; psychological services; case management services; medical services for diagnostic or evaluation purposes only; early identification, screening, and assessment services; health services necessary to enable the infant or toddler to benefit from other early intervention services; social work services; vision services; assistive technology devices and assistive technology services; and transportation and related costs that are necessary to enable the infant or toddler and his or her family to receive early intervention services (U.S. Department of Education, 1993).

The statute specifies that such services are to be provided to "handicapped infants and toddlers," but each state can define this population. In Iowa, for example, these children are defined as functioning at least 25 percent below their chronological age, as measured and verified by appropriate evaluation instruments, in one or more of the developmental areas specified under the law (for example, cognitive development, physical development). Children eligible for early intervention services may also have a diagnosed physical or mental condition that has a high probability of resulting in developmental delay. Examples of such conditions include Down's syndrome and other chromosomal abnormalities; sensory impairments; inborn errors of metabolism; congenital central nervous system disorders; severe attachment disorders, including failure to thrive; seizure disorders; serious chronic illness; traumatic injury; and adverse fetal drug exposure, including fetal alcohol syndrome.

Social workers in health care settings should be aware of the definitions that their respective states use to define the population eligible for services. IDEA requires that every state, having defined the population, implement procedures to ensure that every eligible child and family is identified and assessed for needed services. This identification process is generally referred to as "child find."

Many social workers in health care settings may already be part of their state's efforts to identify the affected population. Many health and human services agencies—maternal and child health clinics; community health clinics; Early Periodic Screening, Diagnosis, and Treatment (EPSDT) sites; Special Supplemental Food Program for Women, Infants, and Children (WIC) sites; and Head Start—are already promoting public awareness of their services, which include screening services to detect developmental delays or disabilities. Increased public awareness through media announcements may further help to identify those who are eligible.

If a potentially eligible child is identified by a social worker or allied health professional, IDEA requires that a referral for evaluation and assessment be made to the appropriate public agency, typically an office of the lead agency, no more than two working days after the child is identified. Such a referral, however, is made only with the advice and consent of the parent. At the time of identification, parents may elect not to participate in the early intervention system. Given their anxieties about the status of their child or fears of system mistreatment, the social worker may use his or her therapeutic skills to evoke, in a nondefensive manner, the paramount concerns or feelings of the parents (Ziolko, 1991). This process may take several weeks, even months, before parents will consider referring their child for further assessment. It is very important for social workers to be fully aware of the entire assessment and intervention process so that they can meaningfully interpret this process to parents.

IDEA, Part H, notes that although states may establish a system of payments by parents for early intervention services, including a schedule of sliding fees, states cannot charge parents for any of the following activities: implementation of child find; evaluation and assessment, including functions related to evaluation and assessment; case management; the development and review of Individualized Family Service Plans (IFSPs); and implementation of the procedural safeguards provided to parents (U.S. Department of Education, 1993).

Once a referral of a potentially eligible child is made to the lead agency, IDEA requires that evaluation and assessment by a multidisciplinary team be completed within 45 days. The assessment process culminates with the development, if appropriate, of an IFSP. Before discussing the IFSP, the role of the health care social worker in assessing family functioning is described. Family assessment is a primary role assigned to social workers under IDEA.

## ASSESSING FAMILY FUNCTIONING

Dunst, Trivette, and Deal (1988) conceptualized the interrelationship among family needs and aspirations, strengths and capabilities, and resources and support as an interlocking set of gears that forms a system that generates energy and power. This conceptualization, they wrote, requires that help givers not take control of the system and define the family's developmental course, but rather "promot[e] the family's ability to negotiate alignment of the gears of the system in a way that makes it operate as efficiently as possible" (p. 55). In the course of his or her assessment, the social worker helps to identify family needs, family functioning style, and sources of support and resources. The worker, with the family's permission, carries this information to the IFSP meeting.

Questions to consider in assessing family needs include
- What are the family's concerns and interests?
- What factors or conditions contribute to these concerns or interests?
- Is there consensus among family members regarding the importance of the needs?
- Are there apparent reasons why other needs are not currently defined as such by the family?
- Are there ways of helping the family see its situation differently so needs become more readily apparent?
- Does the family have the time and energy for meeting needs? If not, why? (Dunst et al., 1988).

Questions to consider in identifying family functioning style include
- Do individual family members demonstrate commitment toward the well-being of one another and the family as a whole? In what ways?
- Do individual family members display appreciation for the small and large accomplishments of other family members? How so?
- Do family members spend time doing things together?
- Are there family beliefs or values that provide direction to the family's life?
- Does the family agree on what needs are important to devote its time and energy to?
- Do family members communicate with one another in a way that reflects positive functioning?
- Does the family use a variety of coping strategies? What are they?
- Does the family engage in effective problem-solving activities?
- Does the family display flexibility and adaptability in division of labor in meeting needs?
- What anecdotes does the family share that reflect different strengths and capabilities?
- What aspects of the physical and social environment reflect family strengths?
- Are there opportunities to help the family rephrase and reframe negative comments in a more positive light? (Dunst et al., 1988).

Finally, in conducting a family assessment, the social worker should pursue questions that identify sources of support and resources for the family. Questions to consider in this process include

- Who are the people with whom the family members have contact on a regular basis or feel close to?
- What social groups or organizations do the family members belong to?
- What agencies or professional organizations do family members come in contact with on a regular basis?
- Which network members constitute resources for meeting identified needs?
- Who are potential but underutilized or unidentified sources of support for meeting identified needs?
- Are there particular reasons or factors (for example, sense of indebtedness) that interfere with procuring necessary resources?
- To what extent does the family feel it can depend on network members in times of need?
- To what extent is the family satisfied with help that is provided by network members? (Dunst et al., 1988).

In addition to these questions, Anderson and Goldberg (1991) posed questions to professionals to ensure that their assessments are culturally sensitive. Among these questions are

- If I have adapted a standardized screening tool, do I know if it has cultural biases or has been normed for this cultural group?
- What do I know about child-rearing practices of this cultural group? How do these practices affect child development?
- Do I know where or how to find specific cultural or linguistic information that may be needed for me to be culturally competent in the screening and assessment process?
- Have I participated in training sessions on cultural competence in screening and assessment?
- Am I continuing to develop my knowledge base through formal training and by spending time with community members to learn the cultural attributes specific to the community and families I serve?

Having gleaned answers to all of these questions, the social worker is uniquely prepared to help the family explore options as it moves toward the IFSP staffing.

## INDIVIDUALIZED FAMILY SERVICE PLAN

Whereas previous planning for children with special needs focused almost exclusively on the child, the intent of IDEA, Part H, is to focus on the entire family. Consequently, planning for the child and his or her family is developed using the IFSP. This plan is developed from the input of the various professionals who have examined the child and interviewed family members. Parents are present at these meetings and play a critical role in defining the short- and long-term goals for the child and family and in deciding which services should be pursued. Services include those necessary to enhance the development of the child as well as the capacity of the family to meet the special needs of the child. The rationale for family-focused intervention is based on clinical observations that parents are better equipped to deal with their developmentally delayed child if their needs are met (Healy, Keesee, & Smith, 1989; Mori, 1983; Odom & Karnes, 1988).

The IFSP should include the following information: the child's present attainments; family strengths; how to enhance development of the child; major outcomes expected, including criteria, procedures, and the time lines to achieve specific goals; specific early intervention services that will help the child and family; projected dates for initiating services and their duration; name of the case manager responsible for helping the family implement and coordinate the plan; and steps to help the child and family with the transition to school services at the appropriate time (Committee on Children with Disabilities, 1992). The IFSP is reviewed at least every six months by the service coordinator and parents, and the entire multidisciplinary team must meet annually to review goals and make modifications. Because of the special health care needs of medically fragile infants and toddlers, the health care social worker may prefer to invite much more than annual multidisciplinary team feedback. Child and family circumstances may mandate a monthly meeting of allied health and human services professionals.

A social worker's obligations during the course of the development of the IFSP are twofold: (1) With the permission of the parents, he or she must help team members understand the strengths and stressors of the family as they formulate the IFSP, and (2) he or she must carefully consider the negative and positive connotations of each IFSP decision.

As suggested earlier, social workers can play a decisive role in multidisciplinary team activities as the team, together with the parents of the identified child, moves toward decision making. The social worker, as decision maker, should thoroughly examine a wide range of alternative courses of action; survey the full range of objectives to be fulfilled and the values implicated by the choice; carefully weigh the costs and risks of negative consequences, as well as the positive consequences; intensely search for new information relative to further evaluation of the alternatives; consider the expert judgment of allied professionals, even when the information or judgment does not support an initial preference for action; re-examine the positive and negative consequences of alternatives before making a final choice; and make detailed plans for executing the decision, including contingency plans if known risks materialize (Janis & Mann, 1977, cited in Golin & Ducanis, 1981). These activities will foster deliberations that recognize that every IFSP has both positive and negative facets that all parents must know about and evaluate as they decide the short- and long-term course of intervention for their child and themselves.

## CASE MANAGEMENT

Case management and coordination can be assumed by any member of the multidisciplinary team involved in the assessment of the child and the development of the IFSP. The decision about who will act as case manager rests with the lead agency, but the case manager generally is designated to be that person who is most involved with the family (Campbell, Bellamy, & Bishop, 1988). In many cases involving a disabled infant or toddler, this would likely be a health care social worker or pediatric nurse practitioner. Case management is assumed to be a mutual responsibility shared between professionals and parents (Radin, 1990). At no time should a case manager act contrary to the desires of the parent.

If a parent believes that a case manager or other service provider is acting contrary to his or her wishes or contrary to the terms of the IFSP, the parent has recourse through a system of procedural safeguards that are required by IDEA, Part H. In Iowa, this includes both informal and formal complaint resolution processes that can be directed to the lead agency or any of the other major agencies that are involved with the family.

Loomis (1988) identified several issues involving case management that are germane to service delivery to children with special needs and their families. The focus of case management under IDEA, Part H, is a medical–social model. According to Loomis, programs in this model are frequently designed to prevent or delay institutionalization of clients; services are provided to maintain clients in their homes. Different organizational settings—large hospitals versus small hospitals versus community-based clinics—play different roles in the provision of case management services. Similarly, the funding source of case management services can dictate the role of the social worker. Because IDEA is an evolving delivery system in most states, social workers in health care settings should advocate the most expansive role of the case manager and the least restrictive funding of this service.

## TRAINING NEEDS

To successfully implement the provisions of IDEA, Part H, all professionals involved with children with disabilities must be educated about the provisions of this legislation and must develop the knowledge, skills, and competencies to effectively provide services to the affected population. Currently, personnel preparation programs are focusing too little attention on service delivery to infants and toddlers with disabilities and their families. Campbell et al. (1988) reported that "dramatic personnel shortages exist in every related profession when analyzed with regard to specific training and skills for working with families and infants" (p. 39). They noted that short-term seminar training has been found to be less effective than long-term field-based training programs. They advocate cooperation among local universities, state experts, and model demonstration centers to implement effective personnel development.

Rooney, Gallagher, Fullagar, Eckland, and Huntington (1992) also identified a shortage of qualified personnel in the early intervention arena. Like Campbell et al. (1988), they called for increased collaboration between state agencies and higher education programs to facilitate progress toward compliance with the personnel preparation component of Part H.

Bailey and Simeonsson (1988) stated that "implementing a family focus . . . will be complicated by the fact that most professionals in early intervention programs have little training in assessing family needs or providing family services" (p. 117). They argued that extensive training; the inclusion of family intervention specialists on early intervention teams; and effective, straightforward assessment tools—like one they developed—are needed to solve this problem.

## CONCLUSION

IDEA, Part H, offers an opportunity to children with disabilities and their parents to secure needed services in a family systems context. Part H also offers the social work profession the opportunity to demonstrate its commitment and competencies on behalf of this underserved, vulnerable population. To realize this opportunity, social workers in health care settings must ensure the following:

- that they are familiar with the implementation of IDEA in their state, the lead agency, the local interagency coordinating council, and the definition of disability their state is using to identify eligible children and families
- that they are knowledgeable about physical and psychosocial disabilities in infants and toddlers and their impact on family functioning
- that they are skilled in family assessment, including knowledge of the unique cultural values and practices of families in their catchment area
- that they are skilled in case management and multidisciplinary collaboration and planning
- that they are knowledgeable about special education resources in their communities, including a working relationship with special education social workers, so that children and parents make the appropriate transition from Part H programs at age 3
- that they promote skill-building resources for social workers invested with this special population in their state through their local NASW office, school of social work, and other training programs
- that they advocate for the most favorable and least-restrictive options for services under Part H within their states to guarantee that all infants and children at risk of developmental disabilities and their families receive the most appropriate services.

## REFERENCES

Anderson, M., & Goldberg, P. F. (1991). *Cultural competence in screening and assessment: Implications for services to young children with special needs ages birth through five.* Minneapolis: Pacer Center.
Bailey, D. B., Jr. (1989). Issues and directions in preparing professionals to work with young handicapped children and their families. In J. Gallagher, P. Trohanis, & R. M. Clifford (Eds.), *Policy implementation and PL 99-457: Planning for young children with special needs* (pp. 97–132). Baltimore: Paul H. Brookes.
Bailey, D. B., Jr., & Simeonsson, R. J. (1988). Assessing needs of families with handicapped infants. *Journal of Special Education, 22,* 117–127.
Campbell, P. H., Bellamy, G. T., & Bishop, K. K. (1988). Statewide intervention systems: An overview of the new federal program for infants and toddlers with handicaps. *Journal of Special Education, 22,* 25–41.
Committee on Children with Disabilities. (1992). Pediatrician's role in the development of an Individual Education Plan (IEP) and/or an Individual Family Service Plan (IFSP). *Pediatrics, 89,* 340–342.
Dunst, C., Trivette, C., & Deal, A. (1988). *Enabling and empowering families.* Cambridge, MA: Brookline Books.
Education of the Handicapped Act, P.L. 91-230, 84 Stat. 175–188 (1970).
Golin, A. K., & Ducanis, A. J. (1981). *The interdisciplinary team: A handbook for the education of exceptional children.* Rockville, MD: Aspen.
Haber, J. S. (1989). *A four-stage approach to early childhood intervention: Educational resources.* Champaign: University of Illinois Press.

Healy, A., Keesee, P. D., & Smith, B. S. (1989). *Early services for children with special needs: Transactions for family support.* Baltimore: Paul H. Brookes.

Individuals with Disabilities Education Act, P.L. 101-476, 104 Stat. 1142.

Janis, I. L., & Mann, L. (1977). *Decision-making.* New York: Free Press.

Loomis, J. F. (1988). Case management in health care. *Health & Social Work, 13,* 219–225.

Mori, A. A. (1983). *Families of children with special needs.* Rockville, MD: Aspen.

Odom, S. L., & Karnes, M. B. (1988). *Early intervention for infants and children with handicaps: An empirical base.* Baltimore: Paul H. Brookes.

Radin, N. (1990). A new arena for school social work practice: At-risk infants and toddlers. *Social Work in Education, 12,* 275–282.

Rooney, R., Gallagher, J. J., Fullagar, P., Eckland, J., & Huntington, G. (1992). *Higher education and state agency cooperation for Part H personnel preparation.* Chapel Hill: University of North Carolina, Carolina Institute for Child and Family Policy.

Trohanis, P. L. (1989). An introduction to P.L. 99-457 and the national policy agenda for serving young children with special needs and their families. In J. Gallagher, P. Trohanis, & R. M. Clifford (Eds.), *Policy implementation and P.L. 99-457: Planning for young children with special needs* (pp. 1–17). Baltimore: Paul H. Brookes.

U.S. Department of Education. (1993). 34 CFR Part 303: Early intervention program for infants and toddlers with handicaps; Final rule. *Federal Register, 58*(145), 40958–40989.

Ziolko, M. E. (1991). Counseling parents of children with disabilities: A review of the literature and implications for practice. *Journal of Rehabilitation, 57,* 29–34.

*This chapter was originally published in the February 1995 issue of* Health & Social Work, *Vol. 20, pp. 39–45.*

# 40

## Funding School-Linked Services through Grants: A Beginner's Guide to Grant Writing

Nancy Feyl Chavkin

**F**unding is at the heart of the school-linked services movement; there is an inextricable relationship between quality services for children and the financing of these services. Farrow and Joe (1992) made a strong case for addressing financing as a first step in developing school-linked, integrated services. Focusing on financing has two clear advantages. First, the methods of funding affect the nature and outcomes of services by determining the priorities, incentives, and usefulness of services to families. The United States is just now beginning to realize the effects of categorical funding; that is, if more dollars go to special education students, suddenly there is an increase in the number of special education students identified. Second, focusing on funding tackles the toughest problem of service integration; administrators must be willing to put their dollars behind shared goals.

Because issues of authority, control, and priorities are part of the financing issue, this article examines the critical components of developing funding proposals. The article discusses the background and context of funding for school-linked services; discusses one part of the issue, seeking external funding; and makes practical suggestions for securing grant funds.

## BACKGROUND AND CONTEXT OF FUNDING

Financing school-linked services is a complicated issue no one has wanted to discuss. No definitive method exists (Farrow & Bruner, 1993). A variety of experiments have used multiple streams of existing and new funding. Hare (1995) described several state-funded initiatives (for example, California, New Jersey, Kentucky, Missouri, Florida), foundation- and organization-funded initiatives (for example, Hogg Foundation, Annie E. Casey Foundation), and federal grants (for example, National Center for Service Integration, Service Integration Facilitation Grants). She listed the major funding services through education, health, and social services, including Title IV-E of the Social Security Act (P.L. 96-272); the Job Opportunities and Basic Skills Training Program (P.L. 100-485); the Alcohol, Drug Abuse, and Mental Health Administration Reorganization Act of 1992 (P.L. 102-321); Title I of the reauthorization of Elementary and Secondary Education Act (P.L. 103-382); and the Individuals with Disabilities Education Act (P.L. 101-476).

Dryfoos (1994) described 16 categorical funding sources that are currently being combined to create comprehensive programs. Some school social work services are funded by Medicaid reimbursements for eligible students; other

412

programs are using Maternal and Child Health Block Grants, Drug-Free Schools money, and funds from child protective services. Congruent with the national picture, the Texas Research League's (1995) *Inventory of School-Linked Services in Texas* lists more than 50 programs in the state, each with a unique combination of public, private, and other sources of funding such as client fees and in-kind support.

Despite the diverse and creative ways schools have funded school-linked services, Kirst (1993) posited that schools alone cannot pay for all noneducational services. The finance issue is a key component of Kirst's definition of *school-linked services:*

> a systemic change that enables parents to better consume and tailor public and private services to their special needs. The systemic change links schools and local public and private social agencies to meet interrelated children's needs. There need to be new attitudes among the service providers as well as sanctions and incentives to collaborate. All levels of government must change their fiscal requirements and incentives to enhance school linkages. The scope of school linkage may vary with the local context but should include a common intake and management information system. (p. 166)

Franklin and Streeter (1995) extended Kirst's ideas by including the funding issue in their summary of the five major approaches to linking public schools with human services. They conceptualized school-linked services along a continuum encompassing informal relations, coordination, partnerships, collaboration, and integration, moving from little or no change to change in the basic philosophy and organization of the system. They examine each approach according to eight dimensions: commitment, planning, training, leadership patterns, resources, funding, scope of change, and impact. The funding issue is of critical importance to each approach but in different ways. For example, in the informal relations approach, only minimal funding is required, whereas in the coordination approach, some additional funds for pupil services are required. When school-linked services have reached true integration, additional funding is required for all systems, and there is greater efficiency because the agencies have been restructured.

In the long run, major changes are needed in how children's health, education, and social services are funded. These changes are integral to the concept of school-linked, integrated services. In the meantime, children cannot wait for the slow wheels of bureaucracy and politics to change the funding mechanisms. Many schools and communities will need to secure grant funds for start-up expenses and pilot projects.

## SUCCESSFUL GRANT SEEKING

### Begin Proactively

Bauer (1995) offered social workers working with school-linked service projects the advice that grant seekers should begin proactively. Too often grant seekers have their own project in mind and then try to fit it into someone else's guidelines within a two-week period. No time is available to develop a relationship with the funding agency; to understand the agenda of the granter; or to prepare a well-conceived, winning proposal. Grant seekers usually begin the negative process of flooding the market with grant requests, hoping that eventually one will be successful.

Drawing on the work of Festinger, Bauer (1995) used the cognitive dissonance theory to develop his own "values glasses theory" of seeking. Understanding the thinking and values of the granter is critical to being successful; too many grant seekers understand only their own beliefs and thus write from a narrow perspective. However, grant seekers should not pander to the granter's values or try to disguise a project. Bauer observed that working proactively does not necessarily mean spending more time on the grant-writing task; rather, grant seekers must use their time well over a longer period instead of trying to produce "a last-minute Herculean proposal effort" (p. 5). Although most grants are written on short notice, those that are funded often were in the planning stages many months before the application was made.

After a relevant funding source is located, grant seekers must read the request for proposals or foundation guidelines thoroughly and follow them exactly. Fine proposals are eliminated at the first stage of the review process because the authors did not comply with the requirements for submission. Grant seekers should know their audience. Key questions to consider are, Who is evaluating the proposal? What kinds of projects does the evaluating group want to fund? What are their interests? It is often beneficial for grant seekers to role-play what it would be like if they were receiving the request for funding.

Grant seekers must be familiar with the criteria for review, especially the points awarded for each section of the proposal. For example, if 25 percent of the points are awarded based on project need, then 25 percent of the narrative should be on project need. Figure 40-1 is an example of review criteria adapted from a U.S. Department of Education proposal.

## Demonstrate Need

One of the biggest problems that beginning grant seekers face is how to separate the need from the solution. For example, school social workers might need a van to transport children to and from afterschool tutoring activities. It is obvious to the school social workers how helpful the van will be. By focusing the proposal on the van, however, they are focusing on the solution and not on the needs the van will meet. It would be better to document the learning needs of the students who will be transported in the van and how the van will help improve learning.

Perhaps the most common error with school-linked services proposals is their exclusive focus on the need for more personnel. For example, many times a school principal's first response to the needs assessment question is, "I need more nurses, social workers, and aides. If I had more staff, the problems would be solved." Most likely there is an element of truth in this statement, but the statement is not a needs assessment. The statement is the proposed solution. A better needs statement would focus on the number of children who are sick or without immunizations, the percentage of children who do not have adequate

*Figure 40-1*

## Sample Proposal Review Criteria

| Selection Criteria | Maximum Points | Points |
|---|---|---|
| 1. National significance | 30 | _____ |
| 2. Quality of project design | 30 | _____ |
| 3. Quality and potential contributions of personnel | 15 | _____ |
| 4. Adequacy of resources | 15 | _____ |
| 5. Quality of management plan | 10 | _____ |
| Total | 100 | _____ |

Highly recommended for funding _____
Recommended for funding _____
Not recommended for funding _____

Each section may also be rated individually according to strengths and weaknesses. For example, under quality of project design, the instructions to reviewers might read:

In determining the quality of the design of the proposed project, consider the following: (1) whether the goals, objectives, and outcomes to be achieved by the project are clearly specified and measurable and (2) whether a specific research design has been proposed and the quality and appropriateness of that design, including the scientific rigor of the studies involved.

**Maximum points:  30**
Excellent   26–30
Good   21–25
Fair   16–20
Poor   1–15
Missing   0

Score _____

supervision, the low level of parental participation in school activities, or the low reading scores. Grant seekers must make the connection between need and solution early in the proposal. Those who begin a proposal with the solution will not convince the reviewer why it should be funded.

Grant seekers should always be asking, Why should the granter fund the project? Grant seekers need to describe the problem and what could happen if it is not funded by considering all possible negative ramifications. For example, the readers should be told of the consequences of low reading or math scores. Painting a worst-case scenario is often useful. Charts, graphs, and facts provide the detail that can help a proposal be specific about needs. One or two brief case vignettes using first names can highlight the human factor in the proposal. References to current literature should be included.

Grant seekers should discuss how the project will be a model for other sites, for example, by explaining how the program addresses the needs of similar schools and could also benefit them. The "upside-down pyramid approach" developed by the author can be useful (Figure 40-2). The proposal should begin with the needs of the project and then describe how meeting these needs will help not only the school, but also the community, the state, and even the nation.

*Figure 40-2*

## The "Upside-Down Pyramid Approach" to Explaining a Project's Benefits

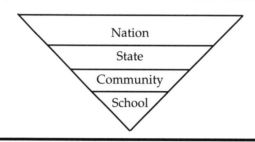

## Describe the Project

Because school-linked services projects involve interrelated needs, they are often difficult to describe. Social workers know that most projects do not follow a linear path, but in a proposal one must explain and link goals, objectives, needs, and resources.

The author developed the worksheets in Figures 40-3, 40-4, and 40-5 as useful guides for beginning grant writers that help them link the goal and objectives to the needs and resources. Grant seekers should begin their thinking with a statement of the problem or issue and then ask the questions, How do the goal and objectives meet the needs? Is the project building on the strengths of the beneficiaries? Is the project using all the strengths and resources of the community and group? (Figure 40-3). Using a sample objective developed by the author, Figure 40-4 breaks the objective statement into a series of questions that many grant writers find useful, and Figure 40-5 presents a linear way to look at goals, objectives, activities, and tasks.

Grant seekers should be clear about the distinctions among goals, objectives, activities, and tasks. The worksheets show a connection between the goals of

*Figure 40-3*

## Describing a Project

1. State problem or issue (whom does this problem affect? how?).
2. Document severity of problem (local, state, and national statistics; hard data needed here).
3. Give beneficiaries of project (whom will it help? why do it?).
4. Give strengths and resources of beneficiaries.
5. Give strengths and resources of community.
6. Give group's strengths and resources.
7. State general goal of project (what you will do).
8. State specific goals.
9. State specific objectives (no more than 3–5).*

*Go to Objectives Worksheet before completing this section.

*Figure 40-4*

## Example of Completed Objectives

**Worksheet Objective 1:** Eighth-grade students at Hometown School who participate in the PATH program will increase attendance at school during the 1996–97 year by 50 percent more than in 1995–96 by the end of the second semester of participation (May 31, 1997).

**Who?** Eighth-grade students at Hometown School
**Do what?** Will increase attendance at school
**When?** By the end of the second semester of their participation (September 1996 to May 1997)
**Under what circumstances?** During their participation in the PATH program
**To what degree?** Fifty percent more than during the 1995–96 school year
**How will it be measured?** By attendance records

the project, the need for the project, the existing resources, and the specific objectives.

## Provide Organizational Capability

Grant seekers should write a clear plan of operation, making a chart of who will do what activity, when they will do it, and where they will do it. This task is especially important for school-linked services projects because organizations are complex regardless of where they fall on Franklin and Streeter's (1995) continuum. Using Figure 40-5, grant writers can begin with the objectives and then

*Figure 40-5*

## The Linear Way to Look at a Proposal

| Goal: | | |
|---|---|---|
| | **How Evaluated** | **By Whom/When/What Instruments/Why** |
| Objective 1 | | |
|   Activity l.a | | |
|     Task l.a.1 | | |
|     Task l.a.2 | | |
|     Task l.a.3 | | |
|   Activity l.b | | |
|     Task l.b.1 | | |
|     Task l.b.2 | | |
|   Activity 1.c | | |
|     Task 1.c.1 | | |
|     Task 1.c.2 | | |
| Objective 2 | | |
|   Activity 2.a | | |
|     Task 2.a.1 | | |
|     Task 2.a.2 | | |
|   Activity 2.b | | |
|     Task 2.b.1 | | |
|     Task 2.b.2 | | |
|     Task 2.b.3 | | |

list each activity that must be done to complete the objective, breaking the activity into tasks. Timelines and organizational charts are helpful.

It must be clear to the readers that the grant applicant is capable of carrying out the project. Grant writers should describe physical resources (for example, office, equipment, library), strong community support (relevant letters of support can be included in an appendix), and previous track record with grants (whether the organization can manage a budget and has been successful with other endeavors). However, some granters are skeptical of applicants who already have many grants. Granters will want to know how a project is different from other previously funded projects and that the new request for funds is not a duplication of previous efforts.

It is helpful to provide concise (paragraph-long) summaries about the qualifications of key staff and how these relate to the proposal. If space permits, one- or two-page vitae of key personnel can be included in an appendix.

A well-done graphic can be worth much more than pages of text. Visual aids can help grant writers get organized and can present a quick, clear picture of the project. Funders look favorably on proposals that include details about timelines and the people responsible for each activity. Figure 40-6 is an example of a Gantt chart, first developed by Henry L. Gantt in the 1900s and still widely used for establishing clear timelines and responsibilities. Grant writers can use other kinds of charts to explain their activities, such as a PERT (Program Evaluation and Review Technique) chart or a project management review chart that links goals, objectives, activities, measurement, data analysis, and outcome.

### Explain Finances

The project's budget should be as specific as possible and should justify any large or unusual expenditures (see Figure 40-7). A section entitled "Budget Rationale" should be included in the proposal. An essential appendix that explains key budget line items is particularly helpful to grant reviewers.

Funders examine a proposal's direct and indirect costs. *Direct costs* usually include personnel (wages and salaries, fringe benefits, and merit and cost-of-living raises), supplies (pens, books, videotapes, computer diskettes, and so forth), equipment (purchase or rental), travel (in-state and out-of-state, broken down by destination, purpose, mileage, or per diem), communication costs (telephone, fax, and e-mail equipment and installation charges and postage), printing (publishing brochures and handbooks and copying costs), contracted services (use of consultants and subcontractors), and miscellaneous (facility rental, repairs, and any expense not included elsewhere). *Indirect costs*— the overhead costs incurred in the administration of a grant—are usually calculated as a percentage of total direct costs. For example, some grants have an 8 percent indirect-cost rate calculated on the basis of all direct costs; others have a 48 percent indirect-cost rate calculated on the basis of only salaries and wages. Some foundations and a few state programs do not allow the inclusion of indirect costs in the budget.

Most funding agencies prefer to have funds go for direct services rather than equipment; grant seekers should check with funding agencies on this issue. If

*Figure 40-6*

## Example of a Gantt Chart

Goal: To develop a training curriculum for school social work interns

| | | Person | Time Frame | | | | | | | | | | | | | | |
|---|---|---|---|---|---|---|---|---|---|---|---|---|---|---|---|---|---|
| | | | January | | | February | | | | March | | | | | April | | |
| Objective | Activity | Responsible | 4 | 11 | 18 | 25 | 1 | 8 | 15 | 22 | 1 | 8 | 15 | 22 | 29 | 5 | 12 | 19 |
| 1. | Develop course objective | J. Addams | | ├──────┤ | | | | | | | | | | | | | | |
| 2. | Prepare outlines of three modules | J. Culbert | | | | ├────┤ | | | | | | | | | | | | |
| 3. | Select teaching methods | E. Abbott | | | | | | | ├────┤ | | | | | | | | | |
| 4. | Prepare workbooks | G. Lee | | | | | | | | | | | ├──────────┤ | | | | | |

*Figure 40-7*

**Example of Budget Summary**

|  | Federal Portion | School Match | Total |
|---|---|---|---|
| Personnel |  |  |  |
| Supplies |  |  |  |
| Travel |  |  |  |
| Equipment |  |  |  |
| Communication |  |  |  |
| Printing |  |  |  |
| Contracted services |  |  |  |
| Miscellaneous |  |  |  |
|  |  |  |  |
| Direct costs |  |  |  |
| Indirect costs |  |  |  |
| Total costs |  |  |  |

possible, the project should secure matching funds or in-kind contributions such as time, personnel, or office space and equipment; some funders require these according to an established ratio. In funding proposals in-kind services should be assigned a dollar equivalency.

**Document Success and Accountability**

If possible, projects should use an external evaluator who provides an objective look at successes and failures. It is not the job of the school social worker to do all of the evaluations, but it is the responsibility of the social worker to make certain that the right questions are being asked. An evaluation might consider questions in each of four areas: planning, implementation, outcome, and economic efficiency. Grant seekers do not have to evaluate every activity or objective but must explain why they chose to evaluate specific parts of the project.

Many kinds of evaluations (not all of them mutually exclusive) are described in reference books (for example, Gabor & Grinnell, 1994; Royse & Thyer, 1996). The kind of evaluation needed depends on its purpose and can examine effort (person hours, visits, meetings), performance (yield, results), adequacy (change in unmet need, decreased absenteeism, increased test scores), efficiency (how efforts were more productive), process (relative success of parts of projects, aspects that were done better), quantitative versus qualitative outcomes, formative versus summative processes, process versus outcome, cost–benefits versus cost-effectiveness, compliance versus quality, effectiveness versus efficiency, and inputs versus impact. Grant writers can seek assistance with statistics, computer programs, survey design, and data collection.

Most important, project evaluation should not fall into the "autopsy" category. Many project coordinators wait until a project is completed before they consider doing an evaluation, when it is often too late to change some of the activities that could have improved the program. Project staff can consider combining a process evaluation with an outcome evaluation.

Grant writers should explain how they will share what works in a project with others (either during or after the program) in both the organizational and evaluation plans. Reviewers look favorably on proposals with a clear plan for dissemination of results.

## ANALYZING THE PROCESS

### Fine-Tuning the Proposal

Writing style is a key factor in selecting the winning proposal when all other factors are equal. Grant writers should write in short sentences and use the active voice, avoiding the abstract and wordy writing that often accompanies the passive voice. Acronyms, jargon, and vague pronoun references should be avoided.

Proposals should include in appendixes supporting documents; essential information needs to be in the text. Appendixes can be useful for history and background of an organization, vitae of personnel, relevant prior studies or projects, copies of support letters, evaluation instruments, or sample lesson plans.

Most important, people outside the project should read and critically review a proposal before submission. It is best to have two types of readers: lay readers and expert readers. Lay readers who know nothing about the project should read a proposal to determine if they understand what is being said. Expert readers who know the field can give feedback on missing research or a discrepancy in organizational plans. Critique and feedback are essential to a successful proposal and are critical to one that has been conceived and written by a team of individuals from different school-linked organizations.

### Trying Again

Very few grants are funded on the first submission; however, many are funded after revisions and resubmissions. Writers of unsuccessful proposals should write a thank-you letter to the funding agency and request to see reviews or a summary of reviews so that the grant application can be revised and improved.

## CONCLUSION

Writing successful proposals is not easy and takes time and commitment. Staff of school-linked services projects who want to obtain funding must take the time to plan and conceptualize what resources are in place, what resources are needed, and how resources will be organized with new funding to accomplish the tasks ahead of them. Farrow's quote in Mellaville and Blank (1993) is an excellent expression of what is required for staff of school-linked services programs to be successful at grant writing: "Fiscal strategies must be driven by a new vision of the service delivery system we are trying to create" (p. 82).

## REFERENCES

Bauer, D. G. (1995). *The "how to" grants manual: Successful grantseeking techniques for obtaining public and private grants.* Phoenix: Oryx Press.

Dryfoos, J. G. (1994). *Full-service schools: A revolution in health and social services for children, youth, and families.* San Francisco: Jossey-Bass.

Farrow, F., & Bruner, C. (1993). *Getting to the bottom line: State and community strategies for financing comprehensive community service systems* (Resource Brief 4). New York: National Center for Service Integration and Columbia University's National Center for Children in Poverty.

Farrow, F., & Joe, T. (1992). Financing school-linked, integrated services. *Future of Children, 2*(1), 56–67.

Franklin, C., & Streeter, C. L. (1995). School reform: Linking public schools with human services. *Social Work, 40,* 773–782.

Gabor, P. A., & Grinnell, R. M., Jr. (1994). *Evaluation and quality improvement in the human services.* Boston: Allyn & Bacon.

Hare, I. (1995). School-linked, integrated services. In R. L. Edwards (Ed.-in-Chief), *Encyclopedia of social work* (19th ed., Vol. 3, pp. 2100–2109). Washington, DC: NASW Press.

Kirst, M. W. (1993). Financing school-linked services. *Education and Urban Society, 25,* 166–174.

Mellaville, A. I., & Blank, M. J. (1993). *Together we can: A guide for crafting a profamily system of education and human services.* Washington, DC: U.S. Government Printing Office.

Royse, D., & Thyer, B. A. (1996). *Program evaluation: An introduction* (2nd ed.). Chicago: Nelson-Hall.

Texas Research League. (1995). *Inventory of school-linked services in Texas.* Austin: Author.

## SELECTED BIBLIOGRAPHY

Coley, S. M. (1990). *Proposal writing.* Newbury Park, CA: Sage Publications.

Decker, L. E., & Decker, V. A. (1993). *Grantseeking: How to find a funder and write a winning proposal.* Charlottesville, VA: Community Collaborators.

Edwards, R. L., Benefield, E.A.S., Edwards, J. A., & Yankey, J. A. (1996). *Building a strong foundation: Fundraising for nonprofits.* Washington, DC: NASW Press.

Foundation Center. (1993). *The national guide to funding for children, youth, and families.* New York: Author.

Ginsberg, L. (1995). *Social work almanac* (2nd ed.). Washington, DC: NASW Press.

Greever, J. C., & McNeil, P. (1993). *The Foundation Center's guide to proposal writing.* New York: Foundation Center.

Lauffer, A. (1983). *Grantsmanship.* Thousand Oaks, CA: Sage Publications.

Martin, M. D., & Landrum, J. W. (1990). *Proposal power: The educator's proposal writing handbook.* Bloomington, IN: Phi Delta Kappa.

National Association of Social Workers. (1990). *Expanding school social work through federal funding in P.L. 100-297.* Silver Spring, MD: Author.

Ogden, T. E. (1991). *Research proposals: A guide to success.* New York: Raven.

Reif-Lehrer, L. (1989). *Writing a successful grant application.* Boston: Jones & Bartlett.

Ries, J. B., & Leukefeld, C. G. (1995). *Applying for research funding: Getting started and getting funded.* Thousand Oaks, CA: Sage Publications.

Soriano, F. I. (1995). *Conducting needs assessments: A multidisciplinary approach.* Thousand Oaks, CA: Sage Publications.

William, H. S. (1991). *Outcome funding: A new approach to public-sector grantmaking.* Rensselaerville, NY: Rensselaerville Institute.

## USEFUL INTERNET ADDRESSES

Federal Information Exchange—http://www.fie.com/cws/sra/resource.htm
Foundation Center—http://fdncenter.org
New York University Medical Center—http://www.med.nyu.edu/nih-guide.html
*Philanthropy Journal*—http://www.philanthropy-journal.org/plhome/plhome.htm
Research Administration Management Systems and Federal Information Exchange—http://www.rams-fie.com

Southwest Texas State University, Research-Sponsored Programs—http://www.rsp.swt.edu
U.S. Department of Education—http://www.ed.gov

## SELECTED REFERENCE WORKS (FOUND IN MOST PUBLIC LIBRARIES)

*Annual Register of Grant Support.* Chicago: Marquis Academic Media.
*Catalog of Federal Domestic Assistance.* Washington, DC: U.S. Government Printing Office.
*Congressional Quarterly Weekly Report.* Washington, DC: U.S. Government Printing Office.
*Federal Grants and Contracts Weekly.* Alexandria, VA: Capitol Publications.
*Federal Register.* Washington, DC: U.S. Government Printing Office.
*Foundation Directory.* New York: Foundation Center.
*Foundation Grants Index.* New York: Foundation Center.
*Grants Magazine.* New York: Plenum Press.
*Grantsmanship Center News.* Los Angeles: Grantsmanship Center.
*National Institute of Health Guide.* Bethesda, MD: National Institutes of Health.
*National Science Foundation Guide.* Arlington, VA: National Science Foundation.

## SELECTED GRANT–WRITING VIDEOS

Bauer, D., & GPN. (Producers). (1991). *Strategic fund raising.* [Available from GPN, 1800 North Third Street, Lincoln, NE 68583; 1-800-228-4630]
Public Broadcasting System. (1996). *Funding educational technology.* [Available from PBS, 1320 Braddock Place, Alexandria, VA 22314-1698; 1-800-344-3337]
University of Nebraska Television. (Producer). (1989). *Winning grants* (Produced in cooperation with the American Council on Education). [Available from GPN, 1800 North Third Street, Lincoln, NE 68583; 1-800-228-4630]
University of Nebraska Television. (Producer). (1992). *Effective grantwriter.* [Available from GPN, 1800 North Third Street, Lincoln, NE 68583; 1-800-228-4630]

---

*This chapter was originally published in the July 1997 issue of* Social Work in Education, *Vol. 19, pp. 164–175.*

# 41

## Combining Mental Health Treatment with Education for Preschool Children with Severe Emotional and Behavioral Problems

Cathryne L. Schmitz and Alan Hilton

Until very recently preschool children with severe emotional and behavioral problems received little recognition in the professional literature, in teacher training, and in service provision. Although the population of preschool children with severe emotional and behavioral problems has grown since the early 1970s, there is considerable evidence that these children are underreferred for services (Swan, Purvis, & Wood, 1986; Walker, Bettes, & Ceci, 1984). Research about or even awareness of this group of children is inadequate (Hilton & Schmitz, 1988).

Early intervention linked to the child's home and community environment are indicated (Freeman & Dyer, 1993). Knitzer, Steinberg, and Fleisch (1990) pointed to the need for mental health as well as education services for children with serious emotional or behavioral disorders, and Fox and McEvoy (1993) discussed the need for interventions that integrate family, school, and community services. This article reviews the characteristics of preschool children with emotional and behavioral problems, discusses existing models of service delivery, and presents a collaborative model for services that integrates mental health treatment and education policy and programming.

## REVIEW OF THE LITERATURE

### Technology

The terms "emotionally and behaviorally disturbed," "emotionally and behaviorally disordered," and "seriously emotionally disturbed" are used interchangeably in the education and mental health literature (Institute of Medicine, 1989; Knitzer et al., 1990). The inference from the literature is that the terms "behaviorally disturbed" or "behaviorally disordered" are used in reference to youths who exhibit acting-out behaviors that fit criteria outlined in the DSM-IV as conduct or attention deficit disorders (American Psychiatric Association, 1994). The terms "emotional disturbances" or "emotional disorders," on the other hand, are applied to youths who exhibit symptoms related to depressive and anxiety disorders or posttraumatic stress disorder. In 1990, the Individuals with Disabilities Education Act (IDEA) (P.L. 101-476) (Knitzer et al., 1990) defined serious emotional disturbance in terms of ability to learn, potential for interpersonal relationships, behavior, feelings, mood, and physical symptoms. The National Institute of Mental Health (Stroul & Friedman, 1986) describes serious emotional disturbance in terms of system involvement, DSM diagnosis, longevity of symptoms, and social functioning in various environments. The various terms are used interchangeably in this article to refer to children with emotional and behavioral problems severe enough to inhibit their ability to learn and to interfere with family, peer, and community relationships.

## Extent of Need

Some researchers have estimated a significant population of children with severe emotional and behavioral problems: 11.8 percent of children have emotional disturbances, and 5.0 percent exhibit severe symptoms (Stroul & Friedman, 1986). Although the identified population is increasing ("Improving Services," 1985), Knitzer (1982) estimated that only one-third of all youths with severe emotional disturbances receive the services they need. Site visits to programs for children and youths with emotional and behavioral problems revealed an inadequacy of services in the education system (Knitzer et al., 1990).

## Resilience and Risk Indicators

Professionals point to the need for early intervention with families of high-risk children (Freeman & Dyer, 1993). Data indicate that behavior disorders are present in very young children (Maselli, Brown, & Veaco, 1984; Thomas & Chess, 1984). The professional literature shows that older children and adolescents with behavior disorders exhibited potential behavior problems at very young ages (Griffin, 1987; Spivack, Marcus, & Swift, 1986; Stevenson, Richman, & Graham, 1985). These early behaviors are strong indicators of later problems (Baenen, Glenwick, Stephens, Neuhaus, & Mowrey, 1986; Thomas & Chess, 1984).

Behavior problems in young children are predictive of later problems in social adjustment (Patterson, Capaldi, & Bank, 1991), and early oppositional behavior is related to conduct disorders later in childhood and adolescence (Kazdin, 1987). A study by Wehby, Dodge, Valente, and the Conduct Disorders Prevention Research Group (1993) found that "children identified as high-risk at kindergarten demonstrate difficulties one year later" (p. 67). Because younger children respond more quickly to treatment, treatment through intensive preschool programs makes therapeutic and financial sense.

The individual, family, and environmental characteristics of children at risk vary widely (Freeman & Dyer, 1993). Practitioners are aware that the population of children and youths is not homogeneous. Children with emotional and behavioral problems exist along a continuum laid out in the education and mental health literature (Institute of Medicine, 1989; Knitzer et al., 1990; Stroul & Friedman, 1986). These children exhibit a range of behavioral, emotional, and neurological symptoms that interact with varying individual and family strengths and risks.

Studies of at-risk children receiving services, including child welfare, mental health, and education services (Anthony & Cohler, 1987; Schorr, 1989) and substance abuse and violence prevention services (Hawkins, Catalano, & Miller,

1992; Smith, Lizotte, Thornberry, & Krohn, 1995; Yoshikawa, 1994), identified a range of factors leading to risk and resilience among youths. These studies pointed out the importance of individualized assessment and holistic intervention. Individual, community, and circumstantial factors influence children's responses to stress (Anthony & Cohler, 1987; Garmezy, 1983).

*Resilience Factors.* Protective factors occur in children, their caregivers, and their environments; these factors interact with stressful events and risk factors to determine a child's level of vulnerability (Werner & Smith, 1982). Significant factors contributing to resilience and risk include parent functioning and education; child's age, developmental stage, gender, physical characteristics, intelligence, health, and temperament; and family characteristics such as family size, support, cohesiveness, perception of the child, discipline style, and stress (Rutter, 1983; Werner, 1987; Werner & Smith, 1982).

Children's self-esteem, achievement orientation, nurturing qualities, and sense of responsibility also affect their resilience (Werner & Smith, 1982). Children's problem-solving skills, coping strategies (Anthony, 1987; Cohler, 1987; Wahlsten, 1994; Werner, 1987; Werner & Smith, 1982), locus of control (Werner, 1987; Werner & Smith, 1982), and interpretation of events (Rutter, 1983) are additional factors. Finally, there is evidence that children who develop constructive coping strategies "have access to resourceful, positive, and stable persons in the environment" (Wahlsten, 1994, pp. 720–721).

*Risk Factors.* Studies indicate that the problems faced by disadvantaged preschoolers are growing increasingly complex (Edlefsen & Baird, 1994). The consequences to children of the economic changes occurring over the past 20 years are clear. Poverty is one of the major risk factors identified as increasing the vulnerability of children and families (Cohler, 1987; Werner, 1987; Werner & Smith, 1982). Children now constitute the poorest age group in the United States (Kealing & Oakes, 1988). The poverty rate among children was 22.7 percent at the end of 1993 (Children's Defense Fund, 1995).

The most dramatic rise in poverty has been among families with young children. Twenty-five percent of children younger than six and 27 percent of children under three now live in poverty. Preschool children from low-income families experience more sociopsychological stressors and enter school with "fewer intellectual, social, and emotional school-readiness skills" than other children (Edlefsen & Baird, 1994, p. 567). Along with increasing poverty rates, children experience increasing rates of homelessness, parental substance abuse, and other major risk factors that contribute to family stress and negatively affect the socioemotional development of children (Children's Defense Fund, 1995).

## EXPLORATORY STUDY TO IDENTIFY TRAITS OF CHILDREN AND FAMILIES SERVED

To understand the traits, characteristics, and needs of preschool children with emotional and behavioral problems, we used an action research plan (see Patton, 1990). Inquiry involved participant observation, conversational interview, and collaborative development. The authors, who have experience and expertise with intervention programs for preschool children with emotional or behavioral disorders, developed an understanding of the traits and characteristics common among preschool children with severe emotional or behavioral problems in collaboration with classroom and program social workers, counselors, and teachers specializing in day treatment with emotionally and behaviorally disturbed preschool children. On the basis of this collaborative process, we developed and refined an initial list of risk factors.

### Sample Sites and Interviewees

Purposive sampling was used to select interview sites. Three sites, including the initial site, were chosen through a combination of theory-based and criterion sampling (Patton, 1990; Rubin & Babbie, 1993). Day treatment programs in two cities in two other geographic regions with demographics similar to the initial site were chosen: These cities had populations of 400,000 to 500,000 and surrounding areas with populations of 1 million to 2 million. Programs serving preschool-age children with severe, multiple emotional or behavioral disturbances were targeted to test the initial findings. One or two individuals from each site were interviewed.

Professionals having experience with young children with severe emotional or behavioral disturbances, familiarity with the characteristics common among preschool children with emotional or behavioral disorders, and knowledge and expertise in intensive preschool day treatment were chosen to review and discuss the criteria. Individuals were interviewed using a combination of the informal conversational and interview guide approaches (Patton, 1990; Rubin & Babbie, 1993). Through in-person and telephone interviews, interviewers shared the list of traits with the interviewees and then discussed how these traits fit with the professionals' experiences. On the basis of input from experts at the subsequent two sites, the list was modified. The final list was then shared with the first center for confirmation.

### Traits Identified

The professionals we interviewed consistently reported that preschool children with severe emotional and behavioral problems exhibit many of the following traits:

- extremely aggressive or withdrawn behavior
- high need for control
- difficulty predicting the future
- difficulty with change, often even the slightest change
- lack of personal boundaries
- difficulty setting and accepting limits
- compulsive or impulsive behavior in work or play
- the tendency to elicit a negative reaction from others
- a wide discrepancy in developmental areas (for example, high in self-help but low in motor and socioemotional development)
- low ability to trust adults or to respond appropriately to classroom structure
- the need to test the environment for five or six months before making any noticeable changes

- cruelty to animals or other children
- lack of empathy or remorse.

Characteristics identified as exhibited by some children included immaturity for their age, involvement with multiple social services agencies, social and developmental disabilities, and an extremely stressful family life with few supports.

Many interviewers noted that not all children with severe behavior disorders had experienced traumatic family histories but that a significant proportion had. For children from troubled homes, the professionals described the typical experience as including several of the following elements:

- a long history of inconsistent parenting and a chaotic home life
- neglect
- physical and sexual abuse
- extreme emotional abuse
- several out-of-home placements
- a history of substance abuse by one or both parents
- family stress caused by poverty
- family stress caused by living with a child who has special problems.

Many of the children served by the professionals also had significant neurological impairments, communication disorders, or delays in motor development.

## EXISTING MODELS OF SERVICE DELIVERY

The structure of traditional systems is inadequate to meet the needs of children with severe emotional and behavioral problems. The children and their families are diverse, and their needs are best met through collaborative service delivery that addresses socioemotional, economic, safety, and educational factors. Successful programs are both child and family centered, are inclusive of families throughout the process, and balance the needs of the child and family.

There are currently two community-based approaches to providing services to children with severe emotional and behavioral disorders involving integrative programming: (1) classrooms in public schools that provide special education and regular education with added support and (2) day treatment programs provided by mental health or other social services facilities (Knitzer et al., 1990).

### Public School Programs

IDEA (1990) requires the legal recognition of special-needs children from birth to six years of age by the education system and mandates services for children ages three and older. The mandates expand the population eligible for special education and related services. To fulfill these mandates, which call for young children with severe behavior disorders to receive appropriate services as close to their peers as possible, increased understanding of service needs and more collaboration among systems are required.

On the basis of reports from site visits, Knitzer and colleagues (1990) cited programmatic difficulties with many school-based programs for children with behavioral and emotional disabilities. They reported "low level academic efforts, simplistic behavioral interventions, inattention to transitions and continuities across grades, and a singular lack of access to mental health services" (p.

117). McEvoy, Davis, and Reichle (1993) also reported programmatic difficulties in serving the needs of young children with emotional or behavioral problems in school-based early childhood programs.

Although programs isolated from the school environment are ill advised for older children (Knitzer et al., 1990), preschool programs are frequently isolated both in schools and in private nonprofit facilities, thus lessening the stigma associated with isolation.

Self-contained classrooms can be effective, but their effectiveness can be diminished by administrative procedures that govern the size and composition of classes (Grosenick & Huntze, 1981). Large class size interferes with effective services. The addition of one extra child with a significant problem may make the classroom impossible to manage. Composition also has a major effect on the functioning of the class; too much diversity in age or level of functioning in a single class can disrupt the flow of the classroom (Stroul & Friedman, 1986).

Some school-based programs are comprehensive and rooted in basic research (Dougherty, Saxe, Cross, & Silverman, 1987; Stroul & Friedman, 1986). Guidelines are available on effective classroom programs that lead to a high rate of placement and maintenance in less-restrictive special education or regular education classrooms (Hilton & Schmitz, 1988). The most effective self-contained programs are multidisciplinary and provide direct services to the student. They involve the family in the change process, support children and families by providing access to a variety of community services, use varied intervention approaches in dealing with children, and include individualized educational programming (Baenen, Stephens, & Glenwick, 1986; Plenk, 1978; Scruggs, Mastropieri, Cook, & Escobar, 1986; Soderman, 1985).

## Day Treatment Programs

Many children receiving support services experience difficulties in traditional education settings. Day treatment can help keep children with serious emotional and behavioral disturbances in local schools or community mental health centers while allowing for continued contact with the family and the community at reduced emotional and financial cost.

Mental health day treatment programs offer nonresidential psychoeducational services incorporating education, counseling, and family intervention. Services are integrated, can be offered in a variety of settings, and frequently involve collaboration among service agencies. The most common settings for mental health day treatment programs are community mental health centers, public schools, special schools, social services agencies, and hospitals.

Programs have an average of eight to 10 students per classroom, with a ratio of one staff member to every two to four students. Most students stay in the program one year or longer. Studies indicate that the programs are effective in mediating behavioral difficulties and addressing academic and preacademic deficiencies (Stroul & Friedman, 1986). The typical cost of day treatment is $10,000 to $15,000 per year per student, whereas residential treatment frequently costs $30,000 to $50,000 per year per student (Stroul & Friedman, 1986).

Research has shown a high degree of effectiveness for day treatment programs (Friedman & Quick, 1983; Friedman, Quick, Palmer, & Mayo, 1982; Wood, Combs, Gunn, & Weller, 1975). Successful programs typically have the following features: a safe and nurturing environment, an individualized educational program that focuses on the child's needs, individualized mental health treatment plans, clearly stated disciplinary procedures, and strong links with the community and the family ("Improving Services," 1985). Other common features of successful day treatment programs include

- small classes
- family services, including family treatment, parent training, and individual counseling for parents
- case management of tangible needs
- family outreach with a psychoeducational focus to help parents understand both the developmental and special needs of their child (Freeman & Dyer, 1993)
- behavior modification for the child skills building and to improve interpersonal problem-solving and practical skills
- recreational art and music therapy to foster social and emotional development
- crisis intervention to provide support and assistance in the development of the family's problem-solving skills ("Improving Services," 1985; Stroul & Friedman, 1986).

Such programs result in positive changes in children's behavior, with most children subsequently entering the regular education system (Baenen, Stephens, & Glenwick, 1986). Although interventions and treatment levels vary, nationally replicated models for the provision of day treatment services include behavior therapy, developmental therapy (Wood et al., 1975), and environmental re-education (Hobbs, 1982).

## COLLABORATIVE MODEL AND INTEGRATED POLICY APPROACH

A number of studies have discussed the advantages of combining the resources, policy supports, and knowledge of education and mental health organizations (Edlefsen & Baird, 1994; Schorr, 1989). Day treatment provided through collaboration between educational and mental health services agencies offers the following advantages: flexibility of services, shared expenses, services that cost much less than residential treatment, and multifaceted treatment in the least-restrictive environment. Integrating service delivery allows the blending of funding streams from education and mental health to provide for enriched service delivery (Edlefsen & Baird, 1994). Additional benefits come from enhanced program development in local education agencies and mental health centers or appropriate child-serving counseling centers.

Collaborative programs function best when they are staffed by multidisciplinary teams, have low student-to-teacher ratios, and use the ecological approaches described in this article and in the literature (Baenen, Stephens, & Glenwick, 1986; Plenk, 1978; Soderman, 1985). Collaborative, multidisciplinary services expand the knowledge base, the ability to respond in a coordinated comprehensive fashion, and the depth of intervention (Mellaville & Blank, 1991; Schmitz, 1995). A successful collaboration requires flexibility, creativity, facilitation, leadership, mutual respect, a commitment to quality services, and frequently a sense of humor.

Collaborations are, however, challenging because of policy limitations, role and time pressures, professional boundaries and competition, and personality clashes (Missouri Linc, 1992; Schmitz, 1995). Not only are professionals from the multiple disciplines trained with separate professional languages, creating communication barriers, but organizations and professions are set up with territorial boundaries designed to establish their expertise as primary. These boundaries take time, training, and commitment to overcome. Bureaucratic structures and regulations must also be overcome. Personalities also play a role in successful collaborations. The individuals involved must be flexible, committed, comfortable with ambiguity, respectful of others' expertise, and willing to share.

## Key Components

The components of successful integrated programs include
- family-inclusive, child- and family-centered assessments and interventions
- classroom services with educational support and treatment for emotional or behavioral disorders
- assessment and treatment of communication and neurological disorders
- consistent disciplinary rules
- environments conducive to the building of positive relationships and trust
- collaborative, interdisciplinary service delivery
- case management
- culturally relevant and culturally sensitive services
- integration of the program into the local community and the child-serving community
- support in the transition to other programs with ongoing services when needed.

An ideal class in a successful collaborative program has approximately 12 children, three professional staff, paraprofessional staff, and professional support. The multidisciplinary classroom teams should include at least one teacher and one social worker and should foster an attitude of mutual respect, both personally and professionally. An expertise in early childhood development is imperative, as are support services addressing health, communication, and physical needs.

Although each child requires two individualized plans—education and mental health—service delivery and policy supports must be integrated. Family members operate best as members of the team. They can become valuable allies in developing plans, participating in educational support, and assisting with transitions. Successful plans also require parent outreach, child development, recreation, and crisis intervention.

## Staff Training

The provision of adequate services to children with serious emotional and behavioral disorders requires the availability of trained and qualified staff from a variety of arenas. These professionals must be able to work well on multidisciplinary teams. Staff members need skills in early childhood education and in mental health diagnosis and treatment. All staff members must be trained in working effectively with parents and families. In addition, staff must be trained in cultural issues so that communication and intervention are appropriate to the community context.

One of the first steps in interdisciplinary training involves the development of a common "jargon-free language" (McEvoy et al., 1993, p. 29). McEvoy and colleagues cited the importance of effective communication among team members, including professionals and parents, for effective assessment and intervention. An investment in comprehensive training that addresses specialized language, professional boundaries and knowledge bases, consensus building, and problem solving has benefits for team building and service delivery (Mellaville & Blank, 1991; Schmitz, 1995).

## Case Example

The Seattle Mental Health Institute (SMHI) preschool day treatment–special education program is an example of a collaborative program that has the necessary components of a successful program. Many young children with developmental disabilities and significant socioemotional developmental delays have been referred to the program by the Seattle public schools; most have entered regular education classrooms after participation in the program. The children served range from those with mild disorders (for example, socioemotional delays caused by psychoneurological impairment, trauma, or environmental factors) to children with severe emotional and behavioral disorders (for example, history of significant trauma and instability and significant neurological impairment).

Classroom services include preschool education, skills building, development of problem-solving skills, and treatment of socioemotional trauma. All classroom staff are trained in early childhood education and mental health treatment. The staff member with primary responsibility for a child in the classroom also works with the child and family outside the class. As a result of the continuity, families feel a sense of commitment and support that is not present when they are in contact with many staff.

Parents are involved as partners throughout the process, assisting in assessment and treatment and participating in the classroom. Outreach to parents involves training in child development and management and family counseling. Case management services help families meet basic needs and acquire additional resources. Staff support is available to help the child's transition into regular classrooms or other programs. The collaborative relationships formed while the child is in the program help establish an ongoing safety net for the child and family.

The preschool program has been integrated into the community through SMHI's Children's Center, thereby fostering a community perception of the program as a preschool center rather than a mental health facility. This perception is important in building a bridge to an ethnically and economically diverse community. The agency has worked to diversify the staff to reflect the composition of the community of families served. The agency is also very active in training staff on cultural issues and needs, including the mental health concerns of diverse ethnic communities.

The program records of staff of the Seattle program who were interviewed for this study indicate success in helping children and families achieve more positive outcomes and improved educational successes and maintain children in the family setting. Of the 36 children served from Seattle Public Schools during the years 1987 to 1989, 53 percent entered regular education programs or less-restrictive special education programs for children with developmental delays. An additional 20 percent entered transition kindergarten classes with fewer emotional and behavioral difficulties. Only one child was placed in a residential program, and staff questioned the appropriateness of that placement. Twenty-seven of the children continued to require intensive day treatment programs or self-contained special education classrooms. These findings are consistent with early, limited indications from other programs that preschool children with severe emotional and behavioral disorders, after exiting intensive and effective intervention programs, can enter regular classrooms (Swan et al., 1986).

## ROLE OF SOCIAL WORK IN COLLABORATIVE PROGRAMS

Social workers must be part of multidisciplinary classroom teams. Because team members cross-train each other, teaching, social work, and counseling staff have overlapping roles in the class, thus allowing for continuity among the educational, support, and counseling needs of the students. Although the teacher takes the lead in developing learning plans, the social worker takes the lead in developing plans to meet the emotional needs of the children. Teachers and social workers may also blend their expertise in reaching out to and working with families, but social workers, in coordination with other counseling staff, frequently have primary responsibility for individual, family, and group treatment and support, skills building, and case management services. The nature of the children's difficulties and the programmatic needs place social workers in a pivotal role (Edlefsen & Baird, 1994) because of their professional expertise in service delivery and systems change.

As program planners, social workers are vital in developing multidisciplinary, holistic, collaborative programs. The flexibility of the social work professionals and their understanding of assessment and intervention set the tone for an inclusive model. Social workers are integral players in the implementation and ongoing functioning of successful programs.

## CONCLUSION

Young children with severe emotional and behavioral problems are in great need of services. Preschool day treatment programs that meet the socioemotional and educational needs of young children and their families through integrated service delivery are the most effective and cost-efficient mechanism for addressing the needs of this special group. Programs must integrate education and mental health treatment; work with families in building on strengths; be collaborative in nature; be based on a solid knowledge of cultural issues; and provide continuity across services, staff, and time.

This article has discussed a general framework; program specifics must be developed by local service providers on the basis of local needs and service patterns. As a profession that trains practitioners in both service delivery and systems change, social work is the ideal field to take the lead in developing collaborative programs serving the needs of high-risk preschool children and their families. Social workers can facilitate relationship building among multiple disciplines, help design and implement collaborative service delivery, train multidisciplinary teams, and take the lead in evaluating programs.

## REFERENCES

American Psychiatric Association. (1994). *Diagnostic and statistical manual of mental disorders* (4th ed.). Washington, DC: Author.

Anthony, E. J. (1987). Risk, vulnerability, and resilience: An overview. In E. J. Anthony & B. J. Cohler (Eds.), *The invulnerable child* (pp. 3–48). New York: Guilford Press.

Anthony, E. J., & Cohler, B. J. (Eds.). (1987). *The invulnerable child.* New York: Guilford Press.

Baenen, R. S., Glenwick, D. S., Stephens, M. A., Neuhaus, S. M., & Mowrey, J. D. (1986). Predictors of child and family outcome in a psycho-educational day school program. *Behavioral Disorders, 11,* 272–279.

Baenen, R. S., Stephens, M. A., & Glenwick, D. S. (1986). Outcomes in psychoeducational day school programs: A review. *American Journal of Orthopsychiatry, 56,* 263–271.

Children's Defense Fund. (1995). *The state of America's children yearbook.* Washington, DC: Author.

Cohler, B. J. (1987). Adversity, resilience, and the study of lives. In E. J. Anthony & B. J. Cohler (Eds.), *The invulnerable child* (pp. 363–424). New York: Guilford Press.

Dougherty, D. M., Saxe, L. M., Cross, T., & Silverman, N. (1987). *Children's mental health problems and services.* Durham, NC: Duke University Press.

Edlefsen, M., & Baird, M. (1994). Making it work: Preventive mental health care for disadvantaged preschoolers. *Social Work, 39,* 566–573.

Fox, J. J., & McEvoy, M. A. (1993). Guest editors' comments. *Behavior Disorders, 19,* 9–10.

Freeman, E. M., & Dyer, L. (1993). High-risk children and adolescents: Family and community environments. *Families in Society, 74,* 422–431.

Friedman, R. M., & Quick, J. (1983). *Day treatment for adolescents: A five-year status report.* Unpublished manuscript.

Friedman, R. M., Quick, J., Palmer, J., & Mayo, J. (1982). Social skills training within a day treatment program for emotionally disturbed adolescents. *Child and Youth Services, 5,* 139–152.

Garmezy, N. (1983). Stressors of childhood. In N. Garmezy & M. Rutter (Eds.), *Stress, coping and development in children* (pp. 43–84). New York: McGraw-Hill.

Griffin, G. W. (1987). Childhood predictive characteristics of aggressive adolescents. *Exceptional Children, 54,* 246–252.

Grosenick, J., & Huntze, S. (1981). *A model for comprehensive needs analysis: Review and analysis of programs for behaviorally disordered children and youth.* Columbia: University of Missouri.

Hawkins, J. D., Catalano, R. F., & Miller, J. Y. (1992). Risk and protective factors for alcohol and other drug problems in adolescence and early adulthood: Implications for substance abuse prevention. *Psychological Bulletin, 11,* 64–105.

Hilton, A., & Schmitz, C. L. (1988, November). *Questions and directions related to the provision of services to preschool children with severe behavior disorders.* Paper presented at the Annual Conference of Teacher Educators of Children with Behavioral Disorders, Tempe, AZ. (ERIC Document Reproduction Service No. ED 312 870)

Hobbs, N. (1982). *The troubled and troubling child: Re-education in mental health, education, and human services programs for children and youth.* San Francisco: Jossey-Bass.

Improving services for emotionally disturbed children. (1985). *Update, 1*(2), 1–10. (Available from the Florida Mental Health Institute, University of South Florida, Tampa, FL.)

Individuals with Disabilities Education Act, P.L. 101-476, 104 Stat. 1142 (1990).

Institute of Medicine. (1989). *Research on children and adolescents with mental, behavioral and developmental disorders.* Washington, DC: National Academy Press.

Kazdin, A. E. (1987). Treatment of antisocial behavior in children: Current status and future directions. *Psychological Bulletin, 102,* 187–203.

Kealing, P., & Oakes, J. (1988). *Access to knowledge: Breaking down school barriers to learning.* Denver: Education Commission of the States.

Knitzer, J. (1982). *Unclaimed children.* Washington, DC: Children's Defense Fund.

Knitzer, J., Steinberg, Z., & Fleisch, B. (1990). *At the schoolhouse door: An examination of programs and policies for children with behavioral and emotional problems.* New York: Bank Street College of Education.

Maselli, D., Brown, R., & Veaco, L. (1984). Aggressive behavior of the preschool child. *Education, 104,* 385–388.

McEvoy, M. A., Davis, C. A., & Reichle, J. (1993). Districtwide technical assistance teams: Designing intervention strategies for young children with challenging behaviors. *Behavior Disorders, 19,* 27–33.

Mellaville, A. I., & Blank, M. J. (1991). *What it takes: Structuring interagency partnerships to connect children and families with comprehensive services.* Washington, DC: Education and Human Services Resources Consortium.

Missouri Linc. (1992). *Interagency cooperation.* Columbia: University of Missouri–Columbia.

Patterson, G. R., Capaldi, D., & Bank, L. (1991). An early starter model for predicting delinquency. In D. J. Pepler & K. H. Rubin (Eds.), *The development and treatment of childhood aggression* (pp. 139–168). Hillsdale, NJ: Lawrence Erlbaum.

Patton, M. Q. (1990). *Qualitative evaluation and research methods* (2nd ed.). Newbury Park, CA: Sage Publications.

Plenk, A. M. (1978). Activity group therapy for emotionally disturbed pre-school children. *Behavior Disorders, 3,* 210–218.

Rubin, A., & Babbie, E. (1993). *Research methods for social work* (2nd ed.). Pacific Grove, CA: Brooks/Cole.

Rutter, M. (1983). Stress, coping, and development: Some issues and some questions. In N. Garmezy & M. Rutter (Eds.), *Stress, coping and development in children* (pp. 1–42). New York: McGraw-Hill.

Schmitz, C. L. (1995). [Collaborative relationships and their impact on the provision of services]. Unpublished raw data.

Schorr, L. B. (1989). *Within our reach: Breaking the cycle of disadvantage.* New York: Doubleday.

Scruggs, T. E., Mastropieri, M. A., Cook, S. B., & Escobar, C. (1986). Early intervention for children with conduct disorders: A quantitative synthesis of single-subject research. *Behavior Disorders, 11,* 260–271.

Smith, C., Lizotte, A. J., Thornberry, T. P., & Krohn, M. D. (1995). Resilient youth: Identifying factors that prevent high-risk youth from engaging in delinquency and drug use. *Current Perspectives on Aging and the Life Cycle, 4,* 217–247.

Soderman, A. K. (1985). Dealing with difficult young children. *Young Children, 40*(5), 15–20.

Spivack, G., Marcus, J., & Swift, M. (1986). Early classroom behaviors and later misconduct. *Developmental Psychology, 22,* 124–131.

Stevenson, J., Richman, N., & Graham, P. (1985). Behavior problems and language abilities at three years and behavioral deviance at eight years. *Child Psychology and Psychiatry, 26,* 215–230.

Stroul, B. A., & Friedman, R. M. (1986). *A system of care for severely emotionally disturbed children and youth.* Washington, DC: National Institute of Mental Health.

Swan, W. W., Purvis, J. W., & Wood, N. J. (1986). *A quantitative study of Georgia SED students.* Unpublished manuscript, University of Georgia, Macon.

Thomas, A., & Chess, S. (1984). Genesis and evolution of behavioral disorders: From infancy to early adult life. *American Journal of Psychiatry, 141,* 1–9.

Wahlsten, V. S. (1994). Development and survival: A study of children at risk of living in adverse psychosocial milieu. *Child Abuse & Neglect, 18,* 715–723.

Walker, E., Bettes, B., & Ceci, S. (1984). Teachers' assumptions regarding the severity, causes, and outcomes of behavioral problems in preschoolers: Implications for referral. *Journal of Consulting and Clinical Psychology, 52,* 899–902.

Wehby, J. H., Dodge, K. A., Valente, E., Jr., & the Conduct Disorders Prevention Research Group. (1993). School behavior of first grade children identified as at-risk for development of conduct problems. *Behavior Disorders, 19,* 67–78.

Werner, E. E. (1987). Vulnerability and resiliency in children at risk for delinquency: A longitudinal study from birth to young adulthood. In J. D. Burchard & S. N. Burchard (Eds.), *Prevention of delinquent behavior* (pp. 16–43). Newbury Park, CA: Sage Publications.

Werner, E. E., & Smith, R. S. (1982). *Vulnerable but invincible: A longitudinal study of resilient children and youth.* New York: McGraw-Hill.

Wood, M. M., Combs, C., Gunn, A., & Weller, D. (1975). *Developmental therapy in the classroom.* Austin, TX: Pro-Ed.

Yoshikawa, H. (1994). Prevention as a cumulative protection: Effects of early family support and education on chronic delinquency and its risks. *Psychological Bulletin, 115,* 28–54.

*The authors thank the Child and Family Program at Seattle Mental Health Institute for its excellent work, which made this article possible.*

*This chapter was originally published in the October 1996 issue of* Social Work in Education, *Vol. 18, pp. 237–249.*

# 42 Appropriate versus Least Restrictive: Educational Policies and Students with Disabilities

James C. Raines

Equality and freedom are deeply held values in the United States, but there are circumstances under which they cannot be pursued as a single goal. One of these circumstances has occurred in the field of educational policy. Providing students with disabilities equal access to education has often meant segregating them in special programs specifically designed to meet their needs. In short, society has improved their access to equal education by decreasing their freedom to associate with their peers without disabilities. This unfortunate state of affairs has forced a re-examination of the balance between an "appropriate education" and an education administered in the "least-restrictive environment."

This article evaluates three very different paradigms for achieving the integration of students with and without disabilities. To put these in perspective, it examines three epochs in the education of students with disabilities. It identifies three current approaches to balancing the two primary mandates of providing an appropriate education in the least-restrictive environment. Finally, this article studies the class action and civil suits brought by parents and interpretations of relevant constitutional amendments by federal courts and the U.S. Supreme Court. The results are important for students with disabilities because they provide guidelines for people with disabilities in U.S. society. They have implications for the inclusion of all excluded or segregated groups in the educational system.

## HISTORY: EXCLUDED AND UNEQUAL

Four early influences led to the practice of categorizing students during the late 19th and early 20th centuries. The first was a large influx of immigrant children from non-English-speaking countries. Although bilingual education had existed extensively during colonial times (Pennsylvania, Maryland, Virginia, and the Carolinas offered education in German), Theodore Roosevelt was committed to the idea of a single-language nation. He suggested that "We should provide for every immigrant by day schools for the young and by night schools for the adults, the chance to learn English; and if after say five years, he has not learned English, he should be sent back to the land from whence he came" (1917, quoted in Allen-Meares, Washington, & Welsh, 1986, p. 181). Thus, when schools were unprepared to teach immigrant students in their own language, special "opportunity" schools were created until they were ready for entry into the regular public schools (Allen-Meares et al., 1986).

The second factor was the industrialization of U.S. society, which provided the vision of a population differentiated by skills (into management and labor). This idea affected both teachers and their students: Teachers were categorized by the subjects they taught, and students were classified by their ability to learn. Pupils who were deemed unlikely to become management material were considered unfit for the investment of educational currency (Allen-Meares et al., 1986).

The third influence was the development of standardized intelligence tests. The Binet–Simon test was developed in France in 1905 expressly to predict school performance. It was translated into English in 1908 by Henry Goddard and was quickly endorsed by the National Education Association as useful for mentally retarded children. It was then revised by Lewis Terman of Stanford University and published as the Stanford–Binet Intelligence Test in 1916. Since then, intelligence tests have been used widely in the United States to track students into ability groupings (Hardman, Drew, Egan, & Wolf, 1990; Reynolds & Birch, 1988).

Finally, in 1922 a group of teachers and other human services professionals established the Council for Exceptional Children. These advocates for children with disabilities found it pragmatic to separate from general education, because it made their students more visible, encouraged philanthropic support, and avoided confrontation with administrators in regular education who wanted to rid themselves of problem students (Reynolds & Birch, 1988).

## TRANSITIONS: SEPARATE BUT EQUAL

### Constitutional Law

*Brown v. Board of Education* (1954) was the turning point in educational policy and law. *Brown* is a landmark case for many reasons. It demonstrated through constitutional litigation that educational issues are social and political issues. It showed that very difficult educational issues can be contested in a civil rights arena. It also illustrated how litigation can provide the bedrock for legislation on both the state and federal level.

*Brown* marked the entry of the federal government into educational policy, an area that had previously been the sole province of state and local governments. In addition, it proved that although the U.S. Constitution did not guarantee public education, its principles of equal protection and due process applied. It typified the kind of case (that is, civil action) used to address inequities in educational law. And by repudiating the "separate but equal" doctrine it had ratified in *Plessy v. Ferguson* (1896), it provided a "right to equal education" for a class of people. If one substituted the word "disabled" for "Negro" and the word "abled" for "white" in *Brown*, then it becomes clear how the Fourteenth Amendment became the constitutional basis for the rights of children with disabilities to be educated (Turnbull, 1993).

### Federal Legislation

Another development in the 1950s was the advances of Samuel Kirk, who started the first teacher preparation and research programs in special education (Allen-Meares et al., 1986). In 1958 Congress passed P.L. 85-926, which authorized

$1 million for universities to train professional educators for mentally retarded students (Reynolds & Birch, 1988). This led a few states (New York, New Jersey, and Massachusetts) to enact mandatory special education legislation. Most states, however, passed legislation that allowed, but did not require, school districts to provide special education services (Hardman et al., 1990).

The federal government finally got directly involved when it passed the Elementary and Secondary Education Amendments of 1966 (P.L. 89-750); these amendments created Title VI, which founded the Bureau of Education for the Handicapped. The bureau established a grants program for innovative educational programs for children with disabilities.

In 1970 Congress replaced Title VI by passing the Education of the Handicapped Act (P.L. 91-230). Part B of the act provided for a grants program with guidelines for states to develop resources and train personnel for special education.

By 1974, however, Congress was becoming impatient with the lack of progress made by the states. Senator H. A. Williams (D-NJ) reported that "the most recent statistics provided by the Bureau of Education for the Handicapped estimate that . . . 1.75 million handicapped children do not receive any educational services, and 2.5 million handicapped children are not receiving an appropriate education" (121 Cong. Rec. 19,486, 1975). With this in mind, Congress passed an interim measure, the Education of the Handicapped Act Amendments of 1974 (P.L. 93-380), which increased funding and required states to adopt the goal of providing full educational opportunities to all children with disabilities. The next year, Congress would pass the most comprehensive legislation for the education of handicapped children.

## Litigation

In 1967 the first school classification case, *Hobson v. Hansen*, was heard. It concerned the misuse of intelligence tests to place predominantly poor black children into the lower tracks of Washington, DC's, educational program. The court ruled that this violated the due process clause of the Fifth Amendment, thus reaffirming *Brown's* contention that a class of people cannot be denied educational rights.

During the 1970s, two landmark cases redefined the public schools' obligation to educate children with disabilities. The first was *Pennsylvania Association for Retarded Children (PARC) v. Commonwealth of Pennsylvania* (1971). PARC, part of a parent movement to advocate for the rights of children with disabilities, relied on four arguments:

1. Expert testimony indicated that all mentally retarded individuals were capable of benefiting from an educational program.
2. The state of Pennsylvania undertook to provide a free public education to all of its children regardless of ability.
3. Therefore, Pennsylvania must provide any mentally retarded child with a free educational program.
4. Further, the state was obligated to place children according to their ability with a preference for placement in a regular public school class rather than

placement in a special public school class or in a nonpublic school program.

The second case was *Mills v. Board of Education of the District of Columbia* (1972), a class-action suit filed on behalf of children who had been suspended or expelled from the schools because of behavior related to their mental retardation, hyperactivity, emotional disturbances, or behavior disorders.

The court required the District to provide a free and appropriate publicly supported education regardless of the degree of disability or the cost involved (even if this meant private tuition). Finally, the school board was forbidden to make disciplinary suspensions for longer than two days unless there was a due process hearing before the suspension and the child's education was continued during the suspension. Thus, the *Mills* case expanded the *PARC* decision by including a broad range of children frequently excluded from the public schools.

## REFORM: INCLUDED AND EQUAL

The Education for All Handicapped Children Act of 1975 (P.L. 94-142) was a watershed for many reasons. It established a "zero reject" principle, which said that the states could not refuse an education to any child within their jurisdiction and must locate previously unserved children. It required nondiscriminatory evaluations by a multidisciplinary team and a battery of nonbiased tests administered in the child's native language or normal mode of communication. The act instituted an appropriate education standard that was to be documented in writing (the individualized education plan [IEP]) and that included the child's present level of functioning, annual goals, specific services to be provided, the extent to which the child would participate in regular education, projected date of initiation, anticipated duration of services, and criteria for determining the achievement of objectives.

P.L. 94-142 also required the maximal use of the least-restrictive environment to reduce the segregation of special education children from their nondisabled peers. It demanded fairness in the form of procedural due process whereby parents must be notified and give their informed consent before any evaluation. It also established a principle of shared decision making whereby parents and professionals communicated and collaborated in the best interests of the child. Finally, it clarified which students were to be regarded as disabled and thus eligible for funds through the federal grant program (for example, learning disabled, yes; culturally disadvantaged, no; severely emotionally disturbed, yes; socially maladjusted, no).

Despite this landmark legislation, several problems remained to be resolved. The two most important were, What does "appropriate" education mean? and What does "least restrictive" mean? The answers were not forthcoming from Congress, so the judicial system decided.

### Appropriate Education

The Supreme Court defined appropriate education in *Board of Education v. Rowley* (1982), the first special education case to reach the high court. The case involved a deaf student with minimal residual hearing but excellent lip-reading skills.

She was placed in a regular kindergarten class and provided with an FM hearing aid. During her first-grade year, her IEP recommended that she be educated in a regular classroom and receive instruction from a tutor for the deaf for one hour each day and three hours of speech therapy each week. Her parents insisted on a sign-language interpreter for all of her academic classes, and the school board balked.

The court declared that the legislative intent was only to provide disabled children the same basic educational opportunities as their nondisabled peers, not maximal development of their potential. Thus, the key to determining appropriateness is "educational benefit." If the student was making progress (not necessarily optimal progress), then the educational program met the standard. The court set forth a process definition that an appropriate education was one that followed the protocol of identification, nondiscriminatory evaluation, and an IEP. If the school district failed to follow these procedures, the education could not be appropriate, but a small mistake would not invalidate the process. Nonadherence to procedures must result in actual or potential harm (Saltzman & Proch, 1990; Turnbull, 1993).

### Least-Restrictive Environment

The principle of least-restrictive environment came from many quarters, including corrections and mental health policies (Turnbull, 1993). It was a reaction against special education's practice of segregating students in separate and unequal education. Children in special education classes were often taught by less-capable teachers in worse facilities with fewer resources and for an indeterminate period of time. Thus, least-restrictive environment became a broad approach designed to correct several inadequacies. It remains ill defined, however, because the law has always allowed for segregation through a broad continuum of placements from inpatient hospital care to the regular classroom. There are three very different interpretations of this principle: mainstreaming, regular education initiative, and full inclusion.

*Mainstreaming.* Neither P.L. 94-142 or its 1990 amendments, the Individuals with Disabilities Education Act (IDEA) (P.L. 101-476), chose to narrow the continuum of services that has made more restrictive programs permissible. Deno's (1973) "cascade model" is a good example of how the most-restrictive placements should serve the fewest number of students and how the continuum should broaden so that the least-restrictive placements serve the greatest number of students. Advocates of this system contend that some students' disabilities are so severe that an appropriate education cannot be achieved in an integrated setting and that the student is more likely to maximize his or her development in a segregated setting, that the inclusion of students with disabilities in the regular classroom deprives nondisabled peers of their right to an appropriate education, that the economic costs of adapting the regular classroom depletes the financial resources available to other students, and that teachers may never be prepared to teach such a diverse group of learners (Kauffman, 1989).

Thus, mainstreaming advocates continued to place children in segregated classes for most of their academic classes but integrated students with disabilities during nonacademic times (lunch, recess, gym, music, and art) and occasionally for an academic class at which the student with a disability excelled. This type of mainstreaming might best be called "physical mainstreaming," because although it brought students together in the same physical space, it did not necessarily lead to social interaction or integrated instruction (Reynolds & Birch, 1988). Under physical mainstreaming, special education teachers were to teach self-contained academic classes while allowing students more freedom of association during nonacademic periods.

*Regular Education Initiative.* Early case law (for example, see *PARC*) indicated a clear preference for educating children with disabilities in regular classrooms in public schools. Indeed, the "separate but equal" concept was repudiated by *Brown* in 1954. Advocates for integration have noted that left to its own devices, special education has become a "second system" for educating children (Wang, Reynolds, & Walberg, 1988). Both P.L. 94-142 and IDEA emphasized the need for special efforts to integrate children with disabilities and their peers without disabilities.

The prescription for what ailed the educational system had three parts: (1) integration, not only of students but also of systems (that is, special education and general education); (2) large-scale mainstreaming into regular education classrooms; and (3) improvement of achievement levels of children with "high-incidence" disabilities such as mild mental retardation, learning disabilities, and behavioral disorders (Fuchs & Fuchs, 1994).

Integration would require special educators and general educators to work together in the best interests of all children, with special educators serving as consultants to regular teachers on a wide variety of students, not just those labeled as disabled. Teachers would have to become skilled at working with a wide variety of students, thereby improving their ability to teach all learners, not just "normal" ones.

Two highly individualized forms of mainstreaming other than physical were envisioned: social interaction mainstreaming and instructional mainstreaming. Some children by the nature of their disability (for example, hearing impairments) have very little social interaction mainstreaming even though they may be able to participate intellectually in the regular educational program. Other children by the nature of their mental disability (for example, learning disorders or mild mental retardation) can participate socially but have difficulty keeping up with the instructional level of the regular class.

To improve achievement levels, several strategies were suggested: continuous assessment of student achievement, use of alternative methods of instruction, availability of a variety of teaching materials, explicit IEPs, student self-management for parts of the school day, peer assistance among students, team teaching by teachers and other support staff, and use of consulting teachers (that is, special educators) (Wang, Anderson, & Bram, 1985).

An important caveat, however, is that the advocates of the regular education initiative have allowed some room for exceptional children to be educated outside of the mainstream. Reynolds and Birch (1988) identified four types of children who should not be mainstreamed: (1) children who are dangerous to themselves or others, (2) children with severe and profound multiple disabilities, (3) children with traumatic injuries that require extensive rehabilitation, and (4) children who require maintenance environments such as mechanical respirators or dust-free living spaces.

*Full Inclusion.* As early as 1968 Dunn had come to the conclusion that

> our past and present practices are morally and educationally wrong. We have been living at the mercy of general educators who have referred their problem children to us. And we have been generally ill-prepared and ineffective in educating these children. Let us stop being pressured into continuing and expanding a special education program that we know now to be undesirable for many of the children we are dedicated to serve. (p. 5)

The IDEA amendments reinforced the concept of full inclusion by placing special emphasis on the integration of students with severe disabilities (Section 1426(a)(3) and (4), cited in Turnbull, 1993). The full-inclusion movement sees only "two roads: the road of inclusion and the road of exclusion. We choose the other road—inclusion. The simple starting point for this road is to include everyone. Educate all children in *regular* classrooms and communities" (Stainback & Stainback, 1992, p. xv).

Advocates of full inclusion accept no compromise because the issue is seen as a moral one, not an educational one. Stainback and Stainback (1992) rejected the term "integration" because it implied previous exclusion, and they rejected the term "mainstreaming" because it inferred a need to fit students into an existing program. They argued that responsibility should be "placed on school personnel to arrange a mainstream that accommodates the needs of all students" (Stainback, Stainback, & Jackson, 1992, p. 4). Whereas the proponents of the regular education initiative aim primarily to include children with high-incidence handicaps, the proponents of full inclusion aim to include children with low-incidence handicaps as well. To achieve this goal, they have taken a radical stance to some revered concepts. First, they take a "social constructivist" approach to curriculum:

> Socialization and friendships are among the major educational goals to enable students to become active members of the community. When adults focus on and foster buddy systems, circles of friends, and other friendship facilitation activities, children start to gain what will be most important to them in their lives—a range of people who genuinely care about them as individuals. Thus, if a child never learns any math, history, or other subject, it is critical that he or she be included. (Stainback, Stainback, & Moravec, 1992, pp. 66–67)

The "standardized" curriculum is rejected for several reasons:

- In a changing society, there is no static body of knowledge that will produce success.
- The standardized curriculum does not accommodate the diversity of learning styles and interests.
- It focuses educators on the content rather than the child.
- It is uninteresting and irrelevant for many students.
- It disempowers teachers who want to use their own approaches.

Full-inclusion advocates want to dismantle the entire special education system. They reason that because all students are in the mainstream full-time, all personnel and resources can be in the mainstream full-time. In addition, valuable resources and time would not be spent classifying, labeling, and making placement decisions: "'General' educators and 'special' educators are able to focus on providing every student challenging and appropriate educational programs geared to his or her unique needs and capabilities" (Stainback, Stainback, & Jackson, 1992, p. 7).

The full-inclusion movement would also like to demythologize the professional disciplines for three reasons: (1) expertise is not a prerequisite for providing educational support, (2) strictly defined boundaries between professions are illusory, and (3) just because two individuals have the same educational degree does not mean that they have the same competencies (York, Giangreco, Vandercook, & Macdonald, 1992). In addition to a de-emphasis on professionalization, there is a focus on peer-assisted learning through cooperative group learning systems, where students are responsible not only for their own learning but also for the learning of every pupil within a heterogeneous group (Villa & Thousand, 1992).

Most important, the full-inclusion movement makes no room for exceptions, even for the physically dangerous child. Educators are encouraged to recognize "disruptive, even dangerous, acts as communication" (Hitzing, 1992). Once the "sign language" is understood, the student should then be taught how to "communicate in ways that are equally effective and adaptive, but are not disruptive or dangerous" (p. 147).

## CLARIFICATION AND CONTROVERSY

The battle among the approaches to creating a least-restrictive environment is clearly related to how one views the right of every student to an appropriate education. Because Congress and the state education agencies have been unable to devise a solution, the judicial system has been forced to develop some guidelines.

### Provision of Nontraditional Services

The Supreme Court has made it very clear that schools must provide heretofore nontraditional related services. In *Irving Independent School District v. Tatro* (1984), a girl with spina bifida suffered from a neurogenic bladder, which prevented her from emptying her bladder voluntarily. She needed clean intermittent catheterization (CIC) every three to four hours to prevent damage to her kidneys. The child's IEP provided early child development classes and physical and occupational therapy but made no provision for CIC. The state argued that CIC fell outside the definition of a related service as defined by Congress, which included only diagnostic and evaluative medical services.

The Court held that CIC was a necessary supportive service for the child to remain in school. Because CIC could be administered by a layperson, the Court did not view it as a "medical service," which required a licensed physician, but a "school health service" that could be performed by a school nurse or other qualified person. Finally, it defined "related services" as those performed by a qualified person, not a requirement for supplying equipment (Lantzy, 1992).

## Cost–Benefit Analysis

The Supreme Court has made it clear that the costs to others can be taken into account when determining least-restrictive environment. In *Roncker v. Walters* (1983), the Sixth Circuit Court of Appeals decided in favor of mainstreaming a student diagnosed as trainable mentally retarded even if the segregated facility was academically superior. The opinion rendered, however, specifically allowed that "cost is a proper factor to consider since excessive spending on one handicapped child deprives other handicapped children" (cited in Turnbull, 1993, p. 186). The court then specified three possible exceptions to the integration requirement: (1) if the handicapped child would receive no benefit from mainstreaming, (2) if it is not feasible for the regular education facility to be modified adequately, or (3) if the handicapped child is too disruptive a force in the integrated setting.

In sum, the court adopted a "competing equities" approach to the issue of least-restrictive environment. This cost-benefit reasoning has several sources. The courts are reluctant to rule on school financing issues. The courts have acknowledged that congressional intent was to leave financing decisions in the hands of the states, not the federal government. The courts also have been reluctant to overstep the natural law that parents have a right to educate their children as they see fit without undue influence by the government (Turnbull, 1993).

## Emphasis on Social Goals

There is growing evidence that courts are placing a greater emphasis on the social goals of the least-restrictive environment provision than the need for educational progress. In *Daniel R. R. v. State Board of Education* (1989), the Fifth Circuit Court of Appeals ruled that a boy with Down's syndrome could be removed from a general education classroom for four periods a day because he was not participating or making progress in his regular class. The court then created a two-pronged test to determine if the least-restrictive environment mandate had been met: (1) whether education in the regular classroom, with supplementary aids and services, could be achieved satisfactorily and (2) if the school district intended to remove the student to a self-contained classroom, whether the school had mainstreamed the student to the maximum extent feasible.

## Further Refinements

In *Greer v. Rome City School District* (1990), the federal court for the Northern District of Georgia cited *Daniel R. R.* in its ruling that a nine-year-old student with Down's syndrome could be mainstreamed in a general education kindergarten class for three years because she was making some progress and was not disruptive to other students. The court then created three more standards to determine what cases met the appropriate and least-restrictive environment demands (Osborne & DiMattia, 1994). First, a school district may compare the benefits received from placement in a regular classroom with the benefits received from placement in a self-contained classroom.

Second, the school board could consider what effect the presence of the disabled child would have on the education of other children in the regular classroom. Last, the school district could consider the cost of the supplemental aids and services necessary for the disabled child in a general education classroom to achieve progress. The school district must balance the needs of each disabled child against the needs of other children in the district (Turnbull, 1993).

## DISCUSSION

It is clear that the move toward integration will continue to move forward. The United States has moved beyond the old medical, economic, and functional definitions of disability to a psychosocial model in which people with disabilities are regarded as a disadvantaged group whose problems in the social environment are not based solely on personal inadequacy but on the discriminatory practices of society (Karger & Stoesz, 1994). Although social workers must support antidiscrimination practices and policies for disabled people, does it logically follow that they must accept full inclusion as an educational mandate? I think not.

### The New Federalism

We should remember where the call for inclusion originated. In 1985 Reagan appointee Madeline Will, the assistant secretary for the U.S. Department of Education, addressed the Wingspread Conference. After affirming Reagan's commitment to excellence in education, she decried the proliferation of federally funded special education programs. Will (1986) reported that over 4.3 million children were eligible for these federally funded programs and asserted the "need to *more efficiently use resources* to accommodate the burgeoning number of students who are failing to learn" [italics added] (p. 413). To meet this need, she recommended that special education form a partnership with regular education to assess and intervene with all children with special learning needs.

There are several reasons to suspect that the rhetoric of academic excellence was actually a guise for the new federalism of disengagement and decreasing financial support. Verstegen and Clark (1988) reported that from 1981 to 1988, federal funding for elementary and secondary education dropped by 28 percent, with the biggest decrease (76 percent) in special education. Albert Shanker, president of the American Federation of Teachers, remarked with skepticism in 1994,

> given the financial situation of our states and school districts, and given the fact that the federal government has never met its commitment to fund its share of education for the disabled, does anybody really believe that the large amount of money that's necessary to provide these services in individual classrooms is going to be made available? (p. 316)

In 1984 the U.S. Department of Education, where Will was the director of the Office of Special Education, recommended to Congress that lawmakers not change the term "emotionally disturbed" to "behavior disorders" because adopting a less-stigmatizing label would increase the number of students eligible for service (Turnbull, 1993). Clearly one of the major reasons behind the Reagan–Bush educational agenda was solely financial and certainly not in the best interests of children with disabilities. This is especially relevant in large, poorly funded cities (Jackson, 1993).

## Naive Liberalism

A second reason to remain cautious about full inclusion has to do with the naive liberal idea that underneath, all people are the same. Stainback and Stainback (1984) argued that there are not two kinds of children—with and without disabilities—but that children are more alike than different. The fallacy of this approach is clear from the racial analogy on which the civil rights of disabled people are based. Multicultural education gave up the "melting pot" idea long ago in recognizing that differences are not just skin deep. Taking such a "color blind" approach to children with disabilities will inevitably lead to failing to provide for their differences (Kauffman, 1989). Although many would agree with the idea that true education involves learning how to learn more than it does learning to recite facts, the fundamental purpose of the education system is to foster learning, not socialization. Socialization must be a shared goal of cultural institutions such as families, religious groups, and communities. It is not the sole province of the school system, and separated from these institutions, it would be doomed to failure.

## Self-Determination

The profession would do well to listen to the people most affected by these educational policies—the families of children with disabilities. Before 1975 parent advocacy groups frequently sued school boards to include their children in regular education classrooms. Presently, parents are as likely to sue to maintain their children in special education classes as otherwise. Clearly, special education is doing something right. A study of five large school districts by Singer and Butler (cited in Kauffman, 1989) reaffirmed this; the study found that parents of special education students were generally very satisfied: "They were satisfied with their children's overall educational program and related services, with their social interaction with other students, with the administration and teaching in the special education program, and with the facilities" (Kauffman, 1989, p. 269). Most parents do not want their children with disabilities mainstreamed because of an abstract agenda, but only after a careful biopsychosocial assessment of their individual child (American Council of the Blind, 1993; Children and Adults with Attention Deficit Disorders, 1993; Consumer Action Network of, by, and for Deaf and Hard of Hearing Americans, 1993; Learning Disabilities Association of America, 1993).

Although many would agree that a student's destructive acts are communicative, they may also interpret them as an indirect request for a more restrictive placement where both the emotionally disturbed student and his or her peers are safe. Few would relish the thought of explaining to the parents of a student who was violently victimized why the school system did not ensure the safety of all the students in the class and school.

## Room for Research

It seems reasonable to study what approaches are most effective for children with various disabilities of various severities. During the 1990–91 school year, the U. S. Department of Education (1993) counted over 4.7 million children with disabilities; of these, 45 percent were diagnosed with specific learning disabilities, 21 percent with speech or language impairments, 11 percent with mental retardation, 8 percent with serious emotional disturbances, and 9 percent preschool children with noncategorical disabilities. Clearly, there are enough children to participate in large-scale studies. In the evaluation research on inclusion so far, the results have been mixed at best (Hepler, 1994; McIntosh, Vaughn, Schumm, Haager, & Lee, 1994; McKinney & Hocutt, 1988).

## CONCLUSION

The success of special education is still in doubt. Of the 248,590 students with disabilities who left the educational system during the 1988–89 school year, only 53 percent graduated from school, whereas at least 27 percent dropped out compared with an average of 11 percent in the general school population (Chronicle of Higher Education, 1994, p. 6). In addition, of the special education students who had been out of high school for more than one year, only 29 percent found full-time employment, and only 17 percent earned part-time wages. Fully 69 percent were still living with their parents, and only 17 percent were living independently, whether alone, in military housing, or in a college dormitory (U.S. Department of Education, 1993).

These percentages provide a strong reason to implement the 1990 IDEA amendments calling for increased transition services as part of an appropriate education. This coordinated set of services is designed to promote a variety of outcomes after graduation, including postsecondary education, vocational training, employment, and independent living. These should be the ultimate "benefits" of an education, and equity should be decided on "the quality of instruction, not the place of instruction" (Kauffman, 1989, p. 258).

These services would also be more in keeping with the spirit of the Goals 2000: Educate America Act of 1994 (P.L. 103-227), which seeks to improve the quality of education for all students, both with and without disabilities, by putting an emphasis on results in eight areas: school readiness; school completion; student achievement and citizenship; teacher education and professional development; mathematics and science; adult literacy and life-long learning; safe, disciplined, and alcohol- and drug-free schools; and parent participation. These are goals social workers can affirm for all students with and without disabilities. Thus, the profession should embrace the regular education initiative in principle and apply it with careful deliberation in practice.

The NASW Standards for School Social Work Services (NASW, 1992) suggest several ways that school social workers should be involved with this issue. School social workers have a responsibility to be ethical professionals. They should stay current on educational policy, including knowing and complying with federal and state legislation, state board of education regulations, and local administrative rules.

Social workers must also be educators to their colleagues. They can provide or arrange in-service training to teachers and other personnel on this issue. School social workers should be systems coordinators by providing creative educational plans that meet the goals of education and socialization through the involvement and collaboration of other community agencies and groups (for example, park districts, libraries, and church programs).

Social workers can act as change agents within various levels of the educational system: the local school, the school district, and state or national organizations. They should regularly communicate problems to the principal, local administrators, or other professionals and work together toward solutions. In addition, social workers can act as mediators between families and the local education agency, helping both avoid expensive and adversarial due process procedures. Conflict resolution strategies can go a long way toward building cooperation. Finally, the profession must advocate for students whose rights have been ignored by the educational system; they must empower families to have a voice in their child's education as well as be a consultant to school personnel about policy issues.

Freeman (1995) noted that "the traditional role of education has changed; its mission cannot be carried out in isolation from the social and economic changes that are occurring in the larger environment" (p. 2097). As a result, there have been changes for school social workers, too. Everything they do within the local school is affected by social and economic policies at state and national levels.

## REFERENCES

Allen-Meares, P., Washington, R. O., & Welsh, B. (1986). *Social work services in schools.* Englewood Cliffs, NJ: Prentice Hall.

American Council of the Blind. (1993). Full inclusion of students that are blind and visually impaired: A position statement. *Braille Forum, 32*(1), 44–47.

Board of Education v. Rowley, 458 U.S. 176, 102 S. Ct. 3034, 73 L. E.2d 690 (1982).

Brown v. Board of Education, 347 U.S. 483 (1954).

Children and Adults with Attention Deficit Disorders. (1993). CHADD position on inclusion. In J. H. Kaufman & D. P. Hallahan (Eds.), *The illusion of full inclusion: A comprehensive critique of the current special education bandwagon* (pp. 319–321). Austin, TX: Pro-Ed.

Chronicle of Higher Education. (1994). *Chronicle of Higher Education almanac.* Washington, DC: Author.

Consumer Action Network of, by, and for Deaf and Hard of Hearing Americans. (1993). Position statement on full inclusion. In J. H. Kaufman & D. P. Hallahan (Eds.), *The illusion of full inclusion: A comprehensive critique of the current special education bandwagon* (pp. 322–328). Austin, TX: Pro-Ed.

Daniel R. R. v. State Board of Education, 874 F.2d 1036 (5th Cir. 1989).

Deno, E. (Ed.). (1973). *Instructional alternatives for exceptional children.* Reston, VA: Council for Exceptional Children.

Dunn, L. M. (1968). Special education for the mildly mentally retarded—Is much of it justified? *Exceptional Child, 35,* 5–22.

Education for All Handicapped Children Act of 1975, P.L. 94-142, 89 Stat. 773.

Education of the Handicapped Act, P.L. 91-230, 84 Stat. 175 (1970).

Education of the Handicapped Act Amendments of 1974, P.L. 93-380, 88 Stat. 579.

Elementary and Secondary Education Amendments of 1966, P.L. 89-750, 80 Stat. 1191.

Freeman, E. M. (1995). School social work overview. In R. L. Edwards (Ed.-in-Chief), *Encyclopedia of social work* (19th ed., Vol. 3, pp. 2087–2099). Washington, DC: NASW Press.

Fuchs, D., & Fuchs, L. S. (1994). Inclusive schools movement and the radicalization of special education reform. *Exceptional Children, 60,* 294–309.

Goals 2000: Educate America Act of 1994, P.L. 103-227, 108 Stat. 125.

Greer v. Rome City School District, 762 F. Supp. 936 (N.D. Ga. 1990).

Hardman, M. L., Drew, C. J., Egan, M. W., & Wolf, B. (1990). *Human exceptionality: Society, school, and family* (3rd ed.). Boston: Allyn & Bacon.

Hepler, J. B. (1994). Mainstreaming children with learning disabilities: Have we improved their social environment? *Social Work in Education, 16,* 143–154.

Hitzing, W. (1992). Support and positive teaching strategies. In S. Stainback & W. Stainback (Eds.), *Curriculum considerations in inclusive classrooms: Facilitating learning for all students* (pp. 143–158). Baltimore: Paul H. Brookes.

Hobson v. Hansen, 269 F. Supp. 401, 514 (D.D.C. 1967).

Individuals with Disabilities Education Act, P.L. 101-476, 104 Stat. 1142 (1990).

Irving Independent School District v. Tatro, 468 U.S. 883, 104 S. Ct. 3371, 82 L. E.2d 664 (1984).

Jackson, D. (1993, April 1). Failure track: Mainstreaming can put kids in over their heads. *Chicago Tribune,* Sec. 1, pp. 1, 18–19.

Karger, H. J., & Stoesz, D. (1994). *American social welfare policy: A pluralist perspective* (2nd ed.). New York: Longman.

Kauffman, J. M. (1989). The regular-education initiative as Reagan–Bush education policy: A trickle-down theory of education of the hard-to-teach. *Journal of Special Education, 2,* 256–278.

Lantzy, M. L. (1992). *Individuals with Disabilities Education Act: An annotated guide to its literature and resources, 1980–1991.* Littleton, CO: Fred B. Rothman.

Learning Disabilities Association of America. (1993). Position paper on full inclusion of all students with learning disabilities in the regular education classroom. In J. H. Kaufman & D. P. Hallahan (Eds.), *The illusion of full inclusion: A comprehensive critique of the current special education bandwagon* (pp. 340–341). Austin, TX: Pro-Ed.

McIntosh, R., Vaughn, S., Schumm, J. S., Haager, D., & Lee, O. (1994). Observations of students with learning disabilities in general education classrooms. *Exceptional Children, 61,* 249–261.

McKinney, J., & Hocutt, A. (1988). The need for policy analysis in evaluating the regular education initiative. *Journal of Learning Disabilities, 21*(1), 12–18.

Mills v. Board of Education of the District of Columbia, 348 F. Supp. 866 (D.D.C. 1972).

National Association of Social Workers. (1992). *NASW standards for school social work services.* Washington, DC: Author.

121 *Congressional Record* 19,486. (1975). (Statement of Sen. H. A. Williams of New Jersey, June 18, 1975)

Osborne, A. G., & DiMattia, P. (1994). The IDEA's least restrictive environment mandate: Legal implications. *Exceptional Children, 61,* 6–14.

Pennsylvania Association for Retarded Children v. Commonwealth of Pennsylvania, 334 F. Supp. 1257, 343 F. Supp. 279 (E.D. Pa. 1971, 1972).

Plessy v. Ferguson, 163 U.S. 537 (1896).

Reynolds, M. C., & Birch, J. W. (1988). *Adaptive mainstreaming: A primer for teachers and principals* (3rd ed.). New York: Longman.

Roncker v. Walters, 700 F.2d 1058 (6th Cir. 1983), *cert. den.* 464 U.S. 864, 104 S. Ct. 196, 78 L. E.2d 171 (1983).

Roosevelt, T. (1917). *The foes of our household.* New York: George Doran.

Saltzman, A., & Proch, K. (1990). *Law in social work practice.* Chicago: Nelson-Hall.

Shanker, A. (1994). Where we stand on the rush to inclusion. *Vital Speeches of the Day, 60,* 314–317.

Stainback, S., & Stainback, W. (Eds.). (1992). *Curriculum considerations in inclusive classrooms: Facilitating learning for all students.* Baltimore: Paul H. Brookes.

Stainback, S., Stainback, W., & Jackson, H. J. (1992). Toward inclusive classrooms. In S. Stainback & W. Stainback (Eds.), *Curriculum considerations in inclusive classrooms: Facilitating learning for all students* (pp. 3–18). Baltimore: Paul H. Brookes.

Stainback, W., & Stainback, S. (1984). A rationale for the merger of special and regular education. *Exceptional Children, 51,* 102–111.

Stainback, W., Stainback, S., & Moravec, J. (1992). Using curriculum to build inclusive classrooms. In S. Stainback & W. Stainback (Eds.), *Curriculum considerations in inclusive classrooms: Facilitating learning for all students* (pp. 65–84). Baltimore: Paul H. Brookes.

Turnbull, H. R. (1993). *Free appropriate public education: The law and children with disabilities* (4th ed.). Denver: Love.

U.S. Department of Education. (1993). *Digest of educational statistics, 1993.* Washington, DC: U.S. Government Printing Office.

Verstegen, D. A., & Clark, D. L. (1988). The diminution in federal expenditures for education during the Reagan administration. *Phi Delta Kappan, 70,* 134–138.

Villa, R. A., & Thousand, J. S. (1992). Student collaboration: An essential for curriculum in the 21st century. In S. Stainback & W. Stainback (Eds.), *Curriculum considerations in inclusive classrooms: Facilitating learning for all students* (pp. 117–142). Baltimore: Paul H. Brookes.

Wang, M. C., Anderson, K. A., & Bram, P. J. (1985). *Toward an empirical data base on mainstreaming: A research synthesis of program implementation and its effects.* Pittsburgh: University of Pittsburgh.

Wang, M. C., Reynolds, M. C., & Walberg, H. J. (1988). Integrating the children of the second system. *Phi Delta Kappan, 70,* 248–251.

Will, M. C. (1986). Educating children with learning problems: A shared responsibility. *Exceptional Children, 52,* 411–415.

York, J., Giangreco, M. F., Vandercook, T., & Macdonald, C. (1992). Integrating support personnel in the inclusive classroom. In S. Stainback & W. Stainback (Eds.), *Curriculum considerations in inclusive classrooms: Facilitating learning for all students* (pp. 101–116). Baltimore: Paul H. Brookes.

*The author thanks Barbara Savitt for her helpful comments and encouragement.*

---

*This chapter was originally published in the April 1996 issue of* Social Work in Education, *Vol. 18, pp. 113–127.*

# Regulating School Social Work Practice into the 21st Century

Isadora Hare

Gazing into a crystal ball is a precarious occupation at best. In attempting to predict the future of social work licensing, school social work certification, and NASW's school social work credential, prognosticators risk failure as circumstances and trends change and new factors enter the situation. Nevertheless, reviewing the legal and professional regulation of school social work practice against the backdrop of health care reform, the expansion of managed health care services, and education reform can be instructive.

Clearly, the environment within which social work services will be delivered in schools is changing quickly and dramatically. Managed care will increasingly be a factor to be reckoned with, whether through Medicaid-funded services, school-based health centers, or child welfare agencies involved in school-linked services. Managed care companies, in their efforts to demonstrate a concern for quality as well as cost containment, place major emphasis on the credentialing and recredentialing of their service providers. The National Commission on Quality Assurance (NCQA, 1996) in its *Standards for the Accreditation of Managed Care Organizations* defined *credentialing* as "the process by which the managed care organization authorizes, contracts with, or employs clinicians who are licensed to practice independently, to provide services to its members. Eligibility is determined by the extent to which applicants meet defined requirements for education, licensure, professional standing, service availability and accessibility" (p. 64). New companies are springing up to undertake credentialing services on behalf of managed care organizations (MCOs). One of these has contracted with NASW for its data on NASW credential holders, including those who have the School Social Work Specialist (SSWS) credential. The American Behavioral Health Care Association will also establish a centralized credentialing service for its member organizations in late 1996. Because of these developments, school social workers will have to pay greater attention in the future to licenses, certifications, and credentials that will be necessary or desirable for social work practice in schools.

## CREDENTIALING IN AN ERA OF EDUCATION AND HEALTH CARE REFORM

### Education Reform

It has been 13 years since the publication of *A Nation at Risk: The Imperative for Educational Reform* (National Commission on Excellence in Education, 1983) propelled the United States into an era of education reform. Although the momentum of reform has slowed somewhat, the national education goals formulated in 1989 remain intact (Hare, 1991). Underlying them is the theme of raising performance standards for teachers and other school staff. One of two goals added to the original six by the Goals 2000: Educate America Act of 1994 (P.L. 103-227) was Goal 4: Teacher Education and Professional Development, which states, "By the year 2000, the nation's teaching force will have access to programs for the continued improvement of their professional skills and the opportunity to acquire the knowledge and skills needed to instruct and prepare all American students for the next century" (National Education Goals Panel, 1995, p. 2).

If we extrapolate this goal to school personnel in a wider sense, it clearly points to the advantage of school social workers achieving and maintaining a national credential that goes beyond entry-level certification. Teachers have developed a private-sector credentialing program that indicates excellence of performance well beyond the entry-level proficiency signified by certification (Carnegie Corporation of New York, 1989). Based in Detroit, the National Board for Professional Teaching Standards (NBPTS) was created in 1987 as an independent, nonprofit, and nongovernment organization "to develop and operate a national voluntary system to assess and certify teachers who meet . . . high and vigorous standards for what accomplished teachers should know and be able to do" (NBPTS, 1996, p. 1). Although NBPTS certification for teachers has thus far received more support from state government than school social work credentialing, it does set an example that school social workers could emulate if they so chose.

## Health Care Reform

The effect of health care reform on schools is another cogent reason for school social workers to consider the advantages of professional social work credentialing. Although President Clinton's health care reform proposals were defeated, the health care delivery system is undergoing major changes nevertheless. These changes are affecting the schools and the context in which school social work is practiced.

*Managed Care.* The past decade has seen the emergence and rapid growth of managed health care in the United States. Contributing to these changes is the fact that health care costs in the United States escalated rapidly during the 1980s. Yet advances in information technology revealed that in spite of its advanced medical technology and huge expenditures, the United States was less successful in improving the health of its citizens than many other industrialized nations (Rice, 1995). *Managed health care* has been defined as "a generic term used to describe a variety of methods of financing and delivering health care services delivery while maintaining a defined quality of care" (Jackson, 1995, p. 1.1). The development of managed care has generated much controversy, partly because for-profit companies dominate the delivery of services, and reports appear periodically alleging that needed services are denied purely for financial reasons.

Yet managed care is an established fact in the United States, and the number of people covered by MCOs for medical and behavioral health services (including mental health and substance abuse services) is growing rapidly. From 1993 to 1995 alone, the number of U.S. citizens in specialized managed behavioral health programs grew from 86 million to 107 million (Oss, 1995). Furthermore, managed care principles are being used in general assistance as well as child and family welfare programs. The Child Welfare League of America (1995) has established a Managed Care Institute "to advance best practice in children's services in a managed care environment and to ensure that all children and families in need have access to high quality, appropriate, affordable, and effective health care, behavioral health care, and child welfare services" (p. 2).

*Medicaid.* Medicaid programs are also moving rapidly toward managed care. Added to the Social Security Act in 1965 as Title XIX, Medicaid is a joint state–federal program to help finance health services for people in poverty. From 1985 to 1995, the costs of Medicaid more than tripled, and increasingly state Medicaid programs have received waivers from the federal Medicaid rules to enable state governments to mandate that Medicaid recipients enroll in MCOs. In 1991 only 6 percent of Medicaid recipients were in managed care plans. By 1994, it was 23 percent. By 1995, 43 states were using managed care companies to deliver Medicaid-funded services to over 8 million beneficiaries (Vandivort-Warren, 1995).

## School-Linked Health-Related Services

The trend in Medicaid-funded health care will increasingly affect schools that have been billing Medicaid for health-related services since the late 1980s. Some states began using Medicaid funding after 1972, when Congress expanded Medicaid to include the Early Periodic Screening Diagnosis and Treatment (EPSDT) Program (NASW, 1995). For example, federal monies were used to provide medical, vision, and hearing screening by school nurses in Louisiana. Later Congress enacted the Medicare Catastrophic Coverage Act of 1988 (P.L. 100-360), which authorized Medicaid funds for education-related health services provided to children with special needs in special education programs.

The Omnibus Budget Reconciliation Act of 1989 (P.L. 101-289) went further and mandated EPSDT health services in all states if they were "medically necessary" to treat a condition found in an EPSDT screening of children eligible for Part H or Part B services to children with disabilities (Danilson, n.d.). Medicaid funding could therefore be used for case management and other social work services authorized by statute. A survey in 1993 revealed that 41 states were using Medicaid as a source of revenue for special education (Malone & Yeater, 1993).

As school-linked services and school-based health centers proliferate, more and more Medicaid dollars are being claimed by school systems and other organizations offering health and social services in school buildings (Advocates for Youth, 1995; Farrow & Joe, 1992; Hare, 1995b). Of the 607 school-based health centers in 41 states and the District of Columbia existing in November 1994, nearly half received Medicaid support, and 28 percent of students using the centers had Medicaid coverage (Advocates for Youth, 1995). However, as more states have initiated Medicaid managed care programs, the process of securing payments for services to Medicaid beneficiaries has become more complicated (Schlitt & Lear, 1995).

As MCOs emphasize the credentialing of their service providers, they are focusing more on provider profiling as a means of ensuring the best quality, cost-effective services to clients (Wadell, 1996). This is an outcomes-oriented approach in which credentialing is but the first step. It goes much further to consider utilization and cost patterns, clinical outcomes, case manager evaluations, incident reports, and patient satisfaction both with the therapist and with the environment in which services are delivered. The goal is to achieve the best match possible between client need and provider skill.

Acquiring and documenting specialized qualifications will therefore become increasingly significant for practitioners. At the same time, it is possible that in the future licensure laws will be amended in the direction of more generalized licensing of mental health professionals. The Pew Health Professions Commission Taskforce on Healthcare Workforce Regulation has issued a set of recommendations to make such regulation more appropriate to the changing environment of health care in the United States (Finocchio, Dower, McMahon, Gragnola, & Taskforce on Healthcare Workforce Regulation, 1995).

## REGULATING SCHOOL SOCIAL WORK PRACTICE

Undoubtedly, the increase in managed care will lead to expanded therapeutic services in schools. Social workers will need to document their special qualifications to provide psychosocial services in this environment. School social workers must understand the many levels of regulation that are used to maintain standards of performance and specialization.

The regulatory system is complex, and this complexity is compounded by the fact that there is no clear nomenclature. The same terms are used interchangeably to refer to different forms of regulation. It is therefore important to gain conceptual clarity, irrespective of the particular titles used. In general, regulation takes two forms: legal and professional.

### Legal Regulation

Legal regulation is undertaken by public bodies at the state level, such as state legislatures, state boards of education, or state departments of education. As Biggerstaff (1995) stated, "Licensing and other forms of legal regulation are an exercise of the state's police power to protect consumers. Legal regulation, a form of public policy that allows government to intervene in the private sector, is protective regulatory legislation implemented through state agencies" (p. 1617). Legal regulation can be divided into two types: (1) regulation of social work practice in general and (2) field-specific regulation of school social work practice.

*Regulation of Social Work Practice in General.* There are three types of legal regulation of social workers: licensing, statutory certification, and registration. Licensing laws establish the minimum standards that practitioners must meet to enter the profession. The primary purpose of licensing is consumer protection, and licensure requirements therefore prohibit unqualified persons from providing the services offered by the profession. Although social work licensing laws can regulate up to four levels of practice, ranging from the baccalaureate level to clinical or advanced levels (which require two to three years of experience), the intent of the law is to establish entry-level standards for each type of licensed practice (American Association of State Social Work Boards [AASSWB], 1995).

Statutory certification and registration laws, unlike licensing laws, are "voluntary statutes applying only to social workers who wish to use a particular title" (Biggerstaff, 1995, p. 1617). According to the AASSWB (1996), a national membership organization of state regulatory boards established in 1979, by 1993 all states had some form of legal regulation. By 1996, 40 states had acts licensing social work practice, and 13 had title protection statutes (the total of 53 includes the District of Columbia, Puerto Rico, and the Virgin Islands). Social work regulatory boards are housed in a variety of state departments such as departments of health or departments of regulation and licensing. In seven states, including Georgia, New Jersey, and Ohio, school social workers are exempted from the requirement of state licensing as social workers per se (AASSWB, 1995, 1996).

*Field-Specific Regulation of School Social Work Practice.* Most school social workers are employed in public school systems, which constitute a major social and governmental institution in every state. Many states have therefore developed governance systems for regulating education professionals who work in the schools (Clark, 1994; Hawkins, 1982). This type of regulation is generally called "certification" (although in some states it is referred to as "licensing" or "credentialing"). An NASW survey conducted for the 1995–96 period revealed that 31 states and the District of Columbia require certification of school social workers, and one additional state, Alaska, has voluntary certification. Twelve states (Delaware, Idaho, Indiana, Iowa, Louisiana, Minnesota, Nevada, New Hampshire, New Mexico, New York, Rhode Island, and Utah) and the District of Columbia require dual licensure; that is, they require practitioners to hold their state license as social workers in addition to their certification as school social workers in public school systems (NASW, 1996b).

## Professional Regulation

Professional regulation comes from the private sector, usually from national professional associations, or boards constituted by members of a particular profession or subspecialty. To differentiate this type of national, voluntary, private-sector regulation from state-sponsored, statutory licensing and certification, this article uses the term "credentialing," although some authorities recommend the use of the term "certification" in this context (Finocchio et al., 1995). Various organizations issue credentials that are relevant to social work practice (for example, the Board Certified Diplomate [BCD] from the American Board of Examiners in Clinical Social Work) and credentials for substance abuse counselors and case managers.

NASW, established in 1955, mandates a credentialing program in its bylaws (NASW, 1993) and reaffirmed the importance of credentialing in its Strategic Plan adopted in 1991. NASW now issues four credentials:

1. The Academy of Certified Social Workers (ACSW) was adopted in 1960 as "the benchmark of practice for practitioners with a master of social work (MSW) degree" (Biggerstaff, 1995, p. 1619). This credential has general applicability and is available to social workers in all fields and methods who

have had two years of approved, supervised post-MSW practice and are members of NASW.

2. The Qualified Clinical Social Worker (QCSW) and
3. The Diplomate in Clinical Social Work are clinical credentials for MSW graduates with two and five years of approved practice experience, respectively. Social workers holding these credentials can be listed in NASW's *Register of Clinical Social Workers,* published biennially since 1976 (Hare, 1995a).
4. The SSWS credential is available to MSW graduates with two years of approved, supervised practice in public schools and other educational settings. (One of these years can be a field placement in the second year of the MSW program.)

## SCOPE AND PURPOSE OF THE SSWS CREDENTIAL

The SSWS credential is a national, voluntary qualification. Initially offered in 1992, it was NASW's first field-specific professional credential, and it requires the necessary supervised practice stated earlier, professional references from a supervisor and a colleague, and adherence to the *NASW Code of Ethics* (NASW, 1996a) and *NASW Standards for School Social Work Services* (NASW, 1992a). Membership in NASW is not required. In addition to these requirements, candidates must achieve a passing score on the National Teachers Examination (NTE) School Social Worker Specialty Area Test.

Why were the specialty test and credential for school social workers created? At the time they were developed, NASW was receiving complaints from school social workers, primarily in the northeast, that to achieve the state certification they needed for their jobs, they were being required to take the NTE core battery, which included a test of professional practice for teachers. Although the full battery of NTE tests contained a variety of specialized tests for pupil services providers, such as school psychologists and speech and language pathologists, there was no test for school social workers.

In collaboration with the Educational Testing Service (ETS), NASW developed the School Social Worker Specialty Area Test, which became a part of the NTE battery of tests; this test is based on the results of a national survey of school social work practice conducted for the 1989–90 period. This survey was the third in a series begun in 1968 by Lela Costin (1969) and continued by Paula Allen-Meares (1977). It used Allen-Meares's 1974 inventory as adapted by a 19-member committee of school social work experts appointed by NASW, with Allen-Meares's advice and consultation. This panel of experts was selected because they had extensive first-hand experience with school social work or had an academic background in teaching courses in school social work. They also represented the gender, ethnic, and geographic diversity of the United States.

On the basis of a return of 862 questionnaires (49.5 percent of the original sample), the survey results provided a rich source of demographic data and data on the tasks performed by school social workers and the knowledge, skills, and abilities required to perform the tasks effectively at the entry level (Allen-Meares, 1994; Nelson, 1990). Such data are essential to ensure the validity and legal defensibility of a test-based credentialing process.

The NTE–SSWS test examines knowledge of social work ethics; social work modalities and procedures; theories of human behavior and development; models of school social work practice; research; multidisciplinary activities; program development and managerial skills; characteristics of pupil populations; public education legislation, case law and due process; and financing. With the exception of a test developed in Illinois, the NTE test developed by NASW in collaboration with ETS remains the only test specifically for school social workers constructed by their professional peers in accordance with standards set by them.

Norms for the test were developed in 1992, when 2,272 candidates took the test and were grandparented into the program if they met all the other criteria for the credential. Presently there are 2,025 active and 823 inactive credential holders.

State departments of education are beginning to adopt the test as a means of certifying school social workers (for example, Colorado, Florida, Louisiana, Missouri, West Virginia, Tennessee, and Washington). Other states such as North Carolina and Oklahoma have expressed interest in the test.

However, the chief purpose of the credential program was to set a national standard of excellence for school social workers over and above the requirements of state certification. It was designed to promote the use of *NASW Standards for School Social Work Services* (NASW, 1992a), to enhance recognition of school social workers' contributions, and to encourage continuing professional development for school social workers. Additional goals included to promote uniform credentialing standards across states, agencies, and training institutions; to ensure a consistent level of training and experience in service providers who earn the credential; and to provide a model for states who are considering the introduction of certification for school social workers (NASW, 1992b). In short, the overarching goal is to promote the professional identity of school social workers as specialists in solving psychosocial problems in schools and their own sense of professional pride. It is interesting to note that these goals are remarkably similar to those enunciated by the National Association of School Psychologists (NASP) for their Nationally Certified School Psychologist program (NASP, n.d.).

## CONCLUSION

Managed care principles are rapidly entering the public child welfare system and are being implemented in the delivery of therapeutic services in schools. Within this environment, professional credentials and high standards for practice are of paramount importance. School social workers would be well advised to look beyond entry-level certification by state departments of education to social work licensing and to professional credentialing that documents their specialized qualifications to provide educationally necessary psychosocial services in the school environment.

## REFERENCES

Advocates for Youth. (1995). *School-based and school-linked health centers: The facts.* Washington, DC: Author.

Allen-Meares, P. (1977). Analysis of tasks in school social work. *Social Work, 22,* 196–201.

Allen-Meares, P. (1994). Analysis of tasks in school social work. *Social Work, 39,* 560–565.

American Association of State Social Work Boards. (1995). *Social work laws and board regulations: A state comparison study.* Culpeper, VA: Author.

American Association of State Social Work Boards. (1996). *Social work laws and board regulations: A state comparison study.* Culpeper, VA: Author.

Biggerstaff, M. A. (1995). Licensing, regulation, and certification. In R. L. Edwards (Ed.-in-Chief), *Encyclopedia of social work* (19th ed., Vol. 2, pp. 1617–1624). Washington, DC: NASW Press.

Carnegie Corporation of New York. (1989). Certifying and rewarding teaching excellence: The National Board for Professional Teaching Standards. *Carnegie Quarterly, 34*(2), 1.

Child Welfare League of America. (1995). *Ensuring quality in the managed care environment* [Brochure]. Washington, DC: Author.

Clark, J. P. (1994). Unraveling the licensing, credentialing, and certification maze: A guide for school social workers. *Iowa Journal of School Social Work, 7*(1), 6–15.

Costin, L. B. (1969). An analysis of the tasks in school social work. *Social Service Review, 43,* 274–285.

Danilson, S. (n.d.). *Medicaid and the schools: The Louisiana experience.* Unpublished paper distributed at the Annual Conference on Medicaid, sponsored by the Department of Health and Hospitals and Medicaid of Louisiana, Baton Rouge, 1992.

Farrow, F., & Joe, T. (1992). Financing school-linked, integrated services. *Future of Children, 2*(1), 56–67.

Finocchio, L. J., Dower, C. M., McMahon, T., Gragnola, C., & Taskforce on Healthcare Workforce Regulation. (1995). *Reforming healthcare workforce regulation: Policy considerations for the 21st century.* San Francisco: Pew Health Professions Commission.

Goals 2000: Educate America Act of 1994, P.L. 103-227, 108 Stat. 125.

Hare, I. (1991). School social work and its social environment. In R. Constable, J. P. Flynn, & S. McDonald (Eds.), *School social work: Practice and research perspectives* (2nd ed., pp. 71–86). Chicago: Lyceum.

Hare, I. (1995a). *Analysis of NASW's credentialing program.* Unpublished manuscript, National Association of Social Workers, Office of Quality Assurance, Washington, DC.

Hare, I. (1995b). School-linked services. In R. L. Edwards (Ed.-in-Chief), *Encyclopedia of social work* (19th ed., Vol. 3, pp. 2100–2109). Washington, DC: NASW Press.

Hawkins, M. T. (1982). State certification standards for school social work practice. *Social Work in Education, 4,* 41–52.

Jackson, V. H. (Ed.). (1995). *Managed care resource guide for social workers in agency settings.* Washington, DC: NASW Press.

Malone, L. D., & Yeater, J. (1993). *States summary: Medicaid billing survey.* Indianapolis: Indiana Department of Education, Division of Special Education.

Medicare Catastrophic Coverage Act of 1988, P.L. 100-360, 102 Stat. 683.

National Association of School Psychologists. (n.d.). *Nationally certified school psychologist: Application and information.* Bethesda, MD: Author.

National Association of Social Workers. (1992a). *NASW standards for school social work services.* Washington, DC: Author.

National Association of Social Workers. (1992b). *School social work specialist (SSWS) credential: Information bulletin.* Washington, DC: Author.

National Association of Social Workers. (1993). *Bylaws of the National Association of Social Workers.* Washington, DC: Author.

National Association of Social Workers. (1995). *Third-party reimbursement for clinical social work services.* Washington, DC: Author.

National Association of Social Workers. (1996a). *NASW code of ethics.* Washington, DC: Author.

National Association of Social Workers. (1996b). *School social work certification requirements from state departments of education.* Washington, DC: Author.

National Board for Professional Teaching Standards. (1996). *Backgrounder.* Detroit: Author.

National Commission on Excellence in Education. (1983). *A nation at risk: The imperative for educational reform.* Washington, DC: U.S. Department of Education.

National Commission on Quality Assurance. (1996). *Standards for the accreditation of managed care organizations* (1996 ed.). Washington, DC: Author.

National Education Goals Panel. (1995). *The National Education Goals report executive summary: Improving education through family–school–community partnerships.* Washington, DC: Author.

Nelson, C. (1990). *A job analysis of school social workers.* Princeton, NJ: Educational Testing Service.

Omnibus Budget Reconciliation Act of 1989, P.L. 101-289, 103 Stat. 2106.

Oss, M. (1995, April). *Trends in behavioral health financing.* Paper presented at the National Managed Health Care Congress, Behavioral Health Care Track, Washington, DC.

Rice, D. P. (1995). Health care: Financing. In R. L. Edwards (Ed.-in-Chief), *Encyclopedia of social work* (19th ed., Vol. 2, pp. 1168–1175). Washington, DC: NASW Press.

Schlitt, J., & Lear, J. G. (Eds.). (1995). *Medicaid, managed care, and school-based health centers: Proceedings of a meeting with policy makers and providers on state and local partnerships to establish school-based health centers.* Washington, DC: George Washington University, Making the Grade: State and Local Partnerships to Establish School-Based Health Centers.

Vandivort-Warren, R. (1995). *Merging managed care and Medicaid: Private regulation of public health care.* Unpublished manuscript, National Association of Social Workers, Office of Policy and Planning, Washington, DC.

Wadell, D. (1996, February). *Provider profiling: A look at today's state-of-the-art approaches.* Paper presented at a Conference on Behavioral Healthcare Provider Profiling, sponsored by Global Business Research, Ltd. (New York), New Orleans.

*The author acknowledges with appreciation the contributions of Marianne Josem, MSW, ACSW, senior staff associate, Quality Assurance, NASW, and Janis Burke, student intern, Radford University School of Social Work, Radford, Virginia, to this article. The views expressed are the author's alone.*

---

*This chapter was originally published in the October 1996 issue of* Social Work in Education, *Vol. 18, pp. 250–258.*

# 44 The Status of School Social Workers in America

Santos Torres, Jr.

As a field of practice, school social work is now nearly a century old, just a few years younger than its parent profession. Simultaneously inaugurated in three eastern U.S. cities around 1906—New York, Boston, and Hartford, Connecticut—early school social workers (referred to as "visiting teachers") were employed by outside agencies to work in the schools (Meares, Washington, & Welsh, 1986). During the next four decades, both privately and publicly supported demonstration projects promoted the growth and expansion of school social work. The relationship between school social work and education became formalized in the 1940s and 1950s, when public school boards began to assume greater responsibility for financing their own social workers to address the needs of students and their families during and shortly after World War II (Winters & Easton, 1983).

Like other human services fields, school social work has historically pursued its own professional identity. As the field has evolved, there has been a growing conviction (supported by both a legal and a political framework) that school social work requires special skills and competencies best served by graduate-level trained professionals (Costin, 1969). How well is this perspective reflected in the real world? A few research efforts have explored this and related issues such as education, training, and certification requirements of school social workers and the availability of social workers in schools throughout the country. This article provides information about the current status of school social workers across 57 education jurisdictions in the United States, including the number of school social workers employed; job titles, descriptions, and related activities; education and training standards; certification requirements within and reciprocity between jurisdictions; institutional and professional organization affiliations; and salary data.

## LITERATURE REVIEW

The literature on the status of school social workers is somewhat limited except in areas such as tasks and certification standards (Allen-Meares, 1994). In 1967 the Interprofessional Research Commission on Pupil Personnel Services, reporting the results from a survey on certification requirements, indicated that only 15 states certified school social workers and that 27 states certified visiting teachers (cited in Hawkins, 1980). Not long after, Venturini's (1974) study indicated a lack of school social work programs in many states, especially in poorer and more sparsely populated regions.

In 1975 NASW launched "a comprehensive study to describe the organization, delivery, and staffing patterns of social work services in schools" (Hawkins, 1980, p. 86) to provide support for maintaining school social work as a profession. All 50 states, the District of Columbia, and Puerto Rico were part of the sampling frame. Hawkins found that school social workers were employed to some degree in 50 to 52 jurisdictions, counselors were employed in 51 jurisdictions, and psychologists were employed in 45 jurisdictions. Certification of school social workers was required by 33 jurisdictions; 19 of the 33 also required a master's degree in social work, four required field work in a school setting or academic courses in education, eight required a bachelor's degree, and 15 required social work experience.

Meares (1977) found that 39 states employed school social workers; of these, nine states, or nearly 25 percent, reported employing only a few school social workers. The remaining 11 states either reported not employing any school social workers or failed to respond to the survey.

In addition to determining how many jurisdictions employed school social workers, Hawkins (1980) found that there was confusion about the definition, role, and requirements of a school social worker; that certification under a single title did not indicate that all school districts within a given system adopted the title; that many different routes to meet training and certification requirements existed between and within states; and that although not widespread, some degree of reciprocity existed among jurisdictions.

## METHOD

A brief 14-item questionnaire was mailed in February 1990 to the chief educational officer of each of the 50 states as well as seven additional U.S. education jurisdictions—American Samoa, Department of Defense Dependents' Schools, the District of Columbia, Guam, Northern Mariana Islands, Puerto Rico, and the Virgin Islands. Forty-five of the 57 surveys were returned for an overall response rate of 78.9 percent. Of those responding, Delaware and Oklahoma reported not providing school social work services, and Missouri returned a blank survey.

## FINDINGS

### Demographic Characteristics

Reliable analysis of demographic data collected in this study beyond the total number of school social workers by education jurisdiction proved difficult. Many jurisdictions reported not collecting such data for their region, or occasionally the figures provided were inconsistent in terms of subtotals. Therefore, because comparative analysis of the data might yield less-than-useful information, it is not included in this article.

### Number of School Social Workers Employed

New York, Illinois, and Puerto Rico were the top three employers of school social workers among the 34 education jurisdictions reporting this data (Table 44-1). The jurisdictions with the fewest school social workers were South Dakota,

*Table 44-1*

**Number of School Social Workers Employed, by Education Jurisdiction**

| Education Jurisdiction | Number Employed |
|---|---|
| Alabama | 11 |
| Alaska | 1 |
| Arkansas | 12 |
| Colorado | 321 |
| Connecticut | 450 |
| Department of Defense Dependents' Schools | 15 |
| District of Columbia | 39 |
| Florida | 539 |
| Georgia | 206 |
| Guam | 3 |
| Hawaii | 40 |
| Illinois | 1,349 |
| Indiana | 190 |
| Kansas | 133 |
| Kentucky | 73 |
| Louisiana | 210 |
| Maryland | 243 |
| Massachusetts | 482 |
| Minnesota | 395 |
| Montana | 8 |
| Nebraska | 37 |
| Nevada | 275 |
| New Hampshire | 72 |
| New York | 1,513 |
| North Carolina | 345 |
| Puerto Rico | 956 |
| Rhode Island | 54 |
| South Dakota | 6 |
| Vermont | 350 |
| Virginia | 449 |
| Washington | 125 |
| West Virginia | 12 |
| Wisconsin | 365 |
| Wyoming | 58 |
| Total (34 jurisdictions) | 9,337 |

Guam, and Alaska. Twenty-one of the jurisdictions employed less than the average of 274 school social workers.

## Job Title, Description, and Activities

Twenty-five of the 42 education jurisdictions that responded to the question used the title "school social worker" when referring to professional staff who provide social work services in education settings (Table 44-2). Fourteen reported using the title "school social worker" or "social worker" in combination with other titles. Only three jurisdictions used unique titles. Florida, Georgia, and Virginia still used the title "visiting teacher."

*Table 44-2*

## Job Titles Used, by Education Jurisdiction

| Job Title | Education Jurisdiction |
|---|---|
| School social worker | Alaska, Colorado, Connecticut, District of Columbia, Idaho, Illinois, Indiana, Kansas, Kentucky, Michigan, Minnesota, Montana, New Jersey, New Mexico, New York, North Carolina, Puerto Rico, Rhode Island, South Carolina, South Dakota, Utah, Washington, West Virginia, Wisconsin, Wyoming |
| Combination of school social worker and other titles | Florida, Georgia, Louisiana, Maryland, New Hampshire,[a] Pennsylvania, Virginia |
| Combination of social worker and other titles | Alabama, Arkansas, Department of Defense Dependents' Schools, Guam, Hawaii, Mississippi, Nebraska |
| School adjustment counselor | Massachusetts |
| School counselor | Nevada |
| Guidance services | Vermont |

[a]New Hampshire reported statewide efforts to incorporate "school social worker" as the job title.

Eleven of the 33 education jurisdictions that responded to the question shared responsibility for writing job descriptions for school social workers (Table 44-3). Washington and Wisconsin were the only jurisdictions that reported school social workers as being the sole source of the job description. State and local education agencies were the most frequent sources of job descriptions.

Content analysis of the job description materials of the 25 education jurisdictions that responded was used to identify the most common school social work job-related activities, tasks, and functions, including casework, liaison, assessment and testing, consultation, referral services, and functioning as a member

*Table 44-3*

## Source of Job Description, by Education Jurisdiction

| Source | Education Jurisdiction |
|---|---|
| Social worker | Alabama, Illinois, Indiana, North Carolina, Puerto Rico, Washington, West Virginia, Wisconsin |
| State department | Alabama, Connecticut, District of Columbia, Guam, Hawaii, Illinois, Kansas, Kentucky, Maryland, Massachusetts, Michigan, Minnesota, Mississippi, Nebraska, Nevada, New Jersey, New York, North Carolina, West Virginia |
| Local education agency | Colorado, Connecticut, Department of Defense Dependents' Schools, District of Columbia, Florida, Illinois, Indiana, Louisiana, Mississippi, Montana, Nebraska, New Hampshire, New Mexico, New York, Puerto Rico, Rhode Island, Vermont, West Virginia |
| Combination | Alabama, Connecticut, District of Columbia, Georgia, Illinois, Indiana, Nebraska, New York, North Carolina, Puerto Rico, West Virginia |

of an interdisciplinary team (Table 44-4). (However, where the name of a given jurisdiction does not appear next to a particular activity in Table 44-4, one should not infer the absence of that activity.) The results of this analysis suggest limited comparability with a recent study on school social worker entry-level tasks conducted by Allen-Meares (1994).

*Table 44-4*

## Job-Related Activities, by Education Jurisdiction

| Activity | Education Jurisdiction |
|---|---|
| Assessment and testing | Alabama, Connecticut, District of Columbia, Georgia, Guam, Kentucky, Michigan, Minnesota, New Jersey, North Carolina, Puerto Rico, Rhode Island, Washington |
| Truancy | Alabama, Florida |
| Member of interdisciplinary team | Alabama, Connecticut, Department of Defense Dependents' Schools, District of Columbia, Michigan, Minnesota, Montana, Puerto Rico, Rhode Island |
| Referral services | Alabama, Connecticut, Department of Defense Dependents' Schools, District of Columbia, Florida, Guam, Massachusetts, Minnesota, Mississippi, New Hampshire, Puerto Rico |
| Record keeping | Alabama, District of Columbia, Guam, North Carolina, Vermont |
| Casework (direct and indirect services) | Alabama, Department of Defense Dependents' Schools, District of Columbia, Florida, Hawaii, Indiana, Kansas, Kentucky, Massachusetts, Michigan, Minnesota, New Hampshire, New Jersey, New York, North Carolina, Puerto Rico, Rhode Island, Vermont, Washington, Wisconsin |
| Liaison (home, school, and community) | Alabama, Connecticut, Department of Defense Dependents' Schools, Florida, Georgia, Indiana, Kansas, Kentucky, Massachusetts, Minnesota, New York, North Carolina, Puerto Rico, Wisconsin |
| Consultation (including court) | District of Columbia, Guam, Hawaii, Indiana, Kansas, Minnesota, New Jersey, New York, North Carolina, Puerto Rico, Rhode Island, Vermont, Washington |
| Advocacy | Connecticut, Indiana, North Carolina, Washington |
| Supervision | District of Columbia |
| Participant in professional development | Georgia |
| In-service training | New Jersey, North Carolina, Puerto Rico, Vermont |
| Program planning, implementation, and evaluation | Connecticut, District of Columbia, Georgia, Guam, Kentucky, Michigan, Minnesota, New Hampshire, New Jersey, New York, North Carolina, Puerto Rico, Vermont |

## Certification and Reciprocity

*Certification*—the credentialing of professionals in a given field—establishes minimum requirements for professional practice and title protection. Of the 57 education jurisdictions in the study, 32 reported that certification was required in their region (Table 44-5). Eight reported having no certification requirements, and 16 either did not respond to the question or did not know if certification existed in their area (respondents may have had incomplete knowledge of certification requirements, certification requirements may have been in transition at the time of the survey, or certification requirements may have been inaccurately reported).

Twenty of the 43 education jurisdictions that responded to the question required a minimum of a master's degree in social work for certification as a school social worker (Table 44-6). Eight jurisdictions permitted individuals with master's- or bachelor's-level training in fields other than social work to be certified as school social workers. Six reported a state-level examination as part of the requirements. Ten identified professional experience and internships as a requirement.

Only six education jurisdictions reported having interstate certification reciprocity agreements: the Department of Defense Dependents' Schools, Louisiana, New York, North Carolina, Rhode Island, and Washington. Twenty of the 26 jurisdictions that responded indicated not having interstate agreements. It is interesting to note that in some cases a jurisdiction reported having reciprocal certification with another jurisdiction, but the identified jurisdiction did not report reciprocity with that jurisdiction.

## Institutional and Professional Affiliation

Respondents selected from four characteristics that described their institutional affiliation: (1) part of the special education department, (2) an independent

*Table 44-5*

**School Social Work Certification, by Education Jurisdiction**

| Certification | Education Jurisdiction |
| --- | --- |
| Required | Alabama, Alaska, Colorado, Connecticut, Department of Defense Dependents' Schools, District of Columbia, Florida, Georgia, Idaho, Illinois, Kansas, Kentucky, Louisiana, Maryland, Massachusetts, Michigan, Minnesota, Montana, Nevada, New Hampshire, New Mexico, New York, North Carolina, Puerto Rico, Rhode Island, Utah, Vermont, Virginia, Washington, West Virginia, Wisconsin, Wyoming |
| Not required | Delaware, Guam, Hawaii, Indiana, Nebraska, Oklahoma, South Carolina, South Dakota |
| Unknown | American Samoa, Arizona, Arkansas, California, Iowa, Maine, Mississippi, Missouri, New Jersey, North Dakota, Northern Mariana Islands, Ohio, Oregon, Tennessee, Texas, Virgin Islands |

*Table 44-6*

## Certification Requirements, by Education Jurisdiction

| Requirement | Field Work | | Course Work | | State-Level Examination |
|---|---|---|---|---|---|
| | Social Work | Other | Social Work | Other | |
| **Education** | | | | | |
| Bachelor's degree | Florida, New Hampshire, New Mexico, North Carolina, Wyoming | Alabama, Florida, Minnesota, New Jersey | Minnesota, North Carolina | New Jersey, North Carolina, Wyoming | Alabama, New Hampshire, North Carolina |
| Bachelor's degree and some graduate course work | Connecticut, Washington | Hawaii | Hawaii | Hawaii | |
| Master's degree | Alabama, Connecticut, Department of Defense Dependents' Schools, District of Columbia, Florida, Georgia, Idaho, Illinois, Indiana, Kansas, Louisiana, Massachusetts, Michigan, Montana, New Hampshire, New Mexico, New York, North Carolina, Utah, Wisconsin | Alabama, Florida, Massachusetts, Nevada, Vermont | Department of Defense Dependents' Schools, District of Columbia, Illinois, Kansas, Mississippi, North Carolina, Wisconsin | District of Columbia, Nevada, New Mexico, North Carolina, Wisconsin | Idaho, Illinois, New York, North Carolina |
| Completion of approved program in social work, academic level not specified | Alaska, Nebraska | | | | |
| Teacher certification | | Alabama, Vermont | | | |

*Continued*

Table 44-6
**Certification Requirements, by Education Jurisdiction**

| Requirement | Field Work | | Course Work | | State-Level Examination |
|---|---|---|---|---|---|
| | Social Work | Other | Social Work | Other | |
| Completion of internship | Connecticut, Department of Defense Dependents' Schools, District of Columbia, Illinois, North Carolina, Utah | | | | |
| Other Experience | Alabama, Connecticut, Department of Defense Dependents' Schools, District of Columbia, Massachusetts, New Mexico, Rhode Island | New Jersey, Vermont | | | |
| U.S. citizenship | Massachusetts | | | | |
| Transcript review | Nebraska | | | | |
| Requirements in process of being changed | Florida | | | | |

component within the school organizational structure, (3) part of the teacher's union, and (4) part of an independent school social work union. Of the 34 education jurisdictions that responded to the question, only two education jurisdictions, Indiana and New Hampshire, indicated that school social workers were typically part of an independent union (Table 44-7). Twelve jurisdictions' school social workers were part of a teacher's union, and those of 22 jurisdictions were typically part of a special education department.

Of the 45 education jurisdictions that responded to the question, 22 reported that they were aware of and 19 reported not being aware of professional school social work state organizations (Table 44-8). School social workers in jurisdictions with such organizations have a greater opportunity to exercise a voice in the policy, planning, and program implementation aspects of educational services to children; to network with colleagues who share similar professional values, goals, and needs; and to participate in professional development and continuing education opportunities relative to certification and licensing requirements.

## Salary

The study sought to obtain aggregate figures on school social worker compensation and did not seek to differentiate according to type of pay scale (for example, teacher or administrator) or length of contract. An assumption made in designing the survey instrument was that aggregate compensation data would be maintained by the state education office in each education jurisdiction. Surveying each local education administrative unit (for example, school district) might have yielded a significantly larger dataset, but any summative results

*Table 44-7*

### Institutional Affiliation, by Education Jurisdiction

| Affiliation | Education Jurisdiction |
|---|---|
| Part of the special education department | Alabama, Alaska, Connecticut, District of Columbia, Guam, Illinois, Kansas, Louisiana, Massachusetts, Michigan, Minnesota, Mississippi, Montana, New Hampshire, New Mexico, New York, Puerto Rico, Rhode Island, South Carolina, Virginia, Wisconsin, Wyoming |
| An independent component within the school organizational structure | Department of Defense Dependents' Schools, Florida, Georgia, Hawaii, Illinois, Kentucky, Nebraska, Nevada, North Carolina, Vermont, Virginia, Washington, West Virginia, Wisconsin |
| Part of the teacher's union | Alaska, Department of Defense Dependents' Schools, Florida, Illinois, Indiana, Minnesota, New York, Rhode Island, Vermont, Washington, Wisconsin, Wyoming |
| Part of an independent school social work union | Indiana, New Hampshire |

*Table 44-8*

**Professional School Social Worker Organizations, by Education Jurisdiction**

| Organization | Education Jurisdiction |
| --- | --- |
| School social work | Alabama, Connecticut, Georgia, Illinois, Indiana, Kansas, Kentucky, Maryland, Michigan, Minnesota, Mississippi, Nevada, New Hampshire, New York, North Carolina, Puerto Rico, Rhode Island, Vermont, Virginia, Washington, West Virginia, Wisconsin |
| School social work and NASW state chapter | Florida, Massachusetts |
| NASW state chapter | Hawaii, Louisiana |
| None or unknown | Alaska, Arkansas, Colorado, Delaware, Department of Defense Dependents' Schools, District of Columbia, Guam, Idaho, Missouri, Montana, Nebraska, New Jersey, New Mexico, Oklahoma, Pennsylvania, South Carolina, South Dakota, Utah, Wyoming |

would have been subject to inaccuracy and inconsistency and would have gone beyond the scope and means of this study.

Twenty-four education jurisdictions reported salary information (Table 44-9). Illinois had the greatest variability in salary range, and Puerto Rico had the lowest salary and the smallest range. An estimated national salary of $28,955, arrived at by averaging the means of jurisdictional salary ranges, is close to the NASW recommended minimum ($30,000) for ACSW-level social work practitioners. The extreme ends of the salary range were occupied by school social workers in Puerto Rico and Maryland, whose average salaries were 57 percent less than and 37 percent more than the estimated national average, respectively. Salaries in northern jurisdictions tended to be better than those in the southern jurisdictions.

## CONCLUSION

Since the 1940s school social workers have made important gains as service providers in their host environments. School social workers have increased their presence; established a professional identity better aligned with the training, education, and tasks traditionally associated with professional social workers; and made significant contributions to and effectively collaborated with other professionals as part of the multidisciplinary teams that serve U.S. schools.

From the study reported in this article, a clearer image of school social work begins to emerge. The job title "school social worker" is being used today more than ever before. Certification and training requirements for people using this title have become more stringent and more universally accepted. Salaries are comparable to the minimum standard set by NASW for ACSW-level social work practitioners.

Finally, ascertaining the total number of school social workers serving all U.S. education jurisdictions is far less important than developing effective strategies to place at least one social worker in every school building across the country.

*Table 44-9*

## Comparison of School Social Worker Salaries, by Education Jurisdiction

| Education Jurisdiction | Rank | Salary Range ($) | Averaged Salary ($) | Difference from Estimated National Average[a] ($) |
|---|---|---|---|---|
| Maryland | 1 | 23,090–56,154 | 39,622 | +10,667 |
| District of Columbia | 2 | 33,980–44,401 | 39,191 | +10,236 |
| Connecticut | 3 | 25,000–50,000 | 37,500 | +8,545 |
| Illinois | 4 | 11,055–61,798 | 36,427 | +7,472 |
| Florida | 5 | 22,000–50,000 | 36,000 | +7,045 |
| Kentucky | 6 | 17,967–50,204 | 34,086 | +5,131 |
| Wisconsin | 7 | 20,000–48,000 | 34,000 | +5,045 |
| New York | 8 | 21,188–45,299 | 33,244 | +4,289 |
| Nevada | 9 | 25,000–40,000 | 32,500 | +3,545 |
| Department of Defense Dependents' Schools | 10 | 22,460–40,045 | 31,253 | +2,298 |
| Washington | 11 | 20,645–38,174 | 29,410 | +455 |
| Minnesota | 12 | 19,000–39,000 | 29,000 | +45 |
| Hawaii | 13 | 21,900–35,976 | 28,938 | –17 |
| Wyoming | 14 | 18,800–38,400 | 28,600 | –355 |
| South Dakota | 15 | 27,497[b] | 27,497 | –1,458 |
| Georgia | 16 | 19,000–35,000 | 27,000 | –1,955 |
| Louisiana | 17 | 21,000–32,000 | 26,500 | –2,455 |
| North Carolina | 18 | 18,330–30,430 | 24,380 | –4,575 |
| South Carolina | 19 | 17,500–30,000 | 23,750 | –5,205 |
| West Virginia | 20 | 16,095–29,488 | 22,792 | –6,163 |
| Guam | 21 | 18,177–24,157 | 21,167 | –7,788 |
| Alabama | 22 | 10,836–29,200 | 20,018 | –8,937 |
| Mississippi | 23 | 11,000–28,000 | 19,500 | –9,455 |
| Puerto Rico | 24 | 10,440–14,652 | 12,546 | –16,409 |

NOTE: Some reported salaries may be based on different standards (for example, nine, 10, or 12 months or teacher versus administrator pay scales).

[a]Based on estimated national salary of $28,955 for 24 jurisdictions reporting. NASW-recommended minimum salaries are as follows: BSW level, $20,000; MSW level, $25,000; ACSW level, $30,000; and DSW/MSW advanced levels, $45,000. These salary figures are purely advisory recommendations and are not intended to suggest any understanding that NASW will or must adopt them. Each member is free to negotiate his or her own salary independently and entirely within his or her own discretion (personal communication with NASW Pennsylvania Chapter).

[b]Reported already averaged salary data.

Implementing these strategies requires finding answers to questions such as, Who should define the role of school social worker? What are the critical linkages to be made with other disciplines within the school as an organizational system? How can state and national organizations be made accountable for advancing school social work as a field of practice?

## REFERENCES

Allen-Meares, P. (1994). Social work services in schools: A national study of entry-level tasks. *Social Work, 39,* 560–565.
Costin, L. (1969). A historical review of school social work. *Social Casework, 50,* 439–453.

Hawkins, M. (1980). Survey of state certification standards for social work practice in schools. In *School social work and the law* (pp. 83–95). Washington, DC: National Association of Social Workers.

Meares, P. (1977). Analysis of tasks in school social work. *Social Work, 22,* 196–211.

Meares, P., Washington, R., & Welsh, B. (1986). *Social work services in schools.* Englewood Cliffs, NJ: Prentice Hall.

Venturini, J. (1974). The school social worker in the United States. *Journal of the International Association of Pupil Personnel Workers, 18,* 215.

Winters, W., & Easton, F. (1983). *The practice of social work in schools: An ecological perspective.* New York: Free Press.

*An earlier version of this chapter was presented at the Pennsylvania Association of School Social Work Personnel Conference, September 1994, Hidden Valley.*

*This chapter was originally published in the January 1996 issue of* Social Work in Education, *Vol. 18, pp. 8–18.*

# About the Editors

*Edith M. Freeman, PhD, is professor, University of Kansas School of Social Welfare, Lawrence. She has an MSW from the University of Kansas School of Social Welfare and a PhD from the Departments of Psychology and Human Development and Family Life. She has practiced as a medical and school social worker and has been published in the area of school–community practice. She was the editor of* Social Work in Education *from 1993 to 1997.*

*Cynthia G. Franklin, PhD, LMSW-ACP, is an associate professor at the University of Texas at Austin, School of Social Work, where she teaches courses on clinical practice and research. She has numerous publications on school social work, clinical assessment, practice theories, and child and family practice. She is coauthor (with Dr. Catheleen Jordan) of the books* Clinical Assessment for Social Workers: Quantitative and Qualitative Methods *and* Family Practice: Brief Systems Methods for Social Work *and is coeditor (with Dr. Paula Nurius) of the book* Constructivism in Practice: Methods and Challenges. *She also serves as editor-in-chief of* Social Work in Education.

*Rowena Fong, MSW, EdD, is associate professor, Social of Social Work, University of Hawaii, Honolulu. She has an MSW from the University of California at Berkeley and an EdD from Harvard University. She has served on the editorial boards of* Social Work in Education *and* Multicultural Social Work.

*Gary L. Shaffer, PhD, is associate professor and director of field education, University of North Carolina at Chapel Hill. He has an MA from the University of Chicago School of Social Service Administration and a PhD from the University of Illinois at Urbana-Champaign. He is a member of the editorial board of* Social Work in Education.

*Elizabeth M. Timberlake, DSW, BCD, is ordinary professor of social work at the Catholic University of America. She teaches clinical social work with children and adolescents, advanced clinical research, practice model development, and philosophical issues in social work knowledge development. Her publications target clinical interventions, school social work, children, personnel issues, and social work education. Her current research addresses the biopsychosocial functioning of homeless children and families and participants in Early Head Start (also, federally funded program evaluation). She has served on the editorial boards of* Social Thought, Child and Adolescent Social Work, Social Work in Education, *and* Clinical Social Work.

# About the Contributors

*Rudolph Alexander, Jr., PhD,* is associate professor, College of Social Work, Ohio State University, Columbus.

*Paula Allen-Meares, PhD,* is dean and professor, School of Social Work, University of Michigan, Ann Arbor.

*Ron A. Astor, PhD,* is assistant professor, School of Social Work and School of Education, University of Michigan, Ann Arbor.

*Robert H. Ayasse, MSW, LCSW,* is social services liaison, Foster Youth Services, Mt. Diablo Unified School District, Bay Point, CA.

*Janet L. Bell, PhD, ACSW,* is assistant professor, School of Social Work, Arizona State University, Tempe.

*Jill Duerr Berrick, PhD,* is director, Center for Social Services Research, School of Social Welfare, University of California, Berkeley.

*Lori J. Brady, MA,* is a school social worker, Fairfax County Public Schools, Fairfax, VA.

*Frances S. Caple, PhD, LCSW,* is associate dean, School of Social Work, University of Southern California, Los Angeles.

*Glenn Carley, MSW, CSW,* is chief social worker, Dufferin Peel Catholic District School Board, Mississauga, ON, Canada.

*Nancy Feyl Chavkin, PhD, ACSW, LMSW-AP,* is professor of social work, Southwest Texas State University, San Marcos.

*Barbara Culton, MSW, ACSW,* is a social worker in private practice, East Lansing, MI.

*Carla M. Curtis, DSW,* is associate professor, College of Social Work, Ohio State University, Columbus.

*Peter De Jong, PhD, ACSW,* is professor of social work, Calvin College, Grand Rapids, MI.

*Jorge Delva, PhD,* is doctoral fellow, Department of Mental Hygiene, Johns Hopkins University, Baltimore.

*Kevin L. DeWeaver, PhD,* is professor, School of Social Work, University of Georgia, Athens.

*Joseph Diament, MRP,* is chief executive officer, Odyssey House, Hampton, NH.

*John di Cecco, MSW,* is coordinating advisor, Integrated Health and Social Service Collaboratives, Los Angeles Unified School District.

*Mark Duerr, MPA,* is president, Duerr Evaluation Resources, Chico, CA.

*Katherine M. Dunlap, PhD, ACSW,* is clinical associate professor and director, Charlotte MSW Program, University of North Carolina at Chapel Hill.

*Barbara Peo Early, DSW, LCSW,* is associate professor, National Catholic School of Social Service, Catholic University of America, Washington, DC.

*Janet Ford, PhD,* is associate professor, College of Social Work, University of Kentucky, Lexington.

*William Ford, MSW,* formerly a probation officer with the New York City Department of Probation, is clinical coordinator, CAP Behavior Associates, New York.

*Cara Frappier, MSW, ACSW,* is a school social worker, Division of Special Education, Ingham Intermediate School District, Mason, MI.

*Mark W. Fraser, PhD,* is John A. Tate Professor for Children in Need, School of Social Work, University of North Carolina at Chapel Hill.

*Harriet Goodman, DSW, CSW,* is associate professor and chair, Protection and Social Justice Field Work, Hunter College School of Social Work, New York.

*Gilbert J. Greene, PhD, ACSW, LISW,* is associate professor, College of Social Work, Ohio State University, Columbus.

*Marion Halim, ACSW,* is executive director, Renaissance West Inc., Kansas City, MO.

*Isadora Hare, MSW, LCSW, SSWS,* is project manager, Healthy Adolescents Project, American Psychological Association, Washington, DC.

*Aminifu R. Harvey, DSW, LICSW,* is assistant professor, School of Social Work, University of Maryland, Baltimore.

*Alan Hilton, EdD,* is special education teacher, Union School District, San Jose, CA.

*Marjorie Witt Johnson, ACSW,* is a retired school social worker and choreographer, Cleveland.

*Dorothy Harper Jones, PhD, ACSW,* is associate professor, School of Social Work, and associate dean of the Graduate School and consultant to the Provost for Multicultural and Racial Issues, Michigan State University, East Lansing.

*Jean C. Karoly, MA, MEd,* is a doctoral student, Department of Psychology, Our Lady of the Lake University, San Antonio, TX.

*Diane Kistner, BSW,* is an MSW candidate, School of Social Work, University of Georgia, Athens.

*Martha Klein, MSW, ACSW, AAMFT,* is a school social worker, Ingham Intermediate School District, Mason, MI, and a social worker in private practice, East Lansing, MI.

*Wynne S. Korr, PhD,* is professor, School of Social Work, University of Pittsburgh.

*Flavio Francisco Marsiglia, PhD,* is assistant professor, School of Social Work, Arizona State University, Tempe.

*John E. McIntosh, Jr., JD,* is an attorney, Crews & Hancock P.L.C., Fairfax, VA.

*Scott D. Miller, PhD,* is president and founder, Institute for the Study of Therapeutic Change, Chicago.

*Christian E. Molidor, PhD, ACSW,* is assistant professor, Graduate School of Social Work, University of Denver.

*Rosemary O'Connor, PhD,* is a school social worker, SOWIC, Joliet, IL.

*Lynne E. Orens, MSW, ACSW,* is a school social worker, Fairfax County Public Schools, Fairfax, VA.

*Janet D. Perloff, PhD,* is associate professor, School of Social Welfare, State University of New York at Albany.

*K. Jean Peterson, DSW, LMSW,* is associate professor, School of Social Welfare, University of Kansas–Lawrence.

*Carolyn B. Pryor, PhD, ACSW,* is associate professor, School of Social Work, Wayne State University, Detroit.

*James C. Raines, MSSW, ACSW,* is a school social worker, Wilmette Public Schools, Wilmette, Illinois, and doctoral candidate, School of Social Work, Loyola University, Chicago.

**Julia B. Rauch, PhD, LCSW-C,** *is professor, School of Social Work, University of Maryland, Baltimore.*

**Barbara Rittner, PhD,** *is associate professor, School of Social Work, University of Georgia, Athens.*

**Arlene Sacks, EdD,** *is academic coordinator, PhD program, and Core Graduate Faculty, Union Institute, Miami.*

**Ramon M. Salcido, DSW,** *is associate professor, School of Social Work, University of Southern California, Los Angeles.*

**Edward J. Saunders, PhD,** *is associate professor, School of Social Work, University of Iowa, Des Moines.*

**Cathryne L. Schmitz, PhD, ACSW, LCSW,** *is assistant professor, Graduate School of Social Work, University of Denver.*

**Carolyn A. Smith, PhD, ACSW,** *is associate professor, School of Social Welfare, University at Albany, State University of New York.*

**Calvin L. Streeter, PhD, LMSW,** *is associate professor and the Meadows Foundation Centennial Fellow in the Quality of Life in the Rural Environment, School of Social Work, University of Texas at Austin.*

**Richard D. Sutphen, PhD,** *is assistant professor, College of Social Work, University of Kentucky, Lexington.*

**David F. Timmer, MSW, AAMFT,** *is a school social worker, Oak Creek–Franklin Joint School District, Oak Creek, WI.*

**Diane Tirado-Lampert, PhD, CSW, BCD,** *is a psychotherapist in private practice, Big Rapids, MI.*

**Santos Torres, Jr., EdD, MSW, ACSW,** *is associate professor and chair, Home and School Visitor/School Social Worker Certificate Program, School of Social Work, University of Pittsburgh.*

**James A. Twaite, PhD, EdD,** *is a psychologist in private practice, Milford, PA.*

**Yvonne M. Vissing, PhD,** *is professor of sociology and National Institute of Mental Health Postdoctoral Research Fellow, Salem State College, Salem, MA.*

**Jack C. Wall, DSW, ACSW, LCSW,** *is associate professor, School of Social Work, Loyola University, Chicago.*

*Brenda Robinson Ward, MSW, CCSW,* is clinical social work specialist, Piedmont Behavioral Healthcare, Concord, NC.

*David Y. H. Wu, PhD,* is professor, Department of Anthropology, Chinese University of Hong Kong, Shatin, New Territories.

# Index

## A

**Multisystem Skills and Interventions
in School Social Work Practice**

Cover design by The Watermark Design Office

Interior design by Bill Cathey

Typeset in Lucida Sans and Palatino by Bill Cathey

Printed by Boyd Printing Company

# ORDER THESE INFORMATIVE RESOURCES ON SCHOOL SOCIAL WORK PRACTICE FROM NASW PRESS

**Multisystem Skills and Interventions in School Social Work Practice,** *Edith M. Freeman, Cynthia G. Franklin, Rowena Fong, Gary L. Shaffer, and Elizabeth M. Timberlake, Editors.* This practical guide will help you meet the emerging needs of students, families, schools, and communities today. You'll learn about the skills and competencies you need to work effectively with new social work consumers. And you'll find out how you can change policies, gain funding, and otherwise influence large systems in the changing sociopolitical climate.

*ISBN: 0-87101-295-2. Item #2952. $35.95*

**Risk and Resilience in Childhood:** *An Ecological Perspective, Mark W. Fraser, Editor.* How is it that some children face enormous odds but prevail over adversity to become successful? How can you develop practice models that foster resilience? You'll find answers to these questions and more in this unique text that introduces and explores the concepts of protection and resilience in the face of adversity.

*ISBN: 0-87101-274-X. Item #274X. $35.95*

**Painful Passages:** *Working with Children with Learning Disabilities, by Elizabeth Dane.* Children with learning disabilities require understanding, knowledge, and skilled intervention to facilitate the growing process. They often find the passage from youth to adulthood painful and perplexing. Dane's text helps social workers, as well as administrators, educators, and parents, respond creatively and effectively to those needs.

*ISBN: 0-87101-175-1. Item #1751. $24.95*

**Helping Vulnerable Youths:** *Runaway and Homeless Adolescents in the United States, Deborah S. Bass, Principal Investigator.* Results of an intensive, year-long investigation undertaken by NASW, with support from the Family and Youth Services Bureau, U.S. Department of Health and Human Services.

*ISBN: 0-87101-221-9. Item #2219. $18.95*

**Social Work in Education.** This quarterly journal publishes new approaches to practice such as full-service schools, research methodology including single-system design and ethnographic client-centered studies, and important topics for today's schools such as multicultural programs and violence prevention.

*ISSN: 0162-7961. Published in January, April, July, and October. Annual rates: NASW Member (#6001) $39; NASW Student Member (#6101) $30; Individual Nonmember (#6201) $62; Library/Institution (#6301) $84*

*(Order form on reverse side)*

# ORDER FORM

| Title | Item # | Price | Total |
|---|---|---|---|
| __ School Social Work Practice | 2952 | $35.95 | _____ |
| __ Risk and Resilience in Childhood | 274X | $35.95 | _____ |
| __ Painful Passages | 1751 | $24.95 | _____ |
| __ Helping Vulnerable Youths | 2219 | $18.95 | _____ |
| __ Social Work in Education | | | |
|     NASW Member | 6001 | $39.00 | _____ |
|     NASW Student Member | 6101 | $30.00 | _____ |
|     Individual Nonmember | 6201 | $62.00 | _____ |
|     Library/Institution | 6301 | $84.00 | _____ |
| | | Subtotal | _____ |
| | + 10% postage and handling | | _____ |
| | | Total | _____ |

❐   I've enclosed my check or money order for $ _____.

❐   Please charge my    ❐ NASW Visa*    ❐ Other Visa    ❐ MasterCard

_____    _____

Credit Card Number                                  Expiration Date

Signature _____

*Use of this card generates funds in support of the social work profession.*

Name_____

Address _____

City _____ State/Province _____

Country _____ Zip _____

Phone _____ E-mail _____

NASW Member # (if applicable) _____

*(Please make checks payable to NASW Press. Prices are subject to change.)*

**NASW PRESS**
**P. O. Box 431**
**Annapolis JCT, MD 20701**
**USA**

**Credit card orders call**
**1-800-227-3590**
(In the Metro Wash., DC, area, call 301-317-8688)
**Or fax your order to 301-206-7989**
**Or order online at http://www.naswpress.org**

*Visit our Web site at http://www.naswpress.org.*      MSIBI98